Business finance

Business finance

Brian Ogley

Longman London and New York

Longman Group Limited
Longman House
Burnt Mill, Harlow, Essex, CM20 2JE England
Associated companies throughout the world

*Published in the United States of America
by Longman Inc., New York*

© Longman Group Limited 1981

All rights reserved; no part of this publication may be reproduced, stored in a retrieval system, or transmitted in any form or by any means, electronic, mechanical, photocopying, recording, or otherwise, without the prior written permission of the Publishers.

*First published 1981
Second impression 1984*

British Library Cataloguing in Publication Data

Ogley, Brian
Business finance.
1. Corporations – Finance
2. Industrial management
I. Title
658.1'5   HG4026   80-42056

ISBN 0-582-29573-4

Printed in Singapore by
Selector Printing Co. (Pte) Ltd.

Contents

Acknowledgements	xi
1 Business finance – a survey	**1**
The need for up-to-date reading	2
Marginal situations	3
The public and private sectors	4
The role of money	6
Planning the start of a private-sector business	10
The two main categories of finance: risk capital (equity) and loan funds	12
2 The main forms available for a private-sector business	**16**
Sole traders	16
Partnerships	19
Companies	21
Company forms: the alternatives available	23
Incorporation of a company: filing of documents	26
The human agents of a company	29
3 The company as a legal person: assets and liabilities	**32**
A new company: a problem of financial security	33
The need for an adequate risk–equity–capital base	34
Profit	35
The meaning and significance of assets	36
Financing the assets of a company	40
Double-entry book-keeping (the dual aspect)	41
The liabilities of a company	42
The capital structure of a company: a preliminary view	44
Gearing: a preliminary view	45
4 The capital needed at the start of a private-sector company	**48**
The initial capital: the options	48

	Capital: yield – a preliminary view	51
	Preparations for the start	52
	The cost of capital	53
	Retained earnings	59
	Do companies seek to maximise their profits?	60
	Weighted average cost of capital	62
	Cost of equity capital: the growth factor	64
	Cost of capital: general comments	66
	Questions	67
5	**Main types of securities issued by companies**	**69**
	Shares	69
	Reserves	73
	Preferred ordinary shares	76
	Deferred shares	76
	Preference shares	77
	Stock	81
	Debentures	81
	Questions	88
6	**Capital structure and gearing**	**90**
	The capital structure	94
	Gearing	100
	The concept of profit	105
	The return on capital	108
	Priority percentage tables (interest and dividend payments)	113
	Questions	118
7	**The working capital**	**121**
	The employees	121
	Stocks suppliers' credits	122
	Credit to customers	123
	Cash and bank balances	124
	The operating cycle	124
	Factors determining the working capital	128
	Estimating the initial working capital	130
	Approximate working capital required for increased scale of activity	131
	Control of working capital: some practical aspects	131
	Questions	137
8	**Budgetary control**	**139**
	Definition	139
	Main objectives	140

Contents   vii

    Budget installation and procedures   141
    Budget forms and reports   146
    Flexible budgets   150
    Capital budgets: a preview   151
    Budgets: some problems   151
    Questions   153

9 Cash forecasts and funds flow statements   **154**
    Cash forecast procedures   155
    Funds flow statements (sources and applications of funds) 164
    Questions   175

10 Short-, medium- and long-term funds   **180**
    Presenting the case   180
    Traditional uses for short-term funds   183
    Main types of short-term finance   184
    Medium-term loans   195
    Long-term loans   197
    Questions   202

11 Government assistance to industry and some private-sector initiatives   **203**
    Assisted areas   204
    Local authority and other public-sector sources   205
    Assistance for small firms   206
    Financial institutions in the public and private sectors 206
    Questions   211

12 The financial strategy   **212**
    The management role: a brief outline   213
    Revenue planning: cost planning   213
    The problem of selling prices   215
    Cost planning   216
    Profit in relation to variable and fixed costs: a preview 219
    The key or limiting factor   220
    Absorption costing   223
    Marginal costing   225
    The key factor: an example   227
    The P/V (profit/volume) ratio   228
    Breakeven charts: breakeven point   229
    The sales mix   233
    Make-or-buy decisions   233
    Should a certain contract be accepted or not?   235
    Questions   239

13 Ratio analysis — 243
- The use of ratios — 244
- Some features of ratios — 244
- Some important ratios — 245
- A summary — 250
- Questions — 254

14 Capital expenditure — 257
- The unevenness of capital expenditure — 258
- Capital expenditure procedures — 258
- Capital investment appraisal: alternative approaches — 261
- The use of tables — 265
- Discounted cash flow methods — 269
- The tax aspects — 271
- Depreciation — 271
- Discounted cash flow methods: advantages and disadvantages — 272
- The profitability index — 273
- Other methods of appraisal — 273
- 'How decisions to invest are made' – Progress Report of the Wilson Committee — 275
- Questions — 285

15 Companies in trouble — 292
- Main reasons for decline or collapse of a company — 293
- A rescue attempt: a practical approach — 294
- Capital reconstruction — 299
- Questions — 301

16 Valuation of a company — 305
- Some relevant factors when valuing a company — 305
- Bases of valuation — 307
- Questions — 322

17 Mergers and takeovers — 326
- Reasons for mergers and takeovers — 326
- Disadvantages of large organisations — 329
- Main types of integration — 330
- Mergers and takeovers: technical aspects — 333
- Legislation or self-regulation? — 336
- The City Working Party: the Takeover Panel — 337
- The Monopolies Commission — 340
- Methods of takeovers — 341
- Advantages and disadvantages of different payment considerations — 342

	Technical aspects of merger or takeover	344
	Reverse takeover (reverse bid)	345
	Valuations in takeovers and mergers	345
	Recent public attitudes	346
	Recent research	348
	Holding companies and groups of companies	349
	Questions	350
18	**Going public**	**354**
	Reasons why some companies have not gone public	355
	Methods of issue	359
	Issues of securities to the public: practical considerations	361
	Introduction	368
	Rights issues	369
	Capitalisation issue (scrip or bonus issue)	374
	Questions	375
19	**Risk and uncertainty**	**378**
	The nature of risk management	379
	Alternative ways of dealing with risks	380
	Questions	387
20	**The nationalised industries and their financing**	**388**
	The economic and political background	389
	The National Enterprise Board (NEB)	391
	The 1960s White Papers	392
	New financial objectives for nationalised industries	394
	Why do governments support certain industries?	400
	The Conservatives and nationalisation	403
21	**Finance for foreign trade**	**407**
	Differences between home and overseas markets	407
	Questions to answer before exporting	408
	Government – and other – support for exporters	409
	Exporting: distribution channels available	409
	Exchange control: export–import regulations	410
	Terms of contract and main documents	410
	Methods of payment	411
	Factors	413
	Methods of finance	414
	The Export Credit Guarantee Department (ECGD)	414
	Foreign exchange	420
	Some other possible options for exporters	421
	Questions	422

22 Financial institutions — 424
- The banking system — 424
- Other financial institutions — 429
- The insurance market — 433
- The Stock Exchange — 436
- The foreign exchange market — 436
- The London gold market — 437
- Commodity markets — 437

23 Investors and their viewpoints: the institutions available to them — 438
- Sources of information — 438
- The investor's viewpoint — 441
- The supply of money — 442
- Short-term investments — 443
- Medium- and longer-term investment: individual and corporate bodies — 454
- Institutions as investors — 463
- Fixed-interest securities — 468
- Equities — 470
- The Stock Exchange: dealings procedures — 475
- Investment analysis — 485
- Questions — 490

24 Protection of assets — 495
- Internal control — 495
- Internal check — 496
- Internal and external audit — 498
- External auditors — 498
- Internal audit — 501
- Questions — 501

25 The Wilson Committee — 505

26 The implications of inflation and taxation — 512
- Inflation — 512
- Current purchasing power and current cost accounting — 515
- SSAP 16 — 518
- The implications of taxation — 520
- Questions — 522
- Revision questions — 523

Further reading — 530

Index — 533

Acknowledgements

I would like to thank the following professional bodies for their kind permission to reproduce past examination questions and I would emphasise that in those cases where questions have been worked, the workings are the sole responsibility of the author:
The Institute of Chartered Secretaries and Administrators (ICSA); The Association of Certified and Corporate Accountants (ACCA), abbreviations signify the paper from which the question was taken: B.M. Business Management, M.A. Management Accounting, Acc 3, Acc 4 Advanced Accounting, other questions are taken from the Financial Management paper; The Institute of Chartered Accountants of England and Wales (ICA); The Institute of Cost and Management Accountants (ICMA); The Society of Company and Commercial Accountants (SCCA).

I thank my wife, Barbara, for dealing with the secretarial and typing work involved, and for her patience and forebearance whilst the book was being written. I dedicate this book to her.

We are also grateful to the following for permission to reproduce copyright material:
The Financial Times Ltd for extracts from 'Rivals to the Banks' *Financial Times* March 13th 1978, 'Sales of Publicly Owned Assets' *Financial Times* July 1979 and 'The Revolution in Portfolio Theory' by Christine Moir *Financial Times* July 16th 1980; The Midland Bank Ltd for an extract from the *Midland Bank Review* Spring 1978; VNU Business Publications for an extract from *Accountancy Age* November 25th 1977 by H. Armstrong.

Chapter 1

Business finance – a survey

The subject of this book is business finance. It is useful to begin with definitions and identify the main features of the subject. A business activity is considered to be one which is concerned in any way with the production or distribution of materials or goods or the performance of services for payment or reward with a view to profit. Conversely, if the object of any activity is a social or charitable one and the question of profit does not arise – for example, the provision of schools or hospitals for which no fees are charged – then, by definition, the activity will be outside the scope of business finance. However, non-business activities cannot be ignored since they are continually in competition with business activities for the limited funds and resources available at any time.

Finance is concerned with money, that money should be available at the time needed, for the period needed and on the best terms possible. Like many of the concepts met in this study the basic principles are simple and easily understood. As a topic is examined in more detail complexities become apparent, but even so a student or a manager who is not a financial specialist but who makes the effort to acquire a reasonable knowledge of the fundamental principles of business finance will find himself able to make an informed assessment of most business situations or problems in financial terms. In practice, adequate 'generalist' rather than specialist knowledge, experience, judgement and common sense count for a great deal when decisions have to be made in relation to financial questions.

However, the bigger the issues at stake the more care will have to be taken in making the appraisals and these can themselves be very costly. Often a team of specialists (e.g. engineers, designers, market researchers, economists, accountants, etc.) will assemble information and will use this to prepare a study which sets out the options available, the implications of each and, usually, recommendations. The total of knowledge and experience brought to bear on a serious issue is thus wide and deep. It will be for the directors of a company, or those who have commissioned the enquiry, to make the final decision and accept responsibility for it, although they may themselves lack technical competence in the main field. When a situation or a problem is efficiently analysed it will usually be found that a number of options are available, but some can quickly be ruled out, and it may finally seem that there is only one option – perhaps to drop an idea altogether – but in other cases the final choice may lie between two or three options and often the choice of any one of them would lead to an acceptable result.

This book is primarily concerned with business finance in relation to activities within the United Kingdom. However, the subject cannot be studied in isolation as business and non-business activities interact in so many ways, and will directly or indirectly be subject to local, regional, national and even international influences, which are dynamic and not static. Moreover, the UK is a member of organisations such as the European Economic Community (EEC) and the Organisation for Economic Cooperation and Development (OECD) and membership has far-reaching implications for business finance as well as other economic activities. Furthermore, many of the principles of business finance apply equally in all countries.

The social, legal, behavioural and economic environments in which businesses operate are powerful factors which can never be ignored but they are largely outside the scope of this book, although an awareness of them will need to be assumed. In the case of students for finals-level professional examinations this is a safe assumption as every examination syllabus requires adequate study of the whole business environment. Readers who do not have an examination in view but who have practical business experience will be familiar with this environment, and not least the important behavioural factors – the fact that people, individually or in groups, often do not seem to act predictably or straightforwardly. Deeper study normally discloses understandable explanations for behaviour which at first may seem irrational.

The need for up-to-date reading

It must be stressed, especially to examination students, that study of textbooks is not enough. In business finance as well as other subjects there is ceaseless change, sometimes with advances and sometimes setbacks. Whilst certain fundamental principles do not change there may be wide fluctuations in interest rates which lead to major changes in market prices of securities and the cost of money. Sometimes money and credit will be readily available, but at other times the supply may be severely restricted. The inflation rate may change from year to year. Government or quasi-government agencies may be created or be ended. Different governments have profoundly different attitudes to financial and taxation questions. Prominent people, governors of national banks or international agencies, academics, analysts, finance ministers, businessmen and others will express opinions which give rise to controversy. Serious students need to keep themselves informed of major changes in fact since the date a textbook went to press, and also keep informed about important areas of intellectual speculation and controversy. Examiners expect evidence to be given of up-to-date knowledge and ability to discuss current controversial matters. Questions are regularly set to test this.

Students can only hope to gain high marks in this subject by combining sound knowledge of fundamentals, with considerable practice in carrying out past examination questions, and with selective and wide reading in relation to current matters. The *Financial Times* is outstanding in this respect and a serious student is advised to take out a subscription and build up indexed and dated files of cuttings related to articles and reports of special interest. *The Times, the Daily Telegraph, Guardian, Sunday Times, Observer, Sunday Telegraph, the Economist* and *Investors' Chronicle and Stock Exchange Gazette* are also publications which give good coverage of financial and investment matters.

Marginal situations

A business activity has been defined as one which has profit as its objective. Many activities do not come within this definition and yet have affinity with those which do. For example, fee-paying independent schools depend on fees and can only survive if their revenues produce a surplus over costs, and the surplus should be such that unexpected emergencies can be survived. Those who manage organisations of this kind, which often complement state owned and financed organisations, must have a management style and outlook in many ways similar to and in other ways different from those who have the making of profits as a main, if not the main, aim of their work. Marginal cases of this kind may be important in themselves but they are comparatively few and thus do not affect the main issues. It seems reasonable to consider their financing as coming within the scope of business finance, especially as company law recognises a special category of limited company, one limited by guarantee. Companies which adopt this form of incorporation normally have non-profit-making objectives, often charitable ones, or, for example, the furthering of the interests of a professional body.

The public and private sectors

Business activities occur within the public and private sectors of the UK economy and the situation is similar in other countries, with the range lying between the extremes of a mainly government- or state-controlled economy in what are known as the socialist Eastern bloc economies, notably the USSR, and the primarily private-sector capitalist economies, of which the USA is the outstanding example. The public sector of the economy is made up of state-owned organisations and institutions, including those owned by local authorities: housing, schools and social services come within this category, as well as the nationalised industries. The private sector is made up of businesses operated by individuals, partnerships or companies, producing and/or selling goods or services with a view to profit; a main distinction between public and private sector businesses lies in the aspects of ownership and control, with more emphasis on profit – and survival – as the major objectives in private-sector business.

Nationalised industries
Nationalised industries in the UK occupy a number of the 'commanding heights of the economy', and they are for all practical purposes wholly owned by the state. Often a nationalised industry is governed by a special statute, or Act of Parliament, but more recently state ownership and control has been made effective through the agency of the National Enterprise Board (NEB), created by the Industry Act in 1975. The chairman and the board of the NEB are under the direction of the Secretary of State for Industry and in effect the NEB is a holding company with particular nationalised industries as major subsidiaries. The concept of a holding company, with one or more operating subsidiaries, which together form a group, is a familiar one in the private sector and will be considered later.

In general, the boards of the various nationalised industries have a mandate from their owners (the state; the community) acting through the government, to operate as far as possible on sound commercial principles, and to generate a surplus of revenues over costs. It is recognised that on occasions a particular industry will have to perform a special service for social rather than commercial reasons, in circumstances which are bound to lead to financial loss. An example could be the operation by British Airways of air services between the Scottish Islands and the mainland, for the social reasons that thriving island communities are desirable but can only exist if there is an adequate travel link with the mainland, but the islanders could not afford normal commercial air fares. In such situations the government may require the airline to operate specified services but the revenues and costs should be identified and any loss made good by the government – in effect, the taxpayers – in the form of a special payment, or subsidy. Another example would be the operation of unprofitable but socially necessary country village bus services operated by the nationalised bus company, on the instructions of the government.

The private sector

A major difference between a public- and a private-sector organisation is that the former will have the resources of the state behind it. Whilst the chairman and the directors of nationalised industries will certainly regard themselves as businessmen and not civil servants, and they will have as many problems and anxieties as their colleagues in the private sector, their problems will less frequently be financial since, in the last resort, the government of the day will ensure that cash will be available at the end of each month to pay wages, salaries, suppliers and other creditors. If the industry cannot generate a surplus of revenues over costs, and it thus incurs losses, the excutive knows that the state will bear the loss in the form of subsidies, paid for by taxes or state borrowing. There will seldom be the continual anxiety about survival which often besets the owners and managers of private-sector businesses. But however reasonable generalisations may be, there will from time to time be exceptions. In recent years the chairmen and boards of British Leyland (BL), of the British Steel Corporation (BSC), and of the British Broadcasting Corporation (BBC) have obviously had serious financial anxieties, and uncertainty as to whether sufficient government support could be relied upon, in a period when they were operating in exceptionally difficult financial environments.

Because public-sector business has state backing there will never be a shortage of experts, money or plans at the start or at any time subsequently and the business concerned will normally be large or comparatively large. There is more variety in the private sector, with individuals, at one end of the spectrum, opening small shops as sole traders and, at the other extreme, groups of major oil companies acting in consortia to have major pipeline systems built, or an exploration and drilling programme carried out, say in the North Sea, when the sums put at risk may run into thousands of millions of pounds.

Small- and large-scale private-sector businesses have a common interest in finance and a trained person, with an adequate briefing, should be able to assess the financial problems and needs of anyone who seeks his advice in relation to a particular problem, whether on a small or large scale. Indeed, examiners make this assumption and set questions to test this ability. However, in 'real life' situations the taxation aspect will normally be very important and this tends to be very complex, and always requiring expert evaluation. For practical reasons, including that taxation arrangements change quite frequently, questions in Business Finance examinations frequently instruct the candidate to 'ignore taxation', who has to take a separate taxation examination.

A special problem of private-sector managers can be to ensure survival. It seems unwise ever to take survival for granted since the records show so many examples of famous companies brought down by unexpected financial collapse. The orginal Rolls Royce Ltd was an outstanding example. Whilst it happens less frequently that a well established company meets financial disaster, and those which do so often fail because a chairman or a board has made a single major miscalculation or error of judgement which may not become apparent until some years later, failure in the early days of a new business is much more common. New businesses have a high 'infant mortality' rate.

Accordingly, the plan of this book is first to deal with business finance in the private sector, beginning with the wish to start a particular business, consideration of the business forms available and advantages and disadvantages of each, the money needed at the start and possible sources from which it may be obtained. Once operations begin, efficient financial control will be a continuing necessity and there are now a number of well-tested techniques which help to ensure this. Later, more complex types of business situations will be considered. Business finance will be examined in relation to the public sector towards the end of the book, and finally finance will be examined from the aspect of investment, the viewpoints of those who are ready and able to put their money at the disposal of others for shorter or longer periods, and the kinds of criteria on which they make their investment decisions. Sources of information for investors will also be considered.

The role of money:

A factor of production

Students of economics will be aware that this subject is a complex and controversial one. Financial managers tend to take a less academic view than economists and to them money has two vitally important roles: firstly, it is an essential factor of production, without which no business activity can begin or continue. Secondly, it is a measure of economic performance, although a very imperfect one. From the first aspect, the possession of money, or assured access to it (e.g. credit facilities) enables the possessor to buy or hire whatever assets he may need for a particular business activity – land, buildings, plant, machinery etc.: it will enable him to employ workpeople and advisers: to acquire whatever raw materials, components, etc., are necessary for the manufacture of whatever goods he intends to make and sell. Money, or access to it, will permit its possessor to mount the sales promotion and advertising campaigns which are now so important in commercial life. Money gives the possessor wide freedom of action within such constraints as the law imposes, and possibly there may be other constraints imposed by powerful interests, such as trade unions.

Credit

Money is not necessarily cash. At present only minor legitimate business transactions are settled in cash as settlement by cheque, giro, bank transfer or cable transfer, etc., is more convenient and avoids the security risk involved in the handling of cash. Exceptionally, in the UK and some other industrialised countries there is now also a substantial unrecorded 'black' or 'parallel' economy. Many people will work only on the basis that they are paid in cash, since this cannot be traced. They then underdeclare their incomes and thereby evade income tax and VAT. When considering money, credit must also be considered as it has a major role in financial management and it is increasingly being used in personal as well as business transactions.

A few years ago it would have been impossible to imagine that an ordinary person, of limited personal resources, could travel around the world by air, stay at the most expensive hotels, use fashionable restaurants, draw cash in different currencies and only be required to make payment a month or so after returning home, merely by holding a piece of plastic, a credit card. The essence of credit is trust, or confidence. There will be at least two parties: the one who requests a credit facility and the one who grants or rejects the request. The party requested to grant credit may be a manufacturer asked by a wholesaler or retailer to supply goods on credit, or it may be a customer of a department store who seeks credit: the list of possibilities is long.

Often the party requested to grant credit will be a bank or a subsidiary of one. In all cases the party able to grant credit – within the limits of its own resources – should operate efficient procedures to check that the applicant is 'creditworthy' – ready and able to honour commitments as they fall due. The enquiries will seek to ascertain that the record of the applicant, whether a person or a corporate body, is good and, for example, that credit-investigating agencies, with their access to computer and other records, report favourably. Important questions will include whether the applicant has a favourable 'cash flow', or, in simpler words, his income exceeds his payments and he should also own assets, property, so that as a last resort a creditor could hope to recover his debt by court action if necessary.

Meanwhile, any organisation which grants credit is limited by the resources at its own disposal. For example, a banker who agrees to grant an overdraft or loan knows that the party to whom this credit facility has been given could at once withdraw cash up to the agreed limit. Whilst bankers know from experience the likely pattern of cash drawings of those to whom facilities have been granted, they must still act prudently and always be able without difficulty to meet their obligations.

Although this is a technical area of finance which is outside the scope of this book the government of the day has a number of means at its disposal either to encourage or discourage the granting of credit by banks and others. The expression 'credit squeeze' is likely to be familiar. At times when money and credit are relatively cheap and abundant, business managers may experience little or no difficulty in obtaining an overdraft or short-term loan to meet a temporary shortage of cash. However, if a similar need arose during a credit-squeeze period the applicant might be unable to borrow except at a much higher price – which is measured by the rate of interest payable: even worse, he might find himself unable to borrow on any terms. At such a time a business may only be able to survive by quick, forced sales of its property in order to have cash to pay wages, salaries, and creditors generally. A feature of forced sales is that property may have to be sold for a fraction of the price it could have fetched if the seller had not been under pressure. A business which does not have properties, assets, which can be sold or offered as 'collateral' – security – to raise cash during a crisis will probably be forced into liquidation. Businesses with competent managers and efficient financial planning and control systems are normally able to avoid cash crises and forced sale or liquidation.

Money as a measure of economic performance
As well as being a main factor in economic activities, money also has a major role as a measure of economic performance. In every business,

managers, workpeople, land, buildings, plant, machinery, materials and money operate together within a defined time scale to produce and/or distribute and sell goods and/or services which, if all goes according to plan, are sold at prices which yield a surplus over costs – a profit. If, through miscalculation or bad luck or bad management the total costs exceed the revenues, the deficit is the loss for the period. There is a common thread which can be discerned in every part of every business. It is that everything used or done can be expressed in terms of money. Indeed, the contributions of the different factors to the total result cannot be effectively measured and compared except by expressing each in the appropriate money terms and using the common factor, money, as the measure of economic performance. The techniques which are available can be astonishingly informative when handled by skilled analysts.

Inflation

Unfortunately, in recent years, the role of money as a measure of economic performance has declined in effectiveness because of inflation. Inflation signifies that prices in general are rising – which means that the value of money is falling. Obviously, a measure, or yardstick, can only be fully effective if it is unchanging over time. This is obviously not now the case with money in the UK. In the past, in the UK the value of money has sometimes remained reasonably stable over extended periods, and sometimes the value of money has risen – prices generally have fallen. In Switzerland at the present time the value of the Swiss Franc remains very stable and although it is a controversial area it appears that measures can be taken to restrain inflation if there is a general will to do this.

Meanwhile, in addition to the many other problems which inflation causes in the UK the accounts of a company which have been prepared in the manner required by law, the Companies Acts, on an historical cost basis, give a distorted view of the situation they are intended to reflect. The same applies when control techniques, such as budgetary control or business ratios, are considered. The best that can now be attempted is to assess and apply adjustments which, as far as practicable, make allowances for the effects of inflation. The whole area of business finance – how to deal with inflation in the accounts and financial records so that the results give a 'true and fair' view – is now the subject of debate, controversy and dispute in academic, professional and business circles, with the government, politicians of all parties, civil servants and the Inland Revenue as participants or spectators. It is evident that so long as inflation persists the problems are insoluble and the best which can be hoped for are partial and compromise solutions which, in each case, may please some but be unacceptable to others. The only satisfactory way of dealing with inflation is to cure the disease itself. The implications of inflation and an outline of the attempts made to devise accounting methods and techniques which take it into account as far as possible will be considered in Chapter 26.

Planning the start of a private-sector business

A new private-sector business will begin with an idea and then a conviction in the mind of a single person. He believes that he has indentified that a profitable market exists, or can be developed for some goods or services he intends to offer for sale. This implies that some need is not being met in the existing market place, or a new product may create new needs. Businesses which start very small, e.g. Marks and Spencer, Tesco, Ford and Sony, may grow into giant companies within the lifetimes of their founders. Others may disappear without trace within one or two years. Between these extremes of astonishing success and total failure, many of the new businesses started reach a certain plateau at which they provide their owners and managers with a comfortable way of life, and employment for a number of workpeople.

In principle, a person who proposes to start a new business – an entrepreneur, an innovator, a risk taker, a person who invests time, money and skill in ventures in the expectation of making profits, but with the knowledge that the outcome may be failure and loss – will first decide upon his objectives and the resources he would need to attain them. The essential basic resources are the same in all cases, although the scale and proportions will vary widely – land and buildings, labour, which includes management, materials, machines, money and time. At the start there may be a single owner/manager, a rented office, or part of the owner's residence, office equipment including a telephone, possibly a typist and a limited amount of money. In all cases, if the business is to succeed, the founder must be clear in mind what he aims to do, and it must be assumed that he has made careful surveys and enquiries before committing himself in any way. If he happens to be an innovator with a patent with important commercial potential, his position will be an exceptionally fortunate one as he will have the advantages of a monopolist position and his options will include approaching major companies in many countries in the expectation that some at least will compete with each other to offer him favourable terms for a manufacturing joint venture project, or to develop and exploit his patent on a licensing basis.

In other cases, when there is not the advantage of a valuable patent, after establishing his objectives and assessing his probabilities of achieving them if he can marshal the necessary resources, an entrepreneur must examine his financial position. If he has sufficient personal wealth, including property which could be offered as security for loans, he could finance a business venture without the need to obtain financial support from any other source. If the venture succeeded he would receive the entire profits, and if it failed, he alone would bear the loss. However, in the majority of cases, an individual who seeks to start a business will experience financial constraints. In some cases it will be apparent to him that whilst he is convinced that he has an idea and a plan for a profitable new business, he could not begin unless he could first find and convince potential backers to put more or less substantial sums of money at his disposal, so that he could buy, or rent or lease land, buildings, plant and machinery, buy materials and engage workpeople – and this word will be used to describe all categories of employees from a managing director to an office cleaner. In some cases it will be apparent that any new business must start on a big scale or not at all. In such cases, if it is soon evident that the necessary finance cannot be raised, the ideas and plans must be abandoned. In other cases, whilst it may seem preferable to start on a fairly big scale if possible, it may still be practicable to start on a much smaller one, if the only available options are to start small or not at all.

In practice an entrepreneur, apart from the special case of one who seeks to exploit a promising patent, will be unable to start even the smallest new business without some personal wealth, or a continuing income. This is because he will need money, or access to it, to live until the new business has been equipped and established and has begun to generate revenue and this always takes some time. If customers are given credit, and sometimes this is a commercial necessity, time will elapse before the proceeds of sale are received as cash. Money will also be needed to buy or hire any assets which will be essential to the running of the business. An asset may be defined as a valuable possession, or an economic resource which is expected to yield future benefits to its owner. If the entrepreneur owns personal possessions such as a residence, a car, or stocks and shares, he could be able to obtain cash either by selling some of these or, alternatively, offering them as security for a loan, which would involve a commitment to pay interest on the loan and in due course repay the principal on the basis agreed. Any failure to honour this commitment would entitle the lender to seize the security and sell it, retaining whatever sum was owing to him.

It is thus evident that whilst a person who takes steps to start a private-sector business does so with the aim of making a profit, his only certainty at first is that he is putting a larger or smaller sum of his money at risk of total loss, as well as his time and effort. The hope and expectation of profit in the future are the inducements to accept this risk of loss and the fact that it is a real one is evidenced by the number of new businesses which fail.

If the intending promoter of a new business assesses that he will be unable to proceed unless he can obtain financial support from others, he will find when he comes to make enquiries, normally beginning with his bank manager, that it is easier to find people or organisations prepared to lend money, against ample security, for shorter or longer periods, and at agreed rates of interest, which may be fixed or variable, than it is to find backers who are willing to make their money available on the basis that they are prepared to accept the risk of loss, but will share the profits in the event that the business is successful. It has been and still is a matter of controversy whether entrepreneurs have had to abandon plans to establish potentially profitable new businesses in the UK through difficulties in raising 'start-up' or 'venture' or 'risk' capital even though such businesses would have been socially desirable through the creation of employment and additional exports. A main reason why the Labour Government in 1977 set up the Wilson Committee was to enquire into this important question. This is considered in Chapter 25.

The two main categories of finance: risk capital (equity) and loan funds

Whilst representatives of financial and investing institutions in the City of London contend that risk capital has always been available for promising new or established businesses there is also evidence, which will be considered later, which challenges these contentions. Meanwhile, it is emphasised that money invested in any business comes within one of two basic categories – it either forms part of the risk capital ('equity') or it is held by the business as a loan – and in this case there is an obligation to pay creditors, which can be enforced in the courts. Suppliers who have granted trade credit are also in this category. There is the now minor category of preference shareholders, which will be considered later, but who are primarily risk bearers. Without doubt it is normally much less difficult for a new business promoter to raise money in the form of loans, against ample security, than it is to raise risk capital.

A promoter of a new private-sector business will be aware that if he makes a major miscalculation he will stand to lose the whole of his investment of capital in the venture and in an extreme case this could mean his whole personal fortune and ruin to an individual who until the failure had enjoyed high material standards of life. It may be objected at this point that in recent years a number of private-sector companies have been 'rescued' by the government. Rolls-Royce, BL and Ferranti are examples. However, only a company which in some ways occupies a position of exceptional importance in the economy is likely to be rescued in this way. It may be a large employer of labour, indirectly as well as directly, with many suppliers dependent on it. The collapse of a large company of this kind could also have strongly adverse effects on the balance of payments. In other cases a company may be a leader, nationally or internationally, in some field of advanced technology. There is a widely held and surely reasonable view that the UK needs more rather than fewer companies which show promise in these difficult, fast-changing and capital-intensive industries and that in special cases it will be desirable to rescue a particular ailing company.

This is evidently a view held by governments in other industralised countries and not in the UK alone. In the USA, in 1980 there was government-sponsored support to rescue the Chrysler Corporation, a leading car manufacturer. If it had been allowed to collapse very many thousands of jobs would have been lost. Moreover, any country which allowed itself to become too heavily dependent on imports, including of advanced technological products, would be giving many hostages to fortune. Indeed, in a study of business finance, as in many others, it will be seen that important decisions are often partially or even wholly based on consideration of political or social factors and by no means solely on business or economic ones. In the real world it could not be otherwise.

In the financial sector, within the private sector a number of secondary banks have received government-sponsored support in the UK. This occurred after the 1974 financial crisis. In some of these cases it was public knowledge that the background was a scandalous one, with numbers of leading people in the business world having enriched themselves either by outright criminal actions or at least by conduct which obviously was morally wrong, and possibly also in breach of the law. In other cases Department of Trade reports following investigations into collapsed or fraudulently operated companies disclosed that numbers of directors of important companies had, at the least, acted with unbelievable weakness and incompetence and had totally failed in their duties, usually by allowing a dominating chief executive to do as he pleased and allowing themselves to be used as 'rubber stamps'.

There has been a further and recurring major scandal in the fact that banks and other companies which collapsed or were rescued with great difficulty and at high cost in the financial crisis following the collapse of the speculative property boom in 1974 had earlier been given unqualified audit certificates by well-known firms of auditors. Not surprisingly, informed members of the public began to question the quality and value of some of the audit work by well-known firms, and whether in some cases the seeming dependence of auditors on the goodwill of directors of their client companies – in order to retain their lucrative accounts – might not lead some audit partners in some cases to close their eyes to matters which should have alerted them to the fact that their duty demanded that they confronted erring, or negligent, or incompetent directors. Many disturbing questions remain unresolved and to many observers it has seemed that the professional accountancy bodies have been far too slow and irresolute in introducing procedures to call their senior as well as junior members before disciplinary committees when it appears that there are serious question marks over their professional competence, judgement or integrity.

In the case of the secondary banks, the government at the time took the view that whatever the merits of their cases – and these were often nil – they should not be allowed to collapse as this would lead to loss of confidence nationally and internationally in the banking system of this country. Accordingly, under the leadership of the Bank of England, supported by the clearing banks, rescue operations were carried out with great skill and at immense cost. They were successful in their objective but many of the parties concerned emerged with diminished reputations for it had been a potentially catastrophic situation which should never have been allowed to arise. In this particular case expensive lessons must have been learned by bankers and others and it will be presumed that they will not be forgotten until the present generation of bankers have retired. It is convincingly said that the basic facts of financial life have to be relearned every generation. Ambitious and able young men emerge, whose reputations are now inflated by the media, and they seem able to prove that the accepted rules do not apply to them. Uninformed investors, and experienced ones who should have known better, show themselves eager to invest heavily in companies promoted by the rising young financiers. Then a sudden crisis occurs and the bubbles burst and the houses of cards collapse and many people find that they or the organisations they represent have lost large sums of money. Financial leaders, including bankers, resolve that the same mistakes must never recur, and they try to see that they do not, but in due course they leave the scene and are succeeded by people who have nev-

Business finance – a survey

er had direct experience of a major financial crisis and the cycle begins once more.

One point must be remembered in relation to rescues of companies by the government or its agencies. It is that the 'risk-bearing' investors, the ordinary shareholders, are not normally rescued, and frequently their shareholdings become valueless. However, the losses of many may still be the gains of the few and it is widely considered that the UK Companies Acts and other legislation still leave too many loopholes and certain offences may be punished by an insignificant fine in the UK, whereas they are liable to be punished by imprisonment in other countries. However, situations and events must be seen in perspective and the financial sector of the UK economy recovered remarkably after the 1974/75 crisis. Probably a large majority of those who operate within this sector maintain high standards of conduct. The problem is the highly intelligent and active minority which do not. It is evident that since 1974/75 tighter controls are being operated and moves are being made towards structural reforms where these are needed.

The fact is that business finance is a subject with as many practical as academic aspects and it involves people and institutions, with their variety, strengths and weaknesses and potential for the future. This book aims to give attention to both practical and academic aspects, including recent and current problems and controversies and possible outcomes.

Chapter 2
The main forms available for a private-sector business

A person who owns, or intends to promote a private-sector business must never forget that one of his main responsibilities will be continually to watch over the financial health of his business. This is true whether he acts alone or with others in a small, medium or large business. His first objective must be survival, which means that he must at all times have cash, which in contexts such as this will include cash equivalents, such as bank balances, or approved overdraft facilities. He must at all times be able to make payments as and when they fall due. If he ever ceases to be in this position his ability to survive will be in danger.

With survival as his first priority the next will certainly be profitability and where there is profitability there will also be potential for growth. Ambitious people tend to seek growth as a major objective at all times but there are many others who look to a business activity to provide them with a financially comfortable way of life, independence, and time to pursue non-business interests and in such cases the emphasis would be on survival and adequate profitability. To ensure these the managements of every business, without exception, need to operate efficient financial controls, paying attention to liquidity and profitability and to securing a cash flow which produces a surplus of receipts over payments. Profitability is essential in the long run but liquidity is essential in both the short and the long run.

Sole traders

Businesses can operate in a variety of forms and in this chapter each main form will be examined briefly. Each form has its own advantages and disadvantages and its own financial implications. It is important that these are known, at least in outline. In practice expert advice would be needed and the taxation implications must always be considered. The taxation aspect can be difficult and is always important and requires expert advice. However, irrespective of the business form adopted, from the aspect of financial management there is a great deal of common ground and the chapters which deal with financial controls are relevant no matter what business form has been adopted, or in what country the business operates.

In the case of the sole-trader or sole-owner form the business is owned by a single person who is usually but not necessarily also the manager or chief executive. It is unincorporated, that is, the business does not have an identity separate and distinct from that of its owner. If the business is to be operated in the name of the owner registration of the name is not necessary but if a modified or special business name is to be used this must be registered with the Registrar of Business Names. The formalities involved are simple and cheap. The Registrar is generally not concerned with whether a name proposed is too similar to a name already registered but he seeks to ensure that misleading or undesirable names are not registered. It is possible that this requirement for registration of names of unincorporated businesses will be abandoned, but this proposal of the government (1980) is being opposed.

The feature of a business operated on a sole-ownership basis is that whilst the owner is entitled to all of the profits he also has unlimited personal liability if losses arise. No special restrictions are placed on persons who seek to operate on this basis and a wealthy person could operate a factory or other large business as sole owner if he chose to do so. He would be subject to the relevant laws in the same way as other businesses and his employees would have the same rights and obligations as they would if they were company employees. The only formalities requiring attention would be notification to the local Inspector of Taxes, and the local rating authority that a new business was being started, and the first accounting date. It is re-emphasised that choice of the latter date has important taxation implications and expert advice will be needed. The choice is by no means as simple as it might seem.

This book seeks to focus attention on the underlying basic principles of business and financial situations since anyone who has a reasonable grasp of these can usually act with judgement in a wide variety of business situations which a person without such knowledge could seriously mishandle. A person who is a good 'generalist' rather than specialist in any subject, including finance, will always be aware of the limitations of his knowledge and when he should seek specialist, expert advice. He needs also to bear in mind that numbers of people put themselves forward as specialists or experts even when their right to do so is open to question. An unfortunate aspect of modern business life is that the calibre of many professional people, accountants, lawyers, doctors included, is poor and it should not always be assumed that advice given is the best advice: it may not even be as objective and disinterested as it ought to be since standards of integrity are too often low and the disciplinary committees of professional bodies tend to be weak and when they can they 'cover up' erring members. In principle, it is desirable that a person seeking advice is able to ask the right questions and have sufficient background knowledge to be able to assess whether the answers given are convincing. Anyone contemplating putting significant sums of money at risk in business situations needs to be aware that he is about to swim in shark-infested waters. Special caution needs to be shown towards suggestions that a particular proposition will offer quick and certain profits. In general it is sound policy to make enquiries and seek recommendations from responsible people before choosing any professional adviser.

Main disadvantages of the unincorporated (sole owner) basis

In practice the unincorporated, sole-ownership business form is seldom acceptable because of the aspect of unlimited personal liability, and also the lack of continuity and corporate form of the business. There is normally difficulty in raising external finance for this type of business and furthermore it would be impracticable for the owner to give deeper personal involvement and incentive in the success of a growing business by giving shares or options to buy shares to senior employees.

Furthermore, an unincorporated business cannot continue beyond the working life of its owner, whereas a company can have a continuing life, although a person operating as a sole owner, or sole-trader business, or a professional practice, and who has established a good name and has regular clients will have built up 'goodwill', and this will normally have a market value which the owner can sell, when he retires, to a prospective buyer who seeks an already established business or practice.

The law and also certain professional bodies require that certain professional practices may only be operated by qualified persons, working alone or with partners. Accountants and solicitors are examples of professional people who may practice only in this way. They may not operate a professional practice as a limited company.

Taxation

A person who works on a self-employed, unincorporated basis should take care to keep the accounts of his business quite separate from his personal accounts – not least because business expenses are allowable as a deduction before tax liability is calculated. A feature of taxation is that a person who practices or operates any type of business in an unincorporated form pays income tax in respect of his profits, under Schedule D. In practice many deductions are allowable before the taxable profits are assessed. A competent taxation adviser will ensure that all possible allowances are claimed and the minimum tax paid.

Partnerships

A partnership may be defined as the relationship which subsists between two or more persons who carry on a business with a view to profit. The main financial implications of this business form are that the partners each have full personal liability for debts incurred to the extent of their entire personal fortunes. Partnerships were common in business in the days before the limited-liability form received the sanction of Parliament in 1855. The dangers and disadvantages of the partnership form are so great that it is understandably avoided in those cases where the alternative of forming a limited-liability company is available. Occasionally there may be taxation advantages in operating as a partnership rather than a limited company and this would be a factor in deciding upon the business form, noting that in certain business activities the inherent dangers of personal unlimited liability can be reduced and kept down to acceptable limits. The principle of a partnership is that normally all the partners participate in the management and share the profits and losses in agreed proportions. Income tax is payable by each partner according to his share of the partnership profits.

The special problem of a partnership is that if the partnership should become insolvent and individual partners also become insolvent, so that they are unable to pay their share of the partnership debts, then if there remained one single solvent partner, he would be called upon to pay the balance of the partnership debts. A wealthy, honest and competent man who formed a partnership with one or more others who proved incompetent or dishonest could therefore find himself called upon to meet heavy liabilities of which he had no prior knowledge. Prudent people therefore normally avoid the partnership form when they can. However, in a few circumstances it cannot be avoided; that is, when qualified people wish to offer professional services but wish to do so as a group rather than as individuals, on a scale beyond the powers of an individual.

Whilst the law normally prohibits a partnership of more than twenty persons it permits certain exceptions, notably partnerships of professional people prohibited either by the law itself or the professional body from forming themselves into a limited-liability company. For example, leading firms of solicitors or accountants operating business on an international scale in the City of London may have fifty or more partners. Sophisticated partnerships of this kind have arrangements so that the continuity of the firm is assured, despite the retirement or death of individual partners. A deed of partnership will invariably be drawn up setting out such matters as how profits will be distributed, losses apportioned, goodwill valued at any time, such as the retirement or death of a partner, or the admission of a new one, as well as any other aspect of their agreement between each other which the partners wish to have set out in writing.

Partnerships: the legal implications
Partnerships are governed by the Partnership Act, 1890. This does not permit partners to limit their liability to the public or their clients but for the most part the Act makes provisions as to the rights and obligations of the partners to each other, and applies only in the event that the deed of partnership, or written or verbal partnership agreement, does not make any other provisions. There is also the Limited Partnership Act, 1907, which provides that so long as there is at least one general partner with unlimited liability a limited partnership may be formed and registered. An ordinary partnership does not need to be registered, except possibly with the Registrar of Business Names. So long as there is strict compliance with the 1907 Act and proper registration, which is open to public inspection, there may be up to nineteen limited partners, whose personal liability is limited to a stated sum. The only rights of a limited partner are to a share of the profits – or losses, but not beyond the limit – and to inspect the books of account. He must not take part in the management, or he becomes liable as a full partner. The Limited Partnership Act, 1907, makes it practicable for a partner to retire from active work without the need to withdraw his capital from the partnership, whose survival might largely depend on this.

In the case of a partnership of professional people the biggest risk will normally be an action brought by a client for damages on the grounds of negligent or otherwise faulty advice, or acts or defaults. Following a pattern which has become evident in the USA, dissatisfied clients in the UK are now tending more frequently to sue professional people if they consider they have been badly served by them. Professional advisers of all kinds can cover themselves against such risks by insurance – professional liability cover – and it would be imprudent not to insure. Even if a claim is not justified, legal proceedings are costly in terms of money and time and a holder of professional liability cover will be spared anxiety about legal arrangements and costs if a case is brought against him.

Companies

The majority of businesses in the UK, even very small ones, including shops, are incorporated as private limited companies. There are a number of alternative company forms and the appropriate choice will depend on the circumstances. Because of the importance of the concept of an incorporated business, one which has an identity separate and distinct from that of its owners, it is necessary to consider it in some detail. Before the invention in the nineteenth century of the limited-liability company form and its sanctioning by Parliament in 1855, people who wished to form and develop a business had to do so on a partnership basis, unless their position was so powerful and exceptional that they could obtain a Royal Charter or a special Act of Parliament. For the vast majority a form of partnership was the only alternative to the sole-ownership form of business. However, a business form such as partnership can only be entered into satisfactorily by people who know each other well and who have confidence in the competence and integrity of the other partners. It is not a form designed to accommodate frequent changes of membership. It is therefore not surprising that partnership proved itself inadequate to meet the business and financial needs of entrepreneurs at a time of quite explosive growth and development of commerce and industry in the UK when the Industrial Revolution was still in progress.

In brief, a new and revolutionary business form was needed, and fortunately it was created and then sanctioned by Parliament. This is the corporate business form, separate and distinct from that of its members, whose liability is limited to the amount unpaid, if any, of the shares for which they have subscribed. This is the central feature of the limited-liability form. It can surely be said that this concept, of the limited-liability company, made possible the industrialisation of the UK and the creation of wealth on a scale which would have been impossible if Parliament had not, in the nineteenth century, passed the first of many Companies Acts and given approval to what at the time was a bold and dangerous step into the unknown. Understandably and inevitably there were at first serious setbacks and abuses as loopholes in the law were found and exploited, but there has been steady evolution and raising of standards and this continues. Even so, there are still weaknesses in the law which are liable to be exploited by unscrupulous company directors, and others, to the heavy loss of uninformed or over-trusting creditors or investors.

The company as a person
An essential feature of a company, using the word in its technical and legal sense, is that it is a legal 'person' which is quite separate and distinct from its human managers and owners. In a legal and, indeed, in a real and practical sense, it has a life of its own. It has a moment of birth and its life can be brought to an end by a process known as liquidation – or there can be a 'takeover' by another company – but so long as all goes well there is no reason why a successful company should not go from strength to strength from one generation to another, being modified and evolving so that it adapts itself to the needs of the changing times.

The separation of ownership from management
A special feature of the company form, and one of immense practical importance, is that it makes possible a separation of the function of ownership of capital from that of management. It may happen that a person with a large personal fortune has an aptitude also to be a successful entrepreneur, manager and administrator. In brief, an entrepreneur is a person who has ideas, vision, imagination and an instinct or flair for sensing that a particular product, or service, or fashion, or style will appeal strongly to the public and will be widely demanded before anyone else senses this. He will be an innovator and a risk taker. Managers and administrators are different. Many regard the latter two words as interchangeable and there is not unanimity about the definitions.

A manager is a person who often has special abilities in some specialist function and who, in addition, is able to plan, organise and employ human and material resources efficiently. In a business environment he will be a man who, whatever his rank – supervisor, foreman or managing director – will have people under his control and he will be expected to produce results as a leader of a smaller or larger team. An administrator is often considered to be a senior manager whose special concern is to ensure that the structure of an organisation is sound and the various office services work smoothly and efficiently. His role may resemble that of a chief of staff of an army command. However, in the public, non-profit orientated type of organisation, the chief executive sometimes has the designation 'administrator', and the UK civil service the Administrative Grade is the most senior.

Successful entrepreneurs are often but by no means always good managers and good administrators, but many good managers are not entrepreneurs. However, a person with substantial capital available for investment in a business venture can lack skill of any kind for business. Equally, there are many potentially good managers, as well innovators and inventors who have no significant personal wealth. It was the limited-liability company which made it possible for wealthy investors, and others with some surplus resources, to come together with inventors, innovators as well as managers, so that the vital elements for a successful business venture could be brought together and a wealth-creating business activity could begin. It would be started with a main objective of making money, profits, for those who took the risks by providing the 'equity' or risk capital, the ordinary shareholders.

The limited-liability company form has made it possible for wealthy persons to provide capital whilst accepting a personal risk limited to the amount of the capital they contribute. Whilst the company itself has unlimited liability in the sense that it would always be called upon to meet its debts up to the limit of its resources, its human shareholders have their personal liability limited to the amount unpaid, if any, on the shares they own. It is this aspect of limited personal liability which makes this company form so attractive to investors. Conversely, it is the aspect of unlimited personal liability of partners which renders the partnership form of business unthinkable except in special circumstances and, not least, when all the partners know and have confidence in each other.

Company forms: the alternatives available

Money put at the disposal of a business, without which it cannot come into being, or operate, takes one of two fundamentally different forms:

(a) The money may be provided as a loan, which involves contractual obligations on the part of the business to the lender. There must be specified and regular interest payments and at the agreed time the loan must be repaid. If these obligations are not strictly met the lender may take court action against the borrower to enforce the obligation.

(b) Alternatively, the money put at the disposal of the business may take the form of 'risk capital'. The party who provides this is not a lender and the basis of the agreement will be that the provider of the risk capital will have a proportionate share in the business and will receive an appropriate share of any profits which are distributed in the form of dividends. In poor years there may be no profits to distribute. There may be losses. There may also be lack of liquidity – cash is not available for distribution.

The persons who provide the risk capital normally control the company (exceptionally, they would not do so if they held 'A' or non-voting shares). In the case of the majority of smaller companies, the private limited company, this may be a single majority shareholder, or it may be a small family group. The limited-liability company form permits abuses: owner-managers may inflict losses on creditors by evading liability and permitting a company to go into liquidation and then beginning again by forming another company. Other abuses include nepotism, or the unfair treatment of minority by majority shareholders, or the wielding of too much power by those who put only money at risk as distinct from their limited working lives – as long-service employees would have done. However, adjustments are made from time to time by legislation in attempts to counteract abuses. Furthermore, the EEC is also active in drafting legislation designed to adapt the company form so that as far as practicable the needs of the state, shareholders, creditors, employees, consumers and other interested parties are reconciled, and there is a growing view that companies, through their directors, should be more 'accountable' to the public interest, and not merely to those of shareholders. United Kingdom and EEC legislation, to which the UK must conform, aim to create a capitalist system which is more humane than the earlier forms. But whatever criticisms may be raised of the capitalist system as it has evolved in Europe, the USA and other parts of the world, it has provided citizens with higher material standards, including of social services, together with comparative freedom and a better quality of life than any alternative form of society has so far been able to achieve for its citizens.

There are several permitted company forms and the form chosen in a particular case will depend on the circumstances and expert advice will be necessary, including on the implications of taxation. The alternative forms from which choice can be made are:

Public companies (*a*) limited by shares;
                        (*b*) limited by guarantee, having a share capital;
                        (*c*) limited by guarantee, not having a share capital;
                        (*d*) unlimited, having a share capital.
Private companies (*a*) limited by shares;
                        (*b*) limited by guarantee, having a share capital;
                        (*c*) unlimited, having a share capital.

Private sector business 25

Some of the above forms are rarely used, and then in special circumstances, and they will accordingly only be examined briefly here.

Unlimited-liability companies
The advantage of an unlimited company over a limited one is that the former does not have to file with the Registrar of Companies copies of its audited accounts, which are then available for public inspection, including by competitors and major clients, as well as by trade union representatives. However, the risks of unlimited liability for shareholders are obviously so great that this company form is only adopted in special and rare circumstances, and normally only when it is practicable to limit the financial risks in practice. An unlimited company form has an obvious parallel with a partnership from the aspect of personal liability of members. The advantage offered by an unlimited company form over a partnership in a particular case might be continuity and the convenience of the distinct and separate identity of the corporate form. The aspect of taxation would also need to be considered.

Companies limited by guarantee
The company limited by guarantee is also a form which is suitable only in restricted and special circumstances, notably when the members consider it essential that their personal liability is limited, but the objects of the company are charitable or professional and expressly state that if any profits are made they will not be distributed to the members, but will be used to further the charitable or similar objectives of the company. Many well-known charities, educational trusts, public schools and professional bodies are incorporated as companies having liability limited by guarantee.

Companies limited by shares: public companies
The company forms with which students of business finance are primarily concerned are therefore: (*a*) public companies and (*b*) private companies limited by shares. As will be more fully considered in Chapter 3, public companies may be: (i) listed (quoted) on the Stock Exchange in the UK, which means that some at least of the securities issued by the company can, in theory if not in practice, be freely bought and sold through the Stock Exchange dealing system; and (ii) unlisted – the directors of such companies have not chosen to apply for the right to have their securities 'listed' and dealt in on the Stock Exchange, with the heavy costs and exacting requirements which have to be met at the outset. This may be because the company has not yet attained a sufficient size for acceptance, or the directors do not yet con-

sider that the company needs to be listed. Unlisted companies may be very large and successful. The Stock Exchange permits limited dealings in the shares of unlisted securities under Rule 163 (2), and an Unlisted Securities Market (USM) is under consideration. Investment bankers M.J.H. Nightingale also operate an 'over the counter' (OTC) market in unlisted securities. For obvious reasons the Stock Exchange does not permit dealings in the shares of unlimited companies. A public company must have at least seven members (shareholders) but six might hold only one share each so that a company can effectively be owned by one person.

Private limited companies
The private limited company is the most popular corporate form of business organisation in the UK and each year many more private than public limited companies are created. However, for technical reasons which need not be considered here, it is now usual for a company to be formed as a private limited company even if there is an intention immediately afterwards to convert it into a public limited company. In brief this procedure reduces significantly the formation formalities, is more convenient for the promoters and results in some savings in initial expenses.

A private company – which is understood to mean a private company limited by shares – is defined in the Companies Act, 1948, as one which, by its articles:
(*a*) restricts the right to transfer its shares;
(*b*) limits the number of its members to fifty, not including persons who are in the employment of the company and persons who, having formerly been in that employment, and having continued after the determination of that employment to be members of the company; and
(*c*) prohibits any invitation to the public to subscribe for any shares or debentures of the company.
It must have at least two members, but one might hold only a single share.

Incorporation of a company: filing of documents

Businessmen who seek the considerable privilege of carrying on their business through the form of a limited-liability company must pay a certain price for this. An important part of what is, in fact, a relatively very small price is that before the company begins operations it mus' 'file' (register) certain documents with the Registrar of Companies. If it is a private company it will receive a 'Certificate of Incorporation' from the Registrar and it may then commence business. A company formed as a public company would also receive this certificate but it could not begin operations until it had complied with certain additional formalities, when it would receive a 'Certificate of entitlement to commence business'. Subsequently every limited company must file prescribed documents, amongst the most important of these are the annual report and accounts. Furthermore, if a lender is given some security by the company for a loan, including a charge over some of its property, details must promptly be filed with the Registrar if they are to be effective against other creditors. These filed documents, including details of any charges, are open for public inspection. The purpose of this requirement of the law is that since the personal liability of the members of a company is limited it is essential that all those outside the company who contemplate dealing with it, or who act as advisers to others – bankers, traders, credit-investigation agencies, financial journalists, etc. – should be able to inform themselves about essential aspects of the company by inspecting the public file. In principle, anyone who does not trouble to do this (or arrange for others to do it for him) has only himself to blame if he deals with the company and later incurs loss because the company is not what he thought it was.

The following documents must be filed with the Registrar of Companies when a company is incorporated (created):
(a) Memorandum of Association;
(b) Articles of Association (which must be printed). Table A is often adopted;
(c) Statement of nominal capital;
(d) Declaration of compliance with the requirements of the Companies Act, 1948. This may be made either by a solicitor engaged in the formation or by a person named in the articles as a director or secretary.

The Notice of the Situation of the Registered Office and particulars of the directors and secretary must also be lodged. The Companies Act, 1948, defines a director as including any person occupying the position of a director, by whatever name called, and as including a person in accordance with whose directions or instructions the directors are accustomed to act (e.g. a majority shareholder who chose not to be a director but who had the power to appoint or dismiss directors). The Act states that a director is an officer of the company and as such will be liable to prescribed penalties if a company is in default of its obligations under the Act. Every public company registered since 1929 must have at least two directors. Every private company must have at least one director, and a sole director may not also be the secretary.

The Memorandum of Association
This is perhaps the most important single document relating to a company and it may be considered the company's charter. It must contain clauses stating:
(a) the name of the company with 'limited' as the last word;
(b) the situation of the Registered Office – i.e. whether in England or Scotland;
(c) the objects of the company;
(d) that the liability of the company is limited;
(e) the amount of share capital with which the company is to be registered, and the division thereof into shares of a fixed amount.

The objects of the company are the purposes it sets out to achieve. It is the custom now for the objects clause to be expressed in very wide terms so that, in effect, the company may in the future enter virtually any new field of activity. Standard model forms are readily available. The Memorandum of a company may be altered within limits set out in the Companies Acts.

The Articles of Association
These are subsidiary to the Memorandum but are still of key importance. They are effectively the by-laws or regulations of the company by which it regulates its internal affairs. They are also the formal mechanism whereby shareholders appoint directors and delegate the necessary powers to them. Subject to certain formalities the Articles of a company can readily be altered. A special resolution is required and this calls for 75% of the votes cast at a general meeting of shareholders. The Articles also operate at all times as a contract between shareholders and the company although the shareholders may not have signed them.

Table A
The First Schedule to the Companies Act, 1948, contains a very comprehensive model set of Articles, applicable to companies limited by shares, Table A, including a model which incorporates the three restrictive clauses which are essential if a company is to be a private company. Table A is optional and not compulsory, but many public as well as private companies are registered which signify that they adopt Table A, either as it stands, or with whatever modifications they choose to make, as their own articles. Earlier Companies Acts incorporated a Table A which was deemed appropriate at that time.

The formalities involved in incorporating a company are by no means unduly onerous. There are regular advertisements in the *Financial Times* wherein reputable advertisers undertake to sell 'off the peg' registered companies, or register a company to order, paying all stamp duties and fees, including a registration fee of £50. In 1980 the price could be well under £100. Law stationers supply model memoranda and articles. The Registrar of Companies also gives guidance, including restrictions with respect to the name chosen. Fuller information is available in *The Chartered Secretaries Manual of Company Secretarial Practice* (Jordan).

The human agents of a company

A company is regarded in law as a 'person' with its own identity, so that John Smith Ltd, is entirely distinct and separate from John Smith, its sole owner. (A fire insurance policy on a building in the name of John Smith would cease to be valid if the building were made over by John Smith to a company owned entirely by him. (*Macaura* v. *Northern Assurance Co. Ltd* (1925)). The insurance company would need first to approve in writing the assignment of the policy. However, whilst a company is a legal person it obviously can act only through human agents. When a company is owned by one or a small number of people, he or they may appoint himself or themselves directors but if there were many part-owners it would be impracticable for them all to share in the management. In brief, the owners of the company – in practice, the ordinary shareholders, whose rights will be set out in the Articles, and Table A is a comprehensive example – delegate their authority to directors, who may or may not themselves be shareholders. Unless the articles so require, it is not essential for a director also to be a shareholder. He may, for example, be a full-time salaried employee. The shareholders could dismiss him whenever they chose to do so, if this were the wish of the majority, but in this case the director could claim damages if he had a service contract with the company and this was breached.

The authority delegated to the directors by the shareholders is technically to them acting together as a board. A problem which seems to arise too frequently is that there is a single dominating director who effectively makes all the decisions, whilst the remaining directors merely take their salaries, fees and other perquisites and act as 'rubber stamps', doing whatever they are told. Normally this situation does not become public knowledge but it is liable to do so if the dominant director miscalculates, over-reaches himself, or commits fraud and the company collapses, or there is some scandal which cannot be covered up. In such cases there may be a Department of Trade enquiry and in due course a report will be published. Reports of this kind often disclose what Mr Heath once vividly described as 'the unacceptable face of capitalism'.

The Articles of Association set out in detail how the directors will be appointed and will regulate their meetings, and so on. They will also authorise the directors to appoint staff and delegate work, duties and authority, and generally do all that is necessary if the company is to operate effectively. All these matters are practical necessities. In this book expressions such as 'the company decides' will be used. The meaning is clear and is technically correct, but the underlying realities must always be borne in mind, that actions or decisions in the name of the company have to be made or carried out by human persons who have been properly authorised to act in the name of the company. Students are reminded that the role of directors, and the type of person who should be appointed, are now matters of public debate, and whether there should be a one-tier board of directors, as is the UK practice, or, possibly, a two-tier board, as is the practice in some EEC countries, and also what the role of part-time non-executive directors should be.

In the UK now it is evident that there are many well-run and successful companies whose directors include men and women of outstanding intellectual and moral stature. Some major companies only have full-time salaried directors, who need not be shareholders. Such directors normally have some special functional responsibilities such as finance, production, marketing, etc. The special attribute of able full-time directors is that they are men who in most cases have risen through ability and they have deep knowledge of their company. There are also part-time, non-executive directors in some cases and, properly chosen, they have the advantage of bringing wide experience and useful outside contacts to their role.

However, it is also evident that there are many incompetent, unqualified directors, often appointed for reasons of nepotism, whose lamentable performance is revealed in the course of an enquiry which is made public and raises the question whether there should be changes in the law, requiring, for example, that a person should have certain qualifications before being eligible for appointment as a director of a company above a certain size, or that directors whose performance is proved to have been seriously inadequate should be liable to financial or other sanctions and penalties. An unqualified person cannot practice as a lawyer, accountant, doctor, airline pilot, and so on. It is therefore arguable that only appropriately qualified people should be eligible to act as directors of companies in which members of the general public have invested money. This is an area of debate and controversy at the present time, and not only in the UK.

Chapter 3

The company as a legal person: assets and liabilities

The concept of the company as a legal person will be re-examined briefly from a most important legal and practical aspect, especially because it is evident that students, who usually have had little or no direct experience of these matters, have real difficulty in grasping the practical implications which flow from this concept. The essential fact is that a company has a separate and distinct identity and, in effect, a life of its own.

A consequence of a company having a separate identity from that of its owners or owner – even when a single person owns every share and the company bears his name, but with the important 'limited' (ltd) as the last word – is that it must operate and deal under its own name, and to do this it must be able, like a human person, to own property and incur liabilities under its own name. How is it able to do this? It is self-evident that no person can purchase anything unless he, she, or in the case of a company, it, first pays for it. How does a company obtain the money to pay for anything at the start of its life, before it has begun to obtain sales revenues in the form of cash? The answer is that it can only do so if human persons first vest money in it: that is, they put money in the form of 'risk', also known as 'equity' capital, or money in the form of a loan, or a mixture of both, in the name of the company, normally in a bank account. The moment that this is done the money becomes the company's own money and remains so unless and until, in accordance with the terms of an agreement which is not contrary to law, the company becomes under an obligation to pay money to any party to whom it has financial obligations.

So that trade creditors, investors and others who have dealings with companies may be protected, the actions of a company and its human agents are subject to specific statutory provisions as well as the general common law. The main statutory provisions are set out in the Companies Acts, but there are also other important statutes, including the

Prevention of Fraud Acts, and the Theft Act. Successive governments have also sanctioned that the Stock Exchange may operate certain controls over listed companies, noting that regulations of this kind can be effective, quicker acting and more flexible than statutes can usually be, and noting that a clever lawyer or accountant will often be able to find ways for people to act within the strict letter of a statute, even when directly against its spirit. Bearing in mind that the right to operate a business in limited-liability company form represents a very considerable privilege, the restrictions and controls imposed by law seem far from being unduly burdensome. Many would consider that they do not go far enough. They are tightened from time to time to meet the needs of changing times and when it becomes apparent that certain businessmen, and their advisers, have detected important weaknesses in the existing laws, and are exploiting and abusing them.

A new company: a problem of financial security

Before it is created a prospective company will own no property and therefore has nothing it can offer as security. At this time, unless its promoter is already well established and highly regarded in business circles, both the company and its promoter will be unknown and there can be no 'track record' and no question of 'goodwill'. Self-evidently, therefore, the new company will not be able to obtain money in the form of loans, as it can offer no security of any kind – neither property which can be the object of a fixed, or floating charge, nor an assured cash flow, a surplus of receipts over payments. At this stage, if money is to be raised at all, it must be in the form of 'risk capital'. Investors must be persuaded that if they make money available to the company on the basis of becoming part owners of it then, whilst they cannot be offered any security or guarantees the probability is that their investment will not only be maintained, but will also grow, as the company grows, and the probability of good profits is so strong that there is justification for expecting that the new company would be able to pay good dividends on risk capital – ordinary share capital. In brief, investors are persuaded to take calculated risks.

Sometimes a new company, without security itself, will be able to obtain a bank loan or overdraft, but on the basis that the promoter has given personal security or an acceptable personal guarantee to the bank – for example, promoters of a small- to medium-sized company may deposit the title deeds of their homes, or stocks and shares, as security for a loan to the new company. It will be evident that in such cases the real nature of money raised in this way is risk capital of the promoters rather than a loan from the bank since, if things go badly, the loss will fall upon the promoters and not the bank. Often, promoters will themselves make unsecured loans to a company, for technical reasons which will be considered later. Such unsecured loans will be seen also to have the nature of risk capital.

The need for an adequate risk – equity – capital base

The following is a proposition of fundamental importance: 'No private-sector business can be created and subsequently operated except on the basis that there is a foundation of sufficient risk capital.' Ordinary share capital is of this nature. When the minimum money needed for the start of a particular business has been decided and obtained, or promised, by the promoters, and then vested in the name of the company – and this will be the risk capital, normally in the form of ordinary shares – the company then owns cash and possibly other property in its own name and if it is then desired to supplement the original risk capital with loans from external sources, then the necessary security can be offered.

Another most important distinction must be remembered. It is that a person who puts risk capital at the disposal of a company is a shareholder and not a creditor. He invests his capital on the basis that he expects that the company will earn profits and he will have a share of these in the form of dividends and, if all goes well, his original investment will appreciate in value. There is a contractual relationship between the shareholder and the company and this is set out in the Articles. However, if the company does badly, and there has been no question of fraud against the shareholders, the ordinary shareholder has no redress against either the company or its promoters or directors. On the other hand, a person who lends money to the company, whether for a few days, or for many years, is a creditor of the company. He will normally lend against a fixed or floating charge as a security, or sometimes without security, on the basis that the company will pay him interest at an agreed rate, and will repay the principal at an agreed time (irredeemable loans are rare). If the company fails to keep its agreement – it defaults – then the creditor can take action through the courts to enforce the agreement or seize and sell the security. A company which defaults may even be forced into liquidation.

In practice, lenders against security normally restrict their loan to 60% or so at most of the market value of their security, since if they

The company as a legal person 35

had to enforce sale of the security there would be legal and other expenses, and a forced sale often realises a poor price, especially if a number take place at the same time. However, lenders are now usually as concerned with the cash flow of a company as they are with their security for a loan. A strong positive cash flow means that there is a probability that the company will be able to pay the loan interest and repay the principal without difficulty, which is what lenders desire.

Profit

Practical justification for profit
No matter how confident investors may feel that their risk capital investment will prove profitable and will give rise to dividend payments, as well as capital growth, they will also recognise that plans can fail, and there will be a risk of loss. Years may pass in which they receive no dividends and finally they could lose the whole of their investment. It is this basic and fundamental relationship between profit and risk which to many seems the primary justification of profit. That is, it would be unreasonable and unrealistic to expect investors to put their money, or resources convertible into money, at risk, when they were under no compulsion to do so, unless they were confident that the reward would be substantial if all went well. It is also logical to consider that the heavier the risk aspect of a projected venture, the higher the reward, in the form of profit, which investors will expect if the venture is successful.

In brief, it is the acceptance of the risk of loss which entitles an investor to a share of profits when all goes well. If it were not for this expectation of profits, risk, or equity, capital would not be available for private-sector business. If equity capital had not been available in the past then the UK and other industrialised countries could not have attained their present levels of prosperity. It is not suggested that there would not have been development and progress in the years since the Industrial Revolution, which began in the UK in the eighteenth century, but rather that progress would have been much slower and might not have gone so far. Indeed, much of the incentive for research, discovery and development, which caused the Industrial Revolution, and which has persisted ever since, has been the expectation of profit.

Profit as an indicator of efficiency
Profit has other major roles. A study of economics and, indeed, simple observation, demonstrates that the factors of production are in relative-

ly short supply everywhere. It is clearly in the general interest that they should all be used efficiently so that the largest practicable output, usually measured in terms of money, is obtained from a given input of resources, also measured in terms of money. Indeed, the definition of 'productivity' is the ratio of output to input. In a business environment the relationship between the profit generated and the capital employed, which will be considered in Chapter 13, is generally regarded as the most important single indicator of the financial and general health of a business although, like all such indicators, it needs to be carefully defined, measured, and then interpreted with caution.

Profit as a main source of new risk capital
Profit has a further major role in both private- and public-sector business. After payment of taxes, and dividends to shareholders in the case of private-sector businesses, the managements of successful businesses invariably retain a substantial proportion of profits earned, and these retained profits now represent the main source of new risk capital for private-sector businesses in the UK (p. 59). It is the making and then retaining of a significant proportion of profits for reinvestment which is a main cause of the growth of successful businesses.

The meaning and significance of assets

The profit motive has been noted as a common factor in every type of private- and public-sector business. Another common factor is that in order to achieve their objectives all businesses need either to own or have the use of assets of different kinds, and the ownership or use of these assets has to be financed by appropriate funds. This is a major theme in the subject of business finance.

An asset may be defined a property in some form. It will almost always have a market value. The three main categories recognised in business are: (*a*) fixed; (*b*) current; and (*c*) liquid assets. Two other less important and less frequently met categories need only be briefly considered. They are: (*d*) intangible; and (*e*) fictitious assets.

Intangible assets
The main example of an intangible asset is 'goodwill' which in practice may have no market value or, on the contrary, it may have an enormous one. Goodwill has many definitions, including a judicial one by

Lord Macnaughten (The Commissioners of Inland Revenue v Muller & Co's Margerine Ltd, 1901):
(goodwill) is a thing very easy to describe, very difficult to define. It is the benefit and advantage of the good name, reputation and connection of a business. It is the attractive force which brings in custom. It is the one thing which distinguishes an old established business from a new business at its first start. Goodwill is composed of a variety of elements. It differs in its composition in different trades and in different businesses in the same trade. One element may preponderate here and another there.

Goodwill may attach itself to the well-known name of a product, or to a particular site, or to a person who has an exceptional reputation in some field. It is not an accepted practice now for a business to attempt to place a value on its goodwill and bring this into its books of account and its balance sheet. Accordingly, when 'goodwill' appears as an item in a published balance sheet the implication is that the company concerned has previously bought another business and, as is normal, has paid a higher price for it than is represented by the book value of the net assets acquired. The buying company will have to record this difference in its books of account and it does so by opening an account designated 'goodwill'. When this account has been opened by a company, it must appear in the balance sheet, unless it has been written off against the profit-and-loss account. As goodwill represents something for which the company has made payment, it must appear as an asset. However, it is clearly something which a company could not sell except as part of a complete sale of the company as a going concern (or an important part of it), and it cannot be regarded in the same way as other assets for which a market value could readily be assessed.

The designation 'intangible' is clearly appropriate for assets which are not readily marketable. Intangible certainly does not necessarily imply negligible value. Whilst goodwill and other intangible assets, notably 'research and development' expenditure (whose appearance in a balance sheet indicates that it has been treated as capital expenditure and not written off as operating expenditure in the profit-and-loss account) may or may not have substantial value, it is widely regarded as prudent that whenever practicable they should be written off to the profit-and-loss account over a reasonably short period. In a particular case, when assets of this type appear in a balance sheet an analyst would ask himself 'do these assets genuinely have the values attributed to them?' and he would be likely to discount them heavily, or ignore them, when making his evaluations. Indeed, the fact that a certain item appears in a balance sheet when it is not usual for it to do so, when it would normally have been written off, will raise a question in the mind of the analyst.

Statements of Standard Accounting Practice (SSAPs)

The fact is that there are Statements of Standard Accounting Practice which prescribe standards of accounting approved by the major accountancy bodies in the UK for application to all financial accounts, and which are intended, *inter alia*, to reduce the scope for manipulation of accounts, and to ensure uniformity and consistency of treatment of certain important matters. These SSAPs, as they are known, are primarily technical and must be studied by students of accountancy rather than business finance at this stage. For example, SSAP 13 deals with Accounting for Research and Development and, in brief, requires that research expenditure should promptly be written off, but development expenditure may be capitalised subject to certain stringent tests, and on the basis that eventual sales revenues will in due course recover this expenditure.

Fictitious (or nominal) assets

A fictitious asset is quite different from an intangible one, and is what its name indicates – an asset which has to appear in the books of account because it has not yet been written off against profits earned, and yet it is totally valueless. When a company has made a profit in a year there will be a credit balance on the profit-and-loss account and any part of this which is not distributed as a dividend must appear in the balance sheet as a liability – that is, something which does not belong to the company: in this case, it belongs to the ordinary shareholders. It will be grouped with the share capital account, as part of the ordinary shareholders' equity. However, if a company makes losses, which cannot be set off against earlier retained profits, or reserves, there will be a debit balance on the profit-and-loss account: that is, the loss appears as an asset, but, obviously, a valueless one (ignoring any possible taxation implications), a 'fictitious' asset. In the same way, when legal and other expenses have to be charged to a company on its formation, and as yet there are no profits against which these expenses can be written off, the relevant debit balance would also appear on the balance sheet, but separated from the other assets, and in the category of fictitious assets. Expenses of this kind should be written off to the profit-and-loss account as soon as possible.

Many balance sheets do not include either intangible or fictitious assets but all will incorporate current and liquid assets and almost always there will be fixed assets as well: often the fixed assets far exceed the current and liquid assets in value.

Fixed assets

Fixed assets may be defined as material items to be used in a business for more than one year and not held primarily for resale. What they are in a particular case will depend on the nature of the business concerned. Common examples of fixed assets are: factories; land; machines; plant; office equipment of all kinds, from mainframe computers to typewriters and smaller items; ships; aircraft; railway engines and carriages; etc. A car or a lorry is normally a fixed asset of a business but it would be a current asset if held for resale by a dealer in cars and lorries. Whilst many companies own all or a large proportion of their fixed assets, having purchased them outright, an increasing proportion do not own all (or even any) of their fixed assets, but instead they lease them. Leasing is considered later (p. 192) but managements of businesses increasingly recognise that it is not the ownership of an asset which is normally important from an operating viewpoint, but rather the right to undisturbed use of the asset for an agreed period. Each case has to be examined in the light of its own circumstances and special factors favouring leasing include the fact that agreed annual payments are made instead of a large initial capital outlay. This benefits the cash flow of a company. The taxation implications need to be considered on each occasion.

Wasting assets

Wasting assets are fixed in nature but are consumed in use or by the passage of time. Examples are a mine or oil well, or a lease. In a sense most fixed assets have a wasting nature since, with the exception of land, all tend to deteriorate or wear out at a slower or faster rate.

Current (or floating or circulating) assets

Current assets are those which do not remain in continuing use, as fixed assets do. They are 'turned over' regularly in the course of a financial year. Current assets include all forms of stock – raw materials; components; 'work in progress'; finished goods awaiting sale; debtors with due provision for bad debts when this seems to be necessary; cash; bank balances; bills receivable, if any; and other near-cash items such as Treasury bills, which a company might own as an interest-earning short-term investment. A company balance sheet may also show 'investments' as assets. If these are held simply as revenue-earning short-term assets, to be sold whenever cash is needed, they may be regarded as current assets. However, 'trade investments' will be shown as such on the balance sheet and are regarded as fixed rather than current assets as they will not be intended for resale. 'Trade investments' are holdings in associated companies such as important customers or suppliers and are held for strategic purposes to give a company a useful although probably not a controlling voice in the policy making and management of associated companies.

Liquid (or 'quick') assets

The essential feature of current assets is that they are continually being 'turned over', being used and renewed. However, stocks are not quickly realisable, or could often only be sold quickly at a loss. Meanwhile, it is always essential that a company pays its debts as they fall due – salaries, wages, overtime, suppliers and other creditors. Liquid assets are components of the current assets but are those which are in the form of cash or bank balances, bills receivable or any other realisable investments. Debtors are also regarded as liquid assets provided that any debtors considered unlikely to pay promptly for any reason are excluded.

Financing the assets of a company

The promoter of a private-sector business, irrespective of size, should always begin with clear objectives and confidence that he will be able to attain these on a profit-making basis. He must have 'done his homework'. It will be assumed that the decision is initially to form and operate a private limited-liability company – the company will include the appropriate restrictive clauses in its articles. The promoter will carefully assess the resources needed at the start, human and material, and will bear in mind that, depending on the business, there will be a short or long period before the company is able to begin operations and sell goods or services so that cash is received in respect of the sales and is itself available towards meeting the liabilities of the company. The promoter will need to consider the assets which the company will need to own (or lease) bearing in mind that everything must be done in the name of the company and not his own name and, in consequence, the company must have the necessary finance vested in it, so that it can finance its operations until it begins to receive cash in respect of sales. The promoter must also bear in mind that the company must also have money at its disposal to meet contingencies, the unexpected, since in practice there are often delays and unforeseen expenses and cost increases. Often promising new companies are unnecessarily forced into liquidation because no provision has been made to deal with contingencies.

Double-entry book-keeping (the dual aspect)

At this point a most important concept will be considered briefly. It is essential for all students of this subject to be familiar with the double-entry principle in accounting – which will be fully explained in any textbook on book-keeping and accounting. In brief, every business transaction has a dual financial aspect. If, for example, a company buys a typewriter – or a steamship, as the principle is the same – it will reduce its asset, cash, to the extent of the cash payment made for the asset, but it will acquire a new asset, a typewriter, and the transactions must be recorded in the books of account so that reference to them will show what has happened. In this simple example, from the book-keeping aspect, the total value of the assets remains as it was before, but there has been a change in the composition of the assets: a current asset, cash, has been reduced by £x, and a fixed asset, a typewriter, has been acquired and is recorded in the accounts at its cost, £x. Transactions are recorded on the basis that the account which gives value – in this case the cash account – is credited, and the account which receives value – in this case the fixed asset, or typewriter account – is debited. A most important point must be remembered. There is a credit entry and an equal debit entry with respect to every transaction recorded in the books of account and the total of the debit and credit entries must therefore always be equal. This does not mean that there must always be the same number of debit and credit entries in the accounts: thus, there may be many individual debits in respect of sales on credit to individual customers, and a single periodic equal and total credit to the sales account.

If an asset is bought on credit, in the first instance it will be the account of the creditor which is regarded as having given value and that account must be credited with £x. The debit entry will be as before. Subsequently, when the creditor is paid, he would then have received value and his account would be debited, and the cash account, having given value, would be credited. The final position would be as when the payment had been made for cash – a credit to the cash account and a debit to the appropriate asset account.

Whilst the underlying principle of double-entry book-keeping is simple, once it has been thoroughly grasped, the applications can be very complex. There is a practical aspect of the utmost importance. When the accounts of a company are prepared, then no matter how small or how vast the company or group of companies may be, the totals of the debit and credit entries must always be equal. If they are not it will be certain that at least one mistake has been made. Planning of the book-keeping system should include as a main aim that locating an error or errors should not be too difficult. Unfortunately, if the totals of the debit and credit entries are equal it is not certain that no mistakes have been made. There could be compensating or certain other types of errors. Textbooks on accounting will give full details.

The balance sheet

Like the limited-liability company, double-entry book-keeping was a brilliant insight, discovery, or invention. The insight was to recognise that every transaction has a dual aspect, and the invention was the means to give practical effect to this – double-entry book-keeping. It is not a recent concept. It was widely used and developed to a high degree of sophistication by Venetian merchants in the twelth and thirteenth centuries. It may have been invented in Arabia. By the sixteenth century it had been exported to all parts of Europe, and yet, even today, some small businesses attempt to operate without recourse to it. A consequence of the double-entry system is the familiar fact that the balance sheet always balances with, in the conventional form, the assets shown on the right and liabilities on the left. The balance sheet is a classified summary of the balances remaining open in the ledgers after the balances on the nominal accounts have been transferred to the profit-and-loss account, and including the balance on that account. The balance sheet represents a 'snapshot' as it were, of the financial situation of a company at one moment in time. It sets out the assets and liabilities (which include capital) of a company in effect at the close of business on the last day of a financial period – the published form usually being the last day of the financial year. A balance sheet should always show this date, e.g. 'Balance Sheet as at 31 December 198 . . .'.

The liabilities of a company

The assets of a business are, of course, what the business owns, and the liabilities are what it owes. Many students are at first puzzled that the capital of a company is shown in a conventional balance sheet at the head of the liabilities. It would seem that the capital of a company is a most important part of what it owns rather than what it owes. However, on reflection, the explanation is apparent. It has been explained that a company cannot begin to acquire assets until money has been vested in its name, so that it can purchase or lease them. Furthermore, in addition to acquiring assets, a company will have to pay promotion and other expenses, such as salaries, etc. People and/or institutions must first put equity, or risk, capital at the disposal of a company before it will be in a position to operate. Self-evidently, the company has an obligation, a liability, to those who provide it with funds – in the form of risk capital or loans – and also to those who supply it with raw materials or other goods or services on credit. As will be seen, the more modern treatment of a balance sheet is to set it out in vertical, tabular form and to describe the assets as 'applications, or uses, of funds', and the liabilities as 'sources of funds'.

Classifications of liabilities

A primary classification of liabilities is according to whether they are redeemable or irredeemable and, if redeemable, the period for which the company may have the undisturbed use of the funds represented by the liability: another classification is whether a particular liability is part of the risk capital, or part of the loan funds.

Permanent liabilities: the capital funds

Permanent liabilities for the most part comprise ordinary shares, which are only redeemable in exceptional and carefully defined circumstances and subject to the approval of the High Court. Preference shares may also be irredeemable in theory if not in fact, but they are seldom issued now and normally in special circumstances. There may also be irredeemable debentures but these are seldom, if ever, issued now.

Long-term liabilities

It is now widely considered that long-term liabilities are debts which do not fall due for repayment until after the expiry of ten years. In the past many companies issued long-term debentures with a life in some cases of between twenty and thirty years. A debenture is defined as a written acknowledgement of a debt by a company, usually under seal, and generally containing provisions as to payment of interest and repayment of principal. It may be either a simple or naked debenture, carrying no charge on assets, or a mortgage debenture, carrying either a fixed or floating charge on some or all of the assets for the time being of a company. For reasons considered later (p. 469), in recent years there has been a marked decline in the value of debentures issued annually in the UK and companies have been having recourse to institutions, such as insurance companies, pension funds and specialist organisations. Recently, clearing banks have also been prepared to lend for longer periods, even up to twenty years in exceptional cases.

Medium-term liabilities

These are now generally regarded as liabilities which fall due for payment not earlier than three years nor later than ten years from the date of the balance sheet under review. Clearing banks are major sources of this type of funds, as are merchant banks, leasing companies, finance houses and institutions such as Industrial and Commercial Finance Corporation Ltd (ICFC) and Finance Corporation for Industry Ltd (FCI) (p. 198).

Short-term and current liabilities

Short-term liabilities are generally regarded as those due for payment between one and three years from the date of the balance sheet, whilst current liabilities are those payable within the next twelve months. Trade creditors come within this latter category, as do taxation liabilities, bank overdrafts and dividends declared but not yet paid.

The capital structure of a company: a preliminary view

The fact that every business must own or have the use of certain assets has been briefly considered, and that the largest proportion of these may be placed in one of two main categories: (*a*) fixed, or (*b*) current assets. The 'mix' will vary from company to company and from industry to industry.

Before the present growth in the leasing of fixed assets, when companies were obliged to own their assets, it could be expected that in a particular industry the ratio of the values of fixed to current assets, and a number of other ratios, would normally lie within fairly well-defined limits which would be well known to competent managers within that industry. However, when, in a particular industry, it becomes feasible to lease rather than own fixed assets then the ratios may lie within much wider limits and ratio analysis becomes more difficult. Meanwhile, it can be stated that when the leasing of fixed assets is feasible, a decision to lease rather than buy will mean that a company will be able to begin operations with a significantly smaller capital than would be necessary if the decision had been to purchase the fixed assets.

The concept of the capital structure of a company is easier to describe than to define. The assets which the company is to own or lease must be financed, employees recruited and paid, at the start, before any revenues from sales begin to be received in cash. It will be a practical necessity that a substantial part of the initial finance will take the form

The company as a legal person

of risk capital, which is of permanent nature. There may then be a 'mix' of long-, medium- and short-term loan finance obtained against the security of assets purchased in the name of the company with its risk capital funds. The capital structure of a company is determined by the relationship between the sources of the company's funds which are made available by creditors (notably lenders and trade creditors) and those made available by the suppliers of risk capital, the ordinary shareholders. There seems to be no single accepted definition of capital structure, which is closely linked with the concept of 'gearing', for which there are a number of measurements and the one(s) chosen in a particular case will depend on whose interests the analyst is serving – ordinary shareholders, debenture holders, bankers, trade creditors, etc.

Gearing: a preliminary view

It has been explained that promoters and other investors put money into ordinary shares, thereby putting their money at risk, in the hope of profit. As will be seen, a main indicator of the performance of a company from the viewpoint of its ordinary shareholders is the 'earnings per share', which will be considered more fully later. In brief, these earnings are measured by dividing the profits of the company after tax by the number of ordinary shares in issue. It is a measure on which analysts focus attention and managements aim for a steadily rising trend in the earnings per share ratio. Whilst the earnings per share (EPS) will rise as operating profits rise at a time when the ordinary shares in issue remain unchanged, they may also be increased independently by skilful financial management of the company, which involves the use of gearing (known as 'leverage' in the USA). A company has to pay for the use of finance, as it has to pay for the use of any resources: it happens that the concept of the 'cost of capital' is a particularly difficult and controversial concept. For the moment, it should be noted that gearing arises when a company has recourse to borrowed money to finance operations, in addition to the employment of risk capital. The cost of this borrowed money is the agreed rate of interest payable for it and in the UK (as elsewhere) this cost is effectively reduced since the Inland Revenue treats interest payments as allowable expenses for taxation purposes. When a company uses borrowed money to finance operations which generate profits which exceed the cost of the borrowings, the surplus – the difference between the costs of these loans and the profits generated by their use – accrues to the ordinary shareholders. It is a surplus which arises from the use of gearing.

The skilful use of gearing can considerably increase the earnings per share of a company. However, its use involves risks and dangers, and reckless use has led to the unnecessary liquidation of numbers of companies. The dangers arise from the fact that when a company borrows, it creates obligations to pay interest and repay the principal in due course, irrespective of whether its affairs are going well or badly. In brief, if a company unexpectedly encounters bad trading conditions the directors could suspend dividend payments to the ordinary shareholders but they must continue strictly to meet their obligations to their creditors. Failure to do so would entitle creditors to initiate court actions, enforce and sell securities, or assume control over the company and, if the debts could be paid in no other way, cause the company to be put into liquidation and its assets sold. In brief, when skilfully and prudently used, gearing can increase the earnings per share of the ordinary shareholders beyond what they would have been without gearing: however, the potential dangers should not be ignored.

The capital structure of a company may and often does change over a period of time. At the start the options available to a promoter may be limited. For the first years he may have to rely on his own personal capital until the company has fixed assets in its name to offer as security, and until he and his company have proved themselves to the point that outside investors, including banks, would be prepared to make loan or debenture funds available on acceptable terms. The company thus begins with a capital structure of equity capital, and no gearing. This risk capital may be supplemented by a bank overdraft and or short-term loan secured against the personal property of the promoter, so that the bank cannot lose, but loans of this type are effectively risk capital of the promoter. However, even in the earliest days a company is likely to receive trade credit.

In due course, if the company were successful, and if external conditions including long-term interest rates seemed favourable, there would be the option of making a major change in the financial structure by adding debentures or long-term bank loans or loans from financial institutions as main long-term sources of funds, especially for financing the purchase of revenue-generating fixed assets or increasing the long-term working capital of a growing company. This option arises because when a company gives proof of being successful, investors who previously would not be prepared to lend to it would now be ready to do so.

In fact, the choice of the capital structure of a developing, or of a mature company may be made within quite wide limits and often the critical factor is the temperament of a promoter, or major shareholder, or

The company as a legal person

dominating chief executive. Some successful businessmen dislike the idea of debt and prefer to finance growth by paying small dividends in the early stages and 'ploughing back' or retaining profits. They accept that growth will almost certainly be slower than it would have been if they had raised additional finance by issuing more ordinary shares or, alternatively, raising long-term loans. Others have quite different temperaments and choose to make the maximum use of gearing despite the risks entailed. There are thus two extremes – an ultra-cautious and conservative chief executive, in a financial sense, who prefers low gearing – a low ratio of debt to equity – and another, with a gambler's temperament, who may be equally able and dedicated, who chooses high gearing, for the chance of higher rewards, and accepts the risks. Most companies choose an intermediate position and it seems that in the UK companies tend to be rather lower geared than their counterparts elsewhere. The Wilson Committee reports (see Ch. 25) present much interesting and first-hand evidence on this very important subject. The Wilson Committee defines the gearing ratio as 'the ratio of bank borrowing and long-term debt to share capital and reserves'.

Chapter 4

The capital needed at the start of a private-sector company

The main theme of this chapter is the assessment of the capital needed to start a private-sector business – the determination of a suitable capital structure. Note that there are no rigid rules in this matter and the choice may be made within quite wide limits. Some important concepts will be examined, notably the cost of capital, and gearing.

The initial capital: the options

Any person who works at a responsible level will continually be faced with the need to make a choice between alternatives. This, indeed, is what decision making is all about. When there is no choice, no decision will be needed. In practice, when considering a particular topic, in this case the start of private-sector business, the starting point is to identify all the possible alternatives, or options, including those which might not be self-evident, but would be known to an alert expert, and then examine each in turn so that, hopefully, the best can be determined and chosen. Often important decisions effectively make themselves. If a particular business can only be started on a large scale, or not at all, then if the intending promoters ascertain that they have no possibility of marshalling the necessary substantial resources, the only real option will be to abandon the project. In real life this often proves to be the situation. Exceptionally, the business might have developed brilliantly and the community will be the poorer because the idea had to be abandoned, but this can never be known for certain. A more usual situation is that if an idea has to be abandoned it is for the reason that it was a 'non-starter' – something which seemed to have possibilities but did not stand up to critical and objective scrutiny.

Questions which should be asked now, but which might not occur to a non-specialist, include 'must this business be set up in the UK and, if not,

Capital for the private sector company

are there governments which offer special incentives to new businesses, e.g. cash grants; interest-free or cheap loans; prolonged tax holidays; etc., and against a background of political stability?' 'Which governments are likely to be helpful and should be approached?' Close to the UK the Government of Eire has been specially successful in attracting new companies to Eire. It offers very attractive 'packages' of inducements and incentives. If it were decided that a particular business should be operated in the UK a question would be 'is special government assistance available in certain locations and, if so, are some more favoured than others, and what exactly is available?' It has been evident that in recent years major multi-national companies have been 'playing-off' one government against others when they have sought to establish a major new factory. Governments have been prepared to offer grants and tax concessions in the effort to persuade the multi-national to establish a major factory in an area of high unemployment in their country. In practice, knowledgeable promoters can obtain significant finance, including risk capital, on favourable terms by presenting a convincing case to an appropriate government agency – in the UK or elsewhere.

In most cases there will not be just two options – start on a large scale, or not at all: more usually there will be several options. There may seem to be an optimum size but if the necessary finance cannot be raised then the business can still be started but on a sub-optimum, smaller scale, or even on a very small scale. In recent years numbers of fast-growing small businesses were started by an executive who decided that he would prefer to be chief executive of his own small company rather than a senior one in a large company. Some large companies, including ICI and Shell, may actively cooperate with managers who act in this way. Some companies now 'hive-off' and sell on concessionary terms subsidiary companies to their existing managements. In such cases the parent company considers the subsidiary to be rather away from the mainstream of its own business, but recognises that it could be profitably developed by its present management team as an independent company. In the present social climate, when the view is widely accepted that small companies create relatively more jobs than larger, more capital-intensive companies can hope to do, it seems certain that in one way or another, governments will create or extend measures to assist the establishment or expansion of small businesses. There is also evidence that sometimes a senior executive of a large company establishes a company without giving up his well-paid job and, indeed, depends on his salary as an important part of his cash flow. In such cases the executive, and possibly members of his family, will be the major or sole shareholder of the new company, which will be managed by a full-time salaried employee who would refer major or policy decisions to the major shareholder. This is a normal pattern for family-owned companies with a non-executive major shareholder.

In practice, it is often a good rather than a bad thing that it is difficult to raise risk capital. Experience has shown that resources can be wasted if large-scale projects are entered into by well intentioned, intelligent, but inexperienced people who have been given too easy access to finance – usually by a government. Governments have easy access to money and politicians and civil servants are never effectively and personally held to account for lack of care, competence or control in the spending of public money. A famous example – there are many more, including the Anglo-French Concorde project – was the East African Groundnuts Scheme of 1946. Shortly after the Second World War expert opinion, which is so often proved wrong by events and was proved wrong on this occasion, was that there would be a serious world-wide shortage of vegetable oils.

The government of the day in the UK, acting through ministers and senior civil servants, decided that it was of national importance urgently to sponsor the cultivation of groundnuts on a large scale on previously uncultivated land in East Africa. Because the whole question was considered from political and not business viewpoints, the normal business tests were not applied and the resources of the state were put at the disposal of the new project. Money was no object. The project was launched on a grand, widely publicised scale and it proved to be an unmitigated disaster, with incompetence, waste and theft on huge scales at many levels and on all sides, and millions of pounds of public money were irretrievably squandered. It produced no groundnuts at all and, in the event, the whole affair proved to be a false alarm, with the experts proved wrong yet again. There was no shortage of vegetable oils. Supply and demand adjusted themselves with remarkably little difficulty through the normal operation of market forces. On this occasion the private sector succeeded where the public sector failed.

In this case, being 'wise after the event', it would have been more sensible to have begun with a small pilot scheme which would have identified the many difficult and unforeseeable problems which inevitably arise in a new and untried venture of this type. This would have allowed assessment of whether a large-scale scheme would have had acceptable prospects of success. However, ministers, politicians and civil servants who, in their different ways, are ambitious for personal success and promotion tend to be interested especially in schemes which give them scope for quick self-aggrandisement, engineered publicity and 'empire building'. Money from the public purse is abundantly available and if things go wrong they are quickly forgotten. Often they are deliberately and successfully 'covered up', so that few are aware of what has gone wrong. When cases of exceptional mismanagement or scandal in the handling of public money are brought to light it is more often than not in consequence of vigilance and skill on the part of journalists, in the UK as well as other Western countries, often allied with leakage of 'inside' information by some disaffected person with access to the facts.

In Eastern bloc, socialist countries, where the press is controlled by the government and the civil service, it is a fair assumption that there are at least as many cases of mismanagement, incompetence or corruption, but they are not allowed to come to light and this must surely be a main reason for the relatively poor economic performance of these countries. It does seem, not surprisingly, that business-type situations are more successfully managed by people experienced in business rather than politicians and civil servants, whose experience and training has been related to different types of activity.

In the same way, it may not be a wholly bad thing that company promoters often have to start on a smaller scale than they would have wished, because of difficulty in raising finance. If they fail, the loss is limited, but if it soon becomes evident that a new company is doing well, with good profits and fast growth, the promoters can then expect to be able to raise finance from external sources with less difficulty and at lower costs than they could have hoped to do before the new company had been able to gain a track record and prove itself.

Capital: yield – a preliminary view

The word 'capital' is frequently used and sometimes with a technical meaning as in expressions such as 'working capital'. Capital is here considered to mean property of any kind which has a market value. The significance of capital is examined in depth in textbooks on economics: often the creation of capital is associated with the foregoing of immediate consumption, or saving. Capital, as property with a market value normally, but not always, has an earning power and in this connection the word 'yield' will be met. Yield may be regarded as the income received from property, usually expressed as a percentage of the current market price, or value. When capital is in the form of money the earning power will vary according to the use of the money which has been decided upon. Capital in the form of land or a building may be rented and the rent will be the measure of the yield.

However, whilst capital in many of its forms has an earning power, or yield, in other important forms it may not have this. For example, wealthy people often hold a proportion of their assets in the form of gold or precious stones, or pictures, or rare postage stamps. Others buy land without agricultural value but with the intention of holding it, without income, in the expectation that in due course it will be sold for building plots at much higher prices. Many wealthy people hold some assets which do not provide income or, in other words, offer no yield, because the investor bears in mind that he will eventually sell these assets and obtain a large capital gain, which may escape tax or be taxable at a much lower rate than the 'top slice' of a large income. An institution, the British Rail Pension Fund, also, for some time, had a policy of buying, with a small proportion of its large income, high-value works of art, accepting that they would not provide a stream of income but with the expectation that after some years they would be sold and provide large capital profits for the Fund.

Another special factor is important in politically unstable countries. Wealthy people who assess that some day they may need to escape from the country at short notice, in addition to holding a proportion of their wealth in secret bank accounts in Switzerland and elsewhere will also hold gold and precious stones. They forego the yield which they could have obtained on other investments for the advantages of holding high-value and easily transportable assets which at any time can quickly be sold anywhere. In a crisis the holding of such assets may make the difference between life and death and will be regarded as a form of insurance policy.

Preparations for the start

A promoter who plans to establish a private limited company will be presumed to have established good relationships with bank managers and other useful business contacts. A good way to do this is to establish a reputation for reliability, integrity and the ability to produce results. The Stock Exchange motto 'my word is my bond' is a good one and worth acting upon. So are three basic rules for the development of a new company from its start: these are: (*a*) be certain that there will be a strong and continuing market for whatever goods or services you propose to sell; (*b*) keep your overheads as low as you can; (*c*) 'plough back' all the profits you can into the business. For examples, successful companies have been started in the home or outbuildings of the promoter:

if suitable premises can be rented rather than purchased, less capital will be needed at the start.

However, when all the essential basic assessments have been made and the signs are considered favourable and it is evident that all the non-financial arrangements can be made satisfactorily, including the employment of a suitable workforce, it will be necessary to marshal the required financial resources. This will entail having careful regard to: (*a*) the suitability, and (*b*) the cost of capital. The suitability of different forms of finance is bound up with the concept of the capital structure, the period of availability of different forms of finance, and likely changes in the future both as regards availability and costs, which will be determined or influenced by prevailing interest rates, which have fluctuated widely in recent years. Gearing must also be considered.

The cost of capital

Fixed-interest loans

The cost of capital of any category is the price which has to be paid for its use. Its nominal cost can be calculated with precision in the case of fixed-interest loans, but not the real cost, which is affected by changes in the value of money. In practice, inflation benefits borrowers since the real cost of the interest payments falls and the principal ultimately repaid has a lower value – purchasing power – than the original sum borrowed. As to the nominal cost, if a loan of, say £100 is considered, and the interest is agreed at 10% p.a. then the borrower is, in effect, hiring £100 and paying £10 p.a. for the use of it – a hire or rent equivalent – and with the obligation to repay £100 in accordance with the terms of the agreement. The principle is the same as for any other hiring.

Tax benefits in respect of loans

A matter of the utmost practical importance is that successive governments in the UK have all allowed interest payments, including debenture interest, as an expense which may be deducted from revenues to arrive at the profit liable to tax. The practical effect of this is that when Corporation Tax stands at 50%, the effective cost of the debenture or loan is only half the nominal cost. Consider the following simple example: two companies, A and B, employ the same total of long-term funds – £4 m. In the case of A this is represented by 4 m. £1 ordinary shares and no loan funds: B has 3 m. £1 ordinary shares in issue and £1 m. as

10% debentures. Both companies have a before-tax profit of £500,000 and Corporation Tax is 50%. The comparison is:

	Company A (£)	Company B (£)
Profits before tax and interest	500,000	500,000
Deduct interest on 10% debentures	–	100,000
Profits before tax	500,000	400,000
Deduct Corporation Tax at 50%	250,000	200,000
After-tax profit	250,000	200,000

Thus, in consequence of the favourable tax treatment, although Company B has paid £100,000 debenture interest, its final after-tax profits are only £50,000 below those of Company A. In this example, the result of the different financial structures of the two companies and the favourable tax treatment of interest payments means that the earnings per share are significantly higher for Company B. Thus, earnings per share: Company A: after-tax profits/number of shares in issue: £250,000/4 m., i.e. £0.0625

Company B: after-tax profits/number of shares in issue: £200,000/3 m., i.e. £0.0667

This major concession in tax treatment, which dates from 1965, has greatly increased the appeal of fixed- (and variable-) interest loans to business managements. In fact, in recent years relatively few debenture issues have been made and there has been more reliance on bank borrowings. An important aspect of the tax treatment of loans should not be overlooked. It is that if a company incurs losses and in consequence there is no liability to tax against which the loan interest can be offset, then the company will have to pay the full nominal cost of the loan at a time when it can least afford to do so.

Bank loans and overdrafts: variable interest

The cost of all fixed-interest funds of this type is calculated in the same manner as just explained, and the favourable tax treatment also applies. However, interest is always payable on overdrafts at a variable rate, linked to the Minimum Lending Rate (MLR). This is the advertised minimum rate at which the Bank of England will discount approved bills of exchange of not more than three months' currency, or grant short-term loans when acting as a lender of last resort. In 1972 MLR replaced the more familiar Bank Rate. Clearly, the cost of capital cannot be calculated with precision beforehand in respect of any funds

Capital for the private sector company

whose costs may move up or down unpredictably in the future. Whilst businessmen will obviously prefer to know with precision what the costs of a particular resource will be for a defined future time, the fact is that in recent years the costs of most resources – materials, labour, energy, etc. – have been largely unpredictable. Variable interest rates add one more element to the risks and uncertainties which businessmen have to accept and try to accommodate.

Interest calculated on (a) original or (b) reducing balances
It is important always to ascertain whether a rate of interest quoted is payable on the original, opening balance, or on the reducing balance: the former is approximately double the latter. Loan interest is usually but not always quoted on the opening balance, whereas in the case of overdrafts it is always quoted on the reducing balance. This is an important reason why overdrafts are so widely preferred by companies as short-term funds.

Current liabilities

A noteworthy feature of credit granted by suppliers and other creditors is that, unusually, it is free, except in two circumstances: (a) if the creditor offers a specified discount for prompt payment; or (b) if the creditor's agreed terms of supply provide that interest will be charged at a specified rate on overdue balances. In the latter case the supplier's credit will be free until the date payment falls due. The value of cost-free creditors' finance in respect of working capital and the operating cycle is apparent in the worked example on page 127. There are now regular complaints that some larger companies, nationalised industries and government departments abuse this facility by delaying payments even for months beyond the due date. Their reasoning must be that their business is so valuable to suppliers that none will press too hard for payment for fear of losing a major customer: however, recently some chairmen of major companies have stated that in order to relieve the liquidity problems of small suppliers they have issued instructions that their invoices should be paid promptly. Meanwhile, smaller companies which delay payments to their suppliers are vulnerable as their creditors would be prepared to lose their business and would press vigorously for payment, including through the courts. In brief, a company management must ensure that liabilities can always be met as they fall due.

Cash discounts
When a supplier offers a cash discount for prompt payment it will

always be important to calculate the value of the discount. It can be so high that it is worth while having even if this entails paying interest on an overdraft. The basic formula is the well-known and easily remembered one used for calculating bankers' discount on bills of exchange. It is:

$$\text{Discount} = \text{principal sum} \times \frac{\text{rate of interest}}{100} \times \frac{\text{number of days}}{365}$$

As an illustration, if a supplier's terms of credit are payment within thirty days but with a cash discount of 2½% if payment is made within seven days, then it is apparent that if a sum of £100 is considered, in effect, the company has the option of paying £97.50 within seven days, or paying £100 at the end of thirty days. This means that the company may have the use of £97.50 for 30 minus seven days, i.e. 23 days, at a cost of £2.50. What is the rate of interest? Let it be x, then:

$$£2.50 = £97.50 \times \frac{x}{100} \times \frac{23}{365} \quad \text{i.e.} \quad x = \frac{£2.50 \times 100 \times 365}{£97.50 \times 23}$$

$$\text{i.e.} \quad x = 40.69\%$$

In this case it would clearly be worth while for a company to make its financial arrangements so that it could take advantage of a discount at such a generous rate. Conversely, this example also illustrates that suppliers should consider very carefully before offering cash discounts. Other less costly alternatives may be available.

Equity capital: difficulties of calculation

The cost of risk capital is a difficult and complex concept and it is a controversial one. In the case of loan funds, the position is clearly defined, but in the case of risk capital there must always be a subjective aspect, a matter of expectations. When a company makes an offer of ordinary shares to large investors or to institutions, or to the public generally, it will do so in a carefully prepared document, a prospectus. The procedures will be considered later but in principle the offer document will go into details about the past results of the company, if it has been established for some time. As these will relate to matters of fact they can be verified independently and this aspect does not present insuperable problems.

However, whilst investors will carefully consider the 'track record' of an established company, not least to assess the quality of its management, they will primarily consider investing new money on the basis of their expectations for the future of the company. The offer document will therefore always state the directors expectations, and these must inevitably be based on a number of assumptions, forecasts and projections. Meanwhile, there can be no certainty that unforeseeable events will not occur so that the results finally achieved will be much worse than those forecast. Possibly, of course, the results will be better than forecast and prospective investors will always be hoping for this outcome.

In practice, those concerned with raising ordinary share capital always pay great attention to timing. Whenever possible money is sought when markets are rising and there is expectation that the rise will continue. In the study of finance, as in other subjects, the behaviour of people, as individuals or as members of a group, must be considered. It has subjective, unquantifiable aspects. When markets are rising even cautious investors are liable to react differently from when they are falling. In brief, they are prepared to grasp quickly at offers and pay a share price which would have seemed excessive a short time earlier. When the market is buoyant and rising investors will prepared to pay relatively high prices in the expectation that prices will rise still further and they could sell at a profit whenever they chose to do so. Buying decisions are often made on intuitive as well as carefully calculated bases and it is this impossibility of being certain how investors will react to a particular offer of ordinary shares at a particular future moment that results in issues sometimes being hugely oversubscribed and at other times heavily undersubscribed.

Meanwhile, in principle, just as in the case of a loan the cost of capital is measured by the rate of interest payable so, when ordinary shares are issued, the directors will consider the cost as being the dividend they expect to pay for a given capital sum invested. Allowance must also be made for the costs involved in making the issue. In the case of ordinary and preference shares there is no favourable tax treatment and the dividends must be paid from profits remaining after payment of tax. This is a reason why preference shares have lost popularity with companies as issuers, as well as investors, since, for example, it costs a company more to meet a 10% dividend on preference shares than it does 10% interest on a loan.

As the dividend payable is not a contractual one – unlike loan interest – and may rise or fall, or be passed, the concept of the cost of capital is a difficult one and different views may be held. However, if directors consider, and are advised, that in order to raise the ordinary capital they seek, they must show convincingly that they expect to pay dividends of, say, 13% then, in their cost-of-capital calculations they will regard the cost of their ordinary share capital as 13%. For a future issue of shares the cost might be more, or less, depending on market conditions and other factors.

A further difficulty in calculating the cost of ordinary share capital is the aspect of growth. A lender is aware that he will receive the agreed interest payments and, in due course, repayment of principal, and no more. Exceptionally, there are sometimes issues of convertible debentures, or debentures with subscription rights (see p. 86). However, an investor in ordinary shares will expect not only dividends but also that he should benefit from the profitable growth of the company, expressed in the form of rising dividend payments and potential capital gains arising from the rising market value of his shares. This growth would be financed by retention of profits and, in many cases, by the skilful use of gearing. The question is whether this expected growth factor can be 'quantified' and taken into account in assessing the costs of capital. Differing views are held on this point.

From the practical aspect, directors may seldom concern themselves with thoughts about the cost of equity capital raised in the past. After a successful issue of ordinary shares the newly raised capital becomes part of the total risk capital: different tranches of risk capital are likely to have been raised at different costs in the past and over the years a substantial proportion is likely to have been accumulated in the form of retained profits. The question of the cost of equity capital may be academic except at times when it seems necessary to raise additional equity capital – normally by means of a 'rights' issue – and the directors and their merchant bank advisers must decide on the terms which should be offered. There will be a number of factors to consider, including the question of timing. For example, if market conditions became buoyant but there were doubts about how long these conditions would persist, it could be decided to seize an opportunity to make a rights issue even when there did not seem an immediate need to raise new capital. The directors might have ambitious plans requiring additional finance in two or three years. If the company were fairly highly geared they could be inclined to seize an opportunity to raise new equity capital on the reasoning that this would 'broaden the equity base' – a favourite expression of company chairmen in the letter they send to shareholders when making a rights issue – broadening the equity base reduces the gearing and gives directors more freedom for manoeuvre in their financial planning. Lower gearing would make it easier for directors to obtain long term loans and possibly make a further rights issue when the time came to embark on a major new project.

J.P. MacArthur, a merchant banker, wrote (*Financial Management Handbook*: Kluwer Harrap, Amsterdam)
In considering rights issues I make the principal point that they are often essential to broaden the equity base to enable the company to

expand further. Recent experience shows clearly that the time to make a rights issue is when the market is prepared to take it. Such opportunities are limited in both time and volume. Once the requirement becomes obvious, therefore, a close watch must be kept on the market in consultation with the company's financial advisers in order that advantage may be taken quickly of what may prove to be relatively short lived opportunities.

Rights issues are considered in detail in Chapter 18.

The question which directors will consider the main one when consider making a rights issue, that is, offering new shares to the existing shareholders in the same proportion as that in which they own their present holdings, will not be 'what will the cost of capital be in this case?' but rather, 'do we need to make a rights issue at all and, if so, should we make it now, or seek to defer it until the market has risen higher? If we ought to make it now, what sum, net of expenses, ought we to seek and what will be the highest price at which we can offer the shares and be confident of a successful issue?'

Retained earnings

When an examination question requires a student to state the main source of new capital for an established company, the majority give the wrong answer. Whilst the position could change, in recent years the largest single source of new capital is retained – 'ploughed back' – profits. These are profits remaining after deduction of tax and dividends paid to the ordinary shareholders (and to preference shareholders, if any). This long-standing practice of company directors paying out only a proportion of the profits available as dividends has been controversial for some time and it is useful to consider the background.

The decision as to what dividend should be declared and what profits should be retained rests with the directors and not the shareholders. The shareholders are required, at a general meeting, to give their approval to the recommendations of the directors. They could overrule the directors and insist on a lower dividend being paid but, not surprisingly, they never do this. They do not have the right to insist on the declaration and payment of a higher dividend. Their right would be to vote the present directors out of office and vote new ones more sympathetic to the shareholders' wishes in their place. In practice it is far from easy for discontented shareholders to overcome the general apathy of the others and obtain a majority which outvotes those supporting the directors. In practice, discontented shareholders of a company tend to 'cut their losses' and sell their shares.

Do companies seek to maximise their profits?

Modern theory about corporate behaviour is that a large company must be regarded as a coalition of very different interests in a dynamic and continually changing environment. Main interest groups may include the ordinary shareholders; preference shareholders, if any; debenture holders and any other lenders; the directors; other groups of workpeople; trade unions; creditors; customers; suppliers; possibly the local community; the government. The most powerful single group is arguably the board of directors. Whilst they can in theory and sometimes in fact be dismissed by a majority of ordinary shareholders the latter can normally only be induced to take united action if they become quite exceptionally aggrieved over some matter. The directors hold the levers of power on a day-to-day basis and arguably one of their main and most difficult tasks is to keep the different interest groups satisfied without paying too high a price to do so. Frequent disruption of production in a particular case would suggest that the directors had been failing in this duty although it would be possible that any other directors would have been defeated by the same problem, possibly a deliberately destructive militant small group of political activists which had infiltrated itself into the general workforce and simply sought to destroy the company as its own contribution to the overthrow of the capitalist system.

Decisions about profit retention are made by directors of companies and there are a number of factors likely to influence them. One is that their life is easier if they are able to put substantial proportions of distributable profits to reserves without effective challenge, so that these form the main source of new capital. When directors need to approach the shareholders for a rights issue, or the capital market generally for additional long-term funds they are required, in effect, to give an account of their stewardship and submit to searching enquiry which could be followed by unfavourable press comment. Profit retention avoids or reduces the need for approaches to the market for new money, and the discipline that this imposes. Some argue that the capitalist system would operate more efficiently if companies were expected to distribute the largest proportion of their available profits as dividends and then go to the market for additional capital whenever needed. The argument is that the most profitable companies would regularly pay the highest rates of dividends and whenever these companies went to the market for new capital they would readily obtain it on the most favourable terms and the most efficient would prosper and the inefficient would decline through the operation of market forces.

In support of their policy of retaining a substantial proportion of distributable profits, directors often state that the finance so retained enables the company to grow at an exceptional rate and that shareholders benefit from this policy. However, independent research, including that by A. Rubner (*The Ensnared Shareholder*. Macmillan, London): I.M.D. Little (*Bulletin of the Oxford University*, 'Higgledy Piggledy Growth') and I.M.D. Little and A.C. Rayner (*Higgledy Piggledy Growth Again*, Basil Blackwell, Oxford), indicates that companies which retain a relatively high proportion of profits do not in general grow faster than companies which distribute a larger proportion of profits as dividends. Directors can also fairly claim that if they had to depend mainly on raising new equity finance in the market it would be difficult and sometimes impossible for them to plan long-term investment programmes since in recent years there have often been huge and unpredictable market fluctuations. At times risk capital has been virtually unobtainable. Investors often take short- rather than long-term views whilst directors who honestly seek the best interests of their company must take long- rather than short-term views and in this respect the interests of the company as a corporate body may be in conflict with the interests of individual shareholders. The duty of directors, as directors, is primarily to their company. Furthermore, when a company has to seek additional equity capital in the market, the costs involved are relatively high and members of the senior management also have to spend considerable time in meetings, discussions, negotiations, etc.

A further practical justification for a policy of substantial profit retention is that directors are aware that the conventional provisions for depreciation, based on historical costs, are now unrealistically low since in due course most of the fixed assets now in use must be replaced by new ones which cost much more. In brief, profits calculated according to the historical cost convention normally appear to be higher than they really are and it is only by following a policy of substantial profit retention that companies can be sure of maintaining their capital stock intact in conditions of inflation. Until the change to the imputation system of taxation in 1973 the tax system in the UK favoured profit retention rather than distribution. Although the imputation system favours distribution, the Labour Government imposed statutory controls on the maximum rates of dividends payable by companies on the principle that without dividend plus price controls, working people and trade union leaders would oppose any attempts to obtain voluntary acceptance of incomes policies.

It also seems that company policies of 'ploughing back' of profits, for the purpose reinvestment, were on the whole widely approved in the prevailing social climate. Many suspected that whilst directors often publicly deplored statutory dividend controls, in private many welcomed them since the controls enabled them to blame the government for a policy which made their lives easier anyway. Meanwhile, social climates, like fashions, can change and then change again. Statutory dividend controls were removed by the Conservative Government in 1979. They could in due course be re-imposed. If the economy should become buoyant again directors could find themselves under pressure to distribute a large proportion of profits as dividends. One must wait and see: of course, payment of dividends requires adequate liquidity and at times of severe liquidity pressure, as in 1980/81, many companies have severe liquidity problems and this factor encourages a conservative dividend policy.

What is the cost of capital in respect of retained profits? Many company directors would consider the question academic and serving no useful purpose. Some argue that retained profits have no cost and that is a large part of their attraction. No costs are incurred in obtaining these funds and profit retention does not involve any breach of contract or commitment in relation to the ordinary shareholders. However, it is arguable that the opportunity costs must be considered. Directors ought not to retain profits as a source of new funds for the company's operations unless they are satisfied that they will be employed efficiently or, in other words, profitably. If the directors wished to retain profits as a precaution, but not for immediate use in the business, then their opportunity cost could be considered to be the return which could be obtained by investing them in gilt-edged or similar short-dated securities. If the company were on the point of seeking new equity capital, or were evaluating new projects, retained profits would probably be regarded as having the same cost as new equity capital, with allowance for the fact that raising new capital gives rise to expenses whereas retaining profits does not. In examination questions which involve calculation of the cost of capital this viewpoint appears normally to be the expected one.

Weighted average cost of capital

When major capital projects are being evaluated, from the aspects of expected costs and revenues, the cost of capital required to finance the

Capital for the private sector company

project will be a major cost. Often the capital to be employed will be a mix of newly raised equity capital, at one cost, plus retained profits at a slightly lower cost since no issue expenses would be incurred, plus long-term loans, assumed in this case to be at a fixed rate of interest. Clearly, when a mix of components is used, the cost of capital must reflect the cost of each component and according to the proportion which each bears to the total of capital required for the project. In brief, a 'weighted average' is used since a simple average cost of capital would be inappropriate: thus, if there were more of a low-cost component the overall cost of capital would be lower than it would be if more of a high-cost component were used.

Example (ACCA adapted)
Directors are considering a project which would require the raising of £600,000 new equity capital. It is estimated that a prospect of 15% dividends must be indicated to investors and the issue expenses are such that an issue of ordinary shares of £1 will result in net proceeds of £0.95 per share. There are retained profits available of £100,000 and £300,000 would be raised by selling 10% loan stock at par. The company has a marginal corporation tax rate of 50%. Calculate the cost of capital.

Workings
As the issue costs are 5% the cost of the new equity capital will be $\frac{0.15}{0.95}$ = 15.8%. (Dividends of 15% would be payable on each £1 nominal of shares issued, but only £0.95 is received in respect of each £1 nominal.) The cost of the retained earnings will be considered to be 15%.

The effective cost of the loan stock will be $10\% \times \frac{100-50}{100}$ i.e. 5%. (If the corporation tax had been, say, 52% the calculation would be: $10\% \times \frac{100-52}{100} = 4.8\%$. This calculation can easily be verified.)

The calculation of the overall weighted average becomes:

	(£) Total (a)	Dividend or interest (b)	a × b
New equity capital	600,000		9,480,000
Retained earnings	100,000	15.0	1,500,000
10% loan	300,000	5.0	1,500,000
	1,000,000		12,480,000

Weighted average: $\dfrac{a \times b}{a}$ i.e. $\dfrac{12{,}480{,}000}{1{,}000{,}000}$

i.e. 12.5% (rounded).

Cost of equity capital: the growth factor

An important difference between investing as a lender and investing in equity, from the viewpoint of the investor, is that in money terms the return on a fixed-interest loan is precisely known but in the case of equity there will be an expected rate of dividends and also an expectation of some capital growth, expressed as a rise in the market price of the ordinary shares of a listed company. M.J. Gordon in *The Investment, Financing and Valuation of the Corporation* (Irwin, Homewood, 1962) developed a formula for calculating the cost of equity capital when the dividend expectation has been indicated and also the expected rate of earnings growth. It is:

$$\text{cost of equity capital} = \frac{\text{dividend expected}}{\text{market price}} + \text{expected growth rate (\%)}$$

This formula would also be applied in calculating the cost of retained profits. It is considered that a limitation of this formula is that it does not take into account the risk involved in investing in different companies. These risks are made up of two main kinds – the business risks, which will be related to the industry within which the company operates and factors internal to the company, and the financial risk, which will be higher for a higher-geared company. The fact is that no theoretical model can be expected to do more than, at best, give very approximate information, which will be useful but must be treated with caution. The following is a comprehensive worked example (adapted from an ACCA question).

Example

The following is the present capital structure of a company, with current particulars relevant to each security. What would you assess the cost of capital to be if the directors sought to increase their long-term funds whilst maintaining their capital structure approximately unchanged?

1. Existing capital structure

	(£000)
Issued ordinary shares (10,000,000)	10,000
Retained earnings	3,000
8% preference shares	2,000
12% Debentures (repayable 1987)	3,000
	18,000

2. 12% Debentures
   (a) Issued in 1972 at par
   (b) Current price £90
   (c) A similar issue made now would need to be made at £89
3. 8% Preference shares
   (a) Preference shares have a par value of £1, originally issued at 94p per share
   (b) Current price 63p
   (c) A similar issue made now would need to be made at 60p
4. Ordinary shares
   (a) The market price of an ordinary share is £6
   (b) £5 m. were paid in dividends this year, representing 75% of earnings
   (c) Earnings are expected to grow at an annual rate of 5%
   (d) If new ordinary shares were issued now costs would represent 20p per share and it would be necessary to offer the new shares at a price of 50p below the market price.
5. Corporation tax may be assumed to be 50%.

Workings
1. Debentures: Marginal cost of capital after tax

$$= \frac{\text{coupon rate}}{\text{proceeds of current issue}} \times (1 - \text{tax rate})$$

$$= \frac{12}{89} \times (1 - 0.50) = 6.74\%$$

2. Preference shares: marginal cost $= \dfrac{\text{coupon rate}}{\text{proceeds of current issue}}$

$$= \frac{8}{60} = 13.33\%$$

3. Ordinary shares: marginal cost

$$= \frac{\text{dividend per share}}{\text{net proceeds of issue}} + \text{growth rate}$$

$$= \left(\frac{50}{530} + 0.05\right) \times 100 = 14.43\%$$

4. Cost of retained earnings: marginal cost
= dividend yield + growth rate = $\left(\dfrac{50}{600} + 0.05\right) \times 100 = 13.33\%$

5. Weighted average marginal cost of capital

	Capital structure (£m.)	Weight	Component cost %	Weighted cost %
Ordinary shares	10	0.55	14.44	7.94
Retained earnings	3	0.17	13.33	2.27
Preference shares	2	0.11	13.33	1.47
Debentures	3	0.17	6.74	1.15
	18	1.00		12.83

Notes: It has been assumed that: (i) the marginal cost of retained earnings is the same as the marginal cost of newly issued ordinary shares except that no adjustments need to be made for expenses of issue, or issue at a discount; (ii) the present dividend/earnings ratio will be maintained; (iii) book values rather than market values give a better representation of the capital structure.

Cost of capital: general comments

This subject is generally regarded as a difficult and controversial one. It has obvious practical importance and has also received much academic and theoretical study in other countries besides the UK. High interest rates in recent years must have stimulated study, as well as the taxation implications. The aspects of business and financial risks and uncertainties are also important. A question which is clearly of interest is whether there is an optimum capital structure for a particular company and, if there is, how can it be determined? Two leading theoretical writers, F.M. Modigliani and M.H. Miller, have argued that decisions as to the proportions of debt and equity in the capital structure of a company do not affect its total value nor, in consequence, the weighted average cost of capital ('The cost of capital, corporate finance and the theory of investment', *American Economic Review*, June 1958). This is a viewpoint which is in conflict with the 'traditional' approach, which is to consider that a weighted average cost of capital can be calculated with fair accuracy in respect of additions to the existing capital – the marginal cost. The powerful arguments of Modigliani and Miller are based on certain assumptions, notably of perfect capital markets and restricted risk and uncertainty. In practice it would seem that working financial managers may not be so much concerned with optimal capital structures as with achieving the best attainable in the circumstances and taking into account temperamental attributes of top managements, notably whether they are risk-seeking or risk-avoiding or, in other words, whether they incline to higher or lower gearing. Readers who wish to study this topic more deeply are referred to J.M. Samuels and F.M. Wilkes, *Management of Company Finance*, Nelson, London, 1975.

Questions

1. Discuss the way in which the cost of capital of a company might be affected by the level of its capital gearing. (ICSA 22 marks)
2. Describe the relative advantages of debt and equity as a source of finance for a listed company and explain the effect which each of these types of finance might have on the overall cost of capital for the company. (ICSA 22 marks)
3. Outline the problems involved in the measurement of capital employed for the purpose of computing return on capital. (ICSA 22 marks)
4. Outline the major objectives which might determine the financial policy of a listed industrial company. In what way might these objectives be different from those of an industrial undertaking in the public sector? (ICSA 22 marks)
5. To what extent may the maximisation of profit be regarded as the main financial objective of a listed company? (ICSA 22 marks)
6. 'Whatever the theorists may say, a business in fact is run primarily for the benefit of its managers: any other parties are only considered insofar as they may be able to threaten the well being of the management.' Discuss the subject of this quotation together with the difficulties experienced in the theoretical analysis of business. (ACCA – Business Management paper 20 marks)
7. N Ltd is entirely financed by equity capital of 1,000,000 ordinary shares of £1 each which have a current stock market price of £4 per share. The annual dividend for the last few years has been 50p per share, earnings per share have been steady at 80p and the stock markets expects these rates to continue.

The directors of the company have proposed an investment project which is expected to show a return of £185,000 per annum indefinitely on an investment of £1,000,000. The company does not have any funds available and does not wish to raise further equity finance.

One of the directors suggests that £1,000,000 should be raised by an issue of 12% debentures at par. He suggests that this would reduce the company's cost of capital sufficiently to make the project worth while.

One of the other directors, however, argues that the overall cost of capital would not be affected by a debenture interest and that, in any case the equity shareholders would require a higher return if a debenture issue were made. You are required to advise the board of directors on the factors which should be taken into account in the acceptance and financing of the project.   (ICSA   34 marks)

Chapter 5

Main types of securities issued by companies

This chapter is concerned with the main types of securities issued by companies and their special features, with comments on advantages and disadvantages from the viewpoints of both companies and investors. A particular company may, of course, never consider issuing certain of the securities described but it is important for students to be informed of the wide choice available. In some cases, but not in all, there may be a presumption that a company would have a Stock Exchange listing, so that its securities could be dealt in freely in the market and, especially, there would be an established market price to which reference could be made. There will always be a need to agree a price by negotiation whenever a dealing in an unlisted security is contemplated.

Shares

Ordinary (equity) shares

A share was defined in a court judgement as 'the interest of a shareholder in the company, measured by a sum of money for the purpose of liability in the first place, and of interest in the second, but also consisting of a number of mutual convenants entered into by all the shareholders *inter se*'. (Farwell, J., Borland's Trustee v Steel Bros & Co Ltd, 1901) The formal procedures for an issue of shares will be more fully considered later. An issue is subject to compliance with the law, notably the Companies Acts, and the law is primarily concerned with protecting members of the public against the minority of fraudulent or too 'sharp' company promoters and their advisers. When shares are to have a Stock Exchange listing – which does not usually apply in the early days of a newly established company – there must also be compliance with stringent Stock Exchange requirements.

The long-term capital of a company may consist entirely of risk capital – ordinary, equity, shares. (The word 'equity' derives from the equitable rights of ordinary shareholders to the residual value of a company after all other claims on it have been met.) It may, alternatively, consist of a mix of different types of shares and also debentures or other long-term loans. As already explained, all lenders are creditors but shareholders are not. The memorandum of association of a company includes a capital clause, which sets out the capital which the promoters have decided upon at the start, or the directors at a later date. The capital clause can be amended without difficulty whenever it is desired to increase the share capital of a company. (Reduction of the issued capital is much more difficult and also requires approval of the court.) The Companies Act, 1948, requires that shares are 'of a fixed amount' and must therefore have a stated nominal value and 'no par value' shares are not permitted in the UK. The nominal value of a share will be as the promoters or directors decide. At the start it is often £1 per share. In the past shares were sometimes issued with a nominal value of £5 or £10 each. However, over the years experience showed that many investors have a possibly illogical but still marked resistance against shares with a high market price with the consequence that such shares become less marketable which, in effect, tends to reduce the overall total market value of a company. Accordingly, it has become the practice of companies to subdivide shares when the market value rises considerably above the nominal value. The formalities involved are simple. Thus if, for example, the market value of a £1 share became £6, the nominal £1 shares could be subdivided into, say, four shares of 25p each. Shares of 25p are common and nominal values of 10p are also met, or even lower.

No par value (npv) shares

Shares of no par value are common in the USA and Canada and elsewhere. There has been desultory, but not overwhelming pressure to have no par value shares sanctioned in the UK. Main arguments in favour of 'npv' shares include:

(a) The nominal value shown on a share certificate may be misleading. Many investors wrongly think that the nominal and market values must be the same. In fact, they may be widely different.
(b) Dividends would be declared at so many pence per share rather than a percentage of the nominal value. This would prevent uninformed people (who are in the majority) from gaining quite wrong impressions, e.g. that excessive dividends are being paid when this is not the case.
(c) An 'npv' share represents a portion of the total equity of the com-

pany and their issue would make the issue of capitalisation (otherwise known as scrip or bonus) issues unnecessary (p. 75).
(d) npv shares can readily be split when a high market price would reduce their marketability, or consolidated if the market price became too low.
(e) Under the Companies Act, 1948, a shareholder remains liable to pay, on liquidation, the amount, if any, unpaid on his shares. Thus, if a person has paid 85p in respect of a £1 share he has a contingent liability of 15p per share. The Companies Act, 1948, also places restrictions on the right of a company to issue shares at a discount on their face value. This can create problems for a company which has been performing poorly but needs to raise new risk capital urgently. This problem does not arise with npv shares.
(f) A company may take over another company and offer its shares as all or part of the consideration. In practice companies are often tempted to overvalue in their accounting records assets acquired in this way: this temptation to overvaluation would be removed if npv shares were involved.

In 1952 the government appointed the Gedge Committee to consider whether the Companies Act, 1948, should be amended to permit npv shares. It recommended the amendment. In 1959 the Jenkins Committee was appointed to consider the whole question of company law reform, including the question of npv shares. This committee also supported the issue. It was later found that there were certain tax complications, which should not be insuperable. It thus appears that informed opinion is in favour of the issue of no par value shares and sooner or later their issue will be authorised by a Companies Act. It is evident that it is not regarded as a high-priority matter on any side.

By far the largest proportion of shares issued by the companies are ordinary shares, of nominal value of £1, or 25p or even 10p. The ordinary shareholders are the main risk bearers of a company in a financial sense. This traditional viewpoint is now often challenged on the argument that there are others, especially long-service employees, as well as customers, suppliers, even a local community, whose financial stake in a company may effectively be much greater than that of many shareholders. As many shareholders buy for short-term speculation, or are institutions holding particular shares as part of a portfolio, it is understandable that the traditional view, that directors should at all times think primarily of the shareholders' interests, should be questioned.

In those cases when there are no deferred or founders' shares, and no preference shares with participating rights in respect either of dividends or assets in the event of a winding up, each ordinary share represents a fraction of the residual value of the assets remaining to a company after all other claims have been met. On the principle that those who bear the risks should exercise control, it is usual for the formal control of a company to be in the hands of the ordinary shareholders, each of whom has voting rights *pro rata* with his shareholding. There are exceptions to this general rule. If the fixed-dividend payments due to preference shareholders, or fixed-interest payments due to debenture holders, or other lenders, fell into arrears, control would be likely to pass to them, at least until the arrears had been paid off. In such cases the position would be set out in the articles or the conditions governing the issue of the security concerned.

'A' (non-voting) ordinary shares

In addition to the above special cases, a relatively small number of companies in the past issued ordinary shares with no voting rights, usually designated 'A' shares. In recent years informed opinion has been that it is wrong in principle that certain ordinary shareholders should not have the same rights as other, whilst bearing the same risks. There was some surprise when the matter was not dealt with in recent Companies Acts. The Stock Exchange will not grant listings in respect of new issues of ordinary shares without voting rights. When the same company has both types of shares in issue, the market price of the 'A' shares is invariably lower – often much lower – than that of the same shares with voting rights. Some companies have recently 'enfranchised' their 'A' shares and others may do so voluntarily in the future. When this happens it is usual for the existing holders of shares with voting rights to be given some compensation by the company since their having to share control with the newly enfranchised 'A' shareholders causes some reduction of their property rights for which fair compensation is appropriate.

Differences between nominal and market prices of shares

Share valuations will be considered later but the nominal, or face value of a share will normally only coincide with the market price at the start of a company. Thereafter the two figures tend to diverge. In the case of an unlisted company the price at which shares are bought and sold will always require negotiation between buyer and seller. The market price of a listed company may fluctuate widely from day to day and will reflect supply and demand. It will be influenced by factors affecting shares as a whole, as well as factors affecting the industry in which the company operates and factors relating to the company itself. In the case of a successful listed company, in buoyant market conditions, the market price will normally exceed the nominal price for several reasons. A main one is that when a company operates profitably it will invariably distribute as dividends only a part of the available profits, retaining the balance as 'ploughed back' profits, normally the major source of new finance.

From the book-keeping aspect, profit for the year will appear as a credit balance on the profit-and-loss appropriation account. A dividend declared will be debited to this account and credited to a dividend account. When paid, the cash account will be credited and the asset, cash, is reduced. The double entry will be completed by a debit to the dividend account, which closes it. However, when profits are not distributed the cash is not reduced through payment of a dividend and the profit will remain in the appropriation account. Clearly, this account will show an increasing balance as it is augmented by retained profits. Rather than permit the balance to accumulate to a very high figure, which would be likely to lead shareholders to press for increased dividends, even if the liquid position of the company did not permit this, the directors of a profitable company now regularly make a simple book entry and transfer a sum from the appropriation account to a general reserve account, or a reserve account with some other name. These reserve accounts consist of profits which could lawfully have been paid out as dividends to ordinary shareholders, but were withheld from them. They clearly belong to the ordinary shareholders and form part of their equity.

This equity comprises the paid-up ordinary share capital (normally the same figure as the issued share capital) plus any credit balance on the profit-and-loss (appropriation) account plus any reserves. If there are no preference shareholders entitled to share in any surplus, this total may also be described as the 'ordinary shareholders' equity': when divided by the number of ordinary shares, the quotient is the net asset value per share. It may stand substantially above the nominal value. It might be expected that the net asset value per share would correspond closely with the market price. Often it does, but for reasons which will be considered later (p. 470), it often stands well above, or well below the market price.

Reserves

Students, and others, often have difficulty in grasping the significance of a 'general reserve' or similarly designated account. In particular they regard the term 'reserve' as implying that the company must have liquid resources readily available but this is often not the case. Often an examination question centres on a company which is obviously passing through a bad period and there is an easily identifiable lack of liquidity and profitability, and the student is required to diagnose the problems and suggest remedies. In a class discussion, students often say 'draw first on the reserves'. This shows a complete failure to understand the position. The fact that there is a reserve account (other than a capital reserve created after a revaluation of a fixed asset, such as land or buildings) indicates that in the past there were profits available for distribution which were not distributed.

The reserve represents a source of funds. If, when it was created or increased, the company had been in a very liquid position – had substantial cash or bank balances – then the cash might have been spent on the purchase of fixed assets, or additional stocks, or financing more debtors, or a combination of these. A loan might have been repaid. When assets are purchased it is the cash balance which is reduced, not the reserves, which remain unchanged. Reserves therefore indicate that a company was doing well in the past but not necessarily that it is still doing well. Reserves certainly do not necessarily indicate that a company has a satisfactory liquid position now. It might be a very bad one. The quick check here is to examine the liquid assets of the company in the latest balance sheet (the current assets less the stock) and deduct the current liabilities from the total. If the latter exceed the former then *prima facie* the company has a liquidity problem. The fact is that a reserve account can never be drawn upon to pay salaries, creditors, etc. These can only be paid with cash or through a bank account.

Capitalisation of reserves

When a company has a 'conservative' dividend policy and each year retains a substantial proportion of distributable profits, if these were left in the profit-and-loss appropriation account (and there is no technical reason why they should not be), the credit balance on this would steadily increase. Shareholders could then form action committees to press for higher dividends: workpeople could protest that they were underpaid and customers that they were being overcharged. The practice of transferring sums from the appropriation account to a reserve is a technically proper one which tends to disarm potential criticism. To many people the word 'profit' is an emotive one whereas 'reserve' is not: it suggests prudence. When directors propose to transfer a sum to reserve a large proportion of shareholders, workpeople, creditors, the public generally do not understand the implications and the sum transferred ceases to be potentially provocative and seems to change its nature and to become respectable and neutral.

Meanwhile, when profits are annually transferred to a general reserve account, this account will also steadily increase. The law permits a transfer from a general reserve back to a profit-and-loss (appropriation) account and if there were a change of directors and the cash position permitted this, the new directors could make such a transfer and pay out large sums as dividends provided that at that time no statutory dividend limitation prevented this.

However, it is now a normal practice, as reserves increase and become 'out of line' with the issued share capital, for the directors to capitalise a proportion of the reserves by making a 'capitalisation' issue – also known as a scrip or, misleadingly, a bonus issue, since uninformed shareholders think that they are being given a 'free gift' of shares, whereas they are not: their proportionate share of the equity is unchanged but is represented by a larger number of shares. The technical aspect is simple. There will be a transfer of a sum from the general reserve account to the ordinary share capital account, a mere book-entry, and the newly created ordinary shares will be distributed to existing shareholders in proportion to their shareholding. In practice, shareholders are sent provisional share certificates which become substantive certificates if the shareholder retains them to the indicated date – some shareholders pass their certificates to a broker with instructions to sell, but any shareholder who does so, whether he realises this or not, reduces his share of the equity of the company.

The reasons why successful companies make capitalisation issues should be understood. For example, if a company never made an issue of this kind, in due course the market price of a £1 share could reach, say, £6 or more. If the directors declared a dividend of 60%, this would represent 10% for a recent purchaser of shares, and would not be excessive, although a declared dividend of 60% sounds high. If there had been a steady policy of making capitalisation issues, a shareholder might now hold, say, six shares, each of £1 market value, instead of a single £1 share with £6 market value. If the directors were declaring dividends of 10% the shareholder would receive the same total dividend, but a declared dividend of 10% does not invite criticism in the way that a 60% dividend is likely to do. Directors sometimes make a capitalisation issue of, say, one for ten and at the same time state that the current rate of dividend will be maintained in the future. In such a case the market price of the share may not fall, and as an individual shareholding will have increased by 10%, the total value will rise by

10% or so. The issue of capitalisation shares tends to be regarded as a 'bullish' factor – an indication that the directors are hopeful that they will be able to maintain a satisfactory rate of dividend in the future. The creditors of a company always welcome a capitalisation of reserves as it strengthens their position. Reserves which have been capitalised cease to be potentially available for distribution as dividends.

Preferred ordinary shares

These shares were sometimes issued in the past, and remain in issue, but new issues are rarely made now. They are essentially ordinary shares which have certain preferential rights in relation to the undesignated ordinary shares. The precise features of a particular security will always be set out either in the articles or the document which sets out the details of the issue. There is no completely standard pattern but shares of this type often provide that holders will be entitled to a specified fixed dividend before the ordinary shares can participate in a distribution. Because of the preference accorded to them in this way, holders of shares of this type must accept sacrifices in other ways. The usual pattern would be that if profits were high the holders of preferred ordinary shares would only participate to a very restricted extent. The conditions of issue might also provide that in the event of a liquidation the holders of preferred ordinary shares would rank above the ordinary shareholders for repayment of capital (but after all other interests). In that event it would be expected that any surplus remaining would belong to the ordinary shareholders. Usually, if a liquidation occurs, the ordinary shareholders lose substantially – often the entire value of their shareholding.

Deferred shares

These are sometimes known as founders' or management shares. They are often issued to the founders of a company in the event that the promoters or founders later sell the company and their interest in it. Founders', or deferred, shares may be issued as part of the purchase price or of the agreed valuation of goodwill. Such shares often do not carry any entitlement to a dividend until an agreed level of payments has been made to the ordinary shareholders. They tend to offer very high returns to their holders when things are going well. Often deferred shares carry a disproportionate share of the voting power and hence control over a company. Many shares of this kind were issued some years ago, when controls, and informed press comment were less effective than they are now, and issue terms often favoured promoters too generously and at the expense of the ordinary shareholders.

Preference shares

There are a number of types of preference shares and many were issued some years ago since in recent years preference shares have largely lost favour both with investors and with companies seeking to raise capital. The principle underlying preference shares is that holders are entitled to a fixed rate of dividend in priority over ordinary and preferred ordinary or deferred shareholders. They rank after creditors but before other shareholders in respect of dividends. Conditions of issue vary widely but common types are listed in the following paragraphs.

Cumulative preference shares
The feature of shares of this type is that if the issuing company 'passes' – fails to declare and pay the fixed dividend on any shares – then any dividend not paid in one or more past years must be paid before any dividend may be paid on the ordinary shares. Unless there are indications to the contrary in the articles or conditions of issue, it will be presumed that preference shares are cumulative.

Non-cumulative preference shares
In this case the holders are only entitled to dividends on a preferential basis over the ordinary shares in the event that there are sufficient distributable profits in respect of the financial year which has just ended. Even if there are profits the law does not compel the directors to declare a dividend with respect to the preference shares. Thus if there should be a sequence of poor years, then the preference and ordinary shareholders would probably receive no dividends. If there were then a sequence of good years the ordinary shareholders could hope for good and rising dividends and a share in the rising equity worth of the company which would be reflected in a rising share price: however, the holders of non-cumulative preference shares would receive only their fixed dividends year by year, and dividends passed in earlier years would not be made good.

The widespread and understandable view of private investors is that preference shares are 'bad buys' and non-cumulative ones are without doubt the worst of all. However, because of favourable taxation treatment, companies may find it worth while to include preference shares as part of an investment portfolio, since the dividends they receive on them are treated as 'franked investment income'. This entitles the company receiving the dividend to take into account the corporation tax paid by the paying company and offset this against its own liability for corporation tax. Study of fixed-interest preference shares in the financial press shows that interest rates vary quite widely. There are two main reasons for this (and the same principle applies in respect of debenture issues). When two companies make issues at the same time the company with the better standing would be able to offer a lower rate: other influencing factors would be the size and conditions of the issue. Timing of the issue is the other major factor. Interest rates now vary quite widely even over short periods and the fixed interest or dividend offered by a company in respect of a security will reflect the prevailing rate at the time of issue.

Participating preference shares

Shares of this type are now rarely encountered. They offer the feature of a fixed preferential dividend and then an additional right to holders to participate to a defined additional extent in the event that the ordinary shareholders receive dividends above a stated rate. Preference shares do not have participating rights unless this fact is expressly stated in the conditions of issue.

Convertible preference shares

The role of specialist institutions which arrange start-up, or venture, or risk capital, as well as loans for promising companies in their earlier stages, will be considered later. These institutions may in appropriate cases make risk capital available to such companies in return for convertible preference shares. This offers advantages to the company and the institution. The latter occupies a preferential position in relation to the ordinary shareholders, although an inferior one in relation to creditors, and it thus accepts special risks. However, the institution will be entitled to a fixed preference dividend before any payment can be made to the ordinary shareholders. The institution would therefore hope for a satisfactory cash flow from the investment and if all went well it would have the right to convert the preference into ordinary shares on a predetermined basis. The intention would be to exercise the option when worthwhile to do so and in due course the institution would plan to sell the ordinary shares at a profit and use the proceeds for reinvestment in another promising but high-risk company in an early development stage.

The advantage to a company of funds of this type is that the money is received on a risk capital and not a loan basis and so the gearing benefits. If results are disappointing in any year the dividend will be passed (but the shares will be on a cumulative basis). Whilst an institution might or might not seek to appoint a director to the board of the company, to watch its interests, if one were appointed he would not involve himself in the day-to-day management and the institution would not seek to gain control of the company. If it duly exercised its right to convert preference into ordinary shares and then sought to sell the latter at a later date, it would offer the shares first to the shareholders of the company and if they were unable to purchase them, the sale would still be made in consultation with them.

Redeemable preference shares
The Companies Act, 1948, provides that if so authorised by its articles a company may issue shares which are redeemable or liable to be redeemed at the option of the company, subject to certain conditions which need not be stated here. This facility was intended to benefit companies which sought to raise fairly long-term but not permanent funds otherwise than on the basis of a loan, and to interest investors who sought an outlet for funds for a predetermined period.

Preference shares – repayment of capital on liquidation
A company may go into voluntary liquidation on the initiative of the directors who would first seek a mandate from the shareholders in general meeting. In such a case it must appear that the company will be able to pay all its creditors in full, including staff for redundancy and other payments due to them. A company may also be put into compulsory liquidation under the control of creditors, and the Court, if it appears that it would not be able to pay its creditors in full.

There are more compulsory than voluntary liquidations and when it appears that there may be insufficient funds to make payment in full the assets realised are applied in the following order: (1) secured creditors with fixed charges realise their security and take payment of their debt from the proceeds. Any surplus is payable to the liquidator and if there is a deficit the creditors rank as unsecured creditors in respect of any debt still due to them; (2) all winding-up costs, including the liquidator's remuneration; (3) preferential creditors (e.g. the Inland Revenue, staff etc.); (4) creditors with floating charges; (5) unsecured creditors; (6) any debts due to members as members (e.g. calls paid in advance); (7) repayment of paid-up capital; (8) surplus, if any, to those entitled – notably, ordinary and possibly preference shareholders.

In the event that neither the articles nor the conditions of issue state the position of a particular security in the event of liquidation then the preference and ordinary shareholders rank equally – at the end of the queue, after all creditors have been paid in full – anything remaining being distributed *pro rata* according to the shareholding. However, more usually, nothing remains to distribute to shareholders. It is often expressly stated in the conditions of issue that in a liquidation the preference shareholders rank immediately after the creditors and before the ordinary shareholders, possibly in respect of arrears of dividend as well as capital. In such cases, in the unlikely event of any surplus, it would be shared only amongst the ordinary shareholders.

Conclusions

In the past the attraction of fixed-dividend preference shares to many investors was that this type of security was regarded as an acceptable compromise between high-risk ordinary shares, with fluctuating dividends, and high-security debentures with relatively low fixed-interest payments. However, from the viewpoint of private investors, inflation erodes the capital values of fixed dividend (or interest) securities, and also of the dividend (or interest) payments. Experience has also shown that these securities are effectively as high risk as are ordinary shares and thus holders of preference shares have the worst of all worlds. As explained, companies may include preference shares in an investment portfolio because of the aspect of the dividends being regarded as 'franked investment income' and preference shares therefore have an important but limited market still. Meanwhile, the issue of preference shares is now also unpopular with issuing companies because of the taxation treatment: whereas interest on loans is allowable as an expense for taxation purposes, dividend payments on preference as well as ordinary shares are not allowable and in consequence have to be paid from the profits which remain after tax. The practical aspect of this is that it is more costly for a company to 'service' preference dividends in comparison with loan interest or, in other words, preference shares give rise to higher costs of capital than do loans.

Because of these factors, issues of preference shares have been relatively few in recent years, apart from the special cases of issues of convertible preference shares to certain institutions. During the period of dividend controls some companies made small issues, with Treasury approval, as a means of circumventing the dividend controls when special circumstances seemed to justify this.

Stock

Readers will be familiar with references to government fixed-interest stocks. A company can also have ordinary stock in issue, instead of ordinary shares. A company is not permitted, by the Companies Act, 1948, to make an original issue of ordinary stock but if it is so authorised by its articles and the company so resolves in general meeting, it may promptly create stock out of fully paid shares, the total nominal value of the stock being the same as that of the shares from which it derives. From a practical aspect there is no significant difference between fully paid-up ordinary shares and ordinary stock, which must always be fully paid up. In the past, company shares had to be numbered, whilst stock does not. Dealing with share numbers was administratively difficult and hence costly and there was consequently advantage in converting shares into stock. However, shares do not now need to be numbered and there is no longer any advantage in converting shares into stock.

Debentures

Some major differences between shares and debentures

The deep differences between the nature of long-term capital obtained by issuing ordinary or other types of shares, and long-term loans, which is what debentures are, must always be borne in mind. A shareholder may sell the shares he has bought to anyone who is prepared to buy them, subject to any restrictions on transfer set out in the articles. If the company is a private one there must be the prescribed restrictive clauses but if it is a listed public company the Stock Exchange will not permit any restrictions on transfer since these make the operation of an efficient market impossible. A sale of shares in a private company must be by negotiation and subject to the approval of the directors who, in practice, can and often do create difficulties or refuse to approve a transfer. A sale through the Stock Exchange will be at a price determined by the forces of supply and demand, influenced by market conditions.

The Companies Act, 1948, prohibits the purchase by a company of its own shares or, subject to certain exceptions, the lending of money to its own officers to enable them to purchase shares in it. (However, the penalties for breach are derisorily low fines and recent court cases and DTI reports have shown that numbers of company chairmen and directors have treated the law with complete contempt.) There are a number of circumstances, which need not be detailed here, when a company may reduce its share capital and may return part of the capital to the shareholders, subject always to the prior approval of the Court. There is also the special provision of the Companies Act, 1948, which permits a company to issue and later to redeem redeemable preference shares. Even in this special case, if a company redeems these shares out of profits and not from the proceeds of a new issue, it must set aside to a capital redemption reserve fund an equivalent sum. This effectively means that when preference shares are redeemed out of profits the company is prevented from distributing that sum in the form of dividends in the future, even if it had ample cash available to do so. In brief, the law endeavours strictly to ensure that the capital of a company is maintained intact and cannot be returned to shareholders except in special circumstances and with the prior approval of the Court. This is for the protection of creditors.

However, when a company obtains long-term finance by issuing debentures, or indeed by means of any other form of borrowing, the position is entirely different. This is so even if the lender is the main or sole shareholder. The company receives the money as a loan, under agreed contractual conditions, and the lender will be a creditor and not a shareholder. The company may issue debentures direct to a lender but this will normally apply only in the case of a large individual loan. More usually, debenture stock will be issued, normally in units of £1 or £100, and there will be trustees on behalf of the debenture holders, a substantial institution, such as a bank, and the trustee will have the duty of ensuring that the company acts strictly in accordance with the terms of its contract and of taking action if the company commits any act of default. However, investors should treat with caution any suggestion that these arrangements mean that their interests are always fully protected by vigilant and efficient trustees. Past lawsuits reveal that there can be loopholes in agreements and if things go wrong it may prove impracticable to obtain compensation from inefficient trustees.

Debentures will almost always be secured, either by a fixed or a floating charge or, less frequently, both. A fixed charge requires that one or more specified assets are designated as security. The characteristics of a floating charge are that the designated security will be a present and future class of assets which will be expected to change in composition in the ordinary course of business and the intention will be that business carries on as usual unless and until an event occurs which causes the charge to 'crystallise'. To be effective, charges must always be registered within strict time limits and the creditor should see that this is done. The technicalities are important but need not be considered here.

If the company commits any act of default, as set out in the terms of the contract, which would include failure to pay interest on time, it would be for the creditor – or trustee, if applicable – to take action to enforce their security. Often a receiver is appointed and he would hold his appointment until the company was no longer in default. He would be in a position to overrule the directors. If the company became unable to continue to operate it would go into liquidation and in that event a liquidator would be appointed to take control. His appointment is a final matter for he supervises the ending of the life of a company. Appointment of a receiver is not necessarily final as the company may recover and the receiver withdraw. However, the appointment of a receiver is often one of the final stages in the decline of a company into collapse and final liquidation.

When a company negotiates a major loan or debenture, the agreement may include a number of restrictive covenants including one that certain key ratios must not be breached. Any breach would entitle the creditors to demand immediate repayment of the whole loan, and if the company could not meet this demand the agreement would authorise the creditors to enforce their security. Major creditors regularly insist upon and in case of need enforce severe covenants. This situation cannot arise if a company is able to persuade investors to provide risk capital by providing money in return for an issue of ordinary shares (or convertible preference shares). The problem is to persuade investors to provide risk capital. If an institution is so persuaded it may or may not impose a condition that its own representative is appointed a director of the company, often with agreed rights of intervention or veto or generally to hold a 'watching brief' and give financial advice and guidance to the management. In practice a situation of this type can offer considerable benefits to a management which may be experienced and competent in, say, marketing and production, but weak in finance. Managers who are aware that they cannot be experts in every function will often welcome support in the vital financial function, especially when this is provided with tact and diplomacy. The employment of factors is also sometimes useful in this respect.

A debenture is a loan, and may be defined as 'a written acknowledgement of a debt incurred by a company. It provides for repayment of the debt together with agreed interest payments, usually twice yearly.' Debentures are normally redeemable although, exceptionally, they may be irredeemable. In recent years there have been few important debenture issues and companies have relied much more on borrowings from banks. Often the precise redemption date of a debenture will not be known beforehand. For example, a security may be listed as '12% debentures (1989/1994)'. In such cases the company has the option to choose whatever date seems most favourable to itself within the exact limits set out in the conditions of issue (say, 1 January 1989 and 31 December 1994). It will be clear that if on the earliest date in 1989, or at any time prior to 31 December 1994 the company could borrow long-term money at, say, 10% p.a., it would redeem the 12% debentures at the earliest possible date, if necessary entering into new borrowing commitments at 10% p.a. in order to raise the cash to make the repayments. However, if in this period money could only be borrowed at, say, 15% p.a., then the company would defer the repayment of the debentures until the latest possible date. In such matters the directors legitimately have regard to the options available and choose the one which is most advantageous to the company.

When debentures of a company are listed on the Stock Exchange, as they normally will be in the case of an important company, then if at any time the market price falls below the nominal price, or face value, the conditions of issue will invariably authorise the directors to purchase debentures on the open market and cancel them if they so wish. In effect, they have repaid the loan in respect of these debentures. This purchase and cancellation of its debentures is not a breach of the law as purchase and cancellation by a company of its own shares would be. Occasionally the terms of issue of debentures may indicate that a certain proportion will be drawn for repayment each year, as for a lottery. There are many possibilities in relation to issue and subsequent redemption. Debentures are sometimes issued at a discount whereas the Companies Act, 1948, forbids this in respect of shares except in exceptional circumstances and subject to the consent of the Court. Debentures issued at a discount may later be redeemed at par, or even at a premium.

When shares are sold by an owner the purchaser must pay stamp duty on the consideration. No stamp duty is payable in respect of debentures and dealing expenses are significantly lower than in the case of shares. However, the government has provided strong incentives for investors to invest in government fixed- (or variable-) interest securities rather than those issued by the private sector. Personal investors who hold a government-issued 'gilt edged' security for a full twelve months before selling it do not pay capital gains tax on any capital profits. Dealing expenses are also significantly lower in respect of government-issued securities.

In principle, book-keeping in relation to the issue and subsequent redemption of debentures is very simple. An issue of debentures represents a source of funds. In the simplest case a debenture account will be opened and credited as and when cash is received and the cash account will be debited. Any expenses of issue will be credited to the cash account as paid and debited to a special account which should promptly be written off to the profit-and-loss account. In due course the repayment would represent an application of funds. Cash would be paid out and the cash account credited and the debenture account would be debited and closed and the debentures would no longer appear on the balance sheet. Even when debentures are not secured, debenture holders would rank as unsecured creditors in a liquidation and would be entitled to repayment in full, including of any outstanding interest payments, before any payment could be made to any category of shareholder.

Special types of debentures

When a particular type of security has been in wide use over a long period, as debentures have been, and when there have been major changes in the economic and financial environments, so that the security is found to have serious limitations which may not have been apparent in the past, modifications will be proposed with the intention of making the security more widely acceptable again. In past years in the UK the value of money tended to remain reasonably stable over long periods and rates of interest on long-term secured loans were low by present-day standards. However, in recent years even the most unsophisticated investors in the UK have become aware that a consequence of inflation is that although the nominal payments of interest and ultimate repayment of capital may be completely secure, they are both insecure in real terms. In brief, at the start a lender lends a certain sum and this has a purchasing power which could be expressed in terms of a certain 'basket' of goods and or services. In times of stable currencies it would be expected that interest payments on the loan and the principal ultimately repaid would have a combined total purchasing power which would significantly exceed that of the original loan. In times of inflation the reverse is true, and the practical position is that borrowers benefit at the expense of lenders. In fact, when the rate of interest is below the rate of inflation the lender receives interest which is negative in real terms – that is, his capital is eroded.

One consequence of inflation is that rates of interest rise and borrowers adjust their attitudes and accept to commit themselves, however reluctantly, to paying historically high rates of interest for a period of years. They presumably believe that inflation will not fall below an annual rate of 10% or so. If it did, people committed to high rates of interest for many years would face heavy problems. Meanwhile, specialists in finance will be identifying problems and then seeking to devise solutions. The devising of variable interest rate securities represents one important attempt to overcome a particular problem by offering an acceptable compromise to borrowers and lenders. The devising of: (*a*) convertible debentures; (*b*) debentures with subscription rights; and (*c*) warrants, represents three further attempts of a different kind.

A feature of these inventions, for this is what they are, is that they are normally invented by people with exceptional skill and experience in financial matters and their main motivation will be self-interest – since finance is a field of activity in which attachment to the profit motive is exceptionally strong – to devise instruments which they can use for their own personal profit, or that of the corporate body they represent, rather than for the benefit of the public at large. In boom periods, when share prices seem bound to go on rising, financial manipulators come into their own. Whilst the newer types of security are sound in conception and enable important gaps to be filled, after the boom years which ended with the stock market collapse in 1974, numbers of unsophisticated investors lost heavily when it became evident that the conditions of issue of some of the newer securities were weighted heavily in favour of the borrowers, and to the prejudice of investors, in a number of debenture issues.

Convertible debentures and convertible unsecured loan stock
There are variations but the underlying principles are that fixed-interest securities are issued which carry an option that the holder may convert these into ordinary shares at a specified future time or times or during a stipulated period and on terms which are fixed in advance and set out in the terms of issue. The attraction of convertible debentures from the viewpoint of investors is that if the market price of the ordinary shares of the company rises to a certain level it would be beneficial for the holder of the convertible debentures (or loan stock) to exercise his option and convert all or part of his debentures into ordinary shares on the agreed basis.

However, if the ordinary shares did not appreciate sufficiently and the market price remained below the price at which it was worthwhile to convert, then the holder would at least still have his holding of fixed-interest securities. The obvious appeal to the investor is that provided the terms are fixed on a reasonable and realistic basis, he obtains a fixed-interest security which, at the same time, offers a 'hedge against inflation'. When offered during boom periods, when it was widely expected that market prices of shares promoted by well-known financiers would rise steadily and indefinitely, buyers were prepared to accept debentures with a fixed interest rate significantly below the rate offered with similar but not convertible securities. Moreover, some of those investors who were no longer normally prepared to invest in fixed-interest debentures because of the aspect of the erosion of the value of money were prepared to purchase convertible debentures because they expected that in due course they would be able to exchange their debentures for ordinary shares of exceptional performance and profit.

Later, in so many cases, it became evident that the ordinary shares were not rising but, on the contrary, they were falling like spent rockets, and the option of conversion was seen to be a worthless one. It then often became apparent that the quality of the debenture itself was not what it had been assumed to be: covenants which usually protect lenders had been omitted. In the event, when the stock market collapsed many holders found that they merely held poorly secured, or not secured, debentures with lower than the prevailing interest rates. Consequently the market prices of these debentures also fell heavily. A feature of convertible debentures is that the holder must make a choice – he must continue to hold debentures, or he must surrender debentures and have them replaced with ordinary shares. He could, if he chose, exercise his option in respect of only part of his holding of debentures and his final holding would then be partly debentures and partly ordinary shares.

Debentures with subscription rights

In this case an inventor who purchases his security at the time of issue – or later, in a market transaction – obtains not only a debenture but, in addition, a right to purchase ordinary shares in numbers related to his holding of debentures, at a price fixed at the time of issue and valid for a specified future period. This means that so long as the holder retained his debentures he would be able profitably to exercise his right to purchase (subscribe to) ordinary shares of the company if, during the validity of the subscription rights, the market price of the ordinary shares rose sufficiently to make the option worth exercising (i.e. if they could be obtained in this way at less cost than by purchase in the market).

The main difference between convertible debentures and debentures with subscription rights is that an investor who chooses to exercise his right to convert all or part of his convertible debentures will receive ordinary shares in exchange for the debentures which he must relinquish. A holder of debentures with subscription rights who exercises his rights will retain his debentures and will obtain the ordinary shares to which he is entitled in return for a cash payment. The rights attaching to a debenture with subscription rights are an integral part of the security. If and when the debenture is sold any rights attaching to it pass to the purchaser at the time of sale. It is normal for both conversion rights and subscription rights to lapse after a prescribed time.

Warrants

These should not be confused with share warrants to bearer. They are entirely different securities. Warrants are documents which entitle the holder to subscribe for ordinary shares of a company at some future date or dates at a price fixed at the time of issue of the warrant. Warrants have been issued relatively infrequently but normally by large companies whose securities are actively dealt in on the Stock Exchange. Particulars about warrants in issue, and prices, are reported daily in the *Financial Times*. The feature of warrants which distinguishes them from convertible debentures or debentures with subscription rights is that they are separable from the security with which they are originally associated and, in consequence, they can be bought and sold as independent securities. They have been described as long-term options and will be listed on the Stock Exchange and freely dealt in.

'The usual reason for the issue of warrants is to make the terms of a takeover bid more attractive without further immediate cost to the bidder. For example, the consideration of a bid may consist of ordinary shares and unsecured loan stock. It is an added attraction if, attaching to the loan stock, there is a warrant entitling the holder to subscribe to ordinary shares at a predetermined price at a future date. From the company's point of view it could be an advantage for capital gearing purposes to issue a non convertible loan stock with long-term warrants attached rather than a convertible loan stock in respect of which conversion rights could be exercised within a few years. There are also cases of warrants being attached to issues of fixed interest stocks with a view to reduce the current market rate of interest that would otherwise be payable on the stock.' (*Chartered Secretaries Manual of Company Secretarial Practice* (Jordon).)

Questions

1. Describe the different types of shares and securities which might be issued by a listed company.   (ICSA   22 marks)
2. What characteristics distinguish convertible loan stock from ordi-

nary loan stock? How do you account for the growth of such issues in recent years? (ACCA 20 marks)

3. What are the distinctive features of the 'convertible' debenture and why has this type of security appeared in recent years? (ICA 20 marks)

4. Distinguish between the various types of long-term loan capital which are available for a listed company and explain their advantages and disadvantages to the lender and the borrower. (ICSA 22 marks)

5. 'The insistence of British and Irish company law on shares of a fixed nominal value in all cases has lead to much needless complexity and misunderstanding amongst the unsophisticated of par value and of dividends expressed as a percentage thereof.' Explain the nature of this apparent problem, preferably with an illustration. Are par value shares really necessary? What steps have been taken to introduce them into the system of company law? (ACCA Acc3 18 marks)

6. E Ltd has share capital issued and fully paid of 5,000,000 £1 ordinary shares. The current market value of the shares is 220p per share, the total pre-tax earnings are £1,100,000 per annum and the gross dividend is £700,000. The company wishes to raise £1,000,000 for a new investment which is expected to generate additional earnings, before tax and interest, of £120,000 p.a. The finance director is considering four methods of raising the £1,000,000:

(i) A rights issue of 1 new share for each 5 currently held at a price of £1 per share.
(ii) A public issue of 500,000 shares at a price of £2 per share
(iii) An issue at par of £1,000,000 11% loan stock 1995. The company has no other debentures outstanding at present.
(iv) An issue at par, made either to the general public or to existing shareholders, of £1,000,000 10% convertible loan stock 1995–2005, convertible into ordinary shares at any time between 1985 and 1995 on the basis of 50 ordinary shares for each £100 debenture.

Required: Comment on the above options from the viewpoint of the company and of its shareholders, consider any other possibilities, and advise the company of the method of finance which should be adopted. In what way would your analysis be affected if the company already had £3,000,000 debentures outstanding? (ICSA 34 marks)

Chapter 6

Capital structure and gearing

In this chapter some matters relating to capital structure and gearing will be more fully examined, with relevant past examination questions. A feature of professional examinations in Business Finance is that they normally take place in the final year, after examinations in advanced accounting and, in some cases, management accounting and costing and they are frequently devised around situations which are similar to those encountered in real life by a financial adviser. The questions tend to assume an adequate technical accounting knowledge and seek to test the ability of the candidate to 'go behind the accounts' and show an awareness of the limitations of published accounts, the fact that they are often not what they seem and could, for example, be manipulated, and hence should be treated with caution. In reality, no experienced adviser would be prepared to recommend a course of action on the basis of a set of accounts, a piece of paper. He would wish to pose and insist on answers to a number of questions, including on non-financial matters. He would wish to know the assumptions on which forecasts and projections were based and, for example, the quality and depth of market research in relation to a proposed new project. In addition to adequate technical knowledge an adviser requires a questioning and analytical approach, wide financial and commercial knowledge, sound judgement, common sense and experience. Examiners try to frame questions which require candidates to show evidence that they have these attributes, although at this stage it must be accepted that they will lack experience.

Example
In early 1973 the directors of ABC Ltd decided to raise £4 m. in order to expand their manufacturing facilities in Wales. It was expected that

Capital structure and gearing

this investment would increase profits by £800,000 before tax and interest. The company had in the past avoided long-term debt because of the degree of fluctuation of its profits, and had financed investment projects from retained earnings and overdrafts.

The project under consideration was too large to be financed by these means and would require an issue either of ordinary shares or debentures. It was estimated that ordinary shares could be issued at £2 each (net of issue costs) while debentures could be issued at 12%.

The directors of the company differed considerably over the method of finance to be adopted:
1. R.G. argued because they would make equity earnings more risky and cause the ordinary shares to become more speculative.
2. J.B. favoured ordinary shares because the project would earn £480,000 after corporation tax of 40%, while dividends paid at the current level of 20% per share would total only £400,000 on the new issue of shares.
3. A.X. thought that the proposed issue price was too low because the net assets per share were about £2.17 and this figure represented book value, which was considerably lower than replacement cost.

Selected earnings and dividend data 1968–1972

	Net profit after tax (£000)	Earnings per share (p)	Dividends per share (p)	Market price high (p)	low
1968	3,360	28	12	350	185
1969	2,400	20	12	195	145
1970	2,400	20	12	220	150
1971	2,940	24.50	12	265	200
1972	3,000	25	20	230	190

Market price of shares at 31.12.1974 was 225p.

Balance sheet as at 31 December 1972

Sources of finance (£000)		Assets (£000)	
Ordinary shares £1 – fully paid	12,000	Fixed assets	9,400
Reserves	14,000	Goodwill	2,000
Current liabilities	8,000	Stock	13,000
		Debtors	8,060
		Cash	1,540
	34,000		34,000

(ICSA 34 marks)

4. S.W. pointed out that earnings per share would be diluted to 24.80p if further shares were issued while an issue of debentures would increase earnings to 27p.

On the basis of this information and that provided below, you are asked to discuss what action should have been taken by the directors. (Ignore the impact of the imputation system of corporation tax.)

Workings and comments

The question indicates that only two alternative methods of finance are to be considered, i.e. (*a*) equity, or (*b*) debentures. In effect, a 'mix' of the two is ruled out. The first step must be to set out clearly the financial implications of each alternative.

(£000)	Ordinary shares	Debentures
Profit before taxation	800	800
Less: debenture interest (£4 m. at 12%)	–	480
	800	320
Less: Corporation tax (40%)	320	128
	480	192
Add: present equity profits	3,000	3,000
	3,480	3,192
Number of ordinary shares initially	12 m.	12 m.
Additional issue	2 m.	– m.
Final number of shares in issue	14 m.	12 m.
Earnings per share	24.80p.	26.60p.

(Note the simplicity of the calculations in this case, once the first step has been decided upon, to set out effectively the financial implications of each option.) Assuming the reliability of the accounts, the indications are of a company in a strong financial position which is run on very conservative lines, as there is no gearing whatsoever and the current and liquid positions are very strong. One sees at a glance that as long as 1968 the earnings per share were as high as 28p and the market price then was at its highest, 350p. It thus appears that the directors have not been able to make satisfactorily productive use of the substantial retained profits. (These can be calculated easily from the information given – they are the difference between the earnings and the dividends paid per share each year, multiplied by the number of shares in issue – 12 m.). Indeed, the comparatively low market price of the shares on 31 December 1972, taking into account the retained earnings − 12 m. × (16 + 8 + 8 + 12.5 + 5)p = £5,940,000 − may be in part an indication of generally poor market conditions and in part a market view that the company is performing inadequately in view of its resources.

The decline in the return on the shareholders' capital can be seen even more clearly from the following calculations: in 1972 the net tangible assets were £24 m., i.e. excluding goodwill, and this sum represents the ordinary shareholders' equity. The after-tax return on this equity capital is £3 m. × 100, i.e. 12.5%. However, in 1968 the shareholders' equity must have been £24 m. − £5.94 m., i.e. £18.06 m. As the after-tax earnings in 1968 were £3.36 m. the after-tax return on the equity must have been £3.36 m. × 100, i.e. 18.60%. The directors would be well advised to investigate the reasons for this decline in performance and also recheck in as much detail as they can the apparent quality of the profit forecasts for the proposed project and the assumptions on which they are based. The strong resources of the company, the fact that there is no long-term debt, the prolonged uninspired performance, and the low market price are classic pointers to the likelihood that sooner rather than later an alert financier will initiate a takeover attempt in order to obtain underemployed assets at a bargain price.

A further indication of the overcautious attitude of the directors is their reason given for not issuing debentures in the past − the degree of fluctuation of the profits. The figures given in the earnings and dividend data for 1968−72 show that the after-tax profits never fell below £2.4 m. These would always have been ample to provide 'cover' for a significant debenture issue, especially when the favourable tax treatment of debentures is taken into account.

It is therefore suggested that, in this case, provided that all is as reported in respect of the proposed project, financing by means of an issue of debentures would be appropriate, and in the interests of the ordinary shareholders. It would introduce a modest element of gearing and since, if all goes according to plan, the cost of the debentures is significantly less than the additional profits generated by their use, the ordinary shareholders would have the benefit of this additional profit, which would boost the earnings per share.

The following are comments on the opinions expressed by the individual directors. They would not form an essential part of an answer to the question.

R.G.: This is surely an overcautious argument against ever issuing debentures. Obviously, judgement must always be used in considering gearing and over-gearing must be avoided. At the moment ABC Ltd goes to the extreme of having no gearing, despite its resources. Even if ABC Ltd issued £4 m. it would still be a low-geared company.

J.B.: The calculations of J.B. are correct but his interpretations are not accepted. It is the earnings per share and not the dividends which are the true measures of the efficiency of the deployment of the shareholders' funds. Falling earnings per share when the rate of dividend remains unchanged mean that the dividend cover is reduced and so is the prospect of capital appreciation of the value of the ordinary shares. All investors in ordinary shares, without exception, will hope for capital gains in respect of their shares, in addition to satisfactory dividends.

A.X.: It is stated that ordinary shares could be issued at £2 net. This implies that the actual issue price would be around 210p., so that after deduction of the not inconsiderable issue costs there would be a net receipt of 200p. This appears to be a rather optimistic assessment for in practice an issue of new shares (a rights issue) must be offered at a price well below the current market price – which could fall before the issue date – since no one would pay the company a higher price for shares than that at which it could obtain the identical shares in the open market. What A.X. is really arguing, possibly without realising this, is that new investors would be obtaining a share of the equity too cheaply. Insofar as existing shareholders exercised their full rights, and maintained their proportionate shareholding in the company, no harm would be done. In effect, A.X. is arguing in favour of obtaining the additional funds by means of a debenture issue since this would not 'dilute the equity'.

S.W. is correct in his statement, as the calculations showed. If debentures were issued and all went according to plan, the earnings per share would increase to 26.60p, which S.W. has evidently rounded to 27p.

The capital structure

The capital structure of a company may and often does change over a period of time. There is no rigid formula and as explained the temperaments of managing directors or major shareholders may often be the major determining factor at any given time. The availability of money, and level of interest rates, and expectations as to future money availability, and whether interest rates are thought likely to rise or fall,

Capital structure and gearing

will also be important factors. Gearing would be expected to be lower in the early days of a company, until it established a good credit standing in the eyes of prospective lenders. The gearing would fall, at least temporarily, at any time when loans were repaid otherwise than by the proceeds of a new loan, or at any time when a rights issue was made. One purpose of a rights issue is to reduce the gearing.

The flow of funds or sources and applications of funds: a preview

Clearly, in order to have the use of, or to own assets, a company must command appropriate resources, or funds. In practice there needs to be a close interrelationship between the types of assets employed and the funds which finance them. The expression sources and applications of funds, or, alternatively, flow of funds, will often be met in a study of business finance and the preparation of flow of funds statements are considered in Chapter 9. Note at this stage that increases in liabilities or, conversely, reductions in assets represent sources of funds, whereas increases in assets or, conversely, reductions in liabilities represent applications of funds.

For examples, the issue of additional ordinary shares, or debentures, represent increases in liabilities and sources of funds The sale of a piece of land, or a machine also, obviously, represents an inflow, or source of funds which, in this case, arises from a reduction in the assets. Meanwhile, the purchase of buildings, or machinery, or stock represent increases in assets, and applications of funds. In this case there has been no change in the total of the assets, but a change in their composition – a purchase of land creates a new fixed asset, with a corresponding reduction in the liquid assets, cash. There can also be an application of funds in the reduction of liabilities – paying of some creditors, for example. In this case a liability will be reduced with a corresponding reduction in the assets, in this case cash, which will have been used to pay the creditors.

It will be apparent, when the implications of double-entry book-keeping are considered, that just as a balance sheet always balances, so, when a funds flow statement is prepared the sources and applications must always equal each other. However, the sources come first in time insofar as the necessary funds must always be available, or promised, before commitments can be entered into.

A modern view is that, despite their limitations, the three key financial statements about a company which an analyst, or creditor, or shareholder, or employee, etc., will wish to study are:

(*a*) the balance sheet which, in effect, shows a 'snapshot' of the financial position of a company at some significant moment in time;

(b) the profit-and-loss account, which is a document credited with the gross profit (or debited with the gross loss) brought in from the trading account, and credited with any other revenue items such as discounts receivable, rents receivable, income from investments, etc., which arise during the period. This account is debited with all the expenses incurred in selling and distributing the goods (or services) and in the general administration of the business. The depreciation of fixed assets over the period is also debited to this account. The balance on the profit-and-loss account represents the net profit (or loss) for the financial period. It is transferred to the capital (or current) account in the case of a sole trader, and to the profit and loss appropriation account in the case of a company;

(c) the funds flow statement.

The importance of the funds flow statement has become widely recognised recently. Its purpose is to explain the movement of funds during a financial period, and to allow assessment of how the change between the opening balance sheet position, and that shown in the closing one has been brought about. Its preparation will be explained in Chapter 9.

A feature of fixed assets is that their introducton into and use in a company is normally only justified in economic and financial terms if they are retained in use for more or less lengthy periods. If they have to be disposed of prematurely for some reason, which could include to raise money in a crisis situation, it is likely that heavy losses would be incurred. It is partly for this reason that decisions about acquiring major fixed assets are always taken at high levels within a company and after detailed evaluations. The issues at stake, in financial and other terms will be substantial. Capital project evaluation is considered in Chapter 14. On the other hand, current, or circulating, assets are 'turned over' as quickly as possible.

It follows that sources of funds which would be appropriate to finance one type of asset could even be dangerously unsuitable to finance another. Above all, short-term sources of funds, liabilities which must be repaid in the near future, are in principle not suitable to finance the purchase of fixed, long-term assets. This is widely accepted as one of the most important and fundamental rules of business finance and breaking it has lead to the compulsory liquidation of many companies in the past and will no doubt lead to the liquidation of many in the future.

Whilst it may seem that rules can safely be broken by exceptional people – and there is evidence that numbers of successful, fast-growing companies in their earlier stages show high profitability, high gearing, serious illiquidity, and unfavourable ratios, and appear to be in danger of failure, and yet they do not fail – the collapse in 1974, first of the property market and then the general equity market, proved, for a generation at least, one hopes, that not even exceptional people can continue to break rules and expect that they will always be able to escape the consequences. A main reason for the market collapse was that property prices were booming and it seemed that they could move only one way – quickly upwards. People in powerful positions in business, who had influence with bank directors and senior managers, bought property on overdrafts or short-term loans, sold the property at a profit and purchased more expensive property with the proceeds, supplemented by further loans. The cycle was a continuing one with sharp people steadily enriching themselves by the use of other people's money (high gearing). Suddenly a new factor arose, the quadrupling of oil prices, and the mood of euphoria vanished overnight. The boom collapsed, as the South Sea Bubble had burst over two centuries earlier. The banks called in overdrafts urgently and there was a liquidity crisis, a shortage of cash. Borrowers against the security of property, and the lenders, found suddenly that properties were unsaleable, or could only be sold at huge losses. Major banks experienced and later quietly wrote off huge bad debts: secondary banks had even larger losses. The Bank of England, with the clearing banks, mounted a 'lifeboat' operation to ensure that numbers of secondary banks were supported, on the principle that if they had been allowed to collapse there would have been complete loss of confidence on the part of investors (one was aware of this at the time), there would have been 'runs on the banks', and a domino effect, with one bank collapse leading to another. In the event, the rescue was handled with great skill and only a tiny number of secondary banks were allowed to collapse, but no depositors lost their money. The secondary bank shareholders did, however.

In business finance it needs to be borne in mind that market psychology can be an important factor. In boom times the view gains ground that the boom will never end and many highly placed, able, energetic and aggressive people act with rapacious greed, and overextend themselves. In most cases they are only able to do so because there are others in positions of authority who act so carelessly, or so incompetently, and with such neglect of their responsibility for the safeguarding of their shareholders' money, that they advance money to them, or approve credit, with astonishing lack of prudence. It seems that every generation there is a major boom followed by an overnight collapse. The 1974 collapse was followed by many individual bankruptcies, but the fact that in one case an individual went bankrupt for a total of over £100 m. and in another case a young man of 28 was given a loan of £17 m., which was never repaid, on a personal guarantee, which proved to be a worthless sheet of paper, showed the extent to which bank directors, managers and others in key positions must have been disregarding the normal rules of commercial and banking prudence during the 'heady' period of the boom. In many cases audit certificates issued by most eminent firms of auditors gave no clue that anything might be wrong.

A usual consequence of a period when people in high or very responsible positions show gross lack of judgement, prudence, competence, and even common sense, is a 'swing of the pendulum' effect. When the extent of their miscalculations and inadequacies become public knowledge (and they 'move heaven and earth' to prevent this from happening, and are frequently experts in having unfavourable matters covered up) then for some time in the future there will be attitudes of special caution, sometimes to the extent that it becomes difficult to obtain loans even for sound projects.

In principle, strong attractions of overdrafts and short-term loans are the relative ease with which they can be arranged and their relative cheapness. However, they are unsuitable finance for the purchase of major fixed assets, since the company may be called upon to repay the overdraft or loan at an inconvenient time, possibly in a credit squeeze, when new loans cannot be raised, or only on usurious terms.

Some problems arising from interest-rate fluctuations and inflation
Recent times have been exceptionally difficult from the aspect of financial management for a number of interrelated reasons. Above all, there is inflation, which varies from country to country and which, *inter alia*, affects currency exchange rates and international trade, on which the UK is very dependent. In the UK itself there is uncertainty from one year to another as to what the rate of inflation will be over the next two or three years. Furthermore, in recent years investors have become more sophisticated and have recognised that to a large extent inflation is an immense confidence trick especially played by governments upon the unsuspecting. In this country, governments and local authorities in the recent past have shown insatiable demands for money and in 1977 a crisis in international confidence arose in relation to the pound sterling. The International Monetary Fund (IMF) had to be requested to arrange support for sterling. In accordance with its mandate the IMF arranged support on the understanding that the UK Government accepted its stringent conditions, designed to impose firm financial discipline. This was a period when there were 'ratepayers' revolts' as

Capital structure and gearing

ratepayers began to show militancy in the face of local authorities which in many cases had been spending public money lavishly and wastefully on ill-considered and unproductive products. Excessive spending of this type is itself considered an important source of inflation.

At the worst point in the sterling crisis in 1976 the minimum lending rate (MLR) rose to 15%, but when the crisis was brought under control it fell to 5% (1977), but thereafter it steadily rose again and in 1979/80 has reached a high point of 17%. Over the years there have been frequent and wide fluctuations in MLR and short- and long-term interest rates. In recent years investors have recognised that fixed-interest securities do not protect the real value of capital, but their position has been eased by the general rise in interest rates, insofar as a part of the rise may be considered a return of capital. For their part, financial managers have been obliged unceasingly to take views as to how interest rates would move in the short-, medium- and long-terms. In principle, when they assess that they will need in due course to borrow for the longer term they pay great attention to timing, for it is obviously to the advantage of a borrower to borrow on a long-term basis at a time when interest rates have reached their lowest point and can subsequently be expected to rise. The problem is to know if and when this point has been reached and experts frequently judge wrongly. Conversely, if they believe that interest rates will fall further, financial managers will seek to avoid committing their companies to long-term borrowing if they can. At such times the temptation to have excessive recourse to overdrafts or short-term loans will be very strong.

In recent years interest rates have regularly been so high that it would have been impossible profitably to use funds incurring such a high cost of capital, and promising investment projects have had to be abandoned. The wide-ranging and unpredictable movements of interest rates in conjunction with a high basic rate is given as a main reason why companies have virtually ceased to issue long-term debentures in recent years and instead have relied much more on bank borrowing. Fortunately, the banks have been generally ready and able to meet the needs. It is argued that high interest rates have come about largely because of continuing and excessive borrowing requirements of the government and public authorities; both are prepared to pay high rates of interest because they are not subjected to the same financial disciplines as private-sector companies: moreover, public sector borrowers have been able to pre-empt an excessive proportion of the available funds because of their ability and readiness to borrow no matter what the rate of interest. A private-sector management, on the other hand, when evaluating a new investment project would be obliged to take the cost of capital into account, and when interest rates make this high, then many projects must be turned down because they could not be profitable, although they might have been if the cost of capital had been lower. The records show that in recent years the after-tax return on capital of UK manufacturing industries has been low – even below 5% p.a. This must surely be a major reason why new investment in manufacturing industry in the UK has often seemed disappointingly low in recent years.

Gearing

Alternative measurements

Main aims of private-sector business include the achievement of profits, survival and growth, and from the financial aspects these require attention to the capital structure and the need for adequate stability and liquidity. As explained, in practice the gearing of a company may lie within quite a wide range and from the aspect of financial as distinct from business risks, a low-geared company will be less risky than a high-geared one, but the attraction of high gearing is that when things go well the earnings per share for the equity shareholders will be high.

The degree of gearing which is feasible tends to vary according to the circumstances of the industry within which the company operates. In principle, if the fixed assets which the company owns have wide alternative uses, and the likelihood of steadily appreciating capital values, so that they are readily acceptable as security, and if the company operates under reasonably stable conditions of demand, with an assured cash flow, then it will be able to operate with higher gearing than would a company whose fixed capital and operating conditions did not have these characteristics. Thus hotel and property companies, and brewing groups, tend to be able to borrow easily, and thus be highly geared, whereas companies which operate in cyclical industries, and with specialised fixed assets such as shipbuilding, mining and gold prospecting companies, have to depend to a greater extent on risk capital, especially when they are still comparatively small.

The concept of gearing is basically simple but there is no complete uniformity in respect of definitions or methods of calculation and students should avoid dogmatic statements and when necessary definitions and methods of calculation employed should be stated. Gearing is frequently considered in relation to the long-term capital structure of the company, the ratio of debentures and other long-term loans, if any, to the shareholders' equity – issued ordinary share capital plus reserves. However, there can be no complete review of the gearing of a company unless all of the borrowing is taken into account, since a main purpose of the measurement of gearing is to assess a major aspect of the financial risks to which a company is exposed. If a company defaults on a bank overdraft or loan the consequences will be the same as for default on any other type of borrowing and this is an argument for including all borrowings in measurements of gearing. Trade credit is also a form of borrowing, of course. Bear in mind, also, the Wilson Committee definition (p. 47).

Gearing: the treatment of preference shares

Many companies do not have preference shares in issue and so no problem arises. If there are preference shares, how can they be regarded in relation to gearing? Insofar as preference shares are fixed-dividend securities, they have a characteristic of loans. However, preference shareholders are not creditors and in this respect they have a main characteristic of ordinary shareholders. They are risk bearers who happen not to enjoy the rewards of risk bearing when things go well. Meanwhile, in many measurements of gearing the convention is to group preference shareholders with lenders because of the aspect of their fixed-dividend security. When gearing is considered from the aspect of its effects on the earnings of the ordinary shares, as it often is, this treatment will be the correct one. However, if the financial stability of the company is being considered, and from the viewpoint of creditors, then preference shareholdings should be regarded – in the view of the writer – as part of the risk capital. In examination questions, when alternative treatments are feasible, as in this case, a student may show his awareness of the position by indicating in a very brief note that there is an alternative treatment.

Gearing measurement

Gearing may be measured on (*a*) a capital basis or (*b*) an income basis, or both. In practice, analysts who examine gearing and other ratios, and financial information in relation to a company will do so for some main reason and this will have an important bearing on their approach. For examples, an analyst paid by a client will take his 'terms of reference', or instructions, from that client; a bank manager would wish to be sure that any loan agreement entered into would be fully honoured, and the cash flow adequate and, in addition, security would be held which, in the last resort, could be sold at a price which exceeded the loan plus the costs of the sale; a financial journalist– analyst would have a particularly wide brief as his readers would represent all types of interests – creditors, shareholders, employees, members of the public, etc.

Widely used measures of gearing include:

1. The debt ratio

$$\frac{\text{Total debt (all loans and other liabilities)}}{\text{Total assets}}$$

The traditional ratio is below 1 : 2. 'Assets' should be valued on a realistic and not 'historical costs' basis, and normally on a 'going concern' basis and not on 'break-up' values, although the latter would be appropriate in critical situations when prospective lenders had to face the fact that even if they made a loan the company might still be moving towards financial collapse.

2. The debt ratio

This is sometimes, alternatively, calculated as

$$\frac{\text{Total debt}}{\text{Shareholders' funds}}$$

It is widely considered that the ratio 1 : 1 should not normally be exceeded. If it is, the implications may be that whereas the ordinary shareholders will enjoy the rewards in the good times, the lenders will be bearing too many unrewarded risks and hence their security appears to be indequate.

3. The borrowing ratio

$$\frac{(\text{Long- + medium- + short-term loans + overdrafts}) \times 100}{\text{Net assets employed}}$$

In this case net assets are considered as the total assets less current and short-term liabilities other than overdrafts. A question is whether overdrafts should be counted as any sums overdrawn when the ratio is calculated, or as the total limit approved. Consistency of treatment is necessary. There is no generally accepted figure for this ratio and the ratio for a particular company would be compared with that calculated on earlier dates, to assess trends, if any: the ratio for the company would also be compared with that of other companies in the same industry.

Capital structure and gearing 103

4. *The gearing ratio*
As an income rather than a capital measure can be

$$\frac{\text{Loan interest payable}}{\text{Earnings before loan interest and taxation}}$$

Lenders will require ample 'cover', so that even if earnings declined considerably the company would still have no difficulty in meeting the interest payments. A ratio below 20% would be wished for.

5. *The gearing ratio*
A commonly used capital measure is

$$\frac{\text{Total debt + fixed dividend share capital}}{\text{Ordinary shareholders' funds}}$$

Measures said to be used by bankers include:
(a) Gross indebtedness (which comprises total creditors of a Gross assets
  company);
(b) Gross gearing (gross borrowings as a percentage of capital employed);
(c) Net gearing (gross borrowings less cash as a percentage of capital employed);
(d) Net short-term gearing (bank borrowings less cash as a percentage of capital employed).

Analysis of gearing is an aspect of ratio analysis, a theme which will be considered in Chapter 13. A non-specialist needs to accept that ratio analysis is difficult and training, aptitude and experience are essential before reliance can be placed in the interpretations of an analyst. There are some special difficulties in measuring and interpreting gearing: (a) not all loan finance may be recorded in the balance sheet – there are 'off balance sheet' items, notably leasing obligations; (b) if a company retains a substantial proportion of its profits as a main source of new risk capital, the gearing will decline over time unless borrowings are increased when important new projects are implemented; (c) if there are significant short-term borrowings the gearing will change when these are repaid; (d) gearing levels will change when redeemable debentures are redeemed, unless there is an issue of new debentures which corresponds exactly with the redeemed issue.

Even in 1975/76, a time of unusual pressures on company liquidity, the gross gearing of UK companies averaged below 33%, a surprisingly low figure. Part of the explanation lies in the increasing practice of companies to revalue their fixed assets at quite frequent intervals. For example, if land and buildings orginally cost £100,000 and stood in the accounts, and balance sheet, at that figure, then if they were revalued by a competent valuer as having a market value of, say £300,000, the book-keeping entries would be simple but important. The land and buildings (or other appropriate account) would be debited with the difference, £200,000, and in order to deal with the dual aspect, or double entry, another account must be credited with £200,000. This would normally be an account with a designation such as 'property revaluation reserve account', and it would be grouped in the balance sheet with the ordinary shareholders' equity – that is, a capital profit belonging to the ordinary shareholders and thus becoming a part of the 'equity base' – the denominator of the ratio which measures the gearing.

The practical implications and the advantages and disadvantages of gearing are illustrated in the following example. To simplify it taxation has been ignored, but the principles are not affected. In practice taxation can never be ignored and each situation must be examined in relation to its own facts. Consider four companies: A, B, C, D.

		A	B	C	D
1.	Long-term capital				
	Debentures (5%)	0	10,000	50,000	90,000
	Ordinary shares	100,000	90,000	50,000	10,000
	Total	100,000	100,000	100,000	100,000
	Profit before payment of interest	20,000	20,000	20,000	20,000
	Debenture interest	0	500	2,500	4,500
	Maximum for ordinary shareholders	20,000	19,500	17,500	15,500
	Return on ordinary share capital	20%	21.7%	35%	155%
2.	Debentures (5%)	0	10,000	50,000	90,000
	Ordinary shares	100,000	90,000	50,000	10,000
	Total	100,000	100,000	100,000	100,000
	Profit before payment of interest	3,000	3,000	3,000	3,000
	Debenture interest	0	500	2,500	4,500
	Maximum for ordinary shareholders	3,000	2,500	500	NIL
	Return on ordinary share capital	3%	2.8%	1%	NIL

Capital structure and gearing 105

Company A represents nil gearing – a capital structure likely to be met in its early days. B is also very low geared. C is a higher than average gearing, but a level which is quite often met in practice. D is an unrealistically highly geared company, which highlights the principle. In practice prudent lenders will impose restrictions which prevent a company from becoming too highly geared. Comparisons between A and C in the above example show clearly how a highly geared company benefits in good times but how heavy the fixed-interest obligation becomes when profits sharply decline. In example 2 company D did not have sufficient profit to cover the interest but in practice this payment must always be made and the cash management must always ensure that the cash is available. If a company has made an operating loss before deduction of interest the effect will be to increase the loss. If reserves had been built up in the past, or a credit balance on the profit-and-loss appropriation account, any final debit balance on the profit-and-loss account for the year would be offset against earlier profits and accordingly the appropriation or the reserve account would be reduced by the amount of the operating loss for the year.

The concept of profit

As a main objective of businesses is to make profits, it is necessary to consider what is meant by 'profit' and how is the adequacy or otherwise of the profit assessed in a particular case? In principle it seems simple. Profit is the surplus which arises when the total revenues exceed the total costs and due allowances have been made for differences in opening and closing stocks, for expenses paid in advance, or payable but not yet paid, with due allowance for the loss in value of capital equipment used in achieving the total revenues and for any sums owing to the business which will remain unpaid because of the defaults of debtors. The determination of the profit for an accounting period requires the matching of costs with related revenues. Revenues and costs are accrued, i.e. recognised as they are earned or incurred and not as money is received or paid.

In practice the determination of profit may be a far from simple matter. The profit for a financial year, in the case of published accounts, will be determined after a number of valuations have been made and this will in many cases include valuations of stocks of raw materials, components, work in progress and finished goods. Stock valuing can be complex and difficult and there will be an important subjective aspect, and it will be necessary to make certain assumptions. The validity of the profit figure will depend upon the quality of the judgement and the validity of the assumptions.

Even when all the parties are acting with the utmost good faith, and, unfortunately, sometimes they will not be, it is possible for different people to calculate independently the profits of a company for a period and to arrive at quite widely differing results and for each result to be acceptable to qualified auditors. When members of a management are fraudulent in intention or act just to keep within the strictest letter of the law, there is scope for considerable manipulation of the figures. The subject is wide and controversial. To sum up, difficulties arise from definitions: many terms are used, e.g. net profit; trading profit; margin; earnings; before tax; after tax; etc. Furthermore, different bases may be used in the calculations and it is sometimes difficult to distinguish between operating and capital expenditure. Use of marginal costing instead of the more usual absorption costing (p. 225) produces different profit figures. There is also the aspect of inflation. Traditional historic cost calculation of profit will produce a significantly different figure from an inflation-adjusted current cost calculation.

It is significant and surely not an accident that the Companies Acts do not define profits, nor how they may be determined, nor that only revenue profits may be distributed as dividends. Table A, which is authoritative but not mandatory, states 'no dividend shall be paid otherwise than out of profits' and this represents the situation as it has been well established by case law. The following comments are a summary only and interested readers are referred to textbooks on company law for details of the legal aspect. In principle, the law requires that the accounts of a company show a 'true and fair' view. (Many competent people consider that this is not now possible unless some form of inflation accounting has been adopted. The law has now begun to require this for larger, listed companies, and the position is set out in SSAP 16. See Chapter 26.) Consistency of treatment is always very important.

Case law has established that dividends may not be paid out of capital and that no dividend may be paid which would operate to deprive creditors of the fund which is available for the satisfaction of their claims. The following general principles appear to be established by case law (as distinct from statute law):

(a) Depreciation of fixed assets, such as plant and machinery, need not necessarily be provided for before the determination of profit available for distribution. (This is a matter in which, unusually, the

Capital structure and gearing

accepted business view is stricter than the law requires. It is that adequate provision must be made for depreciation before the profit is determined.)
(b) Depreciation of current assets must be made before arriving at the profits available for dividends. (Fixed assets of one business may be the current assets of another. Thus cars and lorries are fixed assets for most companies but current assets for car and lorry dealers.)
(c) Capital losses need not be made good out of revenue profits available for distribution.
(d) In cases of dispute it will be for the Court to decide each case on its merits including, in each case, as to what are fixed and what are current assets. This will depend on the asset and the purpose for which it is held.

Capital profits

Unless the contrary is indicated, references to profits are normally to revenue, or operating profits, which have arisen from trading operations. However, clearly, capital profits can also arise, for example, on the sale of land or buildings. Capital profits treatment has been the subject of a number of important Court cases. In summary, Court judgements have ruled that capital profits may be distributed subject to the following conditions:
(a) The articles must permit the proposed distribution.
(b) The surplus must be realised.
(c) The surplus must remain after a *bona fide* revaluation of all the assets.
(d) Any revenue loss must first be made good out of the capital profit before any part of the latter is distributed as dividend.

In practice the management of a company must always distinguish carefully between revenue and capital profits (or losses) including when they are assessing what part, if any, of a revenue or capital profit is available for distribution. The fact is that the two types of profit (or loss) are often viewed differently in law and by the tax authorities.

It is also possible for capital profit to be recorded but not realised. For example, property may increase in value and the appreciation be recorded in the accounts, as already explained. However, a capital profit is only 'realised' if the property is sold at a profit. An unrealised capital appreciation may not be distributed as a cash dividend but provided neither the memorandum nor the articles prevented this an unrealised capital profit could be distributed in the form of capitalisation shares.

The return on capital

The directors of a company will wish to be able to define and then apply objective tests of the levels of efficiency at which the company as a whole, and also its components parts, are operating. It can happen that the overall results appear good but analysis reveals that they are quite poor in certain areas. If these can be improved, the overall results may then become outstanding. The Centre for Interfirm Comparison Ltd has an important role in helping companies to identify areas of strength and weakness. Meanwhile, there is no exclusive test of whether the profits of a company are at an acceptable level, or above or below this. There are a number of indicators and some are subjective or non-financial. Market research and studies of competitors' products may have their place, for example. However, by general consent, there is one measure which, despite some limitations, is of exceptional importance for private- and public-sector businesses. This is a ratio of the rate of return on capital employed. There is no single definition or method of calculation and the measure adopted in a particular case will depend on the purposes of the enquiry. Consistency is always important. It is always important that anyone who uses the ratio ensures that there can be no misunderstandings about the definitions used or manner of calculation in a particular case.

There will be more than one type of capital employed within a business and the outline balance sheet shown here is typical for a long-established company.

Capital employed by a company

Permanent capital
    Ordinary capital
        Paid-up share capital
        Profit-and-loss appropriation account
        Share premium account*
        General reserve account (and any other revenue reserve but not a specific provision against bad debts)
        Capital reserve account
    Ordinary shareholders' equity   A
    Preference capital (if any)   B

Long-term funds (*Repayable after ten years or more*)   C
    Debentures (Secured or Unsecured)
    Any other long-term loans

Capital structure and gearing

Medium-term funds (*Three to ten years*)   D
   Bank or other loans
   Deferred taxation (in certain cases)

Short-term funds (*Repayable within three years – including current liabilities,*   E
i.e. those repayable within one year)
   Short-term bank and other loans and bills payable
   Bank overdrafts
   Trade creditors
   Accrued charges: hire purchase or leasing payments outstanding (if any)
   Current and deferred taxation
   Dividends declared but not paid

---

* A share premium account will be opened when an established company issues ordinary shares at a price above the nominal price. If, for example, 1 m. shares of £1 each are issued at, say, £2 each, the double entry will be:
Debit cash account £2 m.; credit ordinary share account £1 m; credit share premium account £1 m.

Total capital employed (P)	$= A + B + C + D + E$
Medium-, permanent- and long-term capital employed (Q)	$= A + B + C + D$
Long-term and permanent capital employed (R)	$= A + B + C$
Permanent capital employed (S)	$= A + B$
Equity capital employed (T)	$= A$

(*a*) The overall rate of return on the total capital employed is ascertained by adding back any overdraft and or loan interest charged to the profits before tax and expressing this as a percentage of the whole capital employed (P). In most of these measures, but not all, the profits before tax are considered. As tax may change from year to year this results in more consistent and comparable figures, without need for adjustment. (Separate ratios may be calculated to evaluate the efficiency of the tax management.)

(*b*) The return on medium-, long-term and permanent capital employed is ascertained by adding back interest on medium- and long-term and permanent capital employed (Q).

(*c*) The return on long-term and permanent capital employed requires that interest on debentures and long-term loans is added back to the before-tax profits and this is expressed as a percentage of long-term and permanent capital employed (R).

(*d*) The return on the permanent capital employed – profit before tax expressed as a percentage of permanent capital employed (S).

(*e*) Whilst in the case of the ratios (*a*), (*b*), (*c*), (*d*) the before-tax calculation is normally made, in this case the important measure is the 'earnings per share' – the return on the ordinary shareholders' equity. The profit **after** tax (and after deduction of all interest and preference dividends, if any) is divided by the number of ordinary shares in issue. As with all ratios, if this is calculated on a consistent basis, the comparison of the figure for one year with those for earlier years will be on essential element in an analysis. One would like to see a steadily rising trend, and when sudden setbacks occur, one will want to know why. Comparisons can also usefully be made with the results of other companies with a comparable capital structure, especially companies within the same industry. The reasons for any anomalies or disparities would need to be investigated.

Gross and net capital employed
As explained, capital employed may be defined in a number of ways but two of the most widely used definitions are: (*a*) gross capital employed, which comprises the total assets of the business (and this, of course, equals the total of capital plus reserves plus liabilities) and; (*b*) net capital employed, which comprises the total assets less current liabilities (or, alternatively, capital plus reserves plus long term loans).

Profit and profitability
A statement that there has been a profit of, say, £1 m. over a year conveys only limited information in itself. It becomes more meaningful when related to the capital employed in generating that profit. This will permit the appropriately defined rate of return on capital to be calculated. Whether a particular rate of return was considered satisfactory would depend on the circumstances and various comparisons would be made. A higher rate would be expected in a high-risk industry. Furthermore, figures must always be interpreted with caution and preferably with access to material facts. For example, an imprudent manager might achieve exceptional rates of return for a year or so – perhaps if he were planning to sell his business and was doing some 'window dressing' – by working extra shifts with machinery whose maintenance was neglected; or he might avoid new projects because they would reduce his rate of return until they became well established. Good rates of return in the short term would mean too high a price if they resulted in long-term damage, or stagnation.

Undercapitalisation
The concept of the rate of return on capital suggests that a management will normally seek to operate with the smallest practicable capital. Up to a point this is true and a company large enough to afford skilful

specialist financial management would expect this to be an important financial objective and would give attention to such matters as skilful investment of short-term cash surpluses. However, for many smaller companies, which must depend on good, busy, 'generalist' managers, and having no day-to-day access to specialists, the highest theoretical standards represent an ideal which is not even considered, as it would seem impracticable. For example, a feature of recent years has been how quickly financial conditions may change, and normal sources of short- and medium-term funds could suddenly dry up. A manager aiming to attain the highest possible rate of return on capital by skilful 'hand-to-mouth' operations, with minimum capital, could find, in a sudden crisis, that he would have to spend excessive time seeking to arrange new sources of capital, possibly at very high cost, and he might have to neglect development of other and more profitable aspects of his business in which he had greater skills.

An undercapitalised company might be unable to operate efficient buying policies or to take advantage of cash discounts. It might be unable to buy the most suitable fixed assets, although it might be able to lease them. It would probably seek to exploit trade creditors as a major source of cheap finance, but trade creditors would not tolerate this policy for long. They might cease to deal with the company or do so on a cash-only basis. In principle it is desirable to aim for reasonable balance. If the signs are clear that a promising business is undercapitalised then the prudent course of action is to obtain additional risk capital and/or seek medium- or long-term loans. Undercapitalisation will be an aspect of 'overtrading'.

Overtrading

This arises when a business seeks to operate on a scale which cannot be supported by its capital structure, and the assets it is employing. It is trying to do too much with too little. Inflationary conditions and high taxation may be contributory causes, with high interest rates. Overtrading may be especially liable to occur in the early stages of a company which is making and selling an excellent product successfully, but whose management lacks interest in or knowledge of finance. The sequence of events is that sales rise unexpectedly, to the obvious satisfaction of the management. Stocks of materials, components, work in progress and finished goods have to be increased and these give rise to increased financial obligations. Substantial overtime must be worked and paid for. Some of the increased sales are likely to be on credit and so the debtors will increase. Commitments for additional machinery may be entered into without regard to the means of finance. As the company has only limited risk capital and possibly small, if any, long-term loans, it will have recourse to the maximum bank overdrafts it can obtain, and will delay payment to its creditors. The evidence of the apparent profitability of the company will blind its management to its lack of finance and inability to pay its way. Important contributory causes of overtrading may include: (a) too large a proportion of profits distributed and hence too small a proportion retained: (b) too high a proportion of the total capital is in fixed assets; (c) the business being allowed to expand quickly without consideration of the extra fixed and working capital needed and how these will be financed.

Possible danger signals pointing to conditions of overtrading include: (a) a marked increase in the creditors in relation to the sales; (b) an increase in short-term borrowing and an increase in interest payments; (c) gross and or net profits decline; (d) current and liquid assets decrease; (e) stocks increase without a proportionate increase in turnover; (f) the ratios of sales to working capital and sales to capital employed increase significantly; (g) fixed-asset investment is restricted and reduces in relation to the annual depreciation charge; (h) the debtors' ratio (debtors to sales) declines in consequence of pressure to pay put on debtors. If corrective action cannot be taken in time the consequence of overtrading can be compulsory liquidation at the instigation of creditors. Competent financial planning and management are the best insurance policies against avoidable liquidations of this type.

Overcapitalisation

This may arise in two different circumstances:

(a) When a company has initially raised funds on an excessive scale and is unable to employ them profitably. A company may also retain an unnecessarily large proportion of its distributable profits at a time its business is static. The rate of return on capital will decline. The main options open to the company would be to develop profitable new products and/or markets and/or activities, which might be difficult, or to devise a scheme for the return of part of their capital to the ordinary shareholders and obtain Court approval.

(b) When part of the capital is represented by overvalued assets, which are often described as 'watered down'. This situation may arise when a company purchases another business and pays an excessive price for its goodwill, or excessive valuations have been made of fixed assets acquired. The return on capital will be poor, since the true capital employed will be significantly below the apparent capital. The shares of the company will fall in price and the company will have difficulty in raising new capital. Ultimately, the

Capital structure and gearing

best course of action may be a capital reconstruction and a writing off, or down, of unrealistically valued assets against reserves and, if necessary, any balance against the ordinary share capital account. The purpose of a reconstruction would be to 'make a fresh start' with a more realistic capital structure.

Priority percentage tables (interest and dividend payments)

Priority percentage tables are occasionally used to illustrate the relative 'safety' of the payment made in respect of each type of security in issue. The following is an example:

Example

'ABC Ltd has made an after-tax profit of £200,000 and a dividend of 12% has been declared with respect to the ordinary shares. The following are the capital and long-term loans of a company. Prepare a priority percentage table. Ignore taxation.'

	£
£1 Ordinary shares, fully paid (1,000,000)	1,000,000
£1 8% First preference shares (100,000)	100,000
£1 9% Second preference shares (100,000)	100,000
6% Secured debentures (1985/1990)	200,000

Workings

The distributable profit must have been arrived at after payment of the debenture interest, which must therefore be 'written back', i.e. £12,000, and the sum to consider is thus £212,000.

Priority percentage table

	Total (£)	Cumulative (%)
Debenture interest	12,000	0–5.66
8% First preference shares	8,000	5.66–9.43
9% Second preference shares	9,000	9.43–13.68
Ordinary shares (12% dividend)	120,000	13.68–70.28
Reserve account	63,000	70.28–100.00
Totals	212,000	100.00

Interest and dividend cover

In effect, calcuation of interest and dividend cover deals with the same data as the priority percentage table, and has a similar purpose – to assess the relative 'safety' of the interest or dividend paid to a particular category of security holder. Each holder may wish to know how many times the available fund would be sufficient to cover the payments with respect to the security he holds. Self-evidently, the higher the cover the 'safer' the payment for that security seems. It indicates the extent to which the total fund might decline in a bad trading year and yet the payment with respect to the security could still be made. In the above example the cover for the debenture interest is £212,000, i.e. 17.69 times, and this is clearly very high cover. However, in the case of the ordinary shares, after prior interest and dividend payments have been deducted there remains £183,000, i.e. a cover of 1.53 times. This is clearly not ample and in general a cover of 2 for the ordinary share dividends is considered adequate but not excessive. Furthermore, when allowance has been made for inflation it will be found that the real cover is less than the apparent cover.

Dividend equalisation policy

In the above example, if the distributable profit fell by quite a small amount it would be likely that future dividends must be below 12%. However, many companies operate a 'dividend equalisation policy': that is, they seek to avoid wide fluctuations in dividend payments between high in good years and little or none in bad years, but rather to pay a stable rate of dividend from year to year, preferably on a rising trend. There is evidence that a majority of investors prefer this policy to the alternative of fluctuating dividends. When recommending dividends, directors must have regard to the liquidity of the company, as well as the profits available, and to finance needed for planned capital projects. Examination questions which require comment on the financial situation of a company often incorporate a recent balance sheet which reveals lack of liquidity and instability and yet the liabilities include 'dividend declared'. One would ask 'where would the cash come from?' One main reason why directors seek to avoid 'passing' a dividend is that if a company has trustee status, one in which trustees are authorised to invest, it would lose that valuable status if it passed a dividend and would not regain it until five years after the dividend reinstatement. The market rating of the company would suffer and it would have to incur higher costs whenever it sought to raise new funds.

In the example above the balance of undistributed profits is shown as being credited to the general reserve account. This is usual and the

Capital structure and gearing

reserve forms part of the ordinary shareholders' equity. If the company followed a dividend equalisation policy and paid, say, 12% dividend in bad times, and so the total distributed in one year exceeded the profits available for distribution then, in this case, the total column in the priority percentage table could be, say, 120% or more. This would indicate that reserves built up in earlier years must be reduced. The cash position must also permit payment of a dividend, of course, for, as explained, reserves and cash are not synonymous by any means. Payment of a dividend in a bad year, when the cash is available and there are also adequate reserves, does not give rise to a reduction in capital, which would be unlawful unless approved by the Court.

Example

AB Ltd is an engineering company whose 1979 Annual Report and Accounts shows turnover of £3,500,000 and an after-tax profit of £240,000 for the year ended 31 December 1979. The company's balance sheet is summarised as follows:

Balance sheet as at 31 December 1979 (£000)

Ordinary share capital (£1)	600	Fixed assets	1,000
Capital reserve (property revalued)	20	Current assets:	
Revenue reserves	320	Stock	400
Loan funds (12%) (repayable 31.12.1984)	260	Debtors	300
		Bank	10
			710
			1,710
		Less:	
		Current liabiltities:	
		Creditors	400
		Taxation	40
		Proposed dividend	70
			510
	1,200	(payable 1.2. 1980)	1,200

Required. Comment on the following statement put to you by a client who owns shares in AB Ltd:
(i) 'The company seems to be in a very good liquid position because the current assets are well in excess of the current liabilities.'
(ii) 'I compute the earnings on equity capital as 40%. This seems to be a very good performance, doesn't it?'

(iii) 'The Directors' Report says that they propose an issue of bonus shares "fully paid up" – on the basis of one new ordinary share for every three ordinary shares currently held. This is a tremendous benefit for me for it means that the value of my holding will increase by 30%.'
(iv) 'How can the cash balance be as low as £10,000 when the after-tax profit is £240,000?'
(v) 'I've been reading about the risks involved in capital gearing. How do these affect AB Ltd?' (ICSA 34 marks)

Workings and comments
(There is obviously no single 'right answer' to this type of question.)
 (i) 'On the contrary, the liquid position is very disturbing. The excess of **liquid** and not current assets over the current liabilities indicates the liquid position. The liquid assets comprise the debtors plus the bank and cash balances and this assumes that the debtors will pay promptly and in full. The current liabilities exceed the current assets by £200,000. I also note that the directors propose to pay a dividend of £70,000 this February. Where will they find the cash to pay this? They also have to repay £260,000 loan funds within five years. The directors must therefore take action to improve the capital structure in good time and they should consider a rights issue as well as longer term loans.'
(ii) 'The profits are £240,000, which is 40% of £600,000, which is the issued ordinary share capital. However, this is not the equity: the equity consists of the issued capital plus the revenue and plus the capital reserves, which are all attributable to the ordinary shareholders. The equity is thus £940,000 and £240,000 represents 25.5% of this, and not 40%. Even so, 25.5% is an exceptionally high return, but bear in mind that published accounts must always be treated with caution and one cannot form a judgement on the basis of a single balance sheet. It would be desirable to have the accounts for five years or so in order that trends could be considered. In any case, accounts alone do not tell the whole story. One must seek to know more about the company, its standing and the reputation of its products, the quality of its labour relations, etc. Note also that the validity of the profit figure depends on the quality of the valuations of the opening and closing stocks. Mistakes or, even worse, manipulation would result in the profit being misdeclared. Moreover, good management requires attention to the liquidity as well as the profitability of a company. The illiquid state of AB Ltd does not reflect well on the directors.'

(iii) 'It will surely be evident that wealth cannot be created merely by printing new share certificates. The issue of fully paid-up bonus shares, on the basis of one new ordinary share for every three ordinary shares now held, makes no change in the intrinsic value of the individual shareholding in the company. At the present time, assuming the balance sheet figures are realistic, the total shareholders' equity is £940,000, shared amongst 600,000 shares of £1 each. The theoretical asset value of each share would be £1.567. However, if 200,000 additional £1 shares are issued as a capitalisation issue (the term 'bonus' is misleading and should be avoided) all this means is that the same equity is now shared amongst 800,000 shares of £1 each and the asset value of each share is reduced to £1.175. Thus a holder of 3 shares initially had a holding worth $3 \times £1.567$, i.e. £4.7. After the capitalisation issue this would become, in theory, worth $4 \times £1.175$, i.e. £4.7. In fact, sometimes the market does regard a capitalisation issues as a 'bull point' and in this case there could be a small rise in the market value of a holding after this issue.'

(iv) 'This question can only be answered if a flow-of-funds statement is prepared and to do this it would be necessary to have the balance sheets as at the start and at the end of the period, together with the profit-and-loss account for the period. In the present case one can only guess. Possibly additional fixed assets have been purchased during the year, or funds have been applied in acquiring additional stock of financing an increase in debtors: in addition, or as an alternative, a loan may have been repaid or the outstanding obligations to creditors reduced.'

(v) 'Capital gearing is a measure of the extent to which the operations of the company are financed with loans in addition to the essential base of risk capital. In this case the ratio of loans to ordinary shareholders' equity is $\dfrac{£260,000 \times 100}{£940,000}$, i.e. 27.7%. In itself this is not a high ratio. The purpose of capital gearing is largely to improve the earnings per share on the ordinary shares, and requires that the cost of loans, the interest payable on them, which is effectively reduced by the taxation treatment, is more than covered by the net revenues generated by the use of the loans.

However, when loans are used the company must meet strictly all the agreed conditions, both as to interest and to repayment terms. If it fails to do so it becomes liable to fall under the control of the debenture holders, who might appoint a receiver in the first instance. A liquidator might finally be appointed if a company continued in default. The gearing of AB Ltd is potentially disquieting for two reasons. How will the company find the cash to meet the interest payments as they fall due and how will the directors find the money to repay £260,000 principal by 31 December 1984, five years beyond the date of the balance sheet? On the evidence available the profitability of the company suggests that the directors should have a good prospect of improving the liquidity of the company and refinancing the present loan with a new loan nearer the time. But what might the rate of interest be then? It is the fact that the company has been allowed to reach its present illiquid position which is a cause of special anxiety about the management, but if it can be shown that they are aware of the problem and are taking action to overcome it then neither the level of the gearing nor the fact that the principal has to be repaid by 31 December 1984 are causes for undue anxiety in themselves.'

Questions

1. You are required to write adequate notes explaining your understanding of: (a) 'a company being overcapitalised'. How can this situation arise and what are the consequences thereof? (6 marks). (b) 'A company overtrading'. What are its causes and consequences, and what warning signals can be determined from an analysis of its profit-and-loss account and balance sheet? (9 marks). (ACCA 15 marks.)
2. Discuss the matters which have to be taken into consideration when a Board of Directors is formulating its dividend policy. (ACCA 20 marks).
3. A public company is to be established to exploit some newly discovered mineral deposits. It is estimated that £10,000,000 will be required and that this will generate earnings before interest and taxation in the range of £2,000,000 to £2,100,000 p.a. Two proposals are under consideration. The first is to finance the company through an issue of 10,000,000 ordinary £1 shares at par. The second is to issue only 5,000,000 ordinary £1 shares along with £5,000,000 of 9% loan stock. If the all equity financing is used it is estimated that the ordinary shareholders will expect to see the company earn a return after corporation tax of 10%, however, because of the additional risk which will arise if loan stock is used then in this case the shareholders will expect the return to be 15%. Which capital structure would you recommend and why? Make clear any assumptions you make.

Note: 1. Flotation and issue expenses can be ignored.
2. Corporation tax can be assumed to be 50%. (ACCA 17 marks)

4. The summarised balance sheet of G. Ltd, at 31 December 1980, is as follows:

	(£)		(£)
3,500,000 Ordinary shares of 20p each	700,000	Fixed assets	1,550,000
Share premium account	300,000	Current assets	500,000
Reserves	200,000		
10% Debentures	400,000		
Current liabilities	450,000		
	2,050,000		2,050,000

The company intends to maintain the above capital structure and is considering a project which requires an initial investment of £300,000. The project is clearly worthwhile and the main question is the sources of finance which should be used. There is £50,000 of internal funds available and the remainder will have to be raised through the issue of loan stock and/or ordinary shares. It is estimated that if a 20% return on the equity can be offered (present cost of equity is 18%) shares can be sold at 200p (present market price is 210p) to provide net proceeds of 190p. Fifteen per cent stock can be sold at £95. The market price of the debenture is currently £70. The company has a marginal corporation tax rate of 40 per cent. You are required to: (i) Suggest a method of financing the new project and show the balance sheet immediately after the commencement of the new project; (ii) Compute the marginal cost of capital of such a scheme; (iii) Indicate the additional factors which need to be taken into account. (ICSA 34 marks)

5. N Ltd is entirely financed by equity capital of 1,000,000 ordinary shares of £1 each which have a current stock market price of £4 per share. The annual dividend for the last few years has been a steady 50p per share, earnings have been steady at 80p and the stock market expects that these rates will continue.

The directors of the company have proposed an investment project which is expected to show a return of £185,000 per annum indefinitely on an investment of £1,000,000. The company does not have any funds available and does not wish to raise further equity finance.

One of the directors suggests that £1,000,000 should be raised by an issue of 12% debentures at par. He argues that this would reduce the company's cost of capital sufficiently to make the project worthwhile.

One of the other directors, however, argues that the overall cost of capital would not be affected by a debenture issue and that in any case the equity shareholders would require a higher return if a debenture issue were made. You are required to advise the board of directors which factors should be taken into account in the acceptance and financing of the project. (ICSA 34 marks)

6. (*a*) In financing a business it is accepted as good practice not to borrow on short-term for investment in long-term. Explain the reasons for this practice. Give examples of business, commercial or financial organisation, or any special circumstances in which it might be possible to deviate from this practice. (*b*) It is often assumed to be beneficial for a company to have a high-geared capital structure. Explain the circumstances under which this might be true and comment on its validity under current economic conditions. (ICMA 20 marks)

7. Discuss the main problems involved in the measurement of the profit of a listed company. (ICSA 22 marks)

Chapter 7

The working capital

The nature of fixed assets and the need of companies for this type of asset has been considered briefly – the characteristic of such assets being that their working life is expected to last more than a single year. Unless the cost of the asset is small, so that it can be regarded as expendable and not worth including in an asset register, it will be specially recorded as a capital item and a due proportion of the services rendered to the company by the asset will be charged to the revenue accounts for each year of its working life. This is known as depreciation.

However, even when all the fixed assets which a company requires are in place and ready, a number of further arrangements must be made by every company, without exception, before it can begin operations. In brief, every company must have appropriate working capital at its disposal. This is made up of several separate and distinct components and in a company of any size the management of each of these will be the responsibility of a specialist who will be aware of the most suitable techniques, systems and equipment for the efficient management of his own function and he may know little or nothing about the management of the other functions. Net working capital is normally considered to be the total of the current assets less the current liabilities, the latter being those due for payment within the next twelve months. Occasionally a reference will be seen to the gross working capital and in such cases the total of the current assets will be meant.

Before considering the working capital as a concept it may be helpful to consider briefly the constituent parts. These may vary widely between one type of business and another.

The Employees

Some time before a company can begin to receive sales revenues in the form of cash it will need to have recruited a number of workpeople at every level, from chief executive to clerks and operatives. For the start the minimun number will be recruited on the principle that additional employees will be engaged as business increases. A feature of the employment of people is that they expect to be paid their salaries or wages punctually. The cash must be available without fail. Since the company will not be receiving any sales revenues in the form of cash at the start the promoters will have to ensure that the money they will need for the period which must elapse before cash begins to be received from sales on a sufficient scale will be available as part of the initial capital sum needed to establish the company and set it going. They must allow an adequate margin for contingencies since in life things often do not go according to plan and they often go worse rather than better, and due allowance must be made for this.

Stocks

In the case of a manufacturing company, in addition to employing workpeople, it will be essential to obtain adequate stocks of all kinds so that as soon as the signal to start is given production can begin and there will be no stoppages subsequently because of stock shortages. Until cash begins to flow in regularly from sales, the only money available to finance the necessary stocks of all kinds will be that which the promoters make available as part of the initial capital and, as always, there must be due allowance for contingencies. Stocks include raw materials; bought-in components; work in progress; and finished goods.

Suppliers' credits

In the case of raw materials and bought-in components, the position as regards financing is made somewhat easier by the fact that it is the almost invariable custom that suppliers grant credit to business clients. The credit arrangements will vary between industries and may also be a matter for negotiation. Occasionally suppliers offer cash discounts but most do not because of the high cost involved. A new manufacturer will normally approach a number of recommended suppliers and obtain detailed terms and price lists. Prudent suppliers would be expected to deal with new clients on a cash basis unless and until a credit basis had been approved, and efficient credit control would be exercised, including procedures to make searching enquiries before approving credit.

On his side a manufacturer would not only be concerned with the aspects of prices and credit terms but also with the reputation of the supplier for reliability and speed of deliveries and his ability and readiness to take emergency action (to the extent of being able to arrange emergency supplies within hours rather than days or weeks) in the event of a sudden crisis, when the manufacturer finds himself running out of stock of an important item. Suppliers' credits represent an important source of cost-free short-term finance which will be taken into account when the amount of working capital needed is assessed, as well as the cost of capital.

Credit to customers

Every business management will need to consider and decide upon its credit policy. The decision will be influenced or determined by the practice of competitors. If these grant credit, a newcomer which decided to operate on a strictly cash payment basis might find itself without customers. There are a number of financial implications to be considered in relation to a credit policy. If credit is granted the risk of default on some payments will arise and must be allowed for: in many activities 'bad debts' will represent a fairly predictable proportion of the credit sales. It will be necessary to accept the costs of operating an efficient credit-control administration, unless it is decided that factoring is feasible, and is adopted. Granting credit involves a company in financing its customers to some extent and as the receipt of cash by a company in respect of credit sales is delayed it must have sufficient funds to finance itself for the additional periods between the making of a sale and the receipt of cash in respect of it.

Because interest rates have risen so steeply, and perhaps also because there seems to have been a general decline in commercial morality, businesses are now notably more strict than they used to be in resisting attempts by customers to exceed the agreed credit terms. Moreover, it is also usual now for credit agreements to include a clause that the debtor must pay interest on overdue accounts without prejudice to his also being required to pay cash for future supplies. Many companies now also stipulate that they retain title to any goods they have supplied until payment has been made. The implications of this are far-reaching since stocks may not offer as much security to a lender as he might believe. The 'Romalpa' case (Aluminium Industrie Vaassen v Romalpa Aluminium Ltd, 1976) is a leading case in this field but is outside the scope of this book.

Cash and bank balances

A company must also have cash, and in this context 'cash' includes bank current and deposit account balances, not only to pay workpeople and suppliers but also to make payments in respect of rents, rates, telephones, postages, electricity, oil, etc., and there must be cash available to meet contingencies. Agreed overdraft facilities are also the equivalent of cash, but the cost of this facility must be taken into account. In principle a company will aim to have adequate but not excessive cash available. Any significant short-term surpluses should be suitably invested and this question will be considered later.

The operating cycle

The working capital, also known as circulating capital, has been defined. It is often shown in diagramatic form – suppliers supply materials which are converted into goods, which are sold to customers, who become debtors; they pay their debts and the company pays its suppliers, workpeople, and so on in a cycle which continues for the lifetime of the company. This leads to the important concept of the operating cycle, the period from the receipt of the materials from a supplier to the receipt of cash from a debtor. There tends to be an identifiable cycle for a particular industry.

It will be advantageous to a company to keep this cycle as short as possible, provided that relationships with customers and suppliers are not prejudiced, for in this way a company will require less working capital to finance a given scale of operations and hence the return on capital will rise. A shorter operating cycle implies a more intense activity. The cash payments ultimately received by the company from debtors should exceed the earlier payment made by the company because the sales revenues will incorporate the element of profit in the transactions. Because of this profit component in each cycle it will be apparent that the shorter the cycle, the larger the number completed in a financial period and hence the larger the profit will be, assuming that the profit margin in respect of each sale remains unchanged.

Example 1
From the following information prepare a statement showing the estimated working capital needs, in total and for each constituent:

The working capital

Budgeted sales	£520,000 p.a.
Analysis per £ of sales (£):	
Raw materials	0.25
Direct labour	0.45
Overheads	0.20
	0.90
Profit	0.10
	£1.00

It is estimated that: (a) raw materials will be carried in stock for two weeks and finished goods for three weeks; (b) factory processing will take four weeks; (c) suppliers will give four weeks credit and customers will require seven weeks credit.

It may be assumed that production and overheads arise evenly throughout the year.

Workings

Statement showing estimated working capital required:

		£	£
Stock of raw materials:	$\frac{2}{52} \times \frac{5}{20} \times £520,000$		5,000
Work in progress:			
Materials:	$\frac{4}{52} \times \frac{5}{20} \times £520,000$	10,000	
Labour	$\frac{1}{2} \times \frac{4}{52} \times \frac{9}{20} \times £520,000$	9,000	
Overheads	$\frac{1}{2} \times \frac{4}{52} \times \frac{4}{20} \times £520,000$	4,000	23,000
Stock of finished goods:	$\frac{3}{52} \times \frac{18}{20} \times £520,000$		27,000
Debtors:	$\frac{7}{52} \times £520,000$		70,000
			125,000
Less: Creditors:	$\frac{4}{52} \times \frac{5}{20} \times £520,000$		10,000
Estimated total working capital needs			£115,000

Note : It is assumed that the materials enter the work in progress at the start but that the labour costs and overheads accrue evenly during the work in progress and accordingly one-half of those applicable to a completed unit accrue during the work in progress, and hence the multiplier ½.

It will be seen shortly that one of the most important of the management controls is the cash forecast and prior to the commencement of operations, and continually throughout the life of the company, cash forecasts would be prepared. The above calculation of the estimated working capital needs would be used to complement the cash forecast and not as a substitute for it. Note how large a proportion of the working capital needs arise from the financing of debtors, and the financial benefits of taking credit from suppliers will also be evident.

Example 2

(Examination questions are set which give certain essential information and require calculation of the operating cycle.)
From the following information in respect of ABC Ltd, extracted from its published accounts, calculate the cash operating cycle:

	Year 1 (£)
Stock: raw materials	30,000
work in progress	20,000
finished goods	22,000
Purchases	145,000
Cost of goods sold	205,000
Sales	245,000
Debtors	44,000
Creditors	27,000

Workings
In effect, the questions to be answered are: 'How long does the raw material remain in stock before work in progress begins? What is the duration of the work in progress? How long do the finished goods remain in stock? How long do the debtors take to pay? What is the period of credit taken from suppliers?' In fact, the information given above only allows very approximate calculations to be made. The information in respect of the stocks, debtors and creditors must have been extracted from the (end of the year) balance sheet, which shows the position at one moment of time only, and as balance sheets are often 'window dressed' they tend to show the situation in a more than usually favourable light. Any calculations made must therefore be regarded as useful pointers rather than as statements of fact. The stock must be related to the purchases, and so must the credit taken from suppliers – since the total paid or payable to the suppliers in a period will be the total of the purchases. The work in progress will be related to the cost

The working capital

of goods sold and so will the finished goods stock. The credit taken by the customers (the debtors) must be related to the sales and as no indication is given of cash sales it must be assumed that all sales made were on credit.

As the final stock was £30,000 and the purchases for the year totalled £145,000, the average daily purchases were $\frac{£145,000}{365}$. The final stock thus represents $\frac{£30,000 \times 365}{£145,000}$ days purchases, i.e. 76 days. As the sales for the year were £245,000 the average daily sales were $\frac{£245,000}{365}$ and the debtors thus represent $\frac{£44,000}{\frac{£245,000}{365}}$, i.e. $\frac{£44,000 \times 365}{£245,000}$ i.e. 66 days sales. Using similar reasoning for each item, we have:

		Year 1
1. Stock of raw materials	$\frac{30,000 \times 365}{145,000}$	76 (days)
2. Less: Credit from suppliers	$\frac{27,000 \times 365}{145,000}$	68
		8
3. Production period (work in progress)	$\frac{20,000 \times 365}{205,000}$	36
4. Finished goods stock	$\frac{22,000 \times 365}{205,000}$	39
5. Credit taken by customers	$\frac{44,000 \times 365}{245,000}$	66
Operating cycle		149

Comments (not called for in question)
In practice an analyst employed by the company would wish to check trends, to ascertain whether the experience of the company was improving or deteriorating. He would seek to ascertain the operating cycle of other companies in the same industry, for comparative purposes. An external analyst such as a financial journalist is at a disadvantage insofar as he can only make use of such information as the company chooses to publish, or which he can obtain from his enquiries. An internal analyst, who has free access to all the internal accounts and records of the company, can probe more deeply.

When the operating cycle has been calculated, each component would be studied to ascertain whether it seemed acceptable or should be improved. For example, the terms of payment agreed with customers would indicate the period of credit allowed and comparison of this with the average period being taken would be a pointer to whether the credit-control procedures were working efficiently. In principle, a chief executive studying the above calculations and anxious to bring about an improvement would ask himself the following kinds of questions: Would it be practicable to hold smaller stocks of raw materials for shorter periods before beginning to work on them? Would it be acceptable to extend the credit period taken from suppliers? Could the production period be reduced? Could the period that stocks of finished goods are held be reduced? Could the amount and duration of credit allowed to customers be reduced? The full implications of each possible course of action would need to be considered carefully – for example: Might sales decline? Might the goodwill of customers and or suppliers be damaged? Might suppliers' discounts be lost? Might there be a loss of production, or output of the factory, etc.?

Factors determining the working capital

The promoters of a particular company, with expert advice as necessary, will have to assess their working capital needs, amongst many other matters. There are four major factors likely to influence the amount of working capital a company requires to operate at a determined level of activity.

1. The nature and techniques of the business

Every type of business has its own characteristics and these must be studied in each case. Holders of successful agencies may operate with relatively small fixed and current assets. Professional men may be able to insist on substantial advance payments in respect of fees. Normally, for each type of business there will tend to be well known and established ratios between, for example, the fixed and current assets, e.g. a modern chemical factory will be highly automated and capital intensive, and the ratio of working to fixed capital would normally be low, whereas in the case of a high-class department store it would tend to be high, since large, varied and expensive stocks must be held and many customers will require extended credit terms. Managers in a particular business must inform themselves of the various ratios and other yardsticks which are well established as guidelines in that business.

The working capital

2. The period of manufacture

This is clearly a part of the operating cycle. Note that if an additional process or stage of production is introduced this will give rise not only to a need for additional fixed capital but for increased working capital as well. The tendency in modern production is for the manufacturing process to become more complex and more highly automated and hence capital intensive, in which case the ratio of working to fixed capital will decline although the total capital employed may increase. In those cases where there is manufacture carried out to order, as in the construction and shipbuilding industries, the buyer will normally be required to make payments on account at agreed stages and this somewhat reduces the working capital needs. Conversely, when a company is obliged to hold large or varied stocks of materials or finished goods, its working capital needs will be increased.

3. Fluctuations in the supply of raw materials and/or demand for the finished product

Special situations may give rise to a need for additional working capital. If the raw materials and components used in production are always available and in a sudden crisis the supplier is ready and able to cooperate in making special emergency arrangements (and many are), then less working capital will be needed. If a company manufactures an article for which the demand is seasonal and seeks to maintain an even flow of production, it would be necessary to finance the holding of stocks through periods of low demand: this would increase the working capital requirements.

4. The period of credit granted by a company to its creditors

Clearly, a company which does not need to grant credit can operate with less working capital than a competitor which grants credit. However, refusal to grant credit could lead to reduced profits through reduced sales. Some companies have recourse to factoring or invoice discounting, in which the credit provided to customers is financed by specialist companies.

Exports: If a company exports a significant proportion of its goods or services, the UK government, in common with governments of other industrialised countries, helps to make finance available on favourable terms. This includes finance for working capital, provided through the agency of the Export Credit Guarantee Department, whose role will be examined in Chapter 21.

Estimating the initial working capital

In order to estimate the initial working capital needs, budgets and cash forecasts must be prepared and these will be considered in the next two chapters. In brief, the preparation of cash forecasts requires that plans are made, followed by estimates of the payments made to every category of creditor month by month, and with estimates of receipts expected month by month in respect of cash sales, and receipts from debtors. There may be other receipts as well but these two categories are normally the main ones.

Cash forecasts pay attention to the timings of receipts and payments, and ample allowances must be made for contingencies. It is accepted that a high degree of reliability may normally be unattainable and frequent checking and revision will be essential. Even so, the value of careful cash forecasts can not be disputed. When the forecasts indicate that some months hence there is likely to be a cash shortage it will be necessary to take action in good time to ensure that suitable types and sums of finance will be available to meet the expected needs.

In preparing the cash forecast, each component would be considered in turn. If the indications were that an expected cash shortage would be a temporary one and that soon the cash receipts would regularly exceed the cash payments, then the implications would be that adequate overdraft facilities would be suitable finance to meet a temporary cash shortage. However, if the indications were a continuing cash deficit then decisions would need to be taken as to whether short-, medium- or long-term loans should be arranged, and or additional ordinary share capital, or a mixture of these. Furthermore, when a company considers some new project involving capital expenditure it must also make due provision for the additional working capital which would be needed. Conversely, when a project is coming to an end, the working capital invested in it will normally be released. This will be because no new stocks would be needed and existing stocks would be used up or freed for use with other projects: with no more customers no new credit would be needed and the existing debtors should pay their debts. It is a fact that companies tend to have liquidity problems when they are expanding and when trade slackens there tends to be an improvement in liquidity for a time. However, the fixed expenses continue and payment of these presents increasing problems when poor trading conditions persist.

Approximate working capital required for increased scale of activity

When a new or established company plans to expand substantially the sales of one or more products, it will be necessary to calculate the additional working capital needed and to ensure that this will be available. Ratios and other controls will be considered later but it may now be noted that in the present context a useful ratio will be: $\dfrac{\text{Net current assets}}{\text{Sales}} \times 100$ (the working capital ratio). Regular observation usually shows consistency in this ratio and in such cases a simple calculation will give a useful guideline to the approximate additional working capital necessary to finance a predetermined increase in sales. Thus if sales are £500,000 annually and this requires a working capital of £75,000 then the working capital ratio is 15%. If it were proposed to double sales, a 'rough-and-ready' guideline would be that a total working capital of £150,000 would be needed, or an additional £75,000. This would be apart from any additional fixed capital needs and would be on the assumption that the other factors determining the working capital needs would remain unchanged.

Examination questions dealing with the evaluation of projects often state that £x working capital will be needed at the start, and that machinery purchased for £y will have a scrap value of £z. No further mention is made of the working capital. Whilst students invariably and correctly take the final scrap value of £z into account, the fact that the original £x of working capital should be released at the end of the project, as a cash receipt, is often overlooked, with consequent loss of marks.

Control of working capital: some practical aspects

A feature of the working capital is that it is made up of a number of distinct and independent components, and control requires that each is managed efficiently, using the appropriate techniques. In a company of any size, the buying or purchasing function; the storekeeping function; the works management; the marketing and credit-control functions, will each be controlled by a specialist. Each component will be considered in brief outline, from the aspect of the financial management only.

Stocks

There is an expression 'stocks are the graveyard of a business'. Weak managements tend to neglect the vital buying and storekeeping functions and often those in charge of them have relatively low status in the management hierarchy. As many large companies operate a buying budget of many millions of pounds annually, to leave this heavy responsibility to poorly paid people would be shortsighted. Storekeeping is a separate specialist function and a physical inspection of poorly managed stores will reveal that many items which appear in the accounts, and hence in the balance sheet, at cost price are in reality valueless, or nearly so, or they may be missing altogether. The buying and storekeeping functions both give scope for substantial losses, through theft or fraud, as well as inefficiency, unless each is managed with a high degree of competence and integrity.

Stocks represent a tying up of capital and ideally they should be maintained at the lowest possible levels. However, judgement is needed in the assessment of the appropriate minimum stocks, re-order levels and re-order quantities for different items. It would be false economy if production were suddenly halted because stocks of an essential raw material or component had run out. Efficient stock control makes use of specialist mathematical techniques which are fully dealt with in appropriate textbooks. In principle, as far as practicable, standardisation of materials and components should be a main aim. Control is simplified and costs reduced if the variety of items held in stock can be reduced: orders would be for larger quantities, which would result in more favourable quotations from suppliers and the administration involved in the stores and elsewhere is reduced.

As many stores' items are readily convertible into cash, and theft and fraud, including by collusion, are often attempted, it will be essential to operate efficient stores control systems, from ensuring that competitive prices are obtained before orders are placed, to the checking of the goods received at the stores, to the authorisation of payment and also the holding of stores in suitable storage and making issues only against proper authorisation. There needs also to be a procedure for the return to the stores of items issued but found not to be necessary. It is a practical necessity to operate stores control on the perpetual inventory system, with records maintained up to date and with a physical stocktaking of a number of items daily so that all items are checked at least once in the course of the year and more valuable items more often. This is a better arrangement than the old-fashioned annual stocktaking which disrupts work and is also too infrequent to be effective for control purposes. Stock control and new ordering is an area in which the use of carefully programmed computers is relatively inexpensive and can lead to substantial cost savings.

Credit policy and control

If an article is sold on credit and the debtor disappears or does not pay, so that a bad debt is incurred, the article has effectively been given away and that is no basis for business. Decisions about credit policy and control need to be taken at high levels of management and all the implications taken fully into account. The first questions will be whether credit should be allowed and, if it is, what the costs will be. If it is a normal practice of the trade to grant credit there may be no real alternative to doing so. If there is a real choice between selling for cash only or for cash or on credit, then the evaluation will require an assessment of what the sales revenues would be on the basis of cash sales only and what they would be if sales were for cash or on credit. The test would be to relate the profits on the additional sales arising from the granting of credit with the total costs of granting credit. This credit cost would include the salaries and related costs of any credit-control section: the losses arising from any bad debts, and recovery attempts, and the cost of financing the credit, which would be related to the period of credit and the rates of interest. Current overdraft rates would normally be relevant.

If the top management decision is to grant credit, the administration of the credit control will need to be the responsibility of people experienced in this field. The following is a brief outline. In principle, sales to a particular customer should be on a cash basis only, unless and until he has requested credit. He should then be required to complete a carefully drafted credit application form which, *inter alia*, will always require the name and address of the applicant (who will be an individual or a corporate body) and other information designed to indicate his financial substance. The amount of credit requested should be indicated and the form should also state that the conditions of granting credit are: (*a*) payment must be made strictly by a defined date, e.g. 'not later than 30 days after date of invoice'; and the invoice should be despatched without fail simultaneously with the goods; (*b*) failure to pay on time would entitle the company to discontinue the credit arrangements forthwith and their resumption would be a matter for renegotiation; (*c*) interest would be charged at a stated rate on all overdue accounts.

References, including those of bankers, should be called for, and taken up. A company is also well advised to subscribe to a credit-investigating agency such as Dun and Bradstreet, since an agency knows how to keep itself well informed about the day-to-day position and can alert its clients if a particular person or company shows signs of ceasing to be creditworthy. It is usual for the form to state that the company reserves the right to withdraw or change the credit facilities, subject to prescribed notice, which may be short: also, if desired, that it retains the title to goods supplied until payment has been made (the Romalpa case). There should be a final sentence indicating that the applicant applies for credit and, if granted, he accepts all the conditions. The applicant must sign the application form and date it. There can then be no misunderstandings.

Credit-control procedures

A credit-control administration, however small, must always be supervised by a competent person. A list of approved credit customers, with limits in each case, must be maintained up to date, and every order for goods on credit must first be channelled through the credit control. When there is no query the order will be endorsed that credit is approved and the order may be dealt with. If an order would take an account over the agreed credit limit, or the client were in default, or there were some other query or warning sign, the procedures must indicate the further action to be taken. In practice there would be reference to a higher level of management for a decision.

Many companies are inefficient in their handling of credit and bring avoidable trouble on themselves. Often invoices are not prepared and sent promptly, and often there is no prompt or effective follow-up if a credit customer delays payment. Special care should be taken about granting credit (without personal guarantees from individual directors) to small limited-liability companies or to subsidiary companies of a larger company. 'Sharp operators' still too often allow a small company to go into liquidation, causing heavy losses to creditors, and the operators form a new company and the cycle begins again.

Whenever credit procedures operate there must be efficient, up-to-date record keeping so that the state of an account will be available instantly. This is now often computer based. The procedure should provide that customers in default are withdrawn from the approved credit list promptly: there must also be regular analysis of overdue debtors into groups such as: (*a*) up to 1 month: (*b*) 1–3 months; (*c*) 3–6 months; (*d*) over 6 months. Experience shows that the longer a particular account is overdue the greater the risk it will become a bad debt. If there is a genuine dispute or complaint about a particular invoice the company must be ready to examine and resolve this promptly, one way or another, but a dispute over an item would not justify a customer in delaying payment on items not in dispute.

The working capital

The record keeping should be such that the management would be able to keep under review the value of a particular account to them, whether it appeared static, or increasing, or declining, or giving rise to unproductive disputes. In appropriate cases, when the actual or potential volume of business does not seem to justify the administration required for an account, the customer may be notified that credit facilities will be withdrawn. In the event that a debt is written off as bad it is desirable to have a procedure for keeping significant written-off items under periodic review as debtors in default sometimes recover financially and are prepared to pay old debts if approached about them.

Defaulting debtors

When it is evident that a debtor will not pay, a management decision must be taken as to whether the debt should be pursued in the courts, or passed to a debt-recovery agency, or written off. If the sum involved is not large it may save time, trouble and cost to write it off but this decision should only be taken by a specifically authorised manager. The credit controls should incorporate a review procedure designed, *inter alia*, to identify any weaknesses in the arrangements for granting credit. The ratio of bad debts to sales must be kept under scrutiny and the ratio reviewed in relation to the experience of others in the industry. A rising trend would always call for prompt investigations.

Factoring; invoice discounting; cash discounts

The costs of granting credit are significant and expanding companies which are short of capital often have recourse to factoring or invoice discounting, which are considered later. In each case a company would carry out a cost – benefit analysis before making a decision. Cash discounts are an inducement to encourage prompt payment but the costs of a worthwhile discount are high and they seem best avoided. Conversely, when offered to the company, discounts should be evaluated and taken when worthwhile.

Cash and bank balances

Together with reliable debtors, cash and bank balances are liquid as well as current assets. They come within the scope of working capital control. On the one hand a company must be able to pay its debts as they fall due. On the other, it must aim to achieve the highest practicable return on capital. Ample cash and bank balances provide liquidity but a feature of liquid assets is that unless skilfully managed they give rise to little or no return on capital. Cash itself obviously produces no return and large holdings would give rise to security problems and costs. By offering current account and cheque and other transfer facilities, banks render their clients important services and transfer the security problems to themselves. However, they are well paid for their facilities since they have the very profitable use of their clients funds and yet pay no interest on current accounts. This fact is now a matter of some controversy, especially noting the very high profits of the clearing banks recently. In principle, depositors should keep minimum funds in current accounts and at least use deposit accounts, on which interest is paid. Larger companies which can afford specialist cash management and which centralise their cash and bank balances and controls will invest surpluses even in the 'overnight' and very short-period money markets since in recent years high interest rates make this worth while for larger companies. Indeed, it is disturbing that manufacturing companies can sometimes make higher profits through skilful investment of surplus funds in the money market than they can by investing in new machinery and making new products. The topic of investment of short-to medium-term surplus funds on the most rewarding and suitable basis is of practical importance and it also features regularly in examination questions.

Trade creditors and other short-term creditors
The earlier worked examples illustrate the financial benefits of credits offered by suppliers. Price and credit will be two of the several factors considered when a company is selecting its suppliers. From the financial aspect if, unusually, a particular supplier offers cash discounts, the company will calculate the value of the discount, in terms of the effective rate of interest offered. If this exceeds the cost of borrowing on overdraft, or the rate which can be obtained on short-term investments, it will be worth while taking the discount. In other cases the company would be well advised to make fullest use of the credit terms available and should defer payment until just before the end of the credit period, with the proviso that default on the terms of the agreement should be avoided.

It is a characteristic of companies with weak financial managements, which do not operate efficient control or monitoring techniques, that they abuse the credit facilities offered by suppliers and delay payments. In such cases visual inspection of the two most recent balance sheets, with the profit-and-loss account for the period which links them, often reveals that new fixed assets have been financed largely by delaying payment of creditors. This is often a central aspect of an examination question. If a company in this situation gives evidence of operating unprofitably, so that it would be difficult or impossible to attract new

The working capital

funds, then it may be moving towards compulsory liquidation. If it is operating profitably, the directors ought urgently to review the capital structure with a view to reducing the over-dependence on short-term finance. It must be remembered that a creditor who is unable to obtain payment may approach the Court for an order to the debtor to pay. If one creditor makes such an approach others are likely to follow quickly. If a company could not pay its debts and were unable to raise new equity or loan funds, liquidation would be inevitable. Trade creditors may therefore legitimately be regarded as a source of free short-term funds, but one which must be managed competently, carefully and not abused. In brief, the terms of agreements should be honoured strictly. Moreover, in 1980 suggestions began to be made by MPs that the law should be changed so that companies would be entitled by law to claim interest on accounts not settled by the due date. More is likely to be heard of this.

Questions

1. Describe the techniques which might be useful for a company in determining the optimum level of its working capital. (ICSA 22 marks)
2. Discuss the techniques available for optimising the level of working capital in a manufacturing company. (ICSA 22 marks)
3. (a) 'Cash is no different from any other asset – if it is not being utilised properly it is going to result in lower profits.' Discuss this statement in particular referring to the motives for holding cash: (b) The AB Credit Collection Co. Ltd employs agents who collect hire purchase instalments and other outstanding accounts on a door-to-door basis from Monday to Friday. The agents bank the cash collected to be remitted to head office once per week at the end of the week. The budget for the next year shows that total collections will be of the order of £5,200,000 and that the estimated bank overdraft rate is 9%. The collection manager has suggested that a daily remitting system should be introduced for collectors. You are required to comment on the significance of this, stating clearly any assumptions you are required to make. (ACCA 20 marks).
4. Trade credit is one of the most common sources and uses of short-term finance. Discuss the factors which should be taken into consideration in determining the level of trade credit that should be extended to customers. A supplier who had previously been supplying your firm on the basis that all accounts had to be paid within 30 days of receipt of

goods with a 3% cash discount for goods paid within 10 days has notified you that as from the next trading period it is extending the period of payment to 90 days with a reduced cash discount of 1% if paid within 20 days. What are the implications of this as far as your organisation is concerned? (ACCA 17 marks)

5. Your managing director has seen a statement in the financial press which suggests that at all times, but particularly when liquidity is a problem, management should pay particular attention to the cash operating cycle: that is the time between paying for your raw materials and recovering this from your own customers. **Using the following information prepare a memorandum for your Managing Director commenting on the cash operating cycle and suggesting how it might be improved.**

		Year 1 (£)	Year 2 (£)
Stocks:	Raw materials	20,000	27,000
	Work in progress	14,000	18,000
	Finished goods	16,000	24,000
Purchases		96,000	130,000
Cost of goods sold		140,000	180,000
Sales		160,000	200,000
Debtors		32,000	48,000
Creditors		16,000	19,500

(ACCA 25 marks)

Chapter 8

Budgetary control

It is well established that the top management of a company must determine the long-term objectives and plan how these are to be achieved. As money is the common factor in all aspects of the operations and activities, the plans must be expressed in financial as well as physical terms. Plans must be made in advance of events and after they have been drafted, then agreed, and implementation has begun, there will be a need for progress continually to be monitored. This is a function of budgetary control. This resembles the navigation of a ship or aircraft. Before the start the destination is selected and the necessary charts, navigating and other essential equipment and data are assembled, together with highly skilled navigators. The proposed course is charted and the journey begins. The navigators continually check whether the ship or aircraft is on course and on time. If there is a deviation, correcting action will be taken at once and it is normally a simple matter and the destination will be reached on schedule. However, sometimes a major setback occurs, such as a violent storm or engine failure and the plan and destination may then have to be changed quickly. There is an important difference between planning a voyage for a ship or aircraft and planning for a business: the major problem in a business environment is that the journey is always into the future and there are no completely reliable charts or maps available. Risks and uncertainties have to be accepted.

Definition

Budgetary control is a major technique developed so that all who have responsibility for all or part of an activity can be closely and realistically involved in the formulation of those parts of the overall plan which are their direct responsibility, and subsequently in their monitoring. A formal definition of budgetary control, by the ICMA (Institute of Cost and Management Accountants) is 'the establishment of budgets relating the responsibilities of executives to the requirements of a policy, and the continuous comparison of actual with budgeted results either to secure by individual action the objective of that policy or to provide a basis for its revision'. Clearly, the concept of budgeting is a familiar one even to those who are not yet aware of how it is used as a control technique within a company. The fact is that every student who has to live on a laid-down grant has to practise budgeting, as does every person who earns a salary and has to meet the costs of a home and family from his income.

Main objectives

The main objectives of budgetary control may be summarised as:
(a) To express the objectives and plans of the company as a whole, and component parts of it, in financial terms and, where appropriate, also in terms of physical inputs and outputs. When approved, the master budget, and the component parts, represent the approved plan for the period and implementation begins.
(b) To impose the discipline of requiring that all activities in contemplation are studied in detail before their financial implications are incorporated in draft budgets. This process requires that managers identify the options open to them, make evaluations before taking decisions and the probabilities that the resources of the company will be efficiently and economically deployed will be improved. The adoption of budgetary control also permits that lower levels of managers are actively involved in the preliminary planning and subsequent monitoring.
(c) To permit maximum delegation within the company, including to divisions, subsidiary companies, or branches, without weakening the control of the top management.
(d) By continual monitoring of the actual with the budgeted results, to ensure that the approved plans are achieved. In those cases where the actual results differ significantly from the budgeted ones the reasons need to be identified and investigated. When the actual results are better than the budgeted ones it may be found that unexpected opportunities are arising which should be exploited. If actual results are worse than the budgeted ones then as far as possible correcting action must be taken promptly. Sometimes it becomes apparent that the main plan is proving unattainable either because of poor planning, or unfavourable circumstances arising outside the

control of the company. In such cases the plan itself must be revised and, as far as practicable, lessons learned for the future.
(e) To provide relevant and prompt information to all levels of management. Only in this way can managers have effective control over those matters for which they are responsible. Data processing equipment now makes it practicable for important information to be obtained within seconds or minutes rather than after days or weeks.

Budget installation and procedures

In a small, one-man company, the owner-manager will himself be responsible for every important function, sales, production, administration, finance, etc., and he will himself need to estimate in sufficient detail his revenues and costs. In larger companies there will be specialist functional managers. In a company of some size there will be, in effect, a hierarchy. Effective control will be exercised by the board of directors, who are the delegates of the ordinary shareholders and can, in theory more often than in practice, be dismissed by them. A board of directors may sometimes be a mere 'rubber stamp' of a dominating chief executive, who might be the chairman, or the managing director, or who might hold both positions. In the case of major successful companies, boards of directors will be effective ones in which major decisions tend to be taken by consensus rather than by vote. The majority of directors will normally be full-time employees who will individually head a major department, function, division or subsidiary company. With the board at the apex, the lowest levels of management generally comprise supervisors or foremen, employees who have responsibility for the work of subordinates. At the lowest level are clerks, operatives, workpeople who in each case have a direct superior but no subordinates. A feature of budgetary control should be that every manager, however junior, has a role in it.

The informative Industrial and Commercial Finance Corporation (ICFC) booklet 'Budgetary control' observes:

There are six stages in operating a system of budgetary control. The first three take place before the budget is even prepared. The six stages . . . are: (a) to create a clear-cut organisation within the company; (b) to delegate authority and define precisely what each individual is responsible for and the extent of this authority and responsibility; (c) to prepare a series of plans to which the company will work – so ensuring that the company has an overall objective; (d) to prepare and accept budgets, based on the plans; (e) to provide a periodic feedback of actual results and compare them with the budgets; (*f*) to use this information to correct deviations and make new plans.

A company of any size would normally have main and subsidiary organisation charts which indicate visually its hierarchy and structure. There would be a written job description in respect of every job, which would also incorporate details of any authority the holder might have in respect of financial matters, and the limitations on this authority, notably in respect of the sanctioning of capital expenditure. There might be formal standing orders, a procedure manual, including a budget manual. These matters are explained on textbooks on management. Two important practical matters to be borne in mind in respect of budgetary control are:

(*a*) Much of the potential value is lost unless items of revenue and expense can be analysed in sufficient detail, and to permit this it will be necessary to have open a sufficient number of accounts, each with its own identifying code number. Thus, it would not be enough to know that in a period a total value of £x of sales had been achieved. It would be necessary to be able to analyse details of the sales of different product groups, and items, so that the strong and weak selling lines could be identified, and the profit margins on each, etc.

(*b*) The first installation of a budgetary control system is naturally a much more exacting matter than the preparation of budgets in later years, when the system is working satisfactorily and employees have become familiar with it. This initial installation should be supervised by experienced and skilled people. Trade associations and organisations such as the British Institute of Management, etc., would be helpful in providing material, checklists, etc. An essential part of the initial work will be the training and education of all levels of staff, firstly to demonstrate what is to be done and secondly to convince employees of the value of budgetary control to the company and to themselves.

In a company of any size there will normally be a budget committee consisting of the chief executive – or his representative as chairman and functional and departmental heads as members, and an experienced accountant as budget secretary (sometimes known as 'budget controller'). Unless the contrary is stated, budgetary control will be assumed to relate to operating (revenue) as distinct from capital budgets, which are treated separately (see Ch. 14). The key, or limiting factor must first be identified. This is the constraining factor which prevents a company from attaining unrestricted expansion and growth. It may be a shortage of skilled workers – a quite frequent situation in the UK now – or an expensive machine which is working at the limits of its capacity and which can not be added to for some time, either because of lack of availability, or uncertainty whether there would be sustained and profitable demand for a larger output if an additional machine were installed. Normally it is the limits of the market, and competition, so that it will be the sales limits which will be the constraining factor, as will be assumed in this case.

The head of the sales/marketing function would have the responsibility for using market research and other techniques to plan the sales for the approaching financial year, the prices, the distribution and general marketing arrangements. He would express these in the form of budgets – budgeted (*a*) revenues and (*b*) costs, distinguishing between variable, semi-variable and fixed costs. The budget committee would consider the overall plan and then the implications for each department and function. For example, when target sales have been determined the head of production would be able to plan what has to be manufactured and what bought in, but he would need first to know the policy with respect to finished stock holdings. Whilst no rigid rules can be laid down the following is a brief outline of main budgets which are commonly met:

(*a*) *Sales budget*: this would be broken down into products, areas, quantities, prices: the effect of changes in selling prices would have been studied as well as such matters as seasonal factors. Provisions would also be made for flexibility in different contingency situations. Flexible budgeting is often adopted. (p. 150)

(*b*) *Selling cost budget:* this would be based on the sales budget and would include salaries of sales personnel, their travelling and entertaining expenses and commissions; the costs of the sales administration; advertising and publicity expenses (separate budgets would be likely and in a large company the advertising budget alone might be for expenditure of millions of pounds); special packaging; etc.

(*c*) *Distribution cost budget*: this would also be based on the sales budget and would be concerned with all costs, including of employees, related to the storage of finished goods, their packing and transport to the point of sale.

(*d*) *Production budget*: the production head has overall responsibility for the manufacture of the output required and for such matters as stocks of raw materials, the levels of work in progress, storage of finished goods at the factory, warehousing, internal works transport, heating and lighting of the factory, maintenance of works plant, labour, recruitment, welfare and training (in conjunction with the personnel function). The overall production budget would be built up from many subsidiary budgets, e.g. the material requirements and procurement budget; the plant utilisation budget; production cost budget; finished stock budget; etc.

(e) *Administration budget*: this would be built up from subsidiary budgets, as the others are. It would incorporate directors' emoluments, managers and other staff salaries, rents, rates, postages, telephones, stationery, etc.; insurance; security; legal costs; staff training; etc.

(f) *Research and development budget*: this would incorporate relevant salaries, office and laboratory costs, materials used, depreciation of equipment, etc.

(g) *Capital expenditure budget*: this is a major but separate budget which will be considered later (p. 259). Its separateness arises from the fundamental distinction between capital and operating expenditures. It must be remembered that depreciation on capital items must be charged to the appropriate operating budgets.

(h) *Cash budgets*: these have a vital role in financial control and will be considered in Chapter 9.

The above oversimplified and brief summary indicates the diversity and complexity of the activities whose purpose is to give rise to a stream of sales revenues which exceed the costs of achieving these revenues by a sufficient margin, and which is the profit, expressed also in terms of return on capital. On agreeing the operating plan as a whole, each budget committee member would become aware in qualitative and quantitative terms of what should be achieved by the function or department under his control in the approaching financial year, noting that preliminary work on the budget for the next financial year would normally begin three or four months before the end of the current one.

A usual pattern is that preliminary budget meetings are held by the heads of departments or functions with their immediate subordinates who are informed of the operational plan so that each manager is in a position to express the plan in financial terms for that area of work over which he has direct responsibility. Each manager who has subordinate

Budgetary control

managers would hold similar meetings with his direct subordinate managers, so that all managers within the hierarchy become adequately informed. Obviously, in a large multinational company these routines involve large numbers of people, widely dispersed geographically, from the highest to the lowest management levels. Even so, once established, the routines should and do work quickly and effectively.

The initial drafting of the various budget printed forms to be used by a company takes time and must be done by technically competent and experienced people, in consultation with senior employees of the company, who are fully informed about the work and organisation of the company and what it will specially require from budgeting. Whilst operating budgets will be prepared with respect to (*a*) costs, and (*b*) revenues, the fact is that many managers only have costs under their control and in practice there will be many more cost than revenue budgets.

It is well established that each cost (or revenue) budget should be drafted by the manager with direct responsibility for the area under consideration. It would be a mistake to leave the drafting of budgets to accountants, who in most cases could not be expected to have knowledge of the subject matter, which the manager must have. The role of the accountant who is the budget secretary, and other accountants, would be to offer advice and guidance whenever called upon to do so. Experience shows that the best results are obtained when budgets are built up from the lowest management levels upwards, and not when they are imposed by senior managers with little or no consultation. In brief, each manager will first be given guidelines by his superior, as part of the briefings which follow the decision by the board as to what the main plans will be, in detailed terms, for the coming financial year. Each manager then drafts his budget, and sets it out on the preprinted form which will be in use and which is effectively a checklist, so that no item can be overlooked. The draft will be submitted to the direct superior of the manager, who will discuss it and seek clarification or justification for any item, and it will be for the subordinate to convince his superior that his draft is valid for that item, or he must agree to amend it. Both will be aware that managers are tempted to (*a*) overestimate expenses, and (*b*) underestimate revenues, since if they were successful in obtaining approval for a budget drafted on this basis, it would subsequently be more easily attainable and their work would be easier. They would also hope to gain approval in due course as managers who had shown themselves able to perform better than their budget required.

Each manager will incorporate the budgets of his subordinates into his own budget and in this way a draft budget will be prepared for the whole function or department. These will be considered by the budget committee, and the budget secretary would coordinate and amalgamate these drafts and produce draft master budgets. On the basis of these, and using his knowledge of various key ratios, he would also prepare a draft projected profit-and-loss account for the approaching financial year and a projected balance sheet as at the end of it. These drafts would be critically studied by the committee and if, for example, the expected return on capital seemed too low there would be discussions to examine if, how and where costs could be reduced and revenues increased. Where changes were agreed in principle the implications for sub-budgets would also need to be taken into account. Finally, the committee would agree on the drafts, which would then be submitted to the board for approval.

The board might itself call for some further revision but the master budgets would finally be approved by the board. All concerned would then be notified of their approved budget. Each manager, at every level, would now know what he personally had to consider as his targets for the coming year, expressed in financial terms: if all concerned achieved their targets, the company as a whole would do so. Budgetary control involves considerable preparatory work but when this has been done a consequence is that each manager then has considerable freedom of action, to act creatively, within the limits of his authority and within the known policies of the company.

Budget forms and reports

If the full value of budgetary control is to be gained there is a practical necessity to get things right at the start. The printed budget forms and the reporting forms associated with them should be drafted by an expert in budgetary control in consultation with senior managers of the company familiar with its methods and needs. The forms adopted should aim to be comprehensive yet as simple as possible to use and understand since many users, even senior ones, will not be financial experts. If the layouts adopted at the start can avoid simple oversights and omissions there will be the advantage that as time passes it will be practicable to make direct comparisons between later budgets and those of some years earlier, especially for the purpose of identifying trends, if any. If layouts are not initially well drafted their inadequacies will soon become evident and major changes may then become necessary. In such cases comparisons between one period and another can only be made following complex and time-consuming adjustments.

Budgetary control

Budget forms are normally designed to show items of expenditure or revenue in logical groupings and subgrouping in vertical lists, with six adjacent columns headed 'budget'; 'actual'; 'variance'; (or 'deviation'); 'cumulative budget'; 'cumulative actual'; cumulative variance (or deviation)'. Whilst the operating budgets will each cover a financial year, in order continually to monitor progress it will be necessary to break down the annual budget into acceptable shorter periods – often a calendar month or, in many cases, four-weekly periods, since there will then be 13 equal periods in the course of a year: sometimes shorter periods, e.g. a week, are considered appropriate. However, the aspect of cost effectiveness must be considered. Over-administration is counter productive, as the costs will outweigh any possible benefits.

If the sub-budget forms cover four-weekly periods then in respect of those items which do not have a seasonal aspect, e.g. salaries, rents, etc., the entry can promptly be made in the 'budget' column – i.e. 1/13th of the annual operating budget for the item. When there is a seasonal aspect, e.g. heating, lighting, sales, etc., this factor will be appropriately assessed by the manager and the appropriate entries made (the seasonal aspect would have been considered when the original drafts were made). In all cases the total for an item in the operating budget would equal the totals for that item in the 13 sub-budgets. As soon as the budget has been approved as a whole for the next financial year – normally in the month before the new year begins – the 'budget' and 'cumulative budget' figure will be entered against every item in each sub-budget, which will also have provision for subtotals and totals. At the time these first entries are made they will all relate to the future.

The new financial year then begins and the arrangements should be such that as soon as possible after the end of each four-weekly period every manager responsible for a budget is notified of the 'actual' in respect of each item in his budget, normally by the accounts department. In every case the manager, or assistant, will enter each 'actual' alongside the appropriate 'budget' figure and will calculate and enter the 'variance' and 'cumulative variance', i.e. the difference between the 'budget' and 'actual', and this will be 'favourable' or 'unfavourable'. In the case of expenditure a variance will be unfavourable if the 'actual' exceeds the 'budget', and favourable if the 'budget' exceeds the 'actual'. In the case of revenues the reverse is the case, i.e. there will be an unfavourable variance if the 'actual' is below the 'budget' and favourable if the 'actual' exceeds the 'budget'. It is the usual convention that unfavourable variances are shown within brackets, or, occasionally, preceded by a 'minus' sign. The significance of the 'cumulative' columns will be self-evident. As the financial year progresses it will be important to monitor 'actuals' with 'budgets' for each period, and also the cumulative position up to the latest date: exceptional variances in respect of an item in one or two periods could appear in a different perspective when the 'cumulative' position showed 'actual' and 'budget' figures with little cumulative variance.

As soon as he has entered his 'actual' and 'variance' figures for a period, each manager will study his fully entered sub-budget form for the information it conveys to him. When the item is a minor one, or the variance is not significant he will spend less time on it than when the variance, in money terms, is a significant one. If desired, the manager (or his superior, or an auditor) could call for full details of the account concerned, and study every item in it: particular invoices could be identified and called for, e.g. if expenditure under a heading such as 'entertainment' were being queried. There is a most important point to note. Every item in a budget will be either 'controllable' or 'uncontrollable' by the manager concerned. Every item will be controllable by someone, of course, in the sense that there will be a manager responsible for that area, but even he would have no control over a number of external factors. As simple examples, a supervisor would be responsible for authorising overtime worked by his subordinates. Accordingly, if 'actual' overtime costs over a period exceed the 'budgeted' costs, the supervisor would be expected to explain the excess. If his explanation were acceptable, this would end the matter. However, if the excess could not be justified the supervisor would be expected to take action to avoid recurrence. However, often an item in a manager's budget will not be controllable by him. Thus the supervisor of a section working in a part of an office would be charged 'rent' in relation to the space occupied. If the office rents were increased more than expected then the 'actual' would exceed the 'budget' for this item but the supervisor would not be called to account for the variance since 'rent' would not be controllable by him, but by another manager, who would himself have to explain the overall rent variance. The question may be asked whether any useful purpose is served by involving managers with items which they can not control.

A strong argument in favour of treating managers at all levels as people who can respond positively when there are good communications and attitudes of confidence between all levels of management is that experience shows what benefits arise from this policy. For example, years ago major shipping companies considered that ships' captains and officers were only concerned with the technical aspects of sailing their ships and they were not concerned with the financial aspects of voyages. In recent years the general view has become that a ship's captain and

Budgetary control

officers are managers as well as sailors and they are kept informed of the financial implications of what they do and in consequence they can now make significant efforts to increase the revenues or reduce the costs of a voyage. In the case of an office manager or supervisor, awareness of rents, rates, heating and other costs, and the manner in which these are rising could be expected to make an alert manager inform himself of new types of equipment available so that, for example, if he assessed that space requirements could be reduced, and also staffing needs, by installation of new, capital-intensive equipment, he would carry out a cost-benefit analysis and put the case to his direct superior.

An essential part of a budgetary control system is that simple and clear reporting forms are used. As soon as possible after the end of each sub-budget period – certainly within one week – each manager should complete a standard reporting form for submission to his line manager. This form should distinguish between controllable and uncontrollable items and following the 'principle of exceptions' it will focus the attention of the recipient on areas where things are not going according to plan – where variances are significant. In such cases the manager would be required to indicate his explanation and, if appropriate, the action he had taken or was proposing to take. This reporting form is an important formal communication and record between a manager and his superior. The latter also merges the information submitted by his subordinates with the information of his own budget, and he would submit his own standard reporting form to his own superior and there would be a chain of prompt reporting right to the top management.

The reports received by the top management will be in very summarised form but their attention would nevertheless be drawn to areas where things were significantly not going according to plan. A senior manager would then be likely to instruct an assistant to obtain more detailed information on whatever seemed to him to call for more searching investigation. Attention could be focused on a particular subsidiary company, or division or department and in practice an investigation can quickly go into depth and even minute detail if this is required so that, hopefully, problems can be resolved or opportunities exploited.

In practice, experience suggests that when things are going 'according to plan' the managers concerned are normally left alone by their superiors, to get on with their work. However, if significant controllable unfavourable variances arise at any point the manager concerned will find himself under pressure to operate within his budget. If the variances were important enough they would give rise to questions and pressures from the top management to the head of the unit concerned, and if they persisted specialists would be sent to investigate, from the head office. In serious enough cases even chairmen of important subsidiary companies would know that their promotion prospects, or even their continuation in their present post, could be called into question. Budgets are therefore taken very seriously at every level although, naturally, judgement and discretion must be exercised since in unstable and inflationary times there will be occasions when events take control and individuals become powerless. On such occasions experienced senior managers will be able to distinguish between situations when a particular manager responded effectively and did the best that could be expected and when a manager's response was inadequate and suggested that he could not be relied upon in a crisis. In general, it does seem that budgetary control is one of the most important techniques of management and one which makes it feasible for huge multinational companies such as Unilever, Shell, ICI, General Motors, etc., to operate efficiently without intolerable burdens being placed on relatively tiny top managements.

Flexible budgets

The budgets described above are known as fixed budgets as they are based on predetermined levels of activity, notably sales and sales mix. In many circumstances fixed budgets are adequate provided that the level of activity experienced is not too widely different from the planned level. Adequate allowances and adjustments can be made. In operating a system of budgetary control – or any other system – managements should seek cost effectiveness. Unnecessarily complex or sophisticated systems give rise to costs which exceed any possible benefits attainable. However, in certain circumstances, including when there is uncertainty as to the level of activity likely to be experienced, flexible budgets may be prepared. They are complex and will not be considered here except to indicate that a feature of them is analysis of major expenditure items into 'fixed' (remaining unchanged in the short to medium term over wide limits despite changes in the level of activity, e.g. rent and rates); 'variable' (changing directly according to the level of activity, e.g. bought-in components such as TV tubes, to be incorporated in a TV set which is being manufactured); and 'semi-variable' (the cost has two components, one fixed and one variable, e.g. a telephone or telex installation. There is a rental, a fixed cost, and the separate cost of each call, which are variable costs.)

In brief, the feature of a flexible budget is that it is constructed to be effective over a reasonably wide range of activities, noting that the fixed items would be the same throughout the range: the variable items would change but would be calculable for any activity level and in the case of the semi-variable costs, these would be broken down into the fixed and the variable components and each treated appropriately. For any given activity level it should be practicable to read at a glance the budgeted cost for a particular item, or to calculate it easily. Further information on this topic will be found in textbooks on management accountancy.

Capital budgets: a preview

Capital budgets are always kept separate and distinct from operating budgets. A capital item, by definition, is a material item to be used in the business for more than a year and not held primarily for resale. Operating budgets are properly charged with an equitable proportion of the capital asset which relates the year concerned to the expected useful life of the asset. This annual charge to the operating budgets and to the profit-and-loss account is designated 'depreciation'. It would be wrong in principle and misleading and, indeed, impracticable not to distinguish clearly between capital and operating budgets. Capital expenditure, its evaluation and control will be considered in Chapter 14.

Budgets: some problems

The setting up and operating of budgetary control systems involves overcoming problems and these may be (*a*) organisational, and (*b*) behavioural. In respect of (*a*) significant management time will be involved, especially until a system has been well established and 'teething troubles' overcome. A system may be expensive to install. Efficient and rapid information systems will be necessary but this is so in any case, and the availability of relatively low cost data processing equipment and low cost high speed communications make efficient information systems more easily and economically attainable than ever before. Significant extra clerical work may be involved. In brief, there will be costs but experience indicates that the benefits of an efficient system should substantially exceed the costs.

Some hold that the main problems are behavioural ones and suggest that:

(*a*) many managers resent budgetary control and will do their best to undermine and discredit it;

(b) there are difficulties in securing cooperation between the different interests;
(c) tensions can arise because of the need for flexibility on the one hand and the constraints imposed by budgets on the other;
(d) in drafting budgets some managers will overstate their expected expenditures and understate their revenues. If they succeed in obtaining approval for their budget its real value and challenge will be much reduced;
(e) 'awkward' items of expenditure may be charged to the wrong account, or even client, if this account is substantially larger than the correct one, as there will be a strong chance that the wrong entry will pass undetected. If it is detected, it will be passed off as a mistake;
(f) towards the end of a year if 'actuals' are well below 'budgets' some managers will deliberately incur expenditure unnecessarily so that the final variance will be small. The reasoning is that if the year ends with a budget 'underspent' senior managers will rule that that particular item should be substantially cut in the next budget.

C. Argyris has conducted research, published as *Human Problems with Budgets*. This indicated a frequent conflict between the attitudes of people in the non-accounting functions, e.g. sales, production, etc., and accounting people dealing with budgets. He concluded that budgets can be demotivating, arousing hostility, with the viewpoint that budgetary control is primarily a policing device of the management, a means of applying pressure and too lacking in flexibility. Employees with this viewpoint may be expected to manipulate budgets when they can.

Research into budgetary control and behavioural factors has also been conducted by A. Hopwood. In his book *Accounting and Human Behaviour* he concluded:

like architects, accountants must never regard human beings as unsolicited intrusions on their technical activities. It should not be forgotten that these technical activities have themselves no meaning. Accounting systems must always be directed towards fulfilling the needs of managers and employees who are striving to control complex but purposeful enterprises and accordingly their design and operation always needs a sensitivity to attitudes, needs and even passions of the human members of the enterprise.

Other research carried out by Dew and Gee indicated that in some companies budgets were prepared but then put in drawers and in many cases ignored. Commenting on his research, C.T. Horngren wrote 'budgets should not be prepared in the first place if they are ignored, buried in files or improperly interpreted'.

Whatever the experience in some companies may be, the fact is indisputable that in many major companies budgetary control systems certainly can work efficiently and at the same time prove acceptable to staff. Important factors are the 'climate' in the company itself and the calibre of its managers and supervisors, and the quality of the internal communications and training, not least in relation to budgetary control. It is said, and would be understandable, that hostility arises when subordinate managers are not involved in the preliminary drafting stage and their budgets are imposed upon them. Budgets also need to be readily intelligible, logical and internally consistent, as well as being designed so that they are suited to any special characteristics of the company and are not, for example, too rigid in design or interpretation in the case of a company which must adapt quickly if external changes so require.

Questions

1. To what extent is it correct to argue that behavioural factors are likely to undermine a system of budgetary planning and control? (ICSA 22 marks)
2. Describe the organisation and operating of a system of budgetary control, emphasising the importance of behavioural considerations in the development of an effective system. (ACCA MA   20 marks)
3. 'Budgets are sometimes seen as plans for cooperation and sometimes seen as restrictions to be defeated.' What factors would you expect to lead to one view rather than the other? (ACCA BA   20 marks)
4. More and more frequently it is being intimated, even if not overtly suggested, that budgetary control can provide a bridge which links the resources that an enterprise has at its command to the behaviour of people within the enterprise.

Required: Your views on the ability of the budgetary control system to provide such a link. (ACCA MA   20 marks)

5. One of the most difficult tasks facing the financial manager when considering budgeting proposals is to make allowance for inflation. Discuss. (ACCA   15 marks)
6. Describe the key problems associated with assessing the benefits from research and development activities, and exercising financial control over the resources employed. (ACCA BM   20 marks)

Chapter 9

Cash forecasts and funds flow statements

Because a main objective of a private-sector company is to make profits, and press comment on company results will emphasise profits (or losses) and profitability, many people, including students, think that provided that a company is making good profits all must be well. This is not necessarily so, for the reason that whilst profits are of the utmost importance, the cash flow is of equal importance. Clearly, in the same way as an individual, a company must at all times have sufficient cash, or a bank account, which is cash equivalent, or recourse to approved overdraft facilities so that accounts may be paid as and when they fall due. A creditor, or an employee on pay day, is only interested in receiving cash. It would not be acceptable to be told that there was no cause for anxiety and payment would be made sooner or later, as the company owned valuable assets, but was short of cash for the moment. In brief, it is the cash that counts to all those to whom the company is under financial obligations. Liquidity is as important to a company as profitability.

The determination of profit for an accounting period requires the matching of costs with related revenues. Revenues and costs are accrued, i.e. recognised, as they are earned or incurred, and not as money is received or paid.

The maintenance of satisfactory liquidity requires efficient cash management and control at all times. In principle this is not unduly difficult and it is a very practical matter which has an important place within the budget procedures. Paradoxically, experienced people are aware that cash forecasts are unreliable, but this does not reduce their importance: it simply means that they must be kept under constant scrutiny and revised as necessary. The actual cash position will diverge from the forecast (budgeted) position when actual cash sales differ significantly those budgeted and/or debtors do not pay according to the budgeted pattern – usually they pay later than expected. There would be less likelihood of the actual payments differing significantly from those budgeted since managements normally have control over payments to a degree which they do not have over receipts. The internal procedures, for example, should incorporate controls so that individual managers cannot enter into substantial payment commitments without prior approval and the arrangements should include that when this approval is given the cash flow implications will be taken into consideration and recorded.

Cash forecast procedures

A cash forecast is a summary of expected cash inflows and outflows over a period. Whereas a profit-and-loss account excludes items of a capital nature, all expected receipts and payments must be included in a cash forecast irrespective of whether they are of a revenue or capital nature. Whereas 'depreciation' appears in a profit-and-loss account, it does not appear in a cash forecast because no cash movement occurs. The aspect of the loss of value of a capital asset over a period is taken into account since the cost of the asset is incorporated at the start when payment for it is made and if it is sold at the end, even as scrap, the proceeds will be incorporated as a receipt. The difference between the initial payment and the final receipt – if any – represents the loss in value over the whole period of use.

In practice and in examination questions the straightforward clerical aspects must first have attention. Forecast receipts and payments must be grouped logically, so that no category of receipt or payment is overlooked. The opening cash balance will be shown and normally (but not necessarily) monthly periods are considered. The opening cash balance plus the forecast receipts and minus the payments will be the forecast cash balance at the end of the period. It is imperative not to confuse receipts and payments in the clerical work and to distinguish between credit and debit balances. The accepted convention is to show payments or negative balances within brackets, or preceded by a minus sign (–). A negative balance indicates an expected cash deficit, which is unacceptable except insofar as arrangements can be made promptly to ensure that despite this forecast the cash will be available to meet all due liabilities. A company faced with an expected cash deficit would be expected immediately to seek to negotiate overdraft facilities with its bank, or to increase already agreed limits. This would sometimes be part of temporary 'bridging finance' as when a company was making arrangements to sell some surplus assets but there would be some delay before the proceeds were received.

If the deficit appeared likely to be temporary then a prompt approach to a bank manager, with the forecasts and a well-presented case, should normally result in approval for an adequate overdraft facility. However, if the deficit appears likely to persist then prompt arrangements would also need to be made for additional longer-term finance – either an injection of new equity capital or a short-, medium- or long-term loan, as appropriate, or a mix of these. At the same time reductions in cash outlays should be considered where possible, including the deferment of capital expenditures. If a company is basically profitable and has security to offer and is able to overcome a sudden cash shortage, there could be unnecessary damage to its credit status if a crisis were allowed to occur unnecessarily. A financial crisis often signifies that a dangerous situation has arisen which must be dealt with in an impossibly short time. The crisis is often itself the shortness of time available to obtain cash and if there had been more time the arrangements could have been made without fuss, and better terms obtained. A main purpose of cash forecasting is to enable likely cash shortages to be foreseen early, so that precautionary action can be taken promptly. Equally, if it became apparent that there would be temporary cash surpluses, suitable investment arrangements could be made.

Cash forecasting requires that certain assumptions are made as to the pattern of receipts and payments. For a majority of companies the main, often the only, regularly occurring receipts are in respect of cash sales and receipts from debtors, in respect of credit sales. The timings of receipts from debtors should be related to the agreed credit terms and failure of debtors to adhere to these would indicate need for review of the credit control arrangements. The timings in respect of regular payments, such as wages, salaries, rents, rates, etc., should be known accurately. The timings of payments due to suppliers would be related to their terms of sale and should therefore be readily ascertainable. A checklist of headings normally met is as follows:

Receipts	*Payments*
Cash sales	Wages and salaries: overtime
Payments by debtors	Payments to creditors (suppliers); Rent; rates; electricity; telex; telephones; maintenance; heating; lighting; cleaning; etc.
	Insurance premiums

Cash forecasts and funds flow

Non-trading items	
Capital grants	Bank charges
Sale of fixed assets	Tax payments
Proceeds of new share/debenture issues	Dividend payments; interest payments
Loans	Capital expenditure
Dividends receivable	Debenture/loan repayments
Interest/rents receivable	Leasing and hire purchase payments

Because of its importance, cash forecasting is a frequent topic for examination questions. These are not normally difficult provided that the student has acquired speed through practice and loses no time in setting out in blank the appropriate receipts and payments framework, and then entering therein the information given in the question. The maximum marks will be gained quickly and, hopefully, confidence as well, if the simplest items are entered first, those which do not require any calculations, such as salaries, wages, general expenses, intended dividends, etc. Often there is a single item which seems – often unnecessarily – to present difficulties. In the following example the examiner's report indicated that it was calculation of the payments due to suppliers.

Example 1

Newco Ltd has recently been formed to open a furniture shop. It plans to open on 2 October 1980 and has made the following projections for its first year of operations:

(a) Sales (£):

October	20,000	November	28,000	December	55,000
January	30,000	February	20,000	March	25,000
April	30,000	May	30,000	June	30,000
July	25,000	August	25,000	September	20,000

(b) The physical level of stock for each month is to be established at 80% of the predicted sales volume for the following month.
(c) The gross profit margin is expected to be 40%.
(d) It is expected that four-fifths of the sales will be on credit and that customers will take on average two months from the end of the month of sale to pay their bills.
(e) The suppliers of the company have agreed to give one month of credit from the end of the month in which delivery is made. Assume that the initial stock is delivered on 1 October 1980.

(*f*) The shop premises cost £85,000 and shop fittings £36,000, both items to be paid during October 1980. The shop fittings are to be depreciated at 20% per annum.

(*g*) The wages bill is expected to be £5,000 per month and the two directors intend to draw £3,000 each at the end of March and September.

(*h*) General expenses are predicted at £3,500 per month.

Prepare a cash forecast for the first twelve months of operations of the company. The directors have £50,000 available as an initial investment and their bank has agreed to provide overdraft facilities of up to £50,000. Write a short report to the directors explaining how a short-term cash deficit may be financed assuming that the bank is not prepared to allow an overdraft in excess of £50,000. (ICSA 34 marks).

Workings and comments

The detailed workings are set out below. They are straightforward but take time. The only real problem is the calculation of the payments to be made to suppliers. If the position at the start is determined, the calculation for each succeeding month is not difficult, noting that the cost of goods sold will be 60% of the sales revenues and noting also that the opening stock for each month is to be 80% of the sales and accordingly the cost of the opening stock will be 60% × 80% × the sales revenue for the month. As the first month's sales are expected to be £20,000, the cost of the sales will be £12,000: the sales for the next month are forecast at £28,000 and the stock held at the end of the first month must be, in volume, 80% of the expected sales and accordingly the cost will be 60% × 80% × £28,000, i.e. £13,440. The cost of the initial stock of furniture supplied on 1 October 1980 must therefore be £25,440, to be paid by the end of November 1980. The purchases to be paid for at the end of the next month, December, will be the balance of the November sales, i.e. 60% × 20% × £28,000 plus 80% of the December sales, i.e. 60% × 80% × £55,000, i.e. a total of £29,760, and so on. The complete workings are shown and questions of this type (including this one) should be worked in full by students to acquire the necessary speed for examination purposes. The answer requires a short report, which might be on the following lines, noting that the examiner expects the student to show awareness of the options likely to be available, and judgement as to which seem the most promising:

From: Company Secretary   To: The Board of Directors
21 August 1980

Cash forecasts and funds flow

Cash Planning – Newco

1. Attached is a detailed cash forecast for the period 1 October 1980 – 30 September 1981. If all goes according to plan and the sales are as expected and the debtors pay promptly, the projected cash deficit would reach its highest point in January 1981, at £116,200, i.e. £66,200 above the maximum overdraft facility. This allows no margin for contingencies. Additional finance might be obtained in one or more of the following ways:

(i) Obtain a mortgage on the security of the premises and fittings. (Even if it were desired a sale – leaseback would not be feasible in this case: the values are too low).

(ii) If the premises and fittings have not already been purchased, consideration could be given to leasing instead of purchase: hire purchase could also be considered as it would reduce the initial outlay. Suppliers might also be requested to offer longer credit terms, at least until the business becomes established.

(iii) As your sales will be on a retail basis factoring will not be feasible, but invoice discounting may be. In this case cash advances of up to 80% of invoice totals might be obtained promptly, at a cost approximating that of an overdraft. It must be assumed that you will have to offer credit to your customers as this is an established trade practice.

(iv) Provided that a well documented case is made, the bank might be prepared to agree to an additional overdraft but against the personal guarantees and securities deposited by one or more of the directors. It is my view that the bank would raise the question whether the company is not undercapitalised at the start, in view of the commitments entered into and the need for adequate working capital and noting also that the forecast allows no margin for contingencies. A loan might also be obtained from a finance house, but their interest rates tend to be higher than those charged by banks.

(v) Whatever source of finance is decided upon, costs will be involved and a cost – benefit analysis should be made before a decision is taken. The aspect of tax should also be fully considered. Meanwhile, I think it likely that the view of bankers will be that the company is undercapitalised and the shareholders – promoters should start the company with additional risk capital.

John Jones (Secretary)

ICSA: Pilot paper: Question 2: Workings

	Oct	Nov	Dec	Jan	Feb	Mar	Apr	May	Jun	Jul	Aug	Sep
Sales	20,000	28,000	55,000	30,000	20,000	25,000	30,000	30,000	30,000	25,000	25,000	20,000
Credit sales [80% of 1]	16,000	22,400	44,000	24,000	16,000	20,000	24,000	24,000	24,000	20,000	20,000	16,000
Cash sales [1–2]	4,000	5,600	11,000	6,000	4,000	5,000	6,000	6,000	6,000	5,000	5,000	4,000
Material costs [80% of 1]	12,000	16,800	33,000	18,000	12,000	15,000	18,000	18,000	18,000	15,000	15,000	12,000
Closing stock	13,440	26,400	14,400	9,600	12,000	14,400	14,400	14,400	12,000	12,000	9,600	
Subtotal	25,440	43,200	47,400	27,600	24,000	29,400	32,400	32,400	30,000	27,000	24,600	
Less opening stock	–	13,440	26,400	14,400	9,600	12,000	14,400	14,400	14,400	12,000	12,000	
Material purchases	35,440	29,700	21,000	13,200	14,400	17,400	18,000	18,000	15,600	15,000	12,600	

Cash forecast

	Oct	Nov	Dec	Jan	Feb	Mar	Apr	May	Jun	Jul	Aug	Sep
Receipts: Cash introduced	50,000											
Cash sales	4,000	5,600	11,000	6,000	4,000	5,000	6,000	6,000	6,000	5,000	5,000	4,000
Receipts from debtors	–	–	16,000	22,400	44,000	24,000	16,000	20,000	24,000	24,000	24,000	20,000
Total receipts	54,000	5,600	27,000	28,400	48,000	29,000	22,000	26,000	30,000	29,000	29,000	24,000
Payments: Premises	85,000											
Fittings	36,000											
Purchases	–	25,440	29,760	21,000	13,200	14,400	17,400	18,000	18,000	15,600	15,000	12,600
Wages	5,000	5,000	5,000	5,000	5,000	5,000	5,000	5,000	5,000	5,000	5,000	5,000
General expenses	3,500	3,500	3,500	3,500	3,500	3,500	3,500	3,500	3,500	3,500	3,500	3,500
Directors' fees	–	–	–	–	–	6,000	–	–	–	–	–	6,000
Total payments	129,500	33,940	38,260	29,500	21,700	28,900	25,900	26,500	26,500	24,100	23,500	27,100
Balance	[75,500]	[28,340]	[11,260]	[1,100]	26,300	100	[3,900]	[500]	3,500	4,900	5,500	[3,100]
Balance b/f	–	[75,500]	[103,840]	[115,100]	[116,200]	[89,900]	[89,800]	[93,700]	[94,200]	[90,700]	[85,800]	[80,300]
Balance c/f	[75,500]	[103,840]	[115,100]	[116,200]	[89,900]	[89,800]	[93,700]	[94,200]	[90,700]	[85,800]	[80,300]	[83,400]

Note: A balance in brackets [ ] is a debit

Cash forecasts and funds flow

Example 2
The following is a summary of the 1979 accounts of YZ Ltd, a retailing company:

Balance sheet as at 31 December 1979

	(£000)		(£000)	(£000)
Share capital (400,000 shares, of 50p each)	200	Property (at cost)		300
Revenue reserves	130	Fixtures and fittings	500	
		Less: Depreciation	350	150
	330			450
Trade creditors	200	Stock (60,000 units)	180	
Dividend	60	Debtors	260	440
Bank overdraft	300			
	890			890

Profit and Loss Account for the year ended 31 December 1979

		(£000)
Sales (400,000 units)		1,600
Cost of goods sold		1,200
		400
Wages and general expenses	230	
Depreciation	70	300
Profit for year		100
Dividend declared		60
Retained Profits		40
Undistributed at 31 December 1978		90
Undistributed profits as at 31 December 1979		£ 130

YZ Ltd deals in a single product. The following estimates of trading have been made for 1980:
(a) Sales will be 500,000 units at a price of £4.20 per unit. Sales in November and December will be 50,000 per month.
(b) The amount of wages and general expenses will be 20% higher than in 1979.
(c) £100,000 will be spent on new shop fittings during the year. The 1980 depreciation charge will be £75,000.
(d) All sales and purchases will, as in the past, be made on credit for settlement two months after sale or purchase. Wages and general expenses will be paid immediately.

(e) Purchases will be 43,000 units per month at a price of £3 per unit.
(f) An interim dividend of 10p per share will be paid in November 1980.

Required: Budgeted profit and loss account; monthly cash budget and balance sheet for the year 1980. Comment on any trends shown by your figures. (ICSA 34 marks)

Workings and comments

Budgeted Profit and Loss Account for the year ending 31 December 1980

		(£000)
Sales (500,000 units)		2,100
Cost of goods sold		1,500
		600
Wages and general expenses	276	
Depreciation	75	351
Profit for the year		249
Proposed interim dividend		40
		209
Undistributed profit at 31 December 1979		130
Undistributed profit carried forward		339

Budgeted Balance Sheet as at 31 December 1980

	(£000)		(£000)	(£000)
Share capital (400,000 shares at 50p)	200	Property (at cost)		300
Revenue reserves	339	Fixtures and fittings	600	
		Less: Depreciation	425	175
Shareholders equity	539			475
Current liabilities:		Currents assets:		
Trade creditors 258		Stock (76,000 units)	228	
Bank overdraft 326	584	Debtors	420	648
	1,123			1,123

Budgeted Cash Budget: January–December 1980 (£000)

	Jan	Feb	Mar	Apr	May	Jun	Jul	Aug	Sep	Oct	Nov	Dec
Receipts:												
Sales	130	130	168	168	168	168	168	168	168	168	168	168
Balance (monthly)	130	130	168	168	168	168	168	168	168	168	168	168
Payments:												
Purchases	100	100	129	129	129	129	129	129	129	129	129	129
Wages and expenses	23	23	23	23	23	23	23	23	23	23	23	23
Shop fittings*						100						
Dividend	60											
Interim dividend											40	
Balance (monthly)	(183)	(123)	(152)	(152)	(152)	(252)	(152)	(152)	(152)	(152)	(192)	(152)
Net monthly bal.	(53)	7	16	16	16	(84)	16	16	16	16	(24)	16
Balance b/f	(300)	(353)	(346)	(330)	(314)	(298)	(382)	(366)	(350)	(334)	(318)	(342)
Balance c/f	(353)	(346)	(330)	(314)	(298)	(382)	(366)	(350)	(334)	(318)	(342)	(326)

* It is assumed that cash was paid for these fittings in June. Negative balances are shown within brackets ( ).

The following are comments on trends indicated by the figures:
(i) Gross profit margins: 1979   25%; 1980   28.57%
If all goes according to plan there will be an increase in volume and also in gross profit margins. This would be a favourable prospect.
(ii) Net profits (ignoring tax): 1979   6.25%; 1980   11.86%
This also shows a very favourable trend.
(iii) Return on shareholders equity: 1979   30.30%; 1980   46.20%
If this is achieved it will be an extremely good performance.
(iv) The evidence indicates that in respect of profitability the company is doing well and promises to do better. However, the lack of liquidity is disquieting. In financial terms there are two prerequisites for company success – adequate profitability and adequate liquidity. In this case it would even seem doubtful whether a bank would agree to a continuing overdraft which gave no sign of being self-liquidating. The company now appears to need to review its capital structure with a view to having additional funds on a medium-to long-term basis. The company could consider obtaining additional equity capital by means of a rights issue. It could obtain a medium- or long-term loan, or issue debentures. This would provide capital at lower cost insofar as interest payments are allowed as an expense before corporation tax is computed. The ordinary shareholders would benefit from the aspect of 'gearing'. Alternatively, additional long-term funds could be obtained partly by means of a rights issue and partly by means of a loan or debenture. Expert advice would be needed, including as to the tax implications.

Funds flow statements (sources and applications of funds)

Cash forecasting, like budgeting, is a management control technique which is operated internally. It uses information not available to external analysts. Exceptionally, a bank manager or other prospective lender could insist upon being given access to any information he required as a condition before considering a request for a loan. However, when a financial year ends, the law requires that certain financial statements are prepared and made available for public inspection – except in the case of an unlimited company. Before 1929, Companies Acts treated the balance sheet as the most important financial statement of a company.

Cash forecasts and funds flow

The Companies Act, 1929, and subsequent Acts have given equal emphasis to the profit-and-loss account.

It is now expected that the next major Companies Act will give formal recognition to the fact that there is a third financial statement which has comparable importance with the other two – a statement of sources and applications of funds, alternatively known as a funds flow statement. The purpose of this statement is to permit comparison of the balance sheet of one year with that of the previous one in a manner which highlights the relationships between the assets, liabilities and capital of a company and their impact on the working capital and liquidity position. It can then be seen how far the fixed assets have been financed from long-term rather than short-term funds. Similarly, the statement can assist the control of a company's current resources by showing how movements in working capital have come about.

The law does not yet insist upon the publication of this statement but its publication is compelled in practice since in 1975 the recognised accountancy bodies published SSAP 10, which is binding upon practicing auditors. This requires that except in the case of enterprises with turnover or gross income of less than £25,000 p.a., audited financial accounts must include a statement of sources and applications of funds both for the period under review and the corresponding previous period. In the same way, the balance sheet and profit-and-loss account must show the current and the previous period figures, for comparative purposes.

Preparation of a sources and applications of funds statement
SSAP 10 defines the form a statement should take:

it should show clearly the funds generated or absorbed by the operations of the business and the manner in which any surplus of liquid assets has been applied or any deficiency of such assets has been financed, distinguishing the long term from the short term. The statement should distinguish the use of funds for the purchase of new fixed assets from funds used in increasing the working capital of the company.

It indicates that the statement provides a link between the balance sheet at the beginning of the period, the profit-and-loss account for the period and the balance sheet at the end of it, and further requires a minimum of 'netting off' – e.g. the sale of one building should be shown separately from the purchase of another. The items in a statement should generally be identifiable in the profit-and-loss account, balance sheet and related notes: statements in the case of companies with subsidiaries should be based on the group accounts, and any purchases or sales of subsidiary companies should be reflected either as separate items or by reflecting the effects on the separate assets and liabilities dealt with in the statement. In either case the effect should be summarised in a footnote indicating, in the case of an acquisition, how much of the purchase price has been discharged in cash and how much by the issue of shares.

The funds flow statement is also required to show the profit or loss for the period, with adjustments for items which did not use or provide funds – e.g. depreciation – and when material the following sources and applications of funds should be shown: (*a*) dividends paid; (*b*) acquisitions and disposals of fixed and other non-current assets; (*c*) funds raised by increasing or expended in repaying or redeeming, medium- or long-term loans or the issued capital of the company; (*d*) increase or decrease in working capital subdivided into its components, and the movements in net liquid funds. 'Net liquid funds' are defined as 'cash at bank and in hand and cash equivalents (e.g. investments held as current assets) less bank overdrafts and other borrowings repayable within one year of the accounting date'.

The preparation of a funds flow statement is simple in principle although an examination question can be complex if a number of adjustments have to be made. Because of the 'dual aspect' recognised in the double-entry book-keeping system the sources must equal the applications and if, in working a question, they do not, then one or more errors must have been made. Funds are made available from two sources: (i) an increase in a liability, and (ii) a decrease in an asset. Thus, as examples, a main source of funds is normally retained profits, represented by an increase in the credit balance on the profit-and-loss appropriation account, or the proceeds of a rights issue (i above), or the sale of a building or a reduction in the level of stocks (ii above). Equally, funds can be applied in two ways: (i) a reduction in a liability, (ii) an increase in an asset. For examples, paying off a number of suppliers will represent applications of funds (i above) and so would purchase of a capital asset (ii above).

In addition to providing historical data, which is of interest to analysts and others, budgeted funds flow statements can also be used in forward planning to ascertain what additional finance would be needed to support increased sales and provide for long-term investment. By estimating the levels of the various current assets and liabilities it is possible to estimate, approximately, deficiencies of working or of long-term capital which must be sought from outside sources.

It must be borne in mind that depreciation written off fixed assets and charged against profit does not involve a cash outlay. In fact it represents a 'book entry' and is a means of ensuring that the profit for the period is not overstated when it could be followed by cash dividend payments, so that when the time came to replace a worn-out asset it could be found that no provision had been made for that purpose and, in effect, the company had not been maintaining its capital fund intact. The charge for depreciation is therefore a source of funds, in the category of an increase in a liability. It is often not realised that the fact that a provision has been made for depreciation in the accounts does not mean that automatically when the time comes to replace an asset the necessary cash would be available for this purpose, in the same way that creating or increasing a reserve account does not necessarily mean that a company will have liquidity. Cash and liquidity management must also be operated and the controls already explained will be used.

There is also now a further problem in that in inflationary times provisions for depreciation, even when maintained in liquid form, are seldom adequate to meet the increased replacement cost of a worn-out asset. One main reason why companies so often retain a substantial proportion of the distributable profits, crediting the reserve accounts, is to ensure that adequate funds are conserved and, hopefully, can be used profitably so that the cash flow of the company will regularly be sufficient to permit fixed assets to be replaced when necessary.

In the same way, any writings off against profits of 'preliminary expenses' or the transfer of profits to reserves do not give rise to any payments of money and are therefore excluded from any consideration of the flow of funds – the profit figure must be adjusted to what it was before these entries were made by 'writing back'. In answering questions on this topic the implications of each item of information should be assessed and underlying cash movements, if any, identified. For example, if there had been an upward revaluation of fixed assets, with a corresponding increase in the reserve, this would not involve any flow of funds. It will sometimes be necessary to use information supplied for the reconstruction of an asset account in order to determine the cash receipts in the case or a sale, or payments in the case of a purchase.

In order to prepare a funds flow statement for a financial period it will be necessary to have the balance sheet as at the beginning of the period and also at the end, as well as the profit-and-loss account for the period, so that the profit or loss for the period will be known, as well as the depreciation which will need to be 'written back'. Questions may simply require the preparation of a funds flow statement, or they may require an explanation of what has happened to the profits, or how changes in the working capital have come about, or the change in the cash balance from that at the start of the year to that at the end of it. The following summary may be helpful:

Sources of funds	Applications of funds
Profits before taxation	Losses
Depreciation	Decreases in creditors
Increases in creditors	Increases in assets
Decreases in assets	Redemption of debentures or redeemable preference share capital
Increase in share capital (including share premium account)	Payments of dividends and taxation

Sometimes an examination question shows an increase in the issued ordinary share capital and a new, or increased, item 'share premium account'. The share premium account, an increase in a liability, will be a source of funds. The implication will be that shares were issued at a premium over the nominal value, and the premium has to be entered in this special account. The cash received by the company would be represented by the increase in the ordinary share capital and the share premium accounts. The issue expenses would be recorded separately and would be charged against the profit and loss account.

SSAP 10 recommends the basic layout which follows:

Statement of sources and applications of funds: Year ended 31 December 198..

Source of funds		
Net profit before tax		£ X
Add: depreciation		X
Total generated from operations		X
Funds from other sources		
Issue of shares	X	
Issue of loan funds	X	
Sale of fixed assets	X	X
		X
Application of funds		
Dividends paid	X	
Tax paid	X	
Fixed assets purchased	X	X
Increase/decrease in working capital		
Increase/decrease in stock	X	
Increase/decrease in debtors	X	
Decrease/increase in creditors	X	
Increase/decrease in net liquid funds	X	X
		X

Example 1
From the following balance sheets prepare a funds flow statement for Y Ltd reconciling the opening and closing balances of the working capital, and comment on the information revealed:

As at 31 May	1979 (£)	1980 (£)
Issued share capital: £1 ordinary shares	18,000	23,000
Retained profits	7,500	9,200
15% debentures	6,000	7,500
Taxation payable 1 January following	2,900	3,200
Trade and expense creditors	3,200	3,400
Proposed dividends (gross)	500	600
	38,100	46,900
Fixed assets at cost	23,000	25,000
Less: depreciation	5,650	6,200
	17,350	18,800
Stocks	12,000	14,695
Debtors	4,200	4,150
Balance at bank	4,550	9,255
	38,100	46,900

Note: During the year fixed assets were purchased at a cost of £5,600. Fixed assets which cost £3,600 and which stood in the books at £1,500 were disposed of for £2,500 and the profit has been included in the retained profits. (ACCA Acc4 15 marks)

Workings and comments
As the question calls for a reconciliation of the opening and closing balances of the working capital, this must be calculated. It is:

	1979(£)		1980 (£)	
Current assets				
stocks		12,000		14,695
debtors		4,200		4,150
bank		4,550		9,255
		20,750		28,100
Current liabilities				
taxation	2,900		3,200	
creditors	3,200		3,400	
dividends	500	6,600	600	7,200
Net working capital		14,150		20,900
				14,150
Increase in working capital 1979/1980				6,750

(An increase in working capital represents an application of funds – an increase in the assets.)

It is necessary to calculate the trading profit (or loss) for the year as well as the depreciation charged for the year, and to add the latter back to the profit (or to reduce the loss). Using the information given in the question:

	(£)
Cost of fixed assets held on 31 May 1979	23,000
Reduced by the sale of assets (at cost)	3,600
	19,400
Increased by purchase of new assets (at cost)	5,600
Cost of fixed assets held on 31 May 1980	25,000
Depreciation at 31 May 1979	5,650
Less: depreciation with respect to assets sold (£3,600 − £1,500)	2,100
Balance in respect of remaining assets at 31 May 1979	3,550
Balance on depreciation account at 31 May 1980	6,200
Less: adjusted depreciation balance at 31 May 1979	3,550
i.e. depreciation charged during year 1979/1980	2,650
Fixed assets at cost 31 May 1979	23,000
Less: cost price of assets sold during year	3,600
Adjusted cost price of assets held on 31 May 1979 and still held 31.5.80	19,400
Cost price of fixed assets held on 31 May 1980	25,000
Less: adjusted cost of fixed assets held on 31 May 1979	19,400
i.e. cost price of fixed assets purchased during 1979/1980	5,600

As assets held in the accounts at £1,500 were sold for £2,500, the sale resulted in a profit of £1,000 and this is stated to have been incorporated in the retained profits.

	(£)
Retained profits as at 31 May 1980	9,200
Less: retained profits at 31 May 1979	7,500
Retained profits during 1979/1980	1,700
Less: profit on sale of assets	1,000
Operating profits for 1979/1980	700

Cash forecasts and funds flow

Sources of funds: 31 May 1979–31 May 1980 (summarised)

Operating profit		700
Add: depreciation written back		2,650
Funds generated from operations		3,350
Funds from other sources		
Sale of fixed assets	2,500	
new share capital	5,000	
additional 15% debentures	1,500	9,000
		12,350

Application of funds

Purchase of fixed assets	5,600
Increase in working capital	6,750
	12,350

Comment: As the sales for the year are not stated and the information given is limited, comment must also be restricted. It appears that the operating profit was low in absolute terms and in relation to the capital employed. One would need to see details of the expenses charged, including salaries, etc., of directors. Why was additional equity capital raised and also a loan noting that the working capital is relatively high and the company appears to be in an excessively liquid position? The stocks held also seem high. Perhaps the company is about to begin a new capital project, or launch a sales campaign – one does not know as there is insufficient information.

Example 2

F Ltd operates a number of supermarkets in the North of England and has recently greatly increased the number of outlets. The following information has been summarised from their accounts for the last three years. All figures are in £000 and figures in brackets are negative.

Profit statement		Year 1		Year 2		Year 3
Sales		400		600		620
Gross profit		100		132		112
Less: Expenses	36		72		76	
Depreciation	4		12		14	
Interest	–		28		30	
Corporation tax	30	70	10	122	–	120
Profit after taxation		30		10		(8)
Net dividend		24		12		–
Retentions		6		(2)		(8)

Balance sheet

	Year 1		Year 2		Year 3	
Fixed assets		200		500		700
Current assets:						
Stock	120		180		200	
Debtors	80		180		240	
Bank	40	240	–	360	–	440
		440		860		1,140
Current liabilities						
Overdraft	–		152		146	
Creditors	50		220		264	
Taxation	30	80	10	382	–	410
Net assets		360		478		730

Financed by	Year 1		Year 2		Year 3	
Ordinary share capital		200		200		200
Retentions		160		158		150
		360		358		350
10% loan		–		120		380
		360		478		730

You are required:
(a) to produce a statement of sources and applications of working capital for years 2 and 3.
(b) to comment on the changes in the financial position of the company between years 1 and 3.
(c) to suggest a remedial course of action. (ICSA 34 marks)

Workings and comments
The changes in the working capital are (£000):

	Year 2		Year 3	
	Increase	Decrease	Increase	Decrease
Current assets				
Stocks	60	–	20	–
Debtors	100	–	60	–
Bank	–	40	–	–
	160	40	80	–
Net	120		80	
Current liabilities				
Bank overdraft	152	–	–	6
Creditors	170	–	44	–
Taxation	–	20	–	10
	322	20	44	16
Net	302		28	

Cash forecasts and funds flow

Thus: Year 2: Working capital decreased by £302,000 – £120,000, i.e. £182,000

Year 3: Working capital increased by £80,000 – £28,000, i.e. £52,000

Apart from the working capital component, the sources and applications of funds were (£000):

Sources	Year 2		Year 3	
Profit after tax		10		(8)
Depreciation		12		14
		22		6
10% loan		120		260
		142		266
Applications				
Dividend	12		–	
Net increase in fixed assets	312	324	214	214
Change in working capital		(182)		52

Note that the question shows 'fixed assets': this must mean 'at cost less depreciation' since depreciation is not shown separately and the cost of the fixed assets acquired must therefore be the difference between the 'fixed asset' totals from one year to the next plus the depreciation charged for the year in the profit-and-loss account.

(b) The implications of the above sources and applications statement include that in year 2 working capital was heavily drawn upon to finance the purchase of additional fixed assets. In year 3 the working capital was replenished by means of the issue of additional debentures. The changes in the profits before tax and interest payments were (£000):

	Year 1		Year 2		Year 3	
Gross profit		100		132		112
(as a percentage of sales) (25%)				(22%)		(18%)
Less: expenses	36		72		76	
depreciation	4	40	12	84	14	90
		60		48		22

(i) It is evident that the gross profit margins are falling and this always requires urgent investigation. There are a number of possible

reasons and a main one is that the cost of purchases has increased but the selling prices have not been increased in proportion for some reason.
 (ii) Expenses have heavily increased and the 'greatly increased' number of outlets will surely be a main reason for this.
(iii) The overall results are made worse by the high interest costs.
(iv) Although fixed assets have increased considerably the depreciation charge has not increased in proportion and in year 3 is only £2,000 higher than in year 2, despite the substantial purchases of fixed assets in that year. All the foregoing matters now require probing examination.

(c) To suggest a remedial course of action will require study of both profitability as well as liquidity: profit margins, turnover and costs must all be studied.
 (i) It will be necessary to study results over several years, both overall and on a store-by-store basis: relevant ratios must be prepared so that trends can be identified. The figures for F Ltd should also, as far as practicable, be compared with the available figures in respect of other supermarket groups.
 (ii) Profitability of a supermarket depends significantly on skilful central buying as well as on pricing policies and presentation at the point of sale. The local competition will have an important bearing on the results of individual stores. The results of individual stores must be examined and visits made, so that impressions can be formed, including of location and competition. Weaknesses must be identified, e.g. in staffing, training, presentation of goods, etc. Appropriate action must be taken to deal with identified weaknesses. Furthermore, when things go seriously wrong there will be a question mark over the top management. How good are they? In this case it must have been a top management decision to open more stores. How and why was this decision made? Was it a sound one? It seems doubtful.
(iii) A target return on capital should be set and stores which fail to achieve this must be considered as liabilities, to be disposed of promptly. Disposal of unprofitable stores should improve both profitability and liquidity.
(iv) Supermarkets operate on the basis of fast turnover of stock. In the case of F Ltd the stock turnover rate can only be very roughly assessed from the ratio of sales/stocks but it seems low and requires investigation.

(v) The substantial debtors figure is puzzling. A feature of supermarkets is that they operate on a cash basis only. Why is credit being given? Agreeing to grant credit must have been a top management decision. Was it sound and should the policy continue? In any case, the progressive increase in the debtors raises questions about the quality of the credit control. As long as credit is being given it is important that it should be effectively controlled.

Overall, the limited information available raises a number of questions, from the quality of top management decisions to the operational efficiency and competitiveness of individual stores. Fuller investigations would be needed, with free access to information, and visits to stores, if comprehensive proposals were to be made with a view to restoring the performance of F Ltd to more acceptable levels.

Questions

1. 'The most important business objective for the firm is to survive and survival means liquidity. For the management accountant, therefore, the cash and funds flow statement is much more important than the profit statement.' Comment on this statement. (ACCA 15 marks)

2. G Ltd manufactures a single product, H. Below are product data and an extract from the sales forecast for the year to 31 December 1980.

	Apr.	May	June	July	Aug.	Sept.	Oct.
Sales units	800	600	800	1,000	400	800	1,000

H sells at £20 per unit, the total variable cost per unit of £14 being as follows:

Direct material	£10
Labour and overheads	£4

Terms of business etc
Sales: Cash sales; payable in full. Represent 10% of total sales.
Credit sales: collections experience suggests that of the total credit sales in calendar month X, settlement is made by debtors at the end of calendar month:
X + 1 70% then subject to 2% cash discount
X + 2 20% strictly net
X + 3 10% strictly net

Purchases of direct material: accounts for purchases in calendar month X are settled subject to 2% cash discount, by the end of calendar month X + 1.

Direct labour and overheads: these are paid in the calendar month in which they are incurred. Fixed overheads are running at £500 per month, including £50 per month for depreciation.

Production is so arranged that the finished stock of H at each month end is just sufficient to meet the next month's sales forecast. Similarly, the stock of direct materials at each month end is just sufficient to meet the next month's production needs. There is no work-in-progress at any month end. Assume that the ledger balances at 30 June 1980 will be as follows:

	(£)
Bank balance	2,000
Creditors for direct materials	
June purchases	4,000
Debtors for sales	
April sales	1,440
May sales	3,240
June sales	14,400

You are required to prepare a cash forecast for the **three** months to 30 September 1980 showing the bank balance at the end of each month. (ICSA 34 marks)

3. You are given the following information about a wholesaling company which is about to be set up:
(*a*) Plant and machinery is to be purchased for £250,000. It is to be depreciated on a straight-line basis over five years, at the end of which it will be scrapped.
(*b*) Sales for the first two years are forecast at £480,000 p.a. These sales will be seasonal in nature on the basis of the following index:

1st quarter	100
2nd quarter	50
3rd quarter	70
4th quarter	180

(*c*) Gross profit is expected to be 25% of sales revenue.
(*d*) The rate of turnover of debtors is expected to be four times per annum.
(*e*) Goods equal to the expected volume of sales for the following quar-

Cash forecasts and funds flow

ter are purchased half way through each quarter and are paid for two months later.

(f) Wages and other general expenses amount to £5,000 per quarter payable in cash. You are required to calculate the cash deficit at the end of each quarter during the first year and to suggest the best means of financing this (using more than one type of finance if you think fit). Prepare a set of final accounts for the end of the first year incorporating the financing scheme which you recommend.
(ICSA   34 marks)

4. The accounts of ABC Ltd for the years ended 31 December 1979 and 1980 are as below:

	1980 (£)			1979 (£)		
Fixed assets	Cost	Depreciation	Net	Cost	Depreciation	Net
Land and buildings	6,000	500	5,500	3,000	400	2,600
Plant and machinery	8,500	4,000	4,500	5,000	3,000	2,000
	14,500	4,500	10,000	8,000	3,400	4,600
Trade investments			2,000			1,000
Current assets						
Stock		8,000			5,000	
Debtors		5,000			3,000	
Investments		–			4,000	
Cash		100			1,000	
		13,100			13,000	
Current liabilities						
Creditors	9,000			7,000		
Dividends payable	1,000			800		
Overdraft	2,200	12,200	900	–	7,800	5,200
			12,900			10,800
Share capital and reserves			6,000			5,000
Share premium account			2,000			1,000
Profit and loss account			3,000			2,500
			11,000			8,500
Debentures			1,900			2,300
			12,900			10,800

Notes: (i) During the year investments were sold for £5,500 and plant and machinery with a cost of £1,000 and a book value of £800 was sold for £900. The resultant gains were taken to the profit-and-loss account.
(ii) Taxation is to be ignored.

You are required to prepare a statement of sources and applications of **cash** and to comment on the change in the position of the company during the year. (ICSA 34 marks)

5. The treasurer of a large company has to decide what balance he should hold from time to time in cash, as distinct from short-term investments. What are the various factors he should take into account in reaching his decision. (ICMA 20 marks)

6. The balance sheets of ABC Ltd for the years ended 31 March 1979 and 1980 are given below (£000):

	1979		1980	
£1 ordinary shares		4,280		5,080
Reserves:				
Share premium account	–		200	
Retained profits	3,740	3,740	4,384	4,584
		8,020		9,664
Debentures		800		160
Current liabilities				
Creditors	960		640	
Taxation	280		240	
Dividends proposed	428	1,668	508	1,388
		10,488		11,212
Fixed assets				
Buildings (at cost)		2,228		3,308
Plant (at cost)	3,480		3,680	
Less: depreciation	840	2,640	1,000	2,680
Vehicles (at cost)	200		240	
Less: depreciation	64	136	96	144
		5,004		6,132
Investments (at cost)		1,032		1,208
Current assets				
Stock	1,652		2,392	
Debtors	800		1,080	
Cash	2,000	4,452	400	3,872
		10,488		11,212

The profit-and-loss account for the year ended 31 March 1980 included the following (£000):
 (i) Profit on redemption of debentures 10
 (ii) Depreciation of plant 400
 (iii) Depreciation of vehicles 32

Cash forecasts and funds flow

(iv) Loss on sale of plant   80
(v) Provision for taxation   240
    Proposed dividend   508

The loss on sale of plant arose because plant costing £360,000 (accumulated depreciation £240,000) was sold for £40,000.

You are required to:
(a) prepare a statement showing the sources and applications of cash during the year ended 31 March 1980.   (20 marks)
(b) Comment on the use which an investment analyst might make of this information.   (14 marks)   (ICSA   34 marks)

Chapter 10

Short-, medium- and long-term funds

Presenting the case

A prospective borrower of short-, medium- or long-term funds for a company must start by making an effective presentation of his case to a prospective lender and success or failure will depend on this aspect as much as the intrinsic merits of the application. Because of the practical importance of this matter, extracts are quoted from two authoritative articles.

Usually when a banker looks at an application for funds he tends first to look at the person. There are four things he looks for: (1) the character of the person and whether he seems honest and upright; (2) the amount of money that the person is himself prepared to put into the project; (3) the competence of the person to manage the company; (4) the purpose for which the finance is required. I list below the requirements that any institution will look at when considering an application for funds. I realise that it is a long list, but if this is kept updated over a period of time it not only speeds up the application for funds but also helps in the control of the business.

Historical information. This covers the formation of the company, its previous expansion and evolution. More specifically, institutions will require at least three years audited accounts and possibly those for the last five years.

Present information. This covers the present owners of the company and senior management; names and addresses of bankers, auditors, legal advisers; product profile – the most usual method of presentation is trade pamphlets, with price lists, etc.; the markets in which the company operates together with the present order book. Financial information required will be updated accounts if it is more than four months since the last audit: management information concerning future cash flows, and profits statements based on present business. Also, details of existing borrowings and commitments both off and on the balance sheet, including guarantees, indicating how secured, repayments obligations and servicing costs.

Future information. This covers the expansion or the reasons for the requirements for funds. Explicit details of the project should be given including the assumptions made together with incremental cash flow forecasts. (Lord Seebohm, Chairman, Finance for Industry Ltd, 'Sources of Finance for Small- and Medium-Sized Businesses',/*The Accountant*, 29.9.1977)

The second quotation relates to an applicant seeking equity capital as well as loans:

The presentation of the case is so important and the three most important aspects which we consider carefully are: the man, the market and the money. Looking at the man, we pay considerable attention to the following:

Group strength. It is preferable that two to four entrepreneurs are backing a proposition and equally that they should possess complementary skills.

Personal motivation. This must be analysed – without a spark no proposition will ever glow.

Past achievements. The past achievements and the salaries received must be known in detail and be seen to be both worthwhile and relevant.

Commitment. Unless the entrepreneurs have their own shirts on the business an outside backer is unlikely to be impressed.

References. References should be good and should preferably include the last employer.

Education/training. Qualifications are important but, in our view, less so than experience. Overall, it is very important that an entrepreneur seeking funding should be entirely open and honest about his past experience. In the event that this experience is fairly limited there is no point in hiding the fact as it will come out sooner or later – it is possible, too, that even lacking wide experience intermediate funding can be devised so that the budding entrepreneur can have time to prove himself.

Looking now at the market we look closely at the following:

Growth rate. This should be available from existing data. Even in the case of a very new product it should be possible to obtain some data on the growth rate of a product which is broadly speaking similar – if this is also unavailable it must at least be possible to form a view of the likely usage/acceptance which the product will achieve, based on outlets, population, etc.

Exports. With the growth of the Common Market and depreciated pound, it will clearly be less easy in future to forget the export potential – both European and worldwide. Here again, statistics are available although they may be somewhat harder to acquire.

Competition. The strength of the competition must be evaluated in the chosen market. In fact, the strength of the entrepreneur's product must be very accurately analysed against competitive products – not forgetting the many products available abroad. Similarly some attempt must be made to gauge latent competition.

Fashion factor. If this applies the investor will want to know the cycle time – this can be as much an advantage as a disadvantage.

Market size. The ultimate size of the market must be estimated – there may be limitations. The number of customers must be established as the 'hit' rate will be critical if there are but few.

Market volatility. Not all products are stable and many are highly volatile. Some, of course, have a high obsolescence rate such as the computer peripheral field, for example, where technical innovations appear almost daily.

Government policy. No comment is called for other than 'beware'.

In viewing the market section of a proposition report, one should be able to find a fair degree of hard opinion with which to evaluate the chances of success – there is plenty of room also for subjective judgement.

Later in the article the following comment is made:
One further general point worth mentioning is that calculations of the

DCF return and pages of workings for the different accounting ratios are not likely to impress the average backer. This is because in the case of the return the backer will have some very clear views of his own target return and is quite capable of doing his own sums. In the case of ratios the yardsticks usually employed are those for small public companies and the average entrepreneur has little hope, therefore, of a fair match. (H. Armstrong, Managing Director of Small Business Capital Fund (SBCF), in *Accountancy Age*, 25.11.1977)

Traditional uses for short-term finance

It is a recurring theme of business finance that a major cause of problems, and sometimes of disaster, is excessive dependence on short-term funds, especially for the purchase of fixed assets which should have been financed with medium- or long-term funds. Meanwhile, it is accepted that legitimate uses for short-term funds include:

(a) Financing a proportion of working capital. A proportion of the working capital needs of a company are of a permanent nature and need to be financed with equity capital, or, at least, long-term funds. However, as the scale of activities increases there will be a need for additional working capital which may also fluctuate on a seasonal basis. Overdrafts are accepted as suitable for the financing of temporary upsurges in needs for working capital.

(b) Financing seasonal fluctuations. Many businesses experience seasonal fluctuations. Farming is the most obvious example, for there will be an excess of payments over receipts for most of the year and, if all goes well, substantial receipts after harvest. If seasonal fluctuations were financed with equity capital or long-term loans there would be quite long periods when the capital would be unproductive and the overall return would then be unnecessarily low.

(c) For bridging finance. A need for this type arises when it has been arranged to sell one property and purchase another as its replacement. Often the timing presents problems as all or part of the new property may need to be paid for before the proceeds of the sale have been received. An overdraft, or short-term loan, to be repaid when cash is received in respect of the property sold, is the normal means of dealing with this temporary situation.

(d) For purchase of minor fixed assets. Some smaller fixed assets are treated as expendable and as part of the operating expenses.

Main types of short-term finance

Bank overdrafts

Any company seeking short-term finance will include bank overdraft facilities as an important component. They are usually more simply arranged than any other type of loan. The principle is that the holder of a bank current account can draw cheques up to the sum standing to this credit in the account, and if the drawing of a cheque would result in the account of the drawer showing a debit balance, known as being overdrawn, the bank would have the right to refuse to honour the cheque. In practice, banks sometimes do honour cheques which result in an account becoming overdrawn to a small extent even although no prior arrangements have been made. However, a customer who wishes to have the right to overdraw his account up to a specified limit must request his bank to approve an overdraft facility. He would be expected to state his reasons and the maximum overdraft facility required, and its duration. Security might or might not be required. If approved, the bank notes the details of the agreement on the account of the customer, who then has authority to draw cheques up to the overdraft limit on the understanding that the account will be restored to a credit balance by an agreed date. In practice overdrafts are often extended – 'rolled over' – but the liability to repay, and possibly at an inconvenient time, must never be overlooked by the borrower.

Advantages and limitations of overdrafts

Overdrafts can be more quickly and easily arranged by creditworthy borrowers than any other form of loan, and with less formality. Often when an overdraft is requested in the name of a small company the bank may insist upon personal security and/or guarantees being provided by one or more directors. Overdrafts are flexible and relatively economical since interest is only payable on sums overdrawn, calculated on a daily basis. The cost of an overdraft will be expressed as a rate of interest, e.g. 3% or 4% above MLR in the case of an individual or smaller company, but perhaps only 1½% above MLR in the case of a large one. There is some scope for negotiation over the interest rate payable but in practice the scope is limited.

A bank which enters into an agreement to grant overdraft facilities to a customer accepts a commitment which it must take into account when it reviews its overall position. The bank receives remuneration when overdrafts facilities are drawn upon but meanwhile the customer enjoys a valuable right for which he makes no payment if he does not overdraw his account. It would be understandable if banks sought to charge a commitment fee of, say, 1% of the agreed maximum sum, payable even if the facilities were not used. An important advantage of an overdraft for a borrower is that it represents a useful 'stand by' credit, available in case of need.

A serious disadvantage of overdraft facilities is the ease with which an imprudent borrower can overcommit himself, and use the facilities for unsuitable purposes. A management should always consider its cash flow and in its financial planning should plan that in the event of a sudden credit squeeze the company would be able to dispense with the overdraft facility and have recourse to other forms of finance.

Short-term loans

A short-term loan, obtainable from a bank or finance house, is regarded as one with a duration not exceeding three years. Its advantage over an overdraft is that so long as the borrower is not in breach of any of the conditions imposed by the lender, the period of the loan cannot be reduced. In practice the capital structure of a company may comprise a suitable mix of equity capital and different types of loan funds and it would be normal for both overdrafts and short-term loans to be part of the mix. A bank approached for a loan will make its evaluation of the request. If it agrees it will open a special loan account for the borrower and the sum lent will be credited to that account. The agreement may include a number of 'covenants' and will include the rate of interest payable and the duration of the loan. The rate may be fixed but more often it will be variable, i.e. fixed in terms of MLR, which itself is variable. The usual principle is that a fixed proportion of the principal sum, and interest charged on the original sum lent, will be repayable each month, so that if interest rates do not change the whole loan and interest and are repaid by equal instalments, the final payment being made on the final repayment date.

The amount of formality involved in arranging a loan will depend on the amount of the loan, the borrower, the security, the purposes for which the loan is required and the current financial climate. Even in periods of credit squeeze the government indicates to banks that loans for certain purposes should have priority, notably loans related to exports, or to improve manufacturing capacity, or to create additional employment in an area of high unemployment.

Distinction between interest calculated on 'opening' or 'reducing' balance
Care must be taken to ascertain the 'true' rate of interest on a loan. In the case of hire purchase agreements and most loans for fixed periods, interest is calculated on the original sum lent and in such cases the true

rate is approximately double the apparent rate since although the interest is charged on the full original loan or credit, this is only available to the borrower at the start. Thereafter, since each repayment includes a part of the principal, the amount available to the borrower steadily declines, until it is nil when the final repayment is made. The average principal sum available throughout is effectively half of the original total. In contrast, interest on overdrafts is payable on the 'reducing' balance, i.e. on the total outstanding at any time.

Loan agreements often contain 'covenants', restrictive clauses over and above any requirement for security . Usual ones limit loans which a borrower may obtain from other sources and may require that specified financial ratios should be maintained. The loan agreement normally provides that if any covenant is breached the whole loan becomes repayable at once. The negotiation of short-term loans tends to give rise to legal costs, payable by the borrower, and despite the fact that small to medium-sized companies may be required to provide ample security, they will still be charged higher interest rates than large companies of first-class financial standing. Furthermore, the larger companies are in stronger bargaining positions and have more options available.

Because of the different basis of interest payments, and the greater degree of formality involved in arranging a fixed-term loan, companies tend to prefer overdrafts, but as banks find loans more profitable, in practice bank managers are likely to insist that only a proportion of short-term finance needs are met by overdrafts, the balance being met by short-term loans. At times when interest rates are high and are expected to fall, borrowers will seek to avoid committing themselves on a long-term basis at high interest rates and will seek to make maximum use of overdrafts.

Short-term funds may also be obtained from finance houses but their charges are higher than those levied by the clearing banks: they are thus lenders of last resort for many borrowers. However, in special circumstances they may offer short-term funds on competitive terms, notably when a manufacturer is marketing a high-cost product in a very competitive market. The latter may act jointly with a finance house to offer attractive credit terms and a buyer of fixed assets may at such times find the cost of finance cheaper from this source than any other. In fact, the manufacturer will be bearing part of the costs. Vehicle sales are often stimulated in this way.

Credit cards

Banks and subsidiaries , and others, notably the American Express Co., offer credit card facilities. Originally these were orientated towards individuals but they are now being marketed to companies as well, on the basis that the company may nominate as many individuals as it chooses to hold personal cards and no matter how many are issued, the card company will at the end of each month provide the company with a single itemised invoice, showing the purchases by each cardholder, and expressed in sterling if made in some other currency. Without doubt, executives such as salesmen, directors, people who travel widely, find these cards convenient especially, e.g. if a change of plans has to be made on an overseas visit and additional airline tickets obtained. There can be considerable saving in administration work, and some useful credit, for user companies. The card company obtains most (sometimes all) of its revenues from commissions paid to it by the parties from whom the purchases are made.

Acceptance credits

These are widely and increasingly used by larger companies with sophisticated financial managements but less by smaller companies. It is a facility which offers flexibility in use and relative economy. An important advantage is that if a company negotiates a facility for a period of, say, three years, provided the company fulfils the terms of the agreement the facility cannot be withdrawn. The company would have access to an important source of working capital if a credit squeeze occurred at a time when overdrafts were being called in or were unobtainable.

The mechanisms of the facility involve: (a) the granting by a clearing or a specialist bank, a member of the Accepting Houses Committee, of a facility letter granting credit facilities by the bank to the company; and (b) the acceptance of bills of exchange by the bank. The Bills of Exchange Act, 1882, defines a bill of exchange as 'an unconditional order, in writing, addressed by one person to another, signed by the person giving it, requiring the person to whom it is addressed to pay on demand, or at a fixed or determinable future time, a sum certain in money to or to the order of a specified person or to bearer'. The same Act also defines a cheque as 'a bill of exchange drawn on a banker, payable on demand'. (A promissory note is defined as 'an unconditional promise in writing made by one person to another, signed by the marker, engaging to pay on demand, or at a fixed or determinable future time, a sum certain in money to, or to the order of, a specified person or to bearer'.) It is the acceptance by a bank of a bill of exchange which is the mechanism for making funds available.

A company seeking this facility would approach a bank and would be required to complete an application form and accompany this with the type of information indicated at the start of this chapter. The bank would wish to ensure that if it provided this facility it would not rank as a creditor after other banks which had granted overdrafts or loans against security. It would wish to satisfy itself about the cash flow of the company, its gearing and its return on capital and various other ratios.

After approving a facility, the bank concerned would issue a facility letter to the company. This would state: (*a*) the maximum amount drawable at any time, e.g. £500,000. This may be expressed in sterling or other currencies; (*b*) the life of the facility, e.g. 'until further notice', 'one year', 'three years', etc.; (*c*) the purpose for which the facility has been granted, e.g. to finance the purchase of raw materials; (*d*) the rate of charge, known as 'acceptance commission', payable to the bank for accepting bills of exchange, e.g. 1½% p.a.; (*e*) the arrangements for the drawing, accepting and renewing of bills of exchange; (*f*) the security, if any, and any other requirements of the bank. When agreed, the facility letter will signed by the bank and the company and it then becomes effective.

The procedures may be summarised as follows: (i) the company draws a bill of exchange and it may include a short note of the underlying transaction; (ii) the accepting bank endorses its 'acceptance' on the face of the bill and thereby undertakes to pay the bill at the proper time and it is this acceptance which makes the bill an 'eligible bank bill' which may be discounted in the London Discount Market at the 'prime bank bill rate' (which tends to move in step with MLR). In brief, the bill now becomes a negotiable instrument of the highest quality; (iii) a discount house will discount the bill if requested to do so – it would pay over the face value of the bill less a discount calculable from the formula:

Bankers discount

$$= \text{principal sum} \times \frac{\text{number of days}}{365} \times \frac{\text{annual rate of interest}}{100}$$

The rate of interest will be the current prime bank bill rate, which might be well below the current overdraft rate, and the number of days count from the date of the discounting to the date the bill is due for payment; (iv) the accepting bank pays the holder of the bill on the due date; (v) the company puts the accepting bank in funds, in accordance with the terms of the facility letter.

Bill of exchange have featured in foreign trade for many years, their 'tenor' or period often being 90 or 180 days. Some years ago it had been expected that their use would swiftly decline because of improvements in communications and new methods of making payments. In fact, the use of bills has increased, even for inland trade. Reasons for the continuing use of bills of exchange include the efficiency and adaptability of the established discount market to new circumstances: the fact that a bill is itself evidence of an obligation which does not need to be proved by means of other evidence which could possibly be challenged. The acceptance credit facility is an efficient means of augmenting working capital, and having assured access to this, even during periods of credit squeeze is a valuable facility, and the costs are often below those of overdrafts. Moreover, acceptance credits have permitted banks to extend profitable financing activities without breach of regulations or restrictions such as may be imposed by the government when it seeks to impose a credit squeeze.

Credit factoring
This is a financial service which for historical reasons first developed and then expanded in the USA. It was first vigorously marketed in the UK after the Second World War, but many of the earlier users were dissatisfied with their experiences. Subsequently the UK clearing banks, which aim to offer comprehensive financial services within the banking group of which they form a major part, recognised that the factoring service could be useful to their clients and profitable to the banks. The vast financial resources of these banking groups mean that when they decide to offer a service they are in a position to do so on a substantial scale from the start, purchasing established companies as necessary, so that they become subsidiaries, or purchasing shares in others, so that these become closely associated companies. Full use is then made of their 'know-how', contacts and UK and overseas branches, etc.

Credit factors offer three distinct services: (*a*) sales ledger administration and credit control; (*b*) insurance against bad debts; (*c*) if desired, advances of funds of up to 80% of an invoice total, so that the company would have 80% of its money from the date of the invoice and not the date of payment by the debtor, which would depend on the credit agreement and might be six weeks or so after the invoice date even if the debtor paid promptly. Factors' charges for the administration of the sales ledgers and acceptance of the bad-debt risk are said to be in the range of 0.75–2% of the company's factored turnover, depending on the volume of the work, the credit quality of the customers and the average size of each invoice. The optional service of advances against invoices involves a charge to the company of 2½–4% above MLR on the sums advanced, for the period from the date of the advance to the due date of payment. It thus resembles an overdraft charge. Factors will handle UK and/or overseas trade. They are discriminating in their choice of customers, who must sell to other traders and not to final consumers. They would examine a company's approved credit list and would not agree to accept as credit customers any whose status they considered doubtful. In principle, they are interested in working with companies with an annual turnover exceeding £100,000 by a good margin and likely to rise quickly.

Factoring appears interesting to companies whose managements are specialists in marketing and/or production and not finance, and who are selling a profitable product for which the demand is increasing. They may be short of working capital, and with anxieties about overtrading. If factoring seems possibly interesting – and it might be suggested by a bank manager who was being requested to extend overdraft facilities – a cost–benefit analysis would be called for. A bank manager would suggest a factor which was a subsidiary or associate of the bank. Important benefits include the savings on sales administration and credit control and the insurance against bad debts. The management of the company would concentrate on expanding production and sales. Furthermore, if it became evident that the company was outgrowing the capacity of its fixed assets, and it needed long-term funds to finance expansion, the company's banker and the factor would both have an interest in putting their experience and 'know-how', and contacts, at the service of the company. They would introduce the directors to their associated merchant bank and to possible sources of equity capital or long-term loans and would help in the presentation of an effective case.

Disadvantages of credit factoring are said to be that a company may become too dependent on the service and find it difficult to dispense with it if it later wished to do so. Customers might object to their accounts being handled by a factor and there might be loss of contact with customers. These problems seem easily soluble insofar as the company should arrange to maintain customer contact and can point out that the use of factoring is assisting the company in its expansion programme and achievement of delivery dates and high standards of after-sales service, etc. It is also said that banks are more reluctant to approve overdraft facilities if a factor is employed. It would seem reasonable that the bank should take all relevant matters into account, but especially when the bank and the factor are members of the same banking group one would expect the bank manager to be helpful, reasonable and flexible in his dealings with the company.

Invoice discounting

This is a financial service available to companies which might not qualify for credit factoring. It is a long-established service in the UK, offered by finance houses. The company has to undertake its own sales ledger and credit control and bear the risks of bad debts. The service is that the finance house advances up to 80% of invoices and the company repays the advance when the invoice is paid. The charge is normally 2½–4% above MLR. The service is easier to arrange than factoring and tends to be used by smaller companies: there is no problem about ending the service whenever desired as the company is not dependent on the invoice discounter for his sales administration: he will already be doing this himself. In brief, it is a financial option available as a source of short-term funds: use by a company of this service would result in restriction of the bank overdraft facilities available to it.

Hire purchase

This facility is well known because it is so often used by individuals. In effect, an asset may be hired with an option to purchase and the practical arrangements are that the period of the hire purchase, the cash price and the rate of interest are taken into account and a buyer pays equal agreed instalments: each has two components: (*a*) a part of the cost price, and (*b*) interest. It is payment of the final instalment which exercises the buyer's option to purchase and until then the asset belongs to the supplier. The Hire Purchase Acts, devised to protect ill-informed consumers, do not normally cover the more substantial assets purchased by companies, which are presumed able to inform themselves properly of the terms of an agreement. In times of rising prices a company which is short of funds, and does not wish to lease an asset, may find a hire purchase contract beneficial since the asset is acquired at an agreed price which would not be affected by subsequent price rises. Sometimes suppliers or manufacturers offer very favourable hire purchasing terms in order to boost sales. Earlier acquiring of a productive asset may enable a company to generate a positive cash flow earlier than it could otherwise have done. Leasing would have the same effect and often hire purchase and leasing are two interesting options for a company.

A company wishing to examine the options of hire purchase or leasing of an asset which it wishes to acquire quickly but lacks cash for outright purchase must examine the taxation implications, which may be decisive. Hire purchase interest is allowed as an expense against corporation tax and the company would qualify immediately for capital allowances, and regional grants, if any, in respect of the cost price of the asset. Hire purchase is normally quickly and easily arranged, the asset remaining in the ownership of the supplier until the final payment. Hire purchase liabilities would be taken into account by a banker called upon to agree to loan or overdraft facilities, as would be expected. In brief, hire purchase may have a useful but limited role as a source of short- to medium-term finance.

Leasing

Leasing of property has been widespread in the UK for many years but leasing of industrial assets developed first in the USA and began in a small way in the UK in the 1960s. An early prejudice against leasing, which is still sometimes met, arises from the fact that payments must be made continually for the use of an asset and yet a company never owns it, and as the asset does not appear in the balance sheet the total security available for prospective lenders is reduced. It is now recognised that from the operating aspect what is important to a company is not the ownership of an asset but the right to undisturbed use of it for as long as desired. In principle a company which seeks to have the use of a certain asset which is available either for purchase or leasing will have three options: (*a*) to acquire the asset at once by cash payment; (*b*) to acquire it on a hire purchase basis; (*c*) to lease it, accepting that the company would never own the asset.

The evaluation will not be difficult for a technically qualified person and use will be made of discounted cash flow (DCF) methods, taking the timings of cash receipts and payments carefully into account, the rate(s) of interest applicable and the taxation factor, which can be decisive. Examination questions often state that taxation should be ignored but in real situations it can never be, and not least when leasing is being considered. Because the taxation aspect may change from year to year the balance of advantage between purchase, hire purchase and leasing is also liable to change and each situation will require expert evaluation as it arises. Banks are closely involved with leasing for two major reasons: (*a*) to permit the banking group as a whole to offer a comprehensive range of financial services it must include leasing—it is too important and profitable to be ignored; (*b*) it is a major means of legitimately obtaining deferment of payment of large sums of corporation tax, which the banks would otherwise have to pay promptly to the Inland Revenue.

Definitions

The Equipment Leasing Association defines: 'a lease is a contract between lessor and lessee for hire of a specific asset selected from a manufacturer or vendor of such assets by the lessee. The lessor retains ownership of the asset. The lessee has possession and use of the asset on payment of specified rentals over a period.' The Association further comments that within this broad definition there are two sub-divisions, *finance leases* (sometimes known as full pay-out leases) and *operating leases*:

A finance lease is a contract involving payment over an obligatory period (sometimes called the primary or basic period) of specified sums sufficient in total to amortise the capital outlay of the lessor and give some profit. The obligatory period is less than, or at most equal to, the estimated life of the asset. The lessee is normally responsible for the maintenance of the asset. There may be a secondary period. If so, it is optional (at the option of the lessee) and the rentals are reduced in amount. An operating lease is a contract where the asset is not wholly amortised during the obligatory period (if any) of the lease and where the lessor does not rely for his profit on the rentals in the obligatory period. In some operating leases the lessor is responsible for maintenance.

Features of most leases are: (*a*) leases are normally with commercial customers for the use of income producing assets. They are not intended for consumer transactions; (*b*) payments (often called rentals) are usually made in equal amounts and at equal intervals (but many lessors will vary this at the request of the lessee); (*c*) since the asset was acquired at the request of the lessee, the lessor has no responsibility for its suitability or condition; (*d*) it is a condition of most leases that the lessee is responsible for arranging insurance. This may cover not only fire, theft and damage to the asset itself, but possibly also injury to third parties and other risks; (*e*) provided that the lessee punctually fulfils his obligations the lessor may not require accelerated or varied payments, nor terminate the lease; (*f*) when the lessor obtains any grants or allowances arising from the purchase of the asset, he is liable in the event of any breach by the lessee of the conditions under which grants or allowances are available – though by a term of the lease he may seek to recover from the lessee.

Advantages of leasing
In summary, the advantages of leasing include:
(*a*) The need to tie up capital is much reduced and an income generating asset may quickly be brought into use and this income may substantially exceed the leasing and other costs.

(b) Budget planning – the fixed and regular payments involved assist cash flow forecasting and budgeting. As the lessee is not concerned with grants, allowances, depreciation or other calculations it becomes easier for him to evaluate the costs and benefits of a project.

(c) The lessee selects the assets he requires and if he can obtain discounts the lease will reflect this: each lease is tailor-made and the facility, which is of medium-term nature, offers flexibility. Once agreed, a subsequent credit squeeze presents no problems in relation to the asset. Whilst some lessor are prepared to offer flexible terms so that adjustments are made to the leasing payments as and when interest rates change, most lessors and lessees prefer terms fixed at the start.

(d) Sounder replacement decisions may be made. When a machine is owned and continues in use after it has been fully depreciated in the accounts there may be reluctance to replace it with a superior new model whose introduction would lead to improved cash flow. Ownership can blur a clear appreciation of the factors relevant to a replacement decision.

(e) Leasing is a simple and convenient way of financing capital assets, with minimum formality.

(f) There is maximum finance availability as leasing normally provides for 100% of the asset costs.

(g) Risk matching – the lessor retains ownership of an asset, of which the lessee makes productive use. In effect, leasing is a facility which may permit assets to be brought into use despite a lack of risk capital. Even a very high-cost asset such as the 'Concorde' airliner has been marketed primarily on a leasing basis.

(h) Grants, allowances and discounts: as competition between lessors is keen, all benefits obtained by them tend to be passed to the lessees in the form of lower leasing charges in respect of new contracts. The tax allowance treatment is often decisive, not least if a prospective lessee does not have profits liable to tax, in which case he cannot obtain the immediate benefits of capital allowances. In such cases evaluations usually favour leasing.

(i) Tax relief – rentals payable are normally wholly allowable expenses.

(j) Hedges against inflation. This is a most important factor. Leasing allows an asset to be brought into use before prices rise further, and the rental for the future will be fixed and based on the price when the asset was leased.

Disadvantages of leasing
The massive expansion of leasing within the past few years points to the

overall advantages, not least to lessees who may lack funds for outright purchase. However, in 1979 the Bank of England signified that it will be keeping leasing under close review. It is evident:

(a) that the tax aspects have been encouraging profitable companies and wealthy individuals to become lessors merely to obtain tax benefits. The scope for wealthy individuals has already been removed. Meanwhile, the tax liability is deferred rather than eliminated and if there were a sudden downturn in leasing activity many lessors could find themselves called upon to make tax payments for which they were not prepared. An influx of greedy, inexperienced newcomers could lead to instability just as the explosive growth of secondary banks did in the early 1970s.

(b) The ease and convenience of the facility and 'hard selling' of it by inexperienced lessors may result in imprudent managements entering into leasing commitments without proper evaluations and committing their companies to a medium-term liability which fails to generate the expected cash flow. The company has a liability to the lessor who can recover the asset in case of need. Meanwhile, the lessee has a continuing financial obligation which the lessor can pursue through the courts.

(c) Another problem is the treatment of leases in the accounting records. This is a somewhat controversial matter but the majority view appears to be that leased assets should not feature in the balance sheet of a lessee, which should only show owned assets (which, may, in fact, be charged in respect of borrowings). Leases are 'off balance sheet' items and as the law requires that a company balance sheet and profit-and-loss accounts give a 'true and fair' view, this cannot be done if there is concealment of the liabilities. When a company holds significant assets on a leasing basis the position should be indicated in an explanatory note attached to the accounts, and auditors should insist that this is done. It is understood that about 70% of leases are for 3–5 year periods.

Medium-term loans

Competition amongst lenders has been increasing in recent years and an important new element has been provided by the increasing activities of the US banks operating in the City. Apart from the strength of their resources and their worldwide outlets, the American and other overseas-owned banks enjoy an important advantage over the UK clearing banks. They do not have to meet the heavy fixed costs of operating a network of branches in the UK. Consequently they can seek out potential large-scale borrowers of the highest credentials and offer these loans at the lowest rates. In brief, they act as wholesalers rather than retailers of money and can be selective in their choice of clients. They are said to take initiatives and, for example, approach people reported to have obtained important export projects, offering a financial package' and paying more attention to the aspect of cash flow than the security available.

Companies require medium-term finance – which is generally considered as covering a period between three and ten years – for: (a) financing the purchase of assets with a medium-term life, notably much plant and machinery; (b) supplementing working capital likely to be needed for an extended period; (c) funding overdrafts, e.g. especially if a period of credit squeeze is foreseen or a bank manager insists that existing overdraft facilities should be reduced. A special problem of finance managers now is that in recent years interest rates have been (a) at historically high levels, and (b) have fluctuated widely and even within periods of several months only. Companies reporting to the Wilson Committee stressed this problem. They naturally are reluctant to commit themselves to high interest rates for longer periods than necessary if there should be any prospect of their falling and remaining lower in the future. It is equally a difficult time for lenders, who have the opposite viewpoint – they wish to commit themselves to lending on a medium- to long-term basis when they think rates are at their highest and are likely to fall. A feature of times when it is almost impossible to be confident about the future movements of interest rates is that people avoid long-term commitments unless they appear to offer exceptional promise, or cannot be avoided. This is surely a main reason why in recent years so may companies have been limiting their investment in new projects.

Reports to the Wilson Committee also stressed the importance attributed to cash forecasts and 'payback' and the reservations held about the usefulness of evaluations by discounted cash flow methods (DCF), which depend so much on assumptions which cannot now be trusted. Many companies which in the past have issued long-term debentures – say 15 to 20 year terms – now resort to medium-term finance. Main sources of loans are the clearing banks as well as merchant banks, overseas banks and certain other specialist financial institutions, of which FCI and ICFC are well known, the former dealing with larger companies and the latter with medium-sized and smaller ones. Medium-term loans tend to be dearer than short-term loans as the borrower has the benefit that the lender commits his money irrevocably for a longer period, provided that there is no default in any of the agreed conditions. Borrowers and lenders are aware that a major effect of inflation is to reduce the true cost of borrowing to the advantage of the borrower and high interest rates, in inflation-adjusted terms, are seen as involving a partial repayment of real capital. The tax treatment also benefits the borrower – provided he has taxable profits – but, as the Wilson Committee reported, borrowers are deterred by high nominal interest rates despite their awareness that inflation is reducing the real cost of borrowing.

Medium-term loans may give rise to a negotiation fee and legal costs. A degree of formality is involved and an intending borrower would enquire about costs and formalities at the outset. Interest on medium-term loans used to be at fixed rates and may still be, but variable rates are now more common, e.g. at six months Inter Bank Rate and plus 1½ up to 4%, the exact rate depending on the status of the borrower. Borrowers bear in mind that interest rates may fall and in this event they would wish to take advantage of the lower rates available: they may seek to negotiate an early repayment clause in the agreement and if a lender were prepared to agree such a clause he would expect some benefit in return, a prescribed penalty or cost. This would be substantially higher in the case of fixed-interest loans.

Long-term loans

Long-term loans are generally regarded as those which have a duration of 10 years or longer. The pace of change and evolution is indicated by the fact that a few years ago a clearing bank would hesitate to agree to loans of more than 5 years' term. This was extended to 7 years and then 10 and in 1979 the Midland Bank announced that in special circumstances, and for smaller companies, it would consider loans of up to 20 years' duration. Formerly, UK clearing banks were not regarded as possible sources of long-term loans but this position is clearly changing now.

Main reasons for long-term financing

Companies require long-term finance for: (*a*) financing the purchase of major fixed assets with a long life; (*b*) providing the 'hard core' of working capital, the balance being financed with a mix of overdrafts, short- and medium-term finance; (*c*) for financing take-overs or other major long-term extensions of the business. A company will always keep the gearing under close review and if necessary may take advantage of temporarily favourable market conditions to make a 'rights issue', to 'broaden its equity base' prior to raising long-term loans.

Main sources of long-term finance

Main sources of long-term finance include: (*a*) possibly increasingly, the clearing banks – this is a still-evolving situation; (*b*) merchant banks, who tend to act as intermediaries rather than as principals; (*c*) insurance companies; (*d*) pension funds; (*e*) other British and overseas banks; (*f*) specialist institutions such as FCI, ICFC and possibly the National Enterprise Board (NEB) and certain other public-sector institutions. Reports to the Wilson Committee suggested the existence of a gap in the maturity range of long-term loans, the banks being reluctant at present to lend for more than 10 years and the institutions preferring to lend for longer than 20 years. However, Finance for Industry (FFI), through its subsidiaries FCI and ICFC, has been prepared to make funds available for 10 to 20 years but reports that demands for such loans has been limited. It appears that the decline has been on the demand and not the supply side: the institutions have been prepared to lend on a long-term basis as the success of the gilt-edged market shows, but companies have been deterred from long-term borrowing by inflation, uncertainty about the economic outlook and high nominal interest rates. The Wilson Committee were told that the market in industrial loan stocks was unlikely to revive 'unless inflation and long-term interest rates are brought down to single figures'.

Although companies in general may be limiting investment and reluctant to borrow on a long-term basis, there will always be a proportion which is prepared to act against the trend, possibly because of exceptional confidence in their own situation and in some cases because there seems no alternative. In principle, when interest rates are very high it becomes virtually impossible for many projects to show sufficient promise of profitability to justify the risks which would be involved.

A criticism of insurance companies and pension funds as long-term lenders has been that they will only lend in large sums and to large companies of first-class status. This reduces their administrative and monitoring requirements and reduces their costs. Sometimes insurance companies lend to smaller companies provided that directors take out life insurance policies on a 'without-profit' basis, a type of policy which investors should avoid because it is so unrewarding to the holder because of the effects of inflation. In general, the negotiation of a long-term loan takes time – not less than four months should be allowed – and there will normally be legal and negotiation fees. A lender sometimes requires a condition that he must have an option to convert all or part of the loan into equity capital of the borrowing company. A company which owns land and buildings may negotiate a mortgage debenture against the security of these assets. The maximum lent is normally not more than two-thirds of the market value. Against this background it is not surprising that the less formal procedure of leasing has grown so quickly in popularity.

Sale and leaseback

The technique of sale and leaseback has been associated particularly with the late Sir Charles Clore who used it successfully in the 1950s. Companies with substantial properties as fixed assets, notably retail shops, were taken over. Usually the companies taken over had been obtaining poor returns on capital employed and after the take-overs a substantial proportion of the properties were sold to insurance companies on the basis that the seller continued in the occupation and use of the properties – they were leased back – as a tenant and not owner, with the rental terms subject to periodic review. Like many effective ideas it was a simple one. The arrangements offered important advantages for both of the parties. An institution, such as an insurance company or pension fund, will seek to invest a proportion of its long-term assets in good-quality commercial property since this is possibly the best 'hedge against inflation' in the long run. The institution requires income as well as capital appreciation, and good property and tenants, and regular rent reviews, so that rents rise at least in step with general price rises, provide reliable and steadily rising income.

The party which sells the property on the basis that it continues in occupation as a tenant has the advantage that it continues to have the use of an asset, and the capital proceeds of the sale can produce a substantially higher return when utilised to develop and expand the trading activities of the company. The sale proceeds normally include significant capital profit and this, in effect, represents an injection of equity capital without requiring the ordinary shareholders to contribute additional funds. Sales and leasebacks of property therefore continue to occur. A company which is considering selling a valuable property on this basis must naturally evaluate its position carefully before committing itself to an irrevocable decision. As always, the tax aspect must be expertly considered, including the aspect of any capital gains liability. Favourable aspects include that the company would receive a substantial injection of cash and with no ultimate repayment obligation. The asset would continue in use. with an obligation to pay rental, which would be allowable as an expense against tax. Costs would be incurred in the valuing and sale negotiations.

A sale – leaseback gives rise to important balance-sheet changes. At the moment of sale the fixed assets would be reduced and cash would be increased by the same amount, less any expenses which would be written off to the profit-and-loss account. The company would become more liquid but analysts would note that there was now less security available for existing and future creditors. The sale would also mean that the company would no longer own an asset of steadily appreciating value, whose sale would give rise to an even larger capital gain in the future. A company considering a sale-leaseback would also have the option of raising a loan by means of a mortgage debenture. Adoption of this option would result in a cash injection of about two-thirds of the market value of the property, at most. The company would also have an obligation to make interest payments in the future (which could be compared with the rentals) as well as to repay the principal in due course. However, the company would retain the ownership of the property, whose value should steadily increase. A sale and leaseback and a borrowing by means of a mortgage debenture are fundamentally different transactions, of course.

Eurocurrency loans

Business finance is international in scope and larger organisations take advantage of this fact in a way which is not practical for smaller ones. In this field, as in others, there are many advantages arising from size, provided that the organisation concerned enjoys good credit standing and, in the case of a private-sector company, is doing well. There are far more options available to the bigger organisations and they can also raise equity capital or loans at signficantly lower cost than smaller organisations can do, no matter how sound the latter may be. An option open to the UK Government, to nationalised industries and to major companies is to borrow in Europe or the USA – at present the main potential sources of loans. This is a complex subject and conditions are liable to change and evolve steadily. It is a specialist field and students need at least to have an awareness of the background and in their topical reading should take note whenever they see references to significant developments.

Eurobond issues are bond issues which will be underwritten and sold in more than one market simultaneously. The interest rates tend to be lower than the prevailing equivalent rates in the UK. Bonds are normally payable to bearer in accordance with Continental practice and interest is paid gross, except in the case of UK based issues, i.e. tax is not deducted by the borrower for payment by him to the tax authorities, as is normally the case in the UK. It is thus left to the lender to deal directly with the appropriate tax authority and if he evades tax, this is no concern of the borrower.

A major problem and risk of a UK company borrowing in terms of a currency such as the Swiss franc or German deutschmark is that the loan has to be repaid in the currency borrowed, and the interest must also be paid in that currency. If the borrowed currency appreciates in relation to sterling, the loan could prove extremely costly to the borrower, even if the nominal interest rates were very low. In principle a borrower takes great, even potentially ruinous, risks if he borrows sums which are large in relation to his own resources in a currency other than his own, unless he owns assets in the overseas country concerned and has a positive cash flow in it. In that case he would have income and assets which match his currency liabilities. For example, a UK hotel group owning hotels in Switzerland could safely borrow Swiss francs so long as the income in francs was adequate to cover the interest payments and in due course the repayment of the principal.

For a time in 1977/78 when sterling was appreciating in relation to other major currencies it became practicable to issue Eurosterling bonds and some major UK companies did so at interest rates about 2% below the current UK rate. However, when sterling weakened this market virtually collapsed. However, following the appreciation of sterling, as it is now a 'petrocurrency' there are signs of renewed activity. In principle there can only be an active Eurosterling bond market in the event that international investors have confidence that sterling will be able to maintain its value in relation to other major currencies over a period of years.

A common term of issue of a Eurocurrency loan is 5 to 8 years. These issues are often known as 'notes' and issues for a term of 12 to 15 years are known as 'bonds'. Interest rates are normally fixed for the period of the loan but floating-rate issues are also made. UK banks borrow substantially on the basis of floating rates as one of their sources of funds for their overseas activities. In general, Eurobond issues will be to raise a minimum sum of US$10 m. and the maximum sum would be much higher. Issues are arranged by a lead manager, a bank which is a specialist in this field. Large issues may be organised by a consortium of major banks under a lead bank. Issue costs will be very substantial and many are relatively fixed so that they are proportionately much less for a larger loan. This is a main reason why this area of finance is of direct interest only to substantial borrowers. Bond issues are marketable but as the markets are imperfect many are held to maturity.

Questions

1. Discuss the advantages and disadvantages of leasing as a source of finance. (ICSA 22 marks)
2. A company which tends to raise additional funds in the present financial circumstances might do so by mortgaging its freehold commercial property or by a sale and leaseback of the property. Describe these two methods of raising finance and discuss the advantages and disadvantages of each one. (ACCA 20 marks)
3. Explain what you understand by the term 'leasing fixed assets'. Explain the advantages and disadvantages of leasing rather than buying capital equipment. (SCCA 20 marks)
4. Your company is contemplating acquiring an asset and has the choice of the following three methods: (1) ownership, (2) hire purchase and (3) leasing. List the factors for and against each method. (SCCA 20 marks)
5. Businesses frequently have the choice between selling certain of their assets (e.g. sale and leaseback of property, sale of investments) or using them as collateral for advances (e.g. bank loans, mortgages) as a means of raising additional working capital. What factors would you take into account if asked to advise a company as to which course it should follow? (ACCA 20 marks)
6. A successful and expanding company with profits before tax of £150,000 which finds its rate of growth restricted by lack of capital asks your advice as to how and where it may obtain both additional working and fixed capital. Set out the advice you would give, assuming such facts concerning the company as are necessary for your answer. (ICA 20 marks)
7. The board of a manufacturing company has decided to replace machine tools at a cost of £200,000. It has ample borrowing facilities but you are asked whether the machine tools should be leased. What are the main considerations you would present to the board in advising which course to adopt? (ACCA 20 marks)
8. Public corporations, local authorities and companies have raised foreign-currency loans to finance their domestic activities in the UK. What are the advantages and disadvantages of this source of funds from the point of view of (*a*) the borrowers listed above, and (*b*) the United Kingdom economy? (ACCA 20 marks)

Chapter 11

Government assistance to industry and some private sector initiatives

The declining role of the private investor as a source of risk capital and the more cautions attitude of investment managers of institutions towards risk have been considered as well as the controversy as to whether promising ideas for new companies have had to be abandoned because risk capital could not be obtained from any source – main area of study by the Wilson Committee. There is also debate as to why so many – but by no means all – UK manufacturers have difficulty in competing in overseas markets and why so many consumer and other manufactured goods are imported into the UK rather than made by UK companies. The increasing share of imports, including of the newer, profitable high-technology products causes concern because of the adverse effects on the UK balance of payments and also the decline in employment of UK workpeople. There is also the worldwide decline in the older, traditional basic industries, steel, shipbuilding, etc., which, in the UK as well as elsewhere, creates special hardship and social problems as the effects are felt most heavily in densely populated areas where there has been heavy public and private expenditure on the infrastructure in the past but much of this is now below acceptable standards. There is now also, in the UK and elsewhere, a desire to encourage small businesses on the grounds that they will be more labour intensive than larger ones, and more flexible.

This chapter will consider briefly the wide range of government incentives and assistance made available to companies by various means on either a national or regional or local basis. Most governments of industrialised countries now operate schemes designed to induce overseas-based companies to establish factories likely to generate employment, in addition to schemes designed to encourage their own nationals to invest and create more jobs. Indeed, there is ample evidence that major multinational companies on occasion 'play off' one government against another when they are proposing to build a large new factory and it would be feasible for it to be built in any one of several countries. Investors, inventors and others who do not feel necessarily committed to work in their own country may also find it worth while to 'shop around' and ascertain what incentives – grants, tax holidays, interest-free loans, low-rent factories, etc – different countries may be prepared to offer.

This is a changing and evolving field and in the UK changes are liable to occur especially after a change of government, in view of the different political philosophies of the two major parties. Students and others therefore need to be aware of general principles and the sources from which information can be obtained as to the current position.

Assisted areas

In the UK (and other EEC member countries) certain regions and places present special problems. Many are in the North, in areas which had their comparative prosperity during the expansion following the Industrial Revolution, when heavy industries had to be established close to sources of power, at that time coal and, to a lesser extent, water, and raw materials such as iron ore. These areas have now declined since newer, lighter industries can now be concentrated closer to markets and, in the UK, in the more prosperous and congenial South East and London areas. Although workpeople who become unemployed, and school-leavers, are now able to take advantage of state-sponsored training programmes, and mobility is also encouraged, it is not surprising that many older workpeople and their families do not wish to uproot themselves and move homes and, because of housing shortages and costs, it would often be impracticable for them to move to another part of the country even if they were prepared to do so. Accordingly, special government schemes have been designed to bring jobs to people.

Despite the problems and limitations, the measures have met with some, but inevitably limited success. It is open to question whether there has always been sufficient discrimination and attention to cost effectiveness. For example, massive financial benefits have been granted to wealthy oil companies which established terminals in a deep-water harbour in a qualifying area, even though the site would have been chosen anyway because of its natural advantages. Moreover, comparatively little employment was being generated. In principle, government assistance to industry has been specially directed to development and expansion in places of heaviest unemployment and industrial decline, known as 'assisted areas'. There are three types, in decreasing order of priority: (*a*) special development areas (*b*) development areas; (*c*) intermediate areas. In brief, Regional Development Grants, cash payments in respect of capital expenditure on new buildings, plant and machinery, may be available. Under the Industry Act, 1972, loans may be available on preferential terms, together with removal grants, interest relief grants and rent concessions in respect of projects designed to safeguard or improve employment prospects. Loans may also be available from the European Investment Bank. Special and exceptionally generous measures are available for investors who establish qualifying projects in Northern Ireland.

Grants and allowances may be available in respect of workers transferred and whilst these would be payable to individuals they represent costs which the employer would normally otherwise have to meet. The Welsh Development Agency (WDA) and the Scottish Development Agency (SDA) deal with projects in Wales and Scotland respectively and the Highlands and Islands Development Board deals with the Scottish Islands and Highlands areas. These three public-sector bodies may be able to make some equity capital as well as loans available in appropriate cases. They have significant freedom of action, but there are signs that this may be reduced.

Local authority and other public-sector sources

Local councils have powers to offer financial assistance in certain circumstances. These can include improvement grants, derating schemes, industrial site preparation and the provision of advance factories. Naturally, schemes of this type are encouraged in places where the attraction of new industry has a priority. Certain regions have Industrial Development Associations, and there are also a number of New Towns which often place large advertisements in leading newspapers. Comprehensive information is given in the Bank of England's 'Money for Business'.

Whilst special government-funded assistance is made available to encourage UK and overseas industrialists to set up factories in areas with special problems, the fact is that for some years the UK government has been concerned at the relative lack of new industrial investment. Accordingly, special investment incentives are available throughout the country. Two are in respect of tax allowances (a) up to 100% of expenditure on plant and machinery (First Year Allowance) and 50% on industrial buildings (Initial Allowance) can be set against taxable profits in the year in which the expenditure is incurred, and if this exceeds the taxable profits the excess may to some extent be carried back and set off against earlier profits or carried forward and set off against future profits. The effect is (a) to defer tax payments – indefinitely if the company has a heavy capital investment programme each year – and to improve the cash flow: (b) stock appreciation relief – a major problem in inflationary times is the rising cost of holding given volumes of stocks. Stock relief enables a company to set off a large part of any increase in the cost of holding stocks against taxable profits and their treatment is similar to that for capital allowances.

Assistance on a selective basis may be given under Section 8 of the Industry Act, 1972, and there are a number of special schemes, including some designed to assist particularly hard-pressed industries. Special regional or industrial assistance may also be provided by the EEC, to which the UK is a major contributor. Although changes occur it seems a reasonable assumption that government assistance of some kind will always be available, especially at times of high unemployment, such as at present, and a company planning to begin or expand a project would be well advised to obtain the latest information from the Department of Industry.

Assistance for small firms

Following the work of the Bolton Committee in the early 1970s, a good deal of attention has been given in the UK to the needs and problems of small firms. There is a Small Firms Division within the Department of Industry and a number of Small Firms Information Centres sited strategically in England, Scotland and Wales. Expertly written booklets and subsidised consultancy services are also available. The Wilson Committee published a report on 'The financing of small firms' in 1979. As all of the UK political parties support in principle, or pay lip service to the idea of the encouragement of small businesses, which clearly have special problems, not least in respect of raising equity or loans, it can be expected that government and private-sector assistance to this sector will increase rather than diminish. It is an area of debate and a variety of new ideas are now being discussed.

Financial institutions in the public and private sectors

The problems of entrepreneurs and others who wish to raise equity or loans have been considered. It is possible that the change to a

Conservative government in 1979 with a marked emphasis on encouragement of the individual and initiated with massive cuts in the upper levels of income tax, will over a period lead to a re-emergence of individuals as substantial investors and some relative decline in the institutional role: however, it seems certain that the institutions will continue to dominate as sources of finance for the foreseeable future. Within the public sector the National Enterprise Board (NEB) had a major role under the former Labour government, which established it, but its role has been much reduced under the present Conservative government. Initially there were doubts as to whether it would be allowed to survive but it now appears that the NEB will continue to have a significant role not least as an agency available to handle difficult situations whilst the government decides its long-term intentions in respect of a particular company or industry. The Scottish and Welsh Development Agencies have also been noted. All are required to seek an adequate return on capital, recognising that there are bound to be some failures but the profits on the successes will, hopefully, compensate for these. CoSIRA (Council for Small Industries in Rural Areas) has the primary objective of helping the regeneration of rural areas in England and can provide a wide range of financial and other assistance. The British Steel Corporation (Industry) Ltd has been formed by the British Steel Corporation to attract new industry to areas where steelmaking jobs are disappearing in consequence of the Corporation's modernisation programme. A range of financial and other incentives can be provided with the aim of creating new jobs. EEC sources may also make funds available for this purpose and it is evident that there is not enough awareness of what is available.

Finance for Industry (FFI) and its subsidiaries

A number of private-sector institutions may provide loan funds and in some cases equity as well. Financial for Industry (FFI) is the holding company of the Industrial and Commercial Financial Corporation (ICFC) and the Finance Corporation for Industry (FCI), the shareholders being the English and Scottish clearing banks (85%) and the Bank of England (15%). The former specialises in the needs of small and medium-sized companies and the latter in the needs of larger ones. Other FFI subsidiaries are Technical Development Corporation (TDC) which deals mainly with high-risk ventures, and Estate Duties Investment Trust (EDITH) which may provide finance for heirs of major shareholders who have a taxation liability but whose money is tied up in a family-owned company so that time will be needed before cash can be released to meet the liability.

Equity Capital for Industry (ECI)
Equity Capital for Industry (ECI) was formed in 1976 with private-sector capital and partly for the purpose of invalidating left-wing criticism that industrialists were not investing on a sufficient scale in the UK because the finance was unobtainable. (It was at this time that the Wilson Committee was set up in part to examine this question). In brief, ECI was intended to have two main roles: (*a*) to provide finance to viable companies whose needs could not be met through normal market channels; and (*b*) a secondary role of assisting institutional investors by giving advice (for fees) about the effectiveness of the management of a particular company which was giving rise to concern to its institutional investors. Up to 1980 ECI's role appears to have been limited and its future has seemed uncertain. It has been overshadowed by the NEB but this situation could conceivably change.

It was originally envisaged that the types of problems in respect of which ECI might play a constructive role include:

(*a*) Where a company requires equity capital but cannot make a rights issue for technical reasons, for example because the shares stand close to or below par value. It is normally difficult, if not impossible, to make a rights issue successfully in such circumstances. In such cases ECI might subscribe for convertible preference shares, the terms to include conversion at a price somewhat in excess of par.

(*b*) Underwriters might be insufficiently interested because of a very narrow market in the shares e.g. because of large family holdings and the holders could not take up their rights.

(*c*) The company had become overgeared and the amount required to redress the position is more than the market is willing to provide. (The maximum which can normally be provided by a rights issue is 1 for 4 or, exceptionally, 1 for 3). Here again, the device of a convertible preference share might meet the interests of ECI and the present shareholders.

(*d*) Because of an indifferent recent trading record the shares might seem unattractive to underwriters but there seem good prospects of future profitability.

(*e*) The company might lack a Stock Exchange listing and the amount required might be more than could be provided by ICFC or similar institution.

Some problems of institutional investors – ECI
There is also a problem in that when an institution is an important shareholder and it becomes dissatisfied with the performance of a

company its position is technically that of an ordinary shareholder and it has no right to seek or obtain information which is not available to all of the shareholders. It may therefore be difficult for an institutional manager to make effective representations to the top management of a company which is causing concern. Yet if an institution decides simply to 'cut its losses' and sell the shares, the sale itself, of a significant number of shares, could cause a sharp fall in the market price and thus damage the interests of the seller. It was thus envisaged that an important subsidiary role for ECI, possibly in conjunction with the Institutional Shareholders' Committee, could be, on request by one or more institutions, and on payment of appropriate fees, to investigate and advise when there was concern about a company in which there was institutional investment on some scale.

Small Business Capital Funds (SBCF)

SBCF was formed with the financial backing of the Co-operative Insurance Society with the intention of providing risk capital and perhaps also some loan funds for 'young' or even new, promising small companies, which could not obtain sufficient funds from the promoters or normal market sources, or by means of profit retentions. SBCF would be prepared to take a 5–10 year view and would allow interest on loans to 'roll over' and it would not expect dividends in the early years, to assist the cash flow at the most difficult and critical time. SBCF seeks its return through capital appreciation of its equity stake. At an appropriate time, in consultation with the major shareholders, it would sell its equity stake when the company was established and use the cash so obtained for reinvestment in another company which had made a good case for it and the cycle would recommence. However, because of the administrative costs involved SBCF does not invest in very small companies, and the Wilson Committee confirmed that these do have special problems, which were considered in a special report (Ch. 25).

'Moracrest', 'Mentor' and 'Prutech'

In recent years directors of institutions, investment and pension fund managers have been seeking, in small but significant ways, to create new types of organisations which can go some way towards solving problems and meeting identified needs which appear not to be fully met through the normal operation of the market. The situation is complex and evolving. Those closely concerned with the workings of insurance companies, pension funds, etc., are aware that the vast and increasing sums of money under their control are raising politically sensitive issues. At the same time they hold the view that their primary responsibility is to their investors: they seek profitable investment and are ready to take some, but not excessive, risks. 'Moracrest' is an early example of three major and socially aware institutions devising a new type of institution. It was founded in 1977 as a joint venture by the Midland Bank, the Prudential Assurance Company and the British Gas Central Pension Fund. The Pension Fund and the Prudential both have very strong cash flows and need profitable and prudent short-, medium- and long-term investment with adequate diversification. The principle of diversification would permit that a small proportion of the funds, which would still be large in total, could prudently be invested in high-risk situations. A factor influencing the formation of Moracrest was presumably the political climate at the time. Left-wing politicians were claiming that institutional funds were not being managed with a proper sense of social responsibility and a Labour government ought to take powers to direct the investment of funds. Understandably, fund managers found this an unacceptable proposal (as did many Labour supporters who were pension-fund trustees) and, as realists, some of them recognised that the best way to 'defuse' or frustrate left-wing pressures for direction of investment would be to demonstrate that initiatives were being taken and fund managers were making funds available to industrialists with a good case but which nevertheless presented problems and risks.

Until the formation of Moracrest a problem of the major institutions had been lack of machinery to evaluate and then administer and monitor what to them would be small investments but which, to the company invested in, would be large ones. For example, it seems that major insurance companies would not negotiate loans with a company capitalised at less than £10 m. The formation of a new type of joint venture brought together two wealthy sources of funds, which both lacked administrative machinery to deal with comparatively small applicants, with a major clearing bank which by its nature could only put a tiny fraction of its resources into equity investment and long-term loans but which could offer the joint venture great expertise in evaluating and dealing with investment enquiries of every kind, valuable contacts and goodwill and a large number of contact points in its branches throughout the country. Initially Moracrest has been prepared to deal with minimum investments of about £200,000 – a comparatively large sum from the viewpoint of 'small' businesses but in principle a company such as Moracrest offers flexibility and it should not be difficult to consider applications for equity or loan funds of significantly less than £200,000.

Subsequently, another company, 'Mentor', has been formed with the Midland Bank and the Rolls Royce Pension Trust as the major shareholders. The intention is to provide equity capital for the expansion of private companies with successful records. In 1980 the Prudential Assurance Co. took a major initiative by forming a subsidiary company 'Prutech', in partnership with one of the UK's most respected centres of technological research and development, Patscentre, a laboratory and consultancy subsidiary of P.A.International. The Prudential will fund this venture initially with £20 m and will encourage small to medium-sized companies which are working on promising innovatory projects which require significant funds, of a risk-capital nature, which the companies could not afford to fund themselves. Prutech would not be looking for a quick payback: it would fund promising projects which offered no prospect of a return on capital for at least five years.

Questions

1. A company requires £1,000,000 for the next five years. Advise the company on the sources of finance which might be available and explain what further factors should be taken into account. (ICSA 22 marks)

2. An engineer has an idea for a new machine which could well revolutionise the textile industry. He would need about £500,000 to develop the machine and has approached you for advice on the possible sources of finance which might be available. You are asked to write a report advising on the best financial structure for this new operation. (ICSA 22 marks)

Chapter 12

The financial strategy

The creation and starting up of a private-sector company, even of modest size, will require considerable preparatory work, involving people experienced in a number of functions, of which the financial function will be an important one. There is evidence that in the early stages, when a new company is fighting for survival and to gain and then increase a significant market share, it is likely to be aiming for profit maximisation, subject to the proviso that nothing should be done which might damage the long-term prospects of the company. As has been stated, in the case of large, mature private- and public-sector businesses there may be a rather different emphasis. Well-managed large businesses will have exacting profit targets but these may fall short of profit maximisation as it may be decided that some compromises have to be accepted, to satisfy one or more powerful interest groups, and these compromises must be at the expense of profits.

Newly established public-sector businesses which have been directed to operate on commercial principles will also have adequate profitability, as measured by return on capital, as a main aim. Those organisations which do not have profit as an objective, but have to make efficient use of limited resources and with the constraint of working within cash limits, e.g. hospitals, universities, etc., must avoid any use of resources which does not directly increase the usable output and which is not essential for some special reason. In practice it is not difficult for a trained person to make a quick and informed assessment whether a particular company is working efficiently or not. For every industry or activity there are well-established tests or yardsticks which are well known to those working in that field. Financial tests and ratios will always have an important role but they will never be the only ones.

The management role: a brief outline

The promoters of a new company will be assumed to include persons who, when the company begins to operate, will be responsible for what is known as the top management: that is, whilst they may also have a specialist functional role, as head of a division, or function, or department, they will also be concerned with deciding the major overall objectives of the company and its main policies. It will be their responsibility to ensure that at all times the company has all the material and human resources which it needs to pursue its objectives efficiently. Management activities have been analysed into five elements:

(a) Planning, which includes forecasting.
(b) Communicating with people inside and outside the company; whilst lip service is often paid to this concept, in practice it is frequently neglected and if this is so the organisation always suffers. Good communications require that top managers keep workpeople adequately informed and that there is also 'feedback', so that the views of workpeople are known to the management.
(c) Command, including motivation. The right decisions have to be made and then implemented. The role of command has been played down in recent years but it is noteworthy that in wartime good soldiers with poor generals lose battles but as soon as the poor generals are replaced with good ones the same soldiers begin to win their battles.
(d) Coordination – all of the functions of a company must be in step, in harmony with each other. The larger and more complex a company is the more important and difficult the role of the coordinator will be.
(e) Control – in this context the word is used in the sense of monitoring. When plans have been made and targets set and approved and work has begun, it is important that progress in the course set is continually monitored, so that any deviation from course is corrected or, if it is found that the course itself has to be changed, this also can be done promptly.

Revenue planning: cost planning

The survival of a private-sector company requires that cash receipts exceed payments on a continuing basis. In the case of a new company, revenue planning always presents practical problems as there is no previous experience available for guidance. There will be planned sales at planned prices but achievement of these will depend upon how accurately the public taste has been gauged: often forecasts prove to be disastrously optimistic. In other cases there are serious delays in starting and consequently the inflow of sales revenues does not begin until some months after the planned date. It is normally less difficult to plan costs. Sales revenues in a given period are determined by two factors, the price at which each sale is made and the total number of sales made. Revenue is thus a function of price, volume and time. Profit, which is the excess of revenues over costs, is a function of profit margins and turnover. When planning revenues, the company will be able to fix its prices but not the volume of its sales.

In practice considerable market research should be carried out to ascertain, for example, what real confidence can the company have that its proposed goods or services will fill an existing gap in the market? What does the company specially offer which should permit it to establish itself against existing companies; quantitative estimates of the present and future market, the elasticity of demand for the product; what will the distribution channels be? How important is the packaging? How much will need to be spent on sales promotion and advertising and what forms should the campaigns take? What will the 'break-even' sales be, etc.? Sufficiently encouraging answers must be obtained to many questions before commitments are entered into. Obviously, much will depend on the circumstances. A company which at the start would have only a local market would confine itself to local market research. Major multinational companies which are testing a new low-price, large-volume sales consumer item may first carry out intensive market research in a single town regarded as typical of the national market as a whole. Promising results would be followed by further research on a wider basis and if a launch of the product were finally decided upon there would be a massive marketing campaign, beginning with the trade and the trade press and then directed at consumers. The total expenditure on launching a new brand of, e.g. soft drinks or chocolate biscuits, will include television advertising and would cost hundreds of thousands of pounds. It would be carried out like a military operation. It might still fail.

New companies without reserves cannot afford serious mistakes. In this they are unlike well-established companies which can survive occasional miscalculations and failure of a new product launching, such as the tobacco companies experienced when they spent millions of pounds on research and development and then the marketing of tobacco substitutes, whose outcome proved to be a total failure and the substitutes were finally withdrawn from the market and destroyed.

The problem of selling prices

When a company will be making and selling articles of a type already being sold then the existing prices will give useful guidelines as to the price(s) to be charged for the new product. It is an accepted view that it is a mistake for a new company to aim to establish itself by means of selling at lower prices than its competitors since a product sold on the basis of cut prices will gain no customer loyalty and sooner or later will be displaced by a competitive brand selling at an even lower price. It has been noted that many German, Japanese and French companies which command customer loyalty make no concealment of the fact that their prices are high but they stress the style, distinction, reliability after-sales service, etc., of their product.

In the case of a completely new product, perhaps one based on a patent, determination of the selling price will be specially important and difficult. It is a common practice for successful companies to launch new products at high prices initially, when the company will be a (near) monopoly supplier but can expect to enjoy this position for a year or two only, until competitors emerge. In industries in which technological progress is rapid and research and development costs are high and often a small number of successful discoveries and products will have to 'carry' quite a large number of failures, a policy of 'charging what the market will bear' for as long as possible in respect of a new product makes obvious commercial sense. The pharmaceutical and electronics industries have these features and generally appear to follow these policies. A few examples of consumer products launched at comparatively high prices and of which the prices fell dramatically after one to five years are the ballpoint pen, pocket electronic calculators, and battery-operated quartz watches.

When a new product is about to be launched, many decisions would need to be taken including selling prices, distribution channels, discount policies, etc. A special role of the financial manager would be to state the various financial options available, and the financial implications of every option, non-financial as well as financial. Meanwhile, sound pricing is of vital importance. It is said that when the first Morris and Austin 'Minis' were sold a major competitor purchased one, dismantled it and costed every item down to the tiniest component and concluded that the car was underpriced and could not be profitable at the selling price. In the event the car was a huge commercial success but it was later recognised that for many years it had been sold at too low a price and this proved an important factor in the unprofitability and relative decline of the manufacturer. It was a mistake with immensely damaging consequences which could and should have been avoided.

Cost Planning

Cost planning will be studied at the same time as revenue planning. Whilst in some respects costs tend to be more predictable and controllable then revenues, costing is a technically difficult matter, especially in inflationary times. It is worth remembering that profits cannot only be increased by increasing prices and/or sales volumes, but also by reducing costs. Often, in times of easy sales, costs tend to be neglected but when sales decline and attention is focused on reducing costs, the savings prove larger than expected and this is an indication of the lack of control and waste which must have prevailed when sales were buoyant. There are now a number of established techniques available for improving cost control: a single example is value analysis. Usually, small expert teams examine products, materials, components, designs, in detail to ascertain whether savings could be made by making changes here or there but in such a way that the acceptability of the product was not damaged. Efficient cost control would require attention to such matters as the use of energy, the avoidance of wasted materials and rejected products, prevention of pilferage, etc. It is a wide-ranging matter.

The nature of costs

Whilst managers who are not accountants or financial specialists will not need to have detailed knowledge of costing, it will be helpful for them to consider the nature of costs. It will be seen in this chapter that unless certain basic principles are clearly understood it will be possible in certain situations for a management to misinterpret the information available and to make seriously wrong and financially damaging decisions.

Costs can be grouped in a number of different ways which will not be in conflict with each other. One main grouping is to place all costs within one of three broad categories: (*a*) materials; (*b*) labour; (*c*) expenses. Efficient costing requires a sufficient degree of analysis: thus, labour costs would be analysed, *inter alia*, into management, clerical, operative salaries, and according to the department where the work was done; overtime; travelling; entertaining; commissions; etc. For efficient analysis there must be a sufficient number of carefully designated accounts. Since there may need to be many accounts, a numerical code is normally used, which requires an index. Computers and other data processing equipment are being used increasingly because their real costs are falling steeply and they have the capability of carrying out different types of analysis at high speed, in addition to many other uses.

The broad categories of materials, labour and expenses are logical and self-evident. Materials would include bought-in components. Labour would include salaries, wages, overtime, pension contributions, etc., as applicable, for all categories of employees, from the most senior to the most junior, and the coding would permit analysis into appropriate categories, e.g. senior management, clerical, operative, as well as sales, or works or stores department, etc. Expenses will also be put into logical groups and subgroups, e.g. property, with separate accounts for rents; rates; individual properties; maintenance; etc.; transport – petrol, diesel, oil, tyres, licences, depreciation, maintenance, etc., for individual vehicles as well as groups of vehicles. There will be many other expenses requiring analysis – telephones, postage, heating, lighting, printing, etc. When a costing system is being designed and introduced for the first time – and this applies whenever major systems changes occur, such as the introduction of budgetary control – it will be important to try to 'get it right first time' and to do this it will be important to have expert and objective advice: modest expenses at the start may avoid higher ones later.

Fixed and variable costs: indirect and direct costs

There is a further most important distinction between costs when these are analysed in relation to a particular product or service. It is whether a cost should be regarded as fixed or variable. A cost is said to be fixed in relation to a product or service if it is incurred irrespective of whether or not the product or service is produced. Common examples are rent, rates, administration salaries, and those costs which are commonly known as 'overheads'. Variable costs are those which arise only if a particular product or service is produced. For example, if TV sets are manufactured and assembled and 'bought-in' tubes are used, every tube would be counted as a variable (or direct) cost in relation to each set. Thus variable costs rise or fall directly in relation to the production of an item, whereas fixed costs are independent of what is produced and are determined by time. Meanwhile, costing is one of the many subjects about which dogmatic statements and too rigid treatment should be avoided. For examples, although fixed costs are fixed in the short run they are not fixed in the long run, as a company may move to smaller premises and thus reduce rent and rates, or administrative staff may be made redundant and thus salaries reduced, etc.

Although it might not seem difficult to state the costs of materials, in practice there are serious problems. Thus materials and components will be purchased and taken into store and paid for at the prices prevailing at the time of purchase. They then become mixed, in the store, with the same materials or components purchased at different times and prices. By the time they are used in the manufacturing processes the prices may have changed again, and yet again by the time the goods are sold. In these circumstances, what are the prices of the materials used? There are differences of opinion and of practice on this vital question which cannot be considered here. In practice, in inflationary times, alert managements have regard to replacement costs rather than original, historical costs and they seek to raise prices more than in step with price increases of materials and other inputs (they are noticeably slower in reducing prices if materials costs fall).

In the past labour costs were often variable costs whereas they are now increasingly fixed costs. These technical words are pointers to one major aspect of the social revolution which has been occurring in the UK, especially since the Second World War. In the past it was a common practice for employers to select groups of men at the start of each day, to work for that day only, and these workpeople had no security of employment. This was, and is, 'casual labour'. Employers engaged labour only when they were active and did not do so when things were slack. This made life much easier and more profitable for employers but in human terms it was a devastating practice as one can still observe when visiting numbers of developing countries.

In the UK as well as other industrialised countries, in recent years trades unions and legislation have been effective in ensuring greater security of employment for workpeople who, for the most part, are now employed on a 'permanent' basis, which means that their wages and salaries must be paid whether there is work for them or not. The effect of this is that whereas the cost of labour employed on a casual basis can be attributed to a particular job, and is therefore a variable cost, when labour is employed on a permanent basis the costs are fixed costs. Occasionally a labour cost will be partly fixed and partly variable. An example is a salesman who is paid a fixed salary plus a commission on every article he sells, the commission being a variable element when the article concerned is being costed. Often an expense is treated as fixed in those cases where it would be difficult or not worth while to relate a particular cost to a particular article or service. The costs of many types of services are partly fixed and partly variable – for example, telephone charges include a fixed element for rental, but each call made is charged separately.

The use of capital equipment

The services rendered by capital equipment must also be taken into account since these play an essential part in the work done. Having appropriate capital equipment available increases the productivity of a worker, but it gives rise to costs. Thus, the output of a competent typist in a busy office may be much increased if a word processor is available, but this equipment might not be justified in a less busy office. Capital equipment has to be purchased or leased by a company and its costs have ultimately to be recovered through the proceeds of sales. The loss in value of a capital asset through the passage of time, e.g. leasehold offices, or through use and 'wear and tear', or obsolescence, is known as depreciation. It is a complex and controversial topic and depreciation may be calculated in different ways, some being more appropriate in certain circumstances and others at other times, but consistency of treatment is always important. One reason for the importance of the topic is that when major capital expenditure occurs, the depreciation charge may be very high. If assets are leased and not purchased the lessee will not be concerned with the depreciation aspect, but only with the hire charge, which must be recovered through the proceeds of sales of goods or services. The subject of depreciation is examined in detail in textbooks on accountancy and only limited aspects need to be considered in this book. When a profit-and-loss account is prepared for a given period, depreciation will be charged as an expense or, alternatively, the leasing rental will be.

Profit in relation to variable and fixed costs: a preview

Profit is the surplus of revenues over costs, including depreciation. As costs are made up of variable and fixed costs, profit will be the difference between the total revenue and the total of the variable plus the fixed costs. As will be seen, there are occasions when use of this analysis may lead to decisions being made which are right in special circumstances and yet are the direct opposite of the decisions which would have been made if the analysis had not been available. Two important facts are that in complex businesses a substantial proportion of the total costs will be fixed costs and a feature of these is that a company has to commit itself to them in advance of production and sales. In brief, a company requires command over more substantial financial resources as its ratio of fixed to variable costs increases and, moreover, an increase in this ratio signifies that its risks and the problems of its management are also increasing.

The key or limiting factor

The key factor is an important concept with wide practical implications. It needs to be understood. Why is a particular company not able to expand its scale of activity continually and without limit? On examination it will be found that there is a single identifiable reason. If this reason ceases to apply, another will replace it. For example, one company may be unable to expand its sales beyond a certain point because it experiences a shortage of certain skilled workpeople; in another case a certain expensive machine may be a 'bottleneck'. It is working to the limits of its capacity, which could be increased if an additional machine were leased or purchased. However, a prudent management would not commit itself to an additional output without being convinced that the additional output could be sold profitably over the period covered by the life of the machine. There might in any case be a delay of a year or two before an additional machine could be installed. In other cases a certain raw material or component in short supply could be the key factor. Immediately after the Second World War, car manufacturers could quickly sell every car they made and production was then the key factor. Even the largest multinational companies meet a constraint and it will usually be the limits of the available markets and the forces of competition.

In principle, every management should identify the key factor in a situation and also be ready to recognise and reassess the situation in the event that the key factor changes. The basic rule is of vital importance. It is that production should be concentrated on those articles or services which make the most profitable use of the key factor or, expressed formally, it should be concentrated on those articles or services which give rise to the largest contribution per unit of the key factor. 'Contribution' is the difference between the sales revenues arising when an article or service is sold, and the variable costs incorporated in it. The practical implications of this and some other concepts will be considered in this chapter.

Before a new company starts operations, or before the new financial year of an established company, cash forecasts and budgets will be prepared in the light of the plans for the forthcoming period. The plans will be expressed partly in financial and partly in non-financial terms, and as was reported by many companies to the Wilson Committee, because of the many uncertainties in the social and economic environment, plans are treated with caution and reserve, as it is now impossible for anyone to be certain how events will occur over the next weeks, months or years. The farther one tries to look into the future the great-

The financial strategy

er the probability that major mistakes in the forecasts will be disclosed. Even so, the discipline of planning is accepted as having importance. It focuses attention on matters likely to have special importance: problem areas should be identified and considered. Meanwhile, in the normal planning processes it will often be found that the key factor will be the limits of the market, the maximum sales achievable in the next period. In such cases the executive responsible for the sales function will be required to assess what the attainable sales should be, and at what prices and bearing in mind that in inflationary times prices will have to be increased periodically, but if the demand for the product is elastic these price rises could lead to falls in the planned sales and profits would be lower than planned. However, with sales as the key factor, the plans will centre on the sales and sales revenues, and other functional and departmental heads will prepare their own plans in relation to the sales plans. The various budgets will be built up on the basis that there will be sales at certain levels, which will require appropriate production budgets, taking stocking policies and stock levels into account as appropriate.

When detailed sales plans and budgets have been expressed in quantified terms, and agreed, and when there has at every stage been a distinction made between variable and fixed costs, although there will be many items, experienced people will be able to calculate the variable costs for individual items, and the overall totals of these variable costs, on the basis of the assumptions made and the information available. The balance of costs to be recovered before profits begin to accrue will be the fixed costs. A feature of these is that they require prior commitments which, once accepted, cannot be relinquished without financial penalties. Meanwhile, plans have to be made on the basis of various assumptions, not least being the activity levels of the company in the period under consideration. In the light of these assumptions the many items of fixed costs will be assessed and totals made of these. In the case of an established company many of the fixed costs will have to be accepted in the short to medium term even if there is a desire to reduce them. For examples, rents must continue to be paid in accordance with existing agreements: the salaries of employees now on the payroll must continue, etc. In the short term it is often only practicable to make marginal reductions. In practice, fixed costs will, or should, be changed when it becomes evident that the changes in activity level will be of extended duration. For examples, for a long-term increase in activity new employees would be recruited, unless changes in procedures and the use of labour-saving equipment would permit the same work to be done without increasing the workforce. Similarly, a decline in activity which seemed likely to persist would require planned redundancies and, at a later stage, perhaps even a move into smaller premises, in order to save costs.

Another feature of fixed costs is that there is a tendency for certain of them to move in steps – up to a certain point, present employees could handle an increase in activity but a stage would be reached when additional employees would be needed. Flexible budgeting may be used to deal with this feature of costs. It may be helpful here to define a number of specially important terms used in costing and budgetary control: the list is not comprehensive.

Cost unit: A unit of quantity of produce, service or time in relation to which costs may be ascertained or expressed (e.g. jobs, contract, tons of materials, theatre seats, passenger miles, etc).

Cost centre: A location, person or item of equipment, or group of these in, or connected with, an undertaking in relation to which costs may be ascertained and used for purposes of cost control.

Budget centre: A section of the organisation of an undertaking defined for the purposes of budgetary control.

Fixed cost: A cost which tends to be unaffected by changes in volume of output.

Variable cost: A cost which tends to vary directly with changes in volume of output.

Controllable cost: A cost which can be influenced by the action of a manager.

Uncontrollable cost: A cost which can not be influenced by the action of a manager.

Cost allocation: The allotment of whole items of costs to cost centres or cost units.

Cost apportionment: The allotment of proportions of items of costs to cost centres or cost units.

Direct material cost: The material costs which can be allocated to cost centres or cost units. (Direct wages and direct expenses are defined similarly.)

Indirect material cost: Material cost which cannot be alloted but which can be apportioned to or absorbed by a cost centre or cost unit. (Indirect wages and expenses are defined similarly.)

Overhead: The aggregate of indirect material cost, indirect wages and indirect expense.

Prime cost: The total of direct material cost, direct wages and direct expense.

Production costs: The cost of the process which begins with supplying materials, labour and services and ends with the primary packing of the product.

Selling cost: The cost incurred in promoting sales and retaining custom.

Distribution cost: The cost of the process which begins with making the packed product available for despatch and ends with making the reconditioned returned empty package available for re-use.

Administration cost: The cost of formulating policy, directing the organisation and controlling the operations of an undertaking which is not directly related to a research, development, production, distribution or selling activity or function.

Cost of sales: The total cost which is attributable to the sales made.

Total cost: The sum of all the costs incurred.

Gross margin: The difference between the sales value and prime cost.

Gross contribution: The expression of gross margin as a contribution towards fixed costs and profit.

Net margin: The difference between gross margin and total fixed costs.

Absorption costing

A main problem of costing is how to deal with the fixed costs. In principle the variable costs are more straightforward as they can be determined in relation to individual cost units. However, a company does not begin to make profits until its sales revenues cover: (*a*) the total of the variable costs, and (b) the total of the fixed costs. The point at which there is no profit and no loss is known as the 'breakeven' point. It is reasonable to consider that the selling price of every article or service should contain: (a) the full variable cost; plus (b) a fair share of the fixed costs; plus (c) an element of profit.

The traditional costing approach is to examine the main groups and subgroups of fixed costs in relation to whatever is produced and apportion these costs on what seem the most suitable and fair bases so that all the fixed costs will be apportioned to cost centres and finally to cost units. Some of the main bases are: (a) a percentage of direct materials; (b) a percentage of direct wages; (c) a percentage of prime cost; (d) direct labour hour rate; (e) machine hour rate. The most suitable base will depend on the circumstances and cannot be considered here except to note that a difficulty is that apportionment will be based on the assumption that activity will be at a certain level. If the actual activity is below this budgeted level there will be an underrecovery of the fixed costs and the profits will be below the expected levels, or there will be a loss. Conversely, if activity is above the budgeted level there would be an overrecovery of fixed costs and better than expected profits. The latter outcome would obviously be preferred to the former. Insofar as costing is used at all in smaller companies, the methods most often found are: (a) job and contract costing; (b) batch costing; (c) process costing; (d) operating costing. The latter is used by companies which produce services rather than goods, e.g. transport operators.

Standard costing
A sophisticated form of costing which may be justified in larger companies whose sales volumes permit the employment of the necessary costing and other specialists is standard costing:
a system of cost accounting which makes use of predetermined standard costs relating to each element of cost – labour, material and overhead – for each line of product manufactured or service supplied. Actual costs incurred are compared with the standard costs as work proceeds, the differences being known as 'variances': these are analysed by 'reasons' so that inefficiencies may quickly be brought to the notice of the persons responsible for them and appropriate action may be taken.
(J.Batty; *Standard Costing*, Macdonald Evans, London).
The practical applications can be difficult especially when almost all elements of cost become unstable in consequence of inflation.

The financial strategy

Marginal costing

In recent years many managements have begun to look at costing from new and fresh viewpoints. Often, analysis into variable and fixed costs has itself been a recent development and it is the basis of marginal costing: the fact is that when output is increased or decreased by one unit, the increase or decrease in the total costs will be equal to the direct costs of that one unit. This is the simple but central core of marginal costing which is a technique now widely used for decision-making purposes and is of great practical importance. Often students, and even financial managers, do not need to be costing experts, but the fundamental difference between the absorption and the marginal approaches to costing does need to be carefully studied and understood for the same data can be set out and interpreted by two different persons in different ways so that, on the basis of one presentation of the data, a decision would be taken to adopt a certain course of action but a different presentation of the same data would lead to the opposite decision being taken. Marginal costing gives rise to new insights but it is also a potentially dangerous technique if used with more enthusiasm than judgement. Users must be fully aware of, and must always bear in mind, certain pitfalls and dangers in the use of marginal costing.

The contribution

When marginal costing is used the fixed costs are not allocated or apportioned to products but the variable costs of items sold are deducted from the sales revenues and the difference is known as the 'contribution' – an effective and descriptive term. Provided that the selling price exceeds the variable costs – and production should never be undertaken if it does not – then it can be visualised that the proceeds of every sale must in the first place cover the variable costs and, in the second place, any surplus over the variable costs forms a contribution to a fund from which the fixed costs and overall profit must be met.

The following simple example illustrates the different approaches of those who use the traditional absorption costing and those who use marginal costing. A company manufactures and sells four different articles: A, B, C and D, and the total sales revenues are £1 m. and the total variable costs are £½ m. and the fixed costs are £200,000. The details are set out in the table and if it has been decided that the most appropriate way to apportion the fixed costs is in proportion to the prime costs the results will be (£):

	A	B	C	D	Total
Sales revenues	150,000	200,000	300,000	350,000	1,000,000
Prime costs	75,000	135,000	140,000	150,000	500,000
Fixed costs	45,000	81,000	84,000	90,000	300,000
Profit/(loss)	30,000	(16,000)	76,000	110,000	200,000

A manager accustomed to being presented with costing information in this form might understandably say 'as B is giving rise to a loss let its production be discontinued'. However, if discontinuing B did not lead to an immediate and substantial reduction in the fixed costs, and from their nature it would be unlikely to do this, and if the sales of A, C and D could not quickly be increased substantially – and if they could be, why had this not been done already? – then the discontinuing of B would be a bad decision and its implementation would reduce the profit of the company substantially. In brief, a manager who failed to understand the significance of fixed costs, and the assumptions made in absorption costing could make costly mistaken decisions. Presentation of the same information on the basis of marginal costing shows the situation in a different light (£):

	A	B	C	D	Total
Sales revenues	150,000	200,000	300,000	350,000	1,000,000
Prime costs	75,000	135,000	140,000	150,000	500,000
Contribution	75,000	65,000	160,000	200,000	500,000
Fixed costs					300,000
Profit					200,000
Position if production of B is discontinued: deduct contribution					65,000
Profit arising from sales of A, C and D only (in existing situation)					135,000

In practice, companies may use both absorption and marginal costing; one important reason for using the former for general purposes is that a proportion of 'overheads' will be incorporated in stocks and work in progress, which is equitable. Furthermore, it is the generally accepted convention for the preparation of annual and published accounts as well as those used for the computation of tax liabilities. Moreover, the use of absorption costing gives useful guidance when selling prices are being determined: it suggests 'floor prices', but no more than that. Marginal

The financial strategy

costing may be used as a complementary technique and when used with judgement it can be helpful in the following important circumstances:

(a) To assist management in deciding whether to concentrate production and marketing on certain products rather than others and, if so, which ones. If there is a special key factor its identification will be of importance.
(b) In ascertaining at what level of sales the 'break-even' point is reached.
(c) 'Make or buy' decisions – will it be more profitable for a company to make a particular component for itself, or buy it from outside suppliers?
(d) Should a special production contract be accepted or not?
(e) Should certain products be sold, or special contracts accepted, at less than the 'full' price in certain circumstances, notably when there is idle manufacturing capacity; when it is desired to keep a skilled workforce together during a temporary period of shortage of work; when there is a trade recession?

The key factor: an example

The following simple example illustrates the importance of the concept. Suppose that three articles are made and sold and there are no shortages of any kind and the limiting factor is that of the limit of the market and competition. The data are:

Marginal cost statement: sales as limiting factor (£)

		A		B		C
Unit selling price			12		11		10
Unit marginal costs:						
Direct materials	4		2		1	
Direct labour	2		2		1	
Direct expenses	1	7	1	5	1	3
Unit contribution		5		6		7

In this case the most profitable course of action would be to concentrate on the production and sale of C as far as possible since this gives rise to the largest contribution per unit: it offers the highest gross margin.

However, consider the production and sales of three articles X, Y and Z, whose finishing in each case requires the employment of specialist skilled labour and the total available working hours per period of this labour are 7,000 only; other information is as set out below.

Marginal costing statement: special labour as key factor (£)

	X	Y	Z
Unit selling price	100	90	70
Unit marginal costs	30	35	40
Unit contribution	70	55	30
Hours of specialist labour per unit:	7	5	2

At first glance X appears to be the most profitable but this is not so. The key factor has been identified and its implications must be considered. Z is the most sparing in its use of this factor, and the contribution per unit of key factor is: X, £70/7, i.e. £10; Y, £55/5, i.e. £11; Z, £30/2, i.e. £15. Production and sales should therefore be concentrated on Z and this can easily be verified. With 7,000 hours of skilled labour per period, 1,000 of X; 1,400 of Y; and 3,500 of Z can be made and sold, giving rise to total contributions respectively of £70,000 in the case of X; £77,000 for Y; and £105,000 for Z. Z is therefore the most profitable and this fact is apparent only when marginal costing analysis is used. If it appeared that only a limited number of Z could be sold the most profitable course of action would be to produce up to the sales limit for Z and then concentrate on the next most profitable alternative – in this case, Y.

The P/V (profit/volume) ratio

When the selling price and the variable costs per unit remain constant, and in practice they often do so over a fairly wide range, then the contribution per unit will also remain constant. This gives rise to a ratio of considerable practical importance, the P/V (profit/volume) ratio, i.e. unit contribution/unit selling price. It will be seen from this that sales × P/V ratio = contribution.

Example
Suppose that the selling price of Z is £10 and the variable costs are £4 per unit: the contribution per unit is thus £6 and the P/V ratio is

£6/£10, i.e. 6/10 or 60%. If this is the only article sold and the fixed costs of the company are assessed at £20,000, then some useful information can easily be calculated, bearing in mind that:
Total costs = Variable Costs + Fixed Costs
Profit (Loss) = Sales − Total Costs
Contribution = Sales − Variable Costs
Profit = Contribution − Fixed Costs
If, in this example, the planned profit were £22,000, it would be necessary to know what sales would be required to achieve this profit objective. The evaluation is:
planned profit (£22,000) = contribution (X) − fixed costs (£20,000)
i.e. contribution = £42,000. Then, as sales × P/V ratio (3/5) = contribution (£42,000), sales = £42,000 × 5/3 = £70,000. This calculation can easily be verified. With a unit selling price of £10, sales of £70,000 represent sales of 7,000 units. As variable costs are £4 per unit, total variable costs would be £28,000 and with fixed costs at £20,000 total costs would be £48,000. Sales revenues of £70,000 would thus produce the planned profit of £22,000.

Breakeven charts: breakeven point

The concept of the 'breakeven' point of a particular business at a given stage of its development, or for a project which is under consideration, has practical importance. The question is − when fixed costs have to be at a certain level what volume of sales must be achieved so that there is neither a profit nor a loss i.e. what is the 'breakeven' point? Looked at another way, when variable costs have a constant relationship with the selling price, as soon as the breakeven point has been reached every additional sale will give rise to an addition to the total profits of the amount of its contribution noting that, in practice, when sales increase beyond a certain point the fixed costs are likely to need to be increased. In reality it would be unusual but not unknown for a company to sell a single product at a single selling price. There will usually be a number of products at a number of prices. A feature of the sales of major car manufacturers is that a limited number of different models are offered and there is wide choice within each model range, with the low price basic model at one end, to a special Italian-styled model, with many special features, at perhaps treble the price of the cheapest model: profit margins tend to be much higher on the higher-cost models in a range and the manufacturers try to increase the demand for these. In practice manufacturers soon ascertain the usual mix of sales and in any case production can readily be adjusted to meet changes in demand.

Meanwhile, it is useful to have an awareness of the construction and significance of breakeven charts and the starting point must be consideration of a single product. For convenience the example just examined will be considered (see Chart 1). Using ordinary graph paper a starting point, zero, is taken and from this point a vertical axis (y) is drawn and on this both costs and revenues will be shown. From the zero point a horizontal axis (x) is also drawn, on which the level of activity will be shown. These axes are the framework of the chart. The fixed costs will be represented by a horizontal line, parallel with the x-axis and which cuts the vertical axis at the point which corresponds with the fixed costs. This line will be horizontal because, by definition, the fixed costs do not change with the activity level, and when there are no sales, no activity, the total costs will be the fixed costs and so the line representing the total costs will start at the point where the fixed cost line cuts the vertical axis. In the example the total cost line will be straight and will rise to the point which corresponds with the total costs at 100% acitivity. The line representing sales will also be straight but since there will be no sales revenues when there is no activity, the sales line will start at the zero point where the vertical and horizontal axes intercept. It will rise to the point which corresponds with sales revenues at 100% activity.

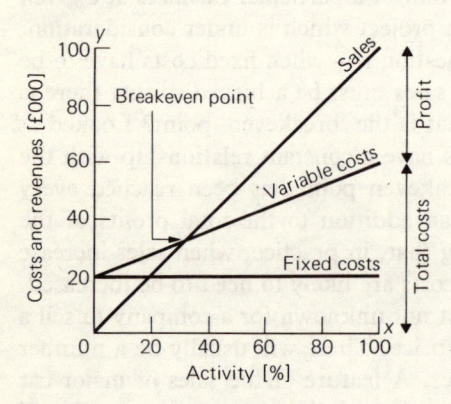

Chart 1

The feature of a breakeven chart is that the point where the lines of total costs and total sales revenues intersect is the point at which there is neither profit nor loss. Reference to the chart shows that it is when the total revenue is about £33,000. It is not possible to read a chart with complete accuracy, of course. Meanwhile, the information on which the chart is based can also be used to make an independent calculation. In this example, the selling price is £10, the variable costs £4 per unit and the fixed costs £20,000. Since at the breakeven point there is neither profit nor loss, this is the point at which the contribution just equals the fixed costs and as the latter are £20,000 the contribution at the breakeven point must also be £20,000. As the contribution per unit is £6, the sales necessary to produce this contribution must be 20,000 ÷ 6, i.e. 3,333 units, representing total sales revenues of £33,333.

The margin of safety

The margin of safety is a measure of the difference between the level of activity at the breakeven point and the planned level of activity. A common characteristic of production before the recent employment protection laws was that it was labour intensive and workpeople could be engaged and dismissed on a casual, daily basis and in these circumstances the labour costs could be treated as variable costs. Breakeven charts then tended to feature relatively low fixed costs and high variable costs whereas now labour costs have become largely fixed costs (since casual engagement and dismissal is no longer feasible) and production has also tended to become more capital intensive. Accordingly, breakeven charts show relatively high fixed costs and low variable costs. The different situations are illustrated in Charts 2 and 3.

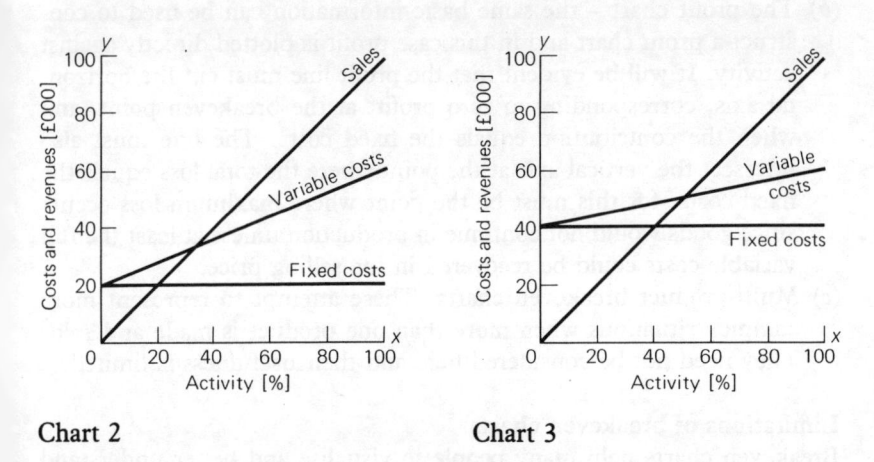

Chart 2

Chart 3

Note that when the variable costs form the higher proportion of total costs the breakeven point occurs at a lower level of activity and hence the margin of safety is higher than when the fixed costs form the higher proportion of total costs. However, when the fixed costs are the higher proportion an important consequence is that after the breakeven point has been reached, a given increase in the number of units sold will give rise to a greater increase in profits. This is an expression of the fact that the P/V ratio will be higher in this case. In such circumstances it becomes specially important to a company to seek a continuing high level of sales and to avoid stoppages of work. The motor car industry is a good example of one which now has a high proportion of fixed to total costs and profits and return on capital can be high when sales are at steady high levels provided that production continues with minimum interruption. Manufacturers are therefore vulnerable to any threat to continuing production.

Other forms of breakeven charts
For deeper study of breakeven charts, their usefulness and limitations, readers are referred to textbooks on management accountancy. Three interesting types are:
(a) Charts in which the variable costs are plotted at the base, in which the total costs line is parallel with that of the variable costs and intersects the vertical axis at the point corresponding to the fixed costs. The advantage of this chart is that it permits a direct reading of the contribution derived from the sales revenue at any level of activity covered by the chart.
(b) The profit chart – the same basic information can be used to construct a profit chart and in this case profit is plotted directly against activity. It will be evident that the profit line must cut the horizontal axis, corresponding to zero profit, at the breakeven point, and when the contribution equals the fixed costs. The line must also intersect the vertical axis at the point where the total loss equals the fixed costs, for this must be the point where maximum loss occurs since goods would not continue in production unless at least the full variable costs could be recovered in the selling price.
(c) Multi-product breakeven charts. These attempt to represent more complex situations when more than one product is made and sold. They need not be considered here and their usefulness is limited.

Limitations of breakeven charts
Breakeven charts help many people to visualise and better understand certain concepts, but they have a number of limitations and, if used, they must be interpreted with caution. In examples normally used it is assumed that the fixed costs include depreciation, but charts may also

be used to show the cash breakeven position which may be specially important in the short term. Breakeven charts are valid, at best, within certain limits, and would be invalid outside these. For example, in practice the sales revenue line will seldom be straight since in order to increase sales it may be necessary to offer special discounts, or make special offers. Similarly, the variable costs may not rise in a straight line for when activity rises additional costs are likely to be incurred, additional overtime at higher rates, materials might involve higher prices, etc. In practice, fixed costs tend to move in steps and not a straight line, e.g. up to a certain level of activity one supervisor might be adequate but the point comes when an additional one would be necessary; larger premises, more machines, etc., may be needed and at any time the management may change the fixed and variable cost relationships, for example by installing a different type of labour-saving equipment. In the case of multi-product breakeven charts it is assumed that the sales mix remains constant but in practice it is unlikely to do so. Meanwhile, when used with judgement and by experienced people the charts may be helpful in focusing attention on the interrelationships between the main factors which largely determine the financial success of a company – the sales revenues, the level of activity, the variable and the fixed costs.

The sales mix

When a company sells a number of products which have different profit –volume ratios, the 'sales mix' will be of great importance. For example, if sales revenues during a budget period were seen to be running close to the budgeted levels it might seem that all was well but if the situation was that articles with a lower P/V ratio were selling better than expected, but articles with higher P/V ratios were not selling so well, then the actual profit would be well below the budgeted profit. A management which concerned itself only with total sales revenues and failed to appreciate the implications of contribution and sales mix and did not practice careful budgetary control could find itself unexpectedly facing severe financial difficulties.

Make-or-buy decisions

Manufacturing companies often 'buy in' a substantial proportion of components which they could manufacture themselves if they chose to do so. As the direct costs arising in the manufacture of a component would usually be lower than the price payable to an outside supplier, how does a manufacturer decide whether to 'buy in' a component or manufacture it? The short answer is that the manufacturer must assess the position in each case. If he could manufacture the component without prejudice to any other work, using his existing machines, management and workforce, he would buy in the component only if the price charged by the outside supplier were lower than his variable costs if he manufactured it himself. He would also wish to satisfy himself that he could expect continuity of supplies from his supplier, at stable prices. However, if some key factor had to be considered within the production process, so that manufacturing the component caused some other work to be displaced, then the component would be bought in if its purchase price were below the variable costs of the manufacturer plus the contribution lost because the component was manufactured by the company instead of an article which could otherwise have been made and sold i.e. the 'opportunity cost' of buying in against manufacture must be taken into account. In practice, pressures on or shortage of managers, or of skilled labour, may be the limiting factors.

Example

Component A can be bought in or manufactured. It could be bought in at a price of £20 per unit. If it were manufactured the variable costs would be £5 per unit, but manufacture would require 2 hours' work per unit on a machine Z which is working at full capacity on an article B which the company makes and sells at £120 per unit. Its variable costs are £40. Producing one unit of B requires 4 hours' work on machine Z. Should the company make or buy component A?

Machine Z, now working at full capacity, is evidently the limiting factor. In the longer term the company may consider installing an additional machine Z but in the short term there are two options – make A but in this case make and sell fewer of B, or buy in A and concentrate on production of B. Which option would yield the higher profits? The contribution of each unit of B is seen to be £80 and this derives from 4 hours' work on Z. The contribution of B per unit of the key factor is therefore £20 per hour of Z. As production of A would require 2 hours' work of Z, thereby giving rise to smaller output of B, the true cost of manufacturing A would be £5 per unit variable costs plus £40 lost contribution of B, i.e. a total cost of £45 per unit. In the stated facts of this case it would be more profitable to buy in component A.

The financial strategy

Should a certain contract be accepted or not?

The following examination question illustrates a situation quite often met in practice.

Example

The XYZ Engineering Co. Ltd has a division which manufactures a range of motor vehicle components. The Board of Directors have been considering an order for £200,000 of special components and a report has been requested from the accounts department to see if the contract should be accepted. The report, which is set out below, advises against acceptance.

		(£)	(£)
Revenue from contract			200,000
Less: Costs	Materials: basic components	41,400	
	additional components	28,600	
	Mouldings	36,000	
	Rackings	9,000	
	Component design costs	5,000	
	Labour costs	72,000	
	Power	6,400	
	Depreciation	21,200	
	Head office administration	10,000	
	Interest on assets employed	3,200	232,800
	Loss		32,800

The following notes accompany the report:
(1) The racking is an old type which cost £18,000 but which the accounts department have written down by half as there was no foreseeable demand for it.
(2) Component design costs are based on an allocation of the time spent by the company's design department on the design of the basic component.
(3) The whole of the labour cost would be paid to workers taken on for the contract with the exception of £3,000 which is an estimate of the proportion of supervisory labour shared with existing work.
(4) Depreciation represents one-fifth of the charge for the whole division as it would take approximately that proportion of the division's machine capacity for one year.
(5) Head Office administration costs are the result of a reallocation designed to give a fair view of the profitability of the contract.

(6) Interest is regarded as the average cost of capital employed by the division.

Required (a) Assuming that the division had idle capacity before accepting the contract: comment on the above report and the suggested rejection of the contract.
(b) Would your position change if the division was operating presently at capacity?   (ICSA   34 marks)

Workings and comments
(a) The heart of the matter is that when a division is operating with idle capacity the continuing fixed expenses must still be paid and therefore, for decision making purposes, these should be separated from those expenses which would arise only if a particular contract were accepted. The first step is therefore simply to restate the information given, showing the revenue to be received if the contract is accepted and deducting from this all the variable (direct) costs. In a question of this kind every piece of information given in the notes must be studied. The restatement becomes:

	(£)	(£)
Revenue from contract		200,000
Less: Variable costs: Materials: basic components	41,400	
additional materials	28,600	
Mouldings	36,000	
Rackings (say)	1,000	
Labour	69,000	
Power	6,400	182,400
Contribution		17,600

As no note is made about the basic components; additional materials; mouldings; and power, these are treated as variable costs. The racking is different. The 'written down' value, £9,000, is an arbitrary one. The question now is 'what is the value to the business of this old type of material?' As there seems to be no foreseeable use for it, its value is taken to be its scrap value. It is assumed here that the scrap value would be £1,000 but any other reasonable and stated assumption on these lines would be acceptable to the examiner.

The notes indicate that in this case the labour costs are part variable and part fixed, £72,000 − £3,000, i.e. £69,000, being variable and the balance, £3,000 fixed, since the £3,000 cost of the supervisory labour would have to be paid anyway. The notes indicate that the design costs, the depreciation, the Head Office administration and the interest on the assets employed are all fixed costs – that is, they would continue irrespective of whether this contract was accepted or not.

The restatement of the information given therefore shows that the company would be £17,600 'better off' if it accepted the contract. The original statement drawn up by the accounts department was a badly drafted statement since it gave the essential facts but obscured the true position. The revised statement has the merit of showing management the full implications of each option open to them – to accept or reject the contract. In this case the management might decide to accept the contract if it were convinced that no early increase in activity could be expected, and if it were satisfied that acceptance of a contract at a low price would not undermine the normal pricing policy. A policy decision would be required which called for the exercise of judgement.

(b) If the division were working at full capacity the situation would be entirely different. The implications would be that buyers would be competing for acceptance of contracts by the division, which would accept those resulting in the highest contributions in a period. The features of special contracts offered on a 'take it or leave it' basis, as this one, are that they make a contribution but an inadequate one and they should therefore only be considered if no more profitable work seemed likely to be offering in the near future. They are also liable to cause difficulties with regular customers who sooner or later learn that work has been done at a very low price for a casual customer and they resent that they have been paying what now seem excessive prices. In brief, when the division was operating at capacity, then capacity would be the key factor and the management must bear in mind that every contract accepted should give rise to a contribution which met its full share of the fixed expenses, and an adequate further margin towards the overall profit. This contract does not do that.

A main practical danger in the use of marginal costing is that certain managers become overenthusiastic about it and consider that provided a contract offers some contribution it is acceptable. This is certainly not the case: the ultimate aim will be a high return on capital, if not profit maximisation, and attainment of this aim will require that most contracts are at a price which provides a contribution which more than covers the variable costs plus an equitable apportionment of the fixed costs noting that there can be no overall profit until the total costs have been met. As a matter of interest the huge and controversial orders of Polish ships accepted by the UK Government in 1977/78 at much below market prices must have been accepted on the basis of marginal costing calculations. There was severe shortage of shipyard work throughout the world and in the UK the underemployed shipyards are mainly in the North, on in Scotland or Northern Ireland, politically sensitive areas of high unemployment.

It appears that many important manufacturers take certain policy decisions on the basis of marginal costings. For examples, supermarkets sell 'own-brand' jams, biscuits, breakfast foods, etc. Many of these are manufactured for the stores by manufacturers whose main products are nationally advertised so that the 'own brands' which they make are sold in competition with their own main products. The decisions whether or not to accept special contracts of this kind will require considered judgement on a major matter of policy. Presumably the manufacturer concerned will have spare capacity and he will accept special contracts provided that each one provides an acceptable contribution and provided that contracts of this type are marginal and not likely seriously to prejudice the sales of the more profitable nationally advertised articles (which are likely also to be based on 'special formulae' and to be in some way rather more appealing than the standard product made for 'own brands'). Another well-known example of this type of situation is the sale of TV programmes overseas by the BBC and ITV (other than high-cost special programmes made on a joint-venture basis at the outset). In principle the party which makes a TV programme will aim to recover the costs of production plus normal profit through showings in the home markets. Because the home and overseas markets are completely separate, selling material overseas in no way prejudices the sales in the home market. It appears that the practice is to charge 'what the market will bear' for such sales, e.g. high prices might be paid by US stations and much lower ones by developing countries in Africa and Asia. Sales of this type are profitable since the variable costs consist of the costs of the tapes concerned plus royalties or agreed fees for performers and others plus any selling costs and commissions. The difference between the sales revenues and the variable costs – the contribution – may be substantial and a useful supplement towards the overall profits of the ITV, and contribution towards the total costs of the BBC. The same principles apply, of course, when US programme makers sell many of their programmes to the BBC and ITV. The costs of such programmes will be significantly less than the costs the BBC or ITV would incur if they made similar programmes themselves, and the sellers also are well satisfied.

The financial strategy 239

Questions

1. A prospective client has asked for your advice as follows: 'I am thinking of establishing the Northern Sales Agency for some highly specialised – and expensive – scientific instruments. I am convinced that the profits will eventually be really big but I am not certain about the first year. I have shares which currently have a sales value of £5,000 and that will certainly cover the initial advertising and sales promotion which will be required. I will not need any premises because I intend working from my home – where my wife will look after the clerical work – but the extra telephone, stationary, expenses, etc., will be about £25 – £50 a month. In addition all stocks will be held by the main distributor in London who will deliver direct to my customers so there will be no storage requirements. In the first year sales will be at least £72,000 and there is no reason why they should not increase substantially thereafter. With a gross profit percentage of 25% therefore, the £18,000 in the first year will pay for the sample instruments I will have to carry around in my car to show to customers. Fortunately I already own my car so there will be no expense other than petrol and oil, etc., which according to the last AA report I read should work out about 10p per mile. My business mileage will be between 10,000 and 15,000 per annum and, of course, I appreciate that the running expenses for this will have to be paid in cash. I will give my customers the usual trade terms, i.e. they will have to pay me at the end of the month following the month in which they received the goods but given the current economic situation some may take an extra month. The money from sales won't come in evenly of course because in the middle two quarters of the year sales will be twice what they are in the other two quarters. I am not sure when I will have to pay the main distributor after he supplies my customers: I know that down South it is within one week of delivery and when they say one week that is what they mean – but in the early stages they have indicated that they will be more lenient as I have got to pay the agency acquisition fee of £10,000 plus 1% commission on all sales payable quarterly in arrears. The initial acquisition fee lasts for five years so after this first payment all I will have is the sales commission charge and then a new deal will have to be negotiated. Do you think there will be enough profits to let me pay my way the first year?'

You are required to draft a letter replying to your prospective client showing:
(*a*) the level of profit anticipated for the first year (assume the year consists of twelve four-weekly periods);

(b) a cash budget for the first year by quarters.
(c) why profit is not synonymous with cash and why in terms of your client's ability to survive the first twelve months a cash flow budget with appropriate quarterly figures is requred; and
(d) a comment on (a) and (b) including the other information you would like to have in order to provide a more satisfactory answer to these. (ACCA   25 marks)

2. Part Works Ltd is a publishing company which specialises in the production of part-work publications. The company recently introduced special single publications to enable it to extend the life of some of its more successful ventures. One such publication is to follow on from the extremely successful *Silver Fingers* part-work. The costing for this single publication, which is as yet unnamed and referred to as Silver Fingers A, is as follows:

(i) Preparation costs, commissioning authors, photographers, composition, blocks, etc., for whatever quantity of the publication is produced will be £3,000.
(ii) Printing costs £8 per hundred up to 25,000 and then £4 per hundred for any further copies, the reduction in costs coming about because of less spoilt work and scrapping of paper during longer print runs.
(iii) Binding and other finishing costs £100 per 5,000, whatever quantity is produced. The publication is to be sold direct to newsagents and similar retailers at a fixed price of 20p each, to retail at a price of 25p.

Required:
(a) A table showing production costs for: 15,000; 20,000; 25,000; 30,000 and 35,000 of Silver Fingers A, together with the average costs per 5,000 copies of each quantity. Show the marginal cost for each increment. (5 marks)
(b) Draw a breakeven chart for the publication and from this derive the breakeven point. Check the accuracy of your graph by calculating the breakeven point. (8 marks)
(c) Part Work Ltd has already printed 35,000 copies of a publication with similar costs to Silver Fingers A. This has not sold as well as expected and the firm has 10,000 copies left which seem likely to remain unsold. A dealer, who specialises in market trading, offers to buy these for £600. What factors should be considered whether or not to accept the offer? What difference would it have made if the offer had been for £100? (7 marks)   (ACCA   20 marks)

The financial strategy

3. The Cost Accountant of Riding Ltd, calculates that the unit cost of producing a new product, the Venture, is £1.89 (it can be assumed that the unit cost of producing a Venture will be unchanged at different levels of production). The Managing Director of the company, in trying to decide upon the selling price for this product, asks his Marketing Manager to provide a forecast of sales for it during the next quarter at each of the following prices: £1.99; £2.19; £2.39. The Marketing Manager has produced the following table of figures:

Price £1.99		Price £2.19		Price £2.39	
Forecast sales	Probability	Forecast sales	Probability	Forecast sales	Probability
10,000	0.2	6,000	0.05	5,000	0.1
8,000	0.6	5,000	0.9	4,000	0.6
6,000	0.2	4,000	0.05	1,000	0.3

Required: Calculations showing the optimal price that Riding Ltd should charge for each Venture: (*c*. 10 marks); an analysis of your computations with comments on any factors which might influence Riding Ltd's final pricing decisions. (*c*. 10 marks) (ACCA MA 20 marks)

4. The divisional managing director is currently reviewing the progress of Splodge, a detergent which is produced and sold by his division. The divisional chief accountant argues that production should be discontinued on the basis of the following operating statement for 1980:

	(£)	(£)
Sales (5 m. units at 10p)		500,000
Operating expenses:		
Materials	150,000	
Labour	100,000	
Distribution	40,000	
Power	25,000	
Advertising	60,000	
Depreciation	80,000	
Group overhead allocation	100,000	555,000
Loss for year		55,000

The figures for distribution and advertising include an allocation of divisional expenditure of £20,000 and £30,000 respectively.

The amount of depreciation represents a 10% straight-line charge on the original cost of the three machines on which Splodge is produced. The relevant data for them is:

	(1) (£)	(2) (£)	(3) (£)
Original cost 1 Jan. 1975	100,000	300,000	400,000
Total depreciation to 31 Jan. 1980	60,000	180,000	240,000
Book value at 31 Dec. 1980	40,000	120,000	160,000

Neither of the first two machines could be used elsewhere in the company and their scrap value would be £15,000 and £60,000 respectively. The third machine could be transferred to the production of a new product which the company is developing. A machine of equivalent performance would cost £250,000. It is unlikely that another opportunity of transferring the machine will occur and it would otherwise only fetch a scrap value of £50,000.

Sales of Splodge are likely to fall by 0.5 m. units p.a. until they reach 0.5 m. in 1989, after which they are expected to cease and the machines would have no value. The divisional accountant argues that the company should take advantage of the high transfer value of the third machine and cease production immediately. This would produce a profit on the sale or transfer of the machines of £5,000 and would also avoid the anticipated continuing losses on Splodge. The company's required rate of return on investments is 15%. Explain in detail whether you agree with the accountant's recommendation. (ICSA 34 marks)

Chapter 13
Ratio analysis

The published accounts of a company will be studied and analysed by a variety of skilled people, depending on the importance of the company and the purpose of the enquiry. Published accounts provide only limited information and will be significantly out of date by the time of publication. Experienced analysts will be aware of the many problems. Many public companies enjoy excellent reputations because of the lucidity of their published accounts and reports and the fact that they publish a good deal more than the minimum required by the law, and the law itself recognises that the competitiveness of a company, internationally as well as nationally, could be damaged if it were compelled to publish information which could be used by competitors. However, at the other end of the spectrum will be the accounts of companies whose managements are not scrupulous and who seek to manipulate their accounts and reports and these manipulations may either be not detected or not challenged, because of the incompetence of auditors or because they did not wish to antagonise directors and risk losing the large fees paid by a client company. There is a further problem that wide differences of viewpoint and treatment of accounts are permissible and leading authorities may genuinely hold strongly differing views as to what the correct treatment should be in respect of many accounting problem areas – not least, inflation accounting.

The fact is, therefore, that for many reasons the results of one company may not be directly comparable with those of apparently similar companies in the same industry. The rule is that 'like must be compared with like' and a number of adjustments may need to be made before comparisons can be made. The Centre for Interfirm Comparison Ltd, a non-profit-making organisation established by the British Institute of Management in association with the British Productivity Council, is of great help in this respect. Subscribers are supplied with definitions of the terms used and instructions as to bases of calculations, so that all subscribing companies within the same industry will work on the same bases and valid comparisons can be made. The arrangements are that each company regularly provides the Centre with a considerable amount of specified data and the Centre analyses this in great detail and sets it out informatively, each company being identified by a number only. The analyses are circulated to subscribers and each knows its own number and can therefore identify itself in the various groupings and note how it compares with the best and the worst in each grouping. It does not know the identity of other subscribing companies since each is identified by a number only. It is the aspect of confidentiality which has encouraged companies to subscribe to the Centre, whose reputation for expertise is very high.

Members of the management of a company have an advantage over external analysts because they have access to all the information available within the company and they will be aware of the different bases on which valuations have been made and any changes in these. Outside parties can occasionally compel a management to supply information beyond that required by law – notably a banker or other prospective lender from whom a substantial loan is sought. However, analysts writing for stockbrokers, journalists, etc., are not in a position to compel disclosure. Even so, it is astonishing how leading professional analysts are able to make detailed evaluations of the health, strengths and weaknesses of a company on the basis of published information only. Analysts keep files on companies and also use information published by companies such as Extel. Recently published data and comments will be considered in conjunction with data and other information on a particular company for earlier years.

The use of ratios

An understanding of business, or financial ratios, their uses and limitations is essential for a student and a financial manager. When a company is being assessed from any viewpoint it will be usual for a number of ratios to be considered as part of a wider study. A ratio is a derived and not an absolute figure and it is calculated by taking one figure as the numerator and other as the denominator. A test of the skill of a ratio analyst is his ability to identify the key ratios in a particular case.

Some features of ratios

Some general comments may be made about ratios:
(a) A principal value of ratio analysis is that it identifies matters which

Ratio analysis

need further investigation. It seldom provides answers to questions by itself.

(b) This is also true if the same ratio is calculated at different times and the later ratio shows an apparent deterioration or improvement. The ratio alone will not identify the cause(s) of the change but merely that it has occurred and there is need for further investigation.

(c) It is a fundamental rule that like must be compared with like. In the case of ratio analysis this requires that the bases from which the figures are derived are strictly comparable. When the same ratio is considered for the same company over a period of years it will be probable but not certain that the basis will not have changed, but an analyst would study the notes attached to each set of annual accounts, and the directors' reports, to satisfy himself on this point. Whenever changes have occurred, adjustments must be made to permit ratios to be validly compared. Over a period of years adjustments would often be necessary for changes in the value of money, and these present special difficulties: in principle, when ratios are considered over an extended period considerable caution must be used in their interpretation.

(d) There are times when absolute figures convey limited information by themselves, but study of these in conjunction with appropriate ratios can be informative as the worked example on the operating cycle shows (p. 127) and the worked example at the end of this chapter.

(e) Ratios alone cannot give financial control but properly used and interpreted they will indicate areas where stronger control is needed. It will be useful to make use of ratios when plans, policies and budgets are being reviewed.

Some important ratios

The following is a list, which is not comprehensive, of a number of important ratios. Each business will have its own key ratios.

Profitability ratios

$$\frac{\text{Net profit before tax and interest}}{\text{Gross capital employed}}$$

The return on capital employed. This is the primary ratio and is a measure of the efficiency of a management in using all the funds available to them, irrespective of source.

$$\frac{\text{Earnings available for distribution}}{\text{Dividend paid}}$$

The 'dividend cover', which indicates how adequately the dividend paid has been covered.

$$\frac{\text{Tax}}{\text{Net profit before tax}}$$

How much has the government taken and is the trend up or down'.

$$\frac{\text{Cost of loan capital}}{\text{Loan capital}}$$

What is the cost of borrowed funds and how does this compare with the return on capital?

$$\frac{\text{Gross profit}}{\text{Sales}}$$

The 'gross profit ratio'. This ratio is carefully studied by analysts, auditors and inspectors of taxes. If the ratio for a company is out of line with that of other companies in the same industry, or if its own ratio changes significantly the reasons will need to be identified. In brief, possible causes of change could include: (*a*) changes in the sales mix; (*b*) understatement of value or quantity of the opening stock or overstatement of the closing stock, or vice versa; (*c*) changes in buying prices or omission or suppression of purchase invoices; (*d*) inclusion of fictitious sales (a fraudulent owner seeking to sell a business at an inflated price might attempt this); (*e*) introduction of new lines or concentration on old lines with higher (or lower) profit margins, (*f*) changes in the pricing policy or failure to make changes; (*g*) changes in demand.

$$\frac{\text{Profit}}{\text{Sales}}$$

The profit ratio, or P/S ratio, the ratio of net income to net sales. It will be considered with the important P/V ratio, which has already been considered.

Liquidity (or solvency) ratios

$$\frac{\text{Current assets}}{\text{Current liabilities}}$$

The 'current ratio'. This is an important ratio. It used to be widely considered that a ratio of about 2 : 1 is desirable but it is now recog-

$$\frac{\text{Liquid assets}}{\text{Current liabilities}}$$

The 'liquid' or 'quick' or 'acid test' ratio. Too high a ratio would suggest that liquid assets were being held which could be more profitably employed in other ways. A ratio of less than 1 : 1 would call for examination but the circumstances would need to be considered. Thus leading supermarket groups have liquid ratios of well below 1 : 1. Often they will have sold fast-turnover stocks for cash well before they pay their suppliers. A company's unused overdraft facilities would also be relevant. The ratio tends to fall in times of improving trade as larger stocks and debtors have to be financed: conversely, the ratio tends to rise for a time when trade is beginning to decline. Purchase of fixed assets could be part of the explanation for a fall in this ratio. It is always important.

$$\frac{\text{Stocks}}{\text{Current assets}}$$

Stocks are the most difficult to realise of the current assets. What percentage of current assets are tied up in stocks? One would wish to consider this ratio for a company over a period and with the same ratio for other companies in the same industry. A rising trend would call for examination.

$$\frac{\text{Debtors}}{\text{Average daily sales}} = \frac{\text{Debtors} \times 365}{\text{Sales}}$$

This is the average time taken by debtors to pay, in days – the collection period. It should be studied with the approved credit terms and would be a pointer to the quality of the credit control.

$$\frac{\text{Creditors}}{\text{Average daily purchases}} = \frac{\text{Creditors} \times 365}{\text{Purchases}}$$

This is the converse of the collection period and is the average time, in days, which a company takes to pay its creditors. As published accounts seldom show the cost of purchases an external analyst could only make an approximate evaluation.

$$\frac{\text{Cost of sales}}{\text{Average stock}}$$

The 'stock turnover ratio'. An internal analyst would be able to compute separate ratios for raw materials, work in progress, finished goods and for different lines and departments. Variations may arise from the seasonal nature of a trade, or bases of valuation. A decrease in this ratio always calls for enquiry. It could point to an accumulation of unsaleable stocks.

$$\frac{\text{Working capital}}{\text{Sales}}$$

The 'working capital ratio'. As explained (Ch. 12), a special feature of this ratio is that it assists an evaluation of the additional working capital necessary to finance a proposed increase in sales.

$$\frac{\text{Net current debt} \times 365}{\text{Earnings before tax}}$$

This ratio is occasionally met and is known as the current liquidity. The net current debt is the current liabilities less the liquid assets. The ratio gives an indication of the number of days required to pay the current debt out of earnings and is a measure of the adequacy of the cash flow. If the liquid assets exceeded the current liabilities the net current debt would be negative but the unusual liquidity of the company would be evident.

Financing ratios

The effect of gearing on the primary ratio – the rate of return on the equity capital – and the earnings per share have been considered as well as the advantages and disadvantages of gearing to the equity holders. Prospective lenders and creditors will in all cases be concerned with the security of their own positions and ratios which will interest them include:

$$\frac{\text{Total debt}}{\text{Total assets}}$$

A ratio above 1 : 2 would imply that the lenders and creditors were providing more finance than the ordinary shareholders and without expectation of a share in any surplus as compensation for this risk bearing.

$$\frac{\text{Total debt}}{\text{Net worth}}$$

In this case a ratio of above 1 : 1 would indicate that the ordinary shareholders were enjoying the rewards whilst taking no more risks than the lenders and other creditors.

Vulnerability

This term is sometimes met. The current assets are related to the current liabilities to ascertain to what extent the current assets, beginning with the most liquid, cash, would need to be realised to meet the current liabilities. If, say, examination showed that all cash and bank balances and all the debtors and 20% of the stock would need to be realised the vulnerability would be described as '20% of stock'.

It is reported that one of the most successful UK industrialists paid special attention to seven key ratios: he had arrived at this short list on the basis of his own experience and on studies carried out in a number of leading US multinational companies. The list is: (1) Profits on capital employed (the primary ratio); (2) Profits on sales (profits as a percentage of sales). This is one of the two major secondary ratios; (3) Sales as a multiple of capital employed. This is the second of the two major secondary ratios; (4) Sales as a multiple of fixed assets. This is a major subdivision of (3). The ability of fixed assets to generate sales is arguably the best measure of their real worth; (5) Sales as a multiple of stocks. This was found to be an area in which US companies tended to show up much better than their UK counterparts. Main reasons were found to be that US companies made much more use of computer-based techniques for stock and production control, and that US middle-managers tended to have had higher levels of education and training relevant to business activities, and are more numerate. Moreover, generally, US companies can rely on better, faster and more reliable services from their suppliers than UK companies can do and they can thus safely work with lower stock levels; (6) Sales per employee; (7) Profits per employee. Clearly, in a profit orientated company the latter two ratios will give useful pointers, especially in comparison with those for other companies in the same industry, and trends over a period.

The relationship between the primary and the two major secondary ratios should be noted. It is:

$$\frac{(a)}{\text{Operating profit (net profit before tax and interest)}}{\text{Capital employed}}$$

$$= \frac{(b)}{\frac{\text{Operating profit}}{\text{Sales}}} \times \frac{(c)}{\frac{\text{Sales}}{\text{Capital employed}}}$$

The return on capital (a) is thus a function of profit margins (b) and of turnover, (c). The top management of a company will pay attention to both profit margins and turnover. A problem is that as margins are raised turnover will be liable to fall and skilful judgement is needed to obtain the mix which gives rise to the highest possible return on capital. Constant vigilance and adjustment will be needed especially in a highly competitive environment, such as supermarkets operate in.

A summary

A special problem of ratio analysis is that proficiency in interpretation can only be acquired by wide study and practice, and experience and familiarity with data from many industries. Published data can be distorted by 'window dressing' but a switch from ownership of assets to leasing them would also have its effect on ratios. Sometimes information in its basic state is almost meaningless, but the situation is quite different when the appropriate ratios have been identified and calculated, as in the examples on pages 126 and 251. Students have a tendency to calculate a mass of ratios of which the majority have little or no relevance. They then make dogmatic deductions which are often wrong, or too sweeping in relation to the limited information available. In principle it is important to identify the quite small number of ratios which are central to the question and concentrate on these. If a question requires assessment of the financial health and prospects of a company, and perhaps of valuation of it, and two or three balance sheets and profit-and-loss accounts are given, it will first be important to make a quick visual appraisal of the absolute figures. For example, what are the sales and costs of sales and are any trends apparent? Are there any other material figures which show trends and, if so, what do these imply? It will normally be essential to calculate the working capital and the liquid position as at the end of each year and consider the implications of changes and trends. Sometimes a funds flow statement may be constructed but if this is not called for and time is limited, visual inspection often indicates that fixed assets have been financed with unsuitable finance, e.g. delaying payments to creditors, increasing overdrafts, etc. A question may require comment as to whether a loan should be made to a company. If evidence shows poor profitability and declining liquidity the company would seem a doubtful proposition and in practice in such situations if a company can possibly be rescued a precondition would almost certainly be a change in the top management. However, if a situation shows poor liquidity but good profitability a management might not have undue difficulty in adjusting the capital structure and switching from shorter to longer term sources of funds by making a rights issue to obtain more risk capital, or to negotiate a medium to long-term loan, or a mix of equity and loan.

Ratio analysis

Example

Reproduced below is a summary of the final accounts of the Shay Key Company, which is a long-established company which many years ago moved from the manufacture of keys into light engineering. The management is concerned at its poor return on capital and asks you to report on the company's performance as revealed by these accounts. Stress in your report any additional information which you would need in order to give a more complete answer.

Profit and loss account (all figures are in £000)

	1977	1978	1979		1977	1978	1979
Dividend declared	700	900	1,300	Profit for year	1,000	1,100	1,200
Profit forward	500	700	600	Profit from last year	200	500	700
	1,200	1,600	1,900		1,200	1,600	1,900

Notes:
(i) Profit for the year is computed after charging the following expenses: (all in £000)

	1977	1978	1979
Wages	4,000	5,800	8,100
Directors remuneration	60	80	100
Depreciation	3,000	3,200	3,250
Interest paid: long term	400	550	900
short term	–	50	200
Audit fee	20	25	30
Rent paid	100	200	500

(ii) The average number of employees was as follows:
  1977 2,000
  1978 2,600
  1979 3,500
(iii) Sales were as follows: 1977 £12,000,000
  1978 £17,000,000
  1979 £28,000,000

Balance Sheet (£000)

	1977	1978	1979		1977	1978	1979
Ordinary shares	10,000	10,000	10,000	Land & Bldgs	5,000	7,000	8,000
General reserve	5,000	5,000	5,000	Plant & Mchy	8,700	13,600	16,600
Profit & loss a/c	500	700	600				
	15,500	15,700	15,600		13,700	20,600	24,600
10% Debentures	4,000	5,500	9,000	Investments	1,000	–	–
Trade creditors	1,500	4,000	8,000	Stock	2,000	3,500	7,000
Bank overdraft	–	2,000	5,200	Debtors	2,500	4,000	7,500
Dividend payable	700	900	1,300	Cash	2,500	–	–
	21,700	28,100	39,100		21,700	28,100	39,100

Notes: (i) Plant and machinery is comprised as follows: (£000):

	1977	1978	1979
Cost	20,000	28,100	34,350
Less: Depreciation	11,300	14,500	17,750
	8,700	13,600	16,600

(ii) Land and buildings are valued at cost and no depreciation is charged. In the opinion of the directors the current market value of the land and buildings is £11,000,000

(iii) The authorised and issued share capital of the company is £10,000,000 divided into 20,000,000 shares of 50p.

(iv) The debentures are secured against the land and buildings of the company. Ignore taxation. (ICSA 34 marks)

Workings and comments

Note that a report is called for and the anxiety is about the primary ratio, the return on capital. Visual examination shows the present dangerously bad liquid position and the heavy increases in the fixed assets which have evidently been financed excessively from short-term sources of funds – trade creditors and bank overdraft. The range of figures is so wide that comparison of the figures as they stand is hardly practicable and it is a situation in which ratio analysis is effectively essential. Visual inspection shows that the expenses list is not complete since the total expenses plus profit must equal the sales revenues and these do not. A student who fails to notice this vital fact – and many fall into this trap – fails to identify the main cause of the troubles. The missing balancing item is clearly the 'cost of materials' plus the obviously minor item of general expenses and it has been calculated and the items in the profit and loss accounts have been calculated as percentages of the annual sales. (The first column shows how the ratio has been arrived at):

1977(£000)		1977(%)	1978(%)	1979(%)
4,000/12,000	Wages	33.3	34.1	28.9
60/12,000	Directors remuneration	0.5	0.5	0.4
3,000/12,000	Depreciation	25.0	18.8	11.6
400/12,000	Long-term interest	3.3	3.2	3.2
	Short-term interest	–	0.3	0.7
20/12,000	Audit fees	0.2	0.1	0.1
100/12,000	Rent	0.8	1.2	1.8
3,420/12,000	Cost of materials & expenses (Balancing item).	28.5	35.3	49.0
1,000/12,000	Profit	8.4	6.5	4.3
		100.0	100.0	100.0

Ratio analysis

Balance sheet ratios

1,000/15,500	Profit/equity capital employed	6.5	7.0	7.7
1,400/19,500	Profit + long-term interest/capital employed	7.2	7.8	8.5
12,000/19,500	Sales/capital employed	0.62	0.80	1.14
1,000/12,000	Profit/sales	8.33	6.47	4.29
1,000/2	Profit per employee (£)	500	423	343
7,000/2,200	Current ratio	3.2	1.1	1.0
5,000/2,200	Liquid ratio	2.3	0.6	0.5
4,000/19,500	Gearing ratio (one of the available measures)	20.5	25.9	36.6
2,000/12,000	Stock as a percentage of sales	16.67	20.59	25.00

(It will be noted how the preparation of ratios improves the informativeness of the absolute figures. Thus, first visual inspection of the question focuses on the large increase in wages paid, but when the wages figures are related to the sales, and expressed as a ratio, they are seen in a new perspective insofar as they have declined as a percentage of sales: there is still a question whether they have declined enough and an analyst would study this aspect.) Other ratios are 'not material', e.g. directors' remuneration and audit fees. In this question the most disturbing ratio is clearly that of the cost of materials and general expenses to sales. Further information and analysis would be needed so that the materials costs could be separately identified and then studied to pinpoint what was going wrong. There is usually more than one cause of weakness. What products are sold? What is the pricing policy? What is the profitability of different lines and what is the sales mix and has this mix been changing? Have prices not been increased in line with rising prices and, if not, why not? What is the buying policy and are competitive quotations sought? What controls are there? What are the storekeeping procedures and controls, including for receipts and issues? What internal checks and controls are operated and is there internal audit? The large increase in sales would have been expected to lead to large increases in profits but this has not happened and there must be serious questions about the efficiency of the operations of different functions of the company. Moreover, if weaknesses of control exist there will be special opportunities for theft and fraud.

The liquid position of the company is unacceptable and pressure from creditors for payment could conceivably result in liquidation or at least forced sales of assets on unfavourable terms. The overall return on capital is below the cost of the borrowed funds and this raises the question of the basis on which the company evaluates and selects capital projects. One would wish to have the accounts, directors' reports, etc., for earlier years to try to pinpoint why and when operations began to be unprofitable. Why is the company paying substantially higher rent charges in view of the purchases of land and buildings? A number of non-financial questions would need to be investigated. Is the company a market leader and what is its market share? What are informed views as to how it stands in relation to competitors? What is its research and development programme and how successful has this been? How are the industrial relations? How effective is the credit control, etc.?

The decline in the return on capital is seen to arise mainly from the fall in the important secondary ratio of profit/sales, which indicates that profit margins have been falling which follows from the startling rise in the ratio of cost of materials to sales. It also appears that in recent years the company has undertaken major new investment projects which have proved to be unprofitable. The expansion has been financed on an unsound basis. These are matters which raise questions about the top management of the company. It would seem desirable that selected consultants should be commissioned to identify weaknesses and propose arrangements to improve all aspects of the operating efficiency and controls. The company's auditors might usefully be consulted. Efforts should be directed to (*a*) increasing revenues, and (*b*) reducing costs. The reasons for the increases in the cost of materials over the period should be investigated as the highest priority, and reasons why these increases were not recovered by appropriate increases in selling prices.

Questions

1. You are required to comment **briefly** on the meaning and practical application of the following ratios: (*a*) capital gearing ratio; (*b*) shareholders' funds/total assets (the proprietary ratio); (*c*) percentage of net trading profit to turnover; (*d*) liquid ratio; (*e*) yields. (ACCA Acciv 15 marks)

2. Define the concept of earnings per share (EPS) and consider its importance in the determination of share prices. (ICSA 22 marks)

3. You are required to give **one** example of a ratio representative of each of the following headings and to comment on its construction and usefulness: (*a*) Primary ratio; (*b*) Secondary ratio; (*c*) Solvency ratio; (*d*) Capital ratio. (ACCA Acciv 12 marks)

4. ABC Ltd is a public company which owns several department stores. Its balance sheet for the year ended 31 December 1978 is shown below with comparative figures for 1977.

Ratio analysis

Balance Sheet of ABC Ltd as at 31 December 1978 (in £1 m.)

		1978		1977
Assets:				
Fixed assets: property		200		180
fixtures		11		10
		211		190
Current assets: stock	80		40	
debtors	60		20	
cash	–		20	
		140		80
Total assets		351		270
Current liabilities: creditors	60		30	
taxation	11		18	
proposed dividend	7		6	
bank overdraft	30		–	
		108		54
Net assets		243		216
Financed by:				
Ordinary shares		70		70
Reserves		142		135
Preference shares		1		1
Shareholders' interest		213		206
Debentures – 10%		30		10
Net capital employed		243		216
Excerpts from the profit and loss account shown in £1 m.		*1978*		*1979*
Sales/turnover		400		300
Purchases		200		130
Operating profit before interest and tax		30		40

You are required to:
(a) comment on the performance and situation of ABC Ltd
(b) write a report on the advantages and disadvantages of ratio analysis. (ICSA 34 marks)
4. The ABC Co Ltd have only recently introduced five-year forward planning and a preliminary meeting has been called to consider the first five-year plan. It has been decided not to formalise the meeting but the **financial manager has been asked to extract the significant aspects – both quantitative and qualitative – of the discussion and produce a summary of them for the next meeting. This is what you are required to do paying particular attention to the financial implications of what is suggested.**
Sales Manager – 'This year our sales reached £5,000,000 for the first time and these is no reason why we should not expect these to continue

increasing. Indeed, I would say that we should achieve sales of £5,300,000; £5,700,000; £6,200,000; £6,800,000; £7,750,000 over the next five years respectively.'

Managing Director – 'Given the inflation rate we are likely to get, that doesn't sound so very impressive to me.'

Sales Manager – 'Oh no – these figures are in present-day prices. Obviously if there is inflation our prices will rise accordingly.'

Managing Director – 'Good – and if we maintain our ratio of net profit after tax to sales to 10% we will be showing a substantial increase in our profits as well.'

Financial Manager – 'If our profits go up our shareholders will expect dividends to go up as well.'

Managing Director – 'Our past policy has always been to have an earnings retention rate of 50% and I see no reason to change this.'

Production Manager – 'This is all very well but while our plant and equipment is fairly modern there will have to be some replacement and there is a limit to what we can put in our present space.'

Financial Manager – 'The same also applies to our working capital needs.'

Managing Director – 'These aspects will obviously have to be worked out in detail but I think you will find that our total net asset turnover which is at present 0.8 times will not vary very much from year to year.'

Financial Manager – 'What about our long-term borrowing?'

Managing Director – 'You know my views on that. I don't think we should ever let our, and by "our" I mean the shareholders', share of long-term funds fall below 70%.'

Financial Manager – 'But we are at that level already.'

Managing Director – 'O.K. – We will consider that along with all other relevant matters at our next meeting.' (ACCA 25 marks)

5. (*a*) Discuss the uses and limitations of accounting ratios to measure the viability and performance of a business. (Use suitable ratios to illustrate your answer). (*b*) Explain any further benefits of ratio analysis which may be gained within a scheme of inter-firm comparison. (SCCA 20 marks)

Chapter 14
Capital expenditure

The distinction between capital and operating expenditure has already been indicated. For the purpose of managing or evaluating any organisation the aspect of time must be taken into account and inevitably the period of a year has been adopted for many purposes as it is a major natural cycle, neither too short nor too long, and allows for a complete cycle of seasonal factors to be included. Cyclical factors are less predictable than seasonal ones and may exert their effects over many years. Furthermore, taxes are everywhere now a fact of life and in most countries taxes on income are with respect to twelve-monthly periods and there will normally be distinctions between taxes on capital gains and taxes on profits, and this in itself makes it essential for accounting records to distinguish between capital and revenue items. In brief, expenditure is regarded as being of an operating – or revenue – nature if the item concerned will be consumed within a year, i.e. will have no residual value after the year ends. Adjustments may need to be made in respect of the stock position or accruals – costs incurred but not paid, or revenues due but not received. Moreover, in the case of minor capital items – items costing less than a stated sum – a company may have a policy of treating these as expendable and not worth the trouble of 'capitalising' them, i.e. recording them in asset registers, depreciating them, etc.

A capital item is one which has a useful life exceeding one year. As explained, an equitable proportion of the cost of the asset will need to be charged as an expense against the revenues of each year, and this is done by means of the depreciation charge. Whilst the concept of depreciation is simple, many complexities arise in practice. A special problem arises in consequence of inflation since the cost of replacing a capital item will normally be much higher than the original cost (but against that, the new asset may be technologically much superior, and more productive). It should be borne in mind that when capital project evaluations are made which are based on cash flows, depreciation is excluded from the cash forecasts since no cash movements arise, but, in fact, the forecasts do take into account the loss in value of a capital item through time since the cost of the asset is treated as an outlay at the start, and an estimate of the proceeds of sale (possibly as scrap) at the end of the project are incorporated in the forecast. The difference between the initial cash outlay and the final cash inflow will be the measure of the loss in value of the asset over the period – this latter estimate may prove to very inaccurate in practice. If a capital asset is leased there will not be a depreciation charge, of course, and the agreed leasing payment – which will be known accurately – will be charged against the project for its duration, and the payments for the year will be charged as an expense in the profit-and-loss accounts for the year.

The unevenness of capital expenditure

Another important distinction between capital and operating expenditure is that whereas the latter tends to have a degree of regularity, capital expenditure may need to be incurred more irregularly and unpredictably. In fact, larger and well-managed companies seek as far as practicable to arrange capital expenditure programmes for ships, vehicles, machines, etc. so that these maintain a reasonably even flow, but even so there are likely to be marked fluctuations from year to year.

Capital expenditure procedures

Acceptance of commitments to capital expenditure, either of major single items or a number of smaller ones, may have far-reaching implications for a company. A major wrong decision can even destroy it. Accordingly, in practice, every well-managed company will exercise strict control over all aspects of capital expenditure. The arrangements often follow a hierarchical pattern with capital expenditure exceeding a specified sum requiring the approval of the full board, and with delegation so that the chief executive can authorise up to a specified and smaller sum, and nominated managers below him authorised to approve smaller sums, in each case up to a maximum in respect of a single item and a specified maximum annual total: the more senior the manager the more authority he will have to authorise significant capital expenditure. Even so, some large companies keep capital expenditure on a very 'tight rein' indeed and only a relatively small number of senior managers have

Capital expenditure

powers to authorise even quite minor expenditure. Practices vary quite widely but tight control is important.

The need for capital expenditure may arise for many reasons – expansion of activity may call for extension of present offices and/or factories, or moves into larger premises, and the acquiring of new machines and/or equipment. At other times, older plant, machines, ships, etc., may become uneconomic to operate, with excessive breakdowns, repairs, losses to production, etc., and sometimes new technologically advanced machines may become available, which may be very labour saving. Skilled evaluation will be necessary to assess whether it will be more profitable to continue with an existing asset or dispose of it ahead of the expected time, replacing it with a more efficient asset. As the Wilson Committee noted, there are many types of investment other than investment in new capacity. A good deal will be needed to replace items which are part of a larger whole and which become damaged or worn beyond economic repair. Other capital expenditure may be necessary for social or legal reasons, such as staff amenities and installations designed to meet health and safety legislation.

It is usual for a company to have two budget committees, with overlapping memberships, one to deal with operating and one with capital budgets. It is recognised now that although companies may seek to make outline plans extending for a number of years into the future, the farther one seeks to look ahead the greater is the margin for error. Even so, companies operating plantations, or electricity generating stations may have to make at least tentative plans extending up to twenty-five years or so in the future. In general, many companies now consider it unrealistic to attempt to plan ahead in detail more than three years or so, and even that will be difficult. Planning, budgetary control and cash forecasting will put emphasis on the next twelve months, and then the year after that. A distinction between an operating and a capital budget is that board approval of the operating budget as a whole will signify approval of all the sub-budgets. This is not so in the case of capital budgets. The board may sanction the proposed capital budget for the next financial year, since it will be essential to take this into account when preparing the important cash forecasts. However, board sanction of the capital budget as a whole does not normally signify approval of each component, which must receive sanction individually.

To permit control and coordination, and so that the cash-flow aspect is always under close scrutiny, those concerned with capital projects will be required to complete carefully designed forms. These will require completion with respect to: (1) general outline of the proposals, and reasons; (2) statement of the estimated total cost of the project, with supporting evidence; (3) breakdowns of the total budgeted outlays over the current and succeeding financial years, noting that many costlier projects extend over several years; (4) reasons for and arguments in support of the project. In the case of smaller projects, expensive feasibility studies would not be necessary but there should always be sufficient material to show, possibly at a later date, that those concerned were not entering into a project carelessly. Naturally, as the sums involved become larger, and the risks greater, the supporting evaluations will be deeper and sometimes extremely costly in themselves. Outside consultants would be employed as required. For a major capital project it will always be necessary to make a number of assumptions. Main ones will be the year-to-year rate of inflation, costs of capital, the various elements of labour and materials costs, selling prices and sales volumes in the case of projects giving rise to revenues.

In principle, assumptions made should always be stated. In appropriate cases mathematical techniques such as the theory of probability, risk analysis and sensitivity analysis will need to be used by competent specialists. It appears that high interest rates and high inflation are major factors in causing industrialists to hold back from approval of projects which they might have approved in more stable and less uncertain times. Indeed, the present high levels of uncertainty in the UK, high inflation and interest rates and the difficulties in recruiting high-calibre and experienced managers and skilled workers may be factors which encourage larger companies seeking to enter new fields of activity to do so by means of agreed takeovers of smaller, well-managed successful companies rather than start from the very beginning themselves.

When a request for a capital sanction approval is prepared by or for a manager who has authority to approve it, he will himself sanction the completed forms and the procedures will include that the identifying details will be passed to the accounts department and also to the budget secretary so that the facts will be recorded in the financial records and, not least, taken into account in the cash forecasts. If sanction could only be given at a higher level of management, as is often the case, the forms would be endorsed and passed upwards to the line manager or appropriate superior, who would either approve or disapprove the proposal, if approval lay within his authority, or he might call for further information. If he approved in principle but the matter exceeded his own authority, he would endorse the proposals and pass them to his superior manager. At the appropriate level the decision would be taken to approve the project, or shelve or reject it. In practice it often happens that when an important project has begun, delays occur and costs increase, often for reasons outside the control of the company. The procedures should include that formal approvals must be sought and obtained for expenditure above what has already been approved and full details and explanations recorded in the project file. Furthermore, the budget committee and the board should be kept informed, the latter normally by means of summarises, with attention drawn to items of special significance: cash forecasts should also be revised promptly.

Capital investment appraisal: alternative approaches

Before a project reaches the stage of detailed appraisal a great deal of work should have been done, including of a non-financial nature, and market research. Then, when all the signs are sufficiently promising the financial evaluations will begin. There are a number of well-established methods and each has its values and limitations and it is usual for important projects, whose acceptance would give rise to significant non-reversible capital expenditure, to be examined under more than one method. The Wilson Committee reported that industrialists informed them that because of the virtual impossibility at the present time of being confident how things would work out in the future, the appropriate management techniques were employed often primarily as disciplines and the final decisions would be made by those concerned on the basis of their judgement and experience, special attention being given to the cash forecasts and the payback period and rather less to discounted cash flow (DCF) projections.

The main commonly used methods are: (*a*) payback; (*b*) the return on investment; (*c*) the net present value (NPV); (*d*) the yield, or internal rate of return (IRR). An important matter must now be considered, which many students find difficult to grasp at first. It is that when significant sums of money are being considered the aspect of the timings of receipts and payments assumes special importance. In brief, £1,000 held today is not the same as £1,000 to be received, say, twelve months from today. This appears obvious in a time of inflation but it is true and important in times of stable prices. The importance of cash forecasting has been emphasised. In the case of operating budgets attempts are made to prepare realistic cash forecasts for the next twelve months and more tentative ones for the next one to two years. In practice the question of how the timings of receipts and payments may affect the value of the money involved is ignored. It is recognised that these forecasts must be approximate only, and are subject to quite large margins of error, and to attempt to introduce an additional factor, if this were not essential, would be to pretend to a degree of accuracy which would be unrealistic.

However, when important capital projects are considered which extend over a period of years, the interrelationships of timings of receipts and payments and the underlying value of money cannot be ignored. This is especially because a main feature of substantial capital projects is that large cash outflows will be necessary at the start to pay for fixed assets and provide working capital: outflows may continue for two or three or even more years and this represents money put at risk. The outflow of cash is sanctioned in the hope and expectation that in due course there will be a net cash inflow which before the project ends will, in total, exceed the total outflows, in which case the project will be likely to have justified itself. There is, however, a problem about measuring the values of the total cash outflows and then inflows because of the fact that the timings of receipts and payments extend over a period of years and sums received later in the project have a lower real value than the same nominal sums received earlier, and noting that it will be the net outflows which occur in the earlier stages and the less valuable inflows – hopefully – in the later stages. This increases the risk aspect of major capital projects.

The timings of receipts and payments

To consider this question from the aspect of first principles, let it be assumed that the value of money is stable, as it has been in the UK in the past, and may be again in the future, and as it tends to be even today in Switzerland. If a person were now offered a choice between £100 now and £100 twelve months from now and the person did not need the money now and had confidence that the option of the deferred payment would be honoured, what would the choice be? It would always be to have £100 now, for the reason that it could always be invested to earn interest, and at the end of the twelve months the £100 invested, with accumulated interest, would effectively have a higher value than £100 paid at the end of twelve months. However, if the offer were a choice between £100 paid now and £110 twelve months from now the choice would depend on an asessment of whether or not £100 received now could be invested so that it accrued to more than £110 at the end of twelve months. There might be certainty as to the outcome or a subjective assessment might need to be made as to how interest rates would move over the next twelve months. In principle, the value of a stated sum of money will be a function of the principal sum, the

Capital expenditure

period of time considered and the rate or rates of interest obtainable during the period.

An important consequence of this fact is that even when prices are stable a given sum of money in a particular currency cannot validly be added to or subtracted from other sums expressed in the same currency: thus, if a payment of £100 is to be made at the end of each year for a period of ten years it is invalid and seriously misleading to state that there will be total payments of £1,000, and yet many businessmen, as well as students, fail to realise this. The fact is that £1 held now is not the same as £1 held twelve months from now. If a student were asked to add sums expressed in a mixture of pounds sterling, Swiss francs, Japanese yen, etc., and to state the total he would unhesitatingly reply that he could not do this unless the currencies were expressed in terms of a single common unit and he would need to be informed of the rates of exchange. On the same principle, present and future units of sterling, or any other currency, cannot validly be added or subtracted until adjustments, or conversions, have been made and the different units are expressed in terms of a common unit, so that like can be compared with like. Is a common unit available? Fortunately, it is. On reflection it will quickly be recognised that by far the most useful and practical concept is the 'present value' of money. People instinctively think in terms of what they know, and the present in preference to the past or future.

In brief, all sums of money to be received or paid in the future have to be 'converted' by use of the appropriate conversion factor, so that all sums under review, future receipts or payments, are expressed in terms of a common unit, the 'present value'. The difference between the totals of the receipts and payments will then be the 'net present value' (NPV). If the receipts exceed the payments it will indicate that the project would be profitable if all the assumptions proved valid. Unfortunately, experience shows that despite the utmost skill and care, major assumptions may prove to be far from valid.

Discounted cash flow (DCF)

An important concept must now be considered which alarms many students quite unnecessarily, so that they often assume, wrongly, that examination questions involving the use of this concept and technique must be the most difficult ones, to be avoided if possible. They can often be easy, provided that the student has had practice and has confidence. The following discussion of the DCF concept will concentrate on the practical applications and will not deal with the mathematical principles. The fact is that reasonable familiarity with and understanding of the uses and limitations of DCF does not require mathematical knowledge. In practice, involved calculations would be done by specialists and an experienced generalist, such as a senior manager would often be, would expect to be able to understand the implications of the calculations, and ask the right questions: he would not feel inhibited because he was not himself trained to understand the underlying mathematics.

In fact, and as will be seen, the underlying work required for DCF evaluations has largely been carried out, once and for all time, many years ago, and has been made available to all who require it in the form of published tables. What is essential for students and managers is familiarity with the use of tables and ability to identify the correct table to use. In examinations either the tables will be supplied or the question will incorporate extracts from tables which will permit the calculations to be made. However, often too much information is supplied in a question in order to test the ability of the student to identify the information he needs. In the past the tables would have been used with logarithmic tables but the latter have effectively been made redundant by the capabilities of pocket electronic calculators, which can now be used in examinations. Naturally, the time factor compels examiners to set rather oversimplified questions, which are designed to test the students' understanding of the basic principles and ability to apply these. Real-life questions can involve many complex calculations, including tax factors, and in practice computers would normally be used.

For those interested, the basic mathematical formula from which much else is derived is the simple one $S = P(1 + i)^n$, where S is the sum to which a given principal sum, P, will accumulate at a given compound rate of interest, i, per period, n. The rate of interest is expressed as a decimal, e.g. 5% becomes 0.05. The period n is usually but not necessarily expressed in years. However, if the period is not a year then the rate of interest used must be appropriate, e.g. if the rate is 12% per annum then the rate per month would be 1%. Banks calculate interest on a daily basis but a computer can easily be programmed to deal with this.

For those not yet familiar with the concept of expressing sums to be paid or received in the future in terms of present values, it may help to consider a simple situation. A student asked what £100 would be worth at the end of a year if it were now invested at a rate of interest of 5% would at once reply '£105'. This seems simple and obvious because people are familiar with the idea of money accumulating through earning interest. However, if the question is put as: '£105 is to be received twelve months from today and the rate of interest is 5%, what

Capital expenditure

is the present value of that £105?' not everyone will answer promptly. The answer is, of course, £100. It will be evident that if the sum to which a given principal will accumulate by a stated date at a given rate of compound interest can be precisely calculated then, conversely, if the sum to be received on a stated future date is known, and the rate of compound interest, then the present value of that future sum receivable can also be precisely calculated.

Students who are acquainting themselves with DCF calculations may find it helpful initially to recheck their workings in the following way – when they have converted several future sums receivable into present values by use of the appropriate table they should satisfy themselves as to the accuracy of their calculation by using the other appropriate table to check that the present sums would indeed accumulate to the future sums receivable, over the same period and at the same rate of interest.

A student familiar with the preparation of cash forecasts should have no difficulty in preparing a DCF statement. In brief, and as explained, a cash forecast is prepared in a simple, unadjusted form because the time period involved is short. For the reasons explained, when longer periods are considered, and the heaviest outflows are at the start, adjustments must be made so that all sums are expressed in terms of a common unit, the present value. In preparing a DCF statement the relevant information must be set out logically, payments and receipts being separated and for a given period the difference between the totals of each group will be the net total, and the net total for each period is shown in a final column. Up to this point the sums shown are in nominal currency units, as yet unconverted. To carry out the conversion from a simple cash forecast to a DCF statement two further columns must be added: the first will be headed 'factor', and will be the figure obtained from the appropriate table, as will be explained. The final column will be headed 'net present value' (NPV) and will be the product of the figures in the two preceding columns – the nominal net cash receipt or payment and the factor. The later worked examples in this chapter should be studied carefully.

The use of tables

To determine differences in the present, or future, value of sums of money arising in consequence of differences of timings of receipts or payments it is necessary to know in each case: (1) the sum involved; (2) the period; (3) the rate of interest. (This is so even when the value of money is stable. Inflation presents problems which need not be considered at this stage, when the emphasis is on first principles.) The use of the appropriate table greatly simplifies the calculations and students will be assumed to use pocket calculators. All the tables are expressed in terms of a value (unit) of 1. This gives them universal application. In the UK the usual unit will be £1. As will be seen, the appropriate factor will be located in the table and will then be multiplied by the number of pounds under consideration and this will be the sum sought. There are four main tables in common use and it is important to understand the significance of each and gain practice in its use.

The compound amount of 1 $(1 + i)^n$

This table permits quick calculation of the sum to which a given sum invested now will accumulate at the end of a stated period and at a stated rate of compound interest, e.g. if £1,250 is invested now at 7% p.a., to what sum will this accrue at the end of 15 years? Take the table with the above heading and look down the left-hand column headed n, which in this case is 15 years. Place a ruler under the horizontal line of figures which has 15 at the left and read the figure vertically beneath the column headed 7%. It will be found to be 2.75903, i.e. (£) I would accumulate to (£) 2.75903, and the answer is therefore £1,250 × 2.75903, i.e. £3,448.7875 or £3,449 (rounded).

Present value of (V_{n_i})

When a sum is to be received at a stated future time and the compound rate of interest is stated, the use of this table permits the present value to be calculated quickly. Thus, if £1,250 is to be received at the end of 15 years and the rate of interest throughout will be 7%, what is the present value? In this case, select the table with the above heading and using a ruler as explained, the appropriate factor will be found to be 0.362446 and the answer is therefore £1,250 × 0.362446 and the answer is therefore £1,250 × 0.362446, i.e. £453.0575 (£453). The difference between the present value of the nominal sum to be received in the future is thus seen to be considerable and this shows how important the DCF concept is when an extended time scale is being considered.

As suggested, the accuracy of the calculations just made can easily be verified. In the first example, £1,250 has been calculated as accumulating to £3,449 after 15 years at 7% interest. In other words, if £3,449 is received 15 years from now and the rate of interest is 7% then its present value must be £1,250. This can be checked. Similarly, from the second example it can be checked that £453 would accumulate to £1,250 at the end of 15 years with an interest rate of 7%.

Capital expenditure

Present value of an annuity of 1 per period (A_{n_i})

A commonly met situation is one in which a regular sum will be received or paid at the end of each period (e.g. an annuity or pension). The present value of an annuity can be quickly calculated by use of the above table, e.g. 'what is the present value of an annuity of £1,250 to be received at the end of each year for 15 years when the rate of interest will be 8% throughout?' Take the table under the above heading and the factor for period 15 will be found to be 8.55948. Accordingly, the answer to this question, found within seconds, is £1,250 × 8.55948, i.e. £10,669.

Amount of annuity of 1 per period (S_{n_i})

This table permits quick calculation of the sum to which a given annuity will accumulate at the end of a stated period at a stated rate of interest, e.g. 'if £1,250 is invested at the end of each year for 15 years at 7% p.a., what will this amount to at the end of that period?' Using the table with the above heading, the required factor will be found to be 25.12902 and the answer is thus £1,250 × 25.12902, i.e. £31,411.

It will be apparent that if at first a wrong table is selected by mistake the figure calculated will be so obviously wrong that the mistake will be self-evident. Thus, the present value of a sum to be received in the future will always be below the nominal future sum. Students should also note that in many DCF questions the first part will require the straightforward preparation of a cash forecast and it will always be essential to distinguish between receipts and payments, for a careless mistake can easily be made by confusing a receipt with a payment so that the conclusions drawn are invalid: receipts should be treated as positive and payments as negative (prefixed by a minus sign, or within brackets). When the net cash flow (in nominal terms) has been calculated for each period, and then converted into 'net present value' terms by multiplying by the appropriate factor, the product will be the 'net present value' (NPV) for that period, and will be positive or negative. The net present value for the whole project will be the total of the final column, the net present value for each period. In brief, a positive total would indicate that if all went according to plan the project would preserve the initial capital intact, would meet the costs of capital, as expressed by the rate of interest used, and would result in a surplus − profit − of the total of the NPV column, and this profit, by definition, would be expressed in terms of present values. Conversely, a negative total would indicate a project resulting in a loss. Naturally, the larger the positive NPV the more profitable, and promising, a project would seem to be. The insuperable problem remains, however, that an evaluation will be no better than the assumptions on which it is based.

Often a capital project has to be entered into which will not give rise to revenues – a new school, or a hospital may be built, or a company decides to improve its staff amenities, etc. In such cases the first test will be whether a proposed project is necessary at all. If the decision is that it is necessary the next step will be to decide the available options, then examine each to determine which should permit the objectives to be achieved efficiently and at lowest cost. A DCF evaluation will often be appropriate for assessing how the real costs of the different options would compare, but the problem would still arise that assumptions would need to be made.

Two important assumptions: year '0'; flows occur at end of period
Two practical points need to be noted: (1) in practice cash flows tend to occur continually throughout the year or, if the business is seasonal, they may be concentrated at certain known times. The tables have all been constructed on the basis that the cash flow occurs at the end of the period. Those concerned regularly with these calculations will have computers at their disposal and in principle there is no real problem since periods of a half year, or a quarter, or even a day could be considered if this were necessary. Examination questions often state that receipts or payments may be assumed as occurring at the end of the year. In other appropriate cases the student may state that he is making this assumption, which would show him to be aware of the point. (2) The starting point of evaluations will usually be 'year 0'. The significance of this is simple. It is that the point in time to which the NPV is related is the moment when the first capital outlays would be made if the project were adopted. This would therefore be the beginning of year 1 and not the end of it. This start of year 1 can be seen as the end of year 0. The point is that, by definition, the present value of money paid out at the present is its present value and, therefore, no matter what the rate of interest, the factor for year 0 will always be 1.0000.

The following example illustrates the application of a DCF approach to a simple situation to which the answer is self-evident. A property is purchased for £1,000 and is rented out at a rental of £100 p.a. payable at the end of each year. It is sold at the end of the fifth year for £1,000. It will be evident that this property gave rise to a return of 10% on an investment of £1,000. A DCF evaluation could be set out thus, the factor having been taken from the table headed 'present value of 1'.

Capital expenditure

Year	Payments (£)	Receipts	Factor	NPV
0	−1,000		1.0000	−1,000
1		100	0.9091	90.91
2		100	0.8264	82.65
3		100	0.7513	75.13
4		100	0.6830	68.30
5		1,100	0.6209	683.01
				0

The '0' NPV indicates that at the stated rate of interest of 10% the project resulted in neither a profit nor a loss in terms of present values, i.e. there was the initial capital outlay, with due receipts of interest at 10% and at the end the original outlay was recovered.

Discounted cash flow methods

There are two main methods of applying the DCF concept, as set out in the following paragraphs.

The net present value method (NPV)
For this method to be used the interest rate applicable must be known and used, e.g. when the cost of capital is known and the appraisal is to determine whether or not a project would be profitable using capital with that cost. For evaluation with this method, cash forecasts will be prepared, with the two final columns, the factor and NPV, as already explained.

The DCF yield method: (the internal rate of return) (IRR)
Sometimes the information available takes a different form, notably when the applicable rate of interest cannot be stated and the calculation is to determine the rate. This involves the use of the DCF yield method which, for reasons which will be apparent, is often known as the 'trial and error' method. It will be evident that when the NPV method is being used, if a project would give rise to neither a profit nor a loss at a predetermined cost of capital then the NPV would be 0. If the NPV were positive then the project would be expected to yield a profit and the implication would be that the project would 'break even' even if capital with a somewhat higher cost were used. Conversely, if the NPV method gave rise to a negative total the implication would be that at the

cost of capital under consideration there would be a loss and for a 'breakeven' to be achieved capital with a rather lower cost must be used. The difference between the approaches of the NPV and yield methods can be simply illustrated by extending the simple example already used. Let the fact that the rate of interest is clearly 10% be ignored, for in practice the figure is not normally self-evident. If the factor for 8% is tried first, the NPV will be positive, indicating that the 'breakeven' rate sought is above this. If the factor of 15% is then taken, the NPV will be negative, indicating that the rate sought is below this. By trial and error in this case it would be found that the rate sought was 10%, i.e.:

Year	NCF*	Factor 8%	NPV	Factor 15%	NPV	Factor 10%	NPV
0	−1,000	1.0000	−1,000	1.0000	1,000	1.0000	1,000
1	100	0.9259	92.59	0.8696	86.96	0.9091	90.91
2	100	0.8573	85.73	0.7561	75.61	0.8265	82.65
3	100	0.7938	79.38	0.6575	65.75	0.7513	75.13
4	100	0.7350	73.50	0.5718	57.18	0.6830	68.30
5	1,100	0.6806	748.64	0.4972	546.90	0.6209	683.01
			79.84		− 167.60		0

* Net cash flow

It will often happen, of course, that the rate sought is not a whole number and the published tables only give details with respect to these. What can be done in such cases, without recourse to mathematical formulae? If the trial-and-error method is used there would be a progressive narrowing of the gap between the positive and negative NPVs until finally it would ascertained that the rate sought was above, say, 16% and below 17%. For most practical purposes it would be enough to state that fact. A closer approximation could be calculated thus: if, say, using factors for 16% the NPV is, say 35 and for 17%, say, −60, then the difference between these two figures is 95 and the figure sought is evidently closer to 16% than to 17%. The approximate figure is $16 + \frac{35 \times 1}{35 + 60}$, i.e. 16 + 35/95 or 16.37 approximately. Because it is recognised that calculations of this type are subject to wide margins of error an approximation such as calculated above is adequate for most situations.

The tax aspects

In practice, in capital project evaluations, the tax aspect will always be of the utmost importance. However, examination questions often state that taxation should be ignored, but the tax aspect is sometimes incorporated in simplified form. If a question states the rate of tax on profits, unless the profits were stated it would be necessary to prepare a profit-and-loss account in order to determine the profits liable to tax. The question would indicate the date for payment of tax, and payment would give rise to a cash outflow on that date. Allowances, if mentioned, do not give rise to direct cash movements but they must be taken into account in computing the tax liability which they reduce, or defer. However, if grants are mentioned, these give rise to cash receipts by the company on the date indicated.

Depreciation

The loss in value of an asset over time is recognised in DCF evaluations by the fact that the initial cost appears as a payment and anything assessed as receivable at final disposal is included as a receipt and the difference between the two figures is the measure of the intervening loss of value, adjusted by conversion into present values by use of the appropriate factor(s). As explained, depreciation is not an item for incorporation in either a cash forecast or a DCF evaluation. However, depreciation must be included as an expense whenever a profit-and-loss account is being prepared. Questions may also state that the fixed expenses, including depreciation, amounted to a stated sum. The implication is normally that the fixed expenses less the depreciation represent the fixed expenses payable in cash and in such cases these must be calculated and incorporated as they represent a cash outflow.

A DCF question will often state that a project will require a stated sum as working capital. It will be necessary to show this as a cash outflow, usually at year 0. However, many students forget that at the end of the project the working capital 'in the pipeline' will no longer be needed and it should therefore be released and shown as a cash receipt, the same treatment as a receipt from sale of scrap, which is not normally forgotten by students.

Discounted cash flow methods: advantages and disadvantages

The main single reason why the appropriate DCF method of capital project appraisal is superior to other methods in theory, and which also makes it important in practice, is that if properly used it takes account of the fact that the value of a given sum of money paid or received in the future is measurably different from the present value of that sum. The main weakness of the alternatives is that they mostly ignore this aspect of timing differences. Of the two DCF methods, where a choice is available the NPV method tends to be preferred as it is simpler to use and puts emphasis on total profits, rather than the aspect of profitability, which the yield method indicates. Furthermore, in the event that there are late negative cash flows in a project, the yield method may produce 'multiple solutions' – more than one rate of return may seem to be indicated. In such cases the method is unsuitable and different techniques must be used, which need not be considered in this book. Often both the NPV and the yield methods will be used as constituents of a more comprehensive review which would also take into account non-financial matters. The NPV and yield methods would complement each other.

The most serious limitations of the DCF methods arise from the fact that in a majority of cases many initial assumptions have to be made and especially in the present uncertain and inflationary times, the quality, reliability and credibility of these are unacceptable to experienced people, who regularly experience or read about the predictions of experts which, in the event, proved totally false. In brief, you cannot build a house on sand and this is what you are trying to do if you make important evaluations on the basis of untenable assumptions. In practice, expert interdisciplinary teams will carry out appraisals which include techniques such as probability and sensitivity analysis. In the latter case many different assumptions are made in relation to each of the main variables, e.g. interest rates, inflation rates, costs of materials, labour, etc., and these will help to indicate the effects on a project if particular variables move a specified amount one way or another. The appraisals will aim to show the worst possible outcomes as well as the most favourable, and the planned outcome. The appraisals are useful disciplines since they compel identification of the main factors and then detailed attention to these before decisions are taken.

As with budgetary control, when projects are being implemented it will be important to have efficient monitoring procedures which should help in alerting management to deviations from plans and also result in useful records being built up which should assist in the identification of strengths and weaknesses in different areas of the business and even of different individual managers.

The profitability index

This is also known as the benefit/cost ratio and requires a DCF appraisal using the NPV method. The ratio is:

$$\frac{\text{Present value of net cash inflow (at cost of capital)}}{\text{Present value of net cash outflows}}$$

When DCF evaluations have been made of several projects, calculation of the above ratio in each provides a useful additional insight. In principle, if the ratio is above unity the project would be profitable if all went according to plan. In situations when the total capital available is limited (or rationed), ranking in order of this index is helpful for decision-making purposes since if all went according to plan (but it seldom does) the projects with the highest profitability ratios which could be financed with the limited capital available would give rise to the highest possible return on the capital available.

Other methods of appraisal

Payback

The payback period is the time which elapses between the initial outlays which mark the start of a project and the moment when the net cash receipts equal the costs incurred in establishing the project – at the 'breakeven' point, when there has neither been a profit nor a loss. The question considered is: 'how quickly do we get our money back?' Projects are selected which have the shortest payback time and what happens afterwards is ignored. The basic objection to the payback method is that it ignores what happens after the critical point has been reached. Thus, one project may build up slowly and then continue to generate a surplus, a profit, for years after the payback point, whereas another might reach the payback point quickly, but end soon after. Under the payback method the second project would be selected although the first would have proved more profitable in the long run. Another criticism is that unlike the DCF method it does not take the timings of receipts and payments into account. This criticism need not be valid since it is a simple matter to make a discounted payback appraisal, as a later worked example shows. This will result in the payback period being seen to be somewhat longer than when calculated by the traditional method.

When the weakness of the payback method is so obvious, why do so many competent and experienced industrialists, many of them qualified accountants, continue to use it? In fact, experienced people do not use one method alone, but a project is evaluated 'in the round' and examined from many aspects, non-financial as well as financial: normally both DCF and payback are two of the several appraisals made. A special merit of payback is that many companies are often short of cash and the attraction of fast payback is that the company should not have to wait too long before the cash receipts overtake the cash payments. If, in the event, a project proves very successful and continues to generate a surplus after the payback point, so much the better. There will be an uncovenanted but welcome bonus. There is also the aspect of uncertainty. Often a DCF evaluation in respect of a high-risk project in a volatile market would be totally unrealistic. It is understandably considered to be more realistic to pay special attention to cash forecasts and flows for a period in the near future and to projects which should achieve payback within three or four years. Not surprisingly, in developing and in politically unstable countries, local entrepreneurs think mainly in terms of projects with short payback periods.

Rate of return on original investment
In this form of appraisal the approach is a traditional one of concern with profit-and-loss concepts rather than cash flows. The annual profit is assessed, with depreciation incorporated as a cost. The total profit expected to accrue is then expressed as a percentage of the original investment.

Rate of return on average investment
In this case the viewpoint is that as the value of the asset falls from its original cost to nil, or to the scrap value over its useful life, and a proportion of the original investment is effectively recovered each year through the depreciation charge, the average investment is approximately half the original investment and the rate of return is approximately double that calculated in respect of the return on the original investment.

Both of these last two forms of appraisal are known as the 'accounting' methods, and except from one aspect it is doubtful if they are much used in practice for decision-making purposes. They ignore the impor-

Capital expenditure

tant aspect of the cash flow and the fact that any profits arising in future years would not have the same value as profits arising in the immediate future. They ignore the aspect of timing. Furthermore, the accounting charge is raised in accordance with accounting conventions and this charge seldom coincides with the actual loss in value of an asset over a period. These accounting methods call for the use of averages, which are often misleading.

However, companies which make their decisions on the basis of wide-ranging reviews, and market research, and judgement may also consider calculations of rate of return on investment in order to examine the possible implications of an important project on the profit-and-loss account and balance sheet. The managers of public, listed companies, especially, tend to be obliged to take short- as well as long-term viewpoints and will always wish to know the likely effects of important decisions on the expected profits over the next two or three years, and the earnings per share.

'How decisions to invest are made' – Progress Report of the Wilson Committee

Companies, trade associations, etc., responded in large numbers to invitations from the Wilson Committee to make submissions to them. The following are two relevant paragraphs (paras 37 and 38) from the 'Progress Report on the Financing of Industry and Trade' (1977), of the Committee:

> The submissions from industry describe various techniques that are used to choose between alternative opportunities, the most common being discounted cash flow and payback period. But many stress the uncertainty of these calculations: they are a guide to decision making and cannot replace the businessman's subjective judgement about the project's prospects. High inflation has greatly increased the uncertainty of business forecasts and has lead some companies to abandon the orthodox DCF technique and place more emphasis on payback period and cash flow. Larger companies use sensitivity tests and other methods to evaluate the effects of risk, but again these are no more than an aid to decision making, since assessment of risk is ultimately a matter of judgement rather than scientific calculation. Moreover, the level of investment in total will reflect businessmens' general view of future prospects, not the method they use to choose between alternative projects.

Several submissions have pointed out that there are many types of investment other than investment in new capacity. Much investment is needed simply to maintain existing capacity and to replace equipment as it becomes obsolete or outworn. There are also forms of capital expenditure which do not directly increase profitability but are required for social or legal reasons, such as staff amenities and installations to meet safety and environmental requirements.

Example 1

'There may be better methods of evaluating the profitability of an investment than payback (or payoff) but it certainly helps in deciding whether or not the investment is too risky to undertake.' Comment on the quotation, making use of the following example, by evaluating the proposed purchase of a new machine, using the payback, net present value and DCF yield methods. A new machine will be purchased costing £100,000 with a life of five years and a scrap value of £5,000. The machine will produce 50,000 units p.a. for which the estimated selling price will be £3 per unit. Direct costs will be £1.75 per unit and annual fixed costs, including depreciation, which is calculated on a straight-line basis, will be £40,000. In years 1 and 2 special sales promotion expenditure, not included in the above cost, will be incurred, amounting to £10,000 and £15,000 respectively and an investment of £25,000 in working capital will be required immediately. The cost of capital is 10%. (*Note*: taxation can be ignored.)

	(10%)	(20%)
Present value of £1: due now (£)	1.000	1.000
due in 1 year	0.909	0.833
due in 2 years	0.826	0.694
due in 3 years	0.751	0.579
due in 4 years	0.683	0.482
due in 5 years	0.621	0.402
due in 6 years	0.564	0.335

(ACCA 20 marks)

Workings and comments
(*Note*: these include explanations which would not be required in an examination answer).
In order to calculate the cash flows it is necessary first to calculate the revenues and also the fixed costs payable in cash. The reference to de-

Capital expenditure

preciation on a 'straight line' basis means that the charge is an equal annual one taking into account the cost price, the expected scrap value and the life of the machine.

Unit selling price		£3.00
Less: Unit direct costs		£1.75
Unit contribution		£1.25
Total annual contribution: 50,000 × £1.25		£62,500
Annual fixed costs (including depreciation)	£40,000	
Annual depreciation: £100,000 − £5,000 i.e. $\frac{£95,000}{5}$ i.e. £19,000		£21,000
i.e. Annual fixed costs payable in cash		
Net annual operating cash flow		£41,500

Year	Capital equipment	Sales promotion	Working capital	Net operating cash flow	Net total cash flow	Factor (10%)	NPV
0	−100,000		−25,000		−125,000	1.000	−125,000
1		−10,000		41,500	31,500	0.909	28,634
2		−15,000		41,500	26,500	0.826	21,889
3				41,500	41,500	0.751	31,167
4				41,500	41,500	0.683	28,345
5	5,000		25,000	41,500	71,500	0.621	44,402
							29,437

(Students should note the simplicity of the layout, which is basically a cash forecast which is then converted, by a simple operation, into terms of present values, when it becomes acceptable for figures for later years to be added to those for earlier ones. Note the entries in year 5 for the (expected) sale of the equipment as scrap, and the release of working capital tied up in the project. It is re-emphasised that great care must be taken to distinguish between receipts and payments: the conventions are either to show payments within brackets, or with a 'minus' sign.)

The NPV method: these show a positive NPV of £29,437. This is quite high in relation to the capital outlay and in principle a favourable sign: however, the outcome would depend on the validity of the underlying assumptions, and also chance factors may arise which could not be foreseen. Furthermore, if the net cash flow of the final year were well below expectations the NPV would be well below £29,000.

The payback period: reference to the net total cash flow column shows that the payback period would be about 3.6 years, assuming an even cash flow. The discounted payback period, which is calculated by reference to the NPV column, is seen to be about 4⅓ years: the discounted payback period is the more conservative calculation, and is also technically more correct. This seems a moderate period in itself but in real situations one would have yardsticks of acceptable periods taking into account the risk factor in each case.

The DCF yield method must also be used in this question and to enable the 'trial and error' method to be applied the examiner has supplied the factor for a rate of interest of 20%. The net cash flows already calculated are now discounted with factor 20%.

Year	Net total cash flow (£)	Factor (20%)	NPV
0	−125,000	1.000	−125,000
1	31,500	0.833	26,240
2	26,500	0.694	18,391
3	41,500	0.579	24,029
4	41,500	0.482	20,003
5	71,500	0.402	28.743
			− 7,594

As the NPV was positive for 10% interest, and negative for 20%, the rate of interest which gives rise to an NPV of 0 must lie between 10% and 20%. In reality additional calculations would be made to narrow the gap between these two figures but this is not practicable in this case, but the approximate rate can be calculated as there is an approximate linear relationship between the rate of interest and the NPV. The calculation is made thus: the range between +29,437 and −7,594 is their total, 37,031. Visual inspection indicates that the rate sought is closer to 20% than 10%. The calculation is: $10\% + \frac{29{,}437 \times 10}{37{,}031}$, i.e. 17.9%, or 18% (rounded). Note that the fraction, $\frac{29{,}437}{37{,}031}$ is multiplied by 10 because the range between 10% and 20% is 10. The question calls for comment on the quotation, which could be on these lines:

(a) A main objection to the payback method is that it is concerned with the breakeven situation and not the profitability of the project over its whole life. Payback is thus a crude and incomplete measure and, if, as is often the case, only the simple non-discounted payback is calculated the time value of money is ignored and so the true payback period is underestimated. However, this objection is overcome by using the discounted payback.

(b) Payback emphasises the aspect of liquidity rather than profitability. It is useful in this respect since liquidity is a vital matter which

Capital expenditure

must never be ignored, but sometimes is. Despite its limitations, payback is helpful when there is a serious shortage of funds or in situations of political instability or rapid technological change.

(c) In this particular case although the DCF, NPV calculation shows quite a high NPV this still depends on the validity of the underlying assumptions, not least with respect to sales. The discounted payback indicates that the breakeven point would only be reached after the fourth year and the ultimate profitability of the project would depend on all going according to plan, including the successful disinvestment of the working capital at the end, and the sale of the machine for scrap. This project would probably be regarded as promising but needing further cautious appraisal.

Example 2

The ABC Co. Ltd has decided to install a new milling machine. The original evaluation for this was done using discounted cash flow techniques which showed a yield of 15%. The machine costs £20,000 and it was estimated that it would have a useful life of five years with a trade in value of £4,000 at the end of the fifth year. A decision has now to be taken on the method of financing the project. Three methods of finance are being considered: (1) purchase the machine for cash, using bank loan facilities on which the current interest rate is 8% p.a.; (2) purchase the machine under a hire purchase agreement. This would require an initial deposit of £5,000 and payments of £4,400 p.a. at the end of each of the next years; (3) rent the machine under a rental agreement which would entail payment of £4,800 to be made at the end of each year for the next five years. You are required to advise the management on (a) the most economic method of finance – figures should be presented clearly and concisely – and (b) any other matters which should be considered before finally deciding which method of finance should be adopted: (*Notes*: Taxation can be ignored in method (1) above; a discount rate of 8% can be used for comparing the different methods of finance.)

Present value of £1 receivable in:		
	1 year	£0.9259
	2 years	0.8573
	3 years	0.7938
	4 years	0.7350
	5 years	0.6806

(ACCA 20 marks)

Working and comments

Note that when the same receipt or payment recurs it takes the form of an annuity and in this case the calculations may be simplified by adding the discount factors and making a single calculation instead of one for each year. In this case the total of the factors is 3.9926. On this basis the calculation for each alternative becomes:

		(£)
(1) Initial cost		−20,000
Trade-in value: £4,000 × 0.6806 (NPV)		2,722
	Net present value	−17,278
(2) Deposit		− 5,000
Instalments: £4,000 × 3.9926 (NPV)		−17,567
Trade-in value £4,000 × 0.6806 (NPV)		2,722
	Net present value	−19,845
(3) Rental £4,800 × 3.9926 (NPV)	Net present value	−19,164

(a) In the conditions stated, alternative (1) gives rise to the smallest negative NPV and is therefore to be preferred; (3) is the next and (2) is the least favourable alternative. However, in the cases of (2) and (3) the precise commitment is known at the start whereas over a period of five years bank loan interest would be likely to fluctuate and in practice this aspect would be considered carefully.

(b) It is assumed that the running expenses are the same under each alternative. If this is not the case appropriate adjustments must be made in the calculations.

(c) Method (1) requires an immediate cash payment of £20,000 and (2) of £5,000, whereas (3) does not require any initial cash payment. The liquidity of the company would need to be considered: if it were unsatisfactory the rental option would be specially interesting.

(d) In alternatives (1) and (2) the trade-in value at the end of the project is material − how reliable is the estimate? In practice the implications of taxation would be important and the implications of each alternative would be considered in relation to the published accounts, the profit-and-loss account and balance sheet, and planned dividend payments. However, as the project does not involve major sums it would be unlikely to have any significant effects on these matters.

Capital expenditure

Example 3

The directors of D Ltd are considering a new type of food mixer which their research department has developed. The expenditure so far on research has been £8,000 and a consultant's report has been commissioned at a cost of £1,500. The report provides the following information:

(a) Cost of production per unit (£):

Materials	4.50
Labour	7.50
Fixed overheads	2.00
(based on the company's normal allocation rates)	

(b) It will be necessary to rent additional premises at £15,000 p.a. and it is estimated that additional fixed costs of £7,500 will be incurred. These are the only anticipated actual changes in fixed costs.

(c) The company would need a new machine which would cost £15,000. Alternatively, it could build the machine itself at a cost of £12,000 representing materials £10,000 (at cost) and labour £2,000. The materials represent items valued at cost which are already in stock and are used regularly for other products of the company. The price of these materials has risen 40% since they were purchased. The scrap value of the machine will in either case be £2,000 at the end of ten years.

(d) A price of £15 is proposed for the new mixer and the estimated demand is as follows:

	Demand (units)	Probability
Years 1–5	20,000	0.10
	10,000	0.65
	6,000	0.25
Years 6–10	12,000	0.20
	8,000	0.50
	2,000	0.30

It is not expected that the commercial life of the mixer will be longer than ten years.

You are required: (i) To state whether the project is worthwhile if the cost of capital to the company is 10%; (ii) To discuss the merits of the method which you have adopted for dealing with the risk involved in the project.

The following are the appropriate discount rates:

	$V_n(10\%)$	$A_n(10\%)$
(n) 1	0.90909	0.90909
2	0.82645	1.73554
3	0.75131	2.48685
4	0.68301	3.16987
5	0.62092	3.79079
6	0.56447	4.35526
7	0.51316	4.86842
8	0.46651	5.33493
9	0.42410	5.75902
10	0.38554	6.14457

(ICSA 34 marks)

Working and comments
(These include explanatory comments not required in an examination answer.)

The expenditure of £8,000 on research and £1,500 on a consultant's report in each case is past expenditure ('water under the bridge') and must therefore be ignored in the evaluation of this project. The only receipts and payments to be considered are those which will arise only if the project is proceeded with.

(*a*) The relevant costs are those which will arise only if the project proceeds. The fixed overheads of £2.00 per unit are therefore ignored since if the project is rejected these overheads will continue but will have to be recovered through other, ongoing production. The direct production costs are therefore £12 per unit – £4.50 for materials and £7.50 for labour.

(*b*) If the project goes ahead, additional annual expenditure of £15,000 rent and £7,500 additional fixed costs will arise (but not if the project is rejected). This annual total of £22,500 must therefore be taken into account as direct fixed costs.

(*c*) If the project goes ahead the alternative of buying a new machine at £15,000 will be preferable to building a machine. The true – opportunity – cost of building the machine would be: materials £14,000 (i.e. at replacement and not at original cost) plus labour, £2,000 i.e. £16,000.

Capital expenditure

The probable level of demand will be:

	Annual demand (units) (a)	Probability (b)	(a) × (b)
Years 1–5	20,000	0.10	2,000
	10,000	0.65	6,500
	6,000	0.25	1,500
		1.00	10,000
Years 6–10	12,000	0.20	2,400
	8,000	0.50	4,000
	2,000	0.30	600
		1.00	7,000

Note: In view of the fact that a large proportion of the payments and receipts are the same from year to year they have the feature of annuities, and the calculations are reduced in number, and time is thus saved, if the A_n column is used. (It should be noted that this is the cumulative total of the V_n column). However, if the V_n column is used the same result would be obtained. In order to illustrate the two methods, both are shown here but in an examination only one method would be chosen, of course.

Alternative (i), using A_n column. It is assumed that cash flows occur at the end of each period and payments are preceded by a 'minus' sign: NPV = net present value.

The NPV is thus £816,537 − £805,866, i.e. £10,671. Thus when the cost of capital is 10% at the end of the ten year period there would be a positive NPV of £10,671 provided that all went according to plan. Alternative (ii) using V_n column:

(i) If the cost of capital to the company is 10% then taking into account the fact that the initial investment in the project is a modest one, and as the discounted payback period should be quite short, between two and three years, the project seems worthy of serious consideration. In practice a decision would never be taken on the basis of a DCF evaluation alone: other factors would be taken into account. This point was made very clear by industrialists giving evidence to the Wilson Committee. It may be noted that in this question when the evaluation is done using the V_n column it becomes apparent that for years 6 to 9 the project would be expected to give rise to a negative cash flow. It would therefore be more profitable, if the project were adopted and all went to plan, if

Year	Machine cost	Rent etc.	Cost of sales	Factor 10%
0	−15,000			1.00000
1		−22,500	−120,000	
2		−22,500	−120,000	
3		−22,500	−120,000	
4		−22,500	−120,000	
5		−22,500	−120,000	3.79079
6		−22,500	− 84,000	
7		−22,500	− 84,000	
8		−22,500	− 84,000	
9		−22,500	− 84,000	
10		−22,500	− 84,000	2.35378
		−22,500 × 6.14457		

the additional premises could be rented for five years only, or another use found for them at the end of the fifth year, and if the additional fixed costs could also be ended then, and the project itself ended at the end of the fifth year.

(ii) This part of the answer is covered within this chapter and in other parts of this book, including the chapter on risk and uncertainty. (Ch. 19). Sensitivity analysis and probability analysis would be employed and it would always be borne in mind that the company should never commit too large a proportion of its resources to a single project or to a single unstable area.

Year	Cost of sales	Machine cost	Rent etc.	Total payments
0		−15,000		− 15,000
1	−120,000		−22,500	−142,500
2	−120,000		−22,500	−142,500
3	−120,000		−22,500	−142,500
4	−120,000		−22,500	−142,500
5	−120,000		−22,500	−142,500
6	− 84,000		−22,500	−106,500
7	− 84,000		−22,500	−106,500
8	− 84,000		−22,500	−106,500
9	− 84,000		−22,500	−106,500
10	− 84,000		−22,500	−106,500

NPV	Factor 10%	Sales	Machine sale	NPV
−15,000				
		150,000		
		150,000		
		150,000		
		150,000		
−454,895	3.79079	150,000		568,619
		105,000		
		105,000		
		105,000		
		105,000		
−197,718	2.35378	105,000		247,147
−138,253	0.38554		2,000	771
−805,866				816,537

Questions

1. Describe the main criticisms which may be levelled against discounted cash flow techniques. To what extent are such techniques still valid? (ICSA 22 marks)
2. To what extent should profit be taken into account in the selection of investment projects? (ICSA 22 marks)
3. Discuss the importance of the search and monitoring processes in the field of project appraisal. To what extent may these processes be regarded as more important than the actual techniques of appraisal? (ICSA 22 marks)

Sales	Sale of machine	Net total	Factor	NPV
		−15,000	1.00000	−15,000
150,000		7,500	0.90909	6,818
150,000		7,500	0.82645	6,198
150,000		7,500	0.75131	5,635
150,000		7,500	0.68301	5,123
150,000		7,500	0.62992	4,657
105,000		−1,500	0.56447	−847
105,000		−1,500	0.51316	−770
105,000		−1,500	0.46651	−700
105,000		−1,500	0.42410	−636
105,000	2,000	500	0.38554	193
				10,671

4. One of the most important decisions which concerns financial management is the decision to incur capital expenditure. Discuss the information which is required in a system for the planning and control of such expenditure. (ACCA 18 marks)

5. (a) What do you understand by the term 'capital rationing'? (b) Give examples of circumstances which might lead to capital rationing? (ACCA 15 marks)

6. The board of an expanding company has authorised capital expenditure projects covering the erection of buildings (on a cost plus fixed profit basis), the provision of services (some being installed by the company's own maintenance department), and the purchase of plant and equipment. Explain how you, as chief accountant, would require the costs of such projects to be collected and controlled. Mention the essential features of a form to report on the monetary progress of projects and describe the type of action you would expect the board to take on the basis of the report. (ICMA 20 marks)

7. A company is considering the acquisition of a new machine which has just become available. Their old machine has a written-down value of £90,000 and a projected remaining useful life of 5 years. The financial manager has produced the following computation to evaluate the project. His working calculations are attached.

Year	Capital expenditure (£)	Costs saved (£)	Discount 15%	P/V(£)
0	−55,000	–	–	−55,000
1		30,000	0.870	26,100
2		30,000	0.756	22,680
3		30,000	0.658	19,740
4		30,000	0.572	17,160
5		30,000	0.497	14,910
6	5,000		0.432	2,160
				47,750

Workings:	Cost savings – Fuel	£12,000
	Labour	8,000
	Depreciation	8,000
	Fixed overheads	2,000
		30,000

Notes: (i) The cost of fuel now used is £132,000 p.a. whereas fuel for the new machine would cost only £120,000.

(ii) The machine is relatively labour-free, and the annual cost of labour would fall from £10,000 to £2,000.

(iii) Depreciation calculated as £10,000 p.a. would be £8,000 less than on the machine used at present which is to be scrapped.
(iv) The new machine could work faster and complete the same volume of work as the old one in 80% of the time involved, so that a smaller apportionment of fixed overheads would be made.
(v) The new machine has a cost of £55,000 and a life of five years and an expected scrap value of £5,000.

You are required to: (a) re-evaluate the project, stating any false assumptions the financial manager has made: (b) explain any factors you would bring to the attention of the management concerning sensitivity analysis and the general viability of this project, illustrating the use of sensitivity analysis. Ignore taxation. Assume a cost of capital of 15% (ICSA 34 marks)

8. The chief accountant of a company has submitted to the managing director the following evaluation of three mutually exclusive investments (net cash outlays in brackets):

	Year 0	1	2	3	4
Project A	(20,000)	12,000	8,000	4,000	2,000
Project B	(40,000)	14,000	14,000	14,000	14,000
Project C	(20,000)	1,000	2,000	6,000	22,000

The approximate internal rates of return are: A = 16%, B = 15% and C = 13%, all of which are greater than the company's cost of capital of 10%. I therefore recommend that project A be accepted because it shows the highest rate of return.

You are required to prepare a report to the managing director which criticises the above recommendation and draws attention to **all** factors which you feel that the chief accountant has overlooked.

n	V (10%)
1	0.90909
2	0.82645
3	0.75131
4	0.68301
5	0.62092

(ICSA 34 marks)

9. M Ltd produces a variety of machine tools and is considering whether one of its products should be discontinued. The profit statement for the product for 1979 was as follows:

	£	£
Sales		320,000
Materials	100,000	
Labour	120,000	
Factory overheads	50,000	270,000
Gross profit		50,000
Interest on capital employed	10,000	
Selling and administrative expenses	30,000	40,000
		10,000

The works manager is arguing that the product should be discontinued on the grounds that material costs are likely to rise by 10% during 1980 and factory overheads by 8%. Furthermore labour costs will rise by 5%, whilst sales remain static in both volume and price. The managing director obtains the following information for the next five years:

(i) Sales will stay at their current level.
(ii) Material costs will rise by 10% in 1980 and at 2% per annum for the next four years.
(iii) Labour costs will rise by 5% in 1980 and will then remain constant.
(iv) Factory overheads are:

Depreciation	£20,000
Share of factory rent and rates	15,000
Direct supervision	15,000
	£50,000

Factory rent and rates are expected to increase by 10% p.a. during the next five years and direct supervision by £1,000 p.a.

(v) The machinery used for the product has a written-down value of £100,000 and a scrap value of £40,000.
(vi) The factory space used by the machinery could either be used for storage purposes or leased out at £5,000 p.a. The present warehouse has a book value of £80,000 and could be sold for £100,000.
(vii) The current rate of interest is 10%.

Capital expenditure

You are required to advise the managing director on whether the product should be discontinued. State any additional information which you feel would be useful for this purpose. (ICSA   34 marks)

n	V_n 10%	A_n 10%
1	0.909	0.909
2	0.826	1.735
3	0.751	2.486
4	0.683	3.169
5	0.621	3.790

10. The following capital projects are under consideration:
 (i) A new product has been proposed and the following forecasts have been produced (£):

Cost of plant and equipment	200,000
Variable costs per unit of product	43
Additional fixed costs per annum	7,500
Selling price per unit	110

£20,000 has been spent on market research, which has resulted in the following probability distribution for the annual sales based on a selling price of £110:

Quantity	600	750	800	900
Probability	0.2	0.4	0.3	0.1

It is considered that the plant and equipment will have a life of 8 years and a residual value of £4,000.

 (ii) An existing department has proposed the manufacture of a new product and has analysed two methods of production:
  (a) The use of a machine costing £220,000. Direct costs are estimated at £60 per unit and the overhead recovery rate is 25% on direct cost. Fixed costs will increase by £46,000 p.a.
  (b) The use of a machine costing £340,000. Direct costs are estimated at £52 per unit, with an overhead recovery rate of 30%. Fixed costs are expected to increase by £32,000 p.a. Sales of the new product have been estimated at 2,200 units p.a. for the next five years reducing to 1,500 units for the following five years. The selling price will be £110 per unit.
 (iii) Further expansion is planned for the future and an opportunity has arisen to purchase land for the sum of £220,000. It is estimated that the land required would cost £340,000 if purchase is delayed for four years when the expansion is planned to take place.

Note: Depreciation is calculated on the straight-line method: taxation is to be ignored: assume that cash flows occur on the last day of the year unless otherwise indicated: cost of capital is 12%.

You are required to explain which project(s) would be approved if the company has unlimited funds available. How would your answer differ if only £350,000 were available? Present value of 1 at 12%:

Year 1	0.893	6	0.507
2	0.797	7	0.452
3	0.712	8	0.404
4	0.636	9	0.361
5	0.567	10	0.322

(ICSA 34 marks)

11. A company is analysing two projects, only one of which can be accepted. It is estimated that the projects will cause the following changes to the budgeted cash flows and reported profits of the company.

	Project A		Project B	
Year	Change in net cash flows	Change in reported profits	Change in net cash flows	Change in reported profits
0	−90,000	−	−20,000	−
1	+20,000	+10,000	−20,000	−12,000
2	+20,000	+18,000	+16,000	−20,000
3	+20,000	+18,000	+16,000	+20,000
4	+20,000	+16,000	+16,000	+24,000
5	+20,000	+16,000	+16,000	+24,000
6	+20,000	+ 8,000	+12,000	+20,000
7	+20,000	+ 8,000		
8	+30,000	+ 2,000		

Given that the cost of capital to the company is 10%, you are asked to answer the following questions: (*a*) If each project could be repeated at the end of its life with an identical project, which should be accepted? How would your answer be affected if this were not the case? (*b*) Reported profits have increased by 10% p.a. in recent years and amount to £100,000. It is estimated that the company's profits for the next three years, excluding these projects, will be £104,000, £112,000 and £120,000 respectively. What impact would the acceptance of each project have on reported earnings and in what way might this influence the choice of project? (c) Discuss the ways in which risk and uncertainty might be taken into account in the selection of capital projects.

n	V_n 10%	A_n 10%
1	0.909	0.909
2	0.826	1.735
3	0.751	2.486
4	0.683	3.169
5	0.621	3.790
6	0.564	4.355
7	0.513	4.868
8	0.466	5.334
9	0.424	5.759
10	0.385	6.144

(ICSA 34 marks)

Chapter 15

Companies in trouble

A company may have a continuing life but often its life ends in consequence of compulsory or voluntary liquidation, or takeover by another company. In the latter case an old and respected company may be taken over by new owners who seek honestly to benefit from the goodwill built up by the original company and to make available larger resources to develop this further, but there are also less scrupulous, including fraudulent, people, who buy a respected company and use it as a 'front' for a different style of operation. It would take some time for members of the public, suppliers, customers, etc., to perceive that things were changing for the worse with the company.

A takeover may benefit all of the parties, including employees, but this is not always so. This chapter outlines situations, and possible reasons for these, when a company may be seen by its management to be moving more deeply into troubles, and action which may possibly be taken to bring about a recovery. In macroeconomic terms it is arguable that it may be in the interests of the community as a whole if inefficient companies are allowed to go into liquidation since in this case the resources they have been deploying will be released for more efficient use elsewhere. However, in real life things are often not so simple. In an area of economic decline the failure of one or more companies means loss of jobs for people unlikely to find new jobs. Offices and factories are left empty and no one wants them. Local shopkeepers lose business and the local authorities lose rates and the central government loses tax revenues. The local decline accelerates. In brief, it can be a matter of satisfaction and challenge for a manager to be asked to take charge of an ailing company and try to restore it to health. If recovery efforts are successful the company could in due course be sold as a going concern on better terms than would be available if it were sold by a liquidator at low 'break-up' values. Moreover, liquidators are themselves very costly to employ.

Main reasons for decline or collapse of a company

There are at least four frequent reasons for the collapse of an established company or even industry:

(a) It sells a single product, or a small range, and the market declines or collapses: there is total failure on the part of the top management to carry out proper research and development and to keep informed of what the public wants. The collapse of the UK motor cycle industry from domination of world markets within little more than a decade is an illustration of this. The Japanese exerted themselves to find what people wanted, but British managements failed to do so and through management complacency, ineptitude and perhaps arrogance, a major market was lost unnecessarily.

(b) There is a general and persisting weakness of top management, well-tried controls are not operated and often a company is near collapse without managers being aware of the fact.

(c) A company may be doing well under an efficient and aggressive management: a major new opportunity appears and is seized and the prospects appear brilliant. It then becomes apparent that a major miscalculation has been made and things go catastrophically wrong, which threaten to destroy, or do destroy, the company. Miscalculations often, but not always, occur when there is a dominating chief executive with a 'rubber stamp' board. He resents and rejects advice. In principle, it is fundamental that a company should never overcommit itself to a single venture or accept a major risk if an unfavourable outcome would seriously damage the company. There needs to be an adequate spread of risks. In the 1960s Rolls Royce Ltd entered into a contract to supply the RB 211 aircraft engine to an American airliner. The agreement was hailed in the UK press as a triumph when it was signed but the development costs of the engine increased beyond expectations (as they always do), but the contract did not allow adequately for price escalation and the company was squeezed between fixed revenues and rising costs. Rolls Royce was effectively destroyed as a private-sector company. Because of the importance of Rolls Royce to the UK economy it was rescued by a Conservative government by massive injections of public money but the ordinary shareholders lost heavily. The Burmah Oil Company is another example. In the early 1970s its widely admired management was seeking to establish it as one of the world's major oil companies and as part of the strategy took an exceptional stake in tanker shipping, in which Greek and

Norwegian shipowners had earlier made vast fortunes. The sudden raising of oil prices caused a total and unexpected collapse of the tanker market. The Burmah Oil Company survived but its shares fell to a fraction of their former market prices.

(d) A fourth reason for company destruction is that it is the victim of a major internal and or external fraud.

If a management has accepted excessive risks and events prove adverse, it will soon be evident whether or not a rescue attempt can be made. It will probably be a similar situation when a company is found to have been the victim of a major fraud, such as came to light in 1979 in respect of the Gray's Building Society, which afforded another example of astonishing failure on the part of auditors to detect frauds committed by the chief executive over a period of forty years. This case also highlighted the dangers of excessive dependence on a single individual, especially when that person holds excessive powers, as an unchecked chief executive is bound to do. In this case members of the building society industry acted promptly to prevent losses from falling on individual investors and to preserve confidence in the industry. In fact, investors as a body bore the £6 m. loss arising from this fraud, since the overall assets of the industry as a whole fell by this amount.

A rescue attempt: a practical approach

The question has to be considered – what, if anything, can be done to prevent the collapse of a company if a management has, even at the last moment, recognised the crisis and that they alone are unable to overcome it? It would seem that in a terminal crisis a company has no practical alternative but to invite a 'company doctor', usually an experienced businessman with an accountancy background, to assume control. A person so invited would not be obliged to accept and before doing so he would insist on obtaining answers to many questions. These would include: whether any guarantees had been given in the name of the company and details of any charges made on fixed or floating assets; contingent liabilities; pending litigation; etc. He would assess whether the company could be saved or whether liquidation now seemed inevitable. The Companies Acts prescribe penalties if directors continue to trade when they are aware that the company is unable to meet its obligations as they fall due and moreover directors then become personally responsible for debts incurred by the company. Account must be taken of current legislation including in relation to redundancy payments. If unions were involved these would also need to be consulted. In this type of situation success requires general preparedness to cooperate and cooperation is best secured by convincing those concerned that it will serve their interests better than opposition. A person who agreed to attempt to rescue a company would insist on being in complete charge of every aspect of the drastic short-term action which would be essential. He will be described here as the acting chief executive (ACE). The following matters would have urgent attention.

Control of cash: liquidity
The essential for survival is cash to pay employees and creditors. The ACE will at once take financial control and arrange that authority to sign cheques is restricted to a very small number of people acting under clear and restrictive orders. Authority to authorise expenditure would similarly be closely restricted and the position made known to all. The ACE would promulgate that no new capital expenditure should be incurred without his authority. Each existing capital commitment would need at once to be re-assessed in the light of its own special facts. Where possible, commitments must be reduced and in principle only essential operating expenditure would be authorised. Because of their position under the Companies Acts, the directors of the company would need to be kept closely informed.

Financial inventory
An inventory must be taken urgently of the present financial resources of the company and its liabilities, and a list prepared of possible options for obtaining access to additional funds. Emphasis must be on the short term since if the company can survive in the short term then longer-term arrangements can be considered at a suitable time. Cash and bank balances and cash forecasts should be reviewed and note taken of any agreed overdraft facilities, their conditions and limits. The possibility of a bank agreeing to grant, or extend, overdraft facilities must also be examined.

Debtors
An up-to-date schedule must be prepared and overdue accounts analysed according to the period overdue: pressure must be put on debtors to pay and court action taken when worth while. The desirability and possibility of continuing to allow credit must be considered: the possibility of recourse to factors or invoice discounting companies could be considered, taking into account costs and benefits.

Stocks

The stock position would need to be examined urgently in respect of all categories – raw materials, components, work in progress, finished goods. Physical or sample checks should be carried out on a selective basis to establish the reliability of the records and the condition of the stores and the procedures assessed and improvements made when these appeared necessary. If evidence pointed to theft or fraud in the stores, or elsewhere in the company, the directors would need to be informed, and the auditors, and probably the police as well. A responsible person should be instructed to sell for cash on the best possible terms any surplus stores disclosed. Special selling efforts should be made in respect of stocks of finished goods, offering reduced prices for slow-moving lines. The emphasis would be on cash sales.

Fixed assets

An urgent review should be made of fixed assets including to determine whether any were not charged and could be charged in return for a loan or could be sold, possibly under a sale-leaseback arrangement, if appropriate and substantial enough. Assets seen to be surplus should be sold promptly to raise cash.

Liabilities: trade creditors

It is essential to check that all creditors, including for PAYE and VAT, have been fully recorded. Consideration should be given to approaching larger creditors to ascertain whether they would relax their terms for a period: if the company were working as a sub-contractor for larger companies, these might be persuaded to assist by themselves supplying or paying for materials used in work done for them, or they might agree to make earlier progress payments. The buying arrangements, including determination of the prices paid for raw materials and components, should be examined as these could prove to be badly or even fraudulently operated in an ailing company. Standardisation and reduced stockholdings in conjunction with more efficient procedures could result in less money being tied up in stocks, and better cash flow.

General review of company activity and prospects

Whilst the tighter controls were being operated, revised cash forecasts would need to be prepared regularly. They would assist assessment of the prospects for survival and give guidance as to additional finance which would need to be sought at any time from external sources. Moreover, under Section 332 of the Companies Act, 1948, directors of a company may have to accept unlimited personal liability for its debts if the Court should form the view that the directors had an intention to defraud the creditors by permitting the company to trade when insolvent. If competently prepared evaluations, regularly updated, indicated a solvent company then the directors could confidently associate themselves with the rescue attempt. However, if the evaluations indicated insolvency, and adequate finance could not be raised from any sources, then the directors should be advised to obtain legal advice as to their positions. In such circumstances the only options would be to put the company into liquidation or quickly find a buyer for it.

Simultaneously with the strict control measures aimed at achieving survival, there would be reviews of the various functions of the company: aims would be efficiency, liquidity and profitability; attention would be given, *inter alia*, to identification of the key factor(s), of the most profitable products and concentration on producing and selling these, and abandonment of uprofitable lines. The variable costs of all products should be ascertained, or checked, and the need to obtain the highest contribution per unit of the key factor would be taken into account. If, for example, a certain machine were found to be a 'bottleneck' and a key factor, in addition to making the most profitable use of this, consideration would be given to such questions as whether output could be increased significantly by working a two- or three-shift system, taking care to ensure that maintenance was not neglected, and accepting that higher shift pay would be required by employees to compensate for unsocial-hours working. There would need to be review of the pricing and marketing and distribution policies; the production and the buying and storekeeping arrangements; the staffing and personnel policies; the research and development. Attention would be given to (*a*) increasing revenues, and (*b*) cutting costs. Aims must include that a factory produces the maximum saleable output from a given input in a given time. Any restrictive labour practices would need to be identified and agreement sought to end these, to improve the company's chances of survival and thus employment prospects. Quality control should ensure minimum wastage of materials and rejected finished goods.

It would obviously be false economy to buy low-priced materials if their defective quality resulted in excessive wastage or rejection or return of finished goods. Equally, it would be wasteful to pay too high a price for unnecessarily high-quality materials. The arrangements for materials handling and efficient work flow should also be examined. It is said that handling adds nothing to a material except costs. Modern equipment, including fork-lift trucks, pallets and conveyors, properly used can result in substantial cost savings. When cash has to be conserved, hire purchase or, more probably, leasing should be considered.

The usage and costs of energy should also be examined as energy costs are now so high and gross waste is often found in practice. There are also government schemes to provide financial assistance for companies seeking to conserve energy.

Employees

It is not practicable in this book to consider such matters as organisation and management structures and personnel matters generally. People are more difficult to deal with than materials and inanimate things, but with the right social environment within the company – and the initiatives must come from management – productivity can be greatly improved. This happens when people work together towards common objectives. However, a company in a crisis situation will be likely to have poor management and industrial relations but a new acting chief executive may be able to obtain a new attitude of cooperation because of awareness that jobs are seriously at risk. The handling of redundancy always requires special care and skill as well as generosity: however, personnel matters are a specialist and sensitive area which need to be studied in depth, noting that legal requirements must always be known and met.

When all the financial and other stocktaking has been done – certainly within a month or so of the ACE taking control – draft revised budgets should be prepared for all functions, with revised cash forecasts, a draft profit-and-loss account for the next financial year and draft balance sheet as at the end of it. If, despite all efforts, the outlook still appears bad then the option of liquidation must be considered. Sometimes there may be the option of substantial contraction or of selling off one part of the business. Major shareholders might also indicate a wish that a buyer could be found for their shareholdings. The ACE would be alert for indications that possible buyers might be interested in the company. Apart from the human aspect of preserving jobs, sale as a going concern, even on relatively unfavourable terms, would almost certainly be a better financial option for the shareholders of a company than liquidation since in the latter case fixed assets and stocks often have to be sold at low, break-up, prices and exceptionally heavy payments have to be made to employees made redundant and in addition there are the heavy costs of liquidation.

It should be evident within at most six months or so of the start of the rescue whether or not it has reasonable prospects of success: if the signs are favourable consideration must be given to the longer term for the company, including the possibilities of sale at a favourable time. The reasons for the decline will have been identified and should be removed: this will often require changes of managers at different levels, especially at the top, since if there had been good top management poor management would not have been tolerated at lower levels. If there is an owner/manager who is a poor manager he would either have to accept to strengthen the management or lose his investment sooner rather than later. A feature of the earlier decline will have been the running down of resources, selling off of assets, etc., and recovery would require an injection of sufficient long-term capital: a proportion of this would be equity and the balance medium- to long-term loans. A practical problem will be that prospective investors will need to be convinced that the company now has good future prospects despite its recent record. All possible sources of equity and loan funds would need to be considered including existing shareholders and the specialist private- and public-sector institutions.

Capital reconstruction

When a company appears to be 'turning the corner' and recovering after prolonged trading and financial ill health, a capital reconstruction is usually essential. For example, if there has been a period of losses there would probably be a debit balance on the profit-and-loss account which, as explained, is a fictitious asset. Dividends would not have been paid and there could be arrears of dividends with respect to any cumulative preference shares and possibly also arrears of interest on loans including debentures: creditors might also have debts overdue for payment. Although creditors for sums exceeding £300 could set in motion liquidation proceedings unless the company paid the debt, creditors may be persuaded to show forebearance, especially if it appears to be in their interest to do so. Moreover, a company may be 'overcapitalised' with some of its fixed assets standing in the accounts at unrealistically high values.

A capital reconstruction is a complex and technical matter which is explained fully in textbooks on advanced accountancy. In brief and in principle, a main aim of reconstruction will be to obtain the agreement of the various interested parties to make certain concessions, and allow the company some time in the expectation that the measures will permit it to survive in the first place, and then proceed to recovery. A feature of an agreed reconstruction will be the requirement of any party who agrees to make a concession to receive an adequate inducement or 'quid pro quo' to compensate for their not pressing for their full rights: otherwise each party involved could insist on seeking to enforce its claims. However, sometimes, and especially if there seemed some doubt as to whether a particular party could be sure of obtaining payment in full in the event of a liquidation, that party may agree not to press for a liquidation but instead take part in discussions on the principle that if the company were able to continue, each party making a concession would in due course receive proportionate benefits from the re-established company in compensation for its forebearance.

In principle a proposed reconstruction scheme would be drafted by skilled people and the drafts submitted to all of the parties whose agreement would be necessary, and to their representatives. The parties involved would include creditors unless provisions could be made for them to be paid in full without significant delay. If the parties concerned were preference and ordinary shareholders, there would be a basic conflict of interest and skill would be needed to draft an equitable scheme, which would need to demonstrate that each party involved would stand to gain more by accepting than by rejecting the scheme and that the proposed benefits going to each party in the future fairly reflected the sacrifices made and the risks taken: the arguments for a scheme will focus on the self-interest of each party involved. It has to be borne in mind that when a company goes into liquidation the ordinary shareholders will get nothing unless and until all the debts of the company have been paid in full and, normally, capital and possibly dividends in arrears have also been paid in full to any preference shareholders. As the ordinary shareholders receive the rewards when all goes well it is equitable that they bear the losses when things go badly. Often when a scheme is drafted the whole of the ordinary capital will have been wiped out by the losses but even so the scheme will allow them some interest, however small, in the reconstructed company for otherwise they would see no point in cooperation and would consider that the company might as well be liquidated if its survival would mean nothing to them.

A scheme would aim to 'wipe the slate clean' as far as possible, so that the company could make a fresh start. The technical treatment centres on the opening of a 'reconstruction account' and fictitious assets such as the debit balance on a profit-and-loss account are closed by transferring the balance to the reconstruction account. Similarly, any overvalued assets will be reduced to more realistic bases by making an appropriate credit entry to the asset account and the corresponding debit(s) to the reconstruction account. When all such transfers had been made to this account it would be apparent by how much the ordinary and preference shares would have to be 'written down'. The mechanism would be that an agreed scheme would involve the issue of shares of lower nominal values to replace the existing shares, which would be cancelled. Preference shareholders could agree to their overdue and unpaid cumulative dividends being written off in return for equity shares in the reconstructed company. When all the entries had been made in the reconstruction account there should be a small credit balance and the reconstruction account would be closed by transferring this balance to a capital reserve account. If a debit balance were allowed to remain on the reconstruction account this would mean a 'fictitious' asset remained, which would be unacceptable in principle and the scheme would need to be revised.

A point to emphasise when a scheme is being drafted is that the writing down of the ordinary shareholders' capital does not indicate that these have made any concessions: it means merely that recognition would have been made of the existing situation. In the event of a scheme being agreed and a recovery achieved it would mean that the ordinary shareholders would have the benefit of this unless, as it should, the scheme ensured that the parties which had made sacrifices to permit the recovery also received appropriate benefits. A practical danger from the viewpoints of interests other than the ordinary shareholders is that unless their negotiators are alert the ordinary shareholders will be liable to benefit by default, as it were. When a scheme is drafted, all of the parties should ensure that their particular interests are represented by a skilful negotiator, otherwise they could make sacrifices unfairly and to the ultimate benefit of the ordinary shareholders. Consideration would need to be given to the effects of the scheme in respect of: (*a*) income; (*b*) capital; and (*c*) voting rights of the party concerned, and it would be necessary to make projections in order to determine whether an equitable share of benefits would accrue to each of the parties which had made sacrifices, in the event of the company making a recovery.

Questions

1. You have been appointed chief accountant to a company which has been operating at a low profit level over a number of years. The company does not operate a budgetary planning system, but based on the present performance plus allowances for price and other cost increases,

a preliminary profit forecast for the next twelve months shows the following:

Estimated sales	£1,750,000
Estimated net profit	£5,000

The managing director is most perturbed and comments as follows: 'It looks as if we are finished. At least £50,000 is needed to replace our old equipment. We have been putting this off for years and we can now delay no longer. We are already overdrawn at the bank and there is nothing to use as security. The directors, who between them own all of the shares in the company, are unable to provide the extra finance required and even if they could it wouldn't be worth while investing for the profit we look like making.'

You are required: (*a*) to comment on the managing director's statement (8 marks); and (*b*) to suggest areas of investigation which might disclose possible sources of finance **within the company** and the matters which would have to be considered in respect of these. (12 marks) (ACCA MA 20 marks)

2. Shown below is a summary of the balance sheet of AL Ltd at 31 December 1979:

	£000		£000
Ordinary shares of £1 each, fully paid	200	Goodwill	100
10% cumulative preference shares of £1 each, fully paid	150	Development expenditure	90
		Fixed assets (net)	150
Share premium account	40	Current assets	60
Current liabilities	60	Accumulated losses	50
	450		450

The company has been trading at a loss for some years and at 31 December 1979 the preference dividend is three years in arrears. The directors have recently reorganised the company and, as a consequence, annual profits available for preference and ordinary dividends are expected to be between £10,000 and £20,000 p.a. in future years. However, many preference shareholders are pressing for the company to be wound up. Preference shareholders are entitled to a 10% cumulative annual dividend and to one vote per share when this is in arrears. Ordinary shareholders have one vote per ordinary share. Preference shareholders have priority on a winding up for repayment of nominal capital and arrears of dividend, but have no rights to any share in additional income or capital.

Companies in trouble

The directors wish the company to continue and have suggested the following scheme for the reconstruction of its capital:

(a) Each ordinary share to be written down to a nominal value of 10p per share.
(b) Each preference share to be written down to a nominal value of 50p per share (but the cumulative preference dividend to be raised from 10% to 15% p.a. which is the current stock-market rate for new preference share capital in this and comparable industries).
(c) The share premium account balance to be written off.
(d) The preference shareholders to receive ten new 10p ordinary shares (fully paid up) for each £1 arrears of 10% cumulative preference dividend at 31 December 1979.
(e) Accumulated losses at 31 December 1979, together with goodwill and development expenditure to be written off.
(f) Fixed assets to be written down to their realisable value (£100,000).
(g) Any surplus resulting from these operations to constitute a capital reserve. Current assets may be assumed to be worth their book value.

Required: A report to the preference shareholders incorporating a revised balance sheet for AL Ltd at 31 December 1979 (as it would look if the proposed reconstruction scheme were put into effect), advising whether they should accept the directors' scheme. Clearly indicate the impact of the scheme on dividends, capital and voting rights. Ignore taxation. (ICSA 34 marks)

3. The following statement summarises the financial accounts of ABC Ltd, for each of the three years ended 31 December 1979:

Year ended 31 December:		1977	1978	1979
Shareholders' funds: 100,000 shares of £1 each		100,000	100,000	100,000
Reserves and profit and loss		50,000	52,000	51,000
		150,000	152,000	151,000
Represented by:	Goodwill	10,000	10,000	10,000
	Freehold property	40,000	40,000	41,000
	Plant less depreciation	48,000	61,000	63,000
	Stock	50,000	65,000	75,000
	Sundry debtors	55,000	60,000	70,000
	Cash in hand	5,000	–	–
		208,000	236,000	259,000

Less: Bank overdraft	–		12,000		30,000
Sundry creditors	48,000		62,000		68,000
Provision for dividend	10,000	58,000	10,000	84,000	10,000	108,000
		150,000		152,000		151,000
Turnover		300,000		330,000		350,000
Less: cost of goods sold		240,000		269,000		287,000
		60,000		61,000		63,000
Less: expenses		45,000		49,000		54,000
Net profit		15,000		12,000		9,000

You have been approached by a finance company to examine the above statement to determine whether you would advise them to lend money to ABC Ltd.

Prepare a report which explains your decision to the finance company and state what additional information you would need for this purpose. (ICSA 34 marks)

Chapter 16

Valuation of a company

A wealthy individual or, more usually, representatives of another company, will often wish to value a company if they are considering attempting to buy it, or a controlling interest in it. Owners of an unlisted company may receive an offer to purchase their shares and they may commission an expert to advise them about the offer and their negotiating position generally. If the company is listed there will in principle be an established market for the shares but this could be a narrow and restricted one, and a wide jobber's turn a feature of dealings. It could not be considered that a realistic valuation of the company could be arrived at by multiplying the number of ordinary shares in issue by the most recent listed price. In practice, when jobbers suddenly begin to receive steady buying orders for a share with a restricted market they will suspect that a takeover attempt may be in progress and will mark up the prices of the shares sharply. Steady purchase orders, invariably in the names of nominees, will lead to sharp price rises and if most of the shares are held by a relatively small number of people, often members of one or two of the founding families of the company, some main shareholders may be determined not to sell at all and others may be ready to sell only if the price rises much higher.

Some relevant factors when valuing a company

It may be presumed that a party seeking to value a company with a view possibly to making a substantial investment would be thinking only in terms of gaining control. The acquiring of a substantial but still minority interest is dangerous since the investor can find himself 'locked in' with a bad investment and powerless to take effective action even if it becomes apparent that the directors are incompetent and ought to be changed or, even worse, are treating themselves to excessive salaries and other benefits. Apart from this aspect, a prospective investor must recognise that whilst the past record of the company, past earnings, dividends, etc., are matters of fact which can be verified, the main concern is the future and not the past and accordingly it will be necessary to make subjective judgements, notably as to the future earning power of the company, what goodwill it enjoys, if any, and which would be indicated by its capacity to generate profits above the average for the industry, often known as 'superprofits'. In practice it may be considered that the value of a company will lie within a range between the lowest price at which the present owners would be prepared to sell and the highest a prospective buyer would be prepared to pay. Even in this aspect the range would be fluid, being at higher levels when market conditions were buoyant and expectations rising and at lower ones when business confidence was low and especially at a time of credit squeeze and high MLR.

In the case of an unlisted company, shares would not have an established market price unless, exceptionally, they were dealt in under Rule 163 (2) by which the Stock Exchange permits certain restricted dealings in unlisted shares, or the over-the-counter market of J.M. Nightingale. A serious prospective buyer would finally be involved in direct negotiations with a small number of major shareholders or their representatives. A purchaser of shares providing just over 50% of the voting power would gain effective control, especially through the power to appoint and dismiss directors. However, it would be necessary to control 75% of the voting power to be sure of being able to pass special as well as ordinary resolutions. In practice all of the parties should be advised by experts, including in taxation, and much would depend on the negotiating skills of those acting for buyers and sellers as well as how anxious the sellers were to sell and the buyers to buy. It sometimes happens that an important company quickly offers a generous price for the shares of a smaller successful company which it wishes to acquire in order to enter a growing market in which the smaller company has an established reputation. In such a case it would be normal for the larger company also to offer attractive service contracts to members of the top management team on the principle that a successful company must be well managed and continuation of its success would best be ensured by the present top management continuing unchanged.

A company being valued from the aspect of control being acquired must be considered from various viewpoints:

(a) Internal – the assets and liabilities, the profit and growth history. The memorandum and articles will be considered and the standing of the company in its own field, with its customers, workpeople,

Valuation of a company

suppliers, etc. The management is always a vital factor and if past success seems mainly attributable to an outstanding individual or team then continuing success would make it desirable that the present top management continues with the new owners and with motivation undiminished. The importance of preparing for the management succession must never be forgotten.

(b) External – a company being valued must be assessed in relation to the industry in which it operates and the business and economic climate, locally, nationally and internationally.

Bases of valuation

Net asset value

No matter how successful a company may be it operates within the constraints imposed by the assets at its disposal. The simplest basis of share valuation is the balance-sheet valuation, using the most recently published information but bearing in mind that it will be siginficantly out of date. The calculation is:

$$\frac{\text{Net tangible assets}}{\text{Number of ordinary shares}}$$

If the company had preference shares any rights of these shareholders in the net assets would need to be taken into account. This basis of valuation is unreliable. The assets of companies as disclosed in balance sheets tend to be understated since balance sheets are prepared on the historic cost convention – although the implementation of SSAP 16 will be changing this somewhat. The tendency to understatement of assets has also been mitigated by the practice of more and more managements to revalue land and buildings more or less regularly, and balance sheets reflect this fact.

A problem with attempts to value assets is that the word 'value' has many meanings, depending on the purposes of the valuation and the viewpoint of its sponsor. A prospective creditor considering assets as security would tend to take an ultra-cautious viewpoint and think in terms of break-up values, which are close to scrap values when the buyer has to pay removal costs. However, a willing prospecive purchaser of a company as a going concern would attribute a much higher value to an asset – its 'value to the business', which would be related to the replacement cost of a similar asset taking into account the age and condition of the existing asset and any improved features of the new version. The range between valuations prepared to meet different viewpoints can be considerable and in all cases expert assistance would be needed – and would be expensive.

In order to determine net assets it is necessary also to determine the liabilities and to ensure that none has been omitted, and taking into account any contingent liabilities arising from possible lawsuits, payments due to employees, and possibly to a pension fund, etc. Assets and liabilities would be adjusted and restated as seemed necessary, on the basis of expert appraisals. In the case of a successful company the net assets valuation omits a vital component, goodwill. In practice, shares are valued on more than one basis and each would be considered and the final decisions would depend on subjective factors, notably the strengths of the wishes of prospective buyers and sellers and the negotiating skills of their advisers.

The dividend yield

An investor who buys shares in an important listed company, such as ICI, Unilever, Shell, etc., through the Stock Exchange knows that his shareholding, however large, will still be relatively tiny. He could not hope to influence the directors in their dividend policy or in any other way. It is arguable that the main concerns of such an investor, apart from possible interest in speculative short-term price movements, must be with: (*a*) dividend yield; (*b*) dividend cover; (*c*) growth prospects. (*a*) and (*b*) are known in respect of the present and past (although the effects of inflation complicate the situation and are often wrongly ignored) but (*c*) is more imponderable and subjective and will only become apparent as time passes. Meanwhile, dividend yield and cover are derived from the fundamental earnings yield:

Earnings yield = dividend yield × dividend cover

Whilst the dividend yield will be a factor which influences the market price of a listed security, it will still only be one factor amongst a number, many of which, including movements of interest rates, will affect market prices in general. Moreover, directors may not continue to recommend the payment of dividends at the same rate in the future as they have in the past.

The formula for share valuation on the basis of the dividend yield is:

$$\text{Share value} = \frac{\text{dividend \%} \times \text{nominal value of share}}{\text{normal market dividend yield}}$$

An unlisted share would be expected to stand at a discount of perhaps 10% to 20% in relation to a comparable listed company share with a

Valuation of a company

similar capital structure and in the same industry. This is because a company which has obtained a listing has been seen to have passed the severe tests imposed by the Stock Exchange, and its shares have the advantage of marketability. However, persons valuing a company with the intention of seeking to acquire control would not be interested in the dividend yield basis of valuation since they could change the dividend policy the moment they gained control. It is the earnings capability of a company which is the fundamental measure.

The earnings yield

The earnings yield effectively takes account of all the resources a company employs, not only its material assets but also the aspect of 'goodwill'. The basic formula is:

$$\text{Earning yield} = \frac{\text{Net (after-tax) earnings per share} \times 100}{\text{Market price per share}}$$

In fact, the imputation system of corporation tax has introduced some complications in practice, depending on the distribution policy of the company and whether a large proportion of its earnings arise overseas. These matters need not be considered here. When determining the earnings an analyst would make adjustments to exclude exceptional items, which would otherwise have a distorting effect since one is concerned with the earnings arising from normal trading operations. A listed share regarded as having special growth potential would tend to have a low earnings yield in comparison with other apparently comparable shares of other companies in the same industry, whereas a high earnings yield would indicate that for one or more reasons market opinion showed misgivings about the shares, particularly doubts as to whether the current level of earnings could be maintained.

Price/earnings ratio

Another important concept is the price earnings ratio:

$$\text{Price/earnings ratio} = \frac{\text{Market price per share}}{\text{After-tax earnings per share}}$$

It should be noted that this is the reciprocal of the earnings yield and also that the ratio measures the number of years of present earnings represented by the current market price. This ratio is by no means fixed or absolute and following the stock market collapse in 1973/4 price earnings ratios fell markedly. The ratio tends to be lower in respect of high-risk industries, and when a company is not highly regarded in the market it will have a low ratio relative to more favoured companies in the same industry.

The principle underlying valuation of a company on an earnings yield basis is that a valuer would assess what after-tax return from capital should be expected from a well-run company in the industry concerned. The results, over a number of years, of a number of listed companies in this industry would be considered as yardsticks, with trends, if any, being taken into account. A share in a listed company would tend to command a premium over a share in an unlisted one, In an examination question if profits were given for several years, an average should be taken and preferably a weighted average so that more weight would be given to results of the most recent years.

The basic principle underlying the calculation is simple. If, say, an after-tax earnings yield of 20% were expected from an investment in a particular company and if, say, the weighted average annual profits over a five-year period had been £150,000 then as an investment of £100 should produce earnings of £20, an investment of £x should produce earnings of £150,000, i.e. $\frac{£100}{£x} = \frac{£20}{£150,000}$ i.e. $x = \frac{£150,000 \times 100}{£20} =$ £750,000. If the valuation were approached from the aspect of the price earnings ratio it would be:

$$\text{Share value} = \frac{\text{P/E ratio} \times \text{earnings}}{\text{Number of ordinary shares}}$$

In this case a subjective judgement would be needed of an appropriate P/E ratio. A guide could be obtained by examining the P/E ratios of representative listed companies in the industry under review and noting that normally shares in an unlisted company would have a lower P/E ratio than shares in a listed company.

Valuation on basis of present value of expected future cash flow

A rather academic but still valid viewpoint is that a purchaser of a security makes a payment in expectation of a stream of income and in due course the proceeds of sale of the security – or an income in perpetuity if it were expected that the security would never be sold. Self-evidently, for appraisal purposes an attempt must be made to express future income streams in terms of present values, and for discounting purposes the cost of capital would be an appropriate interest rate. On the same principle a person valuing a business and informed of the expected net cash flow expected over a number of years (but bearing in

Valuation of a company

mind how uncertain such an estimate must be) could attempt a valuation on the basis:

$$\text{Share valuation} = \frac{\text{NPV on future cash flows discounted at cost of capital}}{\text{Number of ordinary shares}}$$

Like other bases of valuation, this method could only be considered as a pointer, to be used with other methods. In view of the many variables involved, not least as to the cost of capital, the possibilities of error in any attempt to estimate cash flows for many years ahead must be regarded as enormous.

Excess-profits basis of valuation (dual capitalisation)

It has been explained that a limitation of valuing a business on the basis of the net assets value is that it does not take into account the aspect of goodwill. Conversely, if a poorly managed company is achieving below-average results there will be 'badwill' which a prospective buyer would hope to eliminate by improving management, introducing new products etc. The excess profits basis of valuation attempts to redress the limitations of the assets basis: the formula used is:

$$\text{Total valuation} = \text{Net tangible assets} + \frac{\text{Estimated profit} - \text{'normal' profit on tangible assets}}{\text{Target rate of return on non tangible assets}}$$

Example: Valuation of net tangible assets: £1,000,000
Estimated annual profit over next five years: £ 200,000
Estimated annual 'normal' profit on tangible assets: £ 150,000
Target rate of return on non tangible assets 15%
Total valuation on excess profits basis:

$$£1,000,000 + \frac{£200,000 - £150,000}{0.15} = £1,333,333$$

In principle, of course, the negotiators on behalf of the owners would emphasise every available argument or valuation basis which indicated a higher value for the company whereas the negotiators for the prospective buyers would normally emphasise bases which gave rise to a lower valuation. In the end, an agreement would or would not be reached and the outcome would depend on the circumstances and the attitudes of the principals concerned.

Example 1 (see also facing page)

(*a*) I.C.Y. is a small private company which manufactures ice cream. On 31 December 1979 the shareholders receive an offer of £200,000 cash for the entire share capital. On the basis of the information provided state whether you think that the offer is fair. (*b*) Explain clearly what additional information you would require and the use of which this information would be put. Ignore taxation throughout this question. (ICSA 34 marks)

Workings and comments
It is normal for prospective buyers to offer too low a price for the company in their first offer. Equally, the shareholders and their advisers will seek to value the company on the highest possible basis. A main problem in this case is that there were very good results for 1977 and 1978 but very poor ones for 1979. There is thus no trend and the most recent result is the worst.

(*a*) It is proposed to value the company on the two main bases: (i) an assets basis, and (ii) an earnings yield basis. The dividend yield basis is considered irrelevant here since a party taking over the company could easily change the dividend policy. It is the earnings yield which is the more fundamental basis. As instructed in the question the quoted figures will be used.

(i) Assets basis (£):

Land and buildings		150,000
Plant and machinery		100,000
Stock		100,000
Debtors		80,000
		430,000
Less: Trade creditors	50,000	
Bank overdraft	100,000	150,000
Net assets		280,000

In the case of a company to be sold as a going concern, and which is not in imminent danger of liquidation, the assets basis tends to undervalue the company: it ignores the aspect of goodwill, and the dynamism of a profitable company. *Prima facie* the offer is not fair. (*Note*: one can

I.C.Y. Ltd.
(£000)

Years ended 31 December:	1977	1978	1979		1977	1978	1979
Cost of sales	400	500	500	Sales	600	800	700
Administrative expenses	60	100	150				
Directors' remuneration	10	20	30				
	470	620	680				
Profit for year	130	180	20				
	600	800	700		600	800	700
Dividend paid	60	60	60	Profit for year	130	180	20
Profit c/f	100	220	180	Profit b/f	30	100	220
	160	280	240		160	280	240

(£000)

Balance Sheet as at 31 December:	1977	1978	1979		1977	1978	1979
Share capital and reserves				Land & Bldgs (at cost)	150	150	150
Ordinary shares	100	100	100	Plant & Machy	50	60	100
Undistributed profit	100	220	180	(cost less depcn)	200	210	250
Mortgage	100	–	–	Stock	50	60	100
Trade creditors	20	20	50	Debtors	40	50	80
Bank overdraft	–	–	100	Cash	30	20	–
					120	130	180
	320	340	430		320	340	430

see by visual inspection in a few seconds that the offer is, at least, ungenerous: in examination papers which offer a choice of questions it is good tactics to try to choose questions which, as this one does, give clear indications of the right lines of approach to the answer.)

(ii) *Earnings yield basis*: as there is no clear trend and the most recent year was the worst, it is proposed to take a weighted average of the profits, with the heaviest weight on the most recent year. To illustrate the difference between the weighted and simple average, the two are calculated side by side:

		Weighted average			
		Profit (a)	*Weight (b)*	*(a) × (b)*	*Simple average*
Profits before dividend:	1979	20,000	3	60,000	20,000
	1978	180,000	2	360,000	180,000
	1977	130,000	1	130,000	130,000
			6	550,000	330,000

Weighted average $\dfrac{£550,000}{6} = £91,667$

$= £92,000$ (rounded)

Simple average $\dfrac{£330,000}{3} = £110,000$

The fact that it is the most recent result which is the worst is obviously a factor tending to depress the valuation of a company. The weighted average gives effect to this aspect whereas the simple average does not. In answering this question an assumption must now be made and stated – what rate of return would be expected on an investment in this industry and in this particular company? Clearly, a student cannot be expected to show expert knowledge but, rather, a grasp of principles. In this case, taking into account yields obtainable on fixed-interest government securities at the time, and the aspect of risk, it is assumed that an investor would expect an earnings yield – a return on capital – of 20%. A simple calculation will then be: Let x be the value of the company: then, $\dfrac{£100}{x} = \dfrac{£20}{£92,000}$, i.e. $x = £460,000$. If a prospective buyer considered I.C.Y. to be a very risky investment, on which he would require

Valuation of a company

a return on capital of 25% p.a., then $£x = \dfrac{£92,000}{25} \times £100$, i.e. $x = £368,000$. It is thus evident that whatever reasonable earnings yield is considered appropriate, and also taking into account the net assets valuation basis, the offer of £200,000 is **not** fair.

(b) Additional information would be required in respect or both balance sheet and profit-and-loss items over a period of 5 to 10 years, as well as similar information in respect of a number of comparable companies operating in the same industry. Does the company seem to be doing better or worse than competitors and what seem to be the reasons? Valuations of assets; land and buildings – when were these bought and what is the current value? (Current property values are often well in excess of those shown in the balance sheet.) Plant and machinery – more detailed information is needed, notably as to age, condition and suitability. Is depreciation being charged on a realistic and consistent basis and what is the 'value to the business': the physical condition (and existence) of important stock items must be assessed, as well as the stock records. In brief, do the book values of the stock appear realistic or, if not, what adjustments should be made either way? Debtors – has sufficient provision been made for possible bad debts? Creditors – confirm that none have been omitted. On the basis of this review the net asset basis of valuation would need to be recalculated. Revenues and costs: the reasons underlying the key figures must be examined and explained in detail. Questions include – why did the sales fall in 1979? What was the experience of competitors? Detailed study would be necessary with analysis of sales of individual lines, wholesale and retail prices. The cost of sales must be analysed including into direct and indirect costs. If costs of materials have risen, confirm that the increases for major items appear to accord with market movements. Confirm also that the buying arrangements are efficient, and also those for the control of stores. Were selling prices increased in line with cost increases and, if not, why not? Should emphasis be put on increasing sales of the most profitable lines? Explanation would be needed for significant increases in the fixed costs. The heavily increasing administrative expenses need urgent explanation and attention. The substantial increase in directors' remuneration may not be too material but it might call for explanation. (It is a frequent practice for directors of a family-owned business to pay themselves salaries well above the market rate, in conjunction with low dividends since this legitimately reduces their taxation liabilities: taxes on income do not suffer the investment income surcharge.) When this situation exists it would be necessary to make certain adjustments to the accounts with any difference between the remuneration actually paid to the directors and what could be considered a normal commercial remuneration being treated as an appropriation of profits instead of an expense. The effect is that the adjusted profits are above the declared ones. Finally, the review of this company would include the quality of the management and control. If weaknesses were identified and could quickly be corrected there would be good prospects of early restoration of the company to financial health and strong profitability. In any case, it would seem poor and weak tactics to sell this company at a 'give away' price just after one poor year.

Note: Whilst there would probably not be time to incorporate discussion of ratios in the answer the following are three key ratios calculated for each year:

	1977	1978	1979
Profit before dividends (£000)	130	180	20
Shareholders funds (see balance sheet)	200	320	280
Per cent return on shareholders' equity	65	56	7

Profit/sales (%) (margins)
$$\frac{£130{,}000 \times 100 \ (21.7\%)}{£600{,}000} \quad \frac{£180{,}000 \times 100 \ (22.5)}{£800{,}000} \quad \frac{£20{,}000 \times 100 \ (2.7)}{£700{,}000}$$

Sales/total capital employed (turnover)
$$\frac{£600{,}000 \ (1.88)}{£320{,}000} \quad \frac{£800{,}000 \ (2.35)}{£340{,}000} \quad \frac{£700{,}000 \ (1.63)}{£430{,}000}$$

Example 2

Alpha Co. Ltd is a small private manufacturing company. The directors (who own 90% of the shares) have jointly decided to sell the business as a going concern and have set a price of £200,000 on it. The latest balance sheet of Alpha Co. Ltd is as undernoted and its profits before taxation have always been of the order of £10,000 p.a. Beta Ltd is a quoted company with characteristics similar to Alpha. Currently its 100p ordinary shares are trading at 333p and its last dividend of 10% was covered 1½ times.

Valuation of a company

Summarised balance sheet of Alpha Ltd (£)

Capital: 10,000 ordinary shares of £1 each fully paid		10,000	Fixed assets (net)		84,000
Reserves		30,000	Current assets:		
		40,000	Stocks	16,000	
			Debtors	20,000	
Current liabilities:			Prepayments	2,000	
Creditors	76,000		Cash	400	38,400
Accruals	6,400	82,400			
		122,400			122,400

(*a*) Using the above information and assuming a corporation tax rate of 50% is applicable to both buyer and seller, assess the reasonableness or otherwise of the value of £200,000 which the directors have put on Alpha. (16 marks) (*b*) many company valuation models require a projection of future profits. To what extent is the record of past profits as reported in the profit-and-loss account of use in making such forecasts and what qualifications must be placed on the use of the profit-and-loss account for this purpose. (9 marks) (ACCA 25 marks).

Workings and comments

(*a*) A prospective buyer of Alpha Ltd, when told the asking price, would have a number of options: (*a*) to buy Alpha at the price asked; (*b*) to reject Alpha altogether as being of no interest; (*c*) to be interested in Alpha, but only at a lower price, to which the sellers might or might not agree; (*d*) to look for another company to purchase as a going concern; (*e*) to start a new company himself. The asking price of the sellers will normally include an element for goodwill. The question will be whether or not this is priced on a reasonable basis. In the case of Alpha Ltd the net assets appear in the balance sheet at £40,000. If this figure represents a realistic valuation then a buyer who purchased Alpha for £200,000 would need to introduce 'goodwill' into his accounts, as a balancing item, at £160,000. This appears altogether excessive. It is stated that the pre-tax profits have 'always' been of the order of £10,000 p.a., i.e. an after-tax return of £5,000 – for which the sellers are asking £200,000. This would represent an after-tax return on capital of 2½% and a price earnings ratio of £200,000/£5,000, i.e. 40. This is a higher figure than applies to the best 'blue chip' companies in the UK. The asking price appears to be totally unrealistic, even if there should be some favourable factors not evident in the figures given, e.g. are the fixed assets worth, perhaps land and buildings, much more than £84,000? Furthermore, the balance sheet discloses a very disturbing situation, with negative liquidity £22,400 − £82,400, i.e. − £60,000. On the evidence available, Alpha Ltd could only justify a much lower price than £200,000, if it were worth purchasing at all. Alpha Ltd may also be compared with Beta Ltd (which has the advantage of being a listed company. Beta has a dividend yield of $\frac{10 \times 100}{333}$, i.e. 3%. This indicates an earnings yield of 3.0% × 1½ = 4½% (dividend yield × dividend cover = earnings yield). If a listed comparable company has an earnings yield of 4½% one would expect an unlisted Alpha to offer a yield somewhat exceeding 5%, and not a mere 2½%. From the aspect of comparability it appears that the asking price of Alpha is excessive.

(b) Provided that past profits have been calculated realistically and consistently, and appropriate adjustments made for any special factors, and supplementary accounts have been prepared to show as far as possible the effects of inflation, then the record of past profits will give useful pointers about a company if skilfully interpreted. Trends will be apparent, and when comparable information is available with respect to other companies in the industry an impression may be formed of the overall quality of the company and its management and workforce. The record of past profits alone would not be sufficient for full analysis: other financial and non-financial information would be desirable. However, past profits relate to the past and one is concerned with the future. Any projection of past profits implies that essentially things will continue in the future much as they have done in the past but this may be a totally false assumption, especially in times of rapid change. The emergence of a powerful competitor, perhaps from another country, or the invention of new products, could result in future profitability having an entirely different pattern from past profitability. Outstanding managers must sooner or later retire, or die, or resign and will their successors maintain their standards? Study of past profitability is therefore helpful and essential but it must be made with caution and recognising that it can provide no more than a signpost towards a future which is bound to be full of risks and uncertainties.

Example 3

At a meeting of the directors of the Alpha Co. Ltd – a privately owned company – in May 1975 the recurrent question is raised as to how the company is going to finance its future growth and at the same time enable the founders of the company to withdraw a substantial part of their investment. A public quotation was discussed in 1974 but because

Valuation of a company

of the depressed nature of the stock market at the time consideration was deferred. Although the matter is not of immediate urgency the Chairman of the company – one of the founders – produces the following information which he has recently obtained from a firm of analysts in respect of two publicly quoted companies, Beta Ltd and Gamma Ltd which are similar to Alpha Ltd in respect to size, asset composition, financial structure and product mix.

		(£) Beta Ltd	(£) Gamma Ltd
1974	Earnings per share	1.50	2.50
1970/74	Average earnings per share	1.00	2.00
1974	Average market price per share	9.00	20.00
1974	Dividends per share	0.75	1.25
1970/74	Average dividends per share	0.60	1.20
1974	Average book-value per share	9.00	18.00

The chairman asks on the basis of this information what you think Alpha Ltd was worth in 1974. The only information you have available at the meeting in respect of Alpha Ltd is the final accounts for 1974 which disclose the following:

	Alpha Ltd (£)
Share capital (£1 ordinary shares: no variation for 8 years)	100,000
Post tax earnings	400,000
Gross dividends	100,000
Book value	3,500,000

From memory you think that the post-tax earnings and gross dividends were at least one-third higher than the average of the previous five years.

You are required, making **full** use of the information above to: (*a*) answer the question of the chairman (18 marks); and (*b*) discuss the factors to be taken into account in trying to assess the potential market value in a private company when they are first offered for public subscription. (7 marks) (ACCA 25 marks).

Workings and comments
(*a*) The first step is to express the information given with respect to Alpha Ltd in the same form as that given for Beta and Gamma Ltd. It

will then be possible to 'compare like with like'. However, as Alpha Ltd does not yet have a Stock Exchange listing its share value must be presumed to stand at a discount of say 10%–20% of its price if listed. The data for Alpha Ltd is now converted and restated (£):

		Alpha Ltd	Beta Ltd	Gamma Ltd
1974	Earnings per share	4.00	1.50	2.50
1970/74	Average earnings per share	3.20	1.00	2.00
1974	Average market price per share	x	9.00	20.00
1974	Dividends per share	1.00	0.75	1.25
1970/74	Average dividends per share	0.80	0.60	1.20
1974	Average book value per share	y	9.00	18.00

Note: the reader should check the workings: as earnings were £400,000 in 1974 they must have been £300,000 for each of the previous four years, giving average earnings for the five years of £320,000 p.a., similarly the average dividend must have been £80,000. There are thus now two questions to be answered with respect to Alpha Ltd.: (a) 1974 average (market) price per share, and (b) average book value per share. As the book value of Alpha Ltd is £3,500,000 and there are 100,000 (£1) ordinary shares the book value per share must be £35 (y). This leaves only one unknown – x – the likely market price in 1974. This can be examined by using the known information in respect of Beta and Gamma in appropriate ratios and in this way calculating values for x. For this purpose it is assumed first that Alpha is compared directly with Beta and then directly with Gamma. This will lead to a number of values being obtained for x but this is to be expected.

Therefore, depending upon the ratio selected and the company with which Alpha is compared, the lowest value per share of Alpha would be £12 and the highest £38.50 – an enormously wide range. The total value of the company will, of course, in theory be the product of the price per share and the number of shares in issue. However, it is suggested

	Beta	Alpha
1974 Earnings per share (P/E ratio)	$\frac{9.00}{1.50} = 6 = \frac{x}{4.00}$	i.e. $x = £24.000$:
1970/74 Average E.P.S.	$\frac{9.00}{1.00} = 9 = \frac{x}{3.20}$	i.e. $x = £28.80$:
1974 Dividends per share	$\frac{9.00}{0.75} = 12 = \frac{x}{1.00}$	i.e. $x = £12.00$:
1970/74 Average D.P.S.	$\frac{9.00}{0.60} = 15 = \frac{x}{0.80}$	i.e. $x = £12.00$:
1974 Market price/Book value	$\frac{9.00}{9.00} = 1 = \frac{x}{35}$	i.e. $x = £35.00$:

Valuation of a company

that the valuations on the basis of the dividends paid should be disregarded. These merely reflect what the very high book value of the shares also reflects – that Alpha has been paying out very small dividends and retaining an exceptionally large proportion of its profits. If Alpha is to become a public listed company an indication would be desirable that in the future the payout ratio would be increased – a significantly larger proportion of the available profits would be distributed as dividends. With the share price related to dividends disregarded, the range now becomes £24 to £38.50 and if emphasis is given to the earnings per share, as it is the capacity of the company to generate earnings which is perhaps the most critical yardstick, the range becomes £24 to £32 – an average of £28. If about 10% is deducted because Alpha Ltd is not listed, a valuation of £25 would seem a figure the directors could have in mind during discussions. In fact, timing is always of great importance. £25 per share would value the company at £2,500,000 – a figure well below the book value. 1975 was a year when stock market prices were still exceptionally low, after the financial crisis, and directors would have been well advised to avoid selling shares to the public at low prices since the company is clearly profitable and has growth potential. In principle, one should try to 'go public' when market conditions are buoyant. This is what happens in practice.

(b) Directors attempting to place a value on unlisted shares when these are to be offered for public subscription for the first time must bear in mind that there will be three dominant groups of factors to consider: (i) general factors applying to the whole of the equity market; (ii) factors centred on the industry in which the company operates; and (iii) factors centred on the company itself, its capital structure, its past record, the opinions held of its management, etc. It is re-emphasised that timing is of the utmost importance. If a highly regarded unlisted company brought its shares to the market when conditions were depressed and

Gamma	Alpha
$\frac{20.00}{2.50} = 8 = \frac{x}{4.00}$	i.e. $x = £32.000$
$\frac{20.00}{2.00} = 10 = \frac{x}{3.20}$	i.e. $x = £32.00$
$\frac{20.00}{1.25} = 16 = \frac{x}{1.00}$	i.e. $x = £16.00$
$\frac{20.00}{1.20} = 16.7 = \frac{x}{0.80}$	i.e. $x = £13.36$
$\frac{20.00}{18.00} = 1.1 = \frac{x}{35}$	i.e. $x = £38.50$

confidence low, the price obtained would be much lower than it would have been if the launch had occurred at a favourable time. The conditions for a particular industry are likely to be favourable when market conditions generally are buoyant but it also happens that a particular industry, and company, could be regarded with special favour – or disfavour – against the market climate as a whole, and because of exceptional factors. Thus, in 1980 for a time oil shares were rising quickly when the general market was declining. The timing of a launch, and the offer price, are matters in which specialist advice will be decisive, but in this area, as in others, from time to time experts prove astonishingly wrong, notably when shares are offered at unnecessarily low prices, so that issues are hugely oversubscribed, and the profits go largely to 'stags' instead of the company or shareholders. When an issue is announced one of the major factors in its success or failure will be press comment, lead by specialist financial journalists and analysts employed by the press, stockbrokers and others.

Questions

1. The profit-and-loss account and balance sheets of ABC Ltd for the years ended 31 December 1978 and 1979 are as follows (£000):

		1978		1979
Sales		350		450
Less: Cost other than below		250		350
Depreciation on plant	50	100	60	100
Loss on sale of government securities	5		10	
Amounts written off securities and trade investments	–	55	15	85
		45		15
Profit on sales of land		–		30
		45		45
Less: Tax		10		10
Dividends declared and paid		10		12
Profits retained		25		23

Valuation of a company

ABC Ltd Balance Sheets as at 31 December	1978		(£000)	1979
Fixed assets				
Goodwill (at cost)		50		50
Land (at cost)		100		70
Plant (at cost)	400		600	
Less: depreciation	200	200	260	340
		350		460
Trade investments (at cost)		50		50
Current assets				
Government securities (at cost)		40		20
Stock at cost		100		200
Debtors		90		140
Cash at bank		50		(20)
		680		850
Share capital and reserves				
Ordinary shares		400		400
Profit-and-loss account		150		173
		550		573
Future tax reserve		10		12
14% debentures		40		115
Creditors		80		150
		680		850

The total market value of the shares of the company immediately after the publication of the annual accounts was £700,000 in 1978 and £800,000 in 1979. You are required to analyse the accounts of the company on behalf of an investor who is considering buying a large block of the company's shares which is not sufficient to give him control. (ICSA 34 marks)
2. Discuss the effect you would expect each of the following developments to have on the general level of share prices of companies operating in the United Kingdom (or any other country with a developed stock market system with which you are familiar): (*a*) an increase in long-term interest rates; (*b*) devaluation or depreciation of the external value of the currency; and (*c*) an increase in the rate of inflation at the same time unemployment also increases. (ACCA 20 marks).
3. For what reasons should a quoted company continue to be concerned with the market performance of its shares after issue and what action can it take to improve that performance? (ACCA 20 marks)
4. The directors of Black Ltd, clients of yours, have informed you that

they are contemplating the acquisition of the entire share capital of Smith Ltd.

Although they are aware of the three methods of valuing shares:
(1) assets;
(2) prices/earnings ratio;
(3) gross dividend yield;

they are inexperienced and have requested further explanation. You are required to write a letter advising them briefly on (a) each of these methods, and (b) the propriety of each method in relation to a 100% acquisition. (ACCA 15 marks)

5. (a) Explain the term dividend yield in relation to equity investment and why it is in part an unreliable concept. (b) Explain the term price/earnings ratio and its relationship to the dividend yield. (c) The shares of company A which owns and develops commercial property show a dividend yield of 1.5% and a price/earnings ratio 40% while those of company B, a machine tool manufacturer yield 6% with a price earnings ratio of 13. Suggest circumstances which would have accounted for these divergent stock-market ratings during the course of 1971.

6. ABC Ltd is investigating the possible acquisition of XYZ Ltd for diversification purposes and has asked you to advise them on the basis of the following information:

XYZ Ltd, Balance Sheet at 30 November 1979 (£000)

Ordinary shares	1,500	Land buildings	900
Reserves	900	Plant (net of depreciation)	600
10% debentures	750	Investments	450
Creditors	300	Stock	600
		Debtors	600
		Cash	300
	3,450		3,450

Profits 1977 – £350,000   1978 – £300,000   1979 – £450,000

You are also told that:
(i) It is estimated that the investments have a market value of £675,000 and that the stock could be sold for £750,000. The other assets have a value as stated in the balance sheet.
(ii) All of the investments and plant valued at £225,000 would not be needed by ABC Ltd.
(iii) The investments have produced an annual income of £45,000 p.a. and are expected to continue to do so.

Valuation of a company

(iv) ABC Ltd would repay the debentures at par immediately after acquisition.
(v) ABC Ltd requires a return on capital of 10%.
You are required to calculate the maximum price which ABC Ltd should be prepared to pay for XYZ Ltd on each of the following bases:
(a) break-up value;
(b) profitability;
(c) Discounted cash flow, assuming that the cash flows to be discounted are as follows:

1980	£450,000		
1981	£600,000		
1982	£450,000		
1983 onwards	£570,000		
Present value factors at 10%	Year 1		0.90909
	2		0.83645
	3		0.75131
	4		0.68301

(ICSA 34 marks)

Chapter 17

Mergers and takeovers

A company may grow organically because it has an outstanding management, trades successfully, retains profits, uses these efficiently, and this is a factor encouraging growth, which is assisted by the fact that shareholders are prepared to subscribe to rights issues. Other major companies grow in part for these reasons and partly in consequence of mergers and takeovers, which are not new phenomena. Furthermore, it is evident that there are times when mergers and takeovers are specially fashionable and this was a feature of the late 1960s early 1970s. Many were promoted for the financial interests of their promoters who put forward reasons which were not the true reasons. Financiers honestly believed, or pretended, that their aim was to help regenerate UK industries whereas in so many cases the real aim later emerged as 'asset stripping' and quick personal enrichment. The 1973/74 financial collapse exposed many of these people and the fact that their activities caused more harm than good and benefited only themselves. In brief, revulsion set in and even now announcements of proposed mergers or takeovers are regarded by the public with scepticism, as are any public statements made by those concerned.

Reasons for mergers and takeovers

Meanwhile, time has shown that soundly conceived mergers and takeovers can be generally beneficial to all the interests concerned – shareholders, employees, customers, suppliers, the government, local authorities, etc. Time has equally shown that a substantial proportion prove deeply disappointing. Why should there be success in some cases and failure in others? A surmise is that the limiting factor of a company or a group is often the quality of its top management and individuals or small teams of men who might have performed adequately when running smaller companies find themselves 'out of their depth' when attempting to direct much larger ones. It is also evident that the reasons men publicly give for their actions are often not the true reasons, which they keep secret. If the true reason is that a financier wishes to add to his fortune, or a powerful chief executive is an 'empire builder' who pursues expansion because of the extra powers and prestige it confers upon him, then if the proposals have no genuine logic, and there is no real commitment to them, it will not be surprising if they fail, whereas those planned and executed by able men acting with logic and conviction will have a better but still not perfect chance of success.

A frequent reason for an agreed takeover is that a large company or group decides to enter a new market, possibly in another country, as its researches indicate growth potential. In 1978/79 a number of major UK companies, including Unilever, GEC, ICI and major banks made acquisitions of this nature. These moves were facilitated by the relative weakness of the US dollar and share prices on Wall Street, just as in the early post-war period many US companies had found conditions favourable for the takeover of British and other European companies. United Kingdom companies making takeovers in recent times have financed these from internal resources supplemented in some cases by borrowing and or rights issues: because of the standing of the companies concerned they have been able to borrow readily in whatever currency they choose, and not necessarily in sterling. Even so, interest rates are now high even when the standing of the borrower gives access to the lowest available rates.

The logic of many acquisitions of this kind is that the acquirer aims to establish an important presence in a chosen new market with minimum delay, and with a good and experienced management and workforce under his control, as well as appropriate assets and outlets and goodwill. Although a substantial premium will have to be paid for the goodwill of the business taken over, since the agreed price for the shares taken over will be well above the market price for these shares just prior to the acquisition, the benefits should be largely a significant saving of time, and hence earlier access to profits, and reduction of risks. The reduction of risks may be explained as follows. An option open to a company with strong resources is to build up a new business in another country (or in its own) 'from scratch'. It would need to build or rent factories, offices, showrooms, hire managers and workpeople in the open market, etc. Whilst this can be done, it would take some years to build up a presence in this way and in the process exeptional problems could be met, especially in finding and retaining the experienced high-calibre managers required. The option of an agreed takeover, where practicable, appears, to be much the more attractive, not least because the successful company acquired would now be the spearhead for the acquirer in the chosen area of activity, instead of being a fierce competitor.

One point emphasised by the Wilson Committee is that there is ample evidence that larger companies have less difficulties than smaller ones in raising funds, which they can also obtain at lower cost. Recognition of the advantages of size is itself a factor encouraging growth by acquisition and merger. Advantages of size will include some of a financial and others of organisational and technical natures. Financial advantages include: (*a*) readier access to capital on more favourable terms; (*b*) large financial resources can be efficiently managed at a central point and deployed as required to and from operating units, and working capital requirements can be reduced relatively; (*c*) new opportunities can be seized and exploited from a base of financial strength; (*d*) large resources can achieve a reduction in financial risks – for example, whilst self insurance may be justifiable and cost saving for a larger unit, it would be imprudent for a smaller one; (*e*) profitable outlets may be found for surplus funds; (*f*) sometimes new sources of capital may be tapped, e.g. when a bank acquires a smaller bank in a territory where the larger bank has not operated previously; (*g*) a special reason may be the opportunity to offset tax losses of one company against taxable profits of another, thus reducing overall tax liability.

Organisational and technical reasons favouring larger organisations, and which may or may not be socially desirable, include: (*a*) rewards and career prospects can be offered to able managers for all functions; (*b*) there may be effective centralised buying and provision of other specialised functions including research and development, using the best equipment, techniques and high-calibre employees; (*c*) a large company, as represented by its managers, carries more weight in its dealings with authorities, suppliers, etc.; (*d*) there is greater scope for planned and integrated diversification, which can reduce business and financial risks; (*e*) in numbers of industries there are economies arising from large-scale production: (i) the principle of large machines – the capital and operating costs of a machine, e.g. a ship or a lorry, do not increase proportionately to increase in size – in brief, larger machines, when fully utilised, tend to give rise to lower unit costs; (ii) the principle of indivisibility – often a machine has to be above a certain size to be efficient and only larger companies can afford such machines; (iii) the optimum combination of inputs, sometimes called the principle of the least common multiple. Production often involves a number of processes, each with different output capacities; the optimum arrangement will be that which permits each process to operate efficiently so that the lowest attainable unit costs are achieved. In practice, it is often only the larger organisations which can install the most efficient combinations of machines, equipment, processes, etc,; (iv) the principle of massed reserves – manufacturing companies, supermarket chains, etc., must carry large stocks of materials, components, finished stocks, etc., and larger companies can carry parts of these in strategically sited storage. In brief, stocks do not need to increase proportionately as the company grows and thus relatively less capital has to be tied up in stocks: larger units find it worth while to find markets for waste and minor by-products and, for example, to recycle and use heat which would otherwise be wasted.

Disadvantages of large organisations

It is a fact of experience that large organisations tend to be run on bureaucratic lines, which lead to rigidity, lack of flexibility, and inability to make quick decisions even when circumstances demand these. Despite great advances in communications and in data processing, which have put great new capabilities into the hand of top managements, the fact remains that top officials have limited time at their disposal and can only be in one place at one time. There has to be recourse to delegation and this gives rise to problems, and there are also problems of coordination. In 1979 correspondence in the *Financial Times* on the British Steel Corporation (BSC) highlighted that factories such as those at Shotton and Corby were anxious and able to meet specific requests of customers but often were not permitted to do so by their head office controllers: with hindsight, there is a widespread view that BSC might have done much better if there had been half a dozen or so competing and autonomous organisations instead of one monolithic one. There is also evidence in the UK and elsewhere that industrial problems tend to be more frequent and serious in larger than in smaller units, and the larger units also offer more scope for disruptive stoppages organised by small groups of key workers, which may include political extremists. Research and observation suggest that it is often the human factor which places constraints on the size to which an organisation can grow without marked decline in efficiency, and the problems normally centre on the quality of the top management. It is often this problem which prevents a merger or takeover from achieving the results predicted. Often, but not always, of course, there are serious open or concealed personality clashes between senior people and numbers of managers may be quietly obstructive rather than cooperative.

However, despite the problems, in certain industries at least, in the capitalist economies, the movement continues towards an increasing proportion of the world's markets being supplied by a decreasing proportion of giant companies, such as General Motors and Ford of the USA, Fiat in Europe and Toyota in Japan. It is interesting that even in the service industries in the UK there are indications of this trend towards growth: for example, there are now the 'big eight' giant firms of auditors, which operate on an international scale and which have grown significantly by agreed takeovers of and mergers with other auditing firms along the way. It is nevertheless also evident that in all industrialised countries there are still places for smaller, efficiently run companies which meet local needs, or those which do not sufficiently interest the giants. Smaller companies can be more flexible and quickly responsive to market forces and have lower overheads. They may also act as suppliers or subcontractors for larger companies. At any one time a small number of smaller companies are in the early stages of growth into giant companies themselves. Meanwhile, governments everywhere have become more concerned to create a more favourable economic climate for small companies, not least because they tend to be more labour intensive than larger ones, which are increasingly 'shedding' workpeople made redundant by the use of technologically more advanced machines and equipment.

Main types of integration

There are four commonly recognised types of integration. They are: (1) vertical; (2) horizontal; (3) conglomerate; (4) geographical. In the case of vertical integration, companies may move 'upstream', or 'backwards', towards their sources of supply, or 'downstream', or 'forwards', towards their final customers, or both. Main purposes include to protect the sources of supply or to seek surer final markets for products. A major company may also assess that profits are high at some particular point in the production – distribution chain and seek a major share of these for itself. Backward and or forward integration permit more effective planning and control of a larger part of the whole production process by the acquiring company. Even when the management of a smaller company is efficient it may benefit from being acquired by the larger one as it would have ready access to the financial resources of the parent company and also to its high-quality specialist services. The motive of securing reliable sources of supply is particularly strong. It is also a common practice of multinational companies to allow considerable autonomy to subsidiary or associated companies, with emphasis on profit centres and budgetary control. The subsidiary may be permitted to sell at least part of its output on the open market and the major company may also have recourse to outside suppliers.

Horizontal integration involves the integration of companies in the same field of activity. The acquiring company may seek to increase its share of the market, or reduce competition. It may seek to become a 'price leader' and if it assesses that the elasticity of demand is not high, and competition is restricted, it could increase prices and thus profits. An aim could be to obtain the advantages of economies of scale and a spreading of fixed costs over a larger output. The company acquired might have special 'know-how' or patents which could be developed profitably by the acquirer, or the acquirer might be planning expansion and identify an established smaller company whose acquisition would permit it to enter the new market quickly and effectively. On other occasions the acquirer might identify an unprofitable company with poor management, which it could revitalise by introducing new management and then deploying the resources of the company more efficiently and hence profitably.

Some companies have a policy of acquiring smaller companies in widely different fields of activity. Groups of this kind are known as conglomerates. Some years ago conglomerate merger activity was intense in the USA, and articulate entrepreneurs were boosted by the US media and the shares in which they were interested boomed, but later, with the onset of the recession, the results of the groups proved disappointing and reaction set in and conglomerates fell sharply out of favour with investors. Share prices fell. Main criticisms were lack of any underlying logic and the various members of the groups were too unrelated to each other. Individual managements understood only their own business and industry and had nothing to offer to other members of the group. However, the fact remains that there are, in the UK and elsewhere, long established and successful conglomerate groups. Features of some of these are that successful smaller companies have been taken over on agreed bases with their existing successful managements who retain strong financial interest in their own company and have considerable autonomy, whilst the parent company offers access to finance on favourable terms and strong supporting services. Provided that the results of individual companies are considered satisfactory there should be no problems but no doubt the central top management would become more exacting, and would have the last word, in the event that any member companies began to perform inadequately.

Geographical integration occurs whenever there is backward integration with a major company acquiring a supplier of raw materials in a developing country, but in such cases the concern of the acquirer is with the supplier and the location is an incidental matter. However, a feature of multinational companies is the worldwide nature of their activities. Such companies will be concerned with supplies and with ultimate consumers and their vast resources permit them, *inter alia*, to think strategically in global terms and make plans which take into account information obtained from numbers of countries, and to look several years ahead: they have expert advice on such matters as taxation, relative labour costs, and government policies towards expatriate investors. A noteworthy fairly recent development is the creation by multinational car and electronics manufacturers of manufacturing subsidiaries in countries such as Taiwan and South Korea, Brazil, etc., where there are relatively low-paid skilled, hardworking labour forces in economic environments well disposed to the capitalist ethos. Often central and local governments offer strong tax and other financial incentives to companies which establish factories and thereby create local employment. In other cases, and especially with smaller companies, a company holding patents or having manufacturing 'know-how' and wishing to develop sales in a potentially important market in a new geographical area will not itself attempt to establish a presence there but will instead negotiate an agreement with a local company whereby the latter manufactures under license, using the trade name, or patents or processes of the licensor. Franchise agreements may be offered. These are options permitting a company to gain profits with limited capital outlays and risks, and without incurring the costs liable to arise in establishing an operation overseas. Setting up a business overseas in practice always involves unexpected problems and these require the attention and hence the time of top and senior managers. A major company which has successfully used licensing arrangements internationally on a large scale is Pilkington Ltd, the glass manufacturers whose 'Float' glass is manufactured under license on a worldwide basis.

Geographical integration, the activities of multinational companies, transfer pricing questions, declining, employment of people in the heavy traditional industries in the UK, Europe and the USA, often because owners of capital are finding it more profitable to set up modern plants in developing in countries with relatively low labour costs, are already creating problems in the Western industrialised countries. These are likely to intensify in the future as microprocessors come increasingly into use and displace more unskilled labour. It is interesting that a leading multinational company, General Motors of the USA, has appointed for the first time a Director of International Social Action, as the company has the philosophy that multinational companies need to become more directly involved in the human and social problems of the countries and communities in which they operate.

Mergers and takeovers: technical aspects

The distinction between a merger and a takeover can be a narrow one. Generally, a merger occurs when two companies combine their operations to form a new capital and corporate structure and a new company is formed with a new name. However, as the companies concerned will have made heavy investments in advertising and building up the company name and brand names, it will be important not to lose goodwill. Accordingly the new name will often incorporate old and well-known names. Cadbury–Schweppes Ltd is an example. The old brand names are likely to continue in use unchanged.

In the case of a takeover a larger company (normally, but not invariably) acquires a smaller one and the latter loses its identity. Even in this type of situation, however, the identity of the smaller company may be maintained for its trading and operating activities and with a view to preserving the goodwill attached to the well-known name. Takeovers will be considered first. Each will be handled in the light of its own facts and situations and the attitudes of the parties involved. To recapitulate, common reasons for a bid, some considered good and some possibly bad in a social sense include: (*a*) to obtain at bargain prices assets which are not being used efficiently; (*b*) to obtain the use of assets and the management and workforce of a successful company so that the bidder can quickly establish a presence in a new field of activity; (*c*) to obtain at low cost control of a company which has surplus cash; (*d*) to obtain additional productive capacity quickly; (*e*) to move closer to a monopoly position in a market, or one of price leadership; (*f*) to obtain additional sales outlets; (*g*) for the purpose of 'asset stripping' – to take over a company at low price, dismiss the workpeople and sell off the assets for the personal enrichment of the bidders.

The objective of the bidder will often, but not always, be to acquire all of the shares so that the acquired company becomes a wholly owned subsidiary. The bidder will often be satisfied to obtain just over 50% of the vote-carrying shares as this would be enough to give control over the board of directors and thus over the company, and including over any surplus cash it might have. Sometimes the bidder would aim to obtain 75% of the voting power so that he could have a special resolution passed. It may also happen that a larger company wishes to obtain an important but not controlling shareholding in another company, a major customer or supplier, for example, in order that it may be able to influence its policies, have a director on the board, etc. This would not be a takeover, however: when a company has a minority interest in another company, which exceeds 20%, and is concerned with the policies of the other company, the two are associated companies.

The consideration for a bid might be: (*a*) cash, or (*b*) listed ordinary shares of the bidder or even, although unlikely, (*c*) listed loan stock: it could be a mix of (*a*), (*b*) and (*c*). If the company to be acquired is a private unlisted company, the shares will be held privately, normally mainly by members of one or two founding families and with a majority of the shares held by a single individual or a small group, who may or may not be willing to sell. If they were not willing, that would be the end of the matter. If the smaller company were doing badly, the main shareholders might be anxious to sell on the principle that the options were quick sale as a going concern or compulsory liquidation. In such a situation the negotiating position of the bidder would be strong and that of the seller weak. Another common situation arises when the main shareholders of the smaller company have a large part of their capital tied up in the company, no younger family members seek the management succession and the older majority shareholders wish to retire and release their capital. Their company is doing well. The two parties involved, bidders and prospective sellers, would be evenly matched and unless the bidders made a sufficiently generous offer the shareholders would reject the proposals and seek another possible buyer.

In yet another situation the smaller company could be doing well with an able, young and ambitious owner-management and the bidder seeking to acquire the company to integrate it within new fields of activity in which it lacked experience and the bidder would seek to persuade the existing management team to remain. In this situation the position of the smaller company would be strong and the bidder would know this and would make a generous offer at the outset. There is evidence that managements of larger companies often incur considerable expense in seeking to identify smaller companies with high-calibre managements which could be acquired on the basis of a mutually acceptable takeover and the management of the smaller company accepting generous service contracts from the bidding company, and considerable freedom of action within it. Takeovers of this kind are often very successful, with the chief executive of the smaller company at some stage becoming a director of the bidding company and, in some cases chairman of it.

Listed companies
The proposed takeover of a listed company is more complex and gives rise to important special factors. The shares will normally be widely held, by members of the public as well as institutions and, often, members of the founding families of the company. In the years which have elapsed since the first Companies Act, successive UK governments have sought to ensure that current legislation meets the needs of the day and as far as possible prevents dishonest, or merely greedy, company promoters, dealers, bankers, managements and other parties from cheating the public or taking unfair advantage of them. In practice, drafting Companies Acts is extremely difficult and major new Acts, which effectively replace the former major Act, and later supplementary Acts, tend to appear at intervals of twenty years or so. The most recent comprehensive, consolidated Companies Act is that of 1948, which has subsequently been amended or updated by shorter Companies Acts. A new major Act is now well overdue.

Meanwhile, governments of the day have recognised that times change, and also the economic environment and social and political attitudes, and that a Companies Act passed thirty or so years earlier will not be sufficient to regulate matters in a satisfactory way. It has also been recognised that often the parties involved are substantial, can be expected to employ advisers and competently watch their own interests, subject to the protection of the general laws, especially those relating to contract and to misrepresentation and fraud. Those who need protection in the field of investment are members of the general public, who may lack information, or the ability to interpret it and who would be vulnerable to the activities of unscrupulous people.

As it is recognised that the general public who wish to buy or sell shares must in most cases do so through the Stock Exchange, successive governments have considered that the public interest will be substantially protected if it is left to the Council of the Stock Exchange to devise, maintain and strengthen their own rules so that their own members, jobbers and brokers who are subject to direct discipline, will comply with these. They will know that they can be suspended or expelled from membership if they do not. Furthermore, financiers, merchant bankers, company managements, may only be able to operate profitably if the facilities of the Stock Exchange are available to them. Successive Companies Acts leave a number of important aspects of control to the Stock Exchange on the principle that the Council of the latter can quickly amend and tighten its own regulations if the public interest seems to require this.

Takeovers and mergers in relation to listed companies present serious problems of control. A main problem arises from the attitudes of some of the people involved. A small proportion of able and strategically placed people are prepared to be dishonest and ignore the law if the stake is a sufficiently large sum of money. They calculate that the risks of detection are acceptably small and if they are caught they will employ highly paid lawyers and accountants and will have a good chance of acquittal in any court proceedings. In any case, at the first hint of trouble they could take their money and go to the South of France or similar congenial place and escape the law. Many have acted in this way in recent years. In other cases, rather larger numbers of financiers, bankers, businessmen, etc., take the line that whilst they will never break any law, they will take professional advice and do everything they can to press their own financial advantage, keeping just within the strict letter of the law. The intention or spirit underlying a law is of no interest to them.

In practice, every new Companies Act, even a minor one, will set out to close one or more loopholes in the former Act, which have permitted abuses. Stock Exchange regulations are revised rather more frequently for the same purpose. However, when a law, or a Stock Exchange or other regulation is changed, a number of able people, lawyers, accountants, bankers and others, will at once study the wording minutely to see whether there is any loophole which they or their clients can exploit to circumvent the law or regulation without anyone being exposed to any form of sanction of discipline in the process.

Legislation or self-regulation?

There are those who consider that the only way to prevent abuses is to devise appropriate laws, accompanied by severe penalties for those who break them, including imprisonment where appropriate. There are others who have a different viewpoint, arguing that it is virtually impossible in practice to control effectively by legislation and that the main consequence of trying to do so is that heavy costs will be incurred in employing a new army of bureaucrats, including lawyers, and that revising laws is always slow and difficult and can not be otherwise, and that clever lawyers will continue to seek and find loopholes and be ready to exploit them and this would create yet more work for lawyers, accountants and the Courts, at great cost.

The alternative principle of self-regulation is put forward by those who consider that attempts to exercise controls primarily within a legal framework are too rigid, inflexible, costly and impracticable. It is argued that self-regulation can, in practice, be effective and operated more flexibly, quickly, simply and at much lower cost, and proper emphasis can be put on conforming to the spirit as well as the letter of the rules. The view is that the privilege of being a principal in one or more of the activities of issuing or dealing in securities is a valuable one and corresponds to membership of an exclusive club. A person who knows that if his conduct is not acceptable to his fellow members then he will be suspended or expelled from membership, will be careful not to misbehave.

The City Working Party : the Takeover Panel

In 1959 a City Working Party was set up by the Governor of the Bank of England for the purpose of considering good business practice in the conduct of takeovers and mergers. This consisted of representatives of the following bodies: the Accepting Houses Committee; the Association of Investment Trust Companies; the British Insurance Association; the Committee of the London Clearing Banks; the Confederation of British Industry; the Issuing Houses Association; the National Association of Pension Funds; the Stock Exchange; the United Trust Association. The work of this Working Party resulted in the publication of *The City Code on Takeovers and Mergers*, which is regularly revised so that as far as practicable it meets the needs of the times. It also resulted in the setting up of the Panel on Takeovers and Mergers, under a distinguished lawyer chairman and a small but highly qualified permanent secretariat. The following is an extract from the Introduction to the 'City Code' which states the underlying philosphy.

The City Code
The City Code has not and does not seek to have the force of law. It represents the collective opinion of those professionally concerned in the field of takeovers and mergers on a range of business standards. Those who wish to have the facilities of the securities markets available to them should conduct themselves in matters relating to takeovers and mergers according to the City Code, those who do not so conduct themselves cannot except to enjoy those facilities and will find that they are withheld. The privileges and disciplines described herein apply in the first place to those who are actively engaged in the securities

markets in all its aspects, but they will also apply to directors of public companies or persons or groups of persons who seek to gain control (as defined in the City Code) of public companies, and professional advisers (insofar as they advise on the transactions in question) even when they are not directly affiliated to the bodies who are responsible for this document.

The authors of the City Code are satisfied that sufficient advertisement has been given to previous editions and will be given to this edition to make it difficult to plead ignorance as an excuse for non compliance. The provisions of the City Code fall into two categories. On the one hand, the City Code enunciates general principles of conduct to be observed in takeover and merger transactions: these general principles are a codification of good standards of commercial behaviour and should have an obvious and universal application. On the other hand, the City Code lays down a series of rules, some of which are no more than examples of the application of the general principles whilst others are rules of procedure designed to govern specific forms of takeover and merger transactions practices in the United Kingdom. The City Working Party points out that some of these general principles, based as they are on the concept of equity between one shareholder and another, while readily understandable in the City and by those concerned with the securities market generally, would not easily lend themselves to legislation. The City Code is therefore framed in non technical language and is, as a measure of self discipline, administered and enforced by the Panel on Takeovers and Mergers, a body representative of those using the securities markets. The duty of the Panel is the enforcement of good business standards, not the enforcement of law.

The Panel, as the administering body, works on a day to day basis through its executive, headed by the Director General. The Director General or his deputy are available at all times to give rulings on points of interpretation of the Code. Companies and their advisers are invited to make full use of this service. Consultations are confidential. The practice regarding hearings before the full Panel and the Panel's Appeal Committee is set out in the Section on procedure of page 5/6. The City Code is drafted with listed public companies particularly in mind. Nevertheless, the spirit of the City Code and, where appropriate, the letter will also apply to takeovers of unlisted companies. The City Code will not apply, however, to cases where the offeree company is a private company nor will it normally apply to takeovers of companies which are not resident for exchange control purposes in the United Kingdom... Neither the City Code nor the Panel are concerned with the evaluation of commercial advantages or disadvantages of a takeover or merger proposition, which must be decided by the company and its shareholders....

The background reasons for the Panel and the City Code, and the need of the general public for protection, have been outlined. Understandably, the tactics of financiers and others who decide to attempt a takeover of a particular listed company will be to acquire this control as quickly, decisively and cheaply as possible. Secrecy will be important in the early stages. It is also a fact that when the shares of a listed company are widely held a person who acquires 20%–30% of the shares with voting rights can be well on the way to acquiring control in practice. Meanwhile, whenever persistent buying of a share is observed by jobbers the possibility of a takeover attempt will be suspected and journalists and other analysts would soon be reporting the buying activity. Speculators and other investors would assess that the unnamed buyer must have favourable information about the company and there will be widespread speculative buying and a sharp increase in price. The Companies Acts now require that any person who owns 5% or more of the shares of a company must inform it of the fact and the company must record the details in a Register of Substantial Shareholdings, which is open to inspection. To keep within the letter of the law bidders arrange that several persons acquire holdings fractionally below 5% each, in the names of nominees, and hold these until the moment to come into the open has arrived. This practice of building up shareholdings prior to disclosure of the identity of the bidder is known as 'warehousing'.

The moment will arrive when those planning a takeover must openly disclose their intentions and the City Code requires that any offer must first be made to the board of the offeree, to whom the true identity of the bidder must be made known. It must be established that the offer could be fully implemented. The board of the offeree company must obtain independent advice on the offer and must make this known to its shareholders, and whether the board favours the offer. This may be done by means of a press notice. In principle the spirit of the Code is that all shareholders, including minority ones, must be treated on an equal basis, the same information, terms and opportunities being made available to all. Directors should not receive any favourable considerations for themselves, and there must be no privileged 'insider' dealings. Documents circulated to shareholders must be prepared with the same standard of care as is required by the Companies Acts in respect of prospectuses, and information must be given of existing directors' service contracts with indications of how directors' emoluments would be affected by acceptance of the offer. Copies of documents published must be lodged with the Stock Exchange and with the Takeover Panel.

In practice, compliance with the Code requires that both the offeror and the offeree act with expert and costly professional advice at every stage – merchant banks, stockbrokers, lawyers, accountants, etc. A complaint is that an offeree may have to spend very many thousands of pounds to fight off successfully an unwelcome and unwanted bid. Meanwhile, when the board of an offeree company receives a bid the sequence of events will be liable to vary. The board may consider the proposals generous and recommend acceptance, in which case the takeover would probably be successful. However, the board might recommend rejection, either because they opposed the takeover in principle or because they considered the terms unsatisfactory. When a contested takeover attempt occurs the boards of the offeror and offeree companies often place prominent, expensive press advertisements, intending to enlist the support of shareholders and create a climate of opinion, and influence press comment, analysts, advisers, etc. The bidders would make a formal offer in identical terms, accompanied by an acceptance form, to all of the shareholders, by post. They have the right to obtain details of shareholders, with addresses, from the offeree company on payment of charges laid down in the Companies Acts. The offer would be described as being conditional upon acceptances being received in respect of a stated percentage of the shares under offer – the Code requires this to be not less than 50% and by a stated date not less than 21 days ahead, the offer remaining open during that period.

The offer statement will indicate that if the prescribed number of acceptances have not been received by the stated date then the offer will lapse. The acceptance is so worded that it constitutes a transfer of the shares concerned, which becomes effective without further action in the event that the required acceptances are received, in which case the offer becomes unconditional. Sometimes one or more new bidders make offers and in effect an auction develops. In such cases the existing shareholders tend to 'sit back' and wait until they think the highest offer has been made. Sometimes no other bidder emerges but the original bidder only succeeds after he has increased his offer, perhaps more than once, and perhaps changing the 'mix' of cash and shares. Sometimes a bid will fail completely after a costly verbal battle, possibly damaging to one or both sides, including merchant bank advisers.

The Monopolies Commission

When the companies concerned are large and a takeover or merger could result in a single company or group with a near monopoly position, the Monopolies and Merger Act, 1965, gives power to the Department of Trade and Industry to scrutinise and if thought fit refer to the Monopolies Commission for further investigation and report all mergers where the gross assets to be acquired exceed £5 m. or where the acquisition would create or intensify a monopoly. This is at present defined as one quarter of the market. There are, in fact, two tests: (a) size, and (b) market penetration. By no means all large takeover or merger proposals are referred to the Commission. However, reference of a proposal to the Commission may itself cause the proposals to break down because of the time factor. A study always requires several months. Other industrialised countries have legislation designed to protect the general public interest and prevent a single company from acquiring or abusing monopoly powers. In the USA there are the anti-trust laws. It is also normal for governments to be sensitive to the proposed takeover of a major company by a foreign company. Governments in the UK and USA appear generally to have been more tolerant towards foreign takeovers than French, German and Japanese governments have been when one of their major companies has been the object of a takeover attempt by a foreign company. The UK Treasury insists that all foreign bids for UK companies must be in cash.

Methods of takeovers

The following are extracts from the authoritative *Chartered Secretaries Manual of Company Secretarial Practice* (Jordons):

A takeover can be achieved by (a) agreement with the individual members of the company being acquired. This can only readily be achieved when the number of such members is small, as in a private company. (b) Purchases of shares by private treaty and/or on a Stock Exchange. This is unlikely to result in the acquisition of the whole of the share capital but may over a period enable an influential or controlling position to be built up which may satisfy the plans of the acquiring company or be the precursor of an offer for the remainder of the share capital. (c) An offer to all of the shareholders of the company (or a section of them to acquire all or a proportion of their shareholdings. (d) A scheme of arrangement under ss. 206 to 208 of the Companies Acts, 1948. This method requires the agreement of the boards of the companies concerned and is sometimes adopted for technical advantages.

In the majority of cases the acquiring company is an existing company, usually of the same size or larger than the company it acquires though it may be smaller. Sometimes a takeover is effected through the medium of a new holding company which acquires the share capital of two (or more) companies.

Preliminaries
The preliminary stages will involve the offeror company in appraising the project and relating to its appraisal the tactics of the offer and the consideration. The latter may comprise: (*a*) cash; (*b*) debentures (including loan stock) or convertible loan stock; (*c*) shares; (*d*) a combination of two or more of these. In the case of the issue of securities, it may be considered advisable to arrange a cash alternative. In order to achieve this, arrangements are usually made for a financial house to make a separate additional offer to purchase at a fixed price from the acceptors the securities of the offeror company to which the offeree will be entitled. The financial house will usually arrange for its offer to be underwritten.

Prior to 1965 the main or sole consideration to shareholders in the offeree company was normally cash. However, the 1965 Finance Act introduced capital gains on realised gains and accordingly securities of some kind became more acceptable to offeree shareholders as their liability to capital gains tax arose only if and when they sold the securities. Between 1965 and 1973 ordinary shares were popular in principle as they were regarded as hedges against inflation and their market prices were expected to rise steadily. With the collapse of the UK stock market in 1974 and the loss of confidence which ensued, the number and value of takeovers declined and securities became less acceptable than cash to shareholders in offeree companies when takeovers did proceed. Moreover, at this period dividend controls were reducing the popularity of ordinary shares. However, financial fashions change, and with the cancellation of dividend control in 1979 it may happen that shareholders in offeree companies will again begin to find share exchanges at least as acceptable as cash as a consideration, especially at times when the equity market is buoyant and interest rates are falling.

Advantages and disadvantages of different payment considerations

Cash
If the bidder has cash available, cash will be the cheapest consideration in the long term as the acceptor of cash would have no future share in

the equity of the bidder, which would not be 'diluted'. Cash is quantifiable by all of the parties. However, if the liquid resources of the bidder were restricted cash would be expensive in the short term. It might even not be sufficiently available. From the viewpoint of the offeree shareholder there would be an immediate capital gains tax liability (unless he came below the tax threshhold), and he would have no further equity interest in the company and a continuing interest might have benefited him in the longer term. Cash would be available for immediate reinvestment including, if desired, in the shares of the bidder company. However, any capital gains tax liability would need to be considered and also the relatively high dealings costs of a purchase of securities.

Ordinary Shares
The subjective nature of valuations is a main problem. A bidder who proposes a share exchange will seek an agreement which values his shares on a relatively higher basis and those of the offeree company on a lower one. An offeree shareholder who accepts a share exchange may thus relinquish in the company bid for a higher real value than the interest he acquires in the offeror company. It is this aspect which tests the negotiating skills of those acting for the different parties. Meanwhile, a person who participates in a share exchange has a continuing interest in the bidding company. There is no immediate capital gains liability and exemption from stamp duties liabilities on the transfer, and no dealing costs. The offeror company may experience a dilution on the equity and its share price will normally fall somewhat when its takeover attempt is made public, whilst the share price of the offeree company will rise.

Debenture or unsecured loan stock
At a time of high interest rates this would be relatively costly to the bidder but would not dilute his equity. An acceptor would not have an immediate capital gains tax liability but would have a fixed-interest security in place of equity.

Convertible unsecured loan stock
A bidder would be able to offer a lower coupon than for a normal loan stock and possibly also less onerous general conditions, but in the longer term dilution of the equity could arise. From the viewpoint of the offeree shareholder there would be no immediate capital gains tax liability and much would depend on the conversion terms. In principle, and

in view of the record, which shows how issues of this type have been designed to suit the interest of the offeror, offerees should treat them with caution.

Technical aspects of merger or takeover

There are two main ways of carrying out a merger or takeover: (a) the holding company method, and (b) a scheme of arrangement. The holding company method is the more widely used. Often a new, non-trading company is formed, the apex of a group of companies, which could be large. In other cases one of the existing trading companies is the holding company which absorbs the others, which still retain their legal status as corporate bodies, and any goodwill attaching to their trade names. Some of the original shareholders may not accept the takeover terms and thus retain their original shareholding. They then become a minority interest within a group. In certain circumstances a sucessful bidder can apply to the Court for an order which permits it to acquire all of the outstanding shares on the same terms as those accepted by the majority of shareholders. It may also be possible for minority shareholders to apply to the Court to compel the successful bidder to purchase their shares on the same terms as those accepted by the others, although the minority shareholders had rejected the original offer. These are matters of company law which need not be considered here. Whilst in the early stages in might be individuals or corporate bodies representing them, and who have an interest in the bidding company, who, through nominees, purchase shares in a listed company which is an intended victim of a takeover attempt, the formal offers to shareholders of this company will be made by the bidder company. It will thus be a company, and not individuals, to whom the accepting shareholders transfer their shares, and a company from whom they receive consideration in the form of cash and or securities.

Scheme of arrangement
If less than 90% of a bid is in the form of ordinary shares, the forms of acceptance to be signed by the offeree shareholders have to be stamped at the rate of 2% of the market value of the bid. However, under a scheme of arrangement, under Sections 206 to 208 of the Companies Act, 1948, the share capital of the offeree company is extinguished and the capital of the offeror is substituted and there is no document requiring stamping and in consequence substantial savings can be made by the bidder. However, a scheme of arrangement requires 75% of the

votes cast at an extraordinary general meeting of the offeree company and then a slow procedure to obtain Court approval of the scheme. Schemes are therefore only feasible in favourable circumstances and are not necessary if the consideration is cash as stamping is not then required.

Reverse takeover (reverse bid)

Normally a larger company bids for a smaller one but sometimes it is the smaller one which bids for the larger. Main reasons include: (*a*) the smaller company is listed but the larger is not and in order to keep the listing, and without the high costs of obtaining a new one, the smaller, listed company makes the takeover; (*b*) the small company has large undistributed profits, which would effectively be frozen as capital reserves, if the takeover were by the larger company, since the law requires that pre-acquisition profits are treated in this way; (*c*) if the smaller company has an obviously better record and more promising future this course of action could be appropriate; (*d*) it may occasionally be decided that the smaller company would be the administrative unit and the larger company the main trading one.

Valuations in takeovers and mergers

As has already been considered in Chapter 16 this is a specially difficult, subjective area and one in which the reputations of negotiating parties may be made or lost, especially if there is widespread publicity and the original bidder is forced to increase his offer three or four times. Matters to be taken into account from the financial aspects will primarily be the present and expected future earnings; the cash flow; the capital structures and gearing and the quality and nature of the assets; and the present and expected future state of the economy and the industry. Tactical aspects should not be overlooked. Many shareholders will be prepared to accept an offer which shows them a worthwhile profit over the price at which they acquired their shares, either in the recent or more distant past, and they would not necessarily reject an offer which fell significantly below the valuation made by their own negotiators. When a takeover catches public interest, financial journalist and others will publish their own evaluations, which often prove influential. If it appears that a majority intend to accept an offer those who had pressed for its rejection as inadequate may in the end accept it rather than risk being 'locked in' as minority shareholders.

Recent public attitudes

Fashions in finance and business come and go as they do with clothes. In the late 1960s and early 1970s numbers of aggressive young men proved themselves adepts at obtaining media publicity, as well as being brilliant 'wheeler dealers' in financial affairs. They organised successful takeovers, often on the basis that they were about to transform sluggish UK managements. They were widely believed. In the 1973/74 financial crisis it became evident that some of these people had been confidence tricksters on a grand scale, and occasionally criminals who had duped the upper reaches of the financial establishments as skilfully as they had obtained money from the public. Some may have been fundamentally honest but their ambitions exceeded their powers. The achievements of these people were to enrich themselves and their families but the financial crisis of 1973/74 left a trail of devastation. Since that period there has been a less credulous attitude towards takeovers proposed by financiers rather than businessmen with successful records who could show industrial logic for their proposals.

Moreover, in the 1960s and early 1970s a view was widespread amongst people of competence and achievement that amalgamations could lead to important advantages, and furthermore UK companies have to compete internationally with foreign multinational companies which are often themselves of enormous size and financial power. There is an axiom amongst boxers that a good heavyweight can always beat a good middleweight, and this also seems true in business. It was a Labour Government which in 1966 set up the Industrial Reorganisation Corporation (IRC) for the purpose of promoting desirable amalgamations and reorganisations and doing so with minimum interference with the normal workings of the capital market, and seeking the cooperation of industrial, commercial and financial companies and institutions. Three of its main accomplishments were to promote the mergers of GEC and the English Electric Company; of Ransome and Marles, Hoffman Manufacturing and Pollard Ball and Roller Bearing Co. in respect of ball bearings and special steels; and of Associated Fisheries and the Ross Groups Fishing Fleets.

In its own field, each of the above was a major merger which might have been considered to conflict with the objectives of the Monopolies Commission. However, each proposal was considered on its merits and from the aspects of international competition and the national interest. However, in 1970 the incoming Conservative government abolished the IRC on the grounds that it interfered with the normal workings of the markets and also that it was superfluous. Many, including Conservative supporters, at the time and later, regretted this decision to abolish the IRC, for what seemed primarily doctrinaire reasons. There is a widespread view that lack of continuity in the treatment of businesses by successive UK governments, and especially soon after a change of government has occurred, has been one of the factors contributing to the disppointing performance of many UK companies in recent years. It is notable that in 1979 the new Conservative government, despite the attitudes and pressures of influential backbenchers, decided to let the NEB continue, although with much reduced powers and scope.

By the mid-1970s it was practicable to assess how successful the takeovers and mergers of a decade or so earlier were proving. It is evident that a number have achieved all that was expected of them and all parties, including employees, have benefited (a successful takeover usually gives rise to a levelling upwards of salaries scales and conditions of service). However, a number of mergers, including a number which, with hindsight, seem to have been designed to gratify the megalomania of former chief executives, have failed because they lacked underlying logic, and their promoters lacked motivation. Modern technology, notably in the areas of communications and data processing, have made it more feasible than ever before for small groups of men to exercise efficient control over giant multinational corporations. General Motors and Ford of the USA and the UK–Dutch Unilever are examples of what can be achieved. The major oil multinationals seem almost laws unto themselves and seemingly hardly accountable even to governments. From the behavioural aspect it has seemed that ministers and civil servants in the UK have tended to approve industrial concentration into fewer and larger companies because in periods when there is substantial involvement of government in matters relating to business it is easier to deal with small numbers of senior businessmen, chief executives of large companies, and regard them as representative of the whole business community. Labour Ministers may also approve concentration on the grounds that when an industry becomes concentrated into a few of giant companies they would be easier to nationalise when the time seemed right. Many have regarded and some still do regard the clearing banks in this way. From the viewpoint of the public generally, it seems that in the UK many find smaller organisations more agreeable to work in and deal with and the expression 'small is beautiful' has been quoted with increasing approval. Meanwhile, in the late 1970s and early 1980s a viewpoint is becoming widespread – that smaller companies should receive more positive encouragement, not least because they seem likely agencies for the creation of new jobs at a time when the tendency has been for larger and more capital-intensive companies to shed labour on a massive scale. It is also evident (1981) that when the recession ends larger companies will be able quickly to expand production with minimum new recruitment. They have ample scope.

Recent research

A recent major research study *Successful Business Policies* by G.D. Newbould and G.A Luffman (Gower Press, London, 1900) has studied the top 511 listed trading or manufacturing companies of the UK in 1967, of which 302 survived until 1975. Of the original number 169 were taken over either by others within the original group or by companies outside it; 15 were taken over by foreign companies and 25 went into liquidation or were nationalised. General indications of the research were that companies which took over others often damaged the interests of their shareholders and employees and policies of diversification appeared to be no more successful. The authors measured various aspects of each company's published performance, adjusted for inflation. It was assumed that shareholders are primarily interested in total real return on their investment; capital gains or losses; stability of dividends; changes in the company's profit as a proportion of capital employed. It was assumed that employees are primarily concerned with growth in real wages.

Findings of the study were that both shareholders and employees of companies whose boards initiated takeovers on average did worse than shareholders and employees of companies with 'stick in the mud' managements which did not take over others and did not greatly diversify. It appears that the findings did not surprise Mr Newbould, whose earlier studies in 1967/8 had convinced him that most companies which took over others had made no fundamental analysis beforehand of the companies to be taken over and the takeovers met with considerable and unexpected problems afterwards and produced little evidence of 'synergy' – the '2 + 2 = 5 effect', or the whole is greater than the sum of the parts. However, senior managers enlarged their empires and, hence, powers, perquisites and status in the business world and so they personally did very well. A major conclusion of the research was that a policy of acquisition appears to give rise to a conflict of interests between senior management and other interest groups and as it is the former who formulate and implement policies on acquisitions they should be prepared to put forward convincing explanations to justify their policies. The authors conclude: 'either the data are wrong or there needs to be some radical rewriting of business policy'.

Holding companies and groups of companies

A feature of large-scale business in the UK and elsewhere is that the top management of the main company may control the activities of a large number of subsidiary companies. A part of their power to do this derives from the fact that they appoint and can dismiss the chairman and directors of every subsidiary company. This is simply done since at the time of each appointment the executive, who is always a full-time employee, is required to sign an undated resignation form, or blank transfer of his nominal shareholding in the subsidiary. In practice successful subsidiaries are allowed considerable autonomy and freedom of action and dismissals occur infrequently, either after serious clashes have arisen. usually over matters of policy, or the results of the subsidiary have been deemed unsatisfactory. Whilst the top managements of major groups of companies in the UK and elsewhere doubtless act to high ethical standards in most cases, the Companies Act, 1948, gave recognition to the fact that the great powers wielded through the group company form could be abused, and the Act sought to impose effective regulations. In fact, even now unscrupulous directors can, in effect, swindle unalert creditors without breaking any law by the device of lending money against security to a subsidiary, letting the latter receive credit from overtrusting suppliers, foreclosing on the security and allowing the subsidiary to go into liquidation. It then emerges that the holding company has been paid in full, but there is nothing left for the creditors.

The Companies Act, 1948, defines a subsidiary company at length. The core is: 'a company shall... be deemed to be a subsidiary of another if, but only if, (*a*) that other either: (i) is a member of it and controls the composition of its board of directors: or (ii) holds more than half in nominal value of its equity share capital: or the first company is a subsidiary of any company which is that other's subsidiary'. The holding company, which may be seen as the apex of a pyramid, in the case of a large group, is not itself defined in the Act. A definition could be: 'a company which has one or more subsidiaries and is not itself the subsidiary of any other company'.

The Companies Act, 1948, make detailed provisions in respect of group accounts with the intention of ensuring that those who deal with a company or a group of companies have adequate information. Consolidated group accounts have to be prepared and are often seen in summarised form as advertisements in serious business publications. In fact, the preparation of consolidated accounts is widely regarded by students as one of the most if not the most difficult areas of advanced accountancy, and all that can be done here is to draw the attention of the reader to these matters, which need to be studied by those seeking to become qualified accountants. Technical knowledge of them is not essential at this stage in the study of business finance.

Questions

1. The Alpha Co Ltd has operated very successfully over the past few years despite the adverse economic situation. As result the company has a good liquidity position and a relatively advantageous stock-exchange valuation. The Chairman of the company has suggested that because of this it should look for growth through a vigorous acquisition policy. You have been asked to prepare a memorandum outlining the points which should be including in an acquisition strategy which it is hoped to formulate at the next board meeting. (ACCA 15 marks)
2. Compare the management problems which may arise as a result of a policy of growth by takeover or merger with problems arising from a policy of organic growth. (ACCA BM 20 marks).
3. What factors would you take into account in deciding whether to accept a bid on a share exchange basis for a block of shares which you own in a listed company? (ICSA 22 marks)
4. Outline the factors you would expect a board of directors to consider when discussing the possible acquisition of another company. (ACCA 18 marks).
5. The management of a company is anxious to expand the size and range of its activities. In what circumstances would you advise the company to concentrate on (a) internal growth and (b) growth through mergers and takeovers? (ACCA 20 marks).
6. A company which makes an offer for the shares of another company which it wishes to take over, may propose to pay for them either in cash or by means of its own securities. What are the advantages and disadvantages of each form of payment so far as (a) the bidding company and (b) the shareholders of the offeree company are concerned? (ICA 20 marks).
7. 'Many mergers and takeovers do not appear to be very successful on the basis of growth and levels of profitability subsequently achieved.' Comment on this proposition and discuss reasons which may account for the lack of success of some mergers. (ACCA 20 marks).
8. A takeover bid has been made for a quoted company which is not controlled by its directors. If the directors do not support the attempted

takeovers, what means are available to them to resist the bid? (ACCA 20 marks).

9. What is a 'conglomerate'? What are the major problems of this development from the point of view of (a) management and (b) the investor? (ICA 20 marks).

10. The Alpha Co. Ltd is a large distributing company which covers most of the UK. In Area 7 Alpha has never been able to establish itself. One of the reasons for this is the existence of Beta – a partnership between two brothers – which, largely due to the personality of the brothers has built up considerable goodwill in that area. The brothers have decided to retire and have offered Alpha Ltd first chance to buy them out at a price of £500,000 to be payable in cash in two equal instalments, the first six months after the acquisition and the second six months later. The price would include all land and buildings, equipment, stock, debtors and creditors which have book values as noted (£):

Land and buildings	50,000
Equipment	16,000
Stock	80,000
Debtors	26,000
Creditors	22,000

Alpha's Sales Manager after discussions with the partners estimates that if Beta is acquired, additional sales for Alpha will be £250,000 for the first six months of the year ended in 1977 and £300,000 for the second six months of that year. Similar estimates for purchases show figures of £185,000 for the first six months and £195,000 for the second six months. An analysis of Beta's profits for the last five years discloses (£):

Year ended in	1976	1975	1974	1973	1972
Sales turnover	498,000	453,000	411,000	374,000	340,000
Depreciation	8,000	8,000	8,000	6,000	6,000
Profits (before and tax)	66,700	60,000	53,650	50,100	45,000

The above profit has been adjusted to include a notional figure for the salaries of the partners.

It is anticipated that Alpha will be able to apply its control figures to Beta and these are to turn over stock six times per annum, to take six weeks' credit from suppliers and to give four weeks credit to customers.

An examination of the equipment has indicated that it is in good order. Capital expenditure of £15,000 will be required immediately.

The managing director has called a meeting to discuss the purchase of Beta at which he states quite clearly that they have two decisions to take: the first is to decide whether or not Beta is worthwhile acquiring and the second is to discuss the cash implications of this because as he points out in the present economic climate liquidity management is almost as important as profit management.

You are required to analyse and comment on the above information with particular reference to (*a*) **an estimate of the cash flow for the next two six-monthly periods:** (20 marks) **and** (*b*) **the proposed acquisition decision** (15 marks). *Note*: although taxation can be ignored in the analysis it should be referred to in the comment. (ACCA 35 marks)

11. You are the financial manager of a medium-sized engineering firm XYZ Ltd which has just reported record profits of £250,000, after tax and interest, and preference dividends, and declared an ordinary dividend of 15%. Despite the profits record, which maintain the previous pattern of overall growth but with cyclical fluctuations, the company has been facing liquidity problems which have restricted its operational flexibility.

XYZ Ltd has received a suggestion from ABC Ltd that the two companies should consider merging. ABC Ltd is a relatively new company – formed six years previously – which has had a spectacular and consistent growth in profit and whose products complement those of XYZ Ltd. The most recent profit of ABC Ltd were £375,000 after tax and interest, with an ordinary dividend of 10%. The reason for suggesting the merger given by ABC Ltd is that they also have been having liquidity problems and that an enlarged size could help overcome these. ABC's initial approach did not go into any detail but simply suggests that exploratory talks should be opened and that to make these talks purposeful they should assume that both company's profits will increase by 10% in the next period and that for amalgamation purposes a fair PE ratio would be 15 for ABC and 10 for XYZ.

The executive directors have called a meeting to discuss the matter and have asked you to analyse the implications of ABC's suggestion and to list the factors which should be considered at this stage in respect of this analysis.

Mergers and takeovers

The summary of the most recent balance sheets of ABC Ltd and XYZ are as undernoted (£):

Summary of balance sheets for year ended...

	ABC Ltd	XYZ Ltd
Net Assets	3,000,000	2,500,000
Share capital – £1 ordinary shares	750,000	400,000
6% Preference shares		100,000
Reserves	1,500,000	2,000,000
10% Loan stock	750,000	

(ACCA   25 marks)

Chapter 18

Going public

Up to this point it has been assumed that companies under consideration are unlisted – either private limited or unlisted public companies. Although there are important exceptions, experience shows that sooner or later the controlling shareholders of a successful and primarily family-owned company usually (but not invariably) decide to seek a Stock Exchange listing for securities of their company. There are a number of reasons for this, notably:

(a) Shares held in a few hands are not freely marketable nor can a market value readily be established. Often, ageing family shareholders wish to retire and have access to their capital which is represented largely by their shares. A listing enables these to be sold more easily and at better prices.

(b) If a major shareholder of an unlisted company dies suddenly, those dealing with the estate could experience delay and difficulties in establishing tax liabilities with the Inland Revenue, unless the shares were listed, in which case the authorities would accept the market price as published.

(c) There is a special reason arising from UK tax laws, which discriminate against 'close' companies, those controlled by a small group of people, effectively family owners and directors. A company escapes being a close company if at least 35% of its shares are publicly held. When a company is listed it is easy to escape from the close company designation, whilst at the same time retaining family control.

(d) A listing gives a company access to additional sources of capital and this gives it flexibility in raising capital, and possibly on more favourable terms. As well as members of the general public, institutions – insurance companies, pension funds, unit and investment trusts – are now major buyers.

(e) In the UK for high-income people especially, capital gains taxes

have been at a lower rate than income tax. This has provided incentive to many to build up their own company, reinvesting as large a proportion of the profits as possible and then, at a favourable time, obtaining a listing for the company and selling all or a proportion of the shares at a capital profit.
(f) If it were intended at any time that the company would seek to take over other companies using its own securities as part (or all) of the consideration, it would be essential for these shares to be listed and have a known market value.
(g) Obtaining a listing is costly and time consuming but it is a 'once and for all' operation. The procedures require that a company passes a number of severe tests and the fact that it has been able to do this adds to its financial standing, so long as there is also evidence that the company continues to progress.

Reasons why some companies have not gone public

It has been noted that many growing private or unlisted public companies have been choosing not to 'go public' in recent years. This is a situation which may begin to change with a Conservative government sympathetic to private enterprise. Time will show. The following is an analysis which appeared in the *Midland Bank Review* of Spring 1978, in an article on the raising of new capital by companies in 1977:

numerous factors existed which either prevented companies from going public or were sufficient to outweigh the obvious attractions of a listing. These were not new, but it is perhaps worth noting some of the more important of them in order to show why smaller companies in particular, even ambitious ones, could not hope for a successful flotation in what otherwise appeared to be ideal conditions.

Undoubtedly one of the most decisive reasons was the continued absence from the market of the private investor. This point was raised by several bodies in their submissions to the Wilson Committee. For example, the Stock Exchange suggested that the flow of investment funds would be promoted by tax changes designed to encourage personal savings. The Association of Investment Trust Companies concluded that new issues were unlikely to fare well because the institutions which had the money were disinclined to take the risks while private investors no longer had surplus funds for speculative ventures. They warned that companies trying to raise money on the stock market for the first time were handicapped by the fact that 'institutional funds are not well equipped to provide the initial funds for such small ventures...' They wanted a 'proper evaluation of risk'... Since the institutions were mainly interested in enterprises with a market value in excess of £10 m. and, at the same time, the private investor, the traditional source of high risk capital, had had his funds eroded by taxation, a gap existed in the provision for the marketing of small companies. In addition, around £1 m. pretax (and preferably £2 m. in a manufacturing group) was generally regarded as the minimum requirement for profits together with evidence of their growth. A listing was therefore effectively confined to businesses which had already achieved expansion and to mature long established ones that already had a wide and possibly institutional shareholding.

There were, of course, other disincentives. The criteria for new issues remained strict and the costs involved in going public had grown to about 10% of the cash raised. After the listing had been obtained the Stock Exchange's requirements for the protection of investors were still seen in some quarters to be too rigorous and inhibitive. At times when the market was depressed the proprietors of smaller companies were reluctant to seek a quotation, because they did not want to have to provide shares to the market at a price which they regarded as inadequate relative to the value of the underlying assets. Even in the more buoyant conditions of 1977 the stock market rating of companies had increasingly become related to size. For smaller family-owned companies a quotation would no longer ensure marketability of the shares. Small companies had lost status and the market in the shares of many of them was disappointingly quiet. This diminished the appeal of a quotation and undermined the desire to go public. The disenchantment in some cases was so great that they reverted to their private status. Other unquoted companies instead decided to arrange for dealings organised by the investment bankers M.J.H. Nightingale, who operate a market in unlisted securities and whose disclosure requirements were less onerous.

The failure of the rate of new flotations to improve significantly worried the Stock Exchange and lead it to take two steps during the year which effectively relaxed standards. At the beginning of September the minimum proportion of a company's equity capital which must be made available to the public on quotation was cut from 35% to 25%. This was done to counter criticism that this provision deterred many potential vendors as it involved the forced sale of too many shares 'on the cheap', whilst still not guaranteeing an open and active market in a small company's shares. Families generally did not want to part with too much of their capital and selling a quarter of their inheritance was not as painful as over a third. The second move, in what was clearly a response to Nightingale's over-the-counter market, was a decision actively to promote and focus attention on the facility under Rule 163(2) for matching bargains in the shares of unlisted companies without having to fulfil all the regulations in respect of a full listing. However, the Stock Exchange was not prepared to relax its requirements specifically for small companies because, at a time when questionable manoevering in shares was being closely examined, this could have left the way open for a government-sponsored regulatory body.

The power of the Stock Exchange to encourage new listings is clearly limited, but concern over the shrinkage of flotation applications means that it is unlikely to further tighten its rules or do anything else that would increase the fears of private companies. By encouraging the dispersion of shareholdings in sizeable private companies the Exchange is hoping that, in due course, this will create a demand for them to be fully listed. In reality, although it may provide marginal encouragement it could have the reverse effect: a better market under Rule 163(2) may lessen the incentive for a quotation and could cause some companies to allow their listing to lapse. The one positive piece of evidence to emerge on this point was the introduction of Henry Sykes' shares on the Stock Exchange in December, making it the first company to gain a listing via the over-the-counter market. When Sykes shares became dealt in by Nightingales in 1973 it was regarded as the first step to a full quote and in April 1977 a further move in that direction was made by the instigation of dealings under Rule 163(2), from when activity in the shares picked up. However, it was more logical for Sykes to aim for a quote than many others, since unlike most unquoted companies it had no large family holdings: in all it had some 209 shareholders and 14 institutions owned as much as 78% of the equity.

Before any significant improvement in the trend of flotations can be expected, developments external to the Stock Exchange's own arrangements are required. These include a steady revival in the economy, a sustained bull market in which active private investors and institutions become more favourably disposed towards smaller companies, and changes that help reverse the institutionalising of savings.

The change to a Conservative government in 1979 and their first budget, with its move away from direct towards indirect taxation and its drastic cuts in the higher rates of income tax, could conceivably lead to conditions becoming more favourable again to private investors and in due course to increasing numbers of smaller companies seeking a listing.

Detailed information on obtaining a Stock Exchange listing is set out in *The Chartered Secretaries Manual of Company Secretarial Practice* and *Admission of Securities to Listing* (The Council of the Stock Exchange). A listing on the Stock Exchange is sought through a stockbroker alone or in conjunction with one of the issuing houses, which are specialised concerns or departments of the merchant banks. They are known as sponsors. With the help of chartered accountants, the company's finances, its profit and loss accounts, balance sheets, book-keeping and costing systems are examined. The assets and future prospects of the company are the main factors in determining its capital structure and the method of issuing the shares.

The full requirements when a listing for new requirements is sought are available in *Admission of Securities to Listing*. General requirements are:

1. No application will be considered unless the company will have an expected market value of at least £500,000 and any one security for which listing is sought will have an expected market value of £200,000.
2. All applications and documents to be considered or approved by the Stock Exchange should always be submitted at the earliest possible opportunity. Although it is possible for the draft prospectus to be submitted only fourteen days before publication, such a short interval is rarely practicable. Moreover, application to make a placing or an introduction of securities of companies not already listed will usually need to be made at least two or three weeks before the draft prospectus is submitted. When reading documents submitted to it and considering applications, the prime concern of the Stock Exchange is to ensure that sufficient information is revealed to enable a fair view to be taken of the securities involved. The Stock Exchange is also concerned with certain practices and proceedings relating to the distribution of securities.
3. The Bank of England exercises control over the timing of issues, where the amount of money to be raised is £3 m. or more, in order to maintain an orderly new market. In such cases it is necessary for the sponsoring broker to apply to the government broker for a date known as 'impact day' – that is, the first day on which the size and terms of the issue may be made known to underwriters, places and the market.
4. Before granting a listing all companies must sign a Listing Agreement that they will provide certain information about their operations and that they will follow certain administrative procedures. However, a number of the Stock Exchange requirements may be varied if the Stock

Going public

Exchange is satisfied that any of its requirements should not apply in the circumstances of the particular case: specific approval must be obtained. Where it is proposed to increase the authorised share capital, the directors must state in the explanatory circular or other document accompanying the notice of the meeting whether they have any present intention of issuing any part thereof. Where 10% or more of the voting capital will remain unissued (disregarding shares reserved for issue against exercise of subsisting conversion rights or options) the directors must undertake that no issue will be made which would effectively change the control of the company or nature of its business without the prior approval of the company in general meeting.

Methods of issue

Securities may be brought to the Stock Exchange by any one of the following methods:

(a) A prospectus issue, which is an offer by the company of its own securities to the public for subscription.

(b) An offer for sale, which is an offer to the public by an issuing house or broker of securities already in issue or for which they have agreed to subscribe.

(c) A placing, which is the term used to describe the sale of or obtaining subscription for securities by an issuing house or broker through the market and to or by their own clients. This is a concession which, in general, is only allowed where there is not likely to be significant public demand for the securities.

(d) An introduction, which describes an application where no marketing arrangements are required because the securities to be listed are already of such an amount and so widely held that their adequate marketability when listed can be assumed.

(e) A rights offer to holders of securities, which enables those holders to subscribe cash for securities in proportion to their existing holdings.

(f) An open offer to holders of securities, which enables those holders to subscribe cash for securities otherwise than in proportion to their existing holdings.

(g) A capitalisation issue to holders of securities, by which further securities are credited as fully paid up out of the company's reserves in proportion to existing holdings, not involving any monetary payments.

(h) An issue of securities in consideration for assets or businesses acquired by the issuing company (vendor consideration issue).
(i) An exchange for or conversion of securities into other classes of securities.
(j) The exercise of options or warrants to subscribe for securities.

(a) to (j) are quoted from *Admission of Securities to Listing*. The following are brief comments on matters which must, in practice, always be attended to in careful detail by experienced specialists.

The prospectus

The Stock Exchange must approve the prospectus before it is issued and it must be advertised in accordance with the Companies Acts and the Stock Exchange's requirements, which are even more stringent than those required by the law. A prospectus is itself defined in the Companies Act, 1948, as 'a prospectus is any prospectus, notice, circular, advertisement or other invitation, offering to the public for subscription or purchase any shares or debentures of a company'. The Act lays down in detail what must be included in a prospectus and published prospectuses must, under Stock Exchange requirements, state at the head: 'This document contains particulars given in compliance with the Regulations of the Stock Exchange for the purpose of giving information to the public with regard to the company. The directors collectively and individually accept full responsibility for the accuracy of the information given and confirm, having made all reasonable enquiries, there are no other facts, the omission of which would make any statement herein misleading'; 'Application has been made to the Council of the Stock Exchange for the securities to be admitted to the official list'.

In brief, the purpose of a prospectus is to persuade investors to subscribe for securities of a company and for this purpose the company must indicate the sum required, the nature of the securities, the price, the sum payable on application, and the date, and the sum payable on allotment (and, rarely now, on later calls). Information must be given about the past record of the company, an auditor's report, and forecasts of future profits and the assumptions on which these are based. A merchant bank and a firm of accountants would closely monitor the directors' forecasts and the assumptions on which these were based: the accountants write a report and the merchant bank a letter to the company and these are incorporated in the published prospectus. Although the directors have full responsibility for the contents of the prospectus the merchant bankers and accountants will always take the utmost care in their monitoring for if serious public criticisms later arose their reputations could be damaged.

Listing agreement (companies)

When directors seek a listing for a company one of the requirements of the Stock Exchange is that they sign a listing agreement, by which they bind the company in the future to inform the Stock Exchange promptly in respect of a number of specified matters, and also that the company will always follow strictly a number of laid-down procedures. The purpose of the agreement is to ensure that a company gives and later carries out undertakings in relation to its conduct in the future, and if the directors later failed to honour this undertaking the Stock Exchange could use this as grounds to take action against them. A serious problem is that if a listing were granted but later the company did not honour the terms of the listing agreement, the sanctions which the Stock Exchange would have at its disposal, suspension of the listing, would be liable to damage innocent parties, the shareholders of the company. The Council of the Stock Exchange is therefore reluctant to take the action of suspending a listing. In principle, if directors acted improperly and in breach of the spirit or letter of the City Code they would be liable to censure and possibly more severe sanctions by the Panel, just as professional men deemed guilty of unprofessional conduct are liable to disciplinary action by their professional body. In the past these various bodies were widely considered not to be firm enough in taking action against senior members of professions whose actions or failures to act brought discredit on their profession. There is evidence that at least some chairmen and council members of professional bodies are now determined to act more firmly against erring members but members of the public have reservations still. United Kingdom as well as other establishments are practiced and efficient in 'covering up' when one or more of their members behave badly.

Issue of securities to the public: practical considerations

Main ways in which new securities may be issued will be examined briefly, but no matter which way is chosen the timing of the issue will always be of the utmost importance and this is an aspect in which a company managment will always have to be guided by experts in close and daily touch with stock markets. However, as a date has to be decided upon some weeks in advance, and severe price movements may now occur unpredictably, luck will be a factor as well as skill and judgement. In principle, a management will aim to receive the maximum cash, net of expenses, for a given issue of shares (except in the case of a capitalisation issue, when no cash is involved, or when the consideration will be assets and not cash). The most favourable time will be when confidence is rising and markets are buoyant, known as 'bull' conditions. There is still a problem in choosing the right moment for an issue – should it be made soon, or deferred even for some months in the hope that a rising market will go on rising so that a substantially higher price could be obtained for shares issued in, say, twelve months' rather than in two months' time? The problem is that boom markets can and do unexpectedly collapse and if a favourable opportunity is not seized it might be lost and not recur for some years.

Matters to be decided
Ways in which securities may be brought to the Stock Exchange have been described. One or more could be suitable in some circumstances but quite unsuitable in others. In practice the chief executive of a company and probably a small number of the top management would have discussions with the representatives of their merchant bank, their stockbrokers, accountants and lawyers to decide the best course of action. Main questions to decide would include: (1) how much long-term funds are needed and what form should these take and what would the costs be, and the other implications of each alternative? If it were decided to raise equity capital then (2) the amount, manner and terms of the issue, noting that whilst the shares would have a stated nominal value the price at which each would be offered would normally be substantially higher than the nominal price; whether the full amount should be paid on application, or part on application and the balance on allotment and in that case what should the proportions be? In the past it was quite common for part of the value of a share to be left uncalled ('partly paid' shares) but this is no longer the case. It is now usual for shares to be fully paid at the time of allotment.

It must be decided (3) whether shares should be offered directly to the public or issued first to an 'issuing house' with a view of subsequent 'offer for sale'; (4) if an offer for sale is decided upon the terms of issue to the issuing house; (5) whether or not the issue should be underwritten and, if so, the terms. In effect, underwriting is a form of insurance to ensure the success of the issue, since any underwritten shares not taken up by the public will be purchased at the issue price by the underwriter. Underwriting commission is usually about $1¼–2\%$ of the issue price of the shares offered. It will be borne by the company, as part of the issue expenses, when the shares are being offered by the company, and by the shareholders if existing shares are being sold, e.g. by family shareholders. In the case of a large issue the underwriter often arranges sub-underwriters. There is no shortage of these, e.g. pension funds and other institutional investors. However, the main underwriter remains responsible. An issuing house would itself often agree to be the underwriter. 'Underwriting firm' means that the number of shares so underwritten will be allotted to the underwriter even if the public applied for far more than the total number of shares offered, and it requires the prior approval of the Stock Exchange as it can be a means of privileged investors receiving favourable treatment over members of the general public. If a large proportion of a popular issue of shares were underwritten firm, it would mean that the underwriters concerned would obtain their shares at the issue price less their commission, which they could then sell, as 'stags' at a premium, the moment dealings opened. Underwriting commission, when agreed, will always be payable, whether the issue is fully subscribed or not.

It will be decided (6) whether Exchange Control consent will be required (at the present time, it would not be); (7) the timing of the offer and a rough timetable, together with all matters of important detail, such as security printing, advertising, banking arrangements and the rapid physical handling of the applications and issue of allotment letters, letters of regret, splits, renunciations, etc., and then the issue of the securities. Normally, nowadays, the specialist department of the issuing house is the address to which all applications must be sent. An immense amount of accurate, high-speed and specialist work is involved in handling possibly very many thousands of applications arriving almost simultaneously.

Prospectus issue

In this case the company would be issuing new shares and offering them direct to the public. The formalities are onerous and the costs extremely high and this method is rarely used now and only when large and well-established companies are raising exceptionally large sums of money.

Offer for sale

The Stock Exchange normally insists that an issue is by means of an offer for sale when the capitalisation of the company exceeds £1 m. Often the offer will be in respect of new shares issued by the company but it may relate to new shares and also identical shares already owned by existing (family) shareholders who now wish to obtain cash for all or part of their holding. The issuing house normally arranges sub-underwriting. Offers for sale will be advertised in at least two national newspapers and the advertisements, which are prospectuses, will incorporate application forms. Copies of these will also be available at the issuing house, banks, stockbrokers, etc. A small 'brokerage' commission will be payable with respect to allotments made on application forms bearing the stamp of a bank or stockbroker. In the case of an offer for sale the issuing house will make its profits partly from its fees for professional services and partly from the difference it pays the company (and any private shareholders) for the shares and the price at which it issues these to the public. Details of the issue costs are required to be published so that investors, analysts, etc., are aware of the net funds to be raised by the issue and whether the issue costs appear to be reasonable.

Offer for sale by tender
In addition to the question of timing, one of the most difficult decisions in respect of an offer for sale is the price per share at which the shares are to be offered. The difficulty is increased by the fact that sudden and unpredictable changes in market conditions could mean that a price which seemed reasonable on one day could seem unreasonably high or low a few days later, when it would be too late to make changes. The reputation of the issuing house, in the short as well as the long term, will tend to rise or fall in relation to the market's later assessments of the success or failure of those issues for which it has had primary responsibility. On the one hand, if the price set seems too high on the opening date for applications the public response would be poor or bad and the underwriters would be required to pay out large sums in cash to meet their commitments. The company and any family shareholders would receive their money but the market price would stand at a discount when trading in the shares began. The underwriters would have the options of retaining all or part of their shares, to sell them later, if they assessed the market setback to be merely temporary, or they could 'cut their losses' and sell the shares promptly, their loss being reduced somewhat by their underwriting commission. Institutional investors may decide in any case to retain shares allotted to them as long-term investments.

In such circumstances an issue may have an aura of failure in the eyes of all concerned with investment activities. However, there is an equal or worse pitfall if an issue proves to be underpriced and the shares are seen as a 'bargain' by investors, so that on the day the lists open there proves to be a huge oversubscription – applications might be for one to two hundred times the number of shares available, indicating that investors would have been ready to pay a substantially higher price for the shares. With demand heavily exceeding supply on the opening of dealings the shares would stand at a high premium and 'stags', speculators who applied for shares with no intention of retaining them as an investment and with the aim of making a quick sale at a profit, would achieve their aim. In the case of a popular issue it is the practice of stags to send in large numbers of application forms, often under different names, with the intention of concealing their identity and the nature of their activity and in the expectation that if the issue is oversubscribed small applications would be favoured, and also that allotments would be based on ballots, with those making many applications having better chances of receiving allotments.

If events turn out like this it will be evident that members of the top management of the issuing company, and any family members who sold shares, would be displeased at the outcome, considering that parasitic stags had had the profits which should have been theirs, in the form of a successful issue at a higher price. Commentators on the issue would also be critical of it. The problem for the issuing house of getting the balance right – fixing an issue price which does not result in a failure, heavy undersubscription on the one hand, or obvious underpricing and heavy oversubscription, with profits to the stags, on the other – is very great in practice.

Offers for sale by tender have been devised as a means of resolving this problem. In an issue of this type the minimum tender price is stated, but no maximum. Applicants are invited to send their application forms showing the sum they offer for a stated number of shares with their cheque for the appropriate sum, e.g. 25% of the price tendered might be payable on application. In the light of the applications received and the prices tendered, those responsible for the issue decide upon the price which will be fixed and which would be above the minimum if the issue were successful. Some bidders may have tendered well above the selected price but in the event all pay the same price and at the time of allotment adjustments would be made in respect of those whose cheque had been for a larger sum than required: either a refund would be sent to them, or any further sum due from them on allotment would be reduced.

In principle the share price fixed would be such that all the shares offered would be allotted at a price which would result in the highest practicable sum being received with the proviso that some discretion might still be exercised in making the allotment and all the tenders from the highest tenderers might not be accepted in full. Vendors tend to prefer a larger rather than smaller number of allotments since this makes for a more efficient and orderly market, when there are quite a large number of shareholders and, even more important, reduces the number of large individual holdings which could at some stage be the springboard for an unwelcome takeover attempt. Meanwhile, despite their apparent logic offers for sale by tender seem to be relatively infrequent. It appears to be a City viewpoint that this type of offer is primarily justified if the company is operating in a relatively new or unknown field, but otherwise those concerned should be competent to determine a suitable price. A point which may or may not be relevant is that people who work in the City are the main body of those who work as stags, and they can make useful sums of money in this rather stimulating way. It would be understandable if there were reluctance to see opportunities for stagging ended or reduced.

Offer for sale: general
In July 1976 three important offers for sale were made and it happened that market conditions deteriorated suddenly during that month. The offers were in respect of T. Borthwick Ltd, Molins Ltd, and Hambro Life Ltd. Applications were made for only 1.6% of the Borthwick shares, for 23% of the Molins shares, whilst the Hambro Life issue was oversubscribed 1.5 times. The issue price and the price at the end of the first days trading were, respectively: Borthwicks, 80p and 69p; Molins, 120p and 106p; Hambro, 210p and 235p. Thus the undersubscribed shares opened at significant discounts and the oversubscribed one at a premium. In May 1978 there was an offer for sale for Eurotherm, a company in a new technology field. The offer was 100 times oversubscribed and in this case the issue and opening prices were respectively 100p and 148p. The profits for the stags were clearly very high.

Placing
The costs involved in an offer for sale are high and prohibitively so in the case of a smaller company. A large proportion of the costs are almost the same irrespective of the size of the issue, e.g. costs of discussions with merchant bankers, senior accountants, lawyers, etc., advertising costs, etc. The Stock Exchange has recognised this problem and in appropriate cases will approve that a smaller company obtains a listing by means of a placing. The market capitalisation of the company must normally be less than £1 m. but if its name is well known an offer for sale may still be insisted upon. In a placing there is no general

invitation to the public to purchase shares but the issuing house or sponsoring broker accepts shares from the vendor and then 'places' them with its clients, i.e. it sells them to these. In this case underwriting expenses will not arise and costs, including security printing and advertising costs, will be much lower than for an offer for sale. The objection in principle to a placing is that those institutions, wealthy investors, etc., who alone are invited to buy shares on this basis are put in a privileged and hence unfair position in relation to members of the general public. The Stock Exchange Council consider that in a properly regulated market no buyer or seller should normally enjoy privileges denied to others and accordingly placings are only permitted when there seems to be no reasonably practicable alternative. If placings were not permitted smaller companies would abandon the idea of obtaining a listing. Indeed, in recent years many have done this.

The Stock Exchange insists that at least 25% of shares being placed are made available to the market through brokers and jobbers. In appropriate cases it might also approve a placing by a company which already has a listing, notably when it seemed unlikely that there would be wide interest in a particular issue e.g. a loan stock. An advantage of a placing in appropriate circumstances is that it can be arranged quickly and thus the terms should accurately reflect market conditions.

The practical aspects: placing

The following is a brief summary of the mechanism of obtaining a listing by means of a placing.

(a) The company would have discussions with its chosen issuing house or broker and would agree that a placing would be appropriate and the issuing house and/or broker would agree to act for the company.

(b) The type of share, the numbers and the placing price would be agreed after all the implications had been examined, including the issue expenses. The broker or issuing house would provisionally arrange the placing.

(c) The broker would make formal application to the Stock Exchange for a listing. A separate letter would be submitted seeking approval to make a placing and explaining the reasons for adopting this procedure and the proposed marketing arrangements.

(d) An application would formally be made to the Stock Exchange for a certificate of exemption from compliance with the fourth Schedule of the Companies Act, 1948. (The law recognises that in appropriate cases it is reasonable for an abbreviated prospectus – advertisement – to be printed, at the discretion of the Stock Exchange. This is an example of how successive governments, through the Companies Acts, recognise that reliance upon the discretion of the Council of the Stock Exchange permits a degree of flexibility which would otherwise be impracticable.) In practice informal contacts are maintained and stockbrokers would only make a formal application when they were aware that, in principle, it would be approved.

(e) At least 14 days prior to publication, proof prints must be submitted to the Stock Exchange for approval of the prospectus, definitive certificates, memorandum and articles, and two proof prints of the trust deed in the case of a placing of loan capital.

(f) The prospectus must be published in one leading London daily newspaper and abridged particulars published in another: two days before the hearing of the application many additional documents must be lodged with the Stock Exchange, over and above those indicated in (e) above, e.g. copies of newspaper advertisements, certificate of incorporation, board resolutions authorising the issue of securities, a copy of the placing letter, a marketing statement by the broker etc.

(g) When a placing is permitted by the Stock Exchange their listing requirements stipulate the least permitted percentage of a particular security which may be placed and the least percentage which may be made available to the market as a whole. This applies to equity, fixed-interest or convertible securities. The informal contacts maintained by the brokers, issuing-house officials and those of the Stock Exchange would result in questions being resolved as they arose. If there were serious problems, these would become apparent in the early stages, before major expenses had been incurred. The Stock Exchange's formal approvals would only be withheld in the final stages if unsatisfactory information suddenly came to light about the company, or it appeared that important information had been withheld. In practice these arrangements are highly technical and outside the normal experience of a company management which would therefore leave the many important matters of detail to the experienced stockbrokers and merchant bankers to deal with.

Introduction

A public limited company which does not have a listing may have a wide spread of shareholders, possibly 100 or more, with probably a majority of the shares held by a much smaller number within the total. For reasons stated earlier, major shareholders may decide that they wish to sell some of their shares and they wish the shares to be listed. An introduction is a means whereby this can be arranged without the company itself becoming involved in the raising of new capital. The Stock Exchange may approve that a listing is obtained by means of an introduction. The company will need to prepare and advertise a prospectus, for information only, which complies with the requirements of the Companies Act, 1948, and those of the Stock Exchange. However, the public are not invited to apply for shares. The Stock Exchange will require assurances that existing shareholders will make sufficient shares available to the public to justify the granting of a listing by this method. It may also be borne in mind that when 35% or more of a listed company's share capital is held by the public it will not be a 'close company' for taxation purposes.

The Stock Exchange has indicated that in principle introduction procedure could be appropriate when: (a) the securities are already issued on another Stock Exchange; (b) an unlisted company has reached such a size as to fulfil the Council's requirements as to marketability; (c) a holding company is formed and its securities are issued in exchange for those of one or more unlisted companies. 'In cases where a previously listed company, which is seeking restoration of its listing, has increased its size by acquisition, or has changed its business or assets, it will be treated as though applying for a listing for the first time.' However, it is evident that the Stock Exchange carefully reserves its position with respect to introductions and an introduction would not be permitted unless the prospectus included a statement that no change in the nature of the business was in contemplation.

The application for approval will normally be required to include the names and holdings of the ten largest beneficial holders of the security and must state the total number of holders. A copy of the share register may be required by the Council. Particulars of the holdings of the directors and their families must in addition be included. In the case of an equity security, in which no market already exists, an interval before the commencement of dealings is normally necessary to enable a realistic price to be established. Listing will normally become effective to enable dealings to begin on the second business day following that in which the listing is granted.

Rights issues

The Stock Exchange's listing agreement requires that a listed company which seeks to raise additional equity capital must first offer the new shares it issues to the existing shareholders, unless the company in general meeting agrees otherwise. Existing shareholders are given the right to participate in new issues *pro rata* to their existing holdings and for this reason they are known as 'rights issues'. These rights have a money value and a shareholder who does not wish or cannot afford to purchase all or part of the new shares to which he has a right can 'renounce' his rights, that is, sell them through the market of the Stock Exchange. Part of the procedure is that the company posts to all shareholders their rights documentation, which is heavily endorsed, as is the envelope: 'this is not a circular but a document of value'. Despite this, many shareholders take no action, but they are protected by the Stock Exchange since the listing agreement requires that in respect of those shareholders who fail to exercise their rights through the market, the company must after the closing date sell these rights through the market on behalf of the shareholders concerned and then send each such shareholder a cheque for the sum realised on his behalf.

Rights issues, which could be in respect of fixed-interest stock but are normally in respect of equities, are much less expensive than public issues. They are relatively straightforward and do not necessitate many preliminary conferences, but rather informal discussions with the company's brokers regarding the price of the issue, the timing and the aspect of underwriting. The services of an issuing house would not be essential but would probably be used if the company had continuing contacts with its merchant bankers, as is often the case. The press would be supplied with preliminary, follow-up and result information, normally by the publicity or advertising agents of the company. All such press releases must first be monitored by the Stock Exchange. As rights issues are usually in respect of a class of capital already in existence the company does not need to publish a full prospectus but the Companies Act, 1948, requires that shareholders are provided with certain information and in the case of a listed company the Stock Exchange imposes certain additional requirements. This essential information will be supplied by the company in a circular letter which accompanies the 'provisional allotment letter', or it may be embodied in that document. As the provision of rights to renounce the shares to the public means that the circular letter and/or the provisional allotment letter is technically a prospectus, a copy, signed by all the directors, must be delivered to the Registrar of Companies.

There are five important matters to be considered in connection with a rights issue:
(*a*) The exact rights to be offered, e.g. one new share for five existing ones, or two for seven, etc., the ratio being determined by the

Going public 371

amount of new capital required as compared with the amount already issued.
(b) The action to be taken in respect of small holdings, where the shareholder does not qualify for any allotment. In brief, such shareholders must be kept informed, including of their 'nil' allotment.
(c) Fractions of a share may arise. The usual decision is to ignore fractions so far as the shareholder is concerned and the company sells the aggregate fractions on the market for its own benefit.
(d) Excess shares – these are normally sold for the benefit of the shareholders concerned, those who failed to exercise their rights.
(e) Underwritng – there is no hard and fast rule. Some companies do not underwrite rights issues on principle and publicise this fact as showing their confidence that they will receive shareholder support. Others invariably underwrite such issues on the principle that from time to time they will be liable to seek to raise funds in unfavourable financial conditions and they could only expect the support of underwriters in bad times if they used their services in good times, when they did not seem essential. In general, the main factor will be the price at which the issue is made in relation to the current market price of the shares: the new shares must be offered at a price below the current market price in order to make the issue attractive. The farther the price is below the current market price the less important the underwriting aspect will be. If the issue is made in a period when there are many other rights issues there may be a shortage of money for investment, in which case underwriting would be prudent.

Value of rights

Before a rights issue is made of listed ordinary shares the existing shares will have a market value liable to fluctuate from day to day. The company management, advised by its brokers and merchant bankers, if it has an ongoing relationship with these, will have to fix the price at which the shares will be offered to the existing holders, as well as the date when the rights must be exercised. They will wish to raise the maximum cash for the issue of a given number of shares, consistent with a successful issue. To achieve this objective there is a practical necessity for the price to be fixed at a significant discount below the current market price – perhaps 20% or so below this price – in the hope the issue price on the day of issue will be significantly below the lowest point to which the current price could fall, even if market conditions turned unexpectedly unfavourable.

In fact, when a rights issue is made to the existing shareholders (who can sell these rights if they wish), their interests are in no way damaged even when the rights issue price is well below the current market price. This is because the proportion of the equity which an ordinary shareholder owns will remain unchanged provided that he exercises his rights in full. Meanwhile, when new shares have been issued at a price below the current market price the total number of shares in issue will increase and there can only be one market price at any time for all of the shares since the existing and the new shares are indistinguishable. One would therefore expect the market price of the shares in issue to fall after a rights issue and the new market price to be somewhat above the rights issue price. The theoretical fall in the market price can be calculated, as well as the value of the rights to a shareholder who intends to sell all or part of his rights, as the example below shows. In practice the 'ex rights' price may not fall as far as the theoretical price and similarly when rights are sold on the market they may go to a premium over the theoretical price because of demand. A further reason why rights issues may attract interest is because neither the stamp transfer duty arises nor the jobbers' turn, and accordingly dealing costs are significantly reduced.

The procedure in respect of a rights issue of listed shares includes that after the announcement has been made of the impending rights issue the existing shares will be quoted 'cum rights' and in this case the rights will belong to the buyer and the market price will reflect this fact. The shares will then be listed as 'ex rights' from the beginning of an account, and from this time when shares are sold the seller will retain the rights and the market price will fall to reflect this fact. It may be noted that whilst it seems to make little real difference to a shareholder who exercises his full rights whether the rights issue price is at a larger or smaller discount in relation to the current market price, it does make a difference to the company. The interests of the company will be that the discount is as small as possible consistent with a successful issue since in this way it will maximise the cash received for the issue. The interests of the company as a company and that of individual shareholders do sometimes diverge.

A rights issue: an example
(a) Indicate the main sources of information available to an equity investor and outline the type of information he could expect to obtain from each source. (10 marks).
(b) A company with 20 million £1 shares has decided to raise further capital through a 1 for 4 rights issue. Just before the issue is

Going public

announced the market price of an ordinary share was £1.40 and the cost of exercising a right in respect of one share is to be £1.20.

You are required to: (1) calculate the theoretical nil paid value of the rights; (2) advise an existing holder of 10,000 shares of the possible courses of action open to him in respect of his entitlement. (15 marks) (ACCA 25 marks)

Workings and comments
The information relevant to part (a) will be found in Chapter 23.

		(£)
(b) (1) Market price of 4 existing shares at £1.40		5.60
Price of 1 rights share	at £1.20	1.20
Theoretical price of 5 shares after rights issue		6.80

The theoretical ex-rights value of a single share will therefore be $\frac{£6.80}{5}$, i.e. £1.36. As one share with a theoretical ex-rights value of £1.36 can be purchased for £1.20 the theoretical nil paid value of the rights will be 1.36 − £1.20, i.e. £0.16. As this relates to each holding of 4 shares, the value attaching to a single share will be £0.04 in theory.

(b) (2) The holder may be advised that if he wishes to continue to own the same proportionate share of the equity as before, he must exercise his full rights and produce the cash necessary to do this. Alternatively, he may sell all or part of his rights through the market. In this case he will receive cash but his proportionate share of the equity will be reduced. A compromise often chosen by people who are short of cash and who yet wish to retain their proportionate holding of the equity intact as far as they can is to sell that part of their rights which produces the cash necessary to take up as many of their rights as they can without drawing upon their existing resources, i.e. they neither receive nor pay cash in respect of the issue as cash they receive from sale of their rights is exactly expended in taking up part of their rights. The theoretical calculations for the three options are:

Option 1. Exercise of full rights: holding of 10,000 shares: 1 for 4 rights basis − i.e. in this case there is a right to purchase 2,500 shares at £1.20 each: the cost of exercising the rights in full will be 2,500 × £1.20, i.e. £3,000.

Option 2. Sale of all rights: total rights held 2,500 and value of rights £0.16 for 4 shares held: the theoretical selling price will therefore be

2,500 × £0.16, i.e. £400. In this case the theoretical position of the investor would be:
Before sale of rights: holding of 10,000 shares: market price £1.40, i.e. total £14,000.
After: 10,000 shares at £1.36 £13,600
cash received £ 400 total £14,000.

Option 3. The calculation of the third option is rather more difficult. There has to be a sale of part of the rights in such a way that the cash received can exercise the maximum rights without recourse to new cash.
Cost of purchase of 1 new share £1.20
Value of rights £0.16

Number of rights to be sold to produce cash to purchase 1 new share: $\frac{£1.20}{£0.16}$, i.e. 7.50

Thus 7.50 rights must be sold in order to obtain the cash to exercise the right to purchase 1 new share for £1.20, and thus 8.50 rights are involved in a single self-contained transaction.
Total rights available in this case: 2,500

Number of self contained transactions practicable: $\frac{2,500}{8.50}$, i.e. 294.12.

i.e. rights sold 7.50 × 294.12 = 2,205.90 = 2,206 (rounded)
2,206 × £0.16 = £353 cash
rights taken up = 1 × 294.12 $\frac{294}{2,500}$ rights
rights exercised 294.12 × £1.20 = £353 cost

Capitalisation issue (scrip or bonus issue)

It has been explained why directors normally make a practice of keeping the issued share capital reasonably in line with the equity capital employed (Ch. 5.) The mechanism for doing this is simple and involves the capitalising of reserves and/or a share premium account and/or undistributed profits. The issue is made to existing holders of ordinary shares *pro rata* to their present holdings. The listing agreement requires that the Stock Exchange is kept fully informed. As no movements of cash are involved, no prospectus needs to be issued and for administrative convenience companies now normally send a renounceable share certificate to each shareholder according to his entitlement. A shareholder who wishes to retain his full entitlement simply keeps this and does nothing and after a stated date the certificate ceases to be renounceable and becomes the definitive certificate. Before this date, if a shareholder wishes to sell all or part of the shares now issued to him, he sends the certificate with his instructions to his stockbroker and signs a form of renunciation on the back of the certificate.

As the procedures involved are simple, a capitalisation issue can be handled by the company itself, and its external registrar if it employs one. In effect all that is involved are book entries in the accounts of the company – a debit to one or more reserve accounts and/or share premium account and/or profit-and-loss appropriation account, and a corresponding total credit to the ordinary share capital account. Companies often used to use the term 'bonus' issues and unsophisticated shareholders were liable to be misled by the term and wrongly think they were receiving a 'free gift' of shares: as has been explained, the total of the shareholders' equity is not changed by this type of issue and effectively a shareholder who renounced all or part of the shares newly issued to him would reduce his proportionate share of the equity.

In practice, when a successful company announces a capitalisation issue of, say, 1 for 10 or 1 for 9, although in theory the market price of the shares should fall proportionately after the issue, so that the total value of the holding would be unchanged, in fact, the post-issue market price might be little or no different from the pre-issue price. In this case the total value of any holding would be somewhat higher after the issue than it was before. The reason is that the market – investors – may form the view that the company is doing well and is on an improving trend and, in the future, will at least maintain the current rate of dividends per share, including the new shares. The directors often indicate this intention. The total dividend receivable on a given holding would increase.

Questions

1. Outline the advantages for a company of a listing on the UK Stock Exchange. (ICSA 22 marks)
2. Explain the procedure for a placing of shares upon the UK Stock Exchange. (ICSA 22 marks)
3. (Part question). Where an issuing house is employed by a company

to advise and organise and obtain a Stock Exchange quotation, explain the preliminary investigation the issuing house would need to instigate. (ACCA Accs3 6 marks)

4. Describe the mechanics of a rights issue and explain why such issues are normally, but not always, underwritten. (ICSA 22 marks)

5. In recent years there have been relatively few equity issues on the London Stock Exchange and most of these have been rights issues. Why is this so? (ICSA 22 marks)

6. Discuss the factors which a company should take into account in setting the price for a rights issue. (ICSA 22 marks)

7. (a) Consider the advantages and disadvantages to a public company of raising additional long-term finance by means of a rights issue. (b) What factors should the company take into account when choosing between equity and fixed-interest finance? (ACCA 20 marks)

8. 'Not all new issues of shares are underwritten but it is clearly better that they should be if there is any chance that the issue may go badly.' Write a letter to a client, who has little knowledge of finance and whose successful private company is contemplating making a public issue, explaining this statement which appeared in a professional journal. (ICA 20 marks)

9. Discuss the pros and cons of a 'rights' issue from the viewpoint of (a) the issuing company and (b) the shareholder. (ICA 20 marks)

10. For what reasons, other than to raise outside finance, might a private company take the necessary steps to secure a Stock Exchange quotation? (ACCA 18 marks)

11. In recent years there have sometimes been offers for sale of shares by tender, rather than at fixed prices. Describe (a) the main features of an offer for sale by tender; (b) the circumstances in which such offers appear to be most appropriate; and (c) the normal methods of allotment adopted for such offers. (ACCA 20 marks)

12. Consider the means by which a public quoted company can raise additional long-term finance on the equity market. What factors should a company take into account when choosing between equity and fixed interest finance? (ACCA 20 marks)

13. The balance sheet of ABC Ltd at 31 August can be summarised as follows (£000):

Ordinary share capital, 4,500,000 shares of £1 each	4,500
Retained earnings	3,000
Loan capital	6,000
Net book value of capital employed	13,500

Going public

The profit for the year ended 31 August was £1,860,000 after charging loan interest of £600,000. The provision for Corporation Tax based on these profits was £780,000. The board has been studying a number of new opportunities for investment and in particular:
  (i) a project involving an outlay of £3,000,000 and expected to yield £450,000 p.a. additional profits after tax;
 (ii) a project costing £4,500,000 and yielding £540,000 p.a.;
(iii) a project costing £6,750,000 and yielding £607,500 p.a.

The board proposes a rights issue to the ordinary shareholders sufficient to cover one of the above projects and you are asked to advise on the following:

(a) The board wishes to ensure that the market capitalisation of the company increases by at least the amount of the rights issue. Given that the current P/E ratio of 8.33 is normal for this type of business, what is the theoretical maximum amount of capital that could be raised by the proposed rights issue?

(b) (i) Within the total amount eventually agreed for the rights issue, what considerations would affect the number of shares to be issued and the issue price?
   (ii) What, in your opinion, would be the theoretical rights price if the new shares were issued at £1.50 each?
  (iii) What factors might in practice cause a deviation between the theoretical ex-rights price and the actual market price?

(c) Under what circumstances would it be more beneficial to shareholders to take up their rights rather to sell their options in whole or in part? (ICMA 30 marks)

14. Discuss the economic function and structure of the market in unlisted shares in the United Kingdom (ICSA 22 marks).

Chapter 19

Risk and uncertainty

The viewpoint has been put forward that a main justification for profits is that they are a reward for the successful bearing of risks. When loss of the whole investment may be the penalty for failure, it would be unrealistic to expect investment on any other basis than that profits would be the socially sanctioned rewards for success. The question arises – what is meant by risk and can anything be done to eliminate or at least reduce it? There is a technical distinction between two words – 'risk', and 'uncertainty'. Risk is related to probabilities and there are mathematical techniques available to assess and evaluate these and, as the odds can be calculated, so can an appropriate insurance premium. Therefore, in principle, a person can always take out an insurance policy to indemnify himself against a risk which may, in the event, operate against him. Whether all insurable risks should be insured against is another question, which will be considered briefly. A formal definition of risk is 'a situation in which the probability distribution of a variable is known but its actual value (i.e. mode of occurrence) is not'. (A Dictionary of Economics and Commerce: S.E. Stiegler and G. Thomas, Pan, London)

Uncertainty may be defined as 'a situation regarding a variable in which neither its probability distribution nor its mode of occurrence is known'. (*idem*) In brief, uncertainty may be considered an upredictable risk, the odds cannot be calculated and therefore it can not be insured against. Unfortunately, uncertainty is a feature of business situations. Familiar examples are – How will fashions change over the next decade? What will sales be for a new product? Will the company make a profit next year, and if, so, how much? It should be noted that the word 'risk' is often used, including by examiners, when the context indicates that risk and uncertainty, or even uncertainty alone, are intended. A student may indicate his awareness of the distinction and state his own position – for example, that he will consider risk and uncertainty as relating to insurable and non-insurable risks respectively.

Meanwhile, how will a company seek to protect its own position in practice, using the word risk in its accepted dual sense? There must be risk management. In large organisations this may exist as a separate, specialist function. In smaller ones it should be allocated as a specific area of responsibility of a senior administrator, such as the company secretary. In a small, owner-managed company the owner-manager will be responsible for this function: it will be unfortunate for him if he does not realise this fact. One matter is certain. If no competent executive has specific responsibility for risk management, by whatever name called, the function will be neglected and avoidable costs or losses will arise and the existence of the company may even be imperilled, or it may be forced into liquidation.

The nature of risk management

Risk management is concerned with (*a*) the identification of risks; (*b*) the measurement of risk, as far as possible; (*c*) ensuring that individual risks are reduced as far as practicable; (*d*) financing risk-bearing. Risks, including uncertainties, can be analysed into a number of categories and important examples include:

1. Market risks. These are inescapable because of the time which elapses between the planning of a company, or a project, setting it up, starting it and carrying out production and sales. The time interval occurs irrespective of the nature of the business although in some cases it will be much longer than in others. Fashions may change suddenly. A competitor, possibly in another country, may achieve a technological breakthrough. Demand may change unexpectedly. In brief, even with first-class planning and research the outcome may not be as expected. Risks – uncertainties – of this kind cannot be insured against but must always be considered. The old saying 'do not put all your eggs in one basket' is valid and a cardinal rule is that no project should ever be entered into if it is of such a major nature that its failure could lead to the collapse of the whole company. In certain cases a policy of diversification is adopted as a means of spreading risks and, for example, reducing dependence on sales of a limited product range or in an area which is politically unstable.

2. Risks due to human failure. For example ignorance, carelessness, impatience, failure to obey safety instructions, errors of judgement, etc. Risks of this kind sometimes lead to catastrophic loss, including from third-party claims for loss of life or injury. An aircraft crash or the explosion of a supertanker may come into this category. Risks of this kind can and must (or should be) insured against. Product liability insurance is becoming increasingly important, not least in consequence of a number of court cases in the USA when some enormous claims have become payable by companies for defective products.

3. External social hazards. For example strikes, riots, thefts, burglaries, changes in government regulations or laws, taxation changes, etc. Some risks in this category can be insured against, others cannot be.

4. Physical hazards of nature. For example storms, floods, subsidence, earthquakes, etc. These can be insured against, and usually are.

5. Production or marketing risks. For example changes in the availability or productivity of labour; scarcity of raw materials; credit squeezes; etc. These are aspects of market risks and insurance is not possible. Efforts should be made to reduce the risks, or their impact, e.g. by ensuring suitable recruitment and training arrangements and conditions of employment; by not depending on a single source of supply; etc.

6. Fire risks. This is a risk which is always insured against. Moreover, when a serious fire occurs there is not only the aspect of the physical damage but also the disruption, possibly for some months, of normal working. Special 'loss of profits' insurance is available in respect of this and similar risks. Some companies insure against loss of profits but many do not – possibly from lack of awareness that it is available.

Alternative ways of dealing with risks

Specialist techniques

In larger organisations, and some trade associations, specialist mathematical techniques may be used by experts, especially to determine probabilities and to quantify risks. The link between mathematics and risk analysis is not new. In the seventeenth century gamblers approached Pascal and others to calculate the odds for them in respect of various games of chance. Risk analysis, decision theory, decision-tree analysis, etc., have evolved from this earlier mix of theory and practical applications. A new factor is the availability of electronic data processing since although the mathematical formulae are not new it is now practicable for the first time to make many complex calculations, using

Risk and uncertainty

different variables, very quickly. It is now normal practice for specialists to construct theoretical 'models' to represent complex real-world situations. Simple models may be represented on paper or, more usually now, in a computer. A feature of real situations is that there are many variables – factors which may change – e.g. interest rates, power costs, wages rates, materials costs, taxation rates, emergence of competing products, changes in demand, etc. Self-evidently, in a complex situation each variable will be liable to move independently of the others and the range of possibilities in respect of the outcome will be immense. Even the most complex of theoretical models will be oversimplified in relation to real-world situations.

Statistical decision theory

This involves the construction of a table or 'pay-off matrix' in which the alternative decisions which may be made are set out along one row, and columns are headed with the alternative environments or 'states of nature' which may occur. The 'cells' at the intersection of a given row and columns represent the outcome of a given decision and environment. This technique may be used to guide a manager as to the best stock to buy, depending on the probability of the market behaving in any one of the alternative ways, and the criteria the manager wishes to use as the basis of his decision. (*A Handbook of Management*, ed. T.Kempner, Penguin Harmondsworth.)

Decision-tree analysis

Often it will not be feasible for a mangement to make a single decision: a sequence of decisions will be essential, each depending on the one before, and at each step choice will have to be made between options, and each choice will give rise to new options. The situation can be represented by a branching network – 'tree' – setting out the various options – decisions – at every stage and their probable outcomes. Decision-tree analysis will be undertaken, e.g. when a company is considering launching a major new product and many options are available at every stage and the likely reaction of competitors must also be considered. (*The Launch of Persil Automatic and Management Techiques: Unilever Educational Booklets*)

Sensitivity analysis

Sensitivity analysis is important in relation to capital-expenditure decisions. In brief, the effect of changes in key variables is studied, the worst and the best possible outcomes as well as the outcome assessed as the most probable. It is a technique used to highlight the key variables and hence the 'danger' areas. It may enable some risks to be reduced by having contingency plans available.

Probability, correlation and regression
A frequent task of market researchers and other analysts and statisticians is to attempt to assess probabilities. Information may be sought as to whether there is any link between particular variables and, if so, what this is. For example, an ice cream manufacturer would be interested in knowing whether a quantifiable relationship had been established between sales of ice cream, as one variable, and daily hours of sunshine, as together. If analysis and observation over a sufficient period confirmed a quantifiable relationship then, evidently, if reliable long-range weather forecasting were available the manufacturers' risks of loss through either over- or under-production would be reduced. The techniques of correlation and regression analysis are used to estimate the relationship between a variable and one or more others. Meanwhile, as evidence to the Wilson Committee confirmed, top managements of big companies give due weight to expert evaluations but final major decisions are likely to be based even more on their own judgement, intuition and experience, which will be likely to include similar situations in the past and they will recall the problems and outcomes.

Transfer of risks
In appropriate cases it will be practicable and prudent for a company to reduce or eliminate particular risks by making a known payment to a specialist risk bearer with the practical result that what had been a risk now becomes a cost, to be allowed for and recovered in the selling price. Examples include the taking out of an insurance policy, when the risk is transferred to the insurer through payment of an agreed premium. Similarly, an importing or exporting company committed to making or receiving future payments in a foreign currency may transfer to a bank the risks of changes in the exchange rate. The mechanism is that the company enters into a contract with a bank whereby the bank agrees to purchase or sell on an agreed future date a sum of the currency concerned at a rate fixed now (a forward sale or purchase of currency); or a manufacturer who uses a raw material can reduce the risk of loss through price changes in raw materials by means of 'hedging', which involves entering into a 'futures' contract with a specialist commodity dealer or speculator.

Self-Insurance
A risk manager will consciously examine and assess risks and decide

upon those which the company can reasonably bear itself, and those which should be insured against, hedged, etc. This is quite different from the situation when a company does not insure against a particular insurable risk because of an oversight, or lack of awareness that the risk existed, or that it could be insured against. Failures of this kind occur quite frequently but are inexcusable and are examples of management incompetence since, if a manager responsible for insurance is not an expert, he should be aware of this fact and take care to obtain reliable professional advice. Meanwhile, an insurance company sets its premium rates at levels which are aimed to cover: (*a*) its claims costs; (*b*) marketing costs and commissions to agents and brokers; (*c*) heavy administrative costs; (*d*) generous provisions for reserves and contingencies; (*e*) profits. Insurance costs are therefore significant. Some very large companies form or buy an insurance company as a subsidiary, sometimes located in a tax haven, and this then operates as a main instrument for dealing with the insurance needs of the parent company. The subsidiary would reinsure against excess risks as it deemed prudent.

Smaller, but still large companies or groups, which pay large annual sums as premiums quite often form an insurance broking company as a subsidiary. This offers a dual advantage to the parent company, since the broking subsidiary will employ high-calibre insurance specialists who will closely watch the interests of the whole group in respect of insurance matters, and since broking companies obtain their revenues by means of commissions paid to them by the insurance companies, and the party which takes out a policy pays the same premium whether he deals directly with the insurance company or through a broker, a broking subsidiary should be largely self-financing. In other cases it would be the responsibility of the risk manager to obtain reliable insurance cover at the lowest cost consistent with complete security. Normally a broker with first-class local reputation would be employed, noting that the cost to the company is the same, whether it deals with insurance companies directly, or through a broker. A good broker will provide advice and will press the interests of the client whenever claims arise.

In deciding what risks to insure against, the question in each case will be – how serious could a loss be? Records should be kept on a basis which permits quick analysis and over a period should give a useful guide as to the frequency and seriousness of particular types of loss. In principle an insurable risk should always be insured against if a single event, e.g. a fire, or the sinking of a ship, in the case of a shipping company, could give rise to an unacceptable loss. Often a company will obtain lower premiums by accepting to bear the first £x in respect of any claim. A risk manager would also consider such matters as the cash flow – how would this be affected if the company had to find itself the cash to replace a damaged or destroyed asset? If it could have difficulty the risk should be insured against. The larger a company is and the bigger the scale of an activity, the more statistically predictable its loss experience will be. In consequence it tends to be easier and safer for larger companies than it is for smaller ones to contemplate self-insurance against certain types of risk. One would expect supermarket groups to accept self-insurance in respect of breakage of their expensive plate-glass windows, whereas single shops would be likely to insure against this risk.

Elimination or reduction of risks

(a) All practicable steps must be taken to reduce or eliminate a particular type of risk, e.g. by the installation of automatic sprinklers and fire-fighting equipment, burglar alarms, etc. The cost of such installations may be significantly reduced by tax concessions and, in addition, they may be used as strong bargaining counters to negotiate lower than standard insurance premiums. Occasionally government grants may also be available.

(b) Forecasting and research often have an important role – a larger company would employ its own specialists whilst smaller ones may subscribe to appropriate external organisations, e.g. trade associations, universities, etc. Special 'one-off' assignments may be commissioned.

(c) Combination or offsetting of risks – large companies seek, as far as practicable, to have a reasonably stable and assured market and important reasons for mergers and takeovers include to reduce market and related risks, assure source of supply or access to market, etc. The formation of cartels, shipping conferences, price-fixing agreements, etc., must arise partly from a wish to increase profits and partly to reduce risks.

The actions taken by larger companies to diversify may also be seen as part of a strategy towards risk since it is considered that a company will be less vulnerable if its prosperity is built on a wide rather than a narrow base. Tobacco and shipping companies are now specially active in seeking to diversify: in each case, for different reasons, the main activity is recognised as involving specially high risks.

Compensation of risks

In certain cases arrangements may be made so that if a loss should arise

Risk and uncertainty

in one operation there will be a more or less equivalent profit in another. Manufacturers or traders could often make 'windfall' profits from favourable commodity or currency price movements, in addition to their normal trading profits. However, where the chance of a windfall profit arises there is also the chance of a heavy loss if prices move the wrong way. By use of hedging, or forward currency sales or purchases, traders and manufacturers can largely transfer to professional operators these special risk of loss or gain, and they themselves will be satisfied with their normal trading profits.

Ploughing back of profits

One of several reasons why a company ploughs back a substantial proportion of its distributable profits is to reduce risks. This will be especially apparent in the early days of a company. One which distributed profits to the full would have no resources to draw upon in sudden bad times and it could fail. With retained profits in liquid from, the company will have cash available. If these profits had been invested in fixed assets these would be available as collateral security for borrowing. Retained profits may be regarded as a form of insurance against otherwise uninsurable risks.

Laying off of risks

Perhaps the most important single rule in relation to risk management is that a company should never be prepared, alone, to bear a particular risk if it is of such magnitude that an adverse experience would be likely to destroy the company. Risks must be sufficiently spread. All professional risk bearers, including the largest insurance companies, protect themselves against the risk of being overwhelmed by a single huge claim by 'laying off' excess risks – that is, by reinsuring against them. For example, Lloyds underwriters readily agree to insure a supertanker for £30 m. or so, but by means of passing off part of these risks to reinsurers – who operate on an international stage – if a loss occurred the maximum loss falling on an individual underwriter would be unlikely to exceed £5,000. The party taking out the insurance would initially pay a large single premium, normally to a single party, a broker, and the premium would be shared *pro rata* amongst the many who agreed to bear a certain part of the risk. In the same way, when a bookmaker accepts an exceptionally large bet from a gambler he will 'lay off' a more or less substantial proportion of the bet with other bookmakers so that if the gambler's bet won, the bookmaker would pay him the large sum due but would himself collect, as a winner, in respect of the bets he had himself placed with other bookmakers. The action of offsetting risks reduces the chances of large gains and this is the price of keeping the risk of loss to acceptable levels.

Joint ventures and consortia
A feature of modern activity is that some projects require almost unimaginably large capital investment if they are to be undertaken. In the case of the Alaskan pipeline or exploitation of a North Sea oilfield, even thousands of millions of pounds have been involved and the work has to be done at the frontiers of knowledge and technology. In such cases even the largest company may be unable or unwilling to undertake a major project alone, but would be prepared to participate as a member of a joint venture or consortium. Often major consortia or joint ventures will be international in scope and with members who are normally in competition with each other. By acting in this way, immense risks can be reduced to tolerable levels for each party. A very interesting example of this special approach to risks is given by actions taken by those major multinational companies which are now spending vast sums on the high-risk development of video discs. The companies clearly believe that the potential markets for the players and the discs will be enormous and huge sums have evidently been spent on research and development. Unfortunately, three separate systems are being developed and the probability seems that, in the long run, one will succeed and the others will fail, but for the time being each major company will be pressing forward with its own system, hoping it will be the one which succeeds. However, because of the enormous sums which are at stake, major companies which normally compete fiercely with each other are pooling their resources in this particular field, and competing against the other two groups. A layman outside the companies concerned must presume that the present heavy research and development costs of every company involved are amply covered by the massive cash flows arising from the sales of the established products of each company. If, within the next five years or so, it becomes evident that one system has succeeded, the rewards for that group will be enormous, but if the other two systems totally fail then whilst it would obviously represent a setback and disappointment for each of the companies concerned, the setback would not put the survival of any of the companies concerned at risk. They are obviously far too well managed to allow that to happen and none will have put an excessive proportion of its total resources at risk in this venture.

Financial risks
The foregoing may be considered as business risks. There are also

financial risks. A company which adopts gearing accepts a significant financial risk which increases with the level of the gearing. Business risks are evaluated in financial terms and when a management is considering whether or not to adopt a particular project the aspect of 'riskiness' will be taken into account. A project which clearly involves higher than normal risks may only be adopted if it appears to offer a higher than normal return on capital or a shorter payback period. These matters were considered under capital project decisions (Ch. 14).

Questions

1. Explain the relationship between the measurement of risk and attitudes towards risk.   (ICSA   22 marks)
2. Discuss the factors which should be taken into account in evaluating the degree of risk involved in investment projects.   (ICSA   22 marks)
3. Distinguish between corporate risk and project risk and explain how they affect project appraisal.   (ICSA   22 marks)
4. Discuss the relevance of evaluating risk when developing company objectives and in formulating the strategies to be adopted to achieve them.   (ICSA   22 marks)
5. In what ways would you suggest that the riskiness of investment projects should be taken into account by the financial planners of a listed company.   (ICSA   22 marks)

Chapter 20

The nationalised industries and their financing

From the end of the Second World War, a number of UK basic industries in the areas of fuel and power, transport and communications and iron and steel were nationalised. Steel was denationalised in 1954 and renationalised in 1965, although a small number of specialist companies were allowed to continue in the private sector. The supply of gas, coal and electricity is provided entirely by nationalised industries whilst oil, a competitive fuel, is supplied by private-sector international oil companies. The UK government has a large equity shareholding in one of the latter, BP. Whilst successive governments appear always to have avoided involving themselves with the management and control of BP, it may be presumed that chairmen and chief executives of a company in this situation, who are invariably competent and experienced as diplomats, would be unlikely to take a major policy decision which might put it into confrontation with the government unless there had at least been informal discussions beforehand. The government appoints two of the BP directors who presumably will act as channels of communication in case of need. In recent times there has indeed been puzzlement about the alleged roles of BP and Shell in supplying oil to Rhodesia (now Zimbabwe) at a time when there were UK government sanctions against companies trading with Rhodesia, when Rhodesia was under the control of a government in rebellion against the UK but no improprieties were proved against either company. In any case, it is certain that in large organisations things can happen in outlying areas which are not known at the headquarters. In respect of other major undertakings, rail transport is effectively wholly publicly owned but a substantial proportion of the road transport industry is still withing the private sector. British airline operations are partly within the public and partly the private sector. With the election of a Conservative government in 1979 a number of changes have taken place and it is evident that further changes are intended. It is also evident that numbers of less radical

Conservative supporters have reservations about some of the intended changes.

The subject of nationalisation in the UK has for many years been a focus of political controversy. As long ago as 1918 the Labour Party incorporated the often quoted 'Clause IV' in their constitution. An extract is: 'to secure for the workers by hand or brain the full fruits of their industry and the most equitable distribution thereof that may be possible upon the basis of the common ownership of the means of production, distribution and exchange and the best obtainable system of popular administration of each industry or service'.

The economic and political background

It seems to many politically neutral observers that although it could be understandable that the arguments for and against nationlisation could raise strong political feelings some years ago, before the theories had been tried, in recent years the theoretical arguments are primarily live issues to people on the right wing of the Conservative Party or the left wing of the Labour Party. Evidence suggests that the majority of both parties would now prefer continuity of good management and to avoid that key industries are treated as political footballs, liable to experience upheavals after every change of government. In such conditions good management and morale may be unattainable. The background includes that in the inter-war period the coal mines and the railways, *inter alia*, were unable to generate or obtain from the market the capital necessary to operate a profitable industry, with acceptable conditions of employment and price levels. In such circumstances there may be few options – allow the industry to decline, which would be unacceptable for a number of reasons, or have recourse to public ownership with, if necessary, substantial state subsidies. The problems are not confined to the UK: for example, the railway systems in Europe and the USA have proved unprofitable in the private sector and in one way or another the state has intervened to ensure the survival of the industry.

Those who take the view that decision making should reflect the operation of market forces and that railways, for example, should be closed if they cannot operate without subsidies, appear liable to oversimplify the situation. They overlook the hidden subsidies received by road transport operators, whose relatively lightly taxed vehicles use and heavily damage roads provided by taxation at great cost; the unquantifiable social costs of road deaths and injuries or what the situation would be for the next generation if there were no railways at a time when oil was in short supply and petrol prices for cars and public transport buses were rising to unprecedented levels. Similarly, what would the position be if there were no longer a viable coal-mining industry in the UK at a time of worldwide oil shortage? It therefore seems to many that the time has come to cease to view nationalisation from a political aspect, but to regard it as one of the available options. If it appears that a certain industry should survive for social and or strategic and long-term reasons, but private capital is not forthcoming, then nationalisation would be an acceptable option, with the proviso that there should be adequate public debate, with the facts made available, and not concealed, as they so often have been, by ministers of both parties, and civil servants.

The evidence shows that in the first half of this century the supporters of nationalisation for its own sake held the view that when major industries were nationalised there would be a transformation in attitudes and consequently in performance. In theory, managers would no longer be concerned only with making profits for absentee landlords – private-sector shareholders – and they would no longer need to exploit workpeople in order to do so, and the workpeople themselves would have better motivation and would become more productive. In the event, it has not been so simple. Often, managers in a newly nationalised industry, e.g. steel, were aware that a change of government would mean denationalisation. In conditions of complete uncertainty and lack of continuity, proper plans can not be made and no one is likely to work at peak efficiency at any level. Understandably, the ablest managers tend to avoid such situations and whilst the largest organisations in the country needed exceptional management if they were to have real chances of success, the person appointed as chief executive would often be a retired civil servant or academic with no proven record of success as a manager, or a manager obviously below the calibre required. Furthermore, for many years the nationalised industries offered chief executives, and hence other senior managers, far lower salaries than were paid to people in comparable positions in much smaller private-sector companies.

There has also been – and there obviously still is – substantial ministerial and civil service interference with the workings of nationalised industries and it has become evident that for a variety of reasons nationalisation of an industry does not necessarily solve its problems and, perhaps surprisingly, industrial relations have often proved exceptionally bad in nationalised industries. In recent years opinion polls have indicated that enthusiasm for nationalisation as a policy in itself is small and the wish is that the existing industries should be efficient. A special problem in the late 1970s and early 1980s has been the worldwide slump in a number of major basic heavy industries, including steel and shipbuilding, and worldwide overcapacity. In the UK substantial reductions in the labour force have been achieved in part by means of government-funded voluntary redundancy schemes. Indeed, redundant employees in politically sensitive nationalised industries seem to have been more generously treated than most of their redundant counterparts in the private sector. However, recently, the closure of a major steelworks at places such as Shotton and Corby, has obviously caused enormous and still unsolved human and social problems since the works had been by far the largest employer in an area where there was, and is, very little alternative employment.

The National Enterprise Board (NEB)

The position of a nationalised industry may be defined in a special statute, corresponding with the memorandum and articles of association of a private-sector company. This was the earlier practice. In 1975 the Labour government established the National Enterprise Board (NEB) which *inter alia* may act as a holding company for wholly or largely state-owned companies. The NEB was a Labour government creation which permitted established capitalist techniques and mechanisms to be employed with flexibility and sophistication to establish socialist objectives. Whilst the NEB has had a share of failures, it has also had some outstanding successes. In 1975 the major private-sector company Ferranti was unable to obtain funds in the private sector and it was rescued by the NEB with an injection of £15 m. of public money. At this time the action of the NEB was widely criticised, for different reasons, from both sides of the political spectrum.

In the event, the rescue was a complete success and in 1978 Ferranti obtained a relisting on the Stock Exchange by means of an introduction. The NEB profitably sold a part of its shareholding to other Ferranti shareholders, whilst retaining a major shareholding itself in what is now once again a leading UK company in the high-risk field of advanced technology, and one of the main civil and military contractors in Europe. Subsequently, under the Conservative government, the NEB was required to sell its shareholding in Ferranti to shareholders in the private sector. The Labour government had also used the NEB as its instrument and agent in relation to the state's ordinary shareholdings in Rolls Royce and British Leyland. The NEB was critical of management lack of control of Rolls Royce and a major row developed and the government removed Rolls Royce from the NEB control and made it the direct responsibility of the Secretary of State for Industry. The board of the NEB resigned and their viewpoint was apparently shown to be well founded when the annual results of Rolls Royce were published and disclosed a loss of the order of £100 m., which had to be made good from public funds. However, despite clashes between the Conservative government and the NEB, there are many who regard it as an encouraging sign that the NEB has been permitted to survive. It has also been used by the government to assess the prospects of INMOS, a company which originally received financial support from the former Labour government, and promises of further support. INMOS's primary aim is to develop a silicon-chip manufacturing industry in the UK. INMOS has now received £50 m. of public money, of which £25 m. was confirmed by the Conservative government in mid-1980, on the recommendation of the NEB. Many Conservatives expressed criticism of this decision but many others have welcomed it. INMOS appears to be working in a field in which the Americans and Japanese already excel, and the French, German and other governments are giving financial support to national companies which are seeking to establish themselves in this vital field. If £50 m. of public funds to INMOS permit this country also to establish itself in this field, the price will be a very modest one. It seems a risk well worth taking.

The 1960s White Papers

Since the early days of nationalisation there has been awareness of the problems of reconciling commercial and non-commercial objectives, and problems of ensuring adequate accountability without excessive interference in the day-to-day workings of a nationalised organisation. In the 1950s the Government appointed a Select Committee to investigate each nationalised industry. A major change in the financing arrangements followed. The industries were required to borrow from the Treasury rather than directly from the market, as had been the case until then. This introduced an important new element of government central control.

In the 1960s two White Papers defined the financial and economic obligations of the nationalised industries and set out guidelines for their operations. The 1961 White Paper emphasised what must seem a reasonable principle, that although the industries had obligations which were national and non-commercial, they must not be regarded as social services, freed from economic and commercial justification. It was observed that some boards were not making enough provisions to cover the replacement costs of assets, taking inflation into account, or to provide for obsolescence. The White Paper explained how the statutes should be interpreted, with the intention of encouraging boards to increase their revenues and improve their efficiency. Specific financial objectives were subsequently defined for most of the industries, covering periods of up to five years.

However, the financial performances generally continued to be unsatisfactory and this lead to the 1967 White Paper. This required that the industries should be operated on commercial principles, and should aim to allocate and use resources efficiently. Principles were stated in relation to pricing policies and investment decisions. The technique of discounted cash flow was to be used for project evaluation in the investment programmes. Accounting costs were to be recovered and prices were to be considered in relation to long-run marginal costs, and with emphasis on reducing costs and improving efficiency. It latter appeared that the setting out of investment criteria had imposed a useful discipline but a number of fundamental problems remained. Because of their size and the number of people employed, the importance of the services performed or offered and the fact that these may be on a monopoly or near-monopoly basis, all these are matters of public concern. The major nationalised industries are of such central importance in the economy that their investment, their pricing and other policies have political as well as commercial implications.

It seems that no government will, or can, allow the top managements of major nationalised industries the kind of freedom of action which can, up to a point, be claimed by managements of large private-sector companies. For example, in the late 1960s and early 1970s when the government was seeking to reduce inflation by a policy of price and income restraint, nationalised industry price rises were limited, by government orders, to levels below those considered essential by their managements. Self-evidently, when a nationalised industry is not permitted to increase its selling prices at a time when its costs are increasing, and if its efficiency is at the highest attainable levels, the consequence will be that losses will be incurred which will have to be borne by the owners, the community, in the form of higher taxes, which are politically unpopular, or borrowing, which tends to be inflationary. Furthermore, essential capital investment will be cancelled or postponed – a fact which is obvious to rail travellers on the Southern and Eastern Region services of British Rail.

Severe price controls also introduce distortions, as does rationing in wartime. If a service is supplied at an uneconomically low price, demand will be stimulated and will rise and efforts to meet the rising demand will increase the losses. Meanwhile, in 1973 a new factor suddenly arose, the quadrupling of oil prices, which overnight caused the price of energy, on which all economic life depends, to rise enormously throughout the world, and this has been a major factor in bringing about a worldwide recession.

New financial objectives for nationalised industries

In mid-1974 the government of the day decided upon a major change of policy. The objective of the nationalised industries must be to attain operating surpluses. With pricing restrictions removed, heavy increases in the prices of electricity, coal, rail fares, telephone calls, etc., quickly followed. It happened that these coincided with heavy increases in local authority rates, which are levied to cover the costs of services which are provided within the public sector. These rises occurred at a time when UK citizens in general were subjected to income restraint. Predictably, the price and rate rises caused widespread resentment, complaint and public questions about the efficiency of the nationalised industries and whether there is abuse of monopoly powers on the part of mangements, workpeople and trade unions operating within the public sector. The complaints of overmanning and poor discipline have been of long standing, noting that overmanning can be tolerated by a monopoly supplier of essential services, or excessive wage claims quickly agreed since the costs can at once be passed in full to the captive consumers, members of the public.

It is also evident that at least some managements and workpeople in nationalised industries have been seeking to raise standards, to increase revenues without necessarily increasing prices, and to improve industrial relations. The railways are an example: attention has been given to marginal costing techniques and the devising of tariffs to produce additional revenues at off-peak times, when traffic is light but the heavy fixed costs continue. Successful pricing policies of this type make it possible to limit price rises for the high-cost services, notably commuter services in which very large numbers of people have to be carried into city centres around the start of each working day, and away from them at the end of each day. It also happens that British Rail is not a monopoly supplier in the sense that the Post Office telecommunications or the Electricity Generating Board are. The railways were finding that as fares rose customers were switching to private car or bus, or even ceasing to travel altogether, and the point was being reached that an increase in fares could lead to a decline in the number of travellers and hence in total revenues and thus be self-defeating.

Meanwhile, in 1978 the electricity and gas industries and the Post Office produced substantial surpluses, so high indeed that forms of inflation accounting were used which had the effect of producing substantially lower profits than would have been shown by conventional, historic cost accounting. The reaction to the considerable media comment and analysis was public questioning whether the very high profits confirmed that earlier price rises had been excessive. In 1980 matters have gone a stage further. The Conservative government directed the Gas Corporation to increase its prices in order to generate an even more substantial surplus, of which the government would be the beneficiary. The government was elected on a mandate which included the reduction in direct taxes, notably income tax, and one of its first actions after election in 1979 was to reduce substantially the tax payable by wealthy individual taxpayers. It aimed to offset falls in tax revenues from these taxpayers by substantially increased revenues from indirect taxation and at the time when higher levels of income tax were reduced the indirect tax, VAT was increased from the rate of 8% to 15%. In 1980 it appears that the government is seeking to use the profitable nationalised industries, notably the Gas Corporation, as agencies for the generation of indirect taxation, using the mechanism of price rises beyond those which could have been justified by normal commercial criteria. However, this policy may now be giving rise to problems which had not been foreseen by the government. Leaders of a number of major UK industries, which are high consumers of energy, wrote to the *Financial Times* to express anxiety about the trend of this government's policy in respect of energy pricing, since UK energy costs are now substantially above those which prevail in the USA and Western Europe. The consequence is that no matter how efficient they may be, many important UK companies are finding that their costs of production are significantly above those of their competitors and government policies are having the effect of further undermining the structure of manufacturing industry in the UK economy. As a majority of the leaders of manufacturing companies in the UK are known to be strong Conservative Party supporters, it is to be surmised that this powerful and open expression of alarm at the direction of the government's policies will compel the government to review its policies in this and other areas.

It would seem that when major nationalised industries cannot be left out of the political arenal, a major problem is of getting the balance right between extremes. Under previous governments it seemed to many that there was a strong desire to avoid confrontations with organised labour, that managements were not allowed to manage and particular industries were less efficient than they ought to be, with evidence of overmanning, waste, indiscipline. The Conservative government elected in 1979 clearly had a mandate to attempt to raise standards, and partly by imposing firm financial disciplines. A particular problem in dealing with the public service, and monopoly industries is that the discipline imposed when forces of competition operate freely does not apply in these situations. In the private sector, for example, if an employer tolerates waste and slackness he will be unable to sell his products and he will be forced out of business, often because foreign competitors offer a more attractive product at a favourable price. In an effort to find a means of imposing discipline in situations where competition was impracticable, the government has been imposing 'cash limits'. A large part of the intended purpose of cash limits has clearly been to keep public-sector wage claims under control, on the principle that if the employer concerned authorised a claim which could not be met within the laid-down cash limits the only way in which the claim could be honoured would be by reducing the numbers of people employed. Up to a point this cash-limits policy appears to have been working but there are evidently problems which need to be overcome. In brief, the cash-limits policy appears to be operating in a way which is excessively restrictive of capital investment at a time when this has already been neglected for some years (since at times of financial crisis previous governments always cut capital investment programmes rather than attempt to reduce costs in current operations) and, furthermore, at a time of recession, such as the present, when there is widespread unused capacity, the opportunity should be taken to improve the capital stock when this will itself increase the productive capacity of the country as a whole.

For example, it was announced in mid-1980 that towards the end of the year telecommunications charges would be raised by 25% (some calculate that the real increase will be nearer 50%): this will be the second large increase in 1980 and it appears that because of the cash-limits policy the Post Office is having to finance all or nearly all of its massive investment programme out of revenue. Present users will therefore be paying for services which many will not live to enjoy themselves. Similarly, because of the cash limits British Rail is having to operate with a significant proportion of rolling stock which is well below the standard used in most other countries in Western Europe. In the private sector the approach to capital investment has traditionally been quite different, and it seems sounder in principle. It is that retained profits will be an important source of funds for a capital investment programme but if it is not sufficient it may legitimately be augmented by the raising of permanent or long-term capital. Thus a private-sector company would be prepared to borrow on a long-term basis if it were satisfied that the investment programme would result in an improved cash flow which would be ample to take account of the interest on the borrowed funds and the need to repay the principal in due course. If borrowing would result in an unacceptable raising of the gearing ratio a private-sector company would increase its equity capital base by means of a rights issue. No management would ever contemplate attempting to finance a major investment programme from the revenues arising from the sales of the existing products. In a competitive environment it would in any case be a practical impossibility. It would seem arguable that when a government insists that a major industry finances major investment programmes from revenues, and the industry is a monopoly supplier of an essential service, so that there have to be massive price rises which customers cannot escape, then there is a fundamental abuse of power and there ought to be a rethinking of policies.

It may be mentioned that in the case of a publicly owned industry the distinction between equity and loan funds is not so clear, in a practical sense, as it is in the case of private-sector industry. In the past, for example, when the government nationalised a particular industry, which had previously been in private-sector ownership, it raised the money, in many cases, by means of borrowings and paid off the private-sector owners and creditors. The industry's capital structure would, unlike a private-sector company, comprise a liability of indebtedness to the government. In such a situation there would be no point in having equity capital, or so it would seem, since the government would accept responsibility for the funding of the organisation and would be ready and able to ensure its survival. In the case of the railways some years ago there would regularly be an announcement of a heavy loss after taking into account interest due on loans from the government. Subsequently the government announced that it was writing off the loans in question in order to put the finances of the organisation on a more realistic basis. In effect, the relationship of the organisation to the government had throughout been more like that of a company to its equity shareholders than to its creditors. If there had been profits, they would have belonged to the shareholder – the government in this case – but if there were losses the shareholder got nothing. Insofar as nationalised industries have been financed by means of borrowings rather than equity, an interesting consequence – in an academic rather than a practical sense – is that the real net asset values must be very high, noting that they have been financed with money borrowed at negative rates of interest in real terms.

In recent years the government of the day authorised a number of nationalised industries to borrow in the Eurocurrency markets in their own names but with the borrowings guaranteed by the British government. An important reason for this course of action is presumably that it reduced the government's own borrowing needs at the time, both in the UK and overseas, and the overall extent of government borrowings or commitments was at least obscured, even if it was not concealed. The wisdom of these arrangements was questioned at the time because sterling subsequently depreciated against the currencies concerned and this increased the burden of both the principle and the interest since both were expressed in terms of the overseas currency concerned. Meanwhile, in the early 1980s it is evident that a main reason why the government wishes to limit severely, if not prevent, borrowing by nationalised industries even for the purpose of financing revenue-generating investment programmes is to keep to the minimum the public Sector Borrowing Requirement (PSBR) on the grounds that such borrowings increase the money supply and are inflationary. This is now an important area of controversy and debate which is frequently considered in serious newspapers and other media and it is outside the scope of this book. Meanwhile it is evident that there is a view which is gaining support that it should be practicable to make distinction between borrowing to meet current expenditure and borrowing for genuinely productive purposes, especially at a time when there is underemployed manufacturing capacity in the country and orders for capital equipment would ease the unemployment situation, which is itself so demoralising, so wasteful of existing resources which are now under-utilised, and so costly in terms of unemployment payments.

It is evident that for a number of reasons, including the numbers of people they employ and the fact that many are of strategic importance – they occupy 'the commanding heights of the economy'– controversy about different aspects of nationalised industries is inevitable and even informed persons may change their opinions from one period to another. A special problem arises because the interactions of political as well as social, economic and commercial factors make it difficult or even impossible for an outside observer to assess the efficiency of a particular industry , its management and workforce. For example, in the case of the coal industry it is understood that numbers of the more modern pits are very profitable but numbers of the older ones are unprofitable, but they continue to be operated because in the short to medium term closures would cause heavy unemployment in small mining communities where there is no prospect of alternative employment. The losses on the uneconomic pits are recovered from the profits made on the modern ones but the facts in detail are not known to the general public. In the case of the railways, some years ago, under Dr Beeching, there were widespread closures of unprofitable branch lines. Many outside observers claim that because of political pressures at the time the closures were not allowed to go far enough and this is a reason why the railways have continued to experience financial problems. However, other observers have found that years later people whose rail services were cut continue to feel resentment and claim that the quality of life in the country areas concerned has been irreparably damaged. The debate about whether the railway network is now too small or too large continues, with experts supporting each view. In the event, following the rise in oil prices in 1973, and the increasing congestion and carnage on the roads, and the likelihood that real costs of road transport may rise very steeply over the next decades, many neutral observers who had formerly approved the moves towards railway track closures are now glad that they were restricted in past years. The fact that they were restricted in large part because of political pressures at the time is worthy of note and shows that pressures of this kind may lead to benefits in the long run even although this is not apparent at the time.

A feature of the present times is that members of the public, no matter what their political viewpoints, are no longer so respectful towards authority as they were a generation or more ago. People do not believe that the judgements of ministers and civil servants, individually or collectively, are infallible. It is now demanded that governments should make the facts available so that all who wish to do so can study these and thus bring about a widespread exchange of views before major decisions are taken. Hopefully the various options could then be identified and considered. The public have to live with, and pay for, the decisions taken by ministers and civil servants. Technically, major ones may be taken by Parliament, but when a goverment has a large enough majority it may merely 'rubber stamp' approval of a decision taken by a tiny number of people. In the USA there is now the 'Freedom of Information Act' which gives citizens the right to demand information, including access to confidential government files. In the UK the instinct of ministers and civil servants has been and still is – in the overwhelming majority of cases – to fight for secrecy. An example of the consequence of secretive decision making was the commercial production of the Concorde airliner. Whilst this may be technically a superb airliner there was never full and open discussion of what the taxpayer would ultimately have to pay if this too costly aircraft project were proceeded with. In the event, the real costs of the project were concealed since the research and development costs which should be recovered in due course in revenues have in this case been paid by the taxpayer and it is ironic that only rich people or those who travel on expense accounts can afford to fly in this airliner, whose production and operating costs have largely been paid by people who will never be able to travel in it. Again, in 1979 it became evident that the UK was paying a grossly excessive share of the EEC budget and effectively the main beneficiaries were much richer German and French taxpayers. The inescapable implication is that ministers and civil servants who negotiated on behalf of the UK were less capable than their German and French counterparts. Equally, if all the known facts had been properly made public at the time, informed members of the public might have alerted the official negotiators to matters which might have escaped them: even more effective, they might have alerted the media as well.

Why do governments support certain industries?

Examination questions of the professional as well as academic bodies call for a broad financial and commercial general knowledge, as well as technical knowledge of the subject. This general knowledge requires wide and up-to-date reading on a selective basis. An example of a topical question from the ACCA paper 'Industry and Finance' (now 'Financial Management') was: 'Discuss with examples the special characteristics of the so-called "high technology" industries (e.g. computers, aerospace, nuclear reactors) which cause governments to become heavily involved in their support and supervision in countries where such industries exist.'

Special characteristics of these industries in all cases include that effective involvement requires the commitment of large sums of money and highly educated, gifted, trained and skilled men and women to extended research and development programmes whose outcome is uncertain. In a particular country if industrialists in private-sector companies considered that the risks were too great in certain areas of activity then equity capital could not be raised on the scale needed and these areas would not be developed. Governments of industrialised countries appear generally to hold the view that in certain areas, no matter what views private-sector industrialists may hold – and their primary duty, after all, is to their company, rather than to the 'national interest', about which different views may be held – then the government must in some way intervene to ensure that the country maintains a presence in that area. Work is being done at the frontiers of knowledge in the high-technology industries and it is likely that major industries will arise within the next generation or so which become substantial employers and generators of wealth in home and overseas markets. If private-sector companies cannot or will not concern themselves with high-risk projects, work in these areas would be abandoned unless the government concerned interverned, and if ground is lost in a fast-changing technology it may become irrecoverable, and too late if private-sector industrialists suddenly decided to become more venturesome. (It is against this background that one may consider the support given by the UK government to INMOS.)

There is a further assumption that it is dangerous economically for one country to become totally dependent on imports from outside for certain advanced products. It could be 'held to ransom' in respect of prices and furthermore its own manufacturers might find that the most advanced machine tools, components, etc., were reserved for manufacturers in the producer country, with only the second best being available for export. It is also a characteristic of the newer, advanced products that they give rise to a greater 'value added'. This latter is an important concept which may be defined as the wealth a company creates by its own and its workpeople's efforts. It is useful supplementary information in assessing the performance of a company since a high sales revenue may be misleading if a large proportion of the items were 'bought in' as near-finished articles. In brief, successful new advanced-technology products tend to offer employment at high wages to skilled people and at the same time to be highly profitable to the company. Traditional, older declining industries tend to be much less profitable. Governments of industrialised countries also have regard to military and defence requirements and in this respect also decide that their country must maintain a certain independent presence in high-technology industries since these have actual or potential military and defence implications.

From the financial aspect, when a government has decided that its own industry must survive and develop in a high-technology, high-risk field, how does it ensure that the vital finance is made available? There will be several options and political attitudes will also be relevant. The USA is the world leader in the fields under review. The country is vast, wealthy, with abundant natural resources and a large population and so there are large and profitable internal markets which provide bases for aggressive development of overseas markets. These are exceptional natural advantages which arise in a favourable social and economic environment. There is general acceptance of the capitalist system, that profits are socially desirable and wealth creation has priority over wealth distribution. In principle, private-sector industry is preferred and nationalised industry is rare. In the USA, traditionally, vast public funds have been made available to private-sector companies through military and defence contracts, and these permit heavy research and development costs to be incurred and recovered. Major USA multinational companies which expanded, prospered and built up reserves in the years of heaviest military expenditure have developed worldwide markets. In practice if a 'take off' point is reached by a major company it should be able to continue to grow and prosper by serving civilian markets even if the military market declines.

In the UK the position has inevitably been different. The exceptional natural advantages in terms of resources which the USA enjoys, have been lacking, including the large and prosperous home market: social and political backgrounds and attitudes have also been different. The position may have some similarities in individual European countries and it is inconceivable that an individual European company, by itself, could challenge major USA market leaders such as Boeing and IBM. One of the advantages of the EEC, if present inequities can be overcome, would be that European governments and companies could cooperate in the formation of joint ventures in high-technology fields, on the principle that cooperatively pooled European resources should be a match for anything achievable elsewhere. The European Air Bus gives promise of being a commercially successful joint venture of this type, a high-technology commercial production which could not have been successfully produced and marketed as a venture in a single European country.

In the UK itself, with its mixed private- and public-sector economy, there has been and is the option of nationalising a private-sector company or industry, whether or not in a high-technology field, in the event that it cannot survive on any other basis, because it is unable to generate the capital it needs, or obtain capital from the market on tolerable terms. The rescue of Rolls Royce Ltd in 1970 came within this category. Some criticise this policy of rescuing 'lame ducks'. However, there seems to be a widespread, if not universal, acceptance of the idea that certain industries or companies should be enabled to survive and that it is in the short- and long-term national interest that the state should intervene to preserve skilled teams of managements and workpeople, and assets, threatened with dispersion through possibly temporary adverse market forces or a single major miscalculation made by a board of directors. Those who hold this view tend also to believe that if the state, directly or through one of its agencies, puts up equity capital, then is should have the appropriate degree of control – and its due share of profits if these are made in due course. In principle, the party which puts money at risk is entitled to an appropriate share in the supervision and control of venture. On the evidence available it would appear that the NEB is an effective and flexible agency in this respect, and one which should have a role under either a Labour or Conservative government. It would be expected to have a more active role under the former, with generous funding and encouragement to take initiatives, whereas under the latter its role would presumably be a more passive one. Under a Conservative government its role might be that of a provider of capital as last resort, in the event, for example, of a private-sector company in the high-technology field being in imminent danger of collapse and the government wishing to ensure its survival at least whilst all possible options were examined.

The Conservatives and nationalisation

The election in May 1979 of a radical Conservative government with a substantial majority and a clear mandate has set in motion forces which must cause profound changes in relation to nationalisation. It is evident that the philosophy of a majority of members of the government is that business-type organisations, such as the nationalised industries, operate more efficiently and profitably in a primarily private-sector environment than they do as state-owned industries. The clear intention is that the government sells public-sector assets to private individuals and financial institutions but the situation is obviously complex and varies considerably between industries. In many cases legislation would be needed before action could be taken and months would elapse before it could be passed: the size of the government's majority in 1979 is such that it could be confident of passing whatever legislation it chose in this field. Meanwhile, some nationalised companies and industries are unprofitable and private-sector investors would not be prepared to invest in them and in such cases the only options would be continued nationalisation or liquidation.

The word used in 1979 to describe the attitude of the government towards the nationalised industries is 'privatisation'. Sir Keith Joseph, Industry Secretary, commented, 'The whole purpose is to remove responsibility for decision making from Ministers, who are not equipped for the role, to shareholders and their managements. Ministers are specifically eschewing responsibility.' Mr John Nott, Secretary for Trade, said, 'At present, British Airways is in effect controlled by one or two ministers and the odd Treasury official. That is what public ownership often means. I want to give an opportunity for widespread real public ownership.' The situation may be viewed from many aspects: the following are extracts from a *Financial Times* article in July 1979:

Sales of publicly owned assets have an immediate importance to the government. They will make a major contribution to the reduction of the public sector borrowing requirement (PSBR) and to the crusade against the growth of public spending. The sales are an alternative to borrowing which the City finds more palatable for financial as well as political reasons, since it provides investors with equities...; calling public expenditure by another name and selling assets instead of borrowing has no real direct effect on the economy. Nevertheless, the advantages are not purely cosmetic. Using equities rather than fixed interest stock to finance government deficits can reduce the cost of servicing the national debt. Re-allocating industrial borrowing to the private sector can leave a government that is determined to keep public borrowing below a certain level for fear of crowding out private investment, with more headroom for increasing, or at least maintaining, expenditure on genuine public services. ... The end of Ministerial and Treasury surveillance over the running of state industries will have four revolutionary consequences for the financial management of these industries. Each of these of these factors is regarded as an argument in its own right for 'privatisation', though under past Labour Governments, the same arguments have been stood on their heads and used to justify nationalisation. First, management will now make all investment decisions without regard to government macroeconomic and industrial policies. There will be no arm-twisting of the type that British Airways has suffered over its decisions to buy American rather than European aircraft...second, the financial target set for each industry by the Treasury will be abolished. Instead the new companies will simply attempt to maximise profits. In practice this will make little difference to the managements of Airways and Aerospace because they have been hard put to meet the Treasury's financial targets. In effect the last Labour Government accepted that industries operating in competitive international markets, such as airlines and aerospace, should be told to maximise profits in most of their activities. Whereas the present government accepts the need to impose other objectives on monopolies, such as electricity, telecommunications and gas, attempts that have been made to use nationalised industries as instruments of anti-inflation and social policy have disillusioned even supporters of nationalisation.

Third, the new limited companies to be formed will have to borrow without government guarantees. Last year's Labour Government's White Paper on nationalised industries referred to the benefits from industries borrowing through the government on the keenest possible rates but the official view is now that capital markets should not be prejudiced in favour of nationalised industries, so borrowing at market rates is seen as another benefit of privatisation... Fourthly, and most important, the newly private industries will have to stand on their own feet in hard times... It is easy to forget as most of the nationalised industries become more prosperous, that most of them began life in the public sector as lame ducks. While Airways may rise to the challenge of public ownership now, a few years ago its profit record would have made a share sale almost unthinkable. Some aerospace companies like Rolls Royce and Lockheed have needed huge injections of government money in the recent past. Before nationalisation airframe manufacturers owed much of their success to non-economic government purchases of both military and civil aircraft. ....

The wisdom of the whole privatisation campaign depends crucially on the price which the government's assets fetch. The profits of British Gas and the government's capital gains on its BP shareholding will finance a significant part of this year's (1979) tax cuts and public spending programmes. They are a reminder of the financial benefits that can flow to taxpayers from the public assets that the government own, on their behalf. There is a danger that because the government regards 'privatisation' as primarily a political measure, it will overlook the interests of the taxpayers, who now own the assets it wants to sell.

It is evident that the intentions of the Conservative government towards nationalisation are deeply controversial and there is nothing necessarily wrong about that. However, a point of principle is surely that the government stands in the position of a trustee in relation to all the citizens of the country and it would be wrong if it sold publicly owned assets at 'cut price' or 'bargain basement' prices for the benefit of the relatively few wealthy individual or institutional investors who alone could afford to purchase them on a substantial scale. Yet, if the government did not offer assets which, for doctrinaire reasons, it was determined to sell, at prices which excited the greed of investors and speculators (who have shown themselves recently as being risk-averse) the issues concerned would prove total failures, which would be the last outcome the government would want. The misgiving must therefore remain that decisions may be taken for doctrinaire reasons and publicly owned assets may be sold at too low prices, to the benefit of the few but against the true interests of the vast majority of citizens, to whom the assets belong. A test will be how the government deals with the most valuable nationalised organisation of all, the British National Oil Company (BNOC). There is another question, amongst many – if, in later years one of these 'privatised' and former nationalised industries falls on bad times, what will happen? As was the case with Rolls Royce in 1970 it could be considered in the national interest that the company should be rescued by the state, but that would be against the whole principle which this government stands for – that if a company cannot survive in an environment in which decision making is governed by market forces, it must pay the price, which for failed private-sector companies is liquidation. At this stage it is not clear how many matters of important detail will develop. There is no doubt that there will be considerable public debate and it is already evident that numbers of Conservative supporters will focus attention on what they regard as matters of fundamental principle. It must be hoped that the actions finally taken will be demonstrably equitable in relation to the interests of the whole body of citizen of the UK.

Chapter 21

Finance for foreign trade

At some stage many companies find it worthwhile to sell their goods or services in overseas as well as home market. Thus, when a company has heavy fixed costs and excess capacity, contributions obtained from sales overseas will improve the profits. This is a reason why the charge of 'dumping' is often raised. It may be seen that despite the freight and other extra costs involved, some companies sell their products at lower prices overseas than they do at home. Sometimes a specially low price is charged at the start in order to gain acceptance in a new market, but a general guideline is that prices charged in any market should take into account 'what the market will bear' as well as elasticity of demand, amongst other matters.

Meanwhile, when a company plans to export for the first time, many non-financial matters must be considered and experts and specialists consulted at every stage. It is generally accepted that at the start dispersion of effort should be avoided and instead an attempt should be made to identify a potentially good market and concentrate first on establishing a foothold there. Success, and the experience gained, would then improve the prospects of successful extension into further new markets on a step-by-step basis. It is also said that a serious error of judgement on the part of some UK exporters is to seek to gain sales by undercutting prices of competitors. Price cutting never creates loyalty to the product and it is notable that experienced exporters put emphasis in their marketing on such matters as design, effectiveness, reliability, after-sales service, etc., and may even stress that their prices are on the high side, because of the special features they offer.

Differences between home and overseas markets

What are the essential differences between selling in the home and selling in overseas markets? Brief answers are that if certain selling channels are chosen, e.g. a foreign buying house in the UK, or a confirming house, or an export merchant, there is virtually no difference but if an exporter deals directly with buyers overseas then considerable new risks arise even when the overseas buyer is in the minority category of being of the utmost integrity. Firstly, when a currency other than sterling is used there will be a risk of exchange rate changes. There may be problems of exchange control. There may be differences of language as well as laws and trading customs and import and export licenses may be needed. National and local regulations overseas must be known and strictly adhered to. Even a seemingly trivial mistake in the preparation of an invoice can lead to delays through refusal of overseas customs authorities to process the documents, then penal rents and finally a heavy loss on the transaction. However, provided that full use is made of the various highly specialised services available, for which appropriate charges have to be paid, and which must be recovered in the selling prices, the special risks can be transferred to those who are qualified and prepared to bear them.

Questions to answer before exporting

Barclays Bank International suggests in *An Introduction to Exporting* that before attempting to sell in an overseas market a propective exporter should answer these ten question:

1. What is the demand, or potential demand, for my product, bearing in mind local tastes, traditions and even climatic conditions?
2. Who are my competitors, especially those selling under well established brand names?
3. What will be the most effective – or even acceptable – method of presentation in design and packaging?
4. What language is to be used in brochures, packaging, sales and service literature and in correspondence with potential buyers?
5. What is the advisibility of advertising, which media should be used and what will be the cost?
6. What are the means and costs of distribution?
7. Are the products priced competitively in relation to their rivals and to local market conditions?
8. What are the standing and creditworthiness of overseas buyers and or agents?

9. What is the degree of local stability and commercial efficiency and what is the state of the national economy?
10. What is the extent of import restrictions, tariffs and exchange controls?

Government – and other – support for exporters

The UK government, like those of other industrialised countries, seeks to encourage exports and accordingly a great deal of information and help is available from official and other sources. Examples include: the British Overseas Trade Board (BOTB); the Department of Trade; the Export Credit Guarantee Department (ECGD); the Confederation of British Industry (CBI); the London and other Chambers of Commerce; commercial sections of British Embassies and High Commissions overseas; the clearing as well as other specialist banks and institutions. Often when a prospective exporter has conducted his research and enquiries in the UK it will be desirable that he follows these up with a carefully prepared visit to his intended markets. The costs of such visits are quite high.

Exporting: distribution channels available

Whatever criticisms may be made of UK manufacturing industries, its retail and distribution systems are regarded as amongst the world's best. The effect of this, unfortunately, is to facilitate the work of overseas exporters into the UK whereas the work of the UK exporter, who has to make use of less highly developed retail and distribution systems overseas, is more difficult. Meanwhile, a major company may choose the expensive option of establishing a subsidiary company overseas, normally with at least one influential local director. Alternatively, a joint venture might be entered into with an established local company. The options available to smaller exporters may include: (a) A buying agency in the UK. Some US, Canadian and European department stores, *inter alia*, operate their buying agency in the UK. An exporter who makes sales through this channel is effectively selling in the UK and payment would be in sterling. (b) Confirming houses. These act as buying agents for overseas buyers. A UK exporter would deal directly with the confirming house, which would normally pay in sterling and might also attend to the documentation and shipping. (c) Export merchants. These act as 'middlemen', buying on their own account to sell in overseas markets in which they specialise, and normally paying in sterling and attending to the shipping arrangements. (*d*) Overseas importing houses. These may place orders with UK exporters who would be responsible for the shipping arrangements. The currency and mode of payment would be subject to agreement.

From the viewpoint of the exporter the advantages of the foregoing channels are convenience, simplicity and reduction of risk. However, a major drawback is that the exporter has no control over the marketing and if the party buying from him suddenly ceased to do so, the exporter would be cut off from that overseas market. Accordingly, an exporter who wishes to maintain some control over the marketing of his product overseas will normally appoint an agent in the country concerned if he is unable to set up his own organisation there. Choice of a good agent is a decisive matter. Competence, integrity, drive, creativity, reputation, adequate resources, commitment to developing the sales of the product, will be essential qualities. The scope of the authority granted to an agent and the terms would be matters for agreement. Expert advice would be needed.

Exchange control: export–import regulations

An exporter may establish his own export section or he may employ the services of a specialist shipping and forwarding agent, who will be expert in such matters as packing for export and the complex shipping and customs documentation. Certain goods require an export licence before they can be shipped from the UK (e.g. works of art): much more frequently an import licence is required by an overseas country, especially developing countries which are short of foreign exchange. Sometimes the shortage is so severe that not even essential imports can be paid for in transferable currency. A government of an overseas country previously free from restrictions may suddenly impose these. An exporter can cover himself against political and non-commercial risks by insuring through the ECGD.

Terms of contract and main documents

The terms and conditions of the contract must be agreed in advance between the parties. Exports from the UK are normally shipped on a CIF basis (cost; insurance; freight). In this case the exporter or forwarding agent makes the shipping arrangements, pays the freight and marine insurance and is responsible for the goods until they are discharged at the port, or airport, named in the contract: the agreed selling price includes these costs. The essential documents would be: (i) the invoice; (ii) the insurance policy or certificate; (iii) a full set of bills of lading marked 'freight paid' in the case of goods sent by sea, or an air consignment note when they are sent by air; (iv) in most cases, a bill of exchange; (v) occasionally, a certificate of origin. Sometimes additional documents may be required e.g. a certificate of health, import licence, consular invoice, etc. The documents must always be strictly in the correct form, which can not be considered here. Goods imported into the UK are often on an FOB (free on board) basis. In this case it is the importer who is reponsible for making the shipping arrangements and paying the freight and insurance.

Methods of payment

This aspect of exporting is obviously of special importance to a financial manager. The agreement between the buyer and exporter must be clear as to the payment arrangements, which should either be in sterling or a foreign currency which is freely convertible into sterling. (A 'blocked', non-transferable currency should be avoided.) A number of options are available. The main ones are listed below.

Open account

Just as in the case of the home trade there may be approved credit customers, a similar arrangement may be made between an exporter and an overseas buyer of unimpeachable status and integrity. The exporter will consign goods and send documents directly to the buyer. Each party will maintain a current account in the name of the other and the buyer will make payments direct to the exporter, or his bank, on the basis agreed. Payment would normally be by banker's draft – the buyer's own bank issuing a draft on a UK bank in favour of the exporter, or the buyer's bank would make a telex or telegraphic (or, less usually, airmail) transfer to the exporter's bank for the credit of his account. An open account arrangement is only practicable when the exporter has the utmost trust in the buyer.

Goods on consignment

This is common when goods are sent to an agent who undertakes to sell them as best he can, but until sold they remain the property of the exporter. Leading UK banks, with branches or correspondents overseas, will arrange for goods to be stored and insured in the name of the bank, which releases them to the agent in limited quantities and against satisfactory arrangements for payment by the agent to the bank after completion of a sale. This arrangement ties up working capital, involves insurance, storage and heavy bank charges and risk of loss of marketability of the stock and risk of loss if the agent defaults.

Bills and documents for collection
When the export is to an unknown or uncertain buyer, but one who nevertheless has satisfactory references, there are procedures available which provide protection for the exporter insofar as the overseas buyer must pay for the goods before he takes delivery. When the arrangements are for payment against delivery documents, the exporter ships goods addressed to the buyer overseas but consigned to 'order' and the custodian at the destination port will not permit delivery to the addressee, or any other party, until he has produced documentary evidence that they have been 'released' to him by a properly authorised party acting, in effect, as agent for the exporter. In practice the essential part of the procedure is that instead of airmailing the essential documents directly to the buyer, the exporter delivers these to his UK bank, which airmails them to its own or its correspondent branch nearest the address of the importer. The importer (buyer) will only be able to obtain the documents of title to the goods by making payment against the bill of exchange which accompanies the documents if the arrangements are 'documents against payment' (d/p).

A bill of exchange (p. 187) continues to have an important role in the financing of trade. In the event that the buyer has good credit standing, the arrangements may be 'documents against acceptance' (d/a). In this case the documents of title would be handed over to the importer by the local bank as soon as he had formally endorsed his acceptance on the face of the bill. The bill would indicate the due date for payment, e.g. 60 or 90 days 'after sight', or 'after date' or 'after acceptance', the intention being that the goods are released to the importer, who is a creditworthy person, so that he can sell them and, with the proceeds of sale, make the payment due on the bill of exchange.

In practice, exporting under these arrangements may work satisfactorily when the buyers are reasonably reliable. They also work well on a rising market for the goods concerned as the overseas buyer will be anxious to take delivery quickly in order to make a quick and profitable sale. However, if the market price is falling an unreliable buyer may wish to avoid taking delivery of the goods and he would ignore the advice of the bank and not collect his documents. The goods would arrive, would be left unclaimed at the docks, incurring penal rents, which after a month or so might exceed the value of the goods. In theory they might be shipped back to the home port of the exporter, who would have to pay all expenses, including the penal rents, return freight and other charges. In such circumstances exporters often abandon the goods which are then sold by auction by the overseas authorities, often at derisory prices.

Documentary credits
The surest way for an exporter to obtain payment is to insist that the overseas buyer opens an irrevocable and confirmed credit. A feature of this is that when an agreement has been reached none of its terms can be altered except with the agreement of the exporter as well as the buyer, and an overseas and a UK bank also bind themselves to the agreement. The procedure is that the overseas buyer must arrange with his bank that it irrevocably instructs a UK bank to pay a specified sum to the UK exporter provided that the exporter presents to the bank documents which conform in every detail, to the letter, to the instructions and descriptions contained in the documentary credit. If only the overseas bank binds itself, this is an 'irrevocable credit'. The additional feature of an 'irrevocable and confirmed credit' is that a leading UK bank becomes a party to the agreement and warrants to the exporter that the letter of credit will be honoured irrespective of what might happen to either the buyer or the bank overseas, provided that the exporter produces to his bank documents which comply to the letter with the conditions set out in the documentary credit. Naturally, the costs are comparatively high and must in the end be paid by the importer who may therefore seek to obtain agreement to a less costly alternative. Reference may be seen to 'revocable letters of credit'. The feature of these is that an overseas buyer may unilaterally insist upon a change in the terms and because of this they are seldom acceptable to exporters.

Factors

The role of factors in the home trade has been considered (Ch. 10). Factors also offer their services in respect of exports to many countries overseas. They are selective and prefer clients whose business has reached a certain level and gives evidence of expansion. They are naturally also careful as to the buyers overseas to whom they will grant credit. The principles of operation are similar for both UK and overseas services and a company which employed a factor for its UK trade might find it equally worthwhile to use one for its export trade, especially as the factor would have contacts, local knowledge and experience, and would relieve the exporter of many problems, leaving him to concentrate on making sales. Sometimes the same factor will handle the UK and overseas operations.

Methods of finance

Apart from ensuring that payment is duly received, an exporter may also need finance at earlier stages and up to the moment payment is received. In fact, in common with the governments of other industrialised countries, the UK government gives financial support to exporters in a number of ways, which may include making funds available at below full commercial rates of interest. When credit squeezes occur it is an invariable rule that the clearing banks are instructed to give priority to requests for overdrafts and or loans from exporters. Meanwhile, an exporter who has shipped goods overseas against documents for collection receives the cash, less charges, quite soon after the overseas banker has been put in funds by the buyer. Exporters who wish to have an advance of funds in the meantime can normally obtain an advance or overdraft for an agreed proportion of the bills for collection. The bank would have the bills as security and with recourse against the exporter if the buyer ultimately defaulted.

The Export Credit Guarantee Department (ECGD)

The ECGD is a government department, formed in 1919, and since 1930 it has offered credit insurance schemes to UK exporters. It operates on a non-profit-making basis aiming to balance incomes and payments over the years on normal insurance principles. It recently claimed over 11,000 policy holders and to cover one-third of UK exports. Other governments offer their own exporters schemes similar to those of ECGD, which assists exporters in two main ways: (1) it insures them against the risks of non payment, either through default by the overseas buyer, or from economic or political causes in the buyer's country which prevent transfer of currency, or resulting in the cancellation of an import licence; (2) it provides unconditional guarantees of repayment to the banks and enables finance to be provided at preferential rates (except in the case of certain contracts with EEC countries) The ECGD does not cover risks normally covered by commercial insurers, such as fire and marine risks. Premiums depend on the market concerned, the type of policy and, to some extent, also on the exporter as premiums will be increased if the claims experience is unfavourable. The ECGD restricts the cover available to about 90% of the CIF price, on the principle that if exporters are called upon to bear a small part of the risks themselves they will be likely to act prudently. In principle, the ECGD would expect an exporter to insure all his shipments to a particular country, and not only the riskier ones. However, in appropriate cases the ECGD would offer cover in respect of a single shipment. If a particular country showed itself to be a bad risk, the ECGD would discontinue offering cover for future shipments to it.

The ECGD offers a wide range of policies to exporters. A main basic one is the Comprehensive Short Term Guarantee, covering trade of a continuing nature, with regular buyers and where the spread of risks is wide, and the exporter undertakes to cover either the whole of his export business for not less than twelve months, or all his business in an agreed range of good and bad markets for all types of risk. Cover is provided in respect of credit terms of up to six months. The ECGD is not informed of individual transactions unless delays in payments or events likely to cause a loss arise. The exporter must keep his outstandings on each buyer within the agreed credit limit, or advise the ECGD if he wishes to increase the limit, or give credit to a new buyer. For holders of the basic policy additional, optional cover is also available – the Supplemental (Extended Terms) Guarantee. This covers goods sold on credit terms exceeding six months but not normally exceeding five years. Each contract must be approved in writing.

Full details of the up-to-date ECGD policies are available direct from the ECGD and the major as well as specialist banks publish detailed booklets on services for exporters, including the currency aspects. The following is a brief outline of the types of contract for which ECGD cover is available: Suppliers' contracts; specific policies – to cover large, single capital items; sales of aircraft and aero-engines; of ships; leasing contracts; capital goods with deferred payments in sterling or other currency; cover in respect of cost escalation; cover in respect of invisible exports, e.g. giving professional services, as by consulting engineers; performing technical services; royalties on patented inventions or books or copyright fees – either on a comprehensive basis for recurring business or on a specific basis for an isolated large transaction.

ECGD guarantees to banks

The facilities made available to exporters by the ECGD in respect of guarantees to banks represent financial support of great value and at a preferential cost which could not be matched by commercial organisations. In respect of short-term export contracts, ECGD offer: (1) Comprehensive Bankers Guarantee (Bills or Notes); and (2) Comprehensive Bankers Guarantee (Open Account). The goods covered need not be of any particular kind. Under the Bills or Notes scheme credit payments due under the contract must be secured either by promissory notes made by the buyer or by bills of exchange drawn on and accepted by the buyer, and bills must be drawn for sight payments. The length of credit must not exceed two years from the date of shipment of the goods. Under the Open Account scheme, negotiable instruments are not required from the buyer. The length of credit must be stated in the invoice and may range from cash against documents overseas, to six months from receipt of the goods overseas, subject to a maximum shipping time of one month. Under both schemes finance is currently provided by the banks at 5/8% over Base Rate.

The exporter must be the holder of an ECGD Comprehensive Guarantee and must enter into a Recourse Agreement with ECGD since the cover provided by the Bankers' Guarantee (see below) is unconditional and for a higher proportion of the various risks than that provided by the exporter's ECGD policy. For example, where the buyer fails to pay because of insolvency the difference is usually 10% – the margin between the 100% cover under the Bankers' Guarantee and the 90% cover under the exporter's policy, but if non-payment were attributable to the exporter – as when the goods were faulty – the ECGD would take recourse for the whole amount, and must therefore make an assessment of the exporter's standing before issuing a Bankers' Guarantee. A premium is charged by the ECGD based upon the revolving limit for finance and this is payable in advance by the exporter.

Bankers' Guarantees

Under both schemes ECGD issues a Comprehensive Bankers' Guarantee to to the bank, guaranteeing the sums made available and the interest thereon, from the date of the advance or purchase to the date of repayment. The procedures include that an exporter makes a formal application through his bank, accompanied by up-to-date accounts, to the ECGD for one or both of the foregoing guarantees. The bank countersigns this and forwards it to the ECGD with its own confidential report on the exporter, so that the ECGD can assess the recourse risk.

Finance for foreign trade

If the ECGD is then willing to issue the Bankers' Guarantee, the bank will issue its own facility letter, which is in standard form, to the exporter, setting out the terms and conditions under which finance will be made available to the exporter. Whilst in most cases only sterling bills or notes will be covered under the Bills or Notes scheme cover may also be obtained in respect of other specified currencies.

Medium-term guarantees (supplier credit)
Competition often compels a UK exporter to include the option of credit terms and in respect of capital goods a credit period of two to five years is common. The simplest and cheapest method for an exporter to finance such contracts is by arranging a medium-term supplier credit bank facility against an ECGD Bank Guarantee. The exporter must first obtain approval for credit insurance cover from the ECGD either under a Supplemental (Extended Terms) Guarantee or under a Specific Guarantee. At the same time the ECGD must be informed that a Specific Bank Guarantee will be required, unless a Comprehensive Extended Terms Bankers' Guarantee has already been issued. The exporter should also ask his bank to provide finance for the contract subject to the eventual issue of the ECGD Bank Guarantee. Assuming that the ECGD approvals are obtained and the sale contract signed, the bank will issue a facility letter to the exporter. Interest will be charged to the exporter at a fixed rate for the whole facility. It is determined by the UK authorities and is currently $7\frac{1}{4}$ or $7\frac{3}{4}\%$ depending on the buyer's country. These highly preferential rates do not apply for buyers in EEC countries. The bank will also charge fees for providing the finance and an additional premium is payable by the exporter to the ECGD in respect of the Bank Guarantee.

When the exporter negotiates the sale contract with the buyer he must ensure that the credit instalments are secured by valid bills of exchange or promissory notes. These bills or notes will be purchased by the bank without recourse after shipment has taken place. If the bills or notes have not been signed by the buyer when goods are shipped the bank can advance under the facility with recourse to the exporter until valid bills or notes are available. Contracts involving payment in certain foreign currencies can be financed under each of the foregoing Bank Guarantee facilities. In view of the exchange risks involved it is essential to obtain advice from a bank at the earliest possible stage when foreign-currency invoicing is used. Such matters as the suitability of the particular currency, arrangements for forward sale and additional ECGD cover can then be discussed.

Buyer credit guarantees

When large projects are considered it is possible that an ECGD-supported financing facility may be made available direct to a foreign buyer at a preferential fixed interest rate. ECGD buyer credit guarantees are limited to contracts with a UK element of £1 m. or more. In many cases the ECGD will insist on finance being in an acceptable foreign currency – usually US dollars or Deutsch marks – although sterling finance can be considered where contract values are less than £5 m. or where there are special circumstances. To cover such a loan the ECGD would give the bank a full and unconditional guarantee upon payment of a premium by the supplier. While the buyer has the advantage of long-term credit the UK supplier is virtually in the position of having a cash contract, subject to the ECGD's recourse in the event of non-performance of his contract. Furthermore, subject to agreement between buyer and supplier, progress payments can be made from the loan. Normally the buyer monitors such drawings by either sending a representative to the supplier's place of manufacture or by appointing consultants to certify that the work for which payment is claimed has been satisfactorily carried out.

Lines of credit

Lines of credit may be established for general financing of capital goods, for the requirements of a specific industry or for a project where the buyer does not need the services of a main contractor. In general, in the case of a buyer's credit, at the time of underwriting the project the ECGD will specify such security requirements as it considers necessary from the overseas borrower. It will often ask for a guarantee from an overseas bank or from a borrower's parent company(ies). The growing elaboration of international projects has meant that lenders in different markets and their respective credit insurers are moving closer together in coordinating financing, and recently there have been loans where a UK and a non-UK lender have joined in the same loan agreement, coordinating their lending terms, holding security under a common security, under a common agency arrangement and being paid on a *pari passu* basis through a trust account.

Bond support

A feature of substantial contracts can be that an exporter will be required to provide the buyer with a guarantee which covers the buyer against non-performance by the exporter in one way and another. In acceptable circumstances the ECGD is prepared to provide indemnities to banks and surety companies to enable them to issue Tender Bonds,

Performance Bonds and Advance Payment Bonds in sterling or currency for certain classes of exports. This additional security may enable a bank or surety company to issue bonds which might not otherwise have been available. The banks are usually involved in providing the 'on demand' type of bond, where the beneficiary can 'call' the bond without having to prove that the exporter has failed to comply with the terms of the contract.

Eligibility, cost and mechanisms
The following conditions must be satisfied before contracts will qualify for ECGD bond support: (1) the contract must be insured with the ECGD against normal credit risks; (2) the contract must have a value of £½ m. or more; (3) the contract payment terms must be on a cash or near-cash basis; (4) where the bond is of the 'on demand' type the beneficiary must be in the public sector. In respect of cost, in addition to paying the ECGD premium for the issue of the indemnity to the bank, the exporter will be required to meet the bank charge which, in view of the security held, will normally be reduced from the standard fee for issuing bonds. If the bond is issued by a local overseas bank the charges incurred by a correspondent bank will also be for the account of the exporter. The approach for this type of support should be made through the exporter's bank and ECGD approval must be obtained before any commitment is entered into. The ECGD will require the exporter to enter into a Recourse Agreement under which ECGD can make an immediate claim on the exporter for any amount paid over by the ECGD in terms of the unconditional indemnity to the bank. Provided that the exporter satisfies the ECGD that he is not in default or that any failure to perform the contract is due to causes over which he has no control, then the ECGD will consider waiving its recourse to the exporter.

Pre-shipment finance
In case where the exporter is unable to obtain sufficient monies from normal borrowing sources to enable his to finance a large overseas contract during the manufacturing periods, the ECGD is prepared, in certain circumstances, to issue a Pre-shipment Finance Guarantee to the exporter's bank. This will enable the bank to make good any deficit during the pre-shipment period in the exporter's cash flow projection for that particular contract. The main conditions to be satisfied before an exporter would be eligible are: (1) the goods must be of capital or project type. Production goods do not qualify for this type of finance; (2) the contract must be insured with the ECGD against normal credit

risks; (3) the exporter must satisfy the ECGD as to his ability to fulfil the contract; (4) the contract must have a value of £1 m. or more; (5) the exporter must demonstrate that he is unable to obtain finance through normal channels; (6) repayment must normally be made on or before the date on which the goods leave the country. The finance is made available with full recourse to the exporter. The present interest rate is 1% over Base Rate and after meeting the additional bank charges and ECGD premiums the total cost may be higher than the cost of the exporter's normal overdraft borrowing.

Foreign exchange

If the overseas buyer pays in sterling the UK exporter does not bear any exchange risk. However, an exporter may quote his prices in the currency of the buyer, or even another currency. He may do this because of competition or because he considers that the buyer's currency is stronger than sterling. A UK exporter who makes a contract in a currency other than sterling introduces a new types of risk – the exchange risk. He may decide to bear this risk himself and in that case if a currency movement went in his favour he would make his normal trading profit plus a 'windfall' profit on the currency movements. However, if he miscalculated his normal trading profit could be more than wiped out by his currency loss. Many exporters understandably take the viewpoint that their own skill and experience is in trading and accordingly they seek, as far as they can, to avoid the unfamiliar area of currency speculation.

This can largely be done in practice by the exporter entering into a forward foreign exchange contract with his bank, whereby each party agrees to deliver at a specified future time an agreed sum in one currency in return for an agreed sum in another currency. In other words, the rate of exchange to be applied when the trading transaction is paid for in the future ceases to be an uncertain one for the exporter, but becomes a fixed one by means of the exporter's contract with the bank. No cash is exchanged at the time of this contract but both parties commit themselves to a sterling–currency exchange on the maturity date at a rate agreed now. By entering into a forward foreign exchange contract a UK exporter (or importer) can: (*a*) fix at the time of the contract a price for the purchase or sale of a fixed amount of foreign currency at a specified future time (or within an agreed future period); (*b*) eliminate his exchange risk to future foreign exchange rate fluctuations; (*c*) calculate the exact sterling value of an international commercial contract although payment is to be made in the future in a foreign currency.

For it to meet its obligations to a customer, a bank enters into a market commitment to cover its own exchange risk at the time the forward contract is arranged. If, for any reason, the customer fails to meet his contractual obligations on maturity the bank has to buy or sell the foreign currency at the then spot rate to meet its market commitment. This involves a foreign exchange risk on the part of the bank and consequently it allocates limits for customers for forward exchange in the same way as with other banking facilities. In some cases the bank may require a cash deposit as security at the time the contract is taken out. The technical aspects of foreign exchange dealings are, of course, complex and fast changing. At times of currency instability, for example, if a bank offers a contract at a certain rate of exchange the offer may remain open for seconds only. Exchange control regulations may also be applicable.

Some other possible options for exporters

It has been explained that often a major company forms a subsidiary in another country when it assesses that there will be a large and expanding market for its products in that other country (and probably also in its neighbours). Developing countries, in particular, may restrict or prohibit imports, to conserve foreign exchange, but grant inducements, tax holidays, etc., to attract foreign manufacturers to build a factory in their country, so that it uses local materials, adds value to them, creates employement and export opportunities, etc. In other cases a company may enter into licensing agreements, or it may form a joint venture with a local company. There is also a two-way movement of major companies so that, for example, numbers of large UK companies take over US - based companies and vice versa. There are even relatively small numbers of highly gifted multilingual individuals, with a trading flair who have a flair for establishing high-level contacts and make fortunes by arranging large barter deals, often on a government-to-government basis, or government-to-company basis. This occurs especially when one of the countries involved operates strict currency and import and export controls so that normal international trading relationships are impossible. Meanwhile, a company considering forming a subsidiary in another country would consider carefully the special risks likely to be involved, unfamiliarity with the country concerned, risk of changes in taxes and regulations and, not least, the chance at some stage of expropriation on unfavourable terms if, in the future, a hostile government came into power. In principle, a company would prudently only commit a relatively small proportion of its total resources to setting up a subsidiary in another country, and an even smaller proportion if the country concerned appeared to show signs of political instability, or of developing into a hostile environment for some other reason.

Questions

1. Discuss the methods which might be adopted by a company with overseas subsidiaries in order to reduce its exposure to exchange risks. (ICSA   22 marks)
2. What are the major problems and risks associated with export finance and what facilities have been provided to alleviate or reduce them by (a) the government, (b) the financial institutions? (ACCA   20 marks)
3. Just as business has become more and more international, so has financial management. Discuss the role of financial management in an international setting with particular reference to: (a) currency exchange risks; (b) sources of finance; (c) investing in overseas countries. (ACCA   15 marks)
4. Discuss the main factors to be taken into account in the financing and control of a project set up in a developing country by a multinational company. (ICSA   22 mark)
5. What problems would a company face when exporting to buyers in an overseas country which has a floating exchange rate? Suggest ways in which these problems could be reduced.   (ACCA   20 marks)
6. Descibe the main documents that are likely to be presented to a bank with a draft drawn under a documentary credit. What details in them would be given particular attention by a bank and why? (ACCA   20 marks)
7. Consider ways in which banks may help traders in different countries to trade with each other.   (ACCA   20 marks)
8. Describe the main types of ECGD policies available to UK exporters and comment on the risks covered by them. (ACCA   20 marks)
9. Your company is considering the possibility of direct selling into export markets. Discuss the methods by which the risks of non-payment or delayed payment by customers may be minimised. (ICA   15 marks)
10. Your company has the opportunity of making a very large sale of goods to a customer in an overseas country. Due to a shortage of ex-

change, payment would have to be made in the currency of that country.
(a) Under what circumstances do you as financial director consider this business should be accepted?
(b) What would your recommendations or actions be to assist the implementation of your decision? (ICA 20 marks).

Acknowledgements are made to ECGD, Williams and Glyns Bank, Midland Bank International and Barclays Bank International whose publications have been drawn upon for material in this chapter.

Chapter 22

Financial institutions

A student, or anyone with financial responsibilities, needs to have an awareness of the financial environment and the many different institutions which provide the main framework. The factual background is summarised in the current edition of an annual publication: *Britain 1980: an Official Handbook* (HMSO). This short chapter aims to identify leading institutions, or groups of them, and to state briefly some of their main functions and makes use of material published in *Britain 1980*, and acknowledgement is made with thanks of permission to quote from this. However, the subject is a large one and the Further Reading list gives the titles of a small number of books which treat it fully. Outstanding amongst these is the full *Wilson Committee Report* (Cmnd 7939, June 1980, HMSO). The background to this report included that virtually all the leading institutions submitted written and oral material to the Committee, which considered and analysed this, and representatives of various institutions were also interviewed and questioned. The Report, and its Appendices, include descriptions of particular institutions and discussions of their roles, how they have evolved and how they may be developing, together with statistics and factual data. The Report makes a penetrating analysis of the whole financial environment: in the event, its findings in respect of the existing financial institutions and markets proved significantly more favourable and sympathetic than many had expected when the Committee was first formed.

The banking system

The British banking system comprises a central bank; deposit banks which perform the usual main banking services; the British offices of domestic and overseas banks whose main business is in other countries; merchant banks and other specialised institutions.

The central bank: the Bank of England

The Bank of England was established in 1694 by Act of Parliament and Royal Charter as a corporate body; the entire capital stock was acquired by the government under the Bank of England Act, 1946. As the central bank the Bank acts as banker to the government, to overseas central banks and to deposit banks and is the lender of last resort to the banking system; it is the note-issuing authority and the registrar for some 200 government, nationalised industry, local authority, public board and Commonwealth government stocks. As agent for the government, the Bank administers exchange control (when applicable: there is no control at present). On behalf of the Treasury it manages the Exchange Equalisation Account (EEA), which holds Britain's official reserves of gold, foreign exchange and Special Drawing (SDRs) on the International Monetary Fund (IMF). Using the resources of the EEA, the Bank may intervene in the foreign exchange market both to prevent undue fluctuations in the exchange value of sterling and to conserve the means of making payment abroad.

As banker to the government, the Bank examines and seeks to anticipate banking and financial problems and undertakes the appropriate operations in the money, capital and foreign exchange markets; consequently it has a major responsibility for advising the government on the formulation of monetary policy and its subsequent execution. It is also the main channel of communication between the deposit banks and other financial institutions of the City of London on the one hand and the government on the other.

The Bank's implementation of monetary policy is carried out primarily through control over interest rates and through direct controls over the banking system. It administers directly the official discount rate, known as Minimum Lending Rate (MLR), which is the rate at which the Bank will normally provide funds to the discount market as lender of last resort. The Minimum Lending Rate in turn can be expected to have an influence on other short-term interest rates. In addition, the authorities can influence interest rates through their daily operations in the money market and the terms on which they offer gilt-edged stock.

The Bank's direct controls over the banking system include the setting of a 12.5% minimum ratio of specified reserve assets to total eligible liabilities (broadly, sterling deposits drawn from outside the banking system with an original maturity of two years or less plus the banks' net foreign currency liability). Second, the Bank can call for special deposits as a percentage of total eligible liabilities, which generally bear interest at the Treasury bill rate but which do not count as reserve assets and which therefore contract the banks' ability to lend. In addition, a supplementary special deposits scheme can be operated; this requires a bank to place non-interest-bearing supplementary special deposits with the Bank of England for every percentage growth in the interest-bearing element of its eligible liabilities beyond a certain specified rate over a defined period. The Bank of England has also issued qualitative guidance on the direction of bank lending; this provides for priority to be given to the finance required by manufacturing industry, for the expansion of exports and for import saving.

Under the Banking Act, 1979, all deposit-taking businesses which are not specifically excluded require authorisation from the Bank of England and are subject to its continuing supervision. Authorisation may take the form either of recognition as a bank or of a licence to take deposits. The Act also set up a deposit protection scheme to protect the funds of depositors.

The Bank of England has the sole right in England and Wales of issuing bank notes. The note issue is fiduciary, that is to say, it is no longer backed by gold but by government and other securities. The Scottish and Northern Ireland banks have limited rights to issue notes. The provision of coin for circulation is the responsibility of the Royal Mint, a government department.

The deposit banks

The primary business of the deposit banks is the receipt, transfer and encashment of deposits. The principal deposit banks are the six London clearing banks, three Scottish clearing banks and two Northern Ireland banks. Mergers have resulted in the formation of six banking groups, four based in London and two in Scotland. The two Northern Ireland banks are owned by London clearing banks, but two groups of banks based in the Irish Republic also operate in Northern Ireland. In mid-1979 sterling 'sight' and 'time' deposits with these banks from non-bank customers in the British public and private sectors accounted for 74% of the total of such deposits with all banks in Britain, that is including the accepting houses, overseas banks, consortium banks and other British banks. Sight accounts are repayable on demand (current accounts) and no interest is generally paid on them, but on time deposits interest is paid (at a rate below individual banks' base rates). The deposit banks provide full bank services throughout Britain and operate some 14,000 branches. Several of them have interests in British overseas and Commonwealth banks, and in other banks (e.g. consortium banks) which have been formed specially to compete in international markets. They have also acquired substantial interests in hire-purchase finance houses, and some have set up their own unit trusts and merchant banks.

The deposit banks' reserve assets consist of balances at the Bank of England, money at call (mainly loans to discount houses), their holdings of Treasury and some other bills and short-dated British government securities. The banks also hold a proportion of their assets as portfolio (mainly longer-dated British government securities) or trade investments. The banks' profits are largely earned through their advances to customers partly in the form of overdrafts and partly in the form of loans (with or without collateral security). In mid-1979 sterling advances by the London clearing banks amounted to 67% of their sterling deposits. Membership of the London Bankers' Clearing House, which deals with the clearing of cheques and drafts, consists of the Bank of England, and the London clearing banks, together with the Co-operative Bank and the Central Trustee Savings Bank, which became members in 1975.

The bank giro, a credit transfer scheme, and the direct debiting by which a creditor with the prior approval of the debtor may claim money due to him direct from the latter's banking account, have helped to improve the money transmission services. An increasing number of banks have automatic cash-dispensing machines and many are also introducing more automated banking facilities. Credit cards are in widespread use for the settlement of accounts in retail shops and cheque cards enable the card holder to cash a cheque up to a specified credit limit at any office of the major British and Irish banks and at offices of many banks overseas.

National Girobank

The Post Office National Girobank (known as National Giro until 1978) which was introduced in 1968 to provide a low-cost current-account banking and money transfer service, is operated through most post offices in Britain. All accounts and transactions are maintained by means of a computer complex near Liverpool. In addition to its services to individuals, Girobank's services to commerce, industry and the public utilities include a facility whereby organisations with dispersed branches, depots and representatives can rapidly channel receipts into their central account. Some 160 local authorities as well as voluntary housing associations use Girobank's rent collection services. Girobank's international services also provide money transfer facilities in Europe, linking over 19 million account holders in the European Community and other countries in Western Europe. The range of banking services provided by Girobank has been widened progressively to include personal loans, a cheque guarantee card, limited overdrawing for personal customers and overdrafts for corporate customers, deposit accounts, budget accounts, bridging loans, travellers' cheques and foreign currency, *bureaux de change* and the facility to draw cash at 75,000 post offices in Europe.

Overseas banks

Altogether 395 overseas banks and financial institutions were represented in London in 1978, through branches, subsidiaries, representative offices and consortia. There were 308 banks directly represented in London, while 87 banks and financial institutions were represented through a stake in one or more of the 31 joint-venture banks operating in London. They provide a comprehensive banking service in many parts of the world and engage in the financing of trade not only between Britain and other countries but also between third countries.

The merchant banks

The merchant banks have an influence on Britain's financial affairs which is much greater than their size in relation to other financial institutions might suggest. Traditionally they have been primarily concerned with acceptance credits (p. 187) and with the sponsoring of capital issues on behalf of their customers. Today they have a widely diversified and complex range of activites with an important role in international finance and the short-term capital markets, the provision of expert advice and financial services to British industrial companies, especially where mergers, takeovers and other forms of corporate reorganisation are involved, and in the management of investment holdings, including trusts, pension and other funds.

The Discount Market

The Discount Market is an institution which is unique to the City of London. Its function in the monetary system is to provide a financial mechanism designed to promote an orderly flow of short-term funds. The market consists of 11 discount houses, 5 money traders and 2 discount brokers, all of which borrow money 'at call' or short notice and lend for somewhat longer periods. The discount houses have recourse to the Bank of England as lender of last resort. The Bank lends to them generally overnight or for seven days at minimum lending rate although it may charge a higher rate. Most of the market's borrowed funds come from the banks, which are thus provided with a flexible means of earning a yield on surplus funds which they may have at any given time, although an increasing proportion is also coming from industry. The assets of the discount houses mainly consist of Treasury and commercial bills, government and local authority securities and negotiable certificates of deposit denominated in both sterling and US dollars. The discount houses accept as a formal responsibility that they should cover the government's need to borrow on Treasury bills which are offered on tender each week.

National Savings
The National Savings Movement started in 1916, to help finance the First World War by promoting savings. The Department for National Savings is responsible for the administration of Government savings schemes; National Savings Bank accounts; National Savings Certificates; Premium Savings Bonds; and Save as You Earn contracts. Government policy is directed towards encouraging investment, primarily of personal savings, in these schemes, particularly as they represent a major source of funds for financing the public sector borrowing requirement. Facilities are provided by National Savings for the purchase of government stocks (gilts); a selection of about 50 stocks is held on the National Savings Stock Register. Gift Tokens are also available at most post offices. The National Savings Bank provides a countrywide system for depositing and withdrawing small savings at post offices. Ordinary accounts bear a rather low rate of interest but at present the first £70 of annual interest is tax-free. A higher rate of interest is paid on deposits in the Investment Accounts. All deposits carry a government guarantee.

Trustee Savings Banks
The Trustee Savings Banks (TSBs), most of which were founded in the nineteenth century, operate under their own trustees but are subject, under the Trustee Savings Bank Acts, 1969, 1976 and 1978, to the supervision of the Trustee Savings Bank Central Board and the Treasury. In recent years there has been a planned programme of amalgamations and TSBs are now authorised to provide a full range of banking services, including credit services, which include personal loans, temporary overdrafts, bridging loans and home-improvement loans. The TSBs also have their own credit card, Trustcard, which operates within the VISA system and in addition a range of life assurance and unit trust facilities are available. The TSBs have also introduced a pilot scheme offering small-scale commercial loans.

Other financial institutions

Many special financial facilities, which are supplementary to the credit facilities of the banks, are provided through institutions outside the banking system. These include institutions providing credit in specialised forms, such as hire purchase finance companies and leasing and factoring companies; institutions which manage investments on behalf of the public, such as pension funds, life assurance companies, unit trusts and investment trusts; institutions which provide financial services, such as the Stock Exchange, with its associated stock-brokers; commodity markets; the insurance market; and intermediaries which are less dependent on the financial markets in the City of London, such as building societies and credit unions.

Finance houses
Although there are a large number of firms engaged in the financing of hire purchase and other instalment credit transactions, about 90% of all finance house business is accounted for by the 40 firms which constitute the Finance Houses Association (FHA). A substantial amount of new credit extended by finance houses relates to cars and commercial vehicles, including motorcycles and caravans, the remainder relating to industrial and building equipment and other goods. The leading finance houses comply with the authorities' policies on lending similar to those applied to banks, and all finance houses are required to observe term controls affecting the minimum deposits and maximum repayment period for specific goods financed by certain forms of lending.

Leasing companies
Leasing companies buy and own plant or equipment required and chosen by businesses and lease it at an agreed rental (p. 192). This form of finance is growing in importance, partly because the leasing companies can take advantage of investment incentives to the benefit of customers whose tax position would otherwise make them unavailable. In 1978 new assets leased by the 47 members of the Equipment Leasing Association amounted to £1,214 million, some 10% of British investment in capital equipment.

Factoring companies
Factoring companies purchase the trade debts due to a business and provide an accounting and debt-collection service. Services available cover exports from and imports to Britain. In 1978 the eight members of the Association of British Factors handled £1,335 m. worth of turnover.

Finance corporations
These have been described more fully elsewhere in this book, but in

Financial institutions

summary finance corporations meet the need for medium- and long-term capital when such funds are not easily or directly available from traditional sources such as the Stock Exchange or the banks. The roles of Finance for Industry (FFI) and its major subsidiaries FCI and ICFC have been described, and also the National Enterprise Board (NEB) and Equity Capital for Industry (ECI).

There are a number of other important institutions which have been set up to assist in meeting identified special needs, and which are themselves financed by banks, insurance companies and other important commercial interests. In some cases the Bank of England also has a shareholding. Examples include the Agricultural Mortgage Corporation and two institutions which are specially, but not exclusively, concerned with establishing viable projects in Commonwealth (and other developing) countries – the Commonwealth Development Finance Company (CDFC) and the Commonwealth Development Corporation. The Crown Agents for Overseas Governments and Administrations provide financial, professional and commercial services for some 100 governments, mostly of independent countries, and over 200 overseas public authorities and international bodies. The office is not a government department but a public service which is responsible to its principals for its business operations. It is governed by the Crown Agents Act, 1979.

Pension funds

Pension funds are administered by trustees in order to invest members' pension contributions either directly on the market or through intermediaries such as insurance companies. The total market value of funds managed, covering private employers and much of the public sector, was of the order of £40,000 m. at the end of 1978. There is fuller discussion of these funds and their far-reaching implications in the next chapter, and that on the Wilson Committee. Because of the magnitude of the funds involved and the fact that they are steadily growing, and they are managed by relatively small groups who are in theory responsible and accountable only to their trustees and fund members, and in practical terms may hardly be accountable in any real sense, pension funds are a subject of informed public interest, concern and debate to the present time.

Investment trust companies and unit trusts

The theory, which is not always borne out in practice, is that investment trust companies and unit trusts enable investors to spread their risks and obtain the benefit of skilled management. The usual type of investment trust company is constituted as a public company registered under the Companies Acts with limited liability. Its business is to invest its capital in a range of stocks and shares. Like other companies it may issue several types of stocks or shares and may retain part of its profits to build up reserves. Investment trust companies grew to importance in the latter half of the nineteenth century and have been prominent in directing capital towards overseas investment. At the end of 1978 such companies held assets worth £6,7000 m. of which 33% were in overseas securities. With unit trusts and building societies, they will be further considered in the next chapter. They were considered in depth in the Wilson Committee Report.

Unit trusts are entirely different from investment trusts. A unit trust will be constituted by a trust deed between a management company and a trustee company which holds the assets. Normally the managers sell units to the public and must invest the proceeds in a defined range of stock exchange securities. The costs of running the trust are defrayed partly by an initial charge which forms part of the price of a unit, and partly by a half-yearly service charge which is usually taken out of the income of the trust. Until recently the level of both charges was controlled by the Department of Trade, but this particular control is no longer applied and control is left to the forces of competition. In other respects the Department of Trade exercises control over unit trusts and its authorisation is required before units can be offered to the public. This is only granted if the trust deed meets the Department's requirements.

Building societies
Building societies are non-profit-making mutual institutions which borrow mainly short-term (or to a lesser extent up to medium-term) from individual savers, who in the case of short-term investors are able to withdraw money generally on demand. The societies provide long-term loans at variable rates of interest on the security of private dwellings purchased for owner occupation. They also lend to a limited extent to house builders and on the security of business or commercial property. Most societies pay and charge interest on the basis of a structure of rates recommended periodically by the Building Societies Association, the movement's representative body. Building societies account for about 90% of all lending for house purchase in Britain and in recent years they have overtaken the banks as the principal repository for the personal sector's total liquid assets. This growth has been accompanied by a concentration of most of the business in the hands of a few large societies. Building societies have existed in Britain for some 200 years and have been subject to specific legislation governing their operations

(now consolidated in the Building Societies Act, 1962) since 1836. The present legislation is administered by the Chief Registrar of Friendly Societies, to whom the societies must provide regular statements of their financial position and who has discretionary powers to restrict or suspend a society's operations if he considers that the way in which its business is being conducted may put investor's money at risk.

Credit unions

A recent development in the UK has been the creation of credit unions, of which there are now over 50. Credit unions are small savings and loan clubs where members agree to pool part of their savings in order to provide themselves with low-cost credit. The Credit Unions Act, 1979, provides a legislative framework within which credit unions in Great Britain can operate. It requires that members of a credit union have a 'common bond' such as working in the same factory, and provides a system for their registration and supervision by the Chief Registrar of Friendly Societies. In Northern Ireland they are governed by the Industrial and Provident Societies Act (Northern Ireland), introduced in 1969.

The insurance market

The UK insurance industry is a major service industry and is a source of 'invisible' earnings for the economy. It operates nationally and internationally. The London insurance market is still, despite growing competition, especially from the USA, the world's leading centre for insurance where, in addition to most British companies and Lloyd's, a large number of overseas companies are also represented. It is the world centre for the placement of reinsurance and, partly in consequence of this, many British companies have formed close relationships with overseas companies. A certain amount of insurance is provided by friendly societies, banks and trade unions, but most insurance services in the UK are in the hands of mutual or joint stock insurance companies or Lloyd's underwriters.

Insurance companies

The major UK insurance companies are either joint stock companies, listed companies with institutional and personal shareholders, or mutual companies, which do not have outside shareholders. For the most part they undertake general insurance on an international as well as national basis and many undertake life insurance as well. There are also a number of overseas companies authorised to carry out insurance business in the UK. Supervision is exercised overall by the Department of Trade. A feature of modern insurance is that in addition to the numerous conventional policies there are numbers of very large single-risk policies covering, for example, specially designed vessels carrying liquified gas and offshore oil-production policies. Furthermore, individual claims especially in respect of accidental death or injury may now be for extremely large sums, especially when the cases are heard in US courts and there is an allegation that death(s) or injury(ies) arose in consequence of some negligence on the part of, for example, an airline operator or shipowner, or his employees. Some 310 companies belong to the British Insurance Association and these account for about 95% of the worldwide business of the British insurance companies' market. Life assurance is available from 300 authorised insurance companies and certain friendly societies, and a very limited range of contracts is obtainable from certain Lloyd's underwriters. The main types of life policy are whole-life, endowment, unit-linked term assurance and annuities. Many life assurance policies are a form of savings contract – in a tax-favoured form – as well as protection against losses arising (especially to dependents) in the event of premature death.

Lloyd's
Lloyd's is an incorporated society of private insurers in London. The name 'Lloyd's' is derived from Edward Lloyd's coffee house, established in the late seventeenth century, where merchants with maritime and other interests gathered to transact business. Although its activities were orginally confined to the conduct of marine insurance business, a very considerable worldwide market for the transaction of other classes of insurance business in non-marine, aviation and motor markets has been built up. Lloyd's is not a company but a market for insurance, where business is transacted by individual underwriters for their own account and risk and in competition with each other. Insurance may only be placed through Lloyd's brokers, who negotiate with Lloyd's underwriters on behalf of the insured. Only elected underwriting members of Lloyd's, who must transact insurance with unlimited liability and who have met the most stringent financial regulations laid down by the Committee of Lloyd's, are permitted to transact business at Lloyd's: these financial safeguards give security to the Lloyd's policy. In addition to its marine insurance business, Lloyd's has built up a worldwide organisation for the collection and diffusion of shipping intelligence. Lloyd's is regulated by a series of special Acts of Parliament, starting in 1871. The affairs of the Society of Lloyd's in its corporate

capacity are administered by the Committee of Lloyd's. The society does not accept insurance itself. In fact, in recent times Lloyd's has itself been faced with a number of well-publicised difficulties, which are outside the scope of this book. The Fisher Committee has recently conducted an investigation and submitted a report and recommendations which have largely been accepted for implementation. Certainly numbers of Lloyd's underwriters have found their activities much less profitable recently than they were in former times and a complaint has been that they have too often been called upon to meet claims which seemed heavily tainted with fraud. The worldwide decline in commercial morality, assisted by speed of communications, have obviously been important factors in the current problems in Lloyd's, which should be overcome, as history has shown the ability of the institution to adapt itself to changing times.

Insurance brokers
The insurance market is completed by the insurance brokers, acting on behalf of the insured; brokers are an essential part of the Lloyd's market and an important part of the company market. Many brokers specialise in reinsurance business, acting as intermediaries in the exchange of contracts between companies, both British and overseas. The Insurance Brokers (Registration) Act, 1977, provides for the registration of insurance brokers by a Registration Council.

International insurance services
Over 60% of the general, i.e. non-life, business of members of the British Insurance Association is carried on overseas, partly by reinsurance on the London market and partly through branches and agencies established in over 100 countries. The basic principle of this international business is that resources capable of meeting any potential loss are instantly available for use in any part of the world. Behind this large and international volume of business stand the very substantial assets of the companies, in addition to substantial reserves of uncalled capital, and the deposits, underwriting trust funds and other resources of Lloyd's underwriters. In accordance with the Treaty of Rome, insurance and reinsurance in the European Community are regulated by directives addressed to the governments of member states and intended to harmonise the legislation of the various member countries, thus providing a 'common market', which would avoid distortion of competition. Directives in operation cover freedom of establishment to provide services in respect of reinsurance, compulsory motor insurance, freedom of establishment in non-life insurance, and insurance

intermediaries. A further directive on the coordination of regulations relating to Community co-insurance operations came into force in 1980.

The Stock Exchange

The stock exchange of the UK and the Irish Republic amalgamated in 1973 to become 'The Stock Exchange' with its main trading floor and central administration in London. There are also trading floors in Glasgow, Liverpool, Manchester, Birmingham and Dublin. The number and variety of securities officially listed on the Stock Exchange are greater than any other market in the world and its turnover of company securities is roughly equivalent to that of all the European exchanges combined. Some 8,000 securities are quoted on the Stock Exchange. At the end of December 1978 these had a total market value of £323,650 m. About 6,200 securities of companies were quoted, including a number of leading overseas securities (over 470 in December 1978 with a total market value of £193,420 m.) Company issues represented more than four-fifths of the securities at market valuation, the remainder being British, Irish Republic and other overseas government and corporation stocks. Institutional investors, such as pension funds, now own a higher proportion of ordinary shares than individuals. A market in traded share options opened in 1978 on the Stock Exchange. The market, initially in the shares of 10 prominent British companies (now increased to 15), enables investors not only to buy options to purchase shares in future at pre-fixed prices but also to trade in the options themselves. Also in 1978 the Council for the Securities Industry was set up as a self-regulatory body for the securities industry. Its main function is to sustain proper conduct and high standards in the industry. The role of the Stock Exchange is further considered in the next chapter. It was also considered in depth by the Wilson Committee.

The foreign exchange market

The market consists of banks and several firms of foreign exchange brokers which act as intermediaries between the banks. It provides those engaged in international trade with foreign currencies for their transactions. The foreign exchange banks are in close contact with financial centres abroad and are able to quote buying and selling rates for both spot and future delivery. An important function of the market is to engage in arbitrage transactions which serve to eliminate differentials in exchange rates between different centres. The forward market enables traders, who at a given date in the future are due to make or receive a specific foreign-currency payment, to contract in advance to sell or buy the foreign currency involved for sterling at a precise fixed rate. The Bank of England is responsible for granting recognition to broking houses which wish to trade in the foreign exchange and currency deposit market for 'scheduled' currencies, that is, in those currencies for which a specific brokerage scale is laid down by the bank.

The London gold market

All banks may deal in gold but, in practice, dealings are largely concentrated in the hands of the five members of the London gold market. The five members meet twice daily to establish a London fixing price for gold. This price provides a reference point for worldwide dealings in gold. Although much interest centres upon the fixings, active dealing takes place throughout the day. Forward prices may also be quoted upon request.

Commodity markets

Britain remains the principal international centre for transactions in a large number of commodities, although most of the sales negotiated in London relate to consignments which never pass through UK ports. The need for close links with sources of finance and with shipping and insurance services often determined the location of these physical markets in the City of London. There are also futures markets in cocoa, coffee, grains (wheat and barley), rubber, soya bean meal, sugar, wool and non-ferrous metals (aluminium, copper, lead, nickel, silver tin and zinc).

Chapter 23

Investors and their viewpoints: the institutions available to them

Sources of information

A continuing major aim of legislation, including Companies Acts, and also of the Stock Exchange Council, through its listing agreement and other requirements, and of the Panel, through the City Code (p. 337) is to compel directors and others concerned with company promotion, or management, or capital raising, or reorganisation, to disclose to shareholders and prospective investors all the information they need in order to make informed judgements. Modern thinking is also that employees also have a right to information about the company, in which many invest so much of their working lives. The increasing public and media pressures towards openness in the UK supported by awareness of developments in other countries, such as the US 'Freedom of Information' Act, are in conflict with the widespread inclination of UK civil servants, ministers, managers, officials of all kinds towards secrecy in dealings. It is said that the passion for secrecy amongst UK officials is second only to that of Vatican officials. However, despite complaints that too little information is made available in respect of companies, it is evident that many investors are not aware how much information and comment is now published, and the many sources.

Information by itself is often not enough. It may need to be interpreted and commented upon by qualified and experienced persons, noting that sometimes different experts interpret the same information quite differently. There are six major sources of information about companies: (1) the company itself; (2) the Registrar of Companies; (3) the Stock Exchange; (4) government sources; (5) the financial press; (6) various financial specialist sources. The following are brief comments on each category: (1) and (2) – all companies resident in the UK must register with the Registrar of Companies and must file substantial information both at the time of registration and subsequently throughout their lives. A separate file is kept at Cardiff with respect to every company registered in England and Wales, and in Edinburgh with respect to companies registered in Scotland. These files are available for inspection, including in London, on payment of a nominal fee, and microfiche copies may be obtained. For those who are unable to make enquiries in person, a number of companies advertise regularly in the *Financial Times* offering to examine files, send copies, etc., on payment of reasonable fees. Every company is also required to file similar information at its registered or other nominated office and this must also be available for inspection by shareholders and, in some cases, by members of the public.

The requirements of the law are set out in the Companies Act and these may from time to time be extended. A serious investor or supplier of goods on credit could be interested in: the memorandum and articles of association; copies of any prospectus issued, noting that these must always incorporate much detailed information of past results and future expectations, based on stated assumptions; details of any mortgages and charges; the annual report and accounts, which must incorporate the report of the directors, and there is usually also a chairman's report in the case of a listed company; details of directors' shareholdings and dealings in these; register of substantial shareholdings and dealings in these. It may be noted that periodically in a lawsuit, or a Department of Trade enquiry into a failed company, or when a chief executive is charged in a criminal case, time and time again company directors state that they were not aware of the requirements of the Companies Acts, and this is their excuse for their own incompetence or omissions. Published information must therefore in some cases be treated with caution as some companies, through their directors, show much higher standards of competence and integrity than others.

(3) There are a number of Stock Exchange publications dealing with Stock Exchange procedure, e.g. *The New Transfer System*; *The Admission of Securities to Listing*, etc, and others which provide facts about listed companies and government and other securities. A substantial investor would be interested in: (a) the *Stock Exchange Daily Official List*, which provides comprehensive and official information about all listed securities, including prices, yields, etc, in respect of previous days' dealings. (b) the *Stock Exchange Fact Book*, published quarterly and including nominal and market value of all listed securities, in total and also analysed under market sections for the current and two preceding years; classifications of listed securities of UK and overseas companies, distinguishing between loan, preference and ordinary share capital; various analyses; details of all companies granted a listing for

the first time during the quarter; turnover details; etc; (c) the two-volume annual *The Stock Exchange Official Year Book*. The first volume contains comprehensive details of every 'gilt edged' and foreign listed security and of all listed company securities except those in the 'Commercial and Industrial Group' which are dealt with in the second volume. This is an exceptionally full and useful information source and current copies should be available in the reference sections of important public libraries; (d) *Interest and Dividends upon Securities Listed on the Stock Exchange* and *Statistics Relating to Securities Listed in the London Stock Exchange*.

(4) There are many government publications, regular and occasional, and comprehensive statistics. The Bank of England publishes a *Quarterly Bulletin* and other publications. Lists of government publications are available from HMSO. (5) For serious students the *Financial Times* is essential for selective weekday reading. It not only provides all details of previous days' prices of listed securities, and comment, but, in addition, it includes exceptionally authoritative articles on economic, financial and business topics. These articles are essential background reading for generalists as well as specialists. The other serious daily and Sunday newspapers also provide good financial and business coverage and most will also answer readers' specific enquiries on investment and taxation questions. There are also specialist weekly newpapers such as the *Economist* and *Investors Chronicle*. There are also a number of specialist 'newsletters': some advertise widely. Whilst individual newsletters may maintain high standards, they need to be treated with caution as a group. They advertise their successful 'tips' but, understandably, not their disastrous ones and some publishers could use their newsletter to further their own interests, e.g. to 'puff' securities which they hold, or on which they hold options. In general, the serious financial press in the UK plays a role of enormous importance to investors and, indeed, to the community. Regretfully, it must be stated that there is so much evidence that, left to themselves, members of the financial establishment seek to 'cover up' scandals, especially when their senior members are involved: governments and senior civil servants are equally guilty in these matters, and time and time again leading audit firms appear either to have shown astonishing incompetence, or to be condoning serious irregularities. In recent years it has often been an able financial journalist, backed by his newspaper, who has succeeded in exposing a scandal despite all the efforts of establishment members to suppress it.

(6) There are also many financial specialists. A substantial investor might be advised by a merchant bank as well as by stockbrokers, and a less substantial one by a stockbroker alone. Merchant banks and stock-

Investors and their viewpoints 441

brokers are prepared to plan and execute an agreed investment strategy for a client when the fees and commissions would be on a sufficiently profitable scale for them. Accountants and some solicitors may also agree to handle the investments of a client. The quality of performance of financial services will naturally vary widely and presumably exceptional performers will gain an outstanding reputation whilst that of the indifferent ones will decline. The Financial Times Business Service and Extel (Exchange Telegraph Co. Ltd) offer very full information services to subscribers, drawing upon their extensive libraries and specialist staff. Leading stockbrokers often employ outstanding research teams and the reviews they circulate to their clients are taken seriously, including by government policy makers. The major clearing banks also publish quarterly reviews whose contents are wide ranging, expertly written and intended, *inter alia*, to stimulate discussion and debate. In summary, substantial information is continually being made available and many students, investors and businessmen are insufficiently aware of this fact, or how to go about obtaining answers to particular questions. For the student a starting point may be to familiarise himself with a university or college or public reference library which has up-to-date material on financial, business and economic matters. Staff of such libraries are always helpful in explaining how the catalogues and source reference books, etc., should be used.

The investor's viewpoint

The main viewpoint considered so far in this book has been that of a person concerned with the financial planning and management of a business, and whose main concern in relation to the money and capital markets will normally be how to obtain funds from time to time. From time to time there may be surplus funds to invest for shorter or longer periods. However, for every user of funds there must be a provider of funds, and this chapter seeks to identify who are the main providers – investors – and what are the factors which influence them in making their investment decisions, and the mechanisms and institutions which help to equate demand and supply, and what are the main constraints and problems. It is a period of change, of questioning established institutions and practices, and of controversy and a student must keep aware of the varying developments and of the arguments for and against different viewpoints. Selective current reading is essential for this purpose.

The supply of money

The topic of investment is bound up with that of the supply of money, noting that governments create the currency which is in circulation in the form of notes and coin, and which is the basis of the money supply, but they do so subject to constraints insofar as, if the issue is excessive, the currency becomes debased and there is inflation, whereas if the supply is insufficient there will be excessively depressed business activity and unemployment. Because of the interdependence of countries and international trade, Governments are subjected to external as well as internal constraints in their regulation of their money supply. In extreme cases governments operate draconian laws in attempts to seal their country from external factors – even with the death penalty for currency offences. However, the subject of the supply of money is outside the scope of this book and is a part of the syllabus of economics and applied economics. In relation to business finance, the fact is that the government is both a major investor and a major borrower.

A Labour government will be more active as a direct investor than a Conservative one because of the widely diverging political philosophies of the two parties. The NEB is an example of a channel for government investment in commercial-type organisations but governments also invest substantially in non-commercial organisations such as hospitals and schools and it may be noted that in numbers of countries many hospitals and schools operate within the private rather than the public sector. The government is also a major borrower in addition to having the special privilege of raising taxes. Local authorities are also important as investors and borrowers, individually and collectively. They also have the privilege of levying taxes locally on the occupiers of commercial and residential properties within their boundaries. These taxes are known as rates and there is controversy as to whether the present arrangements are equitable or whether different ones would be fairer and at the same time cost effective.

A further important matter is that whilst the government alone can create cash, it is within the power of the banks, and others, to create credit and forms of near money, subject to constraints. In times of speculative activity, for example, investors may obtain overdrafts from banks and use these as a means of financing share purchases. However, the seller will require payment in cash, or cash equivalent, and investment financed by credit is therefore subject to severe constraints insofar as if a government imposes a credit squeeze overdrafts may be called in quickly, especially those intended for speculative purposes. A borrower on an overdraft must then quickly produce cash to repay an overdraft.

To do this he may be forced to sell securities or other properties and possibly at heavy loss if it is a forced, quick sale. The nationwide shortage of liquidity and need for large numbers of heavy borrowers against collateral to raise cash quickly was a main reason for the crash of security and property prices in 1973/74.

In brief, an investor may be considered to have complete freedom of action in making investment decisions only if he owns assets in the form of cash or near cash – if he is 'liquid'. For an individual this would normally represent savings – an excess of income over expenditure – in liquid form, or an inheritance, or the proceeds of a sale of assets, or a gift, or gambling winnings. In the case of a company or other institution, money could be available for short- or long-term investment in consequence of a positive cash flow – an excess of income over expenditure: this is a special feature of insurance companies, pension funds, etc. It could also arise from a sale of surplus assets.

Short-term investments

People and organisations who operate bank current accounts do so for reasons which include security and convenience – security because holdings of cash invite robbery, and convenience (and security) because of the facility of making payments by cheque rather than in cash, which obviously has great advantages. The current-account holder normally foregoes interest on these accounts, deeming that the benefits of security and convenience outweigh the costs, namely the interest foregone by not investing in a deposit or other interest-bearing account. However, alert companies and individuals hold minimum practicable current-account balances and invest any surpluses above this minimum in a deposit account which bears interest. Meanwhile, the banks which receive deposits in the current accounts of their customers, after taking note of their own cash needs, and the need at all times to conform with Bank of England regulations, will deploy surplus funds by lending them in return for an agreed rate of interest. Some of these funds will be lent to the discount houses, in the discount market, on a short, or very short, even 'overnight' basis. The banks will receive the 'going rate', which will be linked with the MLR, and this forms an important source of revenue to them. The main function of the discount houses is to mobilise funds made available to them for very short periods by relending these for rather longer periods to the government, local authorities, commerce and industry. The discount houses provide the goverment with working funds by buying Treasury bills and bonds.

Treasury and other bills: certificates of deposits (CDs)
The Treasury bill is a vital instrument. It is a main means whereby the government raises short-term funds. It is the practice for the government, every Friday, to offer Treasury bills to the market in a volume related to the government's short-term borrowing needs. The discount houses, UK and foreign banks and money brokers tender for these. The bills are redeemable by the Treasury after 91 days, at their face values, and the tenders will therefore be for a price somewhat below the face value, and the discount measures the rate of interest payable by the goverment in respect of the issue. There is a convention that all Treasury bills offered will be taken up by the market and in return the Bank of England acts as a lender of last resort to discount houses which are temporarily short of cash. Treasury bills, which are offered at different face values, up to £250,000, and in different colours to facilitate sorting, are both a means whereby the government can borrow for short periods and one whereby substantial investors, including companies, with temporarily surplus funds, can obtain interest on their funds without risk, including risk of a fall in the market value of the security. The Treasury bill is also readily negotiable and liquid yet interest bearing. Companies and individuals do not tender directly but through a bank or money broker.

The short-term money market is inevitably a fast changing and highly technical and complex one. In recent times, and possibly temporarily, the Treasury bill has declined relatively in importance and commercial, including finance bills have increased in importance and discount houses deal in these as well as local authority bills. A more recent credit instrument is the negotiable certificate of deposit (CD). Negotiable dollar certificates of deposit were first introduced in New York in 1961 by bankers who wished to meet a rise in demand for advances when there was no comparable rise in deposits. The way to attract more money is to offer a higher rate of interest, and the device of issuing CDs permits this to be done without raising interest rates generally. The certificate is exchanged for a fixed deposit until a stated future date. It is negotiable and the purchaser can therefore sell it to a third party at any time, or can hold it until it is redeemed at maturity.

Dollar CDs can be dealt in the UK and in 1968 UK banks were authorised to issue sterling CDs. The minimum denomination is £50,000 and the life varies from three months to five years. Certificates of deposit have attracted to the market funds which previously had been invested elsewhere and substantial numbers will be held at any time by the discount houses, clearing and merchant banks. They are now also a popular form of short-term investment for companies or institutions with temporarily surplus funds, since they have the advantages of negotiability and marketability as well as security. Certificates of deposit have traditionally been fixed rate, but as from 1977 floating rate CDs (FRCDs) have also been issued. For technical reasons relevant to Japanese banking practices, Japanese banks have been specially active in the issue of FRCDs.

The role of the discount houses

A discount house, a member of the Accepting Houses Committee, is a financial institution. It is a company specialising in discounting bills of exchange, in borrowing for short periods and lending for rather longer ones, which appears to have a narrow role. Recently the question has been raised whether the discount houses have outlived their usefulness (in the same way as it has been raised about the role of jobbers). Naturally, when the role of an institution is questioned, those who earn substantial incomes from it will always produce convincing arguments against change. In the case of the discount houses it would be a practicable possibility for the Bank of England to lend directly to the Exchequer instead of operating through the discount market. In evidence to the Radcliffe Committee (1959) a spokesman for the Bank said that the survival of the discount market 'may not be entirely due to the fact that the clearing banks like it so much. It may be because the Bank of England likes it also. We believe it to be the most flexible mechanism for looking after the needs of short-term money that there is in the world.' The banks support the continued existence of the discount houses because they offer a ready made means of earning interest on their very short-term funds as well as a means for the quick rearrangement of their liquid assets.

The authorities recognise that the discount market facilitates the mobilising of idle or other very short-term money and lending this to industry, trade and the government. It also provides a sensitive mechanism by which the short-term interest rates may be regulated, noting that interest rates can only be controlled to a certain point. It is never practicable to act for long against fundamental market forces, and the authorities and all concerned with the market would be too experienced to attempt any course of action they recognised to be unsustainable. The Radcliffe Committee itself reported 'the importance of the work of the discount houses in relation to Treasury bills lies not in any indispensibility... but rather in the fact that they make a highly efficient market in instruments which are very convenient to the Exchequer'.

Bank current and deposit accounts and the money market

The discount market has an important role but a large proportion of those who supply the funds which sustain it do so passively and without an awareness of their role and without themselves obtaining any direct financial return from the use of their funds. This is the position with respect to holders of bank current accounts: holders of bank deposit or building society accounts benefit from receiving interest, but it is an indirect interest and the rate obtained may be well below that available to an active investor in the discount market. For this reason larger companies and institutions with specialist financial management will be likely to operate actively in the discount market by using temporarily surplus funds for the purchase of Treasury bills, CDs, or parcels of commercial bills. Self-evidently, for companies for which direct operation in the discount market is not feasible the use of deposit accounts is a worthwhile alternative. The interest rate obtainable is usually 2% or so below MLR and these accounts offer the advantages of convenience, security and liquidity. Whilst, technically, seven days' notice is required for withdrawal, banks will normally agree to dispense with all or part of this notice, with loss of interest as the only penalty.

Other short-term investment outlets: building societies, NSB; TSB

In past years many individuals maintained large current-account balances in banks. However, in recent years a change has been occurring and this arises largely from the facts that interest rates have risen to historically very high levels, and there is inflation. Even inexperienced investors have become aware of these facts and also of how the real values of their cash or near-cash assets have been eroded through inflation, and all branches of the press give at least simple financial advice and encourage their readers to 'shop around' and invest their short-, medium- and longer-term surpluses in appropriate investments.

Insofar as short-term surpluses are concerned, investors have become better informed as to where, at any time, they can obtain the highest interest rates consistent with security and they are now more ready than formerly to switch quickly from one short-term investment to another. The building societies, together with the Trustee Savings Banks and the National Savings Bank, have developed into important competitors of the clearing banks for the short-, medium- and longer-term surpluses of individuals and of some companies as well. This is in respect of funds which need to be in reasonably liquid form. In evidence to the Wilson Committee the clearing banks showed that their proportion of total funds deposited by UK residents declined from 45.1% in 1962 to 31.1% in 1976, noting that in this period there was also a substantial growth in total deposits. The beneficiaries included the other banks in the UK but the outstanding performance was that of the building societies. In 1962 their deposits by UK residents were only half those held by the clearing banks and only 20% of the total. However, by the end of 1976 the building societies held considerably larger deposits than the clearing banks and 37.6% of the total (*Financial Times*, 18 March 1978).

Main reasons for this fast growth of building society share of deposits include:

(a) For many years all UK governments have given special and favourable tax treatment to building societies and those using their facilities. Thus depositors who pay the basic rate of income tax are not required to pay income tax on the interest they receive: apart from the aspect of convenience, taxpayers in this major category normally effectively enjoy a rather higher return on their deposits with the societies rather than the banks. (However, persons not liable to basic rate income tax for any reason cannot claim tax refunds in respect building society interest and accordingly they should not make deposits with the societies.)

(b) Most banks are closed on Saturday mornings but building society branches are open. This facility is important to many individual (as distinct from corporate) investors.

(c) It was a matter for comment in 1980 that UK citizens are 'the great unbanked'. In comparison with other Western industrialised countries the UK has the lowest proportion of citizens with bank accounts (and the banks are now trying to attract these potential customers): meanwhile, research has shown that many in the UK do not feel at ease in banks but feel at ease in building society branches and therefore use their deposit facilities.

(d) A most important factor is that regular depositors with building societies are given specially favoured treatment in the event that they approach a building society for a mortgage. For this reason many young people save regularly by making deposits with a building society, recognising that obtaining the equity of a house, which invariably shows substantial capital and tax-exempt gains over the years, will often be by far the most important single investment in their lives, and building society facilities enable them to finance this investment largely with borrowed money. Again, because of the favourable tax treatment, the cost of money borrowed for house purchase is well below the normal commercial rates.

Not surprisingly, bank spokesmen have criticised the favourable tax treatment of building societies as being unfair to banks. Whilst building societies do not offer money transfer facilities as the clearing banks do, this is not a major problem for many, especially as accounts can be settled by using the Giro facilities in a post office. The building societies are not truly in the banking business but their role overlaps that of the banks in important aspects – they offer deposit and cash withdrawal facilities and the payment of interest on deposits. The movement was pioneered in the UK in the nineteenth century by working people who chose to work together on a cooperative, non-profit-making basis, to assist individuals in saving towards the purchase of their home, and in making long-term loans in the form of mortgages secured on a house the individual buys and occupies. As the main aim is such a socially acceptable and popular one, not surprisingly the movement has received support and encouragement from successive governments of different political persuasions, subject to certain regulation of the societies. It is notable that although there may be general criticism of the societies for avoidance of competition, and for acting as a cartel, as it were – and the Wilson Committee made far-reaching recommendation that competition between building societies should increase and the recommended rate system should be abolished – and although there is criticism for the manner in which building societies are opening so many branch offices in prime high-street sites, the societies, overall, enjoy high public confidence, esteem and goodwill for the value of the work they do, which has no real counterpart in other countries, and for the financial integrity of their operations. The Gray's Building Society fraud was clearly quite exceptional.

In passing, it is noteworthy that at a time when the clearing banks are putting their branch network under searching scrutiny and expectations are that unproductive branches will increasingly be closed over the next few years, building societies are opening new branches on a wide scale. This extension of branch networks must add heavily to overhead costs, which could only be justified if it led to the generation of sufficient profitable new business. Furthermore, if the opening of a new branch for one society merely took business away from the nearby branch of another society, so that the building society movement as a whole was increasing its overheads but there was not sufficient overall gain of new business, the question would arise whether depositors as a whole would not benefit if there were more rationalisation of the building society movement, more takeovers of smaller societies by larger ones, reduction in the number of branches and hence overheads, and the savings passed on to the supporters of the movement by way of more easily available mortgages, possibly at marginally lower rates of interest, together with rather higher rates of interest for depositors.

Investors and their viewpoints

A feature of building society operations is that the societies borrow largely, but not entirely, for short periods, but lend for long ones. This appears to break a fundamental rule of prudent financial management but it works in practice for a number of reasons, including public confidence and recognition of the social importance of the operations: an essential part of the mechanisms for equating demand for and supply of funds is that lending and borrowing rates are flexible and not rigidly fixed. An important part of the cash flow of building societies arises, of course, from the regular repayments of borrowers, whose repayments contain two components – part interest payment and part repayment of capital.

However, informed observers wonder whether the full financial implications of the growth in relative and absolute importance of the building society movement as a whole are fully understood. In a leading article headed 'Rivals to the Banks' in the *Financial Times* on 13 March 1978, it was stated:

The growth of the movement in recent years has been quite extra-ordinary. The tax privileges of which the banks complain are only part of the explanation. The fact is that over a period of the most stringent credit controls in living memory, the authorities have allowed and even encouraged the growth of what amounts to an unregulated cartel, with near monopoly access to what has proved one of the most important of all outlets for credit. The result, that the building societies now hold larger deposits than the clearing banks themselves, is scarcely surprising. If it were true that the societies – like the life insurance companies, for example – based their activities on genuine long-term savings, invested on broadly similar time scale, then it would be logical to leave them out of account in any question of monetary policy: but this is becoming more and more a caricature of the facts. Not enough is known about the turnover and destination of building society deposits, but certainly their numerous branches are widely used for what are certainly banking purposes. While their lending remains specialised, a proportion at any rate of their deposits are part of the ordinary store of liquidity – not only of shoppers who appreciate Saturday opening but of stock market investors out of the market for the time being.

The societies not only constitute an unmeasured addition to the effective money supply, but their operations distort the growth of the money supply which the authorities do try to control. When interest rates fall, the movement attracts deposits away from the banking system; but it is commonly some months before these are lent in the housing market. A proportion of this rise in deposits is normally invested in public sector debt, and so a large potential rise in the money supply is concealed. The rise in mortgage lending may well therefore have something to do with the rise in the money supply. While the authorities no doubt analyse these changes and try to offset them, no direct control is applied. It is only the banks which have to make special deposits with the Bank of England, or to submit to a limit in the growth of their liabilities. It is much easier to state the privileges of the building society movement than to measure their effect or suggest remedies. Until more is known the safest recommendation is the usual safe anti-climax – a call for further study. This should also extend to the monetary significance of other savings media – the Trustee Savings Banks, which now offer cheque clearing facilities, for example.

The Trustee Savings Banks, which now offer cheque facilities and are also extending into other financial activities, such as hire purchase finance, are competing actively with the established clearing banks. They advertise extensively, including on television, and they evidently seek to appeal to younger people. The National Savings Bank, which operates through the post office and offers two types of account, the Ordinary and the Investment accounts, also competes with the established clearers. As a pointer to how well-informed professionals will seize unexpected opportunities, from January to October 1977, when money market interest rates were falling heavily, the rate on the NSB Investment account was maintained static at 10% and from April 1977 this was higher than the rate which could be obtained elsewhere in the money markets on one-month funds. In May 1977 the gap reached 2½% and institutional managers began to pour their liquid funds into the NSB although this had traditionally been regarded as a 'peoples' bank'. By July 1977 the Department for National Savings was sufficiently alarmed at the size of the inflow that it introduced its £50,000 limit, to deter the institutional investor. In June 1978, when money market rates were again rising, stockbrokers Joseph Sebag made a strong recommendation that substantial investors in NSB Investment accounts should prepare to withdraw their deposits, in order to obtain higher rates elsewhere, notably one-month interbank deposits and one-month sterling CDs. The effect of this advice was dramatic and £180 m was withdrawn from the NSB at the beginning of July 1978. Up to the present it has been characteristic of NSB accounts that interest rates have been changed at infrequent intervals. Accordingly, when NSB rates stand above the market levels it will be flooded with institutional funds, which will equally quickly be withdrawn when the NSB rate stands below the market rates.

Investors and their viewpoints

The money invested in the NSB goes more or less directly to finance the goverment's borrowing requirement and funds are deployed by the National Debt Office in the purchase of gilt-edged securities, Treasury bills and local authority securities, or placed in short-term securities with the local authorities. To the extent that depositors withdraw funds heavily from the NSB, the government will need to sell more gilts or find other means of financing the borrowing requirements. National Savings Bank holdings of short-term deposits and maturing Treasury bills would make cash available to meet at least part of an outflow of funds. In 1978 the *Financial Times* reported that building societies had been amongst the institutions making withdrawl of funds from the NSB and their own depositors were making withdrawals from the societies in order to reinvest their medium- to longer-term funds in National Savings Certificates, whose terms had become attractive relative to competing investment outlets.

Short-term investments – a summary

Because taxation affects individuals and companies in different ways, the former paying income tax and the latter corporation tax, and because different types of institutions are treated differently, some being liable to corporation and capital gains taxes in full at one extreme and, at the other, approved pension and certain insurance funds being exempt from all taxes, it is not possible to make dogmatic general assertions as to which type of short-term investment will be the most profitable. The nature and circumstances of the particular investor must be considered in each case, by a competent person who is also expert in tax matters.

In the case of individuals, if the funds available are substantial their owner would need to be expert himself, or he would presumably employ experts in whom he had confidence, e.g. a merchant bank and or a stockbroker, accountant, taxation adviser, etc. The aim would be to maximise the after-tax and net of expenses return and with assurance that capital invested would be maintained intact, in nominal terms, and would be available, in cash, on the date(s) required. At present, an important feature of UK goverment securities is that an individual who holds them for a full twelve months will have no liability to any capital gains taxes in respect of the transaction. Experts thus normally include in their portfolio of short-term investments gilt-edged securities due to be redeemed at a known price on a known date at least twelve months from the date of purchase, and purchased at a price below the redemption price. The timing will also be important and favoured timing for taxpayers in the higher tax brackets is when the price is low because the buyer will not be entitled to the next interest payment: sale will be timed when the price is at its highest because the buyer will be entitled to the next interest payment. This is arranged so that as far as possible the investor would receive money in the form of capital gains rather than income, bearing in mind that capital gains tax is not payable on holdings of over twelve months, and even when it is payable, it is at a lower rate than tax on income. It may also be noted that dealings costs are lowest with respect to government securities.

Investors with temporary surplus funds sufficient to make careful investment worth while (as distinct from simply depositing the funds with a building society, in the case of a person liable to basic-rate tax), but insufficient to interest professional advisers, would be guided as to the current situation by referring to informed press comment, which tends to be featured in Saturday issues of the serious daily press, as well as the serious Sunday newspapers. For basic-rate taxpayers buildings society deposits have the advantages of liquidity, security, including of capital, and high rate of return. No investment expenses arise and there are minimal formalities. This convenience aspect is important to many. There is the extra advantage that if the investor wished at some future time to borrow for house purchase or improvement, he would be given favoured consideration if he were a regular depositor. Full advantage would be taken of 'index linked' 'Saved as You Earn' schemes and, if applicable, the index-linked goverment scheme for persons of retirement age, as well as the tax-free element of NSB Ordinary accounts. Particular issues of national savings certificates may also be rewarding. Moreover, a number of financial institutions advertise short-term investment opportunities which have been devised by experts to be as tax efficient as possible. The aspect of tax efficiency is of the utmost importance since specially devised schemes may enable an investor to obtain a significantly higher return than he could obtain from direct investment. In principle, short-term investments will never be speculative, by definition, and, in consequence fixed-interest securities whose market prices rise or fall with changes in interest rates would not be chosen. Similarly, private-sector investment, either equity or fixed interest, would be unsuitable since there needs to be certainty that a defined capital sum must be available, in cash, by a specified date: local authority loans or bonds would be possible options.

In the case of a short-term surplus for investment by a corporate body the main criteria for selection are simple to understand and apply. They are:

(1) The sum available; for example, large companies employ financial specialists and one or more would be responsible for the manage-

ment of cash and short-term investment and such person(s) would be experienced in dealing on the money market, with money brokers, etc. In other cases, if a substantial sum became available for a period following the sale of an asset, the merchant bank advisers would be consulted. However, smaller sums which would not warrant expert attention would be held, for example, in a bank deposit account.
(2) The period for which the funds will be surplus and can be invested.
(3) In principle, the highest obtainable return will be sought, taking taxation fully into account as well as the need for complete security of capital and the fact that there must be certainty that the investment(s) may be encashed at the time planned. If there were the possibility that emergencies could arise and cash be needed early, then securities such as Treasury bills, or CDs *inter alia*, would be suitable as they can easily be negotiated at any time. Expectations in respect of interest rate changes could be a factor. If these were expected to rise sharply in the near future then funds would be held in very short-term deposits so that as and when the rise took place maximum advantage could be taken of it. Conversely, if interest rates were expected to fall shortly then, as far as consistent with the short-term investment plans, funds would be invested now in order to have the maximum advantage of the present high interest rates.

Main investments to be considered would include:
(*a*) Very short-term deposits, including 'overnight' money, bank deposit accounts, which would include clearing and merchant and foreign banks, discount houses, etc, depending on which offered the best terms, and only considering institutions of the highest standing (riskier institutions naturally offer higher interest rates but it is imprudent to take unnecessary risks).
(*b*) Treasury and other bills, including first-class commercial bills, CDs, Certificates of Tax Deposits (CTDs). The latter may be purchased from Collectors of Taxes and are government instruments available to corporate bodies and individuals. They bear a fixed rate of interest with a bonus element if they are used in due course in settlement of tax liabilities. They are issued with a minimum face value of £2,000 and can be held for up to six years. There are certain other technical advantages to holders, e.g. if a tax assessment is under appeal, which could be prolonged, CTDs finally tendered in settlement would count from their date of issue and a holder could thus avoid having to pay interest on overdue tax if an appeal went against him. Certificates of Tax Deposits are also

bought when they offer a high fixed interest rate and interest rates are expected to fall. They are widely held.
(c) Local authority deposit receipts – the period ranges from overnight to 364 days. Local authorities also advertise for loans for periods of up to five years or so.
(d) National Savings Bank Investment accounts – deposits are limited to £20,000.
(e) miscellaneous – deposits with building societies (but corporate bodies normally obtain better rates in other investments; government securities with a known and early redemption date; inter-company loans are also quite common and tend to occur when two companies have close working relationships, or there are other special factors).

Medium- and longer-term investment: individuals and corporate bodies

A company may find itself with a cash surplus for which it has no foreseeable needs and in such cases whilst a proportion would be invested on a short-term basis, the deployment of the balance would need to be assessed in the light of the company's own situation. There would be a number of options: (a) the financing of promising new projects or the extension or expansion of existing ones; (b) the development of new markets, including overseas; (c) the takeover of one or more companies, preferably on an agreed basis, as part of a policy of diversification, or entry into new markets; (d) the making of trade investments in appropriate companies. In SSAP 1 a company is defined as being an associated company if, 'whilst not being a subsidiary: (1) the other (investing) company is effectively involved as a partner in a joint venture; or (2) the investing company's interest is long term and is not less than 20% and it can exercise significant influence.' A company often finds it worthwhile to have a close association, with interlocking directorates, with a major supplier and or customer; (e) A real option, but one seldom chosen in practice, is to return a surplus, for which there is no foreseeable use, to its owners, the ordinary shareholders. In order to safeguard creditors, employees, etc., capital can only be returned to shareholders if the proposals have first been approved at a general meeting by the shareholders and then have been sanctioned by the Court. One reason for the rareness of the choice of this option must be that directors prefer to see a continuing increase in the resources they control. An instinct towards 'empire building' is common at all levels of management. There may also be an instinct of prudence: if a company has large reserves with a reasonable proportion in liquid form it would be in a position to withstand prolonged financial setbacks. Ironically, managements can now often obtain very high returns on capital on money invested in the money market – recently well over 15% has been obtainable; this is at a time when the return on capital in manufacturing industry is often less than 5%. In these circumstances it is not surprising that some managements cut down on manufacturing investment and keep money invested in government securities, ignoring the erosion of real values through inflation.

Classes of investors – individuals and institutions
Whilst in the case of short-term investment the funds of many institutional and individual investors will be channelled into banks and the investors will not be required to have active involvement in what is then done with their funds, in respect of medium- and long-term investments deliberate investing decisions will be called for. An individual investor who did not wish to have active involvement in day-to-day investment decision making would entrust his portfolio management to a merchant bank or stockbroker if it were substantial enough to interest them: a smaller investor could consider unit trusts. Investors can be identified as belonging to one of two main groups: (1) individual investors, and (2) institutional investors. A feature of UK investment is how the individual holdings of securities has declined as a proportion of the total holdings, whilst those of institutions have increased. The Wilson Committee Report shows that the distribution of shareholdings by beneficial owner was: 1963 – individuals 54% institutions, 46%; 1975 – individuals 37.5%, institutions 62.5%, and the evidence is that the trend continued up to 1979. However, with the change to a radical Conservative government in 1979 and the sharp reduction in the rates of income tax on high-income individuals it is possible but not certain that there may be more investing by individuals. The new Conservative government lifted the restrictions on dividend payments (possibly to the regret of numbers of boards of directors since they could no longer blame government controls for low dividend declarations). Exchange controls were also lifted and for the time being individuals and institutions can freely invest anywhere they choose. The immediate and longer-term effects of this major change must surely be far-reaching. The Stock Exchange has been pressing for further incentives for equity investors, including reduction or removal of the stamp transfer duty. There is also debate about the tax-favoured positions of different types

of institutions. As long as this continues, the dominant position of the institutions must also continue since so often the most tax-efficient way for an individual to invest on a medium- to longer-term basis is through an institution rather than by direct purchase of shares.

Main regular institutional investors are: pension funds, including those of the nationalised industries; insurance companies; building societies; banks and other financial companies; unit trusts; investment trusts. A feature of those institutions whose role includes regular dealings in securities is that they will employ highly skilled investment managers, who will be concerned with the theory and practice of portfolio management. However, the evidence is that some professional investors, or teams, are much more successful than others and even a highly successful investor may occasionally make a serious miscalculation or misjudgement.

It is not self-evident why individuals have been net sellers of securities. In some cases holdings would represent inherited or acquired capital and securities are sold to supplement current income and maintain standards of living at a time of high personal taxation and rising prices. Retired people, whose earning power has ended, tend to come into this category. In some cases securities would be sold to pay inheritance taxes. In other cases sales could represent a 'switch' from personal holdings of equities, bonds, etc., into a different type of investment, such as property. Other sellers might seek diversification but not wish to be responsible for handling their own investments and such people might reinvest in unit or investment trusts. Others might wish to have more liquid investments and put a part of the proceeds of sales into a building society deposit account, especially if they wished to obtain a mortgage to buy property on a tax favoured basis.

Possibly the most important single reason for the growing importance of institutional investment is the fact that for many years successive UK governments have given a variety of substantial incentives to individuals to invest through institutions rather than personally. It is possible, but not certain, that this Conservative, or a future, government will make major changes in this respect also. An important first step in 1979 was to raise from £1,500 to £5,000 the threshold at which an individual became liable to pay the investment surcharge tax – a tax on income from investments. In many ways this is a most inequitable tax: for example, the inflation-proofed pensions of civil servants, which may be very high, count entirely as earned income, whereas retired small shopkeepers, living largely on income from savings, are liable to pay the investment surcharge on very small investment incomes.) Meanwhile, the current position is that life insurance policies are tax-favoured instruments so that endowment 'with-profits' life insurance policies with carefully selected companies, with good bonus records, are attractive options for medium-to longer-term investors because of the tax relief against premiums. Many individual investors consider that residential property is by far their best long-term investment since it can be lived in and enjoyed, whilst its value rises faster and more consistently than almost any other asset. Successive governments have encouraged borrowing for the purpose of home ownership or improvement by allowing mortgage or other interest payments to be treated as tax-deductible expenses in respect of an indvidual's main residence, thereby reducing income tax liability. Any capital gain arising from the sale of a main residence is exempted from capital gains tax, an extremely important concession.

Furthermore, self-employed persons benefit from massive tax favours when they invest through an approved self-employed pension scheme, operated by an insurance company or other financial institution. Their payments, up to a generous limit, are treated as expenses deductible from profits and the funds held in approved schemes are exempted from all taxes on either income or capital gains. Accordingly, a given annual payment by an individual into an approved pension scheme in due course gives rise to a very much larger return than could have been obtained by the individual if he had invested directly, since direct investment would not give rise to tax favoured treatment. In brief, very substantial funds are being invested indirectly by individuals through the intermediary of various institutions because this is the most tax-efficient way for these investors to invest.

In other cases individuals may buy unit trust certificates or investment trust shares because they recognise their own lack of skill or even interest in investment and prefer to entrust their funds to professional managements. In recent years many stockbrokers have not welcomed the business of smaller investors on the grounds that this gives rise to excessive administration costs in relation to the income derived from it. Furthermore, dealing charges in respect of small purchases or sales are proportionately much higher than for large ones.

The motivation of individual investors

Although at least for the time being direct investment by individuals has declined in relative importance, it is still substantial and important and changes in the form of taxation, and reliefs, could conceivably result in an increase in direct investment in the quite near future. Indirect investment by individuals is also very substantial. It is therefore important to consider the motivation of individual investors and how they may attempt to attain their objectives. Obviously, no individuals are alike in temperament and personal circumstances, and preferences also differ. Even so, it is not difficult to make a useful analysis. In principle, an individual who is considering his investment strategy and policy should first make a rational assessment of his personal position, expectations, needs, obligations and aims. He would establish his objectives clearly, if necessary seeking objective expert advice.

In order to make this personal assessment the following matters would need to be considered: (*a*) the present financial position, taking into account the present cash flow, i.e. sufficient details in respect of income and also expenditure, sufficiently analysed, and the excess of income over expenditure: (*b*) any realistic expectations in relation to income, and to capital, if relevant; (*c*) age – a young person will have a more distant time horizon than an older one and the needs will be very different; (*d*) family responsibilities – a married man with children has heavy obligations towards his dependents and different types of life insurance will be specially important; (*e*) specific future commitments, e.g. if cash is required in the near future for marriage or home purchase, or children's education there must be adequate liquidity; (*f*) pension arrangements – an employed person with adequate or generous pension expectations can accept more risks in his peronal investment programme than a person whose pension expectations are small; (*g*) income, if any, from sources other than employment; (*h*) the 'tax bracket' of the investor and notably his marginal rate of tax – the tax on the 'top slice' of income. A person in a high tax bracket and with investment income surcharge liabilities will seek capital gains rather than income. Indeed, it is simple for competent financial advisers to arrange that a wealthy person receives a continuing flow of tax-free capital gains on gilt-edged securities held for twelve months or longer. In effect, tax-free capital gains are converted into income. The recent income tax reductions – which could be reversed by a future government – may somewhat reduce the emphasis on this factor, but it will still be important; (*i*) temperament. This is an important factor – some enjoy risk taking and active speculation, just as some people enjoy gambling but others loathe it. Speculators buy and sell within an account, sell securities they have not yet acquired (calculating that the price will fall), purchase options, etc. Many other are risk-averse and prefer that other do the worrying. Such persons might invest in a reasonably wide spread of unit trusts; (*j*) personal attitudes – some investors have strong personal views and refuse, for examples, to invest in brewery or distillery groups, tobacco companies, companies with gambling interests, etc.

When the personal position of an individual investor has been assessed and his objectives agreed upon, it would be practicable to determine the appropriate investment strategy. This would be likely to include one or more of the following: (1) maximisation of income with or without preservation of capital, e.g. an older person, without dependents, could seek maximum income and an annuity might be appropriate; (2) guaranteed income for a fixed period of time, e.g. a future commitment to pay school fees and tax-favoured endowment insurance policies are available; (3) a guaranteed income for an indefinite period (but inflation now makes this a less meaningful concept); (4) maximum capital profit with or without protection of capital – for example, an investor might be prepared to accept high risks in respect of a proportion of his available funds, say between 5 and 10%; (5) a guaranteed return of capital on a fixed future date. This is a common objective and securities redeemable on a known future date would be considered: with-profit endowment policies are also a popular means of ensuring that a lump sum will be received on a known future date; (6) adequate liquidity and flexibility; (7) possibly, freedom from personal day-to-day involvement in investment matters; (8) legal constraints may need to be taken into account, e.g. the obligations of a trustee, as set out in the Trustee Investment Act, 1961. Whilst an investor can take whatever risks he chooses in relation to his own money, there is, very properly, more constraint imposed on a person who, as a trustee, is making investments on behalf of others; (9) some investors prefer to invest in UK securities only but others may prefer to invest a proportion of their funds in overseas securities, or in one or more commodities. The simplest and least high-risk way to do this, in the case of a non-expert smaller investor, would be by investment in relevant and well regarded specialist unit trusts.

Diversification

It is a fundamental investment principle, for institutions as well as individuals, that investments should be adequately spread, so that the failure of a single one, or a small number, would be bearable. This is diversification. In the case of an individual, funds would normally be spread amongst: (*a*) fixed- and/or variable-interest securities; (*b*) equities; (*c*) property; (*d*) cash or near-cash; (*e*) possibly, some high risk speculative investments for a small proportion of the total; appropriate life insurance policies and pension funds. Within the fixed- and variable-interest group the securities would be selected mainly from: government 'gilt-edged'; local authority securities; foreign stocks; company debentures; unsecured loan stocks; (possibly) cumulative preference shares. Equities would normally be a selection of ordinary shares of companies operating in a number of industries and listed on the Stock Exchange. Funds invested in properties could be in the form of direct ownership of residential and/or commercial property; the shares of property companies; property bonds; unit trusts specialising in the shares of property companies. High-risk investment would include dealings in commodities, a specialist area in which large sums can be made or lost, notably through the aspect of gearing and trading on margins. When the investment is on a medium- to long-term basis, an appropriate life insurance policy will be amongst the options, especially because of the preferential tax treatment.

Unit trusts and investment trusts
Unit and investment trusts have been mentioned briefly. There are fundamental differences between them. Unit trusts which are authorised to advertise in the UK operate under regulations laid down by the Department of Trade which include the manner of calculation of the daily buying and selling price of units. Unit trusts have (*a*) managers, and (*b*) trustees. Unit trusts are 'open-ended' and intending investors may apply for units at any time. Each unit trust has its own trust deed which defines, *inter alia*, the securities in which the managers may deal and the maximum permitted holding of a single security as a percentage of the total holdings. The trustees will be a financial institution of substance and standing and will be charged with the duty of holding the securities and ensuring that the unit trust managers work strictly within the terms of the trust deed. In addition to 'general' unit trusts there are many specialist trusts, the aim being to offer such variety that every category of investor is likely to find several unit trusts which would be relevant to his personal strategy. Thus some aim for capital growth rather than income, and others for high income rather than growth. Some deal in 'recovery situations' (fairly high risks but possibly quite high returns), or commodities, or property, or Japanese, or US companies, etc. There are also unit trusts linked with life insurance, designed to take maximum advantage of tax concessions in relation to life insurance investment.

There is keen competition between unit trust managements, and a small number of groups offer unit trusts of many categories, each being managed by experts employed by the group. The basic principle is that funds supplied by investors are applied by the managers in the purchase of Stock Exchange listed securities within the range and limits dealt in by that trust. In a period when buyers predominate the inflow of funds to the managers, applied in the purchase of the underlying securities, will tend to cause the prices of these to rise and this will be reflected in the published daily buying and selling price of the unit trusts being dealt it. Conversely, when sellers predominate, prices will tend to fall. Managers need to exercise skill and judgement in deciding upon particular purchases and sales, their quantities and timings and also in balancing investment against liquidity, as they will require to have cash readily available for holders of units who wish to sell. Reasonable liquidity also enables managers to take advantage of investment opportunities. However, over-liquidity could result in a trust being a poor performer in respect of capital gains or income, but in recent years high interest rates have been available on the short-term money markets and professional investment managers take full advantage of this situation, which will be reflected in the performances of their trusts.

Unit trust holders are not 'shareholders' and the value of a unit trust holding on any day is closely related to the market values of the underlying securities. The appeal of unit trusts to certain investors arises from: diversification – even when a speculative trust is chosen there will be a wide spread of holdings and few, if any, would be likely to fail completely; professional management; ease of dealing. A special appeal of the biggest groups is that a holder of trusts in a particular group can normally 'switch' from one trust to another within the group with minimum dealing costs. Criticisms of unit trusts include that insofar as a policy of diversification reduces the maximum loss likely to be sustained, it equally limits the maximum gain likely to be achieved, and so the overall performance can often seem unexciting. It is also a curious fact that when the results of many unit trusts are considered over a period, the performances of many will seem surprisingly poor, so that one questions the skills of the managers concerned. There has been substantial freedom from major scandal and there is confidence that the major groups are operated with strictest probity. In the case of some trusts there have been allegations that dealings have taken place to support the prices of securities in which managers or trustees or associates have been personally interested, or to create a false market in certain securities, or that there have been excessive dealings ('churning'), with managers and certain stockbrokers splitting commissions and the managers benefitting at the expense of unit holders. However, allegations of impropriety have been rare and dissatisfied holders normally complain about poor performance. Sometimes the complaint is not justified and the real cause of the investor's disappointment should be that he personally misjudged his investment timing and bought when the market was high, and wished to sell when it had fallen.

Until 1980 certain aspects of taxation treatment had made it impracticable for unit trusts to be offered based on gilt-edged securites: changes in the law now make such issues feasible and they are being marketed vigorously. A point which investors may overlook is that because of the difference between the bid and offer prices – about 7% – investors who buy and then sell quickly are likely to show losses and as the managers emphasise in their advertisements, unit trust investment is primarily interesting to medium- to long-term investors. The financial press, especially early in the new year, and the publication *Money Management*, once yearly, feature 'league tables', sometimes in considerable detail, showing how individual unit trusts, and different categories of trust have performed over the past twelve months, and over longer periods, and there is also informed comment. In general, investors have ample sources of reliable information in respect of unit trusts and competition between trusts is keen.

Investment trusts

Investment trusts are entirely different from unit trusts. Indeed, the word 'trust' is misleading as an investment trust is a listed public limited-liability company. It is not 'open ended' but has ordinary shares in issue and a prospective investor would place an order with a stockbroker as he would for the purchase of any other listed share. As the market tends to be narrow the 'jobber's turn' may be large and because of the narrowness of the market and the jobber's turn, an investor who bought a particular security might find that he could only sell at a loss. Unlike unit trusts, investment trusts may have gearing, as debentures may be issued, or loans otherwise obtained. The directors of investment trusts have much greater freedom of action than unit trust managers – indeed, a large part of their poor image may stem from this fact. The background is that investment trust companies were first formed over 100 years ago, long before unit trusts. It may be assumed that every investment trust was formed with the intention of producing profitable business for its promoters, who would normally be major shareholders and executive directors. They would offer (and might or might not provide) skilled professional portfolio management, with risk spreading by means of diversification, and the prospect of high returns, partly as a result of gearing. The assets of an investment trust will normally consist largely of holdings of listed companies, but holdings of unlisted companies, properties and other assets are in order. Trusts often specialise in overseas investments. In principle, it is difficult and costly for an individual investor of limited means to invest directly overseas. It is easier (and less worrying) to do so at one remove, primarily now through unit trusts and, to a lesser extent, through investment trusts.

For some years investors appear to have been disenchanted with investment trusts and this is reflected in the fact that market prices of shares regularly stand at a discount of 20%–40% below the net asset values. They do not offer to individuals the tax advantages offered by other forms of indirect investment and performance has been considered generally sluggish. The narrowness of the market makes dealing costs excessive. In principle, investors who prefer to leave their investment management to others consider themselves more satisfactorily served by unit trusts and in recent times a number of investment trust companies have converted themselves into unit trusts. Moreover, in the mid-1970s there was a major scandal involving a former Lord Mayor of London and a pillar of the city financial establishment. An acute financial journalist of the *Investors Chronicle* believed there was evidence of improper conduct on the part of a chairman of several investment trusts and he sought to establish the facts. As so often seems to happen in these cases he seemed to be met by obstruction at too many points, with indications that, typically, a major 'cover-up' was being organised by some influential people. The journalist finally established and published the facts but even so there seemed excessive delays before the authorities acted and, in the event, the chairman at the centre of the scandal died shortly before being arrested to face charges. The disclosing of a scandal and evidence of 'cover-up' activities always leaves an unanswered question – 'how often is this kind of scandal occuring in the City without it ever coming to light?', and confidence is undermined, including in the ability and the will of institutions and individuals in the City to practice 'self-regulation' which, City people claim, serves the public interest better than regulation primarily through statute law and official regulatory bodies such as the SEC in the USA.

Meanwhile, in recent times several investment trusts have been taken over by large pension funds and it is expected that there will be more takeovers of this kind in the future, since a takeover allows fund managers to acquire large blocks of shares and other securities at a cost below the cost of acquiring these securities through the market in the normal way.

Institutions as investors

The reasons why individuals have increasingly been channelling their personal savings through institutions have been considered, including the aspect of tax incentives. In view of the importance of these financial institutions and their key roles in the money and capital markets, those which have not already been considered will be examined briefly.

Pension funds

In 1978 Sir Harold Wilson, Chairman of the Wilson Committee, was reported as stating that the pension fund managers were not aware of their own power as investors and, by implication, neither were the government nor the general public. This situation arises from the continually increasing pension funds available for investment in the UK. Until quite recently it had been a matter for voluntary decisions by an employer whether or not he paid a pension to a retired employee. All employers are now compelled by law either to contribute to a supplementary state pension scheme or themselves to provide a not less favourable one, approved by the Inland Revenue. A feature of the UK schemes, including those operated by the nationalised industries, and which are amongst the largest because of the numbers they employ, but excluding schemes operated by the government itself, is that they must be funded. That is, the employer, and the employee if it is a contributory scheme, or the employer alone if it is a non-contributory scheme, must make regular prescribed payments into a separate fund outside the control of the employer, and the funds are held and invested by trustees and in due course pensions are paid from the fund to retired employees, or their dependents.

The consequence is that pension funds of large employers in the public and private sectors, such as those of the nationalised industries, ICI, Shell, Unilever, etc., will each be huge and the overall totals are enormous and steadily rising. Large funds are invariably self-contained, with their own trustees and specialist managers. Smaller companies, whose funds would not be large enough to justify the expense of expert managers, may make payments into an approved external scheme, which are mostly operated by insurance companies experienced in this field. Approved pension schemes are exempted from liability to tax on their investment income and on capital gains. In due course, pensions are treated as earned income of the recipient and not as investment income liable to investment surcharge tax. Clearly, the ultimate levels of pensions payable from individual funds will be governed by the sizes of the contributions to the funds, the periods of investment, the economic situations over time, and also by the quality of the fund managers, their strategies and tactics over the years. Evidence shows that some funds are much more successful than others.

The sheer size of pension and other institutional funds has been raising political questions. There is awareness of and concern at the lack of accountability of fund managers to anyone except their trustees and members and even this accountability may be more apparent than real. There is also a different fear, that under a Labour government these

Investors and their viewpoints

large centralised funds could be used as a means of 'nationalising by the back door'. Politicians of left-wing views argue that fund managers should have regard to the public interest and that the government should have powers to direct that funds be invested in particular securities, or companies or industries. A main objection to this view, and which is raised by Labour as well as Conservative supporters, is that funds managers could be directed by a Government anxious to 'buy' votes in a marginal constituency to invest in a company or industry which could not raise money through the market for the sound reasons of a bad and unprofitable record, bad labour relations with frequent unofficial strikes, so that the company or industry appeared as a thoroughly bad risk and unacceptable to any prudent investor.

Fund managers argue that their duty is to their trustees and to the ultimate beneficiaries of their funds. There is wide but by no means universal acceptance of this viewpoint. There is also doubt as to how much real accountability there is in practice and concern that increasingly huge sums of money are under the control of relatively small numbers of men whose only qualification for handling them may be that they are very highly skilled in a very narrow field. Because of the relative smallness of the number of senior investment managers, and the fact that a large proportion work in or near the City, they are likely to meet frequently, informally as well as formally, and be subjected to the same influences, including the published views of highly regarded analysts. It has been reported that the turning point towards recovery after the 1973/74 stock market collapse came when a very small group of investment managers, controlling exceptionally large funds, considered that the falls had gone beyond all reason and decided, at an informal meeting, that the time had come to start buying openly in an effort to increase confidence. This aim proved successful and when it was observed and reported that major institutions were buying the tide began to turn and the recovery began.

Assuming the correctness of this report, one wonders where and how the market collapse would have ended and what the social consequences might been if a small group of major institutional fund managers had not decided to act as they did? Meanwhile, in any situations the human aspects must not be overlooked. Investment managers are men and women with highly paid jobs which they wish to keep. A manager who 'plays safe' and avoids going on a quite different course from his colleagues is less likely to be questioned or challenged than one who is ready to 'go it alone', or 'swim against the tide'. When men act together as a herd and a mistake is made, all make the same mistake and it is virtually impossible for trustees to fault seriously an individual manager. However, if a manager were a 'loner', who had a sequence of brilliant successes, but then one or two serious miscalculations, there would be a much stronger chance that cautious trustees would decide that he was too unpredictable and unreliable to be permitted to make investment decisions in respect of large funds. A consequence of a very large proportion of investment decisions being made by relatively small numbers of people is that at any moment buying or selling decisions are predominantly one way. This is in marked contrast to the situation when decisions are made by larger numbers of individuals, who are free to act as they please and are not preoccupied with possible reactions of trustees. When large numbers are involved there is much more likelihood of many decisions being one way, and many the other. The Wilson Committee Report deals in detail with the pension funds. One unanimous recommendation is that there should be more published information available, both to fund members and the public, in the same way as most company accounts have to be prepared in accordance with guidelines set out in the Companies Acts, and then circulated to shareholders, and also made available for public inspection. The Wilson Committee also considered the question whether the investment of pension funds should be liable to government direction in any form. In this case there was a majority view that there should be no direction of any kind, and two separate minority reports recommended the setting up of a new investment institution which could be directed to invest equity capital or loan funds in particular companies or industries and recommended that the pension funds should be significant subscribers of capital to this institution, on the basis that certain government guarantees would be given as well as a minimum rate of return to the pension funds which provided funds. The arguments for each viewpoint are marshalled in the Report, and are interesting.

Time Horizons
A notable feature of the pension and life insurance funds is that the fund managers operate with short, medium, distant and very distant time horizons. New entrants to a fund might not draw their pensions until more than forty years after their first contributions. Accordingly, a proportion of the funds may be invested in long-term securities, e.g. fixed-interest securities redeemable well beyond the year 2000, properties purchased for commercial or industrial letting, equities, works of art, even. Whilst long-dated securities and/or equities are not necessarily bought to hold for long periods, and speculators often buy and sell within an account, institutions may buy an investment or property with a readiness to retain it for many years, or to the final redemption

date. (However, during the 'dawn raids' on stock exchange listed securities in 1980 it was widely reported that when brokers telephoned institutional holders of the shares being 'raided' the holders were often ready to sell in order to gain a quick profit.) Insurance companies are specially concerned with the nominal or face values of their investments as their liabilities are expressed in these terms. However, they are also concerned with real as well as nominal values as these will affect their capital gains, or losses, and their income, and, in consequence, the bonuses they can declare to their 'with-profit' policy holders: they also affect their profitability as companies, and the performance of their shares. Pension funds will have a special concern with real profits and growth as pensions are payable on the salaries received by individuals in the year(s) just prior to retirement, and in inflationary times final salaries will bear no relationship to the much lower salaries paid on entry to the fund.

Insurance companies

A main reason for the growth of insurance company as well as other institutional funds, in real as well as nominal terms, includes the growth of national and international trade and increasing prosperity in the industrial countries, as well as growing awareness of the importance of appropriate insurance. Insurance companies may be divided into two broad groups, life and non-life: the same company may deal with both groups. A feature of insurance is that the premium must always be paid in advance and there will thus always be strong cash flows in respect of premium income (with claims paid as important outflows). In the case of non-life business, premiums are accepted in relation to risks which may or may not give rise to claims in the period covered and the majority of policies taken out in a period do not give rise to claims. However, a feature of life insurance (assurance) is that acceptance by a company of an annual premium in most cases gives rise to a commitment to make a prescribed payment on a known or unknown future date to the policy holder or to his heirs in the event of his earlier death. All insurance companies build up substantial reserves with a sufficient proportion in liquid form so that claims can be met promptly and so that major setbacks and even catastrophes can be survived.

A substantial part of the profits of any insurance company will arise from efficient and successful investment of every type of funds held and full use will be made of the money market, including lending on an 'overnight' basis when appropriate. Advanced mathematical techniques are used to assess risks, and mortality rates, and investment managers will be well informed about portfolio theory even although they may treat it with caution. Clearly, over a period certain companies have been more successful then others in their investment policies and such companies, provided that they are also able to keep their administration costs below average, will be market leaders in respect of the bonuses they can declare to with-profit policy holders. Competition between life insurance companies is keen and their performance is well monitored and publicised in the financial press, and prospective purchasers of policies should study the record before deciding which policy to purchase. In the earlier years of this century many insurance companies concentrated on gilt-edged and other fixed-interest securities and avoided equities as being too risky. However, some investment managers, who must first have obtained the approval of their boards, began to invest significantly in equities. This proved a successful policy which enabled the companies concerned to improve their bonuses, and the more conservative companies then began to follow the same policy. In recent years, the performance of equities has generally been disappointing and companies have been investing a higher proportion of their funds in gilt-edged and similar securities to take advantage of high interest rates. Because it is a period of rapid change all companies must keep their investment strategies and policies under continuing review.

Fixed-interest securities

The following are main types of fixed-interest securities purchasable through the UK Stock Exchange:

(a) British government funds ('gilt-edged') – 'shorts' – (redeemable within the next five years); 'mediums' (redeemable after five but not more than fifteen years hence); 'longs' (redeemable on a specified date more than fifteen years hence); undated, effectively irredeemable, or 'one-way options' – liable to be redeemed but only at the option of the government: thus 3½% War Loan, which is in this category, would be redeemed in the most unlikely event that interest rates fell below 3½% per annum.

(b) Local authority loan stocks.

(c) Foreign and Commonwealth government stocks: miscellaneous loans, e.g. FFI, Agricultural Mortgage Corporation etc.

(d) UK and overseas company debenture or loan stock issues, including convertible debentures and debentures with subscription rights: various types of preference shares.

The terms and conditions attached to fixed-interest securities vary considerably and attention must be given to the 'small print'. Interest (or dividends in the case of preference shares) is normally paid twice yearly in equal instalments.

In general the following factors will be taken into account in assessing the quality and hence the yield expectations in respect of a particular fixed-interest security: (*a*) the financial strength and reputation of the issuer; (*b*) expectations as to ability to redeem on the due date; (*c*) rights of the lender in the event of the borrower's default, and security, if any; (*d*) the size of the issue; (*e*) the marketability of the security; (*f*) prior charges, if any, and types of charge; (*g*) rights on redemption or in the event of liquidation of a company; (*h*) conversion or subscription rights, if any; (*i*) whether interest is payable gross or net (with or without tax deducted and any other taxation implications; (*j*) the country in which the borrower is situated, if overseas; (*k*) expectations with respect to interest rate movements and the date of redemption of the security. Because of the aspect of complete security in terms of nominal values, low dealings costs and favourable taxation implications, UK government securities are specially highly regarded.

Why companies have ceased to issue fixed interest debentures

Subsequent to 1973 UK companies have virtually ceased to issue long-term fixed-interest debentures, and there is now increased reliance on bank loans, or loans from institutions such as FCI and ICFC. Explanations given to the Wilson Committee stressed that companies do not wish to take on long-term debt commitments when interest rates are high, even if the real rate of interest is negative. They pay as much attention to nominal rates as to real rates:

'Since a high nominal rate puts pressure on cash flow in the early years of a project before profits start to accrue; it effectively fore-shortens the period of the loan, since in inflation-adjusted terms most of the interest payment is really a repayment of capital. Moreover, a long-term debt commitment at a high fixed interest rate exposes the borrower to the risk that inflation will **fall** below the level expected, making the real interest burden substantial. We have been told that the market in industrial loan stocks is unlikely to revive unless inflation and long-term interest rates are brought down to single figures.

Yield

An investor who has satisfied himself that a fixed-interest (or dividend) security is safe enough will normally be specially concerned with the after-tax yield it offers. A speculative investor might buy the security in the expectation of an early fall in interest rates, when the market price would rise and he would then be able to sell and make a capital profit he would not then be interested in the yield aspect, but normally the yield is of major importance to an investor. The yield is the financial return on an investment and whilst it is often considered only in nominal terms, adjustment would need to be made in respect of changes in the value of money if it is to be considered in real (purchasing power) as distinct from nominal terms. A higher degree of risk would require compensation by a higher yield. In respect of redeemable securities the yield will be made up of two elements: (a) the flat, or running, yield, which is calculated:

$$\text{Yield} = \frac{\text{Coupon (nominal rate)} \times 100}{\text{Market price}}$$

The market price would include dealing expenses; (b) the yield to redemption. In this case account is taken of the difference between the cost of the security, including expenses, and the amount finally received, net of expenses, on its redemption, and the period of time between purchase and redemption. For example, if, say, a 9% stock (1985) were purchased at 90 exactly three years before the redemption date then, ignoring expenses, the flat yield would be $\frac{9 \times 100}{90} = 10\%$. If the stock were to be redeemed at par, 100, then at the end of three years there would be a capital profit of £10 on a purchase price of £90, i.e. appromimately 11%, spread over three years, approximately 3.7% annually. The redemption yield is the total of the flat yield and the capital profit expressed on an annual basis – in this case 10% + 3.7% i.e. 13.7% (approximately). Analysts, financial journalists and other who wish to calculate the redemption yield with precision take into account the fact that the capital profit would be receiveable on a future date and should therefore be converted into present values by discounting, on the principles followed in DCF calculations (Ch. 14).

Equities

The increased attraction of equities to individual and institutional shareholders has been the prospect of a steadily rising money income, from dividends, together with the prospect of growth and hence of capital gains. Equities are thought to offer a 'hedge against inflation'. However, market prices may fluctuate considerably in both the short and longer periods. Prices move in response to forces which: (a) affect all securities simultaneously; (b) affect securities of a particular industry; and (c) affect the securities of a particular company. At the trough of the 1973/74 stock market collapse even 'blue chip' shares of the highest quality fell to astonishingly low levels, which clearly bore no rational relationship to the intrinsic value of the share in question.

Factors affecting prices

General price movements may have one or more main causes. Sometimes it is reported that prices have fallen, or have been 'marked down' heavily, but there has been little selling. This indicates that jobbers have marked down prices in the expectation that there will be more sellers than buyers, and perhaps also to discourage prospective sellers. Good or bad news of major international events, or expectations, may affect prices at least temporarily. Changes in interest rates are a major factor and security prices tend to move inversely with interest rates. Pressures on liquidity cause price falls, as holders of securities have to sell to obtain cash – during a credit squeeze they might be unable to borrow against the collateral of the securities. Pressure on liquidity was a major factor in the 1973/74 UK stock market collapse and also in the 1929 Wall Street crash in the USA.

There may occasionally be special factors which affect one industry only. Thus an unexpectedly severe tax increase on spirits would cause distillery shares to fall, possibly only temporarily. There are then the factors which concern a single company only, such as a press report of a boardroom dispute and the sudden resignation of directors. For the moment at least, analysts and others would have doubts about the company. In principle, any one or more of the following could have at least short-run effects on the market price of a company's shares: (1) announcement of a capitalisation issue; (2) a rights issue; (3) a dividend declaration; (4) change from a 'cum scrip', 'cum rights' or 'cum div' to an 'ex scrip', etc., position; (5) publication of an interim statement, or the final figures for the year, or the annual report; (6) rumours of a takeover bid either by or for the company – the share price of the company thought likely to be a bid for will rise whereas that of a prospective bidder tends to fall to a greater or lesser extent; (7) announcement of a merger or amalgamation; (8) announcement of new products, patents, etc.; (9) a change in interest rates; (10) a change in taxation; (11) a change in government policy likely to affect the company, or reports of national or international events thought likely to have a similar effect; (12) press comment.

Analysts making a study in depth of a company to assess its likely appeal to equity investors (or other clients) would consider financial and non-financial matters. The following is a summary of matters likely to be of special interest: (1) the dividend yield; (2) the earnings yield; (3) the price earnings ratio; (4) profits – the total, the quality and sources and indications of trends; (5) assets – the net assets per share, the quality, including the location; (6) the capital structure and gearing; (7) various significant ratios, and especially the return on capital, and any trends disclosed; (8) contingent liabilities; (9) capital expenditure commitments; (10) the market share for products and significant changes; (11) the size of the company and the marketability of the shares; (12) general national and international economic prospects, government financial policy, regulations, etc; (13) the assessed prospects of the industry; (14) assessed prospects of the company, development of new products, evidence of successful reorganisation or modernisation programmes, views on the quality of the management, labour relations, etc., (15) any taxation implications; (16) changes in fashion or technology; (17) nationalisation implications (if any), diversification policies; (18) interest rates and expectations.

The equity market in recent years

The behaviour of the UK equity market during the 1970s often failed to conform to forecasts made by experts. The quadrupling of oil prices in 1973 took almost all experts by surprise, although a tiny minority had sounded warnings earlier that huge price increases might occur, but they had been ignored. With hindsight, it is clear that for years energy had been underpriced and sooner or later a readjustment of the kind that took the world by surprise in 1973/74 was inevitable. The speculative property boom which reached its peak in the early 1970s and then collapsed with the oil price explosion in 1973/74 can be seen, in the light of subsequent events and disclosures, not least in official Department of Trade Reports, to have been an outrage, a discredit to capitalism and something which could and should have been prevented if standards of competence and integrity in the City had been a fraction as high as they had been claimed to be, and if self-regulation had been effective. The crash naturally caused a major setback. Even so, puzzling facts remain, notably that during the decade equity shares were becoming relatively cheaper. For example, in 1968 the market price of Beecham shares, a market leader, stood at 29 times earnings, but in 1978 it stood at only 13 times earnings, despite the steady and good growth of the company. Government dividend controls during the period presumably had a generally depressing effect on equity prices. Other important adverse factors must have been, and still are: (*a*) the rise in interest rates; (*b*) loss of confidence of investors in equities as a hedge against inflation, especially in a social climate which, until the change to a radical Conservative government in 1979, seemed largely hostile to capitalism and the interests of shareholders. Subsequent to the change of government there has been the recession, still higher interest rates and pressure on liquidity, continuing inflation and a high sterling exchange rate in consequence of the North Sea oil, and the evident unprofitability of much of UK manufacturing industry; (c) the restructuring of institutional portfolios to increase the weighting of fixed-interest securities in view of their high yields.

Without doubt, in the UK and the USA, at the end of the 1960s the widely held viewpoint was that equities were the 'best buys' for investors, especially as inflation hedges. In Wall Street, market leaders had P/E ratios of 100 or even more, and in the UK up to 40 or so. At these levels, in each country, prices were vulnerable to loss of confidence, and this occurred in 1973/74 with the sudden increase in oil prices. During the decade institutions as well as individuals became disenchanted with equities.

'The real earnings conundrum'
The following is the text of a feature article in the 'Lex' column of the *Financial Times* of 25 June 1979 and which is of special interest

As the equity market wilts at the thought of 17½% inflation by the end of the year it is worth taking another look at the academic arguments going on over the valuation of equities. The basic puzzle continues to be the simple one of why a share in equity does not in practice offer a satisfactory hedge against the ravages of inflation. Why have shares not performed as well in terms of price as houses, or gold or vintage cars? The normal answer is that the acceleration of inflation over the last ten years or so, since share prices in Britain touched a peak in real terms, has coincided with a serious decline in the level of real profitability. The government and other bodies have produced estimates of company profits adjusted for replacement cost depreciation and stock appreciation.

Real returns
Last week, for example, the Bank of England published a real pre-tax rate of return figures for industrial and commercial companies, indicating that returns in the range 10 to 12% had shrunk to less than 5% in recent years. For 1978 the estimate was 4.7%. But the Bank acknowledges that such calculations underestimate the return on the equity interest. High rates of interest containing a premium for inflation are charged as costs, while there is no benefit allowed from

holding assets which are rising in value with inflation and partly financed by debt. The Bank's researches have calculated that the real pre-tax return on equity for 1977 was over 7% and on a still more favourable basis allowing for differential inflation in company assets the return was 9%.

These are pre-tax figures. Bearing in mind that the effective tax burden has been reduced because companies do not pay any tax on unrealised gains and are protected against tax on stock gains (in the UK through stock relief; in the US because of LIFO stock accounting policies) it appears that the comparison with the apparently hugely profitable periods of the 1950s and 1960s is not quite as unfavourable as might appear. In fact, some economists have decided that the purported collapse in real company profitability is a myth. In March Modigliani and Cohn published a paper in the *US Financial Analysts Journal* under the title 'Inflation, rational valuation and the market'. They argued that there was no evidence that the total after-tax return to equity holders had been reduced by inflation, and investors appeared to suffer from a variety of inflation illusions. They concluded that the US equity market was hugely undervalued.

Now an American academic visiting Britain, Professor Basil Moore, has carried out a similar exercise into UK profitability using as his data base the Department of Industry's files containing the aggregated income accounts and balance sheets of over 1000 large quoted companies. He comes to the same conclusion from this UK data as Modigliani did from US evidence. Conventionally adjusted after-tax returns, net of replacement cost depreciation and stock appreciation have fallen sharply since the middle 1960s and even become negative by about 1973. But net after-tax profits, fully adjusted for revaluation gains due to inflation, whilst at times highly volatile, have not shown any evidence of secular deterioration. At this point, however, Moore diverges from the Modigliani theory that investors are behaving irrationally and attempts to find a rational explanation of the stock market's attitude. His explanation boiled down to the view that it is not investors but company managements who have got it all wrong.

Payout ratios
It is a widely accepted theory, at any rate in the US, that a share price reflects the market's valuation of the future earning's stream. The famous Modigliani and Miller theorem, a central proposition of modern financial theory, shows that dividend payout ratios are irrelevant for share prices. But Moore has found that in contrast to the relatively stable trend of adjusted earnings, real dividend payments have been

falling in the UK. He suggests that the connection between inflation and lower payout ratios provides the main explanation for what has been happening to share prices in real terms. The real value of dividends has fallen in most years since 1965, the peak year, and by 1976 the real value had fallen by over a third. Since then there has been a modest recovery. But the downward adjustment of real dividends means that whereas companies paid out over three-quarters of their real after-tax profits in the 1960s they have cut this ratio to about two-fifths in the 1970s. During this period there has been a sharp decline in the so-called valuation ratio, which relates equity market value to the equity interests in corporate assets at replacement cost. In the 1960s it varied between 1.0 and 1.4 but in 1976 it was only 0.68. Companies are not paying high enough dividends to encourage investors to value shares at anything like true net worth.

The removal of dividend controls after 5¾ years at last eliminates one source of distortion. But the question remains whether Moore is right about the trend of real profits (there is much argument about the calculation of after-tax returns) and, if he is, whether it has any relevance to the policies of companies. The concept of fully adjusted profits is based upon accruals, not realisations. This means that companies could only pay out dividends to the full extent of such 'earnings' by borrowing to do so. There is a contrast here with the more limited gearing adjustments of the current cost accounting exposure drafts ED24 which effectively cause only realised gains to be credited to profits. It is only prudent of companies to seek – partly through greater retentions – to reduce their gearing at times of uncertainty, and to build up their dividend cover to provide against the sharp profit fluctuations brought about by rapid inflation. Companies now often talk of having a current cost cover of twice, whereas ten years ago historic cost cover of 1.5 might have been thought acceptable. Prudence has its advantages but it may also have a cost.

As usual when an article of exceptional interest and importance has been published it has given rise to informed correspondence putting forward a number of often sharply divergent viewpoints.

The Stock Exchange: dealings procedures

The Stock Exchange is a secondary and not a primary market. It is not responsible for the issue of securities and the raising of money by companies, although companies which wish to obtain or retain a listing must abide by the rules and regulations of the Stock Exchange. It serves a vital function as it provides a market place where listed securities can be bought and sold in a manner which inspires confidence in the investing public. Experience shows that investors would be reluctant to put money into a company unless they could be confident that shares they bought would subsequently be readily marketable. The Stock Exchange offers marketability. As developing countries industrialise and national companies begin to offer their shares to their own people there soon arises a demand for a national stock exchange so that shares so purchased can readily change hands. Meanwhile, the London Stock Exchange was founded in 1773 and it has been said 'like so many British institutions the Stock Exchange was not suddenly created but developed stage by stage'. In 1973 the London and various provincial exchanges – as well as the Dublin Stock Exchange – came together to form a single Stock Exchange.

Stock jobbers and stock brokers
A feature of the London Stock Exchange, which distinguishes it from that of other countries, is the emergence of two clearly defined functions – stock jobbers who buy and sell on their own account and effectively act as wholesalers, and the more numerous stock brokers who act as agents for clients. Both are required to be members of the Stock Exchange and in consequence are subject to its disciplines, and there are signs that this is now being more strictly enforced than formerly. Stock jobbers can not deal directly with the public but only with other jobbers or brokers. The basic procedure is that an investor who wishes to buy or sell securities will instruct his stockbroker as to his wishes. If he is a new client the broker will need to be satisfied as to his substance and his ability and readiness to meet his commitments. Smaller investors often act through their bank and this does not involve them in higher costs since there is an arrangement that the banker and broker divide the commissions. However, regular investors tend to deal directly with a broker since they then have better control over the important matter of timing.

The client may or may not impose price limits on the broker. If no price limits are stated the broker is expected to deal at the best price he can obtain for his client. This may be specially appropriate in a crisis situation, when prices are either falling or rising very quickly, and the client urgently wishes to buy or sell and has instructed his broker clearly. Otherwise, it is usual for clients to instruct their broker or bank as to the highest price at which they are prepared to buy or the lowest at which they will sell. The broker will approach the jobber(s) dealing in the security and without stating whether he is a buyer or seller, will ask the jobber to state his price. It will be understood that the enquiry relates to a normal-sized parcel, within understood limits. The jobber will state two prices – the lower, at which he will buy, and the higher, at which he will sell. The difference is the 'jobber's turn'. If there is more than one jobber dealing in the security, the broker will approach all and will accept the most favourable quotation provided that it is not outside the limits specified by the client. The jobber and broker each make a note in his notebooks, and inform their office of the details. The brokers send to their client a contract note on their headed paper. This states the name and address of the client, details of the security, including the number of shares, if applicable; the nominal price and the price of the transaction; contract stamp cost; commission; transfer stamp duty, if applicable, (This is payable on the consideration in respect of shares, by the purchaser). The final figure is the total, which is payable by a purchaser (in which case the costs are added) or receivable by a seller (in which case the costs are deducted from the proceeds). A separate contract note is prepared in respect of every transaction and each may be important from the tax record aspect.

The contract note also states the date by which payment must be made or the security supplied (in the case of a sale). The jobber notifies the selling broker of the name in which the transfer is to be prepared. The selling client executes the transfer form and sends the certificate to his broker, if he has not already done so. The buying client pays his broker who, in turn, pays the jobber through the Stock Exchange clearing system. The buying jobber makes payment through the clearing system to the broker from whom he bought, and this broker pays the seller of the security. Whilst brokers will be acting for clients, jobbers act as principals and buy and sell on their own account.

The account

Government securities are dealt in on a cash basis and accordingly are exempt from stamp transfer duty, at present £2% on the consideration, payable by the purchaser. Loan and debenture stocks are also exempt from this duty. Certain transactions give rise only to a nominal payment. Payment of duty is not required when securities are bought and sold within an account period and this reduces the costs of speculators who buy and sell within an account. (Whilst some speculators are 'bulls' and buy securities which they hope will rise in price, so that they can sell at a profit, others take up potentially more dangerous 'bear' positions – they expect price falls and so they sell securities which they do not yet own, intending to make delivery by purchasing the securities at a lower price when the expected price fall takes place. If they miscalculate a 'bear squeeze' may take place, sellers knowing that there are bears who must buy in order to meet their obligations, and so the sellers try to hold out and squeeze the highest possible prices from the bears). In brief, dealings which are not on a cash basis, notably shares, are settled at the end of the 'account'. There are 24 Stock Exchange account periods each year, of which 20 are of two weeks and 4 of three weeks duration, when bank holidays occur within an account period. Every account begins on a Monday and ends on a Friday. Special days within an account are:

(a) Preliminary or contango day (Monday). A purchaser, often a speculator, who wishes to carry over payment, requests his broker to try to make the necessary arrangements, by finding a seller prepared to delay receipt of the payment due. The purchaser has to pay 'contango' interest for this arrangement. 'Backwardation' is the opposite of 'contango' and occurs in a bear market when there is a predominance of sellers and some are prepared to pay a 'backwardation' interest to buyers who are prepared to agree to delay taking delivery of their shares.

(b) 'Making up' day (Tuesday): any contango or backwardation arrangements should be completed.

(c) Ticket day (Wednesday): the buying broker passes a ticket to the jobber with the name of this client: the jobber passes this to the seller's broker (it may be 'split' amongst a number of sellers).

(d) 'Intermediate' days (Thursday, Friday and Monday): these are to allow time for the documentation to be completed.

(e) 'Account day', or 'Settlement day': transactions should be completed, with buyers paying their brokers and securities being delivered to their purchasers. 'New time': transactions entered into on the last Thursday and Friday of an account may be treated as occurring in the following account.

Talisman

The Stock Exchange operates a clearing house and the processes of delivery and payment are facilitated by computer operation in the Central Stock Payment Department. In 1970 a City Working Party on Securities Handling recommended that the present fixed account system should be replaced by a ten-day rolling settlement which would require bargains to be settled on the tenth day after the transaction. In early 1979 'Talisman', the Stock Exchange's new computerised settlement, was inaugurated. The Council considered the existing system to be outdated and to give rise to unacceptable risks of fraud or misappropriation. Talisman is being introduced in phases and should ultimately cover all UK registered stocks. It is expected to streamline the transfer of securities and eliminate a great deal of costly and unproductive paper work, and thus to benefit all the parties. It entailed the setting up of a Stock Exchange nominee company called SEPON Ltd, into which all sold stock will be transferred, and all purchasers will receive their stock by transfer out of SEPON Ltd.

Ariel

Major financial institutions which deal on a large and frequent scale have sought to reduce their costs by participating in a computer-based system in which subscribers can deal with each other rather than through the Stock Exchange. The system was established in 1974 after study of a system operated in the USA. The commission rates are substantially lower than those charged by stockbrokers and the jobber's turn does not arise. The Stock Exchange does not permit its members to transmit business with or through Ariel although, of course, subscribers use the normal facilities of the Stock Exchange whenever they wish. As the fixed costs of Ariel are inevitably high, and this results in a high subscription charge (but relatively low transaction charge), its facilities are only interesting to those who deal on a substantial scale, i.e. institutions. However, in mid-1979 important subscribers were resigning from membership of Ariel on grounds of its failure to meet their needs. Its future is in doubt. Indeed, a fund manager observed that his experience of Ariel lead him to acknowledge the efficiency of the jobber's role in the securities market.

Recent criticisms of the Stock Exchange

The Stock Exchange provides a market for securities which are already in issue. A market has been defined as 'a commodity or group of commodities and the buyers and sellers thereof who are in direct competition with one another'. Whilst a market often involves one or more physical market places it does not necessarily do so and money and foreign exchange markets are examples of markets which operate efficiently without central market places and by means of fast and efficient telecommunications systems. The question arises – is the Stock Exchange a perfect market and, if not, how efficient is it? The prerequisites for a perfect market are considered to be: (*a*) there must be a sufficient number of individuals or firms operating on the market and none on a sufficiently large scale to be able to influence prices; (*b*) there must be freedom of entry into and exit from the market; (*c*) the product(s) dealt in must be homogeneous; (*d*) those dealing in the market must have perfect knowledge of all matters liable to influence prices. In a perfect market there can only be one price for a given commodity at any moment and, in principle, essentials are excellent communications, free competition, negligible dealings costs and wide extent.

In the case of the Stock Exchange particular securities will be homogenous but the supply will be limited, especially in the case of a security with a narrow market. The number of buyers and sellers is also limited and is tending to fall further insofar as the market is increasingly dominated by a relatively small number of institutions. Futhermore, there is not free entry into and exit from the market as dealings costs are relatively high, and tending to increase. The decline in the number of jobbers is another factor raising doubts about the efficiency of the Stock Exchange as a market. Jobbers have for many years tended to specialise in certain securities, industries, etc., but in the past there would normally be enough jobbers dealing in a particular security to offer some competition when a broker sought quotations. Many securities are now handled by one jobber only, or there may be two jobbers who operate a 'joint' book in respect of a particular security – they operate as if they were one firm. With decline in or elimination of competition between jobbers, the jobber's turn has widened and dealing costs in London are now generally higher than in New York. Effects of high dealing costs will be to discourage switching of investments and will also discourage many individuals from Stock Exchange dealings. A special factor arises from 'insider dealings' – those which are improperly made by or on behalf of individuals or institutions who have important information which is only available to a small number of people, e.g. that a takeover bid is about to be made. In many countries proven insider dealing constitutes a criminal offence which is punishable by imprisonment. It has now also been made a criminal offence in the UK but substantial insider dealers would be sophisticated enough to cover their tracks completely, possibly by dealing through overseas dealers and using, e.g. Swiss bank accounts, and secrecy could easily be preserved. Insider dealings present many practical difficulties in respect of definition and control and these aspects, in particular, give rise to continuing controversy.

For highest efficiency a market should operate with efficient and fast communications. Technically, communications facilities are very good and indeed we are living during a communications revolution, the rate of development is so fast. However, there are other aspects which are less satisfactory. For many large-scale operators or speculators, as much secrecy as possible is important. This is facilitated by the facilities which enable individuals and institutions to deal in securities without others becoming aware of their identities. This is by use of nominee accounts, mainly operated by banks on behalf of clients. Many overseas Stock Exchanges require publication of full details of daily turnover of individual securities. This is not a requirement in the UK. A claim often made for the jobbing system is that it makes for steadier prices: it could be, on the other hand, that the jobbing system operates in a manner which inhibits numbers of investors from dealing who otherwise would have done so if more information had been available, including of daily turnover of individual securities.

The present Stock Exchange systems were developed to meet needs which existed in earlier times. The 'twin pillars' of the old and, indeed, the present systems of trading are 'single capacity' and 'competing market makers'. The former establishes that members of the Stock Exchange act either as market makers in specific securities – jobbers – or as agents – brokers – who approach the market makers on behalf of the investing public. They do not act in both capacities. The intention is to minimise the risk that an investor places an order with a dealer who has a vested interest in the price of that security. The second principle is that there should be competing jobbers in respect of each security, otherwise the investor would still be dealing with a party with a vested interest in the price of a security, but at one remove. Because of the reduced jobber competition there is increasing use by brokers of the device of 'put through'. A broker brings together substantial buyers and sellers, normally institutions, and a price is agreed without reference to a jobber. This effectively eliminates the jobber's turn. However, to meet the rules of the Stock Exchange the broker then notifies a jobber and pays him a relatively small fee for recording the risk-free transaction in his books. A further current problem for the Stock Exchange has been that quite substantial business has been by-passing it altogether, mainly to the benefit of international and investment banks. Buyers and sellers are brought together without recourse to a London broker.

Forthcoming developments – the Office of Fair Trading

A new factor has arisen which has been compelling the Stock Exchange Council, and members, to reappraise the role of the Stock Exchange. In 1973 the Fair Trading Act included a provision for the registration of restrictive practices in the services sector and in 1976 the Restrictive Trade Practices Legislation was formally changed to make registration of such practices necessary. In April 1977 the Stock Exchange registered its Rule Book, which defines how British securities are listed and traded, with the Office of Fair Trading (OFT), as required by the legislation. The position with respect to the OFT is that details of all restrictive practices must be registered, and there is a presumption that these are against the public interest unless the organisation concerned, the Stock Exchange in this case, can satisfy the Restrictive Practices Court that the practice concerned will pass through certain 'gateways' which define them as being within the public interest. In practice, an institution which considered that it could not defend its practices before the Court would be likely to abandon them, partly to avoid legal costs and partly to avoid adverse publicity.

In accordance with its practice the OFT began, in 1978, to assemble the facts in relation to the Stock Exchange. It sent a circular to users asking them to comment upon the Stock Exchange's restrictive practices. The letter listed the main restrictions which the Stock Exchange will have to defend. The list referred to 17 restrictions but stated that it was not exhaustive. Questions were posed on the key 'single capacity' aspect, on the fixed minimum commission rates charged by brokers as agents of investors; with respect to the Stock Exchange's listing requirements and the 'club rules' through which it controls its members. For its part, in brief, the Stock Exchange argues that it has four pillars for efficient self-regulation and protection of the public interest. These are: single capacity – to ensure that an investor pays or receives a fair price for his securities; the listing requirement – to ensure that the quality of the listed securities is maintained; a 'compensation fund' – to protect the investor from the consequences of the collapse of a member firm; fixed commissions – to preserve single capacity and the compensation fund.

The purpose of circulating a questionnaire to Stock Exchange users is not to imply that there is cause for criticism and that the matter is being prejudged, but rather to assemble facts and opinions. Users may consider that a practice has weaknesses but still consider that the benefits outweigh these and they cannot think of a better alternative. Compromises are a fact of life. For example, in the mid-1970s the Wall Street Stock Exchange moved from fixed to negotiated commissions as a stimulus to competition. A main consequence was that the major institutions using Wall Street used their bargaining strength to force down the commissions they paid. Competition between brokers became 'cut-throat'. Some went out of business and others merged, but commissions charged to smaller investors, who lack bargaining power, have risen. It appears that many institutional and individual investors would prefer the jobber–broker single-capacity system to survive, in principle, together with the existing regulatory system, and the compensation fund. There is awareness that whilst many who use the Stock Exchange facilities, and their advisers, have integrity, there are others who do not, who are predatory and seek to create and exploit loopholes. It would seem that the public interest could suffer severely if regulatory systems were relaxed or abandoned. There is a widespread but not universally held view that because of the lack of integrity or moral standards of a minority of very able people in all countries, the need is for general tightening rather than relaxation of regulations. Meanwhile, the attitude of the Stock Exchange itself appears to be to regard the OFT enquiry as being unnecessary, time wasting and costly, and the Stock Exchange has shown iself to be capable of adapting itself to changing times through self-regulation. Many who hold the Stock Exchange in good esteem and do not question the good faith of its spokemen still have reservations about the effectiveness of self-regulation. The Wilson Committee Report questions whether the Restrictive Practices Court is well designed for reviewing these matters and considers that the Council for the Securities Industry might be more suited to the task. The latest position is that the matter will in due course be considered by the Restrictive Practices Court.

'Dawn raids' - a 1980 example of the problems of self-regulation

Early in 1980 there were reports of heavy buying by unknown buyers of the shares of a major mining company, Consolidated Gold Fields (CGF). Consolidated Gold Fields became concerned at the implications of the buying because of the scale and the obviously planned secrecy as to the identity of the buyer. On 12 February 1980 leading stockbrokers made very heavy purchases in less than half an hour by what was later christened a 'dawn raid'. They approached institutions with large holdings of CGF shares and offered to make purchases at a substantial premium over the last closing market price. A large number of the institutions accepted the offer. In less than six months the secret buyer had built up its holding of CGF shares to 14% and in the brief 'dawn raid' it increased the holding to 25%. Consolidated Gold Fields formally requested the Department of Trade, under provisions of the Companies Act, 1948, to investigate the identity of the secret buyer. In the event the buyer then disclosed its identity - De Beers Consolidated Mines, a prestigious South African mining company. It also gave reasons for its actions, which were strategic rather than to make short-term profits. Its holding of 25% of CGF equity would be sufficient to prevent any other company, possibly a hostile one, from gaining control over CGF.

The 'dawn raid' was obviously brilliantly planned and executed and it broke no existing laws or Stock Exchange regulations: the holding of the buyer was kept below 30% of the equity, at which level a bid to all the shareholders would have become mandatory. The immediate response of the informed press (with a small number of significant exceptions) was strong criticism of the brokers and jobbers involved (rather than de Beers), for what was seen as action against the spirit of the Stock Exchange, that small as well as large investors should have equality of opportunity. It was also felt to be wrong that managers of companies had to stand by helplessly whilst secret raids were taking place, and the destiny of a company, and its workpeople could be decided by an asset stripper. (This was obviously not the situation in the case of CGF). The Stock Exchange Council and the Council for the Securities Industry (CSI) were subsequently heavily criticised for failing to act quickly and decisively to ban any further 'dawn raids'. Institutional fund managers were also criticised for lending themselves to this type of dealing. In the event there were a number of other dawn raids in 1980 before a temporary ban was imposed by the CSI while new rules were worked out. Meanwhile, the Department of Trade and the Council of the Stock Exchange both investigated and then published reports about the De Beers 'dawn raid'. It is felt that when the Stock Exchange rules and mechanisms come to be examined by the Restrictive Practices Court, the 1980 dawn raids and the failure of the Stock Exchange and the Council for the Securities Industry to act decisively and quickly may prove of lasting embarrassment to the Stock Exchange and its members.

The Council for the Securities Industry: a postscript
Those who support the idea of self-regulation in the City in principle have reservations about the ability and the will of members of the City establishment ever to agree on procedures for self-regulation which would be truly effective. In 1979 the Council for the Securities Industry (CSI) issued a Code of Conduct for the guidance of issuing houses or brokers sponsoring an initial issue of shares. Reports were that behind the scenes influential parties strongly opposed the idea of a code, but when the majority decided that a code was necessary, at least as a face-saving device, it was not accompanied by any effective sanctions or 'teeth' against those who might break it. The following comment was made in the influential 'Lex' coloum of the *Financial Times* on 31 July 1979:

Instead of being a fiery champion of self-regulation in the City the Council for the Securities Industry is turning into a sort of nanny figure. After some quite lively internal debate and a fair amount of reshaping its draft statement on the responsibilities of new issue sponsors, published yesterday, turns out to be hopelessly wet.

Essentially it says that issuing houses should do their job properly, and an appendix gives what amounts to a rather dim child's guide as to what that involves.

It seems clear that the only real reason for a code of this nature is so that it can be brandished on the very rare occasions when some outsider – like a Department of Trade Inspector – might ask whether such a thing exists. As a practical protection for the public it appears to be worthless. The idea is that sponsors should be required prior to the listing to tell the Stock Exchange that they have conducted themselves in accordance with the statement. The is no suggestion that apart from this formal notification there should be any attempt by the CSI or anyone else to administer the code on a day-to-day basis, which is just as well since it would be impossible to oversee such a general statement of behaviour. If only one felt that the City was such a perfect place that time could be spared for such frivolities, and there was no proper work to be done elsewhere.

Investment analysis

Since at any moment fund managers and individuals will be preparing to make important investment decisions there will be a profitable market for investment advice. Investment analysis and advice are services provided by financial journalists, by researchers and analysts employed by stockbrokers and others, by consultants. The basic object of investment analysis will include the forecasting of the performance of securities both as to dividends, in the case of equities, and market price. The subject of investment analysis receives considerable academic and theoretical and mathematical treatment and a problem arises from the fact that distinguished academics often put forward strongly diverging viewpoints, each supported by theoretical arguments. The remainder of this chapter considers briefly a number of important terms and concepts, some of which may give rise to examination questions.

Portfolio theory

Portfolio Theory is concerned with the problem of making a selection of optimal investments in respect of a particular investor, taking into account the anticipated returns and the risks associated with them, and the requirements of the investor in the short, medium and long term and his attitude towards risk. Most approaches to portfolio theory incorporate some statistical measure of the risks involved. An efficient portfolio is one such that no other portfolio exists which offers the same return, but with lower risk, or the same risk but with higher return. A main innovator in respect of portfolio theory was Markowitz, who applied statistical techniques to the assessment of risk. 'He introduced the use of the standard deviation or variance of the return of an investment as a measure of risk and in general introduced the whole concept of statistical measures of risk in the selection situation' (H.M. Markowitz, 'Portfolio selection', *Journal of Finance*, March 1952). The Markowitz model is the name given to the approach which he developed for portfolio selection.

Fundamental and technical analysis
Fundamental, also known as traditional, analysis is based on the viewpoint that examination of the relevant factors in respect of a company or industry will provide a sound guide to future performance, share prices and divident payments; the present and past will be pointers to the future, taking into account both financial and non-financial factors, and internal and external ones. Thus an analyst wishing to apply fundamental analysis to a leading company would study past results in detail, ratios, directors' reports, financial press comments, dividend payments, the past and expected future economic environments, share prices movements, etc. On the basis of this he would form a view as to likely future dividends, earnings and share price movements.

A criticism of fundamental analysis is the practical one that predictions made by practitioners have so often proved to be seriously wrong in the past. There will obviously be differences in the competence and flair of individual analysts and evidence is that those who are most consistently reliable build up large numbers of followers. Problems of analysts arise from the facts that with regard to analysis of past events, they have to depend on published information to large extent and quite often this may not be as full as they would wish. Then there is the aspect of the future: no matter what insights an analyst may have, the future can not be foreseen with accuracy: many assumptions have to be made in forecasting and some at least are bound to prove wrong in the event.

Technical, also known as chart, analysis is based on the viewpoint that past price movements of a particular security, or index, reveal patterns which, if properly understood and interpreted, will enable future price movements to be predicted. Thus technical analysis is concerned with security prices (and not dividend payments). It requires that information is set out in chart form with prices on the vertical axis and dates on the horizontal one. As an example, an important term in technical analysis is 'resistance level'. This occurs where significant buyers and sellers come into the market when a share falls or rises to a certain price. Because of the activity which occurs at these prices there tends to be resistance to further fall, or rise, as the case may be, whenever that price has been reached. There are expressions 'double' and 'triple top' and 'double' and 'triple bottom'. If, for example, a share price fluctuates but reaches its resistance level twice, or even three times, without breaching it, that would be an indication of the strength of that resistance level. However, if a share price moving upwards breached a double or triple top, or going down breached a double or triple bottom, chartists would regard the former as a strong 'buy' and the latter as a strong 'sell' signal. To some extent the advice of chartists can be seen as self-inducing. If they publish 'buy' or 'sell' advice, those who follow this advice will cause prices to rise or fall further, as the case may be, and the signals they give will often be acted upon by investors who themselves do not try to follow the reasoning of the analysts, but only their advice.

Technical analysis has at one extreme its enthusiasts who consider that it makes other forms of analysis superfluous and, at the other extreme, critics who treat it with contempt or who observe that no one has ever met a chartist who has become wealthy by following his own advice. A review in 1979 of a book which featured the Random Walk Theory noted: 'only technical analysis based on past share price data, such as chartism, is dismissed as being absolutely futile'. A few days later an eminent correspondent replied, with searching comment on the book, which included: 'The worst mistake attributed to Mr – 's book is that 'chartism is futile'. It is the only way to try to comprehend fluctuation which is what the Stock Market is all about.' The fact is that technical analysis, or chartism, is a technical and complex matter – it has parallels with ratio analysis in that persons who have only a superficial knowledge can draw dangerously wrong conclusions. In areas where experts can hold opposite viewpoints it is safest for the non-expert to keep an open mind.

The random walk theory
Academic studies in investment in particular, and business finance in general, appear to have been carried out more widely and in greater depth in the USA than in the UK, at least until recently. They appear also to have had more impact on business opinion and action in the USA and reasons for this may include that business, management and financial studies have enjoyed high academic as well as public esteem in the USA, but they have hardly done so in the UK. Consequently much more money has been made available for academic research in the USA,

and much more published data and statistics are available there, and have been for many years. Business subjects are popular options in higher education in the USA and there are high general standards of numeracy amongst senior and middle managers. There has been closer integration of the business and financial and academic environments in the USA, with people moving freely from one to another. Another important factor is that studies based largerly upon statistical evidence tend to require substantial numbers of calculations and sometimes it is only feasible to make these when computers are available. It happens that computers have been in common use in the USA for many years and there is widespread familiarity with them. United Kingdom usage of computers is increasing but is still some years behind that of the USA.

The random walk theory, propounded in the USA, supported by reference to substantial statistical information and advanced mathematical reasoning, has caused widespread controversy in the USA and even anxiety amongst investment managers and analysts as it seems to raise questions about their role and usefulness. In brief, the theory is that in an efficient market, where substantial information is available to investors, who are themselves competent in its interpretation, security prices will respond to all the information now available and at any time the price of a security will take into account all the known factors and in consequence a price or a price index will, in effect, follow a random walk, with each movement independent of previous movements. An implication appears to be that investment success, or an ability to 'beat the index' is more a matter of luck than judgement.

A book review by Christine Moir appeared in the *Financial Times* on 16 July 1980, headed 'The revolution in portfolio theory'. An extract is:

'The investment profession is in the midst of a philosophical revolution', according to Robert Hagin, the vice president in charge of quantitative research at First Boston Corporation in New York (*Modern Portfolio Theory: The Dow Jones – Irwin Guide*, by Robert Hagin. Dow Jones Irwin-Homewars, Illinois, U.S.A). Extensive academic studies of price movements in the stock markets have forced on fund managers across the Atlantic the realisation that the market-place is 'nearly efficient'. In other words it pretty well accurately reflects in its price changes nearly all the extrapolations that can be made from historical data.

So persuasive has the 'efficient market theory' become that investment professionals are abandoning their fundamental analysis –

the detailed investigation of the performance of a company, the sector in which it operates and the overall economy – because it will rarely throw up a prognosis which can be used to pre-empt the market. For the same reason they are also turning away from chartism – the technical analysis of historic patterns of prices because 'there is absolutely no evidence that information of the price and volume movements of a stock over the recent past will aid in predicting the future price behaviour of the stock'. The words are Mr Hagin's. Whether a similar revolution is occuring on this of the Atlantic is doubtful. But certainly, the alternative to fundamental and/or technical analysis – modern portfolio theory – is being eagerly debated by UK fund managers and attendances are good at any seminar on the subject.

Modern portfolio theory, in its crudest form, attempts to replace the uncertain quest for shares which outperform the market with the concept of a portfolio which reduces uncertainty to a mathematical formula. Its twin axioms are 'risk' and 'return'. The new portfolio manager, employing his MPT theorems attempts to balance the risk and return on the basis that he can then forecast his overall performance within an acceptably narrow range. The mathematical jargon is still unfamiliar here. Rumours abound, for instance, that at least one major pension fund has put 65% of its equity portfolio under 'passive managements'. According to Mr Hagin, US professionals would instantly recognise that it was balancing the riskier and safer elements in that proportion of its fund so as to predict an average performance overall. Heated arguments are currently raging over the concept of the 'beta coefficient', which purports to measure the sensitivity of rates of return on a portfolio to general market movements. Afficionados in this country can get away with minimum detailed knowledge because the sceptics are even more ill informed.

Mr Hagin's book then, while possibly dangerously partisan in its support for MPT, is valuable for the scholarly way in which it outlines the investment problems which gave rise to the new investment tool and describes the basic philosophy and applications of the theory. MPT may prove only a passing theory. Meanwhile it has cogent and ardent supporters such as Mr Hagin, who are spreading the word internationally. It must pay to be versed in this vogue.

It is clear from this interesting analysis that investment analysis is a specialist and mathematically orientated area of study and there may not yet be certainties in it.

Questions

1. Indicate the main sources of information available to an equity investor and outline the type of information he could expect to obtain from each source. (ACCA 10 marks)
2. What factors should a listed company take into account in determining its dividend policy? (ICSA 22 marks)
3. What factors should influence the decision of listed companies regarding the amount of profit which should be retained for reinvestment? (ICSA 22 marks)
4. Explain analytically the factors which are likely to affect the share prices of listed companies. (ICSA 22 marks)
5. Describe the procedure by which deals are undertaken on the floor of the United Kingdom Stock Exchange. To what extent would you regard this market as perfect? (ICSA 22 marks)
6. For what reasons is the market price of its shares likely to be important to a listed company? (ICSA 22 marks)
7. Outline the main factors which determine the market value of the shares of a listed company. (ICSA 22 marks)
8. Define the concept of earnings per share and consider its importance in the determination of share prices. (ICSA 22 marks)
9. Outline and explain the relationships between the annual accounts of a listed company and the market value of its shares. (ICSA 22 marks)
10. Advise a listed company which has £500,000 surplus of cash for the next twelve months as to the best way in which to use that surplus. (ICSA 22 marks)
11. Your company's cash budget reveals that cash surpluses will be available. Discuss the matters to be taken into consideration in determining the company's short-term investment policy and describe briefly and **four** possible investments. (ACCA 15 marks)
12. Outline the main arguments which underlie portfolio theory. In what way is this theory relevant to the appraisal of corporate investment projects? (ICSA 22 marks)
13. Discuss the matters which a personal investor should take into consideration when deciding to invest either in unit trusts or investment trusts. (ACCA 15 marks)
14. Discuss the assertion that the most important conclusion of research in security analysis is that the would be investor is well advised to buy and hold a small number of securities selected at random. (ICSA 22 marks)

15. 'Investment is an art, not a science.' A client has asked for your comments upon this statement. (ICA 15 marks)

16. For what reasons should a quoted company continue to be concerned with the market performance of its shares and what action can it take to improve that performance? (ACCA 18 marks)

17. As investment manager for your company's private pension fund you are asked the following questions: (a) What should be the object of your investment policy? (b) Assuming equity management to be permitted it may be desirable for the fund manager to be able to take advantage of short-term changes in market prices. What are the practical difficulties in doing this? (c) How would you calculate at any time the yield to redemption on a long-dated government stock? (d) When the market rate of interest changes, what effect would you expect this to have on the prices of various gilt-edged stocks having different coupon rates and varying lives to maturity? (e) What do you understand by 'technical analysis' and 'fundamental analysis' share prices? Discuss their merits in deciding upon your investment strategy. (ICMA 25 marks)

18. A shareholder in a quoted company is concerned because she receives such small dividends. She has looked at the last annual report and seen that there is a large bank balance. In addition the balance sheet shows the following items which she believes could be used to increase the dividend: (1) a large 'share premium account'; (2) substantial 'unappropriate profits'; (3) a large 'reserve for general contingencies'; (4) a large 'provision for depreciation'; (5) a substantial 'provision for deferred taxation'. You are required to prepare a brief explanation of the nature to these items suitable for this shareholder, indicating which of the items, if any, are relevant to her problem. (ICA 20 marks)

19. 'Institutional funds are usually invested in one or more of the following: (a) bonds, (b) equities, (c) property. Describe briefly each type of investment and outline their advantages and disadvantages in present circumstances. (ACCA 20 marks)

20. The Dick Turpin Unit Trust has two members of its investment department staff, Barnum and Bailey, who are contenders for eventual promotion to general manager of the department. Both candidates are certified accountants who subsequently attended the Branchester Business School where they graduated with the degree of MBA with distinction in finance and investment. The appointment is expected to be made in 15 months' time and to help the board in its decision as to whom to appoint, each man was provided with £150,000 (in December 1975) to invest in dated securities and informed that the basis for the

promotion decision would be their performance in investing the funds over the next 12 months. The record of their performance at the end of 12 months, as prepared by the secretary to the board, is as follows:

Barnum's portfolio

| Treasury 3½% | 1985 £25,000 | bought at 75 ⅗ | Interest due and received £875 |
| Funding 2½% | 1985 £50,000 | bought at 76 ⅕ | Interest due and received £1,250 |

Bailey's portfolio

| Treasury 6% | 1995 £100,000 | bought at 116 ⅘ | Interest due and received £6,000 |
| Treasury 7% | 1979 £30,000 | bought at 110 ⅔ | Interest due and received £2,100 |

Return on investment: Barnum 3.42%; Bailey 5.4%

The secretary recommends to the board that Bailey should be offered the post as general manager of the investment department.

Required. From the information given: (*a*) **Would you agree with the secretary's recommendation? Supporting figures must accompany your decision.** (*b*) **Prepare an estimate of the market values of the portfolios at the end of the 12 month period assuming that interest rates have remained steady throughout the period.** (ACCA 18 marks)

21. Alpha is a company whose assets consist solely of investments in the share and loan capital of other companies. These investments range from complete holdings to very small interests. Alpha is considering investing in the share and/or loan capital of Beta Ltd, a summary of the most recent financial statements of which are undernoted.

You are required to analyse these accounts with a view to reporting upon the significant financial features to which you would draw the attention of Alpha as a potential investor in all or any of Beta's share and loan capital.

Summary profit-and-loss account for year ended 31 December 1976 (£)

Profit before taxation	1,100,000
Corporation Tax (52%)	572,000
	528,000
Preference share dividend	52,000
	476,000
Dividend on ordinary shares (proposed)	400,000
	76,000

Investors and their viewpoints

Summary balance sheet as at 31 December 1976 (£000)

Share capital and reserves				
4,000,000 ordinary shares £1 (fully paid)		4,000	Fixed assets	5,200
800,000 6½ (10%) cumulative preference shares (£)		800	Net Current Assets	4,200
		4,800		
Reserves		600		
		5,400		
Loans: 1,000,000 6% Debentures 1979/80	1,000			
£1,000,000 15% unsecured loan stock	1,000			
£2,000,000 8% convertible unsecured loan stock 1988/90	2,000	4,000		
		9,400		9,400

Notes: (1) At the balance sheet date the various shares and loans in Beta were priced as follows:
- (a) £1 ordinary shares £1.80 each;
- (b) 6½% preference shares £0.50 each;
- (c) 6% debentures: £0.80 per £1 of stock;
- (d) 15% unsecured loan stock: £0.95 per £1 of stock;
- (e) 8% unsecured loan stock: £0.65 per £1 of stock.

(2) the conversion terms for the 8% convertible unsecured loan stock are 3 ordinary shares per £10 of stock.

(3) The forecast pre-tax profits for the next 12 months are £1,500,000

(4) The fixed assets are estimated to be worth £1,000,000 more than book value.

(5) Assume corporation tax of 52% and a basic income tax rate of 35%. (ACCA 25 marks)

22. The following information has been extracted from the most recent public accounts and stock exchange listings of a public company (year ended 31 December 1977). **You are required to analyse this from the points of view of a potential investor in the ordinary shares.**

For this purpose you can assume that a reasonable estimate of next year's profit after taxation will be £33,500 and that there is a 0.5 probability that there will be no increase in the ordinary share dividend and a 0.5 probability that the increase will be 10%. Summary information extracted from the most recent profit-and-loss account (£).

Profit before taxation	63,000
Less: taxation	32,760
	30,240
Extra-ordinary profits	1,420
	31,660

Less: net dividend on preference shares		3,960	
net dividend on ordinary shares		17,820	21,780
Retained profits			£9,880

Share and loan stock	Number	Nominal value (p)	Market value (p)
Ordinary shares	360,000	25	125
Preference shares	75,000	100	58
11% Convertible loan stock (1985/1990)	240,000	100	80

The loan stock becomes convertible in 1982 on terms of 1 ordinary share for each £2.00 of loan stock. (ACCA 25 marks)

23. Calculate from the following information for the year ended 31 December 1975: (1) the basic earnings per share (6 marks); (2) the fully diluted earnings per share (6 marks); your calculations must be presented. The capital of High-Gear Ltd is as follows:

£500,000 in 7% (formerly 10%) preference shares of £1 each.

£1,000,000 in ordinary shares of 25p each.

£1,250,000 in 8% convertible unsecured loan stock carrying conversion rights into ordinary shares as follows:

On 31 December 1976 – 124 shares for each £100 nominal of loan stock

or on 31 December 1977 – 118 shares for each £100 nominal of loan stock

or on 31 December 1978 – 110 shares for each £100 nominal of loan stock

The profit-and-loss account for the year ended 31 December 1975 showed profit after all expenses but before interest and corporation tax – £1,100,000. Corporation tax is to be taken as 45% of the profits shown in the accounts after all expenses and after loan interest. (ACCA 12 marks)

Chapter 24

Protection of assets

The owners and top management of an organisation must self-evidently do all they can to protect their assets against losses through theft, fraud, accidents, mistakes, or for any other reason. In a company of some size three important components of the overall control should be: (*a*) internal control; (*b*) internal check; (*c*) internal audit. A qualified accountant must pass professional examinations in auditing, which is a large subject in itself. In practice the controls discussed in this chapter are largely but not entirely operated by trained accountants. Qualified accountants are those who have passed the final examinations of one of the professional accountancy bodies, who are members of it and therefore subject to its disciplines. These bodies issue statements and other official papers for the direction or guidance of members. Only members of certain accountancy professional bodies are recognised by the Department of Trade as being qualified to carry out the audit of a public limited company. Meanwhile, this short chapter is included in this book as every person concerned with administration, and every manager at every level, should have an awareness of the importance of the protection of assets.

Internal control

Internal control is a key matter. It is defined in Statements on Auditing (U4) as being 'not only internal check and internal audit but the whole system of controls, financial and otherwise, established by the management in order to carry on the business of the company in an orderly manner, safeguard its assets and secure as far as possible the accuracy and reliability of its records'. An effective system should ensure a separation between recording and custodian duties and should provide that information required for control purposes should promptly be available and there should be procedures to ensure that controls are properly implemented and monitored. When a company is started an experienced auditor should be involved in the setting up of an efficient internal control system and similarly when the system is reviewed periodically, as all systems should be.

If a company makes use of a computer in any way, as most companies now do, there need to be special controls in respect of the computer. In recent years computer personnel, even at highest levels, have carried out major frauds, having noted how ignorant senior managers often are about computers and that in consequence there is inadequate control. The main internal controls in respect of computers may be classified as: (*a*) systems development and control; (*b*) organisational controls; (*c*) procedural controls. They are highly specialist and technical matters but a non-accountant chief executive would be prudent to discuss the question fully with the chief accountant and satisfy himself that the controls appeared adequate. Even banks have recently been victims of substantial frauds. It is said that frequently when large companies have found themselves to be victims of a serious computer fraud they have nevertheless not reported the matter to the police, so that their laxity and administration failure should not become widely known. A chief executive who had reservations about the efficiency of the computer control in his company could commission his external auditors, or other specialists, to carry out a special survey and report to him.

Examination of the definition of internal control will indicate its very wide scope. To 'safeguard its assets' a company will need to have proper insurance cover, *inter alia*, and competent people would also need to ensure that unnecessary risks were avoided, e.g. inflammable materials should be suitably stored. The security function may also be involved, e.g. to avert or reduce the risks of sabotage, vandalism, shoplifting, etc.; waste should be avoided since its consequence is to increase expenses and reduce profits; energy saving and other forms of waste avoidance are more important than many realise and should have the attention of a technically competent person.

Internal check

Internal check is not the same as internal control, but it is an aspect, a part, of internal control. It is defined in Statements on Auditing (U4) as 'the allocation of work and authority in such a manner as to afford checks on the routine transactions of day to day to work by means of

Protection of assets

the work of one person being proved independently by another, or the work of a person being complementary to that of another'. One of the main objects of internal check – but not the only one – is to increase the difficulties of a person who plans to carry out a fraud insofar as he would not have all the relevant matters under his control and would need to seek the collusion of one or more people, to share in his criminal activities, if he wished to persist in his plans. Experience shows that many who are prepared to carry out fraud by themselves are not prepared to accept the greatly increased risk of detection or betrayal, which arise when there is collusion. This is not to say that fraud involving collusion never occurs. It often does, but all who are involved should realise that the chances of ultimate detection are greatly increased. One of the parties is liable to speak or act indiscreetly, someone's suspicions are aroused and police or other investigations quietly begin after a 'tip off'. A special problem of internal check is that it is only practicable to a very limited extent in smaller companies and in practice it too often happens that a smaller company is ruined because of continuing undetected fraud by a trusted man or woman employee. An owner–chief executive of a smaller company is well advised to emphasise to his external auditors that he looks to them to bear this aspect well in mind and try to satisfy themselves that no individual in the company is performing his duties in a way which gives rise to questions.

The special problems of internal control, and the fact that internal check may be impracticable in a smaller company, should be well understood by a competent auditor, who should be able so to plan his work that the probability is that any irregularities are brought to light for further investigation. Special investigations could add to the cost of an audit, but could be justified if well done. In principle, in relation to internal control and check, the following areas will have special attention – and any special features of the company would also be considered: (*a*) outgoing cash and cheques; (*b*) incoming monies, received over the counter or by mail; (*c*) payment of wages – uncontrolled, and in a larger company, this offers scope for a variety of frauds; (*d*) debtors' control; (*e*) procedures for paying creditors; (*f*) stock controls; (*g*) control accounts – where practicable, these are very helpful: they are explained in textbooks on accounting; (*h*) petty cash should preferably be maintained on the imprest system; (*i*) staff – where practicable it is good practice to switch clerical staff from one job to another, or from one section to another, without previous warning. There should always be insistence on staff taking annual holidays and indeed signs of reluctance to take holidays should always be regarded as giving cause for enquiry. An employee who is carrying out fraud tends to fear, with good reason, that if he is away from the scene for any reason the fraud will be likely to be detected.

Internal and external audit

Internal and external audit have areas in common and also some important differences and they are independent of each other. Ideally they should complement each other and should never be in conflict. Auditing is defined as

the independent examination and investigation of the books, accounts and vouchers of a business with a view to enabling the auditor to report whether the balance sheet and profit and loss account are properly drawn up so as to show a true and fair view of the affairs and the profit (or loss) of the business according to the best of the information and explanations obtained by the auditor. An audit involves investigation (which may include physical verification of assets, as well as written records) and a report.

External auditors

The Companies Acts make a number of specific requirements as to auditing. The accounts of registered companies (but not of sole traders or partners) are required by statute to be audited and the Acts state who may act as an auditor. In principle, he must be either a chartered or certified accountant who holds a Practicing Certificate from his professional body. The Acts also require that an auditor reports to members of a company in specified form and authorises him to carry out examinations of books, accounts, etc., and seek explanations as he sees fit, so that he can satisfy himself and give the required certificate. If he is not so satisfied and gives a seriously qualified certificate, or states that he cannot give the required certificate at all, there would be immediate press comment in the case of a listed company. Auditors report to members and not directors. An auditor's duties cannot be restricted by a company's directors or officers but they can be extended by mutual agreement. The statutes do not set out in detail how an auditor should work but in the course of years there have been disputes before the courts and consequently important case law has been established.

Protection of assets

The following are short extracts from some famous judgments: 'an auditor is not bound to assume when he comes to do his duty that he is dealing with fraudulent and dishonest people' (*The London Oil Storage Co. Ltd* v. *Seear, Hasbuck and Co.*, 1904); 'He (the auditor) is not bound to be a detective, or to approach his work with suspicion, or with the foregone conclusion that there is something wrong. He is justified in believing tried servants of the company in whom confidence is placed by the company, and is entitled to rely upon their representations provided he takes reasonable care'; and 'The duties of auditors must not be rendered too onerous. Their work is labourious, and the remuneration moderate. I should be sorry to see the liability of auditors extended... they must not be made liable for not tracking out ingenious and carefully laid schemes of fraud, where there is nothing to arouse their suspicions... so to hold would make the position of an auditor intolerable'; and, an auditor 'is a watchdog, not a bloodhound' (in re *the Kingston Cotton Mill Co. Ltd*, 1896).

The position is thus that the responsibility for installing, operating and monitoring procedures and systems rests with the directors and not the auditors. However, public and legal attitudes have been changing, and auditing techniques have been improving, and higher standards of skill and care are now expected of auditors than was the case some years ago.

The auditing scandals which arose in consequence of the 1973/74 financial crash, and the many official investigations and published reports which followed, have given rise to continuing controversy and anxieties. Some of the lapses uncovered – and there are surely many more which have now been successfully 'covered up' and will never become public knowledge – have shown incredible incompetence on the parts of many qualified accountants, including partners in leading City firms, and outside observers expected the accounting professional body concerned to investigate lapses itself quickly and follow up with severe disciplinary action whenever appropriate. This has not happened. In some cases there have been suspicions of worse than incompetence, namely lack of integrity, with audit partners and firms disregarding reports of their staffs and giving unqualified certificates even when there seemed abundant evidence of malpractices on the part of directors, who in numbers of cases were qualified accountants themselves. A main reason why many auditors acted as they did is surely that audit work is highly profitable and very competitive and although in theory auditors report to members and not directors, in practice, if auditors and directors of a company have a strong disagreement, the directors are often successful in forcing a change of auditors. There is a reasonable suspicion that too many auditors have thought more of their profits than their duty and have been too complaisant to aggressive directors for fear of losing the audit account of the company concerned. The weaknesses of the councils of the professional bodies concerned are a cause of continuing public concern. It is claimed that a practical problem is that if an audit partner, or senior employee, were severely disciplined, this would strengthen the position of investors, suppliers, etc., claiming damages against the audit firm for negligently issuing a certificate on the strength of which investments or supplies were made.

The fear which now haunts professional people, accountants, lawyers, doctors, etc., is that the quality of their work is now appraised more rigorously than used to be the case and if it is felt to be poor there may be a successful claim against them for substantial damages for negligence. Clients have been able to sue successfully in the USA for many years and this fact has been noted in the UK and lawsuits are being increasingly initiated. (They are sometimes settled out of court to minimise publicity.) Professional people can and should take out professional liability insurance but premiums have recently and not surprisingly been rising and in a bad case an underwriter might refuse to continue with a policy. Meanwhile, there are grounds for believing that the more active leaders of the accountancy profession feel concern at the poor public image the profession has been acquiring in recent years and unobtrusively they are taking action to compel raising of standards.

In present-day auditing it is recognised that the volume of transactions may be huge and there could be no question of trying to check every transaction: instead, many sample checks are made and selected areas are studied in depth. Procedures and systems are studied and possible weaknesses identified and the attention of the management drawn to these in writing. Samples of individual transactions or operations are taken and checked from the start to finish, to confirm that the procedures or systems laid down are in fact being followed. If it came to light that there was a discrepancy between what was laid down and what was done, this would trigger off a more searching and detailed investigation, particularly in relation to that type of transaction or operation, or the actions of a particular individual might come under close scrutiny. It must be remembered that despite their numbers, scandals are still rare in a relative sense and in the very large majority of cases all the parties, companies and auditors, are honestly and constructively working together to a common end, to ensure that the company organisation is sound, that it is working efficiently and that its assets are protected.

Internal audit

It is not essential for a company to have internal audit and the cost is such that few small companies operate it. If a company which did not employ internal audit wished to have special investigation(s) made, it could ask the external auditor to carry out additional work and a special fee would be agreed. The internal auditor (and staff, if any) is an employee of the company and he must carry out the instructions of the management like any other employee. An internal auditor may or may not be a qualified accountant. When one is employed an important question is – to whom should he be responsible? As auditing is largely an accounting function, performed by an accountant, it is sometimes the practice for the internal auditor to be responsible to the chief accountant, but the disadvantage is obvious. He could be instructed to look into every part of the company except the accounts. The advantage of making the internal auditor responsible to the chief executive or, even better, to the full board, or to the audit committee of the board, if there is one, is that he will have more independence and freedom of action and more standing wherever he does his work.

When there is an internal auditor he may be left to plan his own working programme, but he will also expect to be asked to carry out special assignments on behalf of the management. His role will by no means be confined to the detecting or preventing of fraud. An internal audit will normally be much concerned with efficiency, the identification and rectification of areas of weakness. It is customary for an external auditor to consult closely with an internal auditor and to study his reports and papers. In practice an experienced external auditor would form a mental assessment of the quality of an internal auditor, and his work, and the attitude of the management to it. If all seemed to be well, the external auditor would be likely largely to accept the work of the internal auditor (subject to sample checks) and he would concentrate on those areas less well covered by the internal auditor. The external auditor is the senior partner in the relationship, as it were, and he would decide on his attitudes and course of action in the light of his assessment of each situation.

Questions

(*Note*: these questions are taken from ACCA Auditing (and Investigation) papers, which are not part of the Business Finance syllabus. A few examples are given here because of their interest to financial managers – and students.)

1. A client whom you have known for several years is interested in the purchase of a business which will involve his full-time participation and will provide him with a modest but secure return on his investment. He has been advised by his agents that a small, well-established shop selling newspapers, cigarettes, tobacco and confectionery in West London is on offer for sale and he has accordingly asked you to carry out an investigation. (a) Set out the steps you would take prior to commencing your detailed enquiries; (b) described the work you would carry out in connection with the accounts of the business; (c) specify any other matters which will call for your investigation prior to submitting a final report to your client. (ACCA 20 marks)

2. Your client is proposing to form a company specialising in the provision of tuition for professional law examinations and is about to approach his bank concerning the finance which will be necessary to support the venture during its first two years. He is not certain how the information to be presented to the bank manager should be prepared and has requested your assistance. Set out the matters, both general and financial, which, in your view, are likely to be of particular concern to the bank manager prior to making his decision, and which should therefore be included in your client's presentation. (ACCA 20 marks)

3. The essential stages in an audit have been summarised respectively as 'ascertain; test; compare; review; report'. Outline the purpose of each stage and indicate briefly how you, as the recently appointed auditor of a large industrial concern, would approach each of the stages mentioned. (ACCA 14 marks)

4. The partner in charge of the audit of a manufacturing company gives his staff special instructions at the start of the audit which include the following requirements to: (i) make a critical review of the draft profit-and-loss account, comparing it in detail with that of the previous year; (ii) prepare a schedule giving relevant ratios to assist in the review of the profit-and-loss accounts; (iii) examine the reconciliation of the costing records with the financial accounts; (iv) compare the original budget at the beginning of the year with the actual results for the period; (v) review the nominal and private ledger accounts for unusual entries.

Required. In each of the five specific instructions given above: (a) explain why the partner has told his staff to carry out the tasks concerned; (b) state how the tasks should be carried out; (c) state what

Protection of assets 503

conclusions may be drawn as a result of each task. (ACCA 20 marks)

5. The Shiny Goods Co Ltd manufactures electrical goods. During your audit you review the internal control procedures in operation in the sales department.
Required. (i) State the procedures you would expect to see in operation covering the receipt and acceptance of orders from customers. (ii) How should the prices charged for the goods be determined? (iii) Set out the controls which should operate over the despatch of goods to customers from the warehouse. (iv) Which official of the company should be authorised to write off bad debts? Give reasons for your answer. (v) What controls should be exercised over the issue of credit notes? (ACCA 20 marks)

6. 'The function of an internal control questionnaire (ICQ) is to identify specific areas of weakness: the effect of these weaknesses on the system as a whole, and hence on the accounts must then be *evaluated* by the auditor. Such evaluation work is considerably facilitated by condensing the control criteria for each functional area down to a handful of **key** (or **control**) **questions** whose chief characteristic is that they go directly to the heart of the matter.' The following two typical key questions relate to controls over *purchases*: (*a*) Can liabilities be recorded in respect of goods/services which are either unauthorised or not received? (*b*) Can liabilities for goods/services be incurred but remain unrecorded? **Draft key questions for inclusion in those sections of your firm's evaluation questionnaire which relate to: sales and trade debtors (3 questions); fixed assets (2 questions); and stocks (2 questions).** (ACCA 15 marks)

7. Your client, Lilian, is an elderly retired lady of considerable means and she has been approached by the Managing Director of Harold Ltd, a trading company, for a substantial loan. **What, in general terms, are the matters on which you would make enquiries before being in a position to advise Lilian on the acceptability of the proposition? Wherever appropriate, give reasons for the enquiries you would make.** (ACCA 15 marks)

8. Steel Rings Ltd is a small engineering company of which you are auditor. The books are kept solely by a Miss Brown who has worked for the company for twenty years. She also computes and draws the wages, handles all the banking and draws cheques for directors' signatures.
Required. (i) State four internal control procedures you would hope to find in operation to remove Miss Brown from any temptation to de-

fraud your client. (ii) During the audit, you discover that the directors have been personally retaining the cash received from the sale of scrap received from the company's processes. State the effects that the omission of these amounts will have on the annual accounts. (iii) The system of internal control is designed in part to prevent or rapidly detect frauds. Discuss *three* types of fraud that a system of internal control cannot be expected to prevent. (iv) Internal check is necessarily at a minimum in a company of this size. Therefore, because of this, you will have to rely more upon the representations of management who have exercised supervision. Normally this reliance will not preclude you from giving an unqualified opinion. In what circumstances will the directors' representations be unacceptable? (v) The directors of Steel Rings Ltd are also the shareholders and the managing director suggests to you that the audit is rather a waste of time as the annual accounts you report on are, in effect, sent by the directors to themselves. Briefly state the arguments you would use to counter the managing director's suggestion. (ACCA 20 marks)

Chapter 25

The Wilson Committee

The 1973/74 financial crisis and the collapse of the equity market naturally and properly lead to controversy and recriminations. Main allegations included that the City had been failing the country because banks and other financial institutions, such as insurance companies, had been making finance available for property speculation and development, and had been denying finance to manufacturing industry, which should have had a much higher priority for the national wellbeing. There were calls, *inter alia*, for nationalisation of banks and insurance companies. There was, and still is, a widely held viewpoint that one main reason for the relatively poor performance of UK industry, in comparison with the industry of other countries, has been underinvestment. In fact, this viewpoint is challenged by others who point to data which suggest that many UK industries fail to use efficiently the plant and equipment they already have, and the problem appears to be primarily one of inefficient management and poor industrial and trade union relations. It is an interesting fact that a number of UK industries, including service ones, rank very high by international standards and therefore the problem should not be insuperable. What some can do, others should also be able to do. However, except for their financial implications, these problems are outside the scope of this book.

In the mid-1970s left-wing members of the Labour Party (which then formed the government) and other influential persons were pressing that, in addition to nationalising financial institutions, the government should take powers to direct institutions such as pension and insurance funds to invest a proportion of their funds according to government directives. Persuasive arguments can be put forward to support this viewpoint. However, equally persuasive arguments can be raised against it and it was evident that these suggestions were alarming institutional fund managers, the City establishment generally, as well as Conservative Party supporters and, indeed, many Labour supporters also, not least those who were trustees for the pension funds of workers in the nationalised industries. Accordingly, when the then Prime Minister, Mr James Callaghan, appointed a committee, under the chairmanship of Sir Harold Wilson, the previous Prime Minister, one might have expected a general welcoming of this step. In fact, the appointment of this committee evoked much criticism on many sides. In brief, left-wing Labour supporters complained that urgent action was needed, on the lines they proposed, and an enquiry was merely a pretext to justify delay. At the other extreme, a widely reported City viewpoint was the expected complacent one, that it should be obvious how excellently all City institutions work, how high standards of integrity are and how well self-regulation works: this committee would surely show a left-wing bias and would be hostile to the City.

This short chapter comments briefly on the background and work of the Wilson Committee, as it is known. The official title is: Committee to Review the Functioning of Financial Institutions. It was appointed by the Prime Minister, by a Treasury Minute, on 5 January 1977 with terms of reference: 'To enquire into the role and functioning, at home and abroad, of financial institutions in the United Kingdom and their value to the economy; to review in particular the provision of funds for industry and trade; to consider what changes are required in the existing arrangements for the supervision of these institutions, including the possible extension of the public sector and to make recommendations.' The terms of reference make no reference to taxation although in practice all company financial managers have to take taxation into account as a major factor whenever financial decisions are taken. The Committee consisted of 18 members including the chairman (17 men and 1 woman). All members were eminent in their fields, as industrialists, bankers, trade union leaders, academics and former politicians and senior civil servants.

One strong argument in favour of the appointment of a committee of this stature, with terms of reference of this nature, once in every generation or so, is that the senior people in businesses, corporate and professional and academic bodies, etc., are obliged to pause in their day-to-day activities and examine deeply the work they are doing, their objectives and what they see as their problems and their achievements, and have these set down in writing, accepting that they will be critically studied and public written and oral discussion and probably challenge will follow. In such circumstances people in authority act with great care to ensure that the papers presented on behalf of their organisation reach the highest possible standards. The many papers published thus establish a very large number of facts and opinions at a certain point in time. These remain available for study and reference by academics and other interested parties, and this is apart from whatever usefulness the work, reports and recommendations of the committee itself may have.

The last Committee of Enquiry into the area covered by the Wilson Committee was the Radcliffe Committee, appointed in 1957 and reporting in 1959. This had somewhat different terms of reference: 'To enquire into the working of the monetary and credit system and to make recommendations.' Meanwhile, in the period between 1959 and 1977, certain fundamental changes had been taking place in the UK financial system, including 'the decline of sterling as a reserve and trading currency; the development of the eurocurrency markets; the change in monetary policy introduced in 1971 under the title "Competition and Credit Control"; the rise in and greater volatility of levels of interest rates and inflation; the growth of contractual saving through long-term investing institutions such as insurance companies and pension funds; and the accompanying decline of the private investor'. (The Wilson Committee)

The Committee's approach to its work has been an open one, with emphasis on facts and practicalities, and the Report is lucidly written and easy to read. Every serious student of business finance should examine a copy of the Report and preferably also the volumes of evidence which form part of it. After its first meeting the Committee issued a general invitation to submit evidence either on the priority subject of finance for industry and trade, or any other subject within the terms of reference. The Committee secretariat also wrote to a large number of representative bodies including the main associations representing industrial and financial institutions, inviting them to submit evidence. Government departments, the Bank of England, trade unions and academics working in this field, and prominent businessmen were also invited to submit evidence and both the volume and the quality of the submissions have been impressive. Unlike many committees, the Wilson Committee made evidence public as it went along. The advantages of this include that all the interested parties could publish information at an early stage and comment as they saw fit and debate would thus be stimulated and the Committee itself would have the opportunity to consider interesting ideas or suggestions or viewpoints before making their final report.

The Committee divided potential witnesses into two categories: 'providers of finance' (the various lending and investing institutions) and 'users of finance' (e.g. industry and trade associations), and gave both a list of questions showing the areas to be covered in their submissions. The questions can be summarised as '(i) the parts played by the various financial institutions in providing funds to industry and trade through the banking system and capital markets; (ii) the relationships between users of finance in industry and trade and those who supply it, either directly or as intermediaries; (iii) how decisions to invest or lend money are made – for instance, what are the criteria used to choose between alternative projects or investment opportunities, and what are the conditions which borrowers have to satisfy in order to raise money; (iv) how the criteria for investment and the methods of financing it have changed as a result of higher interest rates and inflation and other changes in economic conditions; (v) how well the banking and investing institutions have met the demands of industry and trade for finance on reasonable terms; (vi) whether there are defects or gaps in the arrangements for raising finance, and if so, how they might be remedied so as to improve the flow of savings into industry and trade and stimulate investment'. (The word investment carries two separate meanings: (1) physical investment in capital assets, and (2) financial investments in financial assets such as company securities.) The Committee was also assisted by an expert Research and a Statistics Panel to attend to and supervise research and statistical work, the preparation of special case studies and reports, etc.

The Committee decided that of the subjects covered in their terms of reference, the provision of funds to industry and trade had highest priority and accordingly they decided to study this, and the evidence on it, first. In 1977 they published *Progress Report on the Financing of Industry and Trade*. (Apart from the final *Report*, June 1980, HMSO, and the various volumes of evidence, other published reports were: *Interim Report on the Financing of Small Firms; Research Reports Nos 1, 2, 3*: (1) *Survey of Investment Attitudes and Financing of Medium-Sized Companies*; (2) *The Financing of North Sea Oil*; (3) *Studies of Small Firms' Financing*.) The following two paragraphs from the *Progress Report* summarise some specially important aspects of the investigations:

19. The main themes of the evidence are these. On the one hand, few in industry or the institutions believe that the way the financial institutions operate has deprived firms of the funds they should have had, or has constrained investment. Low productivity, low demand and problems caused by government policies are regarded as far more important factors behind our poor industrial performance. Industry and the financial institutions both claim that relations between the two sectors are good. Many of the industry associations praise the institutions for the flexibility and efficiency of their services, and the

institutions point out their success as an industry in their own right, especially as earners of foreign currencies.

20. A number of submissions add one qualification to the claim that industries' needs for finance are well served. It is that in some respects the smaller firm may face problems which we summarise in Section 3. But in these cases too it is agreed that other factors such as government policies have had a far more damaging influence than any shortcomings in the financial institutions.

Because the evidence of the special problems experienced by small firms is so widespread, the Committee published a *Special Interim Report* on this subject in March 1979 which included a number of recommendations: these were also incorporated in the final *Report*. Whilst the Conservative government has very different attitudes from its Labour predecessor, the fact is that both the UK major parties, and the Liberals, accept that special measures may be needed to assist the establishment, expansion and, sometimes, the survival, of smaller companies and in the present recession the recommendations of the Committee are likely at least to give rise to careful study. One of the main problems of small firms is access to risk capital, and the Wilson Committee took this into account. In recent years a main difficulty of many individuals in supplying risk capital from their personal resources arose because high personal taxation had greatly reduced their ability to save from income. The substantial reduction of income tax on large incomes in 1979 should make fundamental changes in this situation but the effects may take some time to become apparent. They may not be what the government expect as the beneficiaries of the tax cuts may prefer to spend more on consumption, overseas residences or investment, etc., and investment in high-risk ordinary shares may not appeal to them. Meanwhile, the Committee have identified a number of options which are complementary and not mutually exclusive. These include loan guarantee schemes whereby banks, subject to certain safeguards, could make loans to small firms on the basis that if the firm defaulted the bank would be reimbursed largely but not fully from a public fund. Loans of this kind have the characteristic of equity capital. Similar schemes operate in other countries, including Holland, and in practice the loss experience is surprisingly low. One or two new institutions could be formed: the Committee recommended the formation of an English Development Agency (corresponding to the Welsh and Scottish Development Agencies). However, a Conservative government would seem less likely than a Labour government to approve of the creation of one or more new institutions of this type.

A main problem of people running small businesses is access to various forms of specialist advice. Only big companies can afford to employ full-time taxation specialists, organisation and methods and internal audit teams, management services managers, etc. Small firms must depend on good generalists but from time to time specialist expert advice will be needed. The Committee recommended *inter alia* that big firms might be prepared to cooperate by making their experts available in certain circumstances, and indeed a number are already doing this: there should also be closer cooperation between smaller firms and institutions of higher education, which employ specialists in a number of fields.

The final *Report* of the Committee has shone searchlights into all aspects of the workings of the financial institutions and its findings have been broadly favourable. In relation to the major enquiry, the availability of finance for trade and industry, the findings were 'it is not the availability of external finance that has been the constraint on investment but the depressed level of demand and the low real level of profitability in relation to the perceived cost of capital'. Most of the findings were unanimous – that banks and insurance companies should not be nationalised; that pension funds should be regulated by an Act compelling disclosure, and that there should be a code of practice; that medium- and long-term savings should have the same tax reliefs as life insurance policies; that the building societies cartel should be broken up and their favoured tax position withdrawn. The effects of these proposals, if adopted, would be to put most forms of savings on to a similar tax basis and thus give encouragement to saving by individuals rather than through the intermediary of institutions for the sake of tax benefits. A major proposal is that there should be a new body 'with responsibility for keeping the regulation of all parts of the financial system under regular review'. This 'watchdog' would monitor the financial institutions and report annually to Parliament. The *Report* also recommends that institutions should underwrite a new long-dated tender issue of gilts because 'the present system is widely regarded as unsatisfactory.' It recommends that the government, the Bank of England and industry should experiment with issuing index-linked financial instruments in relation to their inflation-fuelled liabilities. Throughout, the problems arising from high inflation and high interest rates are emphasised.

There is one matter about which the Committee was deeply divided – whether a new investing institution is needed, to provide funds not otherwise available. Some members considered that there is no such need whilst at the other extreme a trade union member commented that the proposal to set up a special institution for this purpose was 'far and away the most important proposal in the Report'. Of those who favour the formation of a special institution, some consider that it should have a funding of £1 bn annually, and others £2 bn. Clearly, this proposal would be more likely to find favour under a Labour than a Conservative government.

The Committee considered in depth the question of regulation primarily by law, or primarily by self-regulation, and decided that there was 'no case for any significant shift in the balance of statutory and non-statutory' methods, but the principle of self-regulating body concerned. Of the Stock Exchange the Committee reported:

(1165) There is little doubt that the Stock Exchange satisfies the basic criteria demanded of a self-regulatory body ... we have no reason to doubt the general efficiency and competence of its administration, though we have some reservations about the extent to which it is member dominated ... Our impression is, however, that it still lags some way behind the Takeover Panel in the forthrightness of its public utterances and there is still some scope for greater openness about issues of current concern including the work of its various committees ...

An extremely important statement of principle is 'The objections to self-regulating governed entirely by the participants themselves have been recognised in certain other areas in recent years by the more direct involvement of the Bank of England.' The view of the Committee is that the Council for the Securities Industry should exercise greater authority over the Stock Exchange, but it should first be strengthened itself, with an increase in membership, some new members 'perhaps in place of some of the existing members'. An observation which will be widely approved is 'If non-statutory regulation is to command general respect those responsible must be prepared to adopt a very robust attitude in publishing the results of their investigations and disciplinary hearings.' The Stock Exchange and the CSI were not felt to have distinguished themselves in their responses to the 'dawn raids' of 1980, and these were subsequent to the publication of the *Wilson Committee Report*.

As is normal, the publication of the *Report* was accompanied by considerable press comment and analysis for a very short time, and then more or less silence. However, although a proportion of the recommendations will be ignored by the government, the value of the *Report*, and the comprehensive information it has made available, remain of the utmost interest and value. It may also be presumed that the influence of the *Report* will be far reaching and profound.

Chapter 26

The implications of inflation and taxation

Inflation

The main purpose of a private-sector business, to operate profitably, has been considered, as well as the need of all organisations to use resources efficiently. When profit is measured in the annual accounts, or for any period, it is presumed that the capital resources of the business are maintained intact. If adequate provision is not made for the replacement of capital assets as they are consumed over time in the production of profit, then what appears to be profit is, in fact, partly profit, and partly consumption of capital. Overstatement of profit implies reduction of capital.

In times of stable prices it is not too difficult to make satisfactory distinctions between capital and revenue items and the 'historical cost' system of accounting produces results which are generally satisfactory to the various parties who wish or need to study the accounts of a company. This is the system used for the preparation of company accounts such as are regularly published in newspaper advertisements, circulated to shareholders, etc. They comply with the Companies Acts. However, as inflation intensifies, the problems become increasingly difficult and irreconcilable. The theoretical and academic aspects of the problem have been apparent for many years throughout the world and its magnitude is emphasised by the fact that despite years of intense debate and controversy no universally accepted solution has been formulated anywhere. What is remarkable is how successfully the managements of many companies have shown themselves able to live with inflation and apparently prosper. A main reason is that at least in rough-and-ready ways managers have been able to identify special problem areas and take appropriate action to deal with these.

For example, recognising that the cost of purchasing new assets in due course to replace existing ones would be much higher than the original costs, companies make substantial appropriations of profits to special reserve accounts for replacement of fixed assets at higher prices. There will be regular reviews of the market value, or of the value to the business, of land and buildings, and often plant and machinery as well, and increases in these over the values recorded in the accounts will be 'written up' – the book value of the assets increased, on the debit side of the accounts, and the corresponding credits being to a capital reserve account, a part of the shareholders' equity. Managements pay special attention to cash flows and monitoring by means of budgets and ratio analysis. When forces of competition, or price controls, or the levels of demand do not prevent this, managements would raise prices as costs rose, in order to maintain, or increase, profit margins. There would also be continuing scrutiny of costs, the use of organisation and methods teams and such techniques as value analysis, with the aim of keeping costs at the lowest feasible levels.

In the 1950s the Retail Price Index rose very slowly by present standards but even then a *Sunday Times* economics correspondent, George Schwartz, wrote constantly about the dangers and immorality of inflation – it is immoral in that governments often welcome a degree of inflation as it effectively permits them to default on their vast borrowings. Schwartz regarded annual price rises of 3% or so as portents of disasters to come. How right he was. But at the time his was rather a lone voice and a widespread view in the UK was that a gentle inflation provided a useful stimulus for business and the economy. There was little anxiety and price rises were regarded as matters which could be ignored for accounting purposes.

During the 1960s and 1970s the menace of inflation became increasingly recognised, including its potentially disruptive effect on the social fabric. The experiences and misery of Germany in the 1920s and the manner in which these led to Hitler and the Second World War were remembered. The leading accountancy bodies therefore cooperated in an attempt to draw up an acceptable Statement of Standard Accounting Practice (SSAP) to cover inflation accounting. As usual, they first published an exposure draft, ED8, a document which set out in detail the reasoning and the proposals for an SSAP and invited comment and criticism, which would be considered and taken into account before the definitive SSAP was agreed and published. SSAP 7 (*Accounting for Changes in the Purchasing Power of Money*) was published in May 1974 and became binding on auditors and thus substantially on companies covered by the SSAP as well, since if a company does not comply with an SSAP its auditor must qualify his audit certificate, which is liable to damage the standing of the company in the eyes of investors.

In the event, SSAP 7 was withdrawn in January 1978. Whilst it had many supporters, it also had too many opponents. Inflation accounting has always been, and remains, a most controversial area, for a number of good reasons.

When accounts are produced on a historical cost basis, inflation introduces a number of serious distortions. These are:

(a) Assets shown at original (historical) cost will be understated in most cases
(b) Because fixed assets are undervalued in the accounts, the conventional depreciation charge, based on the historical cost, will be too low.
(c) Since selling prices will normally be increased to take into account the increased replacement costs of the materials used, but the costs charged in the accounts will be based on the lower historical costs, the published profits will incorporate an element of 'stock profit'. However, this element of profit is not really available for distribution since the funds represented must be available for the purchase of new stocks at higher prices. (It has been noted how there is a need for increased working capital in inflationary times to finance a given level of activity.)
(d) Holdings of cash, bank and debtors' balances steadily decline in terms of purchasing power and accounts prepared on a historical cost basis do not reflect this fact.
(e) Conversely, liabilities expressed in fixed money terms, namely debts of all kinds and trade creditors, steadily becomes less onerous to the borrower as repayments represent a lower command over purchasing power than the original borrowings. This factor is significantly offset by the high interest payments which a borrower normally has to make now.
(f) A consequence of these combined factors is that profit is often overstated in the published accounts.
(g) Apparent growth in sales, profits, etc., is overstated because of the declining purchasing power of the pounds in which they are expressed.

Main problems arise since different industries have different characteristics and different companies within the same industry have different capital structures. Moreover, inflation does not affect all the factors in the same way at any time. Thus certain commodity prices may rise hugely in a period (and might then fall), whilst others rise much less. Skilled and unskilled labour costs may rise at quite different rates, and both of these quite differently from price rises for plant and machinery, or land and buildings. Although attempts have been made to devise formulae so that a system of inflation accounting will take all of the factors properly into account, none have been successful and it has not even proved practicable to devise working compromises which would be adequately applicable to all situations.

Current purchasing power and current cost accounting

There have been two fundamentally different approaches to inflation accounting and both have eminent supporters – and critics. The first, current purchasing power (CPP), was the approach chosen by the accountancy bodies for SSAP 7 in 1974. This involves the translation, or conversion, of all the historical cost (HC) figures for a given balance sheet into currency units of a common purchasing power by multiplying the published figure by an appropriate factor, as is done for DCF evaluations. Price changes, and the appropriate factor, are determined by reference to an index, and the index chosen, as the best available, was the Retail Prices Index (RPI). This approach has the virtue of objectivity since the RPI is widely known and readily available. However, the major disadvantage of this index is that it was devised for a particular purpose, quite unrelated to the needs of businesses. Several specific indices would have been more suitable in principle, but they are not available. In principle, SSAP 7 partly meets the distortions (*a*), (*b*), (*c*), (*f*) indicated earlier in this chapter, and more completely those of (*d*), (*e*) and (*g*). Another objection to SSAP 7 is that the profit determined could include unrealised 'gains' on monetary items and inexperienced users of these accounts could wrongly think the CPP profits to be available for distribution. Supporters consider that the advantages of CPP outweight the disadvantages. It was proposed that mainly listed companies would be required to use SSAP 7 initially, on the basis that the main accounts would be shown on the conventional HC basis and the inflation-adjusted CPP accounts as supplements.

Although SSAP 7 was published by the leading accountancy bodies and received wide support, including that of eminent academics as well as practising accountants, as being a substantial advance over the use of conventional HC accounts alone, and as being the best workable compromise at present available, many other respected accountants, academics, etc., were not convinced about the proposals, on theoretical as well as practical grounds. Those interested in fuller information are referred to textbooks on inflation accounting. As the concept represents such a major change and would require auditors, accountants and businessmen to develop new and unfamiliar viewpoints, it is understandable that preparers and users of accounts are reluctant to make major changes, at least so long as it is evident that there is still widespread disagreement about the acceptability of what is proposed.

Because of the growing awareness of the need to deal with the problems posed by inflation in relation to published accounts, which can now be seriously misleading, the government intervened and formed the Sandiland's Committee (each such committee becomes known by the name of its chairman) in 1973, to work to comprehensive terms of reference. The Sandiland's Committee produced a comprehensive 364 page report in 1975. The various options were each carefully examined but the Committee recommended current cost accounting (CCA) to deal with inflation. This is a fundamentally different approach from that of CCP and SSAP 7. The aim of CCA is to make adjustments in the accounts of individual companies for the effect of specific price changes, and not to use a general index as in CPP. Charges were to be made against revenue of the 'value to the business' of assets consumed. Normally this would be based on replacement costs.

The Sandiland's Committee recommendations appear in principle to remedy the distortions (*a*), (*b*), (*c*) indicated earlier in this chapter but they do not make adjustments for monetary items, which are defined as assets, liabilities or capital the amounts of which are fixed by contract or statute in terms of numbers of pounds regardless of changes in the purchasing power of the pound. Examples are cash, debtors, creditors and loans, including debentures. Accordingly, they do not remedy the distortions (*d*), (*e*), (*g*), and only partially (*f*). A strong practical objection to the CCA approach is the subjectivity which would be involved in making valuations. Self-evidently, wherever feasible a sound objective measure is preferable to a subjective one. (The original price paid for an asset is an example of an objective measure: the valuation of, e.g. a building, by two separate expert valuers, is an example of subjective valuation. Competent and honest experts may value the same object very differently. If an unscrupulous expert is employed, and there are many of these, the problems raised by subjectivity take on new dimensions.) The approach recommended by the Sandiland's Committee has been used in Holland, where it met with general acceptance. It is also compatible with EEC proposals on this subject. The Sandiland's Committee recommended that its proposals should be incorporated in an SSAP and brought into use beginning in 1978, applicable at first only to large companies, and that CCA should replace conventional HC accounting and not merely be a supplement to it.

Inflation and taxation

The Committee's recommendations gave rise to substantial controversy in relation to both the practical and theoretical aspects. There was special concern that the familiar HC accounts should not merely be supplemented but should be replaced by a new, unfamilar and widely disputed type of accounting. Meanwhile, as Sandilands had proposed an SSAP, this had to be drafted in detail and the accountancy bodies accordingly formed the Morpeth Committee to draft this. In the usual way an exposure draft, ED18, was published for comment and debate. This proposed a complex new standard which incorporated the Sandilands proposals and went somewhat beyond them, so that all the distortions arising from inflation were dealt with to some extent. However, the complexities of the proposals and anxiety at the intention to replace a familiar system provoked a strong reaction and two chartered accountants requisitioned a general meeting of their Institute and tabled a special resolution that there should not be compulsory implementation of the proposals set out in ED18. The Council of the Institute of Chartered Accountants of England and Wales appealed to members to vote against the resolution, but their appeal was ignored and the resolution was approved. It is unusual for members of a professional body to overrule its governing council, but the event can equally be seen as showing that the body concerned is a truly democratic one and members have powers provided they take the trouble to act with decision. The exposure draft ED18 was withdrawn in July 1977.

All concerned with published accounts were concerned at the continuing delay in reaching general agreement on some form of inflation accounting and the Accounting Steering Committee (ASC) formed the Hyde Committee, an *ad hoc* group, to produce interim recommendations – proposals of a simpler nature than those set out in ED18, which would meet with general acceptance, so that a start could be made with inflation accounting whilst further and deeper study was given to the whole subject. The Hyde guidelines were published in November 1977 and were generally well received. However, inevitably, limitations were pointed out and it became evident that numbers of important companies, accountants, auditors and academics wished to see a more widely acceptable scheme formulated before decisions were taken to proceed with a particular scheme. The specialist accountancy press was at this time featuring articles by academic accountants, and others, which criticised the professional accountancy bodies, and profitable audit firms for not giving sufficient financial support to basic and fundamental academic research into accountancy problems, as is the practice in the USA. It was pointed out that if the accountancy bodies could not themselves produce proposals which met with general acceptance, the next step would be for the government to take the matter from their control and impose a solution.

Meanwhile, the Morpeth Committee continued its work and took into account comments and suggestions put forward in respect of ED18 and the Hyde guidelines. In April 1979, ED24 was published and the CCA approach continues to be followed. It was proposed that ED24 should apply to all listed companies and to all companies with a turnover exceeding £5 m. p.a., with a target date of 1 January 1980. They would be required to publish a supplementary profit-and-loss account and balance sheet, on a CCA basis, with the main published accounts on the conventional HC basis. Insurance, property investment and dealing companies and investment and unit trusts were to be excluded on the grounds that CCA did not appear to be wholly appropriate to them and further discussion and research would be necessary.

SSAP 16

Exposure draft ED24 was generally well received and a viewpoint had developed that as no proposals could overcome all objections, the time had come to make the best of any reasonable proposal put forward, and try to make it work, not least as the alternative seemed a government-imposed solution. As usual, ED24 invited comment and suggestions, for consideration before a definitive SSAP was prepared. This SSAP 16 (*Current Cost Accounting*) was issued in March 1980, to become effective as soon as possible, and for annual statements of the companies covered relating to accounting periods starting on or after 1 January 1980. It is mandatory and applies to all listed companies and larger unlisted ones and with the exceptions indicated in ED24. The working of SSAP 16 may be reviewed after a period of not less than three years from its inception. SSAP 16 is not a lengthy document and all concerned with business finance should have a copy and familiarise themselves with it, not least because the financial environment is deeply affected by inflation and it therefore has practical as well as theoretical importance. The objective of CCA is 'to provide more useful information than that available from historical accounts alone for the guidance of the management of the business, the shareholders and others on such matters as: (*a*) the financial viability of the business; (*b*) return on investment; (*c*) pricing policy, cost control and distribution decisions; and (*d*) gearing.' In briefest outline, the starting point, in the preparation of the CCA profit-and-loss account, would be the historical cost profit before tax and interest. This would be reduced by deducting: (i) a depreciation adjust-

Inflation and taxation

ment; (ii) a cost of sales adjustment; (iii) monetary working capital adjustment (MWCA) which allows for the effect of price changes on the company's monetary working capital. (i) and (iii) are intended to allow for the difference between the 'value to the business' and historical costs of the fixed assets and stocks consumed during the period. These three adjustments provide the current cost operating profit (or loss), and are a measure of the performance of the company. Where the company has 'net borrowings' a gearing adjustment has to be added to the current cost profit attributable to the shareholders – they benefit from net borrowings because their liability becomes less onerous in real terms as the purchasing power of money falls. The CCA balance sheet based on the conventional HC balance sheet would incorporate a capital maintenance reserve to reflect: (*a*) revaluation surpluses (or deficits) arising from (i) price changes in respect of fixed assets and (ii) price changes in respect of stock and investments other than those included as current assets, to the extent that they are not already included in the historical cost accounts; (*b*) the monetary working capital adjustment; and (*c*) the gearing adjustment.

In 1979 the Conservative government indicated that it regarded the finding of acceptable solutions to the problems of inflation accounting as urgent and that future company taxation would take inflation into account. Meanwhile, important reliefs of an *ad hoc* nature given by the previous government included capital allowances of up to 100%, which deferred the taxation liabilities of companies with an active investment programme, and stock appreciation relief. Both of these measures reduced pressures on company liquidity. Other measures taken by companies themselves have been considered elsewhere in this book and, in summary, include regular revaluation of fixed assets and putting the increase into a capital revaluation reserve; putting to reserve a substantial proportion of the distributable profits, which compensates for the tendency of HC accounting to overstate profits; attention to cash flow and cash forecasting and requiring short payback periods when evaluating capital projects which are not essential. There is also greater emphasis on the control of all components of working capital, with stock maintained at lowest practicable levels. The pressures on liquidity have been reduced by many companies by leasing instead of purchasing fixed assets.

An interesting fact is that although in theory borrowing is advantageous to borrowers (although high interest rates reduce this advantage), in practice many managements show great caution about borrowing to finance growth. This emerges clearly in the *Survey of Investment Attitudes and Financing of Medium-Sized Companies* (Research Report

No. 1) of the Wilson Committee. The experience of many in the 1973/74 crisis was traumatic and showed that highly geared companies may have the utmost difficulty in surviving a sudden credit and liquidity squeeze. Many do not survive. Meanwhile, from the examination aspect, it would seem that detailed and technical knowledge of inflation accounting is called for in the financial and management accounting papers. Business finance papers have tended to require candidates to show an awareness of the nature of inflation and the problems it poses and their implications and the possible means of dealing with the problems, rather than detailed technical knowledge.

The implications of taxation

Taxation, like auditing, is a large subject in itself. Because of its complexities and the fact that skilful understanding and interpretation of the strict letter of the law can substantially reduce the liability of a company to tax, leading taxation specialists command large fees and incomes. For multinational companies there are the special problems of activities giving rise to taxation liabilities in more than one country, double taxation agreements between countries, etc. Companies rightly insist on their taxation planning being carried out by experts, so that their tax liabilities are minimised. For those who are not aware of this, there is a vital distinction between tax avoidance and tax evasion. Tax avoidance entails meticulous, expert study of the strict letter of the law and taking fullest advantage of what the law permits. It has therefore been regarded as an entirely proper and lawful activity, including by the Courts, although many regret it in a social sense. Tax evasion, however, is entirely different. It entails deliberate deception, misdeclarations and, in one way or another, fraudulent actions on the part of a taxpayer, and is a criminal activity punishable as such.

In recent times it has become apparent that some tax-avoidance schemes marketed at high prices to very wealthy corporate or individual taxpayers have been extremely artificial, and the Labour government and the Inland Revenue showed signs of increasing hostility towards tax-avoidance schemes which appeared to be going too far, with ingenious specialists able to defeat the obvious intentions of Parliament. Many Conservative Party supporters also felt distaste for obviously artificial tax-avoidance schemes, not least because if the very wealthy can pay little or no taxes through tax avoidance, the remainder, who cannot afford expensive expert advice, have to pay more. Meanwhile, the Labour government began to 'change the rules of the game' by closing loopholes in the law by means of retrospective amendments of the Finance Acts. The retrospective effect meant that those who thought they had escaped tax could now find themselves caught. The Inland Revenue, under the Conservative government, has continued to make life difficult for tax avoiders using schemes of which it does not approve. It appears that the attractions of these schemes has sharply declined. Meanwhile, taxation law is so complex that some practising accountants decide to work only in the field of tax, and others decide to avoid tax as far as they can and specialise in other areas and take the advice of tax specialists when they need it.

However, in principle, all responsible businessmen, as well as accountants, need to have an awareness of the implications and importance of taxation. Adequate awareness will alert a manager to the importance of seeking the opinion of a tax expert on the taxation implications of significant decisions or situations. Taxation has implications for the cash flow, for the liquidity and also for the profitability of a business. In respect of cash forecasting and budgeting it will be important to take into account both the values and timings of cash payments (and receipts), including in respect of PAYE and VAT when the company or trader acts as a collecting agent for the government. The company, or individual, will know beforehand the precise dates when receipts or payments should occur. Taxation implications may be important when deciding whether an asset for use in a business should be purchased outright, or on deferred terms, or leased.

Taxation will be important when making investment appraisals. It will affect both the profitability and the timings of cash inflows and outflows. Tax allowances and grants, if any, will need to be known and taken into account. Taxation also has important implications for the cost of capital, noting especially that the net cost to a business of borrowed money is reduced by the fact that interest payments may be deducted as an expense before arriving at the profits liable to tax, whereas dividends on preference (and ordinary) shares must be paid out of the profits which remain after tax. Taxation also affects the net return which shareholders receive and will need to be considered when the company is comparing the cost to it of retained earnings *vis a vis* rights issues. In brief and in principle, a management must seek to be tax efficient – that is, in given circumstances and levels of activity the overall tax liabilities should be at a minimum. An interesting fact is that in many aspects of business, including finance and administration, and in the board itself, the competent generalist has an important role. However, in the field of taxation a practitioner must be an expert, and one who must keep himself informed as it occurs of every change in laws or regulations which may have a bearing on the taxation liabilities of the organisation which he serves.

Questions

1. How might inflation be taken into account in the appraisal of new projects? (ICSA 22 marks)
2. Explain the impact which inflation has upon the financial policies of UK companies in recent years. (ICSA 22 marks)
3. To what extent is current cost accounting likely to assist financial decisions in an industrial company? (ICSA 22 marks)
4. Discuss the effect which a rate of inflation of 30% p.a. might have on the financial requirements and the sources of finance of a large manufacturing company. (ICSA 22 marks)
5. In recent inflationary conditions companies have had to invest much higher amounts in stock and debtors. In what ways may these be financed? (ICSA 22 marks)
6. The financial manager in his day-to-day decisions must take into consideration the impact of inflation. However, for long-run decisions such as the appraisal of capital projects he can ignore this because in the long run an average inflation rate applied to all the variables will produce the same answer as if inflation had been ignored. Comment. (ACCA 15 marks)
7. 'What is vitally needed is a generally acceptable system of accounting both for management purposes and for reporting which shows the effect of changing prices levels' said the preface to ED18. The introducing of the document continued that 'management needs up to date information of costs and values for the proper running of the business. The system of current cost accounting described in the Exposure Draft will help to provide such information in the management accounts of companies and in their published annual accounts. If more realistic information is to be available to management than is provided by historic cost accounts, the change to current cost accounting needs to be made at the basic management accounting level. . . . As long as industry uses historical costs for management accounts, it may unknowingly undercost, with dangerous consequences for the business.' **Required**. Briefly explain why the use of historic costs for management accounts may have dangerous consequences for a business, and discuss in more detail the aspects of those dangers associated with depreciation and the cost of material consumed. (ACCA MA 20 marks)
8. Proposals for changes in financial reporting stress the distinction be-

tween 'operating' and 'holding' gains. In what ways may these different forms of gains be reflected in the managerial functions of a company? (ACCA BM 20 marks)
9. One of the most difficult tasks facing the financial manager when considering budgeting proposals is to make allowances for inflation. Discuss. (ACCA 15 marks)
10. Inflationary conditions may make it necessary for organisations to formalise within their management accounting systems, methods which enable them to cope with price level changes. **Required**. In general terms explain how inflation may affect the decision-making, planning and control aspects of management accounting. (ACCA MA 20 marks)
11. Discuss the arguments for and against allowing companies to calculate their tax liabilities on the basis of accounts adjusted for the effects of inflation. (ACCA 20 marks)
12. 'An understanding of taxation is almost as important for the financial manager as it is for the tax planner'. Comment on this statement indicating at least three areas of financial management where taxation can have a significant effect. (ACCA 15 marks)

Revision questions

1. Define return on capital employed and assess its efficacy for the measurement of performance of the various divisions of a divisionalised company. (ICSA 22 marks)
2. Examine the main problems of financial control likely to arise in a decentralised (divisionalised) manufacturing firm, and discuss possible solutions to these problems. (ICSA 22 marks)
3. Write brief notes on **four** of the following: (1) sensitivity analysis; (2) random walk; (3) profitability index; (4) portfolio theory; (5) simulation; (6) synergy; (7) capital rationing. (ACCA 15 marks)
4. Write brief notes on **four** of the following: (1) conversion premium; (2) Markowitz model; (3) random walk; (4) weighted average cost of capital; (5) prospectus; (6) eurobond; (7) chartist. (ACCA 15 marks)
5. What advantages may arise from the use of 'value added' in the measurement of business efficiency, as opposed to profits or sales revenues? (ACCA BM 20 marks)
6. Write brief notes on **four** of the following: (1) sensitivity analysis; (2) decision tree; (3) synergy; (4) stags; (5) factoring; (6) net terminal value; (7) transfer pricing. (ACCA 15 marks)
7. Write brief notes on **four** of the following: (1) fundamental and

technical analysis; (2) financial leverage/gearing; (3) profitability index; (4) terminal value (net); (5) capital rationing; (6) factoring; (7) opportunity cost. (ACCA   20 marks)

8. Write brief notes on **four** of the following: (1) contango (2) efficient portfolio; (3) resistance level; (4) sensitivity analysis; (5) issue by prospectus, issue by tender; (6) diluted earnings per share; (7) added value. (ACCA   15 marks)

9. The terms 'cost control' and 'cost reduction' frequently appear to be used synonymously. **Required**: an explanation of the distinction between these two terms, together with a consideration of the major techniques involved in their operation. (ACCA MA   20 marks)

10. What is meant by the term 'value engineering' or 'value analysis'? Indicate the importance of this technique for a manufacturing concern. (ACCA BM   20 marks)

11. In his reports the management accountant may present quantitative information expressed in physical quantities, monetary values, or a combination of both. **Required**: (*a*) Examples of reports showing how each of these measures may be used. Discuss the advantages and disadvantages of drawing up reports in each of these different ways (12 marks) (*b*) Discuss situations where consideration should be given to qualitative information in decision-making and suggest ways in which details of such information may be brought into decision analysis. (8 marks) (ACCA MA   20 marks)

12. Discuss how far it is sensible to use historical data for the purposes of making forecasts about the future. (ACCA BM   20 marks)

13. Define the term 'profit gap' in the context of corporate planning and discuss its relevance to the planning process. (ACCA BM   20 marks)

14. Discuss the use of probability theory in the context of annual sales forecasting. (ACCA BM   20 marks)

15. How far does pricing policy rely upon data external to the firm and how far upon internal considerations? (ACCA BM   20 marks)

16. Discuss the role of financial management as part of the management process of a company. (ACCA   15 marks)

17. Cost affects supply and demand affects revenue. **Required**. A discussion of the factors that would affect price setting in both (*a*) a competitive market and (*b*) an oligopolistic situation. (ACCA MA   20 marks)

18. Business balance sheets have often been criticised in disparaging terms in recent years. Why do you think that their meaningfulness is being questioned and to what extent do you think that adverse criticism is justified? (ACCA Acc3   12 marks)

19. The fundamental assumption underlying published company accounts has been, in the past, that the information, like all other activities of the company, is primarily designed to benefit the equity shareholder. What evidence is there to suggest that this assumption may be mistaken, and that new lines of responsibility are being recognised? (ACCA BM 20 marks)

20. Many traditional management accounting practices are criticised because they fail to include assumptions about human behaviour: **Required**: For **two** of the following areas: (*a*) budgetary control; (*b*) absorption costing; (*c*) installation of a costing and management accounting system; Discuss with reference to practical situations how the effects of human behaviour should be recognised in the introduction and operation of the system. (ACCA MA 20 marks)

21. The managing director of Worried Ltd has been informed that last year the stock turnover ratio, based on sales over average stock, for Similar Ltd was 12 and for Different Ltd 8, while this ratio for his own company was only 7. Similar Ltd is in the same industry as Worried Ltd, however, Different Ltd is not. Furthermore, the managing director of Worried Ltd understands that the stock turnover ratio for Similar Ltd has improved from 9 for the year before last to the 12 of last year. The managing director of Worried Ltd expresses concern that his firm is inefficient in its stock control procedures. **Required**. Assume that you have no other reason to believe that Worried Ltd is less efficient than either of the other two firms, and that the change in Similar's ratio is not due to any change in its level of efficiency during the years concerned. **Write a report to the managing director of Worried Ltd**, explaining the full range of likely possibilities which could account for the differences in these ratios. (ACCA MA 20 marks)

22. The summarised balance sheet of MacSuit and Coat Ltd, together with extracts from its revenue account for the year ended 31 March 1976 are given below. This small company manufactures clothing and is managed by two young, capable, energetic directors with a good knowledge and experience of the trade. They have made loans to the company to the full extent of their personal resources and currently require funds to finance a large contract worth £60,000 from reputable first-class buyers for a quantity of suits. They have applied to their bank for an unsecured overdraft limit of £15,000 to finance the contract. They have offered the bank manager their personal guarantees and postponement of their own loans. They do not wish to offer a secured debenture as they feel this would precipitate action from the company's creditors.

You are employed by the bank in its regional office as accountant adviser to bank managers in respect of loans such as this. **You are**

required to write a report to the bank manager: (a) analysing the information available to you in the context of the request made, and (b) advising him of the risk to the bank in granting the overdraft.

MacSuit and Coat Ltd, balance sheet as at 31 March 1976 (£).

Share capital:	Ordinary shares of £1 fully paid		3,000
	Profit-and-loss account		500
			3,500
	Loans by directors		5,500
Current liabilities:	accrued expenses	5,000	
	trade creditors	55,000	60,000
			69,000
Fixed Assets:	Plant and machinery (cost less depreciation)		10,500
	motor vehicles (cost less depreciation)		1,500
	goodwill		1,800
			13,800
Current assets:	cash at bank	11,800	
	trade debtors	17,000	
	stock and work in progress	23,500	
	prepayments	2,000	
	preliminary expenses	900	55,200
			69,000

Extracts from the Profit and Loss Account for the year ended 31 March 1976 (£)

Sales £ 230,000	Purchases of stock	£ 140,000	
Profit for the year (after all expenses including those below)			4,550
Provision for corporation tax			Nil
Provision for depreciation of fixed assets			1,800
Provision for directors' remuneration			6,400

(ACCA Acc4   20 marks)

23. The balance sheet of Plan Ahead Ltd as at 31 March 1976, together with its projected balance sheet as at 31 March 1977 and profit-and-loss account for the year ending on that date is as follows (£):

	31 March 1976		31 March 1977	
Ordinary share capital in £1 shares (fully paid)		200		250
Capital reserve – share premium account				25
Revenue reserves: general reserves	30		40	
profit and loss a/c	40	70	68	108
		270		383

Represented by: Fixed assets					
Freehold premises – cost			60		90
Plant and machinery (cost less depreciation)			48		125
			108		215
Current assets: stock		140		170	
debtors		100		120	
cash		1		2	
		241		292	
Less: Current liabilities					
Trade creditors	40			64	
Accrued expenses	1			2	
Corporation tax	16			26	
Proposed dividends	16			20	
Bank overdraft	6	79	162	12	124	168
			270		383

Budgeted profit-and-loss account (extract) for the year ending 31 March 1977 (£000):

Trading profit for the year (**after** charging all expenses including depreciation of plant and machinery (£28,000) but before taxation)		84
Less: corporation tax		26
Profit after taxation		58
Add: Balance of profit unappropriated last year b/f		40
		98
Appropriations (£000): Proposed dividend to ordinary shareholders	20	
transfer to general reserve	10	30
Profit unappropriated c/f		68

Note: No disposals of fixed assets were anticipated for the year ending 31 March 1977. **You are required to produce as part of the planning information a sources and applications of funds statement for the year ending 31 March 1977.** You should bear in mind the objectives of SSAP 10 and choose a presentation format which will demonstrate clearly the manner in which the operations of the business will be financed and the utilisation of its financial resources. You should highlight the excess or deficiency of internally generated funds over the disposition thereof and end your statement with the variation in the company's liquid resources. Marks will be awarded for form and presentation. (ACCA Acc4 14 marks)

24. 'The question of whether to buy or lease cannot be determined solely by the apparent impact on profitability'. **Comment on this statement making use of the following information.**

The ABC Food Processing Company Ltd is required under new legislation to introduce an additional sterilising machine into one of its factories. Two machines FA (fully automatic) and SA (semi-automatic) are available. The FA machine has a purchase price of £15,000 and will have a life of 7 years with annual running costs of £1,400 and a nil scrap value; SA on the other hand has a purchase price of only £8,000 with annual running costs of £1,500 in the first year increasing at the rate of 10% p.a. Machine SA has a life of 5 years and again a nil scrap value. As an alternative to buying either FA or SA, these can be leased for £375 and £250 per month respectively. If the machines are leased the operating costs will be reduced by £300 and £160 p.a. for FA and SA respectively. The company's target net of corporation tax return is 15% and its current net of corporation tax long-term borrowing rate is 10%.

Notes:
(1) Both machines can be assumed to attract a 100% first-year depreciation allowance and the corporation tax rate can be assumed to be 50%.

(2) Present value of £1 due in 1 year's time at:

Year	10%	15%
1	0.909	0.870
2	0.826	0.756
3	0.751	0.658
4	0.683	0.572
5	0.621	0.497
6	0.564	0.432
7	0.513	0.376
8	0.467	0.327
9	0.424	0.284
10	0.386	0.247

(3) For calculation purposes it can be assumed that cash outflows other than any initial capital expenditure take place at the end of each year. The tax benefits can be assumed to be obtained in the year in which the expenditure is incurred. (ACCA 20 marks)

25. **Discuss the factors to be considered in the formulation of a policy for credit control management, and use the following information in your discussion.**
A study of the debtors of the XYZ Co Ltd has shown that it is possible

Revision questions

to classify all debtors into certain classes with the following characteristics:

	Average collection period (days)	Bad debts (%)
A	15	0.5
B	20	2.5
C	30	5.0
D	40	9.5

The average standard profit/cost schedule for the company's range of products is as follows (£):

Selling price		2.50
Less: Material	1.00	
Wages	0.95	
Variable cost	0.30	
Fixed cost	0.05	2.30
	Profit	£0.20

The company has the opportunity of extending its sales by £1,000,000 split between categories C and D in the proportions 40 : 60. The company's short-term borrowing rate is 11½. (ACCA 15 marks)

26. **You are required to analyse the following information from the viewpoint of the implications it has for working capital policy.**

	Position as of now (£)	Budget position one year from now
Sales	250,000	288,000
Cost of goods sold	210,000	248,000
Purchases	140,000	170,000
Debtors	31,250	36,000
Creditors	21,000	30,000
Raw material stock	35,000	60,000
Work in progress	17,500	30,000
Finished goods stock	40,000	43,000

N.B. Assume all sales and purchases are on credit terms. (ACCA 20 marks)

Further reading

Ansoff, H. I., *Corporate Strategy*, Penguin, 1970
Anthony, Vivian, *Britain's Overseas Trade*, H.E.B., 1976
Anthony, Vivian, *Banks and Markets*, H.E.B., 1979
Archer, S. H. and **d'Ambrosio, C. A.**, *The Theory of Business Finance*, Collier-Macmillan, 1967
Argenti, J. I., *Corporate Planning: A Practical Guide* (Studies in Management), London, 1968
Argyris, C., *The Impact of Budgets on People*, Controllership Foundation, 1951
Batty, J., *Management Accountancy*, Macdonald and Evans, 1975
Briston, R. J., *The Stock Exchange and Investment Analysis*, Allen and Unwin, 1975
Briston, R. J. and **Dobbins, R.**, *The Growth and Impact of Institutional Investors*, Institute of Chartered Accountants, 1978
Britain – A Handbook (an annual publication), HMSO
Brown, J. L. and **Howard, L. R.**, *Principles and Practice of Management Accountancy*, Macdonald and Evans, 1975
Chambers, R. J., *Financial Management*, Sweet and Maxwell, 1970
Committee to Review the Functioning of Financial Institutions: Report (The Wilson Committee), Cmnd 7937 HMSO 1980
Davies, Brinley, *Business and Finance and the City of London*, H.E.B., 1979
Davies, J. R. and **Hughes, S.**, *Pricing in Practice*, H.E.B., 1975
Dickinson, G. M. and **Lewis, J. E.**, *Financial Management Handbook*, Kluwer-Harrap, 1979
Financial and Economic Obligations of the Nationalised Industries, Cmnd 1337, HMSO, 1961
Gibbs, J., *A Practical Approach to Financial Management*, HFL (Publishers), 1978
Glautier, M. W. E. and **Underdown, B.**, *Accounting In a Changing Environment*, Pitman, 1974

Further reading

Gregory D. and **Ward, H.**, *Statistics for Business*, McGraw Hill, 1978
Harper, W. M., *Operational Research*, Macdonald and Evans, 1975
Harper, W. M., *Management Accounting*, Macdonald and Evans, 1977
Hartley, W. C. F., *An Introduction to Business Accounting for Managers*, Pergammon, 1969
Hopwood, A., *Accounting and Human Behaviour*, Haymarket Press, 1974
Horngren, C. T., *Introduction to Management Accounting*, Prentice-Hall, 1978
Howard, L. R., *Principles of Auditing*, Macdonald and Evans, 1977
Inflation Accounting: Report of the Inflation Accounting Committee (The Sandilands Committee), Cmnd 6225, HMSO, 1975
Kempner, T. (ed.), *A Handbook of Management*, Penguin, 1976
Lamaison, M., 'Fundamentals of finance', *Certified Accountant*, 1978
Lucey, T., *Investment Appraisal: Evaluating Risk and Uncertainty*, Institute of Cost and Management Accountants, 1971
Merrett, A. J. M. and **Newbould, G. D.**, *Equity Issues and the London Capital Market*, Longman, 1967
Merrett, A. J. M. and **Sykes, A.**, *The Finance and Analysis of Capital Projects*, Longman, 1973
Modigliani F. and **Miller, M. H.**, 'The cost of capital, corporate finance and the theory of investment', *American Economic Review*, June 1958
Modigliani, F. and **Miller, M. H.**, 'Dividend policy, growth and the valuation of shares, *Journal of Business*, October 1961
Money for Business, Bank of England, 1980
Money for Exports, Bank of England, 1979
Morison, A. M. C., **Burden, R.** and **Crabtree, M. G.**, *Understanding Modern Business Mathematics*, Accountants Publishing Co., 1971
National Economic Development Office, *Finance for Investment*, HMSO, 1975
Nationalised Industries. A Review of Economic and Financial Objectives, Cmnd 3437, HMSO, 1967
Oyert, R. M. and **March, J. G.**, *A Behavioural Theory of the Firm*, Prentice-Hall, 1963
Prais, S. J., *The Evolution of Giant Firms in Britain*, Cambridge University Press, 1976
Rockley, L. E., *Finance For the Non Accountant*, Business Books, 1979
Robichek, R. A. and **Myers, S. C**, *Optimal Financing Decisions*, Prentice-Hall, 1965
Samuels, J. M. and **Wilkes, F. M.**, *Management of Company Finance*, Nelson, 1980

Sizer, J., *An Insight into Management Accounting*, Pitman, 1979
Small Firms: Report of the Committee of Enquiry (The Bolton Report), Cmnd HMSO, 4811, 1971
Stafford, L. W. T., *Business Mathematics*, Macdonald and Evans, 1979
'The cost of capital finance and investment', *Bank of England Quarterly Bulletin*, June 1976 and June 1977
Tomkins, C., *Financial Planning in Divisionalised Companies*, Haymarket Press, 1973
Watts, B. K. R., *Business and Financial Management*, Macdonald and Evans, 1978
Watts, B. K. R., *Elements of Finance for Managers*, Macdonald and Evans, 1978
Whiting, D. P., *Finance of Foreign Trade and Foreign Exchange*, Macdonald and Evans, 1976
Wood, F., *Business Accounting*, Longman, 1979

Index

A (non voting) shares, 24, 72
absorption costing *see* costing
acceptance, 188
acceptance commission, 188
acceptance credits, 187–9, 428
Accepting Houses Committee, 187, 445
account, the 477–8
accountants, 18, 336, 362, 495
accounting date, 17
Accounting Steering Committee, 517
acid test ratio *see* ratios
Act of Parliament, 21
administration cost *see* costs
administrator, 22
admission of securities to listing, 358–9
advance payment bonds, 419
air consignment note, 411
allowances, 194, 205
Aluminium Industrie Vaassen v Romalpa Aluminium Ltd, 1976, 123
analysis
    fundamental, 486–7
    investment, 485–9
    portfolio, 458, 485–6
    technical, 486–7
annual report and accounts, 27
applications (or uses) of funds, 166–7
Argyris, C., 152
Ariel, 479
Armstrong, H., 183
articles of association, 27–8, 30, 72
assets 11, 36–40, 111, 307–8
    current (or floating or circulating), 39–40
    fictitious (or nominal), 36, 38, 299–300

fixed, 36, 39, 44, 100, 296
intangible, 36–7
liquid (or quick), 40
protection of, 495–501
registers, 257
wasting, 39
assisted areas, 204–5
associated company, 334, 454
audit certificates, 14, 98, 498
    definition, 498
    external, 498–500
    internal, 498, 501
audited accounts, 25
auditing, statements on, 495–6
auditors, 14, 296, 495, 499–500

backwardation, 478
bad debts, 123, 189
balance sheet, 42, 95, 200
bank balances, 16, 135, 295
bank borrowings, 54, 99, 469
bank giro, 427
bank loans, 54
Bank of England, 14, 54, 205, 207, 337, 358, 425–6
Bank Rate, 54
bankers' discount formula, 188
Banking Act, 1979, 426
banking system, 424
banks, 14, 424–9
barter deals, 421
batch costing *see* costing
Batty, J., 224
bears, 477
benefit cost ratio, 273

bills and documents for collection, 412–13
bills of exchange, 54, 187, 412, 416, 444
Bills of Exchange Act, 1882, 187
bills of lading, 411
black economy, 7
Bolton Committee, 206
bonds, 201
bonus issue *see* capitalisation issue
Borland's Trustee v Steel Bros & Co., Ltd, 1901, 69
borrowers, 85–6
borrowing ratio, 102
Borthwick, T. Ltd., 366
breakeven chart, 229–33
breakeven point, 224, 227, 229–31, 273
break up value, 307
bridging finance, 155
British Gas Central Pension Fund, 210
British Institute of Management (BIM), 243
British National Oil Corporation (BNOC), 406
British Overseas Trade Board (BOTB), 409
British Productivity Council (BPC), 243
Britsh Rail Pension Fund, 52
British Steel Corporation (Industry) Ltd, 207
brokerage commission, 364
brokers *see* stockbrokers
budget, 139
budget centre, 222
    flexible, 150–1
    forms, 146–50
budgetary control, 139–53
building societies, 432–3, 446–50
bulls, 477
Burmah Oil Company, 293
business finance, 1
business risks *see* risks
buying agency, 409

Callaghan, Mr James, 506
capital, 23, 51–2, 257, 299, 512
capital allowances, 192, 194, 205, 519
    budgets, 151, 258–61
    cost of, 45, 53–67, 260

equity, 12, 23–4, 32–5, 43, 50, 55, 70, 356
expenditure, 257–76, 295
gains (tax), 84, 257, 342, 354–5, 451
profits, 84, 107
project, 258–61
rationing, 273
reconstruction *see* reconstruction
capital redemption reserve fund, 82
capital, risk, or venture, or start-up, 32–5 *see also* capital, equity
capital structure, 44–5, 53, 94–5, 100–1, 111
capitalisation issue, 75–6, 374–5
capitalisation of reserves, 74–6, 374–5
case law, 106, 498–9
cash, 7, 16, 124, 135, 154, 295–7, 342, 442
cash discounts, 55–6, 122, 135–6
cash flow, 16, 35, 154–7, 188, 191, 194, 258, 275
cash forecasts, 154–64, 196, 258–9, 261, 274, 295
cash limits, 396
Centre for Interfirm Comparison Ltd, 108, 243–4
certificate of deposit (CD), 444, 453
certificate of entitlement to commence business, 27
certificate of exemption, 367–8
certificate of incorporation, 27
certificate of tax deposit (CTD), 453–4
charge, 82
chart analysis *see* analysis, technical
Chartered Secretaries Manual of Company Secretarial Practice, 358
chartism *see* analysis, technical
cheques, 136, 187
churning, 461
circulating capital *see* working capital
City Code (on takeovers and mergers), 337, 361, 438
City Working Party, 337, 361, 438
civil servants, 50
Clause 1V, 389
clearing banks, 14, 43, 44, 136, 186, 189, 196, 197–8, 207, 347, 426–7, 443, 446
Clore, Sir Charles, 199

Index

collateral, 8
collection period, 247
collusion, 497
command, 213
Commissioners of Inland Revenue v
    Muller & Co's Margerine Ltd,
    1901, 37
commodity markets, 437
Commonwealth Development
    Corporation (CDC), 431
Commonwealth Development Finance
    Company (CDFC), 431
communicating, 213
Companies Acts, 9, 15, 21, 27, 32, 70, 79,
    81, 106, 165, 294, 296, 335, 344,
    349, 367, 439
company, 21-31
company, close, 354, 369
company
    doctor, 294
    limited by guarantee, 25
    limited by shares, 25-6
    listed, 25
    private, 26
    public, 25-6
    unlimited, 25
    company directors *see* directors
competing market makers, 481
components, 122
comprehensive short term guarantee
    policy, 415
computer controls, 496
Concorde (project), 50, 194, 399
confirming houses, 409-10
conglomerates, 330-2
Conservative government, 207, 293, 346,
    355, 357, 395, 403-6
consideration, 334
consolidated accounts, 349-50
Consolidated Gold Fields, 483-4
consortia, 386
contango, 478
contingent liabilities, 308
contract note, 477
contribution, 220, 225-9, 297
control, 213
controllable cost *see* cost
convertible debentures, 86-7
convertible preference shares, 78, 208

convertible unsecured loan stock, 343-4
Cooperative Insurance Society, 209
coordination, 213
corporate form, 21-2, 29
corporation tax, 53, 78, 191-2
cost
    administration, 223
    controllable, 222 direct, 222
    direct material, 222
    distribution, 223
    fixed, 222
    indirect, 222
    indirect material, 223
    prime, 223
    production, 223
    selling, 223
    total, 223
    variable, 217-22
cost allocation, 222
cost apportionment, 222
cost benefit (analysis), 190
cost centre, 222
cost insurance freight (CIF), 410-11
cost of sales, 223
cost planning, 213-14, 216-19
cost, uncontrollable, 148-9
cost unit, 222
costing
    absorption, 223-4
    batch, 224
    contract, 224
    job, 224
    marginal, 225-9
    operating, 224
    process, 224
    standard, 224
costs, 219-23
Council for Small Industries in Rural
    Areas (CoSIRA), 207
Council for the Securities Industry (CSI),
    436, 483-4
Court(s), 12, 43, 79, 82, 106-7, 137, 297,
    336, 344-5
covenants (restrictive), 83, 185-6
cover, 103
credit, 7-8, 55, 123, 442
credit cards, 7, 186
credit control, 134-5, 189
credit factoring, 189-90

credit policy, 123, 133–5
credit sales, 123
credit squeeze, 8, 414, 442, 520
credit unions, 433
creditors, 12, 34, 45–6, 79, 82, 112, 296, 300, 349
Crown Agents, 431
cumulative preference shares, 77
current or floating or circulating assets *see* assets
current cost accounting (CCA), 515–20
current costs, 106
current liquidity, 248
current purchasing power accounting (CPP), 515–20
current ratio *see* ratios
cyclical industries, 100

dawn raids, 483–4
Daily Telegraph, 3
De Beers Consolidated Mines, 483–4
dealing expenses, 84
debentures, 43, 54, 81–8, 99, 196, 343
debentures
  convertible, 86–7
  fixed interest – why companies have ceased to issue, 469
  with subscription rights, 87–8
debt ratio, 102
debtors, 123, 295
decision making, 48
decision tree analysis, 381
deed of partnership, 20
deferred (or founder or management) shares, 76–7
Department of Industry *see* Industry, Department of
Department of Trade *see* Trade, Department of
deposit accounts, 136, 446
deposit banks, the, 426–7
depreciation, 61, 106, 121, 151, 155, 167, 219, 257, 271
derating schemes, 205
development areas, 204–5
direct costs *see* costs
direct debiting, 427
direct material costs *see* costs

directors, 27, 30–1, 59, 61, 294–7, 305, 349
discount, 54, 194, *see also* cash discount
discount houses, 188, 444
  role of, 445–6
discount market, 187–9, 428–9, 444–6
discounted cash flow (DCF), 196, 261–76
distribution, 107
distribution costs *see* costs
diversification, 210, 379, 459–60
dividend control, 342
dividend cover, 114, 246, 308
dividend equalisation policy, 114
dividend yield, 308–9
dividends, 24, 33–5, 45–6, 59–62, 74–7, 106–7, 299
documentary credits, 413
documents against acceptance (d/a), 412
documents against payment (d/p), 412
double entry book keeping, 41, 95
dual capitalisation valuation basis, 311
dumping, 407
Dun and Bradstreet, 133

earnings per share (EPS), 45–6, 54, 100–1, 109–10
earnings yield, 308–9 *see* also yield
East African groundnuts scheme (1946), 50
economic performance, 8–9
economies of scale, 331
Economist, 3
Eire, Government of, 49
elasticity of demand, 331
eligible bank bill, 188
employees, 121–2, 298–9
English Development Agency, 509
entrepreneur, 10–11, 21–3
Equipment Leasing Association, 192–5
equity *see* capital, equity
Equity Capital for Industry (ECI), 208–9
equity market in recent years, 472–5
Estate Duties Investment Trust (EDITH), 207
eurobonds, 200–2
eurocurrency loans, 200–2
European Economic Community (EEC), 2, 206–7, 402

Index

European Investment Bank (EIB), 205
Eurotherm, 366
excess profits basis of valuation, 311
exchange control, 363, 455
Exchange Equalisation Account (EEA), 225
Exchange Telegraph Co Ltd (EXTEL), 244, 441
Export Credit Guarantee Department (ECGD), 129, 409, 414–20
  bond support, 418–19
  buyer credit guarantees, 418
  comprehensive short term guarantee policy, 415
  guarantees to banks, 416–19
  lines of credit, 418
  pre-shipment finance, 419–20
  supplemental (extended terms) guarantee, 415
exporters, other options for, 421–2
export licence, 410
export merchants, 409–10
exports, 129, 407–22
  methods of finance, 414–20
exposure draft (ED), 513
ED8, 513
ED 18, 517
ED 24, 518
EXTEL (Exchange Telegraph Co Ltd), 244, 441

facility letter, 187–9
factors of production, 6–7
factoring, 129, 135, 189–90, 295, 413–14, 430
Farwell, J., 69
Ferranti Ltd., 391
fictitious (or nominal) assets *see* assets
finance, 1, 12
Finance Corporation for Industry (FCI), 44, 196, 198, 207
Finance for Industry (FFI), 207
finance houses, 44, 186, 191–2, 430
financial institutions, 424–37
financial risks *see* risks
Financial Times, 3, 29, 404, 439, 447–51
Financial Times Business Service, 441

financing ratios *see* ratios
finished goods, 122
first year allowance, 205
fixed assets *see* assets
fixed charge, 43, 82–3
fixed costs *see* costs
fixed interest loans, 53–4, 197
fixed interest securities, 468–70
flexible budgets *see* budgets
floating charge, 43, 82–3
floatations, 356–7
flow of funds (statement), 95–6, 154, 164–8
foreign exchange, 420–1
foreign exchange market, 437–8
foreign trade, 407–9
forward foreign exchange contract, 420–1
franchise, 332
franked investment income, 78–80
fraud, 294, 296, 496–8
free on board (FOB), 411
Freedom of Information Act (USA), 399
fundamental analysis *see* analysis

gearing, 45–7, 53, 58, 95, 100–5, 188
gearing measurement, 101–5
gearing ratio, 47, 103
Gedge Committee, 71
General Motors, 333
gilt edged, 84, 459
going concern value, 307
Gold Market, London, 437
goods on consignment, 411–12
goodwill, 18, 33, 36–38, 76, 292, 308–9, 311, 317, 327, 333
Gordon, M.J., 64
governments, 50 98, 335, 347, 400, 442
grants, 194, 204–5
Grays Building Society, 294
gross capital employed, 110
gross contribution, 223
gross margin, 223
gross profit ratio, 246
gross working capital, 121
growth, 16, 35–6, 47, 58, 100, 308
growth factor, 64–6
Guardian, 3

Hagin, Robert, 488
Hambro Life, 366
hedge (against inflation), 86, 194, 199, 342, 382, 470
Henry Sykes Ltd, 357
Highlands and Islands Development Board, 205
hire purchase, 191–2, 297
Hire Purchase Acts, 191
historical cost (accounts), 9, 61, 106, 512, 515
holding company, 344, 349
Hopwood, A., 152
Horngren, C.T., 152
Hyde Committee, 517

impact day, 358
import license, 410
improvement grants, 205
incentives, 204, 332, 441
income tax, 19, 355, 520–2
incorporated business, 21–3
incorporation, 26–9
indirect costs *see* costs
indirect material costs *see* costs
Industrial and Commercial Finance Corporation Ltd (ICFC), 44, 196, 198, 207
Industrial Development Associations, 205
Industrial Reorganisation Corporation (IRC), 346–8
Industrial Revolution, 21, 35, 204
industrial site preparation, 205
Industry Act, 1972, 205–6
Industry, Department of, 8, 206, 341
inflation, 9–10, 53, 61, 85, 98–100, 106, 197–8, 224, 257, 260–1, 275, 308, 512–20
information, sources of, 438–41
initial allowance, 205
Inland Revenue, 192, 520–2
INMOS, 392
innovator, 10, 22
insider (dealings), 339, 480
Inspector of Taxes, 17
institutional investors, 206–11, 355
Institutional Shareholders Committee (ISC), 209
insurance, 198–9, 209, 382, 432–6, 467–8

brokers, 435
market, 433–6
intangible assets *see* assets
integration, 330–3
inter bank rate, 197
interest, 53–6, 191
  cover, 114
  rates, 98–100, 198, 250, 469
interest free loans, 204
intermediate areas, 205
internal check, 496–8
internal control, 495–6
internal rate of return (IRR), 261, 269–70
International Monetary Fund (IMF), 98
introduction, 358–9, 368–9
investment(s), 39, 275–6, 335, 459–60
investment analysis *see* analysis
investment trusts, 431–2, 460–3
investments
  medium and longer term, 454–68
  short term, 443–54
investment surcharge tax, 456
investors, 15, 22–3, 32–3, 61, 84–5, 204, 438–41
  classes of, individuals and institutions, 455–7
  motivation of individuals, 457–9
  viewpoints of, 441, 455–60
Investors Chronicle, 3
invoices, 189, 191, 246
invoice discounting, 129, 135, 191, 295
irrevocable and confirmed credit, 413
issue (of securities), 361–9
issuing house, 358, 363–4, 367

Jenkins Committee, 71
job costing *see* costing
jobbers, 305, 339, 367, 476–7
jobbers turn, 305, 372, 477, 481
joint ventures, 386, 421
Joseph, Sir Keith, 403

Kempner, T., 381
key factor, 143, 220, 227, 234, 237, 297
Kingston Cotton Mill Co Ltd, 1896, 499

Labour Government, 12, 207, 210, 346, 404

Index

lead manager, 201
leasing, 39, 44, 192–5, 258, 297
leasing companies, 44, 430
lenders, 12, 34–5, 65–6, 82, 86, 300
leverage, 45
liabilities, 42–4
licensing, 332, 421
limited company *see* company
limited liability company form *see* company
Limited Partnership Act, 1907, 20
limiting factor *see* key factor
liquid (or quick) assets *see* assets
liquid ratio *see* ratios
liquidity ratios *see* ratios
liquidator, 83, 292
liquidation, 22, 46, 79, 112, 137, 292–9
liquidity, 16, 24, 100, 135, 154, 295, 297, 443
listed companies *see* companies
listing (Stock Exchange), 69, 72, 208, 354–69
listing agreement, 358, 361
Little, I.M.D., 61
Lloyds, 434–5
loan (funds), 11, 23, 32–3, 43
local authorities, 98, 205, 442
local authority loans, 454
locked in, 305, 345
London Discount Market, 188, 445
London Oil Storage Co Ltd v Seear, Hasbuck and Co, 1904, 499
long term loans, 197–202
loss, 12
Luffman, G.A., 348

MacAura v Northern Assurance Co Ltd, 1925, 29
Macnaughten, Lord J., 37
main residence, 457
make or buy decisions, 233–4
management, 22, 213
manager, 22
margin *see* profit margins
margin of safety, 231–2
marginal costing *see* costing
market, perfect, 479
market price, 72–3, 470–1
market research, 214
marketability, 309

markets, differences between home and overseas, 407–8
Markowitz model, 486
medium term loans, 195–7, 299
memorandum of association, 27–8, 70
Mentor, 209, 211
merchant banks, 44, 196, 198, 358, 362, 368, 428
mergers, 326–53
methods of issue, 359–61
Midland Bank, 197, 210–11
Midland Bank Review, 355
Minimum Lending Rate (MLR), 54, 99, 188, 425
minority shareholders, 305, 345
Modigliani, F.M., 66, 474
Moir, Christine, 488
Molins Ltd, 366
money, 1, 6–10, 32, 40
'Money for Business', 205
money, supply of, 442–3
Monopolies Commission, 340–1
Monopolies and Merger Act, 1965, 341
Moore, Prof B., 474
Moracrest, 209
mortgage debenture, 198–200
Morpeth Committee, 517–18
Multinational companies, 49, 203, 214, 249, 331–2, 346

National Enterprise Board (NEB), 4, 198, 207, 208, 347, 391–2, 403
National Girobank, 427–8
National Savings Bank, 429, 446, 450–1
National Savings schemes, 429
nationalisation, 4–5, 403–6
nationalised industries, 4–5, 388–406
negotiable instrument, 188
net asset value, 73, 307–8
net capital employed, 110
net current debt, 248
net margin, 223
net present value (NPV), 261, 263, 269–76
net working capital, 121
new time, 478
new towns, 205
Newbould, G.D., 348
Nightingale, M.J.H., 26, 306, 357
no par value shares (NPV shares), 70–2

nominal value, 72–3
nominees, 339, 481
non cumulative preference shares, 77–8
Northern Ireland, 205
notes, 201
Nott, Mr John, 404

Observer, 3
offer for sale, 359, 363–4, 366
   by tender, 364–6
Office of Fair Trading (OFT), 481–3
open account, 411
open offer, 359
operating costing *see* costing
operating cycle, 124–8
opportunity cost, 62, 282
options, 360
ordinary share capital, 32–6, 43, 56–60, 301, 343
ordinary shareholders, 15, 23, 29, 45–7
ordinary shareholders equity, 73
Organisation for Economic Co-operation and Development (OECD), 2
original (opening) balances, 55, 185–6
'over the counter' market (OTC), 26
overdraft, 16, 44, 54–5, 124, 184, 295
overcapitalisation, 112–13, 299
overhead, 223
overseas bank, 195–8, 428
overtrading 111–12
ownership, 22–3

P A International, 211
Panel *see* Takeover Panel
parallel economy, 7
participating preference shares, 78
partly paid shares *see* shares
partnerships, 19–21
Partnership Act, 1890, 20
Patcentre, 211
patent, 10
payback, 196, 211, 261, 273–6
payout ratios, 474
pension funds, 198–9, 209, 431, 464–7
performance bonds, 419
perpetual inventory, 132
person, a company as a, 22, 29
Pilkington Ltd, 332

placing, 358–9, 366–8
planning, 213
'ploughing back' of profits, 59–60, 385
politicians, 50
portfolio management, 456
portfolio theory, 485–9
preference shareholders, 77–80, 301
preference shares, 77–80, 301
preferred ordinary shares, 76
present value of expected future cash flow, 310–11
Prevention of Fraud Acts, 33
price/earnings (p/e) ratio, 309–10
price leader, 331
prices, 9–10, 213–16
prime bank bill rate, 188
prime cost *see* costs
principle of exceptions, 149
priority percentage tables, 113
private companies, 24–6, 354–9
private investors, 355, 455–60
private sector businesses, 5–6, 10–15, 16–31, 35, 100, 212
'privatisation', 403–6
probability, theory of, 260, 272, 382
process costing *see* costing
production costs *see* costs
productivity, 36, 298
professional advisers, 18, 20–1
professional liability cover, 21
profit, 1, 12, 19, 23–4, 35–6, 59–62, 74–7, 100, 105–10, 154, 214, 219, 257, 355, 512
profit and loss account, 42, 96, 299
profit and loss appropriation account, 73–4
profit margins, 246, 249
profit ratio, 246
profit/volume (p/v) ratio, 228–9
profitability, 16, 110, 154, 212, 276, 297
profitability index, 273
profitability ratios, 245–6 *see also* ratios
promissory note 187, 416
promoter, 12, 13, 33, 40, 46, 51–2, 77, 213
prospectus, 360–1
prospectus issue, 359, 363
Prudential Assurance Co, 210–11
Prutech, 209
public companies, 24–9, 354–75

Index

Public Sector Borrowing Requirement (PSBR), 398, 404
public sector businesses, 4–5, 212, 388–406
put through, 481

quick ratio *see* liquid ratio

Radcliffe Committee, 445, 507
Random Walk Theory, 487–9
rate of return on average investment, 274–5
rate of return on original investment, 274
rating authority, 17
ratio(s), 83, 188, 243–54
ratio, acid test, 247
ratio analysis, 243–54
ratio(s)
　borrowing, 248
　current, 246–7
　financing, 246, 248
　liquid, 247
　liquidity, 246–8
　profitability, 245–6
　solvency, 246–8
raw materials *see* materials
Rayner, A.C., 61
receiver, 83
reconstruction, 113, 299–301
reconstruction account, 300
redeemable preference shares, 79, 82
reducing balances, 55, 185–6
regional development grants, 205
Register of Substantial Shareholdings, 339
Registrar of Business Names, 17, 20
Registrar of Companies, 25, 27, 29, 438
renounceable share certificate, 375
rescue operations, 14, 292–301
research and development expenditure, 37–8, 293
reserve account, 73–6
restrictive practices, 481–2
Restrictive Practices Court, 482
Retail Prices Index (RPI), 515
retained profits (or earnings), 47, 59–60
return on capital, 108–10, 135, 212, 249
return on investment, 261, 274–5
revenue (planning), 213–14, 220, 257

reverse takeover (reverse bid), 345
revocable letter of credit, 413
rights, cum, 372
rights, ex, 372
rights issues, 58, 95, 198, 208, 359, 369–74
rights
　renouncing of, 370
　value of, 371–4
risk(s), 12, 35, 139, 262, 275, 293, 327, 378, 485
　alternative ways of dealing with, 380–6
　analysis, 380–2
　business, 386
　categories of, 379–80
　compensation of, 384
　elimination or reduction of, 384
　exchange, 408, 420–1
　financial, 386–7
　laying off of, 385–6
　management, 378–87
　taker, 10, 22
　transfer of, 382–3
Rolls Royce Ltd, 293, 391–2, 402
Rolls Royce Pension Trust, 211
'Romalpa' case, the, 123, 134
royal charter, 21
Rubner, A., 61
Rule Book (Stock Exchange), 481–3
Rule 163 (2) (Stock Exchange), 306, 357, 481

'safety', 114
sale and leaseback, 199
sales ledger administration, 189–90
sales mix, 233–46
Sandiland's Committee, 516–17
Schedule D (income tax), 19
scheme of arrangement, 344–5
Schwartz, George, 513
Scottish Development Agency (SDA), 205
scrip issue *see* capitalisation issue
Sebag, Joseph, 450
secondary banks, 13–15
security, 33–4, 100, 307
Seebohm, Lord, 181
self insurance, 382–4
self regulation, 336–7, 484–5, 511

selling costs, 223 *see also* costs
sensitivity analysis, 260, 272, 275, 381–2
Sepon Ltd, 479
share premium account, 168, 374–5
shareholders, 34–5, 59–62
shares, ordinary, or equity, 69–77
    factors affecting prices, 471–2
    partly paid, 362
short term finance, 183–6
simple average, 314
single capacity, 481
size, 328
Small Business Capital Funds (SBCF), 209
Small Firms Division, 206
small firms, 206, 209–10, 332, 347, 356–7, 509–10
Small Firms Information Centres, 206
sole traders, 16–19
solicitors, 18, 336, 362
solvency ratios, 246–8 *see also* ratios
sources and applications of funds (statements) *see* flow of funds
special development areas, 205
special resolution, 28
sponsors, 358
stags, 322, 363, 365
stamp transfer duty, 84, 344, 372, 455, 477
standard costing, 224 *see also* costing
statement of nominal capital, 27, 70
Statements of Standard Accounting Practice (SSAPs), 38
    SSAP 1 (Accounting for the Results of Associated Companies), 454
    SSAP 7 (Accounting for Changes in the Purchasing Power of Money), 513–16
    SSAP 10 (Statements of Sources and Applications of Funds), 165–8
    SSAP 13 (Accounting for Research and Development), 38
    SSAP 16 (Current Cost Accounting), 106, 518–20
statistical decision theory, 381
Stiegler, S.E., 378
stock, 246
stock appreciation relief, 206, 519
stockbroker, 358, 362, 367–8, 441, 476–81

Stock Exchange, 26, 33, 52, 69, 72, 81, 84, 308–9, 335–7, 354–9, 436, 438–40, 511
Stock Exchange Daily Official List, 439
Stock Exchange dealings procedures, 475–9
Stock Exchange Fact Book, 439
Stock Exchange Gazette, 3
Stock Exchange, obtaining a listing, 359–69
Stock Exchange Official Year Book, 440
Stock Exchange, recent criticisms and developments, 479–85
stock jobbers *see* jobbers
stock turnover ratio, 248
stocks, 105, 122, 132, 296
subsidiary (company), 349
Sunday Telegraph, 3
Sunday Times, 3
superprofits, 306, 311
suppliers, 12, 296
suppliers' credit, 122–3
survival, 16, 100, 213, 296
synergy, 348

Table A, 28, 106
tables (mathematical), 264–5
takeover, 22, 260, 292, 305, 326–53
Takeover Panel, 337–40, 438, 511
Talisman, 478
tax avoidance, 520–1
tax efficient, 457
tax evasion, 520
tax holidays, 204, 421
taxation, 17–18, 53–4, 191–2, 194, 271, 451, 457, 521–2
taxation liabilities, 44
technical (chart) analysis *see* analysis
Technical Development Corporation (TDC), 207
tender bonds, 418
tenor (bill of exchange), 188
Theft Act, 33
Thomas, G., 378
time horizons, 466–7
The Times, 3
timing, 262, 272–5, 321, 358, 361, 451
total costs *see* costs
track record, 33

Index

trade credit, 12, 46, 55–6
trade creditors, 32, 44–5, 136–7, 296
Trade, Department of, 13, 30, 81, 341, 409, 432, 483
trade investments, 39–40
transfer form, 477
transferable currency, 410–11
Treasury bills, 429, 444, 453
trustee, 82, 459
Trustee Investment Act, 1961, 459
Trustee Savings Banks, 429, 446, 450
trustee status, 459
turnover, 214, 249

uncertainties, 139, 260, 274, 378–87
uncontrollable cost, 148–9, 222
undercapitalisation, 110–11
underwriters, 208, 364, 371
underwriting (commission), 362, 371
underwriting firm, 363
Unilever Educational Booklets, 381
unit trusts, 431–2, 460–2
US banks, 195–6
unlimited liability, 17, 296–7
unlimited liability companies, 25
unlisted companies, 26, 306, 354–8
Unlisted Securities Market (USM), 26
unsecured loans, 34–5, 86–8, 343–4

valuation of a company, 305–25
valuation ratio, 475
valuations, 105–6
value, 307–8
value added, 401

'value to the business', 307, 516
variable costs *see* costs
variable interest, 54–5, 197
variables, 381
variances, 224
vendor consideration issue, 306
volume, sales, 214, 260
vulnerability, 249

warehousing, 339
warrants, 88, 360
wasting assets *see* assets
'watered down', 112–13
weighted average, 62–4, 314
weighted average cost of capital, 62–4
Welsh Development Agency (WDA), 205
White Papers, 392–4
Wilson Committee, 12, 47, 196–7, 203, 206, 208, 209, 259, 261, 275, 328, 355, 424, 464, 466, 505–11
Wilson Committee, terms of reference, 506
Wilson, Sir Harold, 506
without profits insurance policy, 198
work in progress (WIP), 122
working capital, 55, 121–37
working capital ratio, 248

year 0, 268–9
yield, 51–2, 469–70
yield, flat or running, 470
yield, redemption, 470
yield method (discounted cash flow), 261, 269–70, 276–9